Depression and the Social Environment

Depression and the
Social Environment

Research and Intervention with Neglected Populations

Edited by
Philippe Cappeliez and
Robert J. Flynn

McGill-Queen's University Press
Montreal & Kingston • London • Buffalo

Legal deposit second quarter 1993
Bibliothèque nationale du Québec

Printed in Canada on acid-free paper

This book has been published with the help of a grant
from the Social Science Federation of Canada, using funds
provided by the Social Sciences and Humanities Research
Council of Canada. Publication has also been supported
by grants from the Faculty of Social Sciences and the
School of Psychology, University of Ottawa.

Canadian Cataloguing in Publication Data

Main entry under title:
Depression and social environment : research
and intervention with neglected populations
Includes bibliographical references.
ISBN 0-7735-0960-7.
1. Depression, Mental—Social aspects.   2.
Depression, Mental.   I. Cappeliez, Philippe,
1951-   .   II. Flynn, Robert J. (Robert John),
1942-   .
RC537.D47 1993   616.85'27   C92-090722-9

---

*To my mother, Madeleine, and my late father, Charles,
and to my wife, Patricia – PC*

*To the memory of my parents, Anna and Maurice,
and to my wife, Geneviève – RJF*

Contents

Tables

Figures

Acknowledgments

The editors gratefully acknowledge the financial support received for the publication of this volume from the Aid to Scholarly Publishing Programme, Social Sciences Federation of Canada; the Faculty of Social Sciences, University of Ottawa; the School of Psychology, University of Ottawa; and McGill-Queen's University Press. We also wish to thank the members of the Teaching and Research Secretariat of the University of Ottawa's School of Psychology, especially Ms. Kibeza Kasubi, for their excellent help in the preparation of this manuscript.

Contributors

HARVEY ARMSTRONG, M.D., Department of Psychiatry, University of Toronto, Ontario

GORDON E. BARNES, Ph.D., Department of Family Studies, University of Manitoba, Winnipeg, Manitoba

CAROLYN BOULOS, M.D., Department of Psychiatry, Sunnybrook Health Science Centre, University of Toronto, Ontario

PHILIPPE CAPPELIEZ, Ph.D., School of Psychology, University of Ottawa, Ottawa, Ontario

GRANVILLE A. daCOSTA, M.D., Child and Family Studies Centre, Clarke Institute of Psychiatry, Toronto, Ontario

JAN E. FLEMING, M.D., Department of Psychiatry, McMaster University, Hamilton, Ontario

ROBERT J. FLYNN, Ph.D., School of Psychology, University of Ottawa, Ottawa, Ontario

JUDITH FRIEDLAND, Ph.D., Department of Rehabilitation Medicine, University of Toronto, Ontario

PREM S. FRY, Ph.D., Department of Educational Psychology, University of Calgary, Calgary, Alberta

DORIS HANIGAN, Ph.D., Laboratoire de recherche en écologie humaine et sociale, Université du Québec à Montréal, Montreal, Quebec

STAN KUTCHER, M.D., Department of Psychiatry, Sunnybrook Health Science Centre, University of Toronto, Ontario

MARY ANN McCOLL, Ph.D., Department of Rehabilitation Medicine, University of Toronto, Ontario

PETER MARTON, Ph.D., Department of Psychology, Sunnybrook Health Science Centre, University of Toronto, Ontario

E. ANN MOHIDE, Ph.D., Faculty of Health Sciences, McMaster University, Hamilton, Ontario

DAVID R. OFFORD, M.D., Department of Psychiatry, McMaster University, Hamilton, Ontario

JANET M. STOPPARD, Ph.D., Psychology Department, University of New Brunswick, Fredericton, New Brunswick

DAVID L. STREINER, Ph.D., Faculty of Health Sciences, McMaster University, Hamilton, Ontario

MICHEL TOUSIGNANT, Ph.D., Laboratoire de recherche en écologie humaine et sociale, Université du Québec à Montréal, Montreal, Quebec

"Four months after the Germanys reunited, depression is widespread ... All the major life changes that can cause depression in an individual have been unleashed by the absorption of East Germany into West Germany: unemployment, marital problems, uncertainty about the future, financial difficulty, identity crisis, loss of status in society, lack of purpose in life."

– N. Morris, "After Euphoria, East Germans Plagued by Depression," *The Ottawa Citizen*, 14 February 1991

CHAPTER ONE

An Integrative Cognitive-Environmental View of Depression

ROBERT J. FLYNN AND PHILIPPE CAPPELIEZ

Variously defined as a symptom, a syndrome, a single condition, or a spectrum of biopsychosocial manifestations, depression is the most common mental disorder in industrialized societies (Jablensky 1987). Although there is diversity at the conceptual level as to the nature of the disorder, there is consensus at the descriptive level concerning the unique importance of dysphoria as a sign of depression. Dysphoria, found in over 90 per cent of depressed persons (Lewinsohn et al. 1985), is reflected in the common conceptualization of depression as a "negative mood."

The importance of depression is heightened by the fact that its prevalence appears to be increasing and is expected to continue to do so on a worldwide basis (Sartorius 1978). Klerman et al. (1985) found that, among 2,289 relatives of depressed Americans, successive birth cohorts had experienced rising rates of depression since the beginning of the twentieth century. They also found a progressively earlier age of onset for both males and females in each birth cohort, as well as a greater rate of depression for females than males in all birth cohorts. That female-male difference was least apparent, however, in the more recent cohorts, largely because of the increase in male rates. Hagnell et al. (1982), comparing the period 1957-72 with that of 1947-57, reported a ten-fold increase in the risk of moderate or severe depression among Swedish males twenty to thirty-nine years of age.

ETIOLOGICAL IMPORTANCE OF THE SOCIAL ENVIRONMENT

Such data, showing that depression is increasing in incidence or prevalence, or both, clearly suggest that the environment is etiologically significant, even if its mechanisms of influence are poorly understood. Klerman et al. (1985) speculated that a complex, as yet unknown, form of gene-environment interaction was responsible for the temporal birth-cohort trend they observed. Hagnell et al. (1982) couched their environmental explanation of their findings in terms of lifestyle and other social changes.

Other research on psychosocial factors in the etiology of depression confirms the importance of the environment. Brown and colleagues, for example, showed that a provoking agent could be identified in 80 to 89 per cent of all episodes of depression in nonhospitalized community samples; they termed the provoking agent "severe" in 65 to 73 per cent of cases (Brown and Harris 1978; Brown and Prudo 1981). Moreover, they found a relapse to be especially likely when such provoking factors as aversive life events occurred in the context of an unsupportive interpersonal environment (Brown and Prudo 1981). In a study dealing with the refining of the assessment of life-event stressfulness, Shrout et al. (1989) reported that, for patients with diagnoses of major depression, the odds of experiencing a fateful, disruptive event were more than three times as large as for respondents within the community-at-large. The findings of this study suggest that uncontrolled, disruptive life events constitute risk factors for both the onset and recurrence of major depression. More recently, longitudinal data from the New Haven (Connecticut) Epidemiologic Catchment Area Study have indicated that, with controls for other background factors, living in poverty is associated with a greater than twofold increase in the risk of major depression (Bruce et al. 1991).

Clearly, much remains to be learned about the specific linkages between psychosocial variables and individual responses. Also, the wide variability in the responses of individuals to stressful life events should not be minimized. Nevertheless, the literature in the area does indicate that stressors that disrupt functioning, such as social losses, unemployment, economic deprivation, and interpersonal conflict, have an important relationship with the development of distress and depression.

INTRAINDIVIDUAL FOCUS IN CONTEMPORARY RESEARCH ON DEPRESSION

There is now substantial evidence that many psychotherapies are effective in treating depression. Moreover, the various therapies actually studied (behavioural, cognitive, interpersonal, and psychodynamic) have shown equivalent therapeutic effectiveness (Elkin et al. 1989; for reviews, see McLean and Carr 1989; Robinson et al. 1990).

Cognitive therapy, as initially formulated by Beck and colleagues (Beck et al. 1979), has generated considerable interest in recent years. Indeed, most comparative outcome studies have suggested that cognitive therapy performs as well as antidepressant pharmacotherapy (for reviews, see Dobson 1989; Hollon et al. 1991), even though, as Hollon et al. (1991) pointed out, the studies' methodological limitations temper this conclusion. Research on the processes that mediate outcome has gradually developed, in conjunction with these efforts, to assess the efficacy of cognitive therapy for depression (for example, DeRubeis et al. 1990; Hollon and Garber 1990). New developments in cognitive therapy seek to integrate cognitive and interpersonal approaches in order to achieve a better understanding of the process of psychotherapeutic change (Safran and Segal 1990).

Cognitive theorists place a critical emphasis on cognitive processes for understanding and alleviating depression (for example, Beck 1983; Beck et al. 1979; Abramson et al. 1978). These theorists also posit a relatively enduring cognitive vulnerability to depression. For Beck and his colleagues, for instance, depressive symptoms result from the systematic interpretation of reality in self-defeating ways through the operation of negatively biased thought processes, such as arbitrary inference, personalization, and catastrophizing. These negative thought patterns are believed to result from the reactivation, by adverse life events, of enduring belief systems and attitudes. Abramson et al. (1978), on the other hand, point to a depressogenic attributional style (that is, an habitual tendency to perceive internal, stable, and global explanations as causes of adverse events) as a key source of vulnerability for depression. Such theories reflect the contemporary perspective on stress that views adaptation to stress as determined by, to a large extent, how individuals appraise the meaning of stressful situations, their coping strategies, and their coping-related efficacy beliefs (for example, Bandura 1986; Lazarus and Folkman 1984; Kessler et al. 1985).

Although cognitive theories of depression emphasize intraindividual cognitive-personality variables, they are fundamentally diathesis-stress models. That is, they imply that some individuals have a "predisposition" to develop depression when confronted with a particular life stressor. Both dysfunctional attitudes and beliefs and a depressogenic attributional style are hypothesized to increase the probability of depression, but only in conjunction with stressful life events. Unfortunately, there has been a tendency in such theories for the central focus on cognitive vulnerabilities to overshadow the importance of negative life events in the genesis of depression. In addition to specifying the person-environment transactions that predict the onset, maintenance, exacerbation, or recurrence of depression (for example, Alloy et al. 1988; Beck 1983; Hammen et al. 1989a; Hammen et al. 1989b; Robins 1990; Segal et al. 1989), cognitive theories need to focus more explicit attention on the individual's actual social context (Coyne and Gotlib 1983; Oatley and Bolton 1985; Robins and Block 1989).

INTEGRATING COGNITIVE AND
ENVIRONMENTAL PERSPECTIVES

The main purpose of this book is to supplement the dominant intraindividual focus of contemporary cognitive models of depression by presenting the role of the social environment, particularly as it applies to groups whose members have a greater than average likelihood of experiencing adverse life circumstances. The term "social environment" refers to a wide range of situations and experiences, from the general and remote (for example, social class, ethnic background, gender) to the specific and immediate (for example, major life events, chronic adverse conditions, key social relationships, and daily hassles [see Monroe 1988]). In this broad sense, the social environment encompasses the social, cultural, and economic conditions and influences that impinge upon people's everyday lives.

The renewed emphasis on the role of the social environment implied by an integrative cognitive-environmental perspective is congruent with today's new thinking apropos mental health policy. In *Mental Health for Canadians: Striking a Balance* (Health and Welfare Canada 1988), for example, the federal government of Canada recently adopted a health-promotion perspective on mental health. The new policy defines mental health explicitly in terms of individual-environmental interactions, justice, and equality, while emphasizing prevention, enhancement of individual coping abilities, and reduction of social inequalities. These themes recur throughout this volume.

Lewinsohn et al. (1985) have provided a useful vehicle for integrating the cognitive and environmental approaches which we see as necessary. Because their model of depression development integrates many of the single-factor "mini-theories" that abound in the literature, it is proposed here as a useful heuristic device. With its conception of depression as the end result of environmentally initiated changes in behaviour, affect, and cognition, their multifaceted approach has considerable explanatory potential. It allows for many causes, each of which is contributory but none of which is essential. After sketching the model, we shall use it to introduce and link the various contributions to this book.

Figure 1, adapted from Lewinsohn et al. (1985), shows the variables involved in the occurrence of depression. The chain of events culminating in depression begins with a stressor, such as experiencing marital problems, losing one's job, or suffering from chronic illness and disability. These stressful life situations, typically associated with chronic strain, may place individuals at particular risk for depression. Stressors, to the extent that they disrupt interpersonal relationships, major social roles, and patterned behaviours, are postulated to lead to depression. The stressful event and its immediate consequences trigger a generalized and negative emotional reaction. This negative emotional response, aggravated by the emotional impact of the individual's

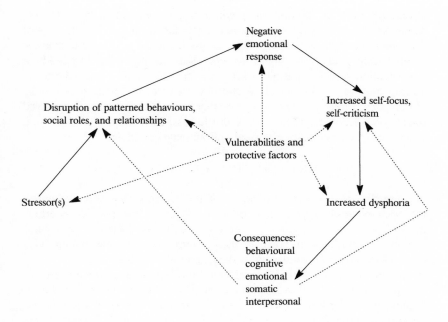

Figure 1
Schematic representation of variables involved in the occurrence of depression (adapted from Lewinsohn et al. 1985). The solid lines refer to the main chain of events in depression and correspond to the description in the chapter. The dotted lines refer to a) the vulnerability factors that influence most components of the sequence of events, and b) the feedback loop (secondary influences).

inability to reverse the effects of the stress, leads in turn to a heightened state of self-awareness. The elicitation of this state increases the person's awareness of his or her failure to meet expected standards of coping and, in turn, engenders self-denigration, social withdrawal, and further dysphoria. The experience of increased self-awareness and dysphoria brings about many of the cognitive, behavioural, emotional and interpersonal changes typically associated with depression: negative self-evaluation, low self-reinforcement, pessimism about the future, internal attributions concerning negative experiences, ruminations about past negative experiences, poor social competence, and negative impact on others. The model includes several "feedback loops" that are seen as important mechanisms for determining the severity and duration of a depressive episode.

Predisposing characteristics (vulnerabilities and protective factors) are postulated to exist within either the person or the person's environment (probably both) to explain why individuals have varying probabilities of experiencing depression and why depressive episodes may be long or short. Lewinsohn et al. (1985) list the following as predisposing vulnerabilities: being female, being between the ages of twenty and forty, having a previous history of depression, having poor coping skills, having increased sensitivity to aversive events, being poor, being highly self-conscious, having a low threshold for the evocation of depressogenic beliefs and attitudes, having low self-esteem, scoring high on interpersonal dependency, and having children below the age of seven. Protective factors, on the other hand, include high self-perceived social competence, high learned resourcefulness, high frequency of pleasant events, and the availability of a close and intimate confidant.

THE CONTRIBUTION OF THIS VOLUME

Because the influence on depression of the larger socioeconomic context has been relatively neglected to date, the tendency has been to overlook the difficulties encountered by certain groups in our society. This volume focuses on depression in some of these groups, with a view to improving our understanding of assessment, etiology, and intervention.

Barnett and Gotlib's (1988) recent review of research on the antecedents of depression underlined the importance of disturbances in interpersonal functioning, particularly low social integration, in the etiology of the disorder. Several contributors to this volume actually show how the larger social conditions, such as social and economic inequalities, lead to low social integration, conflictual interpersonal relationships, and ultimately to depression. For example, in his overview of the empirical research on depression among Native Indians in Canada (a topic that has received little empirical attention to date, but which promises to become much more prominent in the future), Armstrong suggests that major improvements in Native people's social and economic environment will be needed to address their high rates of depression and suicide. Similarly, daCosta's discussion of depression among immigrants and refugees (another topic that, although it has received little systematic research attention in the past, seems likely to grow rapidly in the future) identifies a number of factors – unsatisfactory immigration policies; the stresses that often accompany migration and resettlement; prejudice; and discrimination at the hands of the host society; and uncoordinated, sometimes insensitive, health and social services – as potential contributors to family conflict, social isolation, underutilization of services, and depression. Finally, Flynn's chapter on the impact of unemployment shows that joblessness often creates financial strain, loss of time structure, loss of purpose in life, lessened self-esteem, and increased family conflict – all of which have considerable potential for increasing depressive affect. In light of the frequency of periods of high unemployment in modern societies, it is surprising that the impact on depressive symptomatology of being without a job has not been grasped more clearly by mental health professionals and policymakers.

The role of the social environment in causing depression in women has often been underestimated as well. Epidemiological studies of mental health disorders (for a review, see Nolen-Hoeksema 1987) and a recent longitudinal study on risk factors for depression (Lewinsohn et al. 1988) have both demonstrated that women are more likely than men to experience depression. Not surprisingly, much of our present knowledge about the social, psychological, and biological aspects of depression has been based on studies of clinical and subclinical samples in which women greatly outnumber men. Paradoxically, however, this same literature does relatively little to explain gender differences in incidence rates or gender influences on etiology, symptomatology, and intervention. In this volume, Stoppard attempts to shed some light on women's heightened vulnerability to depression by looking at the implications of sex-role development and adult sex-role actualization.

Because many studies of depression have been conducted with young adults, other age groups have been neglected. In the case of children, for example, the possibility that children might experience depression was recognized only recently. Yet inasmuch as depression is often a recurring condition, improved knowledge about childhood depression will only enhance our understanding of the early developmental determinants of depression and of its relapse prevention. In this volume, Fleming and Offord provide a comprehensive discussion of the literature on childhood depression.

The impact of adolescents' relationships with peers and parents makes the social dimension of depression especially crucial in this age group. In this book, Tousignant and Hanigan suggest that the study of depression in adolescents provides a unique point of entry into the investigation of societal differences and changes as they influence the mood and morale of a population. Kutcher, Marton, and Boulos point out the profound effects of depression during adolescence, a lifestage marked by important personality developments and affective and vocational choices. The recent epidemiological data mentioned earlier, that suggest a trend toward a decreasing age of onset for depression among the more recent birth cohorts, provide an additional reason for focusing on depression in adolescents and young adults.

As for the growing interest in depression among older citizens, it is fueled by the realization that society is rapidly aging and that this segment of the population, although most often in need of treatment, is one of the least likely to receive it. In complementary chapters, Cappeliez and Fry rebut several misconceptions in this area, viewing depression among elderly persons in the context of the latter's often difficult life circumstances and challenges. Cappeliez and Fry both proceed from an integrative view of depression that results from the interplay of a person's stressors and personal and environmental resources. Both emphasize the importance of the individual's appraisal of stressors, as well as his or her coping responses. In line with the new policy direction in the mental health area articulated by Health and Welfare Canada (1988), both chapters emphasize that interventions should concentrate largely on maintaining elderly people's health and building their coping capacity through community-based services.

Mohide and Streiner analyze the situation of family members who care for an impaired older person and who, in turn, may themselves require intervention for depression. As the authors point out, the current tools are inadequate for identifying the needs, and assessing the emotional burden, of these family caregivers. Appropriate instruments need to be developed before interventions can be properly planned and evaluated.

Today, people are generally better aware of the physical challenges of living with a physical disability than was once the case. However, as McColl and Friedland point out in their chapter, awareness of the psychological and social aspects of physical disability lags far behind. By addressing these issues as they relate to depression, McColl and Friedland attempt to explain why some people adjust well to disability while others suffer from depression.

It is widely acknowledged that many depressed persons make their way to general practitioners rather than to mental health specialists. This phenomenon, however, has rarely been investigated. Although, as Barnes points out in this volume, well-known vulnerability factors appear to be operating (for example, being female or of low socioeconomic status), much remains to be learned about this group of depressed individuals. Only a fraction of these patients are likely even to be correctly identified as depressed and treated appropriately. The recurring nature of many depressive episodes makes this problem still more serious.

A FINAL COMMENT

The goal of researchers is to develop and disseminate knowledge. Unfortunately, this knowledge too rarely influences the thinking of politicians and policymakers. In countries such as Canada, policies in such areas as mental and physical health, child care, unemployment insurance, welfare, and tax reform are often developed largely on the basis of political considerations, with relatively little attention paid to theory or scientific data. We hope that the present book will be able to bridge the two worlds of scholarship and action. Although not primarily about policy, the volume contains much empirical information and many recommendations of direct relevance to social policy and practical intervention.

BIBLIOGRAPHY

Abramson, L., Seligman, M., and Teasdale, J. 1978. Learned helplessness in humans: Critique and reformulation. *Journal of Abnormal Psychology* 87: 49–74.

Alloy, L.B., Abramson, L.Y., Metalsky, G.I., and Hartlage, S. 1988. The hopelessness theory of depression: Attribution aspects. *British Journal of Clinical Psychology* 27: 5–21.

Bandura, A. 1986. *Social foundations of thought and action: A social cognitive theory.* Englewood Cliffs, N.J.: Prentice-Hall.

Barnett, P.A., and Gotlib, I.H. 1988. Psychosocial functioning and depression: Distinguishing among antecedents, concomitants, and consequences. *Psychological Bulletin* 104: 97–126.

Beck, A.T. 1983. Cognitive therapy of depression: New perspectives. In *Treatment of depression: Old controversies and new approaches*, edited by P. Clayton, and J.E. Barrett, 265–90. New York: Raven Press.

Beck, A.T., Rush, A.J., Shaw, B.F., and Emery, G. 1979. *Cognitive therapy of depression.* New York: Guilford Press.

Brown, G.W., and Harris, T. 1978. *Social origins of depression.* London: Tavistock.

Brown, G.W., and Prudo, R. 1981. Psychiatric disorder in a rural and an urban population: 1. Aetiology of depression. 2. Sensitivity to loss. *Psychological Medicine* 11: 581, 601–16.

Bruce, M.L., Takeuchi, D.T., and Leaf P.J. 1991. Poverty and psychiatric status: Longitudinal evidence from the New Haven Epidemiologic Catchment Area Study. *Archives of General Psychiatry* 48: 470–74.

Coyne, J.C., and Gotlib, I.H. 1983. The role of cognition in depression: A critical appraisal. *Psychological Bulletin* 94: 472–505.

DeRubeis, R.J., Evans, M.D., Hollon, S.D., Garvey, M.J., Grove, W.M., and Tuason, V.B. 1990. How does cognitive therapy work? Cognitive change and symptom change in cognitive therapy and pharmacotherapy for depression. *Journal of Consulting and Clinical Psychology* 58: 862–69.

Dobson, K.S. 1989. A meta-analysis of the efficacy of cognitive therapy for depression. *Journal of Consulting and Clinical Psychology* 57: 414–19.

Elkin, I., Shea, T., Watkins, J., Imber, S.D., Sotsky, S.M., Collins, J.F., Glass, D.R., Pilkonis, P.A., Leber, W.R., Docherty, J.P., Fiester, S.J., and Parloff, M.B. 1989. NIMH Treatment of Depression Collaborative Research Program: 1. General effectiveness of treatments. *Archives of General Psychiatry* 46: 971–82.

Hagnell, O., Lanke, J., Rorsman, B., and Ojesjo, L. 1982. Are we entering an age of melancholy? Depressive illnesses in a prospective epidemiological study over 25 years: The Lundby study, Sweden. *Psychological Medicine* 12: 279–89.

Hammen, C., Ellicott, A, and Gitlin, M. 1989a. Vulnerability to specific life events and prediction of course of disorder in unipolar depressed patients. *Canadian Journal of Behavioural Science* 21: 377–88.

Hammen, C., Ellicott, A., Gitlin, M., and Jamison, K.R. 1989b. Sociotropy/autonomy and vulnerability to specific life events in patients with unipolar depression and bipolar disorders. *Journal of Abnormal Psychology* 98: 154–60.

Health and Welfare Canada. 1988. *Mental health for Canadians: Striking a balance.* Ottawa: Minister of Supply and Services.

Hollon, S.D., and Garber, J. 1990. Cognitive therapy for depression: A social cognitive perspective. *Personality and Social Psychology Bulletin* 16: 58–73.

Hollon, S.D., Shelton, R.C., and Loosen, P.T. 1991. Cognitive therapy and pharmacotherapy for depression. *Journal of Consulting and Clinical Psychology* 59: 88–99.

Jablensky, A. 1987. Editorial: Prediction of the course and outcome of depression. *Psychological Medicine* 17: 1–9.

Kessler, R.C., Price, R.H., and Wortman, C.B. 1985. Social factors in psychopathology: Stress, social support, and coping processes. *Annual Review of Psychology* 36: 531–72.

Klerman, G.L., Lavori, P.W., Rice, J., Reich, T., Endicott, J., Andreasen, N.C., Keller, M.B., and Hirschfield, R.M.A. 1985. Birth-cohort trends in rates of major depressive disorder among relatives of patients with affective disorder. *Archives of General Psychiatry* 42: 689–93.

Lazarus, R.S., and Folkman, S. 1984. *Stress, appraisal, and coping.* New York: Springer.

Lewinsohn, P.M., Hoberman, H.M., and Rosenbaum, M. 1988. A prospective study of risk factors for unipolar depression. *Journal of Abnormal Psychology* 97: 251–64.

Lewinsohn, P.M., Hoberman, H., Teri, L., and Hautzinger, M. 1985. An integrative theory of depression. In *Theoretical issues in behavior therapy,* edited by S. Reiss, and R. Bootzin, 331–59. New York: Academic Press.

McLean, P.D., and Carr, S. 1989. The psychological treatment of unipolar depression: Progress and limitations. *Canadian Journal of Behavioural Science* 21: 452–69.

Monroe, S.M. 1988. The social environment and psychopathology. *Journal of Social and Personal Relationships* 5: 347–66.

Nolen-Hoeksema, S. 1987. Sex differences in unipolar depression: Evidence and theory. *Psychological Bulletin* 101: 259–82.

Oatley, K., and Bolton, W. 1985. A social-cognitive theory of depression in reaction to life events. *Psychological Review* 92: 372–88.

Robins, C.J. 1990. Congruence of personality and life events in depression. *Journal of Abnormal Psychology* 99: 393–97.

Robins, C.J., and Block, P. 1989. Cognitive theories of depression viewed from a diathesis-stress perspective: Evaluations of the models of Beck and of Abramson, Seligman, and Teasdale. *Cognitive Therapy and Research* 13: 297–313.

Robinson, L.A., Berman, J.S., and Neimeyer, R.A. 1990. Psychotherapy for the treatment of depression: A comprehensive review of controlled outcome research. *Psychological Bulletin* 108: 30–49.

Safran, J.D., and Segal, Z.V. 1990. *Interpersonal process in cognitive therapy.* New York: Basic Books.

Sartorius, N. 1978. Depressive disorders, a major public health problem. In *Mood disorders: The world's major public health problem* edited by F.J. Ayd, and I.J. Taylor, 1–8. Baltimore: Ayd Medical Communications.

Segal, Z.V., Shaw, B.F., and Vella, D.D. 1989. Life stress and depression: A test of the congruency hypothesis for life event content and depressive subtype. *Canadian Journal of Behavioural Science* 21: 389–400.

Shrout, P.E., Link, B.G., Dohrenwend, B.P., Skodol, A.E., Stueve, A., and Mirotznik, J. 1989. Characterizing life events as risk factors for depression: The role of fateful loss events. *Journal of Abnormal Psychology* 98: 460–67.

CHAPTER TWO

Childhood Depression

JAN E. FLEMING AND
DAVID R. OFFORD

Over a decade ago, knowledge concerning childhood depression was such that a journal editor felt called upon to preface a publication about childhood depression with the following cautionary statement: "The Editor feels it necessary to stress extreme caution (1) in identifying any child as having a depressive illness and (2) in prescribing any medication for such a disorder" (Weinberg et al. 1973; 1065). This statement was justifiable at the time, given the paucity of carefully designed studies dealing with depressed children. Since then, the field of childhood depression has come into its own, and, today, it is supported by a vast body of knowledge. The present chapter will attempt to review critically the literature on childhood depression in the following six areas: diagnosis, assessment, epidemiology, etiological/risk factors, clinical course/outcome, and treatment approaches. Most of the studies reviewed were generated from a computer search of the literature on childhood depression since 1980. However, additional selective reference is made to papers presented at scientific meetings, unpublished manuscripts, and papers published before 1980.*

Because adolescent depression is covered in another chapter of this book, we only reviewed studies that included preadolescents. Note particularly that the topic of childhood bipolar disorder has not been examined.

*One chapter author, J.E. Fleming, was supported by an Ontario Mental Health Foundation Research Fellowship.

DIAGNOSIS

An adequate classification system for childhood depressive disorders is a prerequisite for any investigation of these disorders, particularly for studies that deal with etiology, prognosis and treatment of the condition. The system adopted must be sufficiently reliable to ensure that it can be used in a uniform way by most investigators; otherwise, scientific communication concerning these conditions would be impossible. In addition, the classification system must be both valid and useful, capable of conveying information not only about the symptoms of the children in question, but about the etiology, natural history, or response to treatment of their disorder.

The criteria from adult diagnostic systems such as the Research Diagnostic Criteria (RDC) (Spitzer et al. 1978), the *Diagnostic and Statistical Manual of Mental Disorders–Third Edition* (DSM-III) (American Psychiatric Association 1980), or *Diagnostic and Statistical Manual of Mental Disorders–Third Edition, revised* (DSM-III-R) (American Psychiatric Association 1987) are becoming firmly entrenched in the diagnosis of affective disorders in children. Witness the fact that the majority of studies reviewed in this chapter used these tools. For the most part, too, these studies have found that the adult systems are reliable, although the most recently introduced diagnostic system, DSM-III-R, allows three modifications of its adult criteria for children and adolescents' depressive disorders. That is, for a major depressive episode and dysthymia, an irritable mood can be substituted for a depressed mood; for a dysthymic disorder, a duration of one year instead of two years is possible; and for a major depressive episode, the failure to make expected weight gains can be substituted for weight loss or anorexia. A number of additional descriptive statements are included under "age-specific features" as well: (1) that prepubertal depressed children frequently have somatic complaints, psychomotor agitation, and mood-congruent hallucinations; and (2) that adolescent depression may be accompanied by "negativistic or frankly antisocial behavior and use of alcohol or illicit drugs"; "feelings of wanting to leave home or of not being understood and approved of," as well as "restlessness, grouchiness, and aggression"; "sulkiness, a reluctance to cooperate in family ventures, and withdrawal from social activities, with retreat to one's room"; "school difficulties"; and "inattention to personal appearance and increased emotionality, with particular sensitivity to rejection in love relationships" (American Psychiatric Association 1987 220). There is, thus, an acknowledgement of age-specific differences, although they have not been considered important enough to incorporate into the diagnostic criteria.

Nevertheless, and despite the widespread usage of adult diagnostic systems, there is controversy. The concern is that the application of adult criteria to children does not take into account possible developmental differences in the phenomenology of depression in children (Carlson and Garber 1986; Garber 1984; Rutter 1986). For example, Rutter (1986), who commented on the paucity of data available concerning the development of children's social cognitions, self-perceptions, and ability to experience depressive affects, concluded that "perhaps the most basic need of all is to determine how the manifestations of depression vary with age" (508). On the other hand, four years earlier, Puig-Antich (1982b) had already concluded that the research evidence suggests no marked developmental changes in depressive symptoms after age six or seven. Several recent studies have helped to shed some light on this controversial matter. Two studies of clinical samples found depressed children and adolescents to be very similar symptomatically (Mitchell et al. 1988; Ryan et al. 1987), although one study did find enough differences between the age groups to suggest that "some minor age-dependent changes in the diagnostic criteria may be justified in the future" (Ryan et al. 1987, 859). Carlson and Kashani (1988), in their comparison of three samples of depressed subjects spanning the age range from preschoolers to adults (including the sample of Ryan et al. above), also concluded that "the basic symptom picture of serious depressive disorder was relatively unchanged regardless of age" (1225). On the other hand, based on their analyses of parent- and child-rated behaviour and depression checklists, Weiss and Weisz (1988) have concluded that important differences may exist between childhood and adolescent depression.

Although there seems to be some consensus among investigators that age-specific manifestations of depression do exist, the question remains as to whether these differences are sufficiently significant to warrant changes in the current diagnostic systems, changes that would have to be shown to improve the validity of the current categories of depression used for children. According to a preliminary report from the group working on the revision of child psychiatric diagnoses for the *Diagnostic and Statistical Manual of Mental Disorders–Fourth Edition* (DSM-IV), age specific criteria for mood disorders are not required (Shaffer et al. 1989).

ASSESSMENT

The issue of diagnosis, or classification, is closely tied to the strategies used to assess the presence of disorders. And assessment, in turn, is very much a matter of the available instrumentation. In the area of childhood depression, it is assessment that has perhaps generated the most attention and research to date. Indeed, assessment techniques in childhood depression have been the subject of several recent reviews (for example Costello 1986; Costello and Angold 1988; Edelbrock and Costello 1984; Kazdin 1981; Kazdin and Petti 1982; Kovacs 1980–1981) that reported, in depth, the psychometric properties of the available depression scales and diagnostic interviews. Unlike the assessment of depression in adults, where self-report is often the only and most valid source of information, assessment of depression in children is complicated by the use of multiple, often conflicting, sources of information. In this section, we briefly review the assessment measures before discussing the issue of informant variance. Check-lists and interview measures are described separately.

Check-lists

PARENT- AND CHILD-RATED. The parent- or child-rated check-lists (at times both) that measure childhood depression are described in Table 1. In their recent review of scales assessing child and adolescent depression, Costello and Angold (1988) pointed out that scales should be evaluated according to the purpose they were meant for, which is usually either to count symptoms or to differentiate among groups of normal, depressed, and nondepressed patients. In the first instance, "content validity" is important; in the second instance "criterion-related validity" is the issue. Apropos content validity, Costello and Angold note that the available scales vary considerably, with the Children's Depression Inventory (CDI) (Kovacs 1985a) and the Mood and Feelings Questionnaire (MFQ) (Costello and Angold 1988) providing the most comprehensive coverage of the DSM-III-R criteria for depression. Apropos criterion validity, they state that only sparse data are available for most of the scales and that when available, they are often conflicting, owing to lack of consistency in defining the criteria for a "case" of depression. Nevertheless, it appears that most data pertaining to criterion validity, although conflicting, are available for the CDI (Carey et al. 1987; Doerfler et al. 1988; Knight et al. 1988), and that data for the MFQ are sparse but promising (Costello and Angold 1988).

PEER-RATED. The Peer Nomination Inventory of Depression (PNID) (Lefkowitz and Tesiny 1980) is a twenty-item questionnaire that asks schoolchildren to identify their classmates who are best described by each item. The score for any given child is the sum of the item scores, as determined by the sum of the child's nominations for each item divided by the number of classmates. The PNID has potential usefulness as an adjunct in epidemiological studies and as a tool for predicting clinical outcome (Hoier and Kerr 1988).

TEACHER-RATED. Although teachers have been used as sources of information in several studies of childhood depression, the instruments they used to assess depression have varied considerably and, for the most part, were never designed specifically to measure depression (Hoier and Kerr 1988). For example, the Teacher Nomination Inventory for Depression (TNID), which was modified from the PNID, lacks any reported psychometric properties (Hoier and Kerr

Table 1
Parent- and child-rated scales for assessing childhood depression

Scale	Age range	No. of items	Scoring	Time frame	Rated by
Children's Depression Inventory (CDI) (Kovacs 1985a)	7-17	27	3-point scale	Past 2 weeks	Child/ parent
Short CDI (SCDI) (Kovacs and Beck 1977)	7-17	13	4-point scale	Past week	Child
Children's Depression Scale (CDS) (Lang & Tisher 1978; Rotundo and Hensley 1985)	9-16	66	5-point scale	Past week	Child/ parent
Center for Epidemiologic Studies – Depression Scale for Children (CES-DC) (Weissman et al. 1980)	6-17	20	4-point scale	Past week	Child/ parent
Depression Self-Rating Scale for Children (DSRSC) (Birleson 1981)	8-14	18	3-point scale	Past week	Child
Children's Depression Rating Scale (Joshi et al. 1987)	5-13	38	5-point scale	Not stated	Child
Mood and Feelings Questionnaire (MFQ) (Costello and Angold 1988)	8-17	31 (long form); 11 (short form)	3-point scale	Past 2 weeks	Child/ parent
Personality Inventory for Children - Depression Scale (PIC-D) (Wirt et al. 1977)	3-16	46	True-false	Not stated	Parent

1988). Also, even though several studies did develop their own global rating scales of depression for teachers, the psychometric properties of these scales, like the TNID, were never stated (Blumberg and Izard 1986; Reynolds et al. 1985; Sacco and Graves 1985). Inasmuch as teacher data have obviously not been given priority in assessing childhood depression, this valuable source of information has been vastly underused. This situation can only be remedied with the development of valid and reliable measures of teacher-rated depression. Apparently, the development of a structured teacher interview is underway (Hoier and Kerr 1988).

Interview Measures

These instruments require a direct interview of the child or other informant by an individual trained in the use of the particular interview. Two interview measures were designed specifically to assess depression in children. The first, the Bellevue Index of Depression (BID) (Petti 1978) was developed from the operational criteria of Weinberg et al. (1973) and later revised by Kazdin et al. (1983a,b). The second, the revised Children's Depression Rating Scale (CDRS-R) (Poznanski et al. 1985) is a clinician-administered interview for use with six- to twelve-year-olds. Although it was not meant as a diagnostic tool, researchers have reported that a score of forty or more suggests the presence of a major depressive disorder (Poznanski et al. 1985). The CDRS-R was based on the Hamilton Psychiatric Rating Scale for Depression (Hamilton 1960), which is often used in drug efficacy studies of adult patients as a quantitative measure of change in depressive symptomatology. Both the CDRS-R and its earlier version, the CDRS (Poznanski et al. 1979), have been used in studies of tricyclic antidepressants in children (Preskorn et al. 1987; Geller et al. 1986); they are probably most valuable as measures of severity of depressive symptoms.

Interview measures that include, but are not specific for, affective disorders are described in Table 2. Comprehensive reviews of their uses and psychometric properties are available elsewhere (Edelbrock and Costello 1984; Gutterman et al. 1987). Although these instruments have come a long way in helping to reduce information variance in the diagnostic assessment of children and adolescents, at least five major issues remain unresolved. First, given that most of the instruments are periodically revised to improve psychometric deficiencies and incorporate changes to diagnostic criteria, insufficient reliability and validity data have been accumulated for these interviews. Second, there is no accepted "gold standard" against which to assess the validity of a structured interview. Third, evidence exists that structured interviews are unreliable with younger children (Edelbrock et al. 1985; Shaffer et al. 1987). Fourth, parents and their children disagree about the presence of symptoms in the children (see next section) and, to date, there is no mutually satisfactory way of handling these discrepancies. Fifth, children who meet criteria for depressive disorders based on structured interviews are not necessarily considered as "cases" of depression. Information with regard to various forms of social and academic impairment and the perceived need for treatment, for example, are used in addition to diagnostic criteria, to determine "caseness." But, because this is not done in a consistent way across studies (especially epidemiological studies), the comparability of the findings is jeopardized (Fleming and Offord 1990).

Finally, we agree with the conclusion of Gutterman and colleagues, who state: "Although psychiatric research among children and adolescents has been enriched by diversity among the available interview schedules, it has also been encumbered by lack of a clear rationale for many of these options ... Consolidation of available instruments into fewer but better choices is a worthy goal" (Gutterman et al. 1987, 629).

Table 2
Structured diagnostic interviews that yield DSM-III depressive diagnoses

Instrument*	Type	Age range	Clinical judgment required	Time frame
Children's Assessment Scale (CAS) (Hodges et al. 1982)	Semi-structured	7–12†	Yes	Present
Diagnostic Interview for Children and Adolescents (DICA) (Herjanic et al. 1975)	Highly structured	6–17	No	Present, past
Diagnostic Interview Schedule for Children (DISC) (Costello et al. 1984)	Highly structured	6–18	No	Present, past 6 months, past year
Interview Schedule for Children (ISC) (Kovacs 1982)	Semi-structured	8–17	Yes	Present, past 6 months
Schedule for Affective Disorders and Schizophrenia in School-Aged Children (Kiddie-SADS) (Puig-Antich and Chambers 1978; Puig-Antich et al. 1980)	Semi-structured	6–17	Yes	Separate forms for present and lifetime

* Parent and child versions are available for all instruments except the Kiddie-SADS which uses the same version for parent and child.
† An adolescent version is also available (Hodges et al, 1987)

Informant Variance

Disagreement among raters, or "informant variance," is pervasive in the assessment of childhood depression and childhood psychiatric disorder in general (Offord et al. 1989). Indeed, disagreement occurs whether check-lists or interview measures are used. Table 3 summarizes the results of studies that have examined the correlation between parent- and child-rated depression in the child via several different check-lists. In both patient and non-patient samples, whether one uses the same or different measures in the child and parent, the correlations are either nonsignificant or slightly significant, except for two studies (Knight et al. 1988; Wierzbicki 1987).

Studies that have included teacher-rated depression scales have all been carried out on non-patient samples (see Table 4). In two particular studies, either a nonsignificant correlation between teacher and child ratings (Saylor et al. 1984) or a significant negative correlation (Sacco and Graves 1985), was found; yet two other studies found significant, positive teacher-child correlations (Reynolds et al. 1985; Wierzbicki 1987). Interestingly, teacher-peer and teacher-parent correlations were not only significant in all studies,

Table 3
Correlations between parent- and child-rated depression scales in children from patient and nonpatient samples

Study	N	Age/ grade(s)	Status	Parent measure(s)*	Child measure(s)	Correlations between parent and child measures
Kazdin 1983a	120	7-13	Inpatients	CDI	CDI	(Mother) n.s.† (Father) .4 $p<.001$ (Mother and father)
1983b	104	5-13	Inpatients	CDI	CDI	n.s.
				DS-CL	DS-CL	n.s.
Kazdin 1987	185	7-12	Inpatients	CDI	CDI	n.s.
				CDS	CDS	n.s.
Knight et al. 1988	57	8-12	Outpatients and non-patients	CDI	CDI	.49, $p<.001$
				CDS	CDS	.59‡, $p<.001$
Leon et al 1980	138	7-12	Nonpatients	PIC-D	CDI	.33, $p<.05$
Moretti et al. 1985	60	8-17	In and outpatients	CDS	CDS	.35, $p<.05$
Reynolds et al. 1985	166	Grades 3-6	Nonpatients	CDI	CDI	(Mother) .26, $p<.01$ (Father) n.s.
				CDS	CDS	(Mother) .26, $p<.01$ (Father) n.s.
Stavrakaki et al. 1987a, b	130	6-16	In and outpatients	CBCL-D	CDI	n.s.
Wierzbicki 1987 study 1	50	8-14	Nonpatients	CDI	CDI	(Time 1) .37, $p<.01$ (Time 2) .59, $p<.001$
study 2	96	6-16	Nonpatients	CDI	CDI	.66, $p<.001$
Weissman et al. 1980	28	6-18	Children of psychiatrically disturbed parents	CES-DC	CES-DC	n.s.

* CDI - Children's Depression Inventory; DS-CL - Diagnostic and Statistical Manual of Mental Disorders - Third edition symptom checklist; CDS - Children's Depression Scale, except for Reynolds et al. 1985, where CDS is Child Depression Scale; PIC-D - Depression scale of the Personality Inventory for Children; CBCL-D - Depression factor based on DSM-III items from the Child Behavior Checklist; CES-DC - Center for Epidemiologic Studies - Depression Scale for Children
† n.s.- a non-significant correlation was obtained
‡ for the Total Depression subscale; significant correlations were also obtained for all other subscales except "Death" subscale

but also generally higher than reported teacher-child and parent-child correlations.

Studies using interview measures have also shown substantial rater disagreement. Using the BID-R, Kazdin et al. (1983a) found significant but small correlations between parent and child total symptom scores for their inpatient sample. Mokros et al. (1987) found similar significant but small correlations between parent and child versions of the CDRS-R in both nonpatient and patient samples. They also examined parent-child agreement on specific items and found mostly low kappa values, ranging from -.09 to .48. Results of studies using the Diagnostic Interview for Children and Adolescents (DICA), the Diagnostic Interview Schedule for Children (DISC), and the Schedule for Affective Disorders and Schizophrenia in School-Aged Children (K-SADS) are summarized in Table 5. It can be seen that the studies differed in terms of sample characteristics, parent(s) interviewed, and interviewer strategy (same or different interviewer(s) for the parent and child). Despite these important differences, the finding of low parent-child agreement is remarkably consistent, except for one study that used the DICA (Welner et al. 1987) and one that used the K-SADS (Orvaschel et al. 1982). Mother-father agreement was also low in the two studies that reported that information.

So far, attempts to understand the factors contributing to rater disagreement must be considered preliminary. In an exploratory study of children of U.S. Army personnel, Jensen et al. (1988b, c) found that interrater agreement on child psychopathology was affected by parents' gender and psychiatric symptoms, as well as by various child and family characteristics. Weissman et al (1987b) noted that findings regarding the effects of both the parent's sex and the child's age and sex on interrater agreement have been inconsistent across studies. The effect of parental depression on the rating of depression in children has aroused a great deal of interest as well, although the findings have conflicted: some studies found that depression in parents correlated positively with the parents' ratings of depression in their children (Friedlander et al. 1986; Jensen et al. 1988b; Moretti et al. 1985); others found the opposite (Ivens and Rehm 1988; Kashani et al. 1985). Finally, it has been hypothesized that parents are less aware of (or perhaps bothered by) their children's internal feelings and symptoms than their overt behaviours and are thus less likely than their children to report depression or anxiety symptoms (for example, Edelbrock et al. 1986; Kashani et al. 1985). This hypothesis is supported by the fairly consistent finding that children report more of their own depressive symptoms and diagnoses than their parents report about them (Angold et al. 1987; Edelbrock et al. 1986; Herjanic and Reich 1982; Ivens and Rehm 1988; Kashani et al. 1985; Reich et al. 1982; Weissman 1987). In the only two community studies to report on this issue, McCracken (1987) found more child reports of major depression in nine-year-olds and more parental reports of dysthymic disorder, while

Table 4
Correlations between teacher-rated and self-, parent-, or peer-rated depression scales in children from patient and nonpatient samples

Study	N	Age/ grade	Teacher measure*	Other measure(s)† (source)	Correlations with teacher measure
Sacco and Graves 1985	62	9-11	7-point global scale	CDI(self)	-.27, $p<.004$ (for vegetative symptoms only)
Saylor et al. 1984	133	Grades 2-8	TNID	CDI(self) PNID(peer)	n.s. .48, $p<.001$
Reynolds et al. 1985	166	Grades 3-6	5-point global scale	CDI(self) CDS(self) PIC-D(mother) PIC-D(father)	.38, $p<.001$ .33, $p<.001$ .51, $p<.001$ .34, $p<.01$
Wierzbicki 1987	72	6-16	CDRS	CDI(self) CDI(parent)	.43, $p<.01$ .64, $p<.001$

*TNID = Teacher Nomination Inventory for Depression; CDRS = Children's Depression Rating Scale
†CDI = Children's Depression Inventory; PNID = Peer Nomination Inventory for Depression;
CDS = Child Depression Scale (NOT Children's Depression Scale); PIC-D = Personality Inventory for Children - Depression Scale

Fleming et al. (1989) found that twelve- to sixteen-year-olds reported more depression about themselves than did their parents. Two more factors still to be considered in future studies of interrater agreement are community (or clinic) status and type of depressive disorder.

Although the phenomenon of rater disagreement clearly exists, it is often the practice, for research purposes, to combine information from all available sources so as to arrive at a "best estimate" diagnosis. This method presumes, however, that childhood psychiatric disorder is a unitary phenomenon, the study of which is hampered by lack of knowledge about the best way to integrate discrepant information from multiple sources. Offord et al. (1989) have presented compelling evidence suggesting that it may be more useful to consider childhood psychiatric disorders as source specific. In their community survey of four childhood psychiatric disorders (see Epidemiology), they found that certain sociodemographic, family and child correlates of disorders studied differed in important ways as a function of the identifying source. They recommend that future research focus on validation of source-specific disorders by examining differences in etiology, family history, natural history and response to treatment.

Table 5

Agreement by source on depressive diagnoses using structured diagnostic interviews

Instrument	N	Age(s)	Status of children	Parent(s) interviewed	Same or different interviewer(s) for parent and child	Kappa for parent - child or mother-father agreement on major depressive disorder (unless otherwise indicated)
DICA						
Kashani et al. 1985	50	7-17	Children of affectively ill parents	Mostly mothers	Same	-.07
Reich et al. 1982	307	6-16	Pediatric and psychiatric outpatients	Mothers	Different	.36(PD)†
Sylvester et al. 1987	91	7-17	Children of psychiatrically disturbed or normal parents	Mothers and fathers	Different	.11
						.31 (mother vs father)
Welner et al. 1987	84	7-17	Psychiatric outpatients	Mothers	Different	.63†
DISC						
Edelbrock et al. 1986	299	6-18	Psychiatric outpatients	Mostly mothers	Different	.28‡
McCracken 1987	149	9	Nonpatients	Mostly mothers	Different	.27
						.49(DD)§
K-SADS						
Ivens and Rehm 1985	38	8-12	Children attending a child guidance centre	Mothers and fathers	Different	-.02 (child vs father)
						.05 (child vs mother)
						.17 (mother vs father)
Orvaschel et al. 1982	17	6-11	Psychiatric outpatients	Mothers	Same	.66‖
Weissman et al. 1987b	220	6-23	Children of affectively disturbed and normal parents	Mostly mothers	Same	.39 (for children <age 13)
						.47 (for children 13-18)
						.11 (for children 19-23)

* PD - possible depression (Feighner criteria); also, an earlier version of the DICA was used

† "Probable" affective disorder was included (i.e. one symptom lacking for "definite" disorder or duration uncertain)

‡ correlation between parent- and child-rated total symptom depression score (kappa not reported)

§ DD - dysthymic disorder

‖ average kappa value for 14 individual depression symptoms (range: .21 - 1.0)

Note: DICA = Diagnostic Interview for children and adolescents; DISC = Diagnostic Interview Schedule for Children; K-SADS = Schedule for Affective Disorders and

EPIDEMIOLOGY

This section will cover three topics: the community prevalence of childhood depression, sex differences in prevalence rates, and comorbidity.

Community Prevalence Studies

Table 6 outlines prevalence studies that used interview techniques and included only younger children (up to age twelve). It can be seen that the community prevalence of major depression in these studies ranged from 0.5 per cent to 2.7 per cent (child-reported), whereas the prevalence of dysthymic disorder ranged from 1.3 per cent (child-reported) to 4.0 per cent (parent-reported). Furthermore, although all the studies used RDC or DSM-III criteria to diagnose depression, they used diverse methods internally to combine information from sources and to define a "case" of depression. Only McCracken (1987) reported prevalence rates separately by source.

Self-report scales have generally not been used in prevalence studies. One exception was a Canadian study in which 112 fifth-grade children were screened for depression using the CDI (Stavrakaki et al. 1987c). Using a cutoff score of nineteen or more on the CDI, 7 per cent of the children were classified as depressed. These children were then interviewed using the DICA, and 72-per-cent concordance was found between the DICA and the CDI. Because a randomly selected group of children not identified by the CDI were not interviewed with the DICA, it was impossible to assess the sensitivity and specificity of the CDI as a screening measure; however, this work is now underway (Stavrakaki et al. 1987c). In an American sample of 486 fourth-, fifth- and sixth-grade students, almost twice as many children (12.6%) as in the Canadian sample (7%) scored nineteen or higher on the CDI (Mullins et al. 1985). Differences in sample characteristics such as age, sex and socioeconomic status (SES) distribution may account for this discrepancy.

Table 7 describes four community surveys of child psychiatric disorders that included children aged four to eighteen years of age. Because the methodology of these studies varied considerably, it is described in more detail below. In the first study, conducted in Puerto Rico, psychiatrists employed clinical judgment to combine information obtained from children and their parents (using the DISC) to arrive at DSM-III diagnoses (Bird et al. 1988). To be considered a "definite" case, a child had to meet DSM-III criteria for one or more disorders and be functionally impaired as measured by the psychiatrist-administered Children's Global Assessment Scale (CGAS). "Possible" cases met the same criteria but scored as "less functionally impaired." Although the sample was too small to provide separate prevalence estimates by age and sex, multiple regression analyses did find only age to be sig-

Table 6
Community prevalence studies of depression in preadolescent children

Study (location)	N	Age	Method of assessment	Source(s)	Prevalence (sources combined except where indicated as separate)	Percentage of depression MDD*	DD*	Significant sex effect
Anderson et al. (1987) (New Zealand)	792	11	DISC†	Child parent‡ teacher‡	12-month	.5	1.7	Not stated
McCracken (1987) (USA-midwest)	149	9	DISC†	Child parent	Current child	2.7	1.3	Not stated
					Current parent	1.3	4.0	Not stated
Kashani et al (1983) (New Zealand)	641	9	K-SADS-E§	Child parent‡ teacher‡	Current	1.8	—	None
Kashani and Simonds (1979) (Missouri)	103	7-12	Clinical interview	Child parent	Current	1.9	—	Not stated

* MDD = major depressive disorder; DD = dysthymic disorder

† DISC = Diagnostic Interview for Children

‡ Checklist information only

§ K-SADS-E = Schedule for Affective Disorders and Schizophrenia in School-Aged Children.

Table 7
Community prevalence studies of depression in children and adolescents

Study (location)	N	Age range	Instruments	Source(s)	Prevalence of depression (%)
Bird et al. (1988) (Puerto Rico)	777	4-16	DISC CGAS*	Parent, self	*Major depression/dysthymia (6 months)* 5.9
Kashani et al. (1989) (USA-midwest)	210	8,12,17	CAS	Parent, self	*Major depression (current)* Parent Self age 8,12 0.7 1.4 age 17 2.9 5.7
Velez et al. (1989) (New York state)	776	9-18	DISC	Parent, self	*Major depression (current)* age 9-12 2.5 age 13-18 3.7
Fleming et al. (1989) (Ontario)	2852	6-16	SDI†	Parent, teacher‡ self§	*"DSM-III-like" major depression (6 months, sources combined)* High DC‖ Med DC‖ Low DC‖ age 6-11 0.6 2.7 17.5 age 12-16 1.8 7.8 43.9

* cgas = Clinical Global Assessment Scale

† sdi = Survey Diagnostic Instrument

‡ for 6- to 11-year-olds only

§ for 12- to 16-year-olds only

‖ dc = Diagnostic Certainty: high, med (medium), low

nificantly associated with depression. The association was strongest for the twelve- to sixteen-year-olds.

In the second study, conducted in the U.S. midwest, clinically experienced doctoral students administered a structured interview to parents and children separately to arrive at DSM-III diagnoses based on symptom counts alone. No significant age or gender differences were found in the prevalence rates (Kashani et al. 1989).

In the New York state study, children and their parents were assessed by different lay interviewers (Velez et al. 1989). Computer algorithms gave parent and child responses equal weight, combining them at the symptom level to determine DSM-III-R diagnoses. Normative responses to a depression scale based on DISC items were used in determining "caseness." Major depression was found to be more common in girls than boys in the older age group.

In the Ontario study, 1,869 families, including 3,294 children aged four to sixteen were interviewed to determine the prevalence of four childhood psychiatric disorders: conduct disorder, hyperactivity, emotional disorder, and somatization (Boyle et al. 1987). The Child Behavior Checklist (Achenbach and Edelbrock 1983) furnished the basic pool of items used to measure the diagnostic criteria (based on DSM-III) with some additional items generated to describe each criterion adequately. The resulting check-list was termed the Survey Diagnostic Instrument (SDI) and separate versions were completed by parents, teachers, and youths aged twelve to sixteen. Details of the measurement and prevalence of the four disorders are provided elsewhere (Boyle et al. 1987; Offord et al. 1987). Although the category "emotional disorder" included symptoms of anxiety and depression, a separate measure of depression was not originally included. The SDI, however, does measure all the symptoms required for a DSM-III diagnosis of major depression. A depression measure was thus devised that required a report of depressed mood, plus four or more additional depressive symptoms (Fleming et al. 1989). Diagnostic certainty (DC) was manipulated by varying the level of symptom severity required; three levels of certainty (high, medium, and low) resulted, with a high DC requiring the greatest degree of symptom severity and a low DC requiring the least degree of symptom severity. Tables 7 and 8 summarize the prevalence rates of depression in six- to sixteen-year-olds, with sources both combined and separated. Prevalence rates were seen to decrease as DC increases. Rater disagreement was high, however, with only a few cases identified by both sources (Table 8). For six- to eleven-year-olds, teachers identified fewer depressed children than did parents in the low DC group, more depressed children than did parents in the medium DC group, and equal numbers in the high DC group. To our knowledge, this is the first community survey to report a separate teacher-identified prevalence rate. There was also a significant effect of age for all three levels of DC, with higher rates in the adolescent group. Prevalence rates varied significantly by sex only for those adolescents in the low DC group, with a higher rate for females than males. To assess the concurrent validity of the three levels of DC, it would have been helpful to have had interview measures of depression in the children. Because this step was not feasible, the following external validators were examined: use of mental health or social services (MH/SS), comorbidity, parent's perception that the child needs professional help, poor school performance, and problems getting along with others. The findings for these variables are presented in Table 8, where it can be seen that the greater the degree of DC, the more likely the child was to have had the external validator. Thus was support lent to the validity of these levels of DC. Furthermore, the overall, combined prevalence rates for six- to eleven-year-olds in the high and medium DC groups (0.6 and 2.7 %, respectively) fall within the range of rates found in the other reported studies, whereas the rate of 17.5 per cent for the low DC group does not. Considering all the evidence, it is most likely that the prevalence of major depression in six- to eleven-year-olds in Ontario is between 0.6 and 2.7 per cent.

In a recent review, Fleming and Offord (1990) conclude that, because of deficiencies and inconsistencies in the methodologies of the studies reviewed, the current literature cannot provide a firm answer to the question of degree of prevalence of childhood and adolescent depression in the general population. They point to the need for reliable and valid instruments (with standardized methods of administration) for measuring depression and for determining "caseness" (including handling of data from multiple sources), as well as to the need for carefully chosen samples, representative of the general population of children and adolescents.

Sex Differences in Prevalence Rates

In adults, depression has been found to be more common in women than in men (Weissman and Klerman 1977; Weissman et al. 1984), although this discrepancy apparently lessens in old age (Jorm 1987). The many theories, including biological and psychosocial, that have been advanced to explain the female preponderance of depression are reviewed by Weissman and Klerman (1977).

Community prevalence studies of preadolescent depression have found either no sex effect (Bird et al. 1988; Fleming et al. 1989; Kashani et al. 1983) or a greater prevalence of depression in boys than in girls (see Table 6). Anderson et al. (1987), who found an approximate male to female ratio of 5:1, concluded that the higher number of depressed boys reflected this age group's high comorbidity of depression with externalizing disorders, such disorders being more prevalent in boys than girls.

Table 8

Depression in the Ontario Child Health Study: Prevalence and measurement validators

a. Prevalence (per 100) by source, age and level of diagnostic certainty

Source*	Level of Diagnostic Certainty					
	High		Medium		Low	
	Age 6-11	Age 12-16	Age 6-11	Age 12-16	Age 6-11	Age 12-16
Parent	0.3	0.2	0.5	1.0	9.0	5.0
Teacher or self	0.3	1.3	2.2	6.4	7.4	30.3
Both	0	0	0.1	0.2	1.8	8.5

*Teacher or self = teacher for 6- to 11-year-olds; self for 12- to 16-year-olds

Both = parent *and* teacher or self

b. External validators of the depression measure

External validator	Per cent of Depressed Children Scoring Positive at Each Level of Diagnostic Certainty (DC)		
	High DC	Medium DC	Low DC
Used MH/SS in last 6 months*	21.5	12.7	9.3
More than one disorder†	95.8	63.2	34.9
Needs professional help (parent report)	33.3	31.4	15.0
Poor school performance	29.2	20.0	10.3
Problems getting along with others	66.7	40.9	17.0

*MH/SS = mental health or social service

†disorder = conduct disorder, hyperactivity, emotional disorder or somatization (in 12- to 16-year-olds)

As for sex differences in adolescent depression, they are beyond the scope of this chapter. Nevertheless, it should be pointed out that the finding of a greater prevalence of depression in adolescent girls than boys has not been consistent across all studies (see Fleming and Offord 1990; Fleming et al. 1989). Thus, because we know that depression is more prevalent in adult women than men, the challenge will be to determine the actual age of onset of this sex effect, as well as the factors, such as those associated with puberty, related to its onset.

Comorbidity

In a large epidemiological survey of adult psychiatric disorders, the presence of major depression was found to increase significantly the risk of having another disorder (Boyd et al. 1984). Childhood depression, moreover, is associated with a high degree of comorbidity. Several of the community prevalence studies already discussed have addressed the issue of comorbidity. For example, Anderson et al. (1987) found that 79 per cent of their depressed sample had coexisting disorders. Corresponding percentages for the remaining studies are 68 per cent (Bird et al. 1988), 63.2 per cent and 95.8 per cent for the medium- and high-DC groups, respectively (Fleming et al. 1989); and 100 per cent (McCracken 1987). Much as was found in community studies, Alessi and Magen (1988) found significant comorbidity with depression in their inpatient sample; that is, every child with a depressive disorder had at least one coexisting disorder and 52 per cent had three or more coexisting disorders. The most common overlapping disorders in all the above studies were anxiety, attention deficit, and conduct disorders. These three comorbid disorders are discussed separately below.

ANXIETY DISORDERS. A vast literature exists on the relationship between depression and anxiety in adults, including two recent books on the subject that include chapters dealing with the childhood aspects of this relationship (Kendall and Watson 1989; Maser and Cloninger 1990).

Kovacs et al. (1989), in their longitudinal study of depressive disorders in referred children, found that 41 per cent of their depressed children had a comorbid anxiety disorder, mostly related to separation anxiety. They also found that their subjects had a lifetime risk (.47) of developing an anxiety disorder by age eighteen, and that the comorbid anxiety did not affect the length of an episode of primary major depression. Interestingly, Puig-Antich et al. (1987) found that the presence of separation anxiety did not influence the response to imipramine in children with major depressive disorder (see Treatment Approaches). Puig-Antich and Rabinovich (1986) had earlier determined that separation anxiety had no influence on either the psychobiological correlates of prepubertal depression or the familial aggregation of major depression in relatives of depressed children.

Strauss et al. (1988), in a study of children referred to an anxiety disorders clinic, found that children with coexisting anxiety and depression were more likely than children with pure anxiety to be older, have more severe anxiety symptomatology, and have more diagnoses of obsessive-compulsive disorder and agoraphobia. In their sample of chronic school refusers, Bernstein and Garfinkel (1986) found that 69 per cent of the sample had a depressive disorder, 62 per cent had an anxiety disorder, and 50 per cent had both.

In terms of severity of anxiety and depressive symptoms, the children with coexisting anxiety and depressive disorders were similar to children with depression alone; they also scored higher on these measures than the children with anxiety alone. Finally, Mitchell et al. (1988) found more severe depressive symptomatology in those young people, especially adolescents, who had combined depression and separation anxiety rather than depression alone.

In summary, evidence to date indicates that children with coexisting anxiety and depressive disorders suffer more severe anxiety symptoms than do anxious children without depression; they also may or may not suffer more severe depressive symptoms than depressed children without anxiety. In addition, the presence of anxiety does not seem to influence recovery rate from a depressive episode in depressed children, nor their long-term outcome, response to imipramine, family history of affective illness, or biological correlates. Together, this evidence suggests that depression coexisting with an anxiety disorder is not likely to constitute a distinct subgroup of childhood depression.

ATTENTION DEFICIT DISORDER. The association between hyperactivity and depression in children has been noted for some time (Brumback and Weinberg 1977; Weinberg et al. 1973). Brown et al. (1988) found that children with attention deficit disorder (ADD) as well as their parents, scored higher on self-report measures of depression than normal controls and their parents. They concluded that this finding represented a "demoralization syndrome" in ADD children and their families. Another study found a significantly higher prevalence of past and current episodes of affective disorders in a group of boys with ADD than in a group of normal controls (Biederman et al. 1987; Munir et al. 1987). In addition, relatives of the ADD probands had higher rates of affective disorders than relatives of the normal controls. Surprisingly, relatives of probands with coexisting ADD and depression did not have higher rates of affective disorders than relatives of nondepressed ADD probands. Jensen et al. (1988a) have speculated, based on their findings of affective symptoms in children with ADD, that ADD children may suffer from a subclinical form of bipolar disorder and might benefit from treatment with antidepressant drugs.

CONDUCT DISORDER. As noted earlier, the DSM-III-R states that antisocial behaviour frequently accompanies adolescent depression. Other researchers have found antisocial behaviour to be common in both pre- and post-pubertal depressed children (Geller et al. 1985a; Mitchell et al. 1988; Ryan et al. 1987). Yet these findings conflict not only with regard to a sex effect for conduct disorder (CD) or antisocial behaviour in depressed children, but with regard to the temporal relationship between behavioural symptoms and depression. For example, whereas depressed girls and boys in some cases did not differ in number of conduct symptoms (Geller et al. 1985a; Kovacs et al. 1988), in other cases, there were more depressed boys with comorbid CD than girls (McGee and Williams 1988; Mitchell et al. 1988; Puig-Antich 1982a). Mitchell et al. (1988) also found that equal numbers of depressed adolescent males and females had comorbid CD. As for the temporal relationship, conduct symptoms have been found to both precede (Anderson et al. 1987; Marriage et al. 1986) and follow the depression (Geller et al. 1985a; Kovacs et al. 1988).

Two studies (see Clinical Course and Outcome) examined, longitudinally, the association between CD and depression. First, in their follow-up of a clinic sample, Kovacs et al. (1988) found that comorbid CD did not affect the length of either the depressive episode in children, or symptom-free intervals between episodes of major depression. They also found in children with childhood-onset depression a cumulative risk of .36 for the development of CD by age nineteen. Due to small numbers, their analyses were inadequate in terms of statistical power, and the results should therefore be considered "preliminary." Second, in their longitudinal community sample, McGee and Williams (1988) found a long-term association between antisocial behaviour and depression in boys only. As always, conflicting findings in the above studies can be attributed, in part, to differences in sampling and methodology.

As pointed out by Alessi and Magen (1988), disorders may coexist for three reasons: (1) a disorder may predispose to, or cause, the development of another; (2) disorders share a common diathesis; or (3) they co-occur by chance. At this point, because research into the association between affective and nonaffective disorders in childhood is in its infancy, there is little evidence to support any hypothesis over another. Future research must therefore address the extent to which pure and comorbid disorders differ in terms of etiology, course, natural history, and response to treatment. A careful assessment of the range of childhood psychiatric disorders in study samples will be essential.

ETIOLOGICAL OR RISK FACTORS

Risk factors are defined as those variables associated with an increased probability of disorder (Offord 1989). Such factors must predate the disorder and must plausibly and directly contribute to the occurrence of a particular disorder. Identification of etiological or risk factors for childhood depression, a necessary prerequisite for primary prevention, may provide valuable clues concerning how and why a disorder develops. This section summarizes the evidence for including each of the following variables as etiological or risk factors for depression in children: genetics, parental psychopathology, cognitive vulnerability, life events, socioeconomic status, and biological factors.

Genetics

In his review of the genetics of affective disorders, Gershon (1983) cites evidence from family studies that strongly supports a genetic contribution to affective illness. The majority of these studies examined the adult relatives of adult probands and, hence, strongly support a genetic component to adult affective illness. Similar studies of childhood depression are few in number.

Three small uncontrolled, and two larger controlled, studies examined the family histories of affectively ill children. In the first uncontrolled study, Puig-Antich (1980) assessed the relatives of twenty-six prepubertal major depressives. The lifetime morbidity risk for major depressive disorder in their first-degree relatives, older than sixteen years of age, was found to be higher than that reported for the relatives of adult probands, suggesting a higher genetic loading for prepubertal than for adult major depression. In the second study, Livingston et al. (1985) interviewed the families of twenty-three children, six to twelve years of age, who had previously been hospitalized for treatment of a depressive or anxiety disorder. Information was obtained from twenty-two first- and thirty-six second-degree relatives of eleven children with a depressive disorder. Seventy-two per cent of these relatives were given psychiatric diagnoses, mostly affective disorders and alcoholism. Because the findings were similar for the anxious children, the authors suggest the possibility of a familial association of affective and anxiety disorders. In the third uncontrolled study, Dwyer and Delong (1987) included only bipolar subjects age four to eighteen years of age, all of whom were outpatients. They evaluated 71 first-degree and 178 second-degree relatives of twenty probands via a structured family-history method. The existence of affective illness on one or both sides of the family was found for every proband. About 63 per cent of the parents of probands had a history of major affective disorder.

Only two studies have included control groups. Mitchell et al. (1989) administered the Schedule for Affective Disorders and Schizophrenia – Lifetime version (SADS-L) to most mothers and about half the fathers of eighty-seven depressed children and adolescents and thirty nondepressed psychiatric controls. Not only did they find a high lifetime occurrence of major depression in the mothers of both the depressed and control children, they also found that the mothers of the depressed children had significantly higher rates of anxiety and substance-use disorders than the mothers of the control group. There were no significant findings for fathers. Puig-Antich et al. (1989a) compared depressed children to both anxious and normal controls, assessing mostly mothers directly with the SADS-L and fathers and second-degree relatives indirectly with the Family History RDC method. Similar to the Mitchell et al. study, lifetime morbidity risks for major depression in the first- and second-degree relatives of children with major depression were not significantly higher than for children with anxiety disorders; however, they were higher than for normal controls. Rates of alcoholism, on the other hand, were significantly higher for the relatives of the depressed group than for members of either control groups. The findings from both these controlled studies raise questions about the specificity of transmission of psychiatric disorders, as well as about the nature of relationships among depressive, anxiety, and substance-abuse disorders.

Parental Psychopathology

Whereas the previous section dealt with studies of the relatives of depressed children, this section looks at the children of psychiatrically disordered parents. Strong evidence exists that childhood psychiatric disorders are associated with parental psychopathology (Rutter and Quinton 1984). Recently, interest has focused on disorder specificity; that is, on which parental disorder is associated with which disorder in the child. In particular, the literature on the children of affectively disturbed parents has been growing quickly.

The first comprehensive review of twenty-four studies in this area found consistently high rates of psychiatric impairment, especially affective disorders and symptoms, in the children of affectively ill parents (Beardslee et al. 1983). However, as noted by the authors, methodological shortcomings were abundant in these studies: they suffered from small numbers, absence of control groups, lack of follow-up of children at risk, and inconsistencies in assessing parental illness.

Since the publication of this 1983 review, several methodologically sound studies have been completed. The largest is a study by Weissman et al. (1987a) of 220 six- to twenty-three-year-old children of fifty-six probands with major depression and thirty-five normal controls. A best-estimate diagnostic procedure was used for both children and adults, combining information from structured interviews and several other sources. Weissman et al. found that the offspring of depressed parents had significantly higher rates of major depression (37.6%) and substance abuse (16.8%) than did the offspring of normal parents (24.2% and 7.9%). Nevertheless, they did not have significantly higher rates of attention deficit disorder, conduct disorder, or anxiety disorders, although they did have a significantly higher mean number of diagnoses (2.4) than children of normals (1.7), as well as significantly higher overall psychopathology scores. Another important finding was that the children's age of onset of depression was related both to the status of the proband parent (depressed versus normal) and to the age of onset of the parent's depression (Weissman et al. 1988). That is, those children whose parents' own depression had had an early onset (before age 20) experienced the earliest mean age of onset of depression (11 years), followed by those children whose parents had had a later age of onset of depression (20 years old or older) and whose own mean age of onset was 13.6 years; finally, the latest mean age of onset (16.7) was in children of normal parents. These findings suggest the possibility that prepubertal-onset depression has the highest genetic loading. But, as noted by the authors, this type of family study design cannot determine the relative influence of genetic versus environmental factors in explaining the increased risk of affective illness in children of depressed parents.

Rutter and Quinton (1984) suggested the possibility of three environmental mechanisms underlying the association between parental and child's psychiatric illness. The first involves direct effects of the parent's illness, such as hostility or aggression directed toward the child; the second involves indirect effects of the parent's illness, such as interference with parenting skills; the third involves effects derived from correlates of the parent's illness, rather than the illness itself, such as marital discord (which often precedes illness in the parent).

Several researchers have attempted to explore environmental mechanisms underlying the association between parental affective illness and depression in the child. For example, Hammen et al. (1987) hypothesized that the stress associated with having both an ill family member and a currently depressed parent (a depressed mood) may work independently of parental psychiatric status to increase the risk of psychiatric disorder in the child. To examine this hypothesis, they compared three groups of children: children of women with chronic or recurrent affective disorders, children of women with chronic medical illness, and children of normal women. Mothers were given lifetime diagnoses of psychiatric illness based on a structured interview; as well, their current mood was assessed by a self-report depression inventory. The rating of "lifetime depression status" was based on the number of major depression episodes and hospitalizations. A summary score for "chronic strain" was based on ratings of the difficulties experienced for at least six months in such areas as marriage and finances. Altogether, eighty-four children of fifty-eight women were assessed twice, six months apart, using the K-SADS. Rates of psychiatric disorders were significantly higher in children of affectively and medically ill mothers (69%) than in children of normal mothers (29%). Rates of affective disorders were highest in children of affectively ill mothers (71%), next highest in children of medically ill mothers (44%), and lowest in children of normal mothers (17%), although the statistical significance of these differences was not reported. From multiple regression analyses, it was found that a mother's lifetime depression status was a unique predictor, but only of the child's lifetime diagnoses. On the other hand, the mother's current mood contributed in a unique way to most outcome variables, including mother and teacher ratings of current behavioural and school functioning. Although chronic strain contributed uniquely to several outcome variables, current mood contributed to a higher number. Additional reports from the above study indicate that the currently depressed women were more critical and negative toward their children during an interaction task than nondepressed women (Gordon et al. 1989); the study also showed that children of mothers with affective disorders harbour more negative views about themselves, suggesting a possible psychological mechanism for vulnerability to depression in these children (Jaenicke et al. 1987). Incidentally, a follow-up study to test this latter hypothesis is described in a section on cognitive vulnerability (Hammen et al. 1988). In still another study, Keller et al. (1986) found that the more severe and chronic a parent's depressive disorder, the poorer would be the current adaptive functioning and the more prevalent would be the lifetime psychiatric diagnoses in the children. Although it was reported that parents from 38 per cent of the families were currently depressed, the effect of current mood on childhood outcome was not assessed separately.

Investigators have found that the presence of comorbid nonaffective illness in affectively disturbed parents, as well as the presence of psychiatric illness in their spouses, may both have important roles to play in the development of depression in their children. For example, Welner and Rice (1988) found that 65 per cent of the affectively ill cohort's spouses had DSM-III diagnoses. In a multivariate analysis of their data, they noted that whereas maternal depression had the largest relative risk for affective disorder in the child – followed by paternal, then maternal, alcoholism – paternal depression was not associated with depression in the child. Similarly, using a younger subset of Weissman et al.'s (1987a) sample described above, Merikangas et al. (1988) found that 69 per cent of their depressed probands' spouses, compared to 37 per cent of the normals' spouses, had diagnoses of depression, anxiety, or alcoholism. They noted, too, that comorbid lifetime diagnoses of anxiety and secondary alcoholism were common in the depressed probands. Merikangas et al. identified maternal alcoholism as the strongest predictor of major depression in the offspring; they also found that parental concordance for diagnoses, especially for anxiety disorders, increased the risk of major depression and anxiety disorders in their children significantly. Finally, they showed that when both parents were ill, there was a greater history of divorce, global severity of both parents' current symptoms and marital discord, as well as poorer family functioning, than when only one or no parent was psychiatrically ill, thus suggesting the need to explore environmental as well as genetic factors to understand the associations between parental concordance for psychiatric illness and psychiatric illness in their children.

Finally, Rolf et al. (1988) found children of recovering alcoholics to have higher mean ratings of depression on parent- and self-rated depression checklists than children of nonalcoholics, while also being more likely to score very high on these scales. Parental depression, however, was not measured.

In summary, there is evidence that children of parents with depression, anxiety and alcoholism are at risk for depression. It seems, however, that the magnitude of the risk may be related to the parent's sex, to parental concordance for psychiatric disorder, and to the parent's age of onset of depression. Furthermore, some progress has been made in understanding the environmental mechanisms that play a role in the association between parental affective illness and psychiatric illness, although not specifically depression, in their children. All in all, the relationship between parental psychiatric illness and depression in children is clearly very complex. Future studies should be undertaken to examine the past and current psychiatric status of mothers, fathers, and their children, including the presence of non-affective disorders. In addition, longitudinal studies that measure the chronicity and severity of parental illness, as well as family functioning and other potential contributing factors to a depressive outcome in the child, are required to better elucidate the mechanisms involved. Finally, the actual strength of the parental psychiatric illness needs assessment, as a marker or risk factor for depression in children in community populations. Preliminary work suggests that children of psychiatrically and affectively ill parents in the community may be at as great a risk for psychopathology as the children of ill parents from referred samples (Beardslee et al. 1988; Canino et al. 1990).

Cognitive Vulnerability

In adults, cognitive models of depression have received support from countless studies and have formed the basis for specific treatment methods for depression (Beck et al. 1979; Williams 1984). The literature that attempts to examine similar cognitive theories of depression in populations of children and adolescents is growing as well. Most studies have addressed two separate hypotheses: first, that depressed children evaluate themselves negatively in a variety of ways; and, second, that depressed children either perceive a total lack of control over events in their lives (externality), or a lack of control over positive events in tandem with responsibility for negative events (internality). These negative "cognitive sets" are believed to be enduring characteristics of a group of children who are, thus, predisposed to develop depression in the face of adversity. Nevertheless, although cross-sectional studies examine the association between cognitive set and depression, only longitudinal studies can establish a causal link between them. Results from these two types of studies are reported in separate sections, below.

CROSS-SECTIONAL STUDIES OF SELF-ESTEEM AND SELF-EVALUATION. Support for the hypothesis that depressed children evaluate themselves more negatively than do nondepressed children has come from four studies of school children and two of psychiatric patients that all used the CDI to assess depression. Kaslow et al. (1984), for example, who established a strong negative relationship between self-esteem and depressive symptoms, found that depressed children evaluated their performance on a task more negatively than nondepressed children. Similarly, Sacco and Graves (1984) reported that depressed children not only assessed their performance as poorer than that of their peers, but were also less satisfied with their performance than nondepressed children. Altmann and Gotlib (1988) found that their depressed children had more negative self-perceptions of their social, scholastic, and athletic competence, of their appearance and conduct, and of their global worth as a person, than nondepressed children. Using a picture-sequencing task, Meyer et al. (1989) reported that depressed, compared with nondepressed, children had consistently negative views of themselves, their experiences, and their future. Finally, in samples of both in- and out-patients, Weisz et al. (1987; 1989) found CDI scores to be correlated with low levels of perceived competence in dealing with problems at home and at school.

Four studies have used the K-SADS to determine diagnostic status. McCauley et al. (1988) found depressed children to have significantly lower self-concept scores than both children with nondepressive psychiatric disorders and children whose depression had resolved at the time of testing. In two separate studies of inpatients, Asarnow and colleagues found that children with depressive diagnoses scored lower on measures of global self-worth and perceived scholastic competence than children with nondepressive diagnoses (Asarnow et al. 1987; Asarnow and Bates 1988), as well as on measures of perceived athletic competence and physical appearance (Asarnow and Bates 1988). Additionally, children who were currently depressed scored lower than children whose depression had remitted on measures of global self-worth and perceived scholastic and athletic competence (Asarnow and Bates 1988). Most recently, in three separate school and referred samples, Kendall et al. (1990) found that depressed, compared to nondepressed, children evaluate themselves less favourably on school performance, popularity, and athletic prowess despite having comparable performance standards.

In summary, whether depression is assessed by self-report or direct interview and whether subjects are schoolchildren or psychiatric outpatients or inpatients, depression has been found to be associated with low self-esteem and negative self-evaluation. These findings are more evident for children who are currently depressed than for children whose depression has resolved or who have nondepressive diagnoses.

CROSS-SECTIONAL STUDIES OF PERCEIVED CONTROL OVER EVENTS. Seven studies have used the Children's Attributional Style Questionnaire (CASQ), a tool that measures the extent to which children make internal, global, and stable attributions for positive and negative events. The first four studies, which included 324 schoolchildren, found that the more depressive the symptomatology the children reported on in the CDI, the more likely they were to make internal, stable, and global attributions for failure, and the less likely they were to make these same attributions for success (Blumberg and Izard 1985; Bodiford et al. 1988; Kaslow et al. 1984; Seligman et al. 1984).

The next three studies used the K-SADS to assess psychiatric disorder in outpatients or inpatients (or both); the CASQ difference scores (difference between composite scales for positive and negative events) were used to measure the depressive attributional style overall. The first study found currently depressed children to have a more depressive attributional style for positive events, as well as overall, than formerly depressed children, but not more than for children with nondepressive disorders (Asarnow and Bates 1988). Self-reported depression, however, was significantly associated with a depressive attributional style for negative events, as well as overall. The second, larger study found currently depressed children to have a more depressive attributional style overall, as well as for positive events, than a combined group of formerly depressed children and those with nondepressive disorders (McCauley et al. 1988). Self-reported depression was significantly correlated with an overall depressive attributional style. Finally, the third study found depressed children to have a more depressive attributional style overall than nondepressed clinic patients and normal controls (Kaslow et al. 1988). An additional important finding from this latter study was that no relationship could be found between children's attributional style and that of their parents, thereby lending no support to the hypothesis that children learn their "negative cognitive sets" from their parents.

Three studies have used the Nowicki-Strickland Children's Locus of Control Scale (CLOC), a tool that measures the tendency of children to perceive an external locus of control over their life events (separate scores are not given for positive and negative events) (Lefkowitz et al. 1980; Mullins et al. 1985; McCauley et al. 1988). The first two studies of 978 schoolchildren found self-reported depressive symptoms to be significantly correlated with an external attribution for events. The third study found currently depressed children to have a more external locus of control than formerly depressed and nondepressed children.

Four additional studies measured control-rated beliefs in children, using less common measures than those of the CASQ and CLOC. First, Leon et al. (1980), who used the Cognitive Processes Inventory for Children, found that depressed children attributed positive events to external causes significantly more often than nondepressed children. In addition, they noted that high scorers on the CDI were more likely than low scorers to attribute negative events to internal causes. Second, examining the effort subscale of the Intellectual Achievement Responsibility Scale, Fincham et al. (1987) found that effort attributions were inversely related to depression scores. In other words, depressed children inferred less effort for an outcome, implying a perceived lack of control over the outcome. Third, Haley et al. (1985), using the Cognitive Bias Questionnaire (CBQ), reported that children with a major depressive disorder had higher "depressed-distorted" scores on the CBQ than children with dysthymic or nonaffective disorders. Although the authors of the study stated that the CBQ probably does not measure external locus of control, it is not clear what the questionnaire does measure. Finally, Weisz et al. (1987, 1989) found CDI scores to be consistently correlated with low levels of perceived control in their outpatient and inpatient samples. In addition, the higher the CDI score, the more likely the children were to have a low level of belief in themselves as a cause of success. High CDI scores were also related to the children's uncertainty concerning the cause of either positive or negative outcomes.

In summary, despite different methods of diagnosing depression and assessing cognitive style, studies of referred and nonreferred children are remarkably consistent in finding specific patterns of perceived control over events in depressed children. In most cases, this depressive attributional style is not evident in children whose depression has resolved or in children with nondepressive disorders.

LONGITUDINAL STUDIES OF COGNITIVE VULNERABILITY. Two such studies have made an attempt to examine the causal link between cognitive style and depression in children. In the first study, conducted by Hammen et al. (1987) and described earlier (see Parental Psychopathology), children completed only the negative event items of the CASQ. Although the researchers, when controlling for initial diagnostic status and for depressive symptoms measured by the CDI, found they could not say that a depressive attributional style for negative events would predict a depressive diagnostic status six months later (Hammen et al. 1988), Hammen (1988), herself, subsequently found that negative self-concept did contribute significantly to the prediction of depressive diagnoses. The second longitudinal study was completed by Seligman et al. (1984). Here, ninety-six elementary schoolchildren completed the CDI and CASQ twice, six months apart. Although a depressive attributional style for negative events with initial level of depression held constant predicted subsequent depressive symptoms, a depressive attributional style for positive events did not. Also, children's attributional style for negative events, as well as their depressive symptoms, correlated with maternal, but not paternal, attributional style and depressive symptoms. As noted earlier, Kaslow et al. (1988) found no relationship between child and parental attributional style, although they did not present the findings separately for mothers and fathers.

While there seems little doubt that attributional style is a correlate of depression in children, further work is required to tease out the temporal relationship between cognitive characteristics and depression.

LIFE EVENTS. Five studies have examined the relationship between life events and depression in children. First, Beck and Rosenberg (1986), using a parent-rated life events scale, found that depressed children had experienced more recent positive and negative life events than behaviourally disturbed or normal children and, furthermore, that they had experienced more family disruptions such as parental divorce and death in the family. Second, Mullins et al. (1985), who used the same life-events scale as above but examined the children's reports instead of the parents', found a significantly positive relationship between level of self-reported depressive symptomatology and number of negative life events in the preceding year. This relationship did not hold for positive events, however, and the investigators did not look specifically at family disruptions. Third, in an elegant study of psychiatrically disturbed children and community controls, Goodyer et al. (1988) administered the Newcastle Child and Family Life Events Schedule to mothers, measuring seventy-two different life events, grouped into eight classes, that had occurred one year before onset of disorder in the "cases" or one year before the interview day in the controls. Emotional disorder was diagnosed on the basis of clinical interview, and the subjects were subclassified as "predominantly depressed" or "predominantly anxious." It was found that recent undesirable life events were significantly associated with both subtypes of emotional disorder. In a logistic regression analysis, it was also found that maternal distress, poor maternal confiding relations, and recent stressful life events exerted independent effects on the probability of having an emotional disorder. Fourth, Kashani et al. (1990) found that inpatient children diagnosed with a major depressive disorder on the DICA reported significantly more negative, but not positive, life events in the past year than nondepressed psychiatric inpatients. However, because depressed children had more comorbid diagnoses than nondepressed children, the possibility exists that the presence of multiple disorders or severity of disorder in general could account for the association between negative stressors and depression. Fifth and finally, in the study by Hammen et al. (1988) already described, children and their mothers were interviewed retrospectively, at follow-up, about the occurrence of twelve classes of life events during the preceding six months. Negative stressors, when controlled for initial depression, were found to predict depression at follow-up. Of interest, high stress interacted both with negative attributional style and negative self-concept to predict nonaffective diagnoses at follow-up, a finding which was not true for affective diagnoses. The researchers noted, however, that some children with nonaffective diagnoses also had coexisting affective diagnoses.

In summary, recent negative life events, as rated by children or their parents, appear to be correlates of self-reported, or clinically diagnosed, depression in children. Whether this finding is specific to affective disorders, and whether certain types of negative life events are more strongly associated with depression than others, requires further clarification. In addition, some evidence has appeared that negative life events may exert their effect in conjunction with other factors such as maternal distress, poor maternal confiding relations, and possibly cognitive factors. Finally, prospective longitudinal studies are required to determine the existence of a causal relationship between life events and depression.

Socioeconomic Status (SES)

In his extensive review of the literature on correlates of childhood psychiatric disorders, Boyle (1988) concluded that there was little evidence of an association between social class and emotional disorders (which include anxiety and depressive symptoms).

The evidence for depressive disorders is conflicting. Lefkowitz and Tesiny (1980) studied 944 fourth- and fifth-grade students, from all SES levels, attending ten urban public schools. They found a highly significant inverse relationship between family income and three measures of depression in the children (peer-, self- and teacher-rated). Mullins et al. (1985), using only a self-report measure of depression in a group of 134 students, nine to twelve years of age, from one public grade school in a midwestern U.S. city, found only a modest negative correlation between depression and father's occupational status. Yet, when students were classified as depressed or not depressed based on their self-report scores, no significant difference in SES emerged between the groups. In the two community prevalence studies of depression in nine-year-olds, described earlier (Kashani et al. 1983; McCracken 1987), the measures of SES of families of depressed children did not differ from those of families of nonaffectively disordered or normal children. On the other hand, in Puerto Rico, depression in four- to sixteen-year-olds was associated more with Hollingshead's class V than with classes I through IV (Bird et al. 1988). In the only longitudinal study to examine SES, Velez et al. (1989) found that a composite measure of low SES, including low income and low parental education, was not a risk factor for the development of major depression eight years later (at ages nine through eighteen), although the individual component of low maternal education was. This relationship, however, did not hold two years later when the children were aged eleven to twenty. These conflicting results are not surprising, given the vast differences in methodology and sampling among studies. A tentative conclusion can even be drawn, to the effect that a strong relationship between SES and depression in children does not exist.

Biological Factors

Biological abnormalities in depressed patients may have etiological significance or simply be state markers of depressed mood or other psychopathology. Most of the studies reported here are cross-sectional in nature and therefore cannot address the issue of causality. The following section reviews studies of depressed children that examined abnormalities in cortisol, thyroid-stimulating hormone, melatonin, growth hormone, and polysomnography.

CORTISOL. Abnormalities in cortisol regulation have been studied extensively in adult affective disorders via the dexamethasone suppression test (DST). In their review, Arana et al. (1985) found that over 10,000 subjects had been studied with the DST during a five-year period. The overall sensitivity of the test in major depression was about 44 per cent based on 5,000 cases. Although the test's overall specificity came to over 90 per cent when patients with major depression were compared to 1,100 normal subjects, it fell to 76.5 per cent when those patients were compared to 1,207 others with other psychiatric disorders. Studies of the DST in depressed children have been much fewer in number, but have established results similar to those of the adult studies. The results of eight studies that included only preadolescents are presented in Table 9. Sensitivity of the DST ranged from 14 to 87 per cent, averaging 65 per cent across studies (129 of 199 depressed patients were nonsuppressors); specificity ranged from 53 to 91 per cent, averaging 80 per cent across studies (99 of 124 nondepressed subjects were suppressors). The Pfeffer et al. (1989) study was particularly important for its investigation of both the optimum dose of dexamethasone and the criterion value of cortisol for nonsuppression in prepubertal youngsters on the DST. The DST has shown some promise for predicting clinical response to imipramine in children (Preskorn et al. 1987) and for predicting clinical outcome in depressed children after five months of unspecified treatment (Weller et al. 1986).

Hypersecretion of cortisol by depressed adults has also been demonstrated by elevated mean 24-hour plasma levels (Puig-Antich et al. 1989b). This abnormality was not found, however, in an elegant study that compared depressed prepubertal children to nondepressed psychiatric and normal controls (Puig-Antich et al. 1989b). The authors speculated that age differences in cortisol secretion and the low-stress environment of the study probably contributed to the negative results.

THYROID-STIMULATING HORMONE. In their review, Loosen and Prange (1982) reported that in forty-one studies of 917 depressed adult patients, the thyroid-stimulating hormone (TSH) response to thyrotropin-releasing hormone (TRH) was deficient in about 25 per cent of cases. Puig-Antich (1987) stated that his group found no differences between prepubertal depressives and controls in the TSH response to TRH, although details of the work were not provided. Clearly, this is an area that requires further study.

MELATONIN. Having noted that decreased melatonin levels have been found in depressed adults, Cavallo et al. (1987) measured melatonin levels in nine

Table 9
Dexamethasone suppression test (DST) in prepubertal children*

Study	Age	Number with MDD†	Nondepressed psychiatric comparison group (n)	Sensitivity (%)	DST‡ Specificity (%)
OUTPATIENTS					
Geller et al. 1983	5-12	14	none	14	-
Poznanski et al. 1982	6-12	9	9	56	89
INPATIENTS					
Fristad et al. 1988	6-12	63	14 (21 normal controls also)	67	91
Livingston et al. 1984	6-12	4§	11	75	64
Petty et al. 1985	5-12	13‖	17	87	53
Pfeffer et al. 1989	6-12	20	31§	53	87 (at 8 A.M.)
				31	94 (at 4 P.M.)
Weller et al. 1984	6-12	20	none	70	-
Yaylayan et al. 1989	mean 9.3	59	21	73	76

* All studies used dexamethasone .5 mg except study #1 which used $20\mu g/kg$; dexamethasone was given at 11 or 11:30 P.M. and serum cortisol levels drawn the next day at 4 P.M. (also at 8 A.M. in studies 3, 6, 8; and at 11 P.M. in studies 5 and 6).

† MDD - major depressive disorder by DSM-III criteria

‡ criterion for nonsuppression - $5\mu g/dl$ of cortisol

§ one patient had schizoaffective disorder, depressed by Research Diagnostic Criteria

‖ some patients with dysthymic disorder

depressed and ten nondepressed seven- to thirteen-year-olds. They found a significantly lower, mean 24-hour melatonin concentration and a significantly lower, mean night-time concentration in the depressed group.

GROWTH HORMONE. Puig-Antich et al. (1984c) have noted that adult studies of endogenously depressed patients found hyposecretion of growth hormone (GH) in response to the insulin tolerance test (ITT). In their studies of prepubertal depressed children, these researchers found a significant hyposecretion of GH in response to the ITT in endogenously depressed, compared to nonendogenously depressed and nondepressed, children (Puig-Antich et al. 1984c). They also found significantly increased GH secretion during sleep in depressed, compared to nondepressed, children (Puig-Antich et al. 1984a). When these abnormalities persisted up to four months after clinical recovery, the authors concluded that GH abnormalities might be markers of either past episodes of depression or traits for prepubertal major depression (Puig-Antich et al. 1984b, d). This persistence of GH abnormalities contrasts with the normalization of the DST after clinical recovery (Weller et al. 1986) and suggests that the pursuit of GH as opposed to cortisol, abnormalities might prove fruitful in the search for biological risk factors in prepubertal depression. More recently, Jensen and Garfinkel (1990) also found hyposecretion of growth hormone in response to both clonidine and L-dopa challenges in depressed pre- and early-pubertal boys compared to normal controls.

POLYSOMNOGRAPHY. As summarized by Emslie et al. (1987, 1990), several polysomnographic abnormalities have been consistently found in adult depressives. As well, conflicting results have been shown in five studies of electroencephalogram (EEG) sleep in depressed children. The earliest study by Kupfer et al. (1979) examined the effects of imipramine on the sleep EEGs of twelve hospitalized children aged six to fourteen. When compared to previously published normative data for children, the depressives, although they did not differ in sleep continuity, did have a shorter rapid eye movement (REM) latency (statistical significance was not reported). In their study of children age seven to thireen, Young et al. (1982) found that, compared to twelve-age-matched normal controls, depressed children showed no differences apropos sleep EEG measures. Similarly, Puig-Antich et al. (1982) found no significant differences in the sleep EEGs of fifty-four depressed prepubertal children, compared to twenty-five nondepressed neurotics and eleven normal controls. They hypothesized that maturational factors accounted for the absence of polysomnographic findings in this age group. On the other hand, in a later study, Puig Antich et al. (1983) found that recovered prepubertal depressives had both a significantly shorter REM latency and more REM periods, as compared to themselves when ill, as well as to ill, nondepressed, neurotic children and normal children; the authors therefore concluded that a shortened first REM latency might be a trait marker for depression or a marker of past episodes. In a preliminary study, comparing data from seventeen depressed inpatients (aged nine to fourteen) to previously published control data for twelve- and thirteen-year-olds, Emslie et al. (1987) found a significantly shorter REM latency and increased REM density as well as several other differences. The conflicting results of these early studies are not difficult to understand considering the vast differences among the various studies' sample characteristics, diagnostic criteria used for depression, use of control groups, and definitions of the various sleep parameters. In a recent, carefully conducted study, Emslie et al. (1990) found a significantly shorter REM latency in twenty-five hospitalized depressed children compared to twenty healthy controls. Not only were the findings significant using two different scoring criteria for REM latency (including the method used in the earlier study by Puig-Antich and colleagues [1982]), but several other findings were significant as well, including longer sleep latency and increased REM time for depressed children.

In summary, although evidence from cross-sectional studies apparently supports an association between depression and most of the hypothesized risk factors examined here, the examination was limited to four longitudinal studies. We found that negative self-concept and negative stressors in children of depressed mothers predicted future depression, that a depressive attributional style for negative events predicted depression in school children, that low SES did not predict depression, and, finally, that abnormal GH secretion and sleep parameters were present in recovered prepubertal depressives. Offord and colleagues (1988) recently completed a four-year follow-up study of their community sample of Ontario children and are currently examining the data for various sociodemographic and familial risk factors of depression in children. Also, the Pittsburgh group (Puig-Antich, 1988) has launched a study of the biological risk factors of childhood depression.

CLINICAL COURSE AND OUTCOME

As noted by Rutter (1986), "the validation (or rather part-validation) of depressive syndromes in childhood relies on the demonstration that depressed children are more likely than children with other forms of psychiatric disorder to develop major depressive disorders in adult life" (510). Apart from this scientific purpose of syndrome validation, a practical need has surfaced. That is, the course of childhood disorders must be examined so that persistent and severe disorders receive the currently scarce treatment and research resources.

Few studies have examined the course of childhood depression. Several follow-up studies of clinic and nonclinic populations and of children of depressed parents are described below. Six are clinic-based studies. Although the first two predicted a poor four- to eleven-year outcome for depressed children, they both suffer from several methodological flaws: the first study (Poznanski et al. 1976) was small; the second (Eastgate and Gilmour 1984) had a large sample loss; and both studies lacked rigorous criteria for the diagnoses of depression, a blind follow-up evaluation, and control groups. The third, a more rigorous study (Kovacs et al. 1984a,b; Kovacs, 1985b) located in a psychiatric outpatient clinic, followed three cohorts of children with different DSM-III diagnoses of depression: adjustment disorder with depressed mood (ADDM), major depressive disorder (MDD), and dysthymic disorder (DD). The first group, ADDM, had the best prognosis with a median recovery time of about five months; after nine months, 90 per cent of the children had recovered from the adjustment disorder and no child developed a major depression during the five-year follow-up period. The MDD cohort, in contrast, had a median recovery time of about seven months and a maximum recovery rate of 92 per cent from the depressive episode by eighteen months; at five-year follow-up, a 72-per-cent risk of a second episode of major depression had emerged. The DD group had by far the worst prognosis. Not only was the patients' median recovery time three and one-half years, but they took more than six years to reach the maximal recovery rate of 89 per cent. They also had a high probability of developing a first episode of major depression in a five-year period. Nevertheless, and although this last study is the most rigorous to date, it still suffers from lack of blind follow-up evaluations and failure to match the depressed and control subjects on nondepressive symptoms. The fourth study (Zeitlin 1986) found that a symptom pattern analogous to childhood depression correlated highly with a comparable symptom-pattern in adult life; that is, thirty-one of thirty-seven patients (83.8%) with the syndrome during childhood went on to have the syndrome during adulthood. This study, however, has three major weaknesses or limitations; first, the sample is restricted to those who attended the psychiatric departments of the same hospital as children and adults; second, no formal category of clinical depression existed at childhood admission; and third, the data (both child and adult) were based on existing clinical records. In a fifth and much more methodologically rigorous study, Harrington et al. (1990) assessed, as adults (mean age 30.7), fifty-two matched pairs of subjects who had attended a child psychiatric clinic as children (mean age: about 12.7). Each child with a depressive classification was carefully matched, in terms of several background variables, nondepressive symptoms, and indicators of severity of disorder, to a child with a nondepressive classification. The results were striking: a clear continuity existed between childhood and adult depression. The main limitation of this study was that the childhood diagnoses were not made according to current diagnostic systems, although the authors gave reasonable evidence for the validity of their diagnostic approach. The last of the clinic studies (Asarnow et al. 1988) followed up on hospitalized children with major depressive and dysthymic disorders for one to six years after discharge, comparing them to children with schizophrenia and schizotypal personality disorder. Despite treatment with psychotherapy and pharmacotherapy in the majority of cases, the risk of rehospitalization for depressed children reached 45 per cent after two years, greater than for children with schizophrenia spectrum disorders, controlling for a variety of sociodemographic and clinical variables. The majority of depressed children were rehospitalized for suicidal behaviour or increased depression. In addition, 15 per cent of depressed children were placed outside their homes in the year after discharge, significantly fewer than those with schizophrenia spectrum disorders.

Three studies examined the natural history of childhood depression using nonclinical populations. These studies are important inasmuch as the generalization of data from clinic to nonclinic populations is unknown. The first (Chess et al. 1983) was a longitudinal study of the behavioural development of 133 subjects from early infancy to early adult life. The Diagnostic assessments were carried out if, during one of the routine interviews, a child was reported by the parent to have a behavioural deviation and was considered by the interviewer to require psychiatric consultation. On this basis, six subjects were identified with DSM-III depressive disorders, only two of whom (boys) had onsets of depression before age twelve. Both these boys had persistent or recurrent depression up to the last assessment, at age twenty-two. Although this study provides good clinical descriptions of the course of depressive disorders in the identified children, it suffers from a lack of reliable and valid, blind diagnostic assessments of all children at specified points during the follow-up period.

The second study (McGee and Williams 1988) presented data pertaining to childhood depression from the Dunedin Multidisciplinary Health and Development Study. Three groups of nine-year-old children identified as having current depressive disorder, a past depressive disorder, or no depressive disorder were studied at ages eleven and thirteen. At all three ages, data were collected from parents, teachers, and the children themselves. The results indicate that those children identified at age nine as having a current depressive disorder continued to show emotional and behavioural difficulties at ages eleven and thirteen. In terms of depressive symptoms, these children, themselves, reported significantly more of such symptoms at both later ages, as compared with children who were not depressed at age nine. Their parents reported high levels of depressive and internalizing symptoms in their children at ages eleven and thirteen. Two other findings should be noted: depression was more persistent among the boys than the girls, and there was a long-term association between depression and antisocial behaviour in the boys but not the girls. The third study (Pfeffer et al. 1988), while actually intended to examine the two-year outcome of suicidal behaviour in a normal population of six- to twelve-year-olds, also provided information about depressive diagnoses. That is, four of six children were found to have persistent dysthymic disorder. Although the use of blind follow-up evaluations was a positive feature of this last study, the sample was not representative of the population from which it was drawn; also over half of the children with dysthymic disorder were lost to follow-up, limiting the generalizability of these findings.

Two studies have reported on the long-term outcome of children of depressed parents. The first study (Apter et al. 1982) followed up, three to five years later, eighteen children with a mean age of ten years at the time of initial assessment. Of the children with a depression at initial evaluation (by Weinberg's criteria), 83 per cent had a psychiatric diagnosis at follow-up (70% depressive, 30% nondepressive). Although outcome assessments were blind, this study is nevertheless limited by its smallness and uncontrollability. The second study, conducted by a Canadian group, followed up children of bipolar parents (Laroche et al. 1987). The original sample included thirty-nine children, aged five to eighteen years of age, of twenty-two families in which one parent had a bipolar affective disorder (Laroche et al. 1985). When 85 per cent of these children were followed up three to seven years later, only one of the children originally diagnosed with affective disorder had still not shown any evidence of the disorder since (Laroche et al. 1987). As noted by the authors, this study suffered from a small sample and lack of a control group.

Much more work needs to be done in learning about the course of childhood disorders in general (Robins, 1979), and depression in particular. The data, limited as they are, indicate three tentative conclusions. First, childhood depression is persistent for a significant proportion of cases over a period of several years. Second, the outcome studies of childhood depression should not restrict their measures only to depression; they should include other diagnoses, since depressed children seem to be at increased risk for a number of psychiatric diagnoses. Third, the relationship between comorbid disorders and depression deserves further examination. Finally, the validation of childhood depressive syndromes, using outcome data, awaits more long-term studies that follow children into adulthood.

TREATMENT APPROACHES

This section will review the evidence for the efficacy of pharmacotherapy, electroconvulsive therapy (ECT), phototherapy, and psychosocial interventions in depressed children.

Pharmacotherapy

In a recent review of tricyclic antidepressants in the treatment of prepubertal depression, Weller and Weller (1986) noted the lack of any published double-blind, randomized, placebo-controlled studies. Since then, major advances have been made with the publication of three such studies (Geller et al. 1989; Puig-Antich et al. 1987; Preskorn et al. 1987). In the following sections, we will discuss, separately, the evidence for the efficacy of several tricyclics, tetracyclics, and lithium. No studies to our knowledge have yet examined the efficacy of monoamine oxidase inhibitors (MAOIs) in childhood depression.

Tricyclics

IMIPRAMINE. Early 1987 saw the publication of two placebo-controlled studies of imipramine in prepubertal depression. One study by Puig-Antich et al.

(1987) included thirty-eight prepubertal inpatients and outpatients diagnosed with the K-SADS as having a major depressive disorder. Children in the drug group received imipramine of up to 5 mg/kg/day. Pediatricians made dose adjustments taking cardiac and other side-effects into consideration. Outcome was measured with a K-SADS assessment for the fifth week of treatment. For a child to be considered a responder, both depressed mood and anhedonia had to be scored as only minimally present. Although the original plan was to recruit sixty subjects, the trial was terminated early when preliminary analyses of the first thirty-eight patients did not find imipramine superior to the placebo. In fact, a high placebo response rate of 68 per cent was found, as compared to the imipramine response rate of 56 per cent. Further analyses found that the drug group's response was related to total drug-plasma level. Eighty-five per cent of children who achieved a plasma level above 150 ng/mL responded to imipramine, whereas only 30 per cent of children with a plasma level below 150 ng/mL responded. Drug dose was not associated with plasma level. A poor response was also found in children with psychotic symptoms. The only side effect reported significantly more often in the drug group than in the placebo group was a flushed face on exercise.

The second controlled study by Preskorn et al. (1987) included twenty-two hospitalized children age six to twelve. To be included in the depressed group, a child had to meet DSM-III criteria for a major depressive disorder, based on responses to an open clinical interview and the DICA. In addition, they had to obtain a score of at least twenty on the CDRS-R and be symptomatic for at least thirty days prior to the study. Children with attention deficit disorder and psychotic symptoms were excluded. Adjustments to imipramine dosage were made to achieve drug-plasma levels in the range of 125 to 250 ng/mL. Outcome was measured in terms of mean per cent change from baseline on the CDI, CDRS-R, and Clinical Global Impressions (CGI) scale. Unlike the first study, imipramine was found to be superior to placebo after twenty-one and forty-two days of treatment. This significant drug effect was limited to children who were nonsuppressors on the DST. No serious side effects were reported.

It is interesting to compare the above two studies. With drug-plasma levels above 150 ng/mL in the first study and between 125 and 250 ng/mL in the second study, the drug response rate was high (85% and 80%, respectively). However, the placebo response rate was much higher in the first (68%) than in the second (20%) study. This latter finding deserves some attention, for it would be clinically helpful to be able to predict which patients would be more likely to respond to drugs than to a placebo. Differences in sampling may account, in part, for the differential placebo response in these two studies. The first study, for instance, included outpatients and inpatients, whereas the second study included only hospitalized children. In addition, the requirements for diagnosing depression were more stringent in the second study, which used duration and severity criteria over and above those required by DSM-III. The inclusion of less severely depressed children in the first study may help explain the high placebo response rate as well.

In children who are likely to respond to imipramine, it would be advantageous to achieve an adequate plasma level as early in treatment as possible. This cannot be done using a traditional mg/kg dosing strategy, for the same dose of imipramine in children has been found to yield a sevenfold difference in the steady-state, total tricyclic plasma level (Preskorn et al. 1983). Moreover, the presence and degree of side-effects cannot be used for dose titration because reports of nuisance side effects, such as dry mouth, have been found to be unrelated to imipramine plasma levels (Preskorn et al. 1983). Sallee et al. (1986) described a method for estimating the dose required to achieve a steady-state plasma level of 200 ng/mL: the patient is given a test dose of 25 mg, the plasma level is measured twenty-four hours later, and the resulting value is put into a regression equation that yields the required dose. Using this method, the investigators were able to predict the steady-state plasma level successfully 80 per cent of the time. They caution, however, that this method is not as accurate for patients with an elimination half-life of less than eight hours. They state, as well, that sensitive and specific assay methods are required that may not be available in all laboratories. It should be noted that, based on their assessment of the cardiac side effects of imipramine, Preskorn et al. (1983) concluded that children can be safely treated with imipramine at plasma levels below 225 ng/mL. This same group of investigators (Preskorn et al. 1988) have also determined a relationship between supratherapeutic plasma levels of tricyclics in children and central nervous system toxicity, especially when levels exceed 450 ng/mL. The same researchers have also recommended that imipramine be prescribed in three roughly equivalent daily doses, although twice-a-day dosing is apparently adequate (Preskorn et al. 1987).

A third controlled trial of imipramine in children, although carried out, was too small to yield statistically meaningful conclusions (Petti and Law, 1982). The results did, however, support the efficacy of imipramine over placebo, in that all three of the drug-treated children improved, whereas two of the three placebo-treated children actually got worse. The marked withdrawal reaction of one child in this study when imipramine was discontinued and the limited withdrawal reactions in the other two children constituted important findings, the suggestion being that discontinuation of imipramine should be accomplished by a gradual tapering of the dose.

NORTRIPTYLINE. In an open trial of nortriptyline in twenty-two depressed outpatients (aged six to twelve years), Geller et al. (1986) found an overall drug response rate of 64 per cent, with the best response occurring at a plasma level of at least 60 ng/mL. Based on these findings, the same group conducted a randomized controlled trial of nortriptyline, using a fixed plasma-level design and a two-week placebo wash-out period (Geller et al. 1989; Geller et al. 1992). Subjects were required to have a DSM-III diagnosis of MDD, to be nondelusional, and to have a CDRS score of at least forty and a duration of illness of at least two months. Subjects were considered responders if their CDRS scores decreased to twenty or less and their MDD items from the K-SADS were rated as "absent" or "very mild." Contrary to the positive findings of the open trial, this trial terminated early (after completion by 50 of 60 subjects) due to poor results. The drug response rate of only 31 per cent was not significantly greater than the placebo response rate of 17 per cent. As well, no correlation existed between drug-plasma level and clinical response. The conflicting findings of the above two studies are a good demonstration of the need for care in interpreting the results of open medication trials. Before concluding, however, that nortriptyline is ineffective in depressed children, two major limitations of the latter study must be considered. First, the sample was probably unrepresentative of most clinic populations, in that it consisted primarily of boys from small, intact, suburban, middle- to upper-class families. Also, most of the subjects had been ill for two or more years and 50 per cent had had MDD for five or more years. Perhaps the choice of "acute" *versus* "chronic" will be an important predictor of antidepressant response in future studies. Second, the optimum plasma level chosen for the study may have been too low.

Extensive work has also been done on the pharmacokinetic parameters and electrocardiographic (ECG) effects of nortriptyline in depressed children. From this work it was found that there is a two-fold variation in the drug half-life in prepubertal younsters and that the mean half-life is short enough that twice-a-day dosage is recommended for prepubertal children (Geller et al. 1984). Similar to adults, steady-state plasma levels are achieved after approximately seven days and are stable over time (Geller et al. 1985b). At plasma levels of 50 to 100 ng/mL, clinically significant ECG effects are absent (Geller et al. 1985d). Clinicians may be interested to know that the therapeutic dose of nortriptyline can be predicted for an individual child in a manner similar to that already described for imipramine (Geller et at, 1985c).

AMITRIPTYLINE. To date, only one placebo-controlled study of amitriptyline has been conducted using subjects as their own controls in a crossover design (Kashani et al. 1984). In this study of nine hospitalized children, aged nine to twelve, with major depressive disorders, a positive but nonstatistically significant drug response was found in six of the nine children. Doses were low, reaching a maximum of 1.5 mg/kg/day and plasma levels were not reported. Apart from a hypomanic reaction in one eleven-year-old boy, side-effects were minimal.

Tetracyclic Compounds

MIANSERIN. Although this tetracyclic antidepressant is unavailable in Canada, it has been used for several years in Europe and other countries. One uncontrolled study has examined its use in childhood depression (Mouren et al. 1983). Nineteen depressed children, eight to twelve years of age, were given a dose of 1 mg/kg/day. Fifty-six per cent of the children recovered, 32 per cent improved, and 12 per cent were unchanged. A statistically significant decrease in CDRS scores occurred after twenty-one and thirty-five days of treatment. Side effects were minimal, with somnolence and weight gain most frequently reported.

MAPROTILINE. One uncontrolled study reported on the use of this tetracyclic in depressed children and adolescents (Minuti and Gallo, 1982). Twenty children, aged four to fifteen, were treated with a mean daily dose of 32 mg of maprotiline for four weeks. There was a 54 per cent reduction in depressive symptomatology reported. Somnolence and tremor were reported in two cases.

Lithium

The efficacy of lithium in the prevention of manic recurrences in adult bipolar disorder has already been established (Prien 1983). Good evidence also exists for its use in the prevention of depressive recurrences in adult bipolar and unipolar disorders (Prien et al. 1984). Although there is some evidence for its efficacy as an antidepressant in the acute phase of adult unipolar depression as well, such usage remains controversial (Peet and Coppen 1980). As yet, no controlled trials have examined the antidepressant effect of lithium in children (Delong and Aldershof 1987). One series of cases, however, did report an overall success rate of only 14 per cent for lithium usage in the treatment of twenty-one children with unipolar depression (Delong and Aldershof 1987).

Few guidelines exist for the proper use of lithium in children. Although it is known that lithium has a higher renal clearance in children than in adults (Jefferson, 1982) and that children report fewer side effects than adults (Lena 1979; Khandelwal et al. 1984), little information is available concerning the long-term side effects of lithium in children. Khandelwal et al. (1984) studied four adolescents who had been treated with lithium for three to five years. No impairment in renal function was found in these children, whose serum levels of lithium had been maintained between 0.5 and 1.0 meq/liter.

In summary, evidence regarding the efficacy of drugs in the treatment of childhood depression is preliminary. Further confirmation of the promising results that have been found for imipramine is needed. Also required are carefully controlled trials of other tricyclics, tetracyclics, MAOIs, lithium, and the newer serotonergic drugs such as fluoxetine.

ECT

A small number of case reports have shown improvement in childhood depression treated with electroconvulsive therapy (Bertagnoli and Borchardt 1990; Guttmacher and Cretella 1988). A case of major depression comorbid with anorexia nervosa in a prepubertal boy, however, did not respond to ECT (Guttmacher et al. 1989). There is clearly a need for more systematic study of this treatment modality in depressed children.

Phototherapy

Seasonal affective disorder (SAD) is characterized by recurrent winter depressions that respond to light therapy (Rosenthal et al. 1984). Two preliminary studies examined the use of phototherapy for children with SAD. The first, an open trial of six children and adolescents with SAD, included three children twelve years of age or less, all of whom had symptomatic relief with varying degrees of exposure to either bright full-spectrum light or dim yellow light (Rosenthal et al. 1986). The second study, a randomized, single-blind crossover study of nineteen children and adolescents, comparing the use of bright environmental light and relaxation training, found that phototherapy led to relief from neurovegetative symptoms in children with SAD (n=5), but not in children with nonseasonal major depression (n=9), attention deficit disorder (n=5), or no disorder (n=5) (Sonis et al. 1987). Furthermore, relaxation training was effective only for nonseasonal major depression.

Psychosocial Treatments

Two studies have systematically studied the efficacy of various forms of group psychotherapy in depressed children. In the first study (Stark et al. 1987) twenty-nine children, age nine to twelve years, who scored thirteen or higher on the CDI, were randomly assigned to one of three groups: selfcontrol therapy (SC), behavioural problem-solving therapy (BPS) and a waiting-list control group (WL). The SC therapy combined cognitive and behavioural-skills training based on Rehm et al. (1984), while the BPS therapy combined self-monitoring, pleasant activity scheduling, and the acquisition of problem-solving skills, partially based on Lewinsohn et al. (1980). The CDI, CDS and CDRS-R were administered before and after treatment. Although significant within-group differences were found between the pre- and post-treatment scores for both treatment groups on all dependent measures, between-group comparisons were not as supportive of a treatment effect. The only statistically significant finding was that post-treatment depression scores on the CDI were lower for the SC than the WL group. The main limitation of this study was the use of a self-report measure solely to determine entry to the depressed group. Only 56 per cent of the SC group, 20 per cent of the BPS group, and none of the WL group were actually depressed prior to treatment on the psychologist-administered CDRS-R. The authors of the study recommend that future studies use interview-derived DSM-III diagnoses of depression.

In the second study to examine psychosocial treatment of depressed children, it is even less likely that a depressive syndrome was being measured (Butler et al. 1980). In this study, 562 fifth- and sixth-grade children in five Toronto schools were screened using a "self-report Depression Battery." The battery included four self-report questionnaires of which only one, the CDI, was a direct measure of depression. The other three were measures of self-esteem, cognitive distortions, and locus of control. Children were included in the depressed group if they attained a score 1.5 standard deviations above the mean on two or more of the four measures, or scored 1.5 standard deviations above the mean on their summation. In addition, the children had to be identified by their teachers as displaying "low self-esteem, poor social skills, academic underachievement, helplessness in stressful situations, and withdrawn or acting-out behavior" (114). On the basis of these criteria, fifty-six children were selected and assigned (randomness not stated) to one of four conditions: role play (RP), cognitive restructuring (CR), attention-placebo (AP), and classroom control (CC). The RP category involved teaching the skills required for problem solving and social interaction; the CR category included teaching how to recognize and deal with negative thoughts; the AP category involved learning a group approach to problem solving; the CC category received no intervention at all. The first three treatments were administered in ten one-hour sessions, and the "Depression Battery" was readministered after the tenth session. Significant improvement was seen on all four measures for the RP group, on two measures (self-esteem and CDI) for the CR group, on no measure for the AP group, and on the CDI for the CC group. Although this study lends support to using role play and possibly cognitive restructuring for a subgroup of disturbed children, it is not clear what diagnostic category, if any, this group of children would fall into.

Despite the diagnostic issues raised for the above two studies, these studies do represent the only systematic attempts to evaluate group-administered psychosocial treatments in children with depressive symptoms. To our knowledge, there have been no similar attempts to evaluate individual psychotherapy or family therapy in depressed children.

In conclusion, there is very little firm evidence for the efficacy of any treatment modality in childhood depression. How, then, is the clinician to develop a rational approach to treating a depressed child? Published opinions on this matter vary widely, depending on the theoretical orientation of the author(s). For example, Wilkes (1987), who has also written on the use of cognitive therapy for depressed adolescents (Wilkes and Rush 1988), recommended family therapy as the treatment of choice, followed by antidepressants if this fails. On the other hand, Puig-Antich (1984), who pioneered research in the psychobiology of childhood depression, recommended that antidepressants be used to treat the depressive episode, followed by psychotherapy to treat any residual psychosocial deficits. Cytryn and McKnew (1985) recommended an individualized approach that took into account the child's age, severity of illness, and family circumstances. Similar to Wilkes' approach, they suggested that psychosocial interventions should precede pharmacotherapy. Our own experience is that concurrent pharmacotherapy and psychosocial interventions can often prove effective. Carefully controlled studies of single and combined treatment modalities are required to further clinicians' understanding of the best approach to treating childhood depression.

CONCLUDING REMARKS

Previous sections have identified both significant gains in the scientific knowledge base and major unresolved issues in the field of childhood depression. This final section will attempt to summarize the implications of what has been learned to date–that is, for practitioners, the training of professionals, and for policymakers–and to indicate priorities for future research.

Practitioners

Although the clinical implications for practitioners that can be derived from the existing research are numerous, three stand out. First, the assessment of a child for depression must be comprehensive, to address the issue of comorbidity, and should include information from multiple sources. Second, treatment planning should be comprehensive, addressing specific diagnostic and etiological factors. Practitioners should look at such important etiological factors as the child's recent stresses, the parents' psychiatric status (past and present), and the child's cognitive characteristics. Lack of strong scientific evidence for the efficacy of any one treatment approach means that treatment decisions must continue to be guided by sound clinical judgment. But the clinician should bear in mind the positive relationship found between plasma levels of certain tricyclic antidepressants and clinical response, as well as the existence of a significant placebo response in some children. Third, close follow-up of children with major depression and dysthymic disorders is warranted, given the evidence for a severe and relapsing course for these disorders.

Training of Professionals

Only a minority of children with emotional problems, including depression, are seen in mental health settings; the majority are seen by family physicians (Fleming et al. 1989; Offord et al. 1987). These findings suggest that childhood depression should be part of the curriculum for medical students and family-practice residents, as well as for students of the mental health professions. Today in Canada, the number of "experts" in childhood depression is insufficient to provide this kind of training. Students in university departments of psychiatry and clinical psychology therefore need to be encouraged not only to pursue this area but to seek financial support for travel to relevant conferences.

Policymakers

In the policy area, funds are required for at least two purposes. First, specialty clinics in childhood and adolescent affective disorders are needed so that expert consultation, teaching (including education for families and school professionals), and research will take place. Second, coordinated, multicentre projects, with common research designs and instrumentation, are needed to address important research problems.

Research Priorities

All aspects of childhood depression require further research. Although most of the critical research questions have already been mentioned in preceding sections, three will be repeated here to emphasize their importance. First there is a basic need for a better measure of "caseness," one that takes impairment into account. Second, there is a need for the identification of risk factors and the assessment of natural history and clinical course through longitudinal studies of both community and clinical samples of children. Finally, need is urgent for randomized, controlled trials of different treatments, and combinations of treatments, for depressed children. For the latter two questions, the impact of comorbid nonaffective disorders must be addressed.

BIBLIOGRAPHY

Achenbach, T.M., and Edelbrock, C.S. 1983. *Manual for the child behavior checklist and revised child behavior profile* Burlington, Vermont: University of Vermont, Department of Psychiatry.

Alessi, N.E., and Magen, J. 1988. Comorbidity of other psychiatric disturbances in depressed, psychiatrically hospitalized children. *American Journal of Psychiatry* 145: 1582–84.

Altmann, E.O., and Gotlib, I.A. 1988. The social behavior of depressed children: An observational study. *Journal of Abnormal Child Psychology* 16: 29–44.

American Psychiatric Association. 1980. *Diagnostic and statistical manual of mental disorders* 3d ed. Washington, D.C.: American Psychiatric Association.

American Psychiatric Association. 1987. *Diagnostic and statistical manual of mental disorders* 3d ed., rev. Washington, D.C.: American Psychiatric Association.

Anderson, J.C., Williams, S., McGee, R., and Silva, P.A. 1987. DSM-III disorders in preadolescent children. *Archives of General Psychiatry* 44: 69–76.

Angold, A., Weissman, M.M., John, K.R., Merikangas, K.R., Prusoff, B.A., Wickramaratne, P., Gammon, G.D., and Warner, V. 1987. Parent and child reports of depressive symptoms in children at low and high risk of depression. *Journal of Child Psychology and Psychiatry* 28: 901–15.

Apter, A., Borengasser, M.A., Hamovit, J., Bartko, J., Cytryn, L., and McKnew, D.H. 1982. Four-year follow-up of depressed children: Preventive implications. *Journal of Preventive Psychiatry.* 1: 331–35.

Arana, G.W., Baldessarini, R.J., and Ornsteen, M. 1985. The dexamethasone suppresion test for diagnosis and prognosis in psychiatry. *Archives of General Psychiatry* 42: 1193–1204.

Asarnow, J.R., and Bates, S. 1988. Depression in child psychiatric inpatients: Cognitive and attributional patterns. *Journal Of Abnormal Child Psychology* 16: 601–15.

Asarnow, J.R., Carlson, G.A. and Guthrie, D. 1987. Coping strategies, self-perceptions, hopelessness and perceived family environments in depressed and suicidal children. *Journal of Consulting and Clinical Psychology* 55: 361–66.

Asarnow, J.R., Goldstein, M.J., Carlson, G.A., Perdue, S., Bates, S. and Keller, J. 1988. Childhood-onset depressive disorders: A follow-up study of rates of rehospitalization and out-of-home placement among child psychiatric inpatients. *Journal of Affective Disorders* 15: 245–53.

Beardslee, W.R., Bemporad, J., Keller, M.B., and Klerman, G.L. 1983. Children of parents with major affective disorder: A review. *American Journal of Psychiatry* 140: 825–32.

Beardslee, W.R., Keller, M.B., Lavori, P.W., Klerman, G.K., Dorer, D.J., and Samuelson, H. 1988. Psychiatric disorder in adolescent offspring of parents with affective disorder in a non-referred sample. *Journal of Affective Disorders* 15: 313–22.

Beck, S., and Rosenberg, R. 1986. Frequency, quality and impact of life events in self-rated depressed, behavioral-problem, and normal children. *Journal of Consulting and Clinical Psychology* 54: 863–64.

Beck, A.T., Rush, A.J., Shaw, B.F., and Emery, G. 1979. *Cognitive Therapy of Depression* New York: The Guilford Press.

Bernstein, G.A., and Garfinkel, B.D. 1986. School phobia: The overlap of affective and anxiety disorders. *Journal of the American Academy of Child Psychiatry* 25: 235–41.

Bertagnoli, M.W., and Borchardt, C.M. 1990. A review of ECT for children and adolescents. *Journal of the American Academy of Child and Adolescent Psychiatry* 29: 302–07.

Biederman, J., Munir, K., Knee, D., Armentano, M., Autor, S., Waternaux, C., and Tsuang, M. 1987. High rate of affective disorders in probands with attention deficit disorder and in their relatives: A controlled family study. *American Journal of Psychiatry* 144: 330–33.

Bird, H.R., Canino, G., Rubio-Stipec, M., Gould, M.S., Ribera, J., Sesman, M., Woodbury, M., Huertas-Goldman, S., Pagan, A., Sanchez-Lacay, A., and Moscoso, M. 1988. Estimates of the prevalence of childhood maladjustment in a community survey in Puerto Rico: The use of combined measures. *Archives of General Psychiatry* 45, 1120–26.

Birleson, P. 1981. The validity of depressive disorders in childhood and the development of a self-rating scale: A research report. *Journal of Child Psychology and Psychiatry* 22: 73–88.

Blumberg, S.H., and Izard, C.E. 1985. Affective and cognitive characteristics of depression in 10- and 11-year-old children. *Journal of Personality and Social Psychology* 49: 194–202.

– 1986. Discriminating patterns of emotions in 10- and 11-year-old children's anxiety and depression. *Journal of Personality and Social Psychology* 51: 852–57.

Bodiford, C.A., Eisenstadt, T.H., Johnson, J.H., and Bradlyn, A.S. 1988. Comparison of learned helpless cognitions and behavior in children with high and low scores on the Children's Depression Inventory. *Journal of Clinical Child Psychology* 17: 152–58.

Boyd, J.H., Burke, J.D., Gruenberg, E., Holzer, C.E., Rae, D.S., George, L.K., Karno, M., Stoltzman, R., McEvoy, L., and Nestadt, G. 1984. Exclusion Criteria of DSM-III: A study of co-occurrence of hierarchy-free syndromes. *Archives of General Psychiatry* 41: 983–89.

Boyle, M.H. 1988. Evaluating scales to measure childhood psychiatric disorder: Findings of the Ontario Child Health Study. Ph.D. thesis, Toronto, University of Toronto.

Boyle, M.H., Offord, D.R., Hofmann, H.G., Catlin, G.P., Byles, J.A., Cadman, D.T., Crawford, J.W., Links, P.S., Rae-Grant, N.I., and Szatmari, P. 1987. Ontario Child Health Study: I. Methodology. *Archives of General Psychiatry* 44: 826–31.

Brown, R.T., Borden, K.A., Clingerman, S.R., and Jenkins, P. 1988. Depression in attention deficit-disordered and normal children and their parents. *Child Psychiatry and Human Development* 18: 119–32.

Brumback, R.A., and Weinberg, W.A. 1977. Relationship of hyperactivity and depression in children. *Perceptual and Motor Skills* 45: 247–51.

Butler, L., Miezitis, S., Friedman, R., and Cole, E. 1980. The effect of two school-based intervention programs on depressive symptoms in preadolescents. *American Educational Research Journal* 17: 111–19.

Canino, G.J., Bird, H.R., Rubio-Stipec, M., Bravo, M., and Alegria, M. 1990. Children of parents with psychiatric disorder in the community. *Journal of the American Academy of Child and Adolescent Psychiatry* 29: 398–406.

Carey, M.P., Gresham, F.M., Ruggiero, L., Faulstich, M.E., and Enyart, P. 1987. Children's depression inventory: Construct and discriminant validity across clinical and nonreferred (control) populations. *Journal of Consulting and Clinical Psychology* 55: 755–61.

Carlson, G.A., and Garber, J. 1986. Developmental issues in the classification of depression in children. In *Depression in Young People*, edited by M. Rutter, C.E. Izard and P.B. Read, 399–434. New York: The Guilford Press.

Carlson, G.A., and Kashani, J.H. 1988. Phenomenology of major depression from childhood through adulthood: Analysis of three studies. *American Journal of Psychiatry* 145: 1222–25.

Cavallo, A., Holt, K.G., Hejazi, M.S., Richards, G.E., and Meyer, W.J. 1987 . Melatonin circadian rhythm in childhood depression. *Journal of the American Academy of Child and Adolescent Psychiatry* 26: 395–99.

Chess, S., Thomas, A., and Hassibi, M. 1983. Depression in childhood and adolescence: A prospective study of six cases. *Journal of Nervous and Mental Disease* 171: 411–20.

Costello, A.J. 1986. Assessment and diagnosis of affective disorders in children. *Journal of Child Psychology and Psychiatry* 27: 565–74.

Costello, A.J., Edelbrock, C.S., Dulcan, M.K., Kalas, R., and Klaric, S.H. 1984. *Report to the National Institute of Mental Health on the NIMH diagnostic interview schedule for children* Bethesda, Md.: NIMH.

Costello, E.J., and Angold, A. 1988. Scales to assess child and adolescent depression: Checklists, screens, and nets. *Journal of the American Academy of Child and Adolescent Psychiatry* 17: 726–37.

Cytryn, L., and McKnew, D.H. 1985. Treatment issues in childhood depression. *Psychiatric Annals* 15: 401–03.

Delong, G.R., and Aldershof, A.L. 1987. Long-term experience with lithium treatment in childhood: Correlation with clinical diagnosis. *Journal of the American Academy of Child and Adolescent Psychiatry* 26: 389–94.

Doerfler, L.A., Felner, R.D., Rowlison, R.T., Raley, P.A., and Evans, E. 1988. Depression in children and adolescents: A comparative analysis of the utility and construct validity of two assessment measures. *Journal of Consulting and Clinical Psychology* 56: 769–72.

Dwyer, J.T., and Delong, R. 1987. A family history study of twenty probands with childhood manic-depressive illness. *Journal of the American Academy of Child and Adolescent Psychiatry* 26: 176–80.

Eastgate, J., and Gilmour, L. 1984. Long-term outcome of depressed children: A follow-up study. *Developmental Medicine and Child Neurology* 26: 68–72.

Edelbrock, C., and Costello, A.J. 1984. Structured psychiatric interviews for children and adolescents. In *Handbook of psychological assessment*, edited by G. Goldstein, and M. Hersen, 276–90. New York: Pergamon Press.

Edelbrock, C., Costello, A.J., Dulcan, M.K., Kalas, R., and Conover, N.C. 1985. Age differences in the reliability of the psychiatric interview of the child. *Child Development* 56: 265–75.

Edelbrock, C., Costello, A.J., Dulcan, M.K., Conover, N.C. and Kala, R. 1986. Parent-child agreement on child psychiatric symptoms assessed via structured interview. *Journal of Child Psychology and Psychiatry* 27: 181–90.

Emslie, G.J., Roffwarg, H.P., Rush, A.J., Weinberg, W.A., and Parkin-Feigenbaum, L. 1987. Sleep EEG findings in depressed children and adolescents. *American Journal of Psychiatry* 144: 668–70.

Emslie, G.J., Rush, A.J., Weinberg, W.A., Rintelmann, J.W., and Roffwarg, H.P. 1990. Children with major depression show reduced rapid eye movement latencies. *Archives of General Psychiatry* 47: 119–24.

Fincham, F.D., Diener, C.I., and Hokoda, A. 1987. Attributional style and learned helplessness: Relationship to the use of causal schemata and depressive symptoms in children. *British Journal of Social Psychology* 26: 1–7.

Fleming, J.E., and Offord, D.R. 1990. Epidemiology of childhood depressive disorders: A critical review. *Journal of the American Academy of Child and Adolescent Psychiatry* 29: 571–80.

Fleming, J.E., Offord, D.R., and Boyle, M.H. 1989. Prevalence of childhood and adolescent depression in the community: Ontario Child Health Study. *British Journal of Psychiatry* 155: 647–54.

Friedlander, S., Weiss, D.S., and Traylor, J. 1986. Assessing the influence of maternal depression on the validity of the Child Behavior Checklist. *Journal of Abnormal Child Psychology* 14: 123–33.

Fristad, M.A., Weller, E.B., Weller, R.A., Teare, M., and Preskorn, S.H. 1988. Self-report vs. biological markers in assessment of childhood depression. *Journal of Affective Disorders* 15: 339–45.

Garber, J. 1984. The developmental progression of depression in female children. In *New Directions for Child Development: Childhood Depression*, edited by D. Cicchetti, and K. Schneider-Rosen, 29–58. San Francisco: Jossey-Bass Inc.

Geller, B., Chestnut, E.C., Miller, D., Price, D.T., and Yates, E. 1985a. Preliminary data on DSM-III associated features of major depressive disorder in children and adolescents. *American Journal of Psychiatry,* 142: 643–44.

Geller, B., Cooper, T.B., and Chestnut, E.C. 1985b. Serial monitoring and achievement of steady state nortriptyline plasma levels in depressed children and adolescents: Preliminary data. *Journal of Clinical Psychopharmacology* 5: 213–16.

Geller, B., Cooper, T.B., Chestnut, E., Abel, A.S., and Anker, J.A. 1984. Nortriptyline pharmacokinetic parameters in depressed children and adolescents: Preliminary data. *Journal of Clinical Psychopharmacology* 4: 265–69.

Geller, B., Cooper, T.B., Chestnut, E.C., Anker, J.A., Price, D.T., and Yates, E. 1985c. Child and adolescent nortriptyline single dose kinetics predict steady state plasma levels and suggested dose: Preliminary data. *Journal of Clinical Psychopharmacology* 5: 154–58.

Geller, B., Cooper, T.B., Chestnut, E.C., Anker, J.A., and Schluchter, M.D. 1986. Preliminary data on the relationship between nortriptyline plasma level and response in depressed children. *American Journal of Psychiatry* 143: 1283–86.

Geller, b., Cooper, T.B., Graham, D.L., Fetner, H.H., Marsteller, F.A., and Wells, J.M. 1992. Pharamcokinetically designed double-blind placebo-controlled study of nortriptyline in 6- to 12-year-olds with major depressive disorder. *Journal of the American Academy of Child and Adolescent Psychiatry* 31: 34–44.

Geller, B., Cooper, T.B., McCombs, H.G., Graham, D., and Wells, J. 1989. Double-blind, placebo-controlled study of nortriptyline in depressed children using a "fixed plasma level" design. *Psychopharmacology Bulletin* 25: 101–8.

Geller, B., Farooki, Z.Q., Cooper, T.B., Chestnut, E.C., and Abel, A.S. 1985d. Serial ECG measurements at controlled plasma levels of nortriptyline in depressed children. *American Journal of Psychiatry* 142: 1095–97.

Geller, B., Rogol, A.D., and Knitter, E.F. 1983. Preliminary data on the dexamethasone suppression test in children with major depressive disorder. *American Journal of Psychiatry* 140: 620–22.

Gershon, E.S. The genetics of affective disorders. 1983. In *Psychiatry update: The American Psychiatric Assoication Annual Review. Vol.* 2, edited by L. Grinspoon, 434–57. Washington, D.C.: American Psychiatric Press, Inc.

Goodyer, I.M., Wright, C., and Altham, P.M.E. 1988. Maternal adversity and recent stressful life events in anxious and depressed children. *Journal of Child Psychology and Psychiatry* 29: 651–67.

Gordon, D., Burge, D., Hammen, C., Adrian, C., Jaenicke, C., and Hiroto, D. 1989. Observations of interactions of depressed women with their children. *American Journal of Psychiatry* 146: 50–55.

Gutterman, E.M., O'Brien, J.D., and Young, J.G. 1987. Structured diagnostic interviews for children and adolescents: Current status and future directions. *Journal of the American Academy of Child and Adolescent Psychiatry* 26: 621–30.

Guttmacher, L.B., and Cretella, H. 1988. Electroconvulsive therapy in one child and three adolescents. *Journal of Clinical Psychiatry* 49: 20–22.

Guttmacher, L.B., Cretella, H., and Houghtalen, R. 1989. Dr. Guttmacher and colleagues reply. *Journal of Clinical Psychiatry* 50: 106–7.

Haley, G.M.T., Fine, S., Marriage, K., Moretti, M.M., and Freeman, R.J. 1985. Cognitive bias and depression in psychiatrically disturbed children and adolescents. *Journal of Consulting and Clinical Psychology* 53: 535–37.

Hamilton, M. 1960. A rating scale for depression. *Journal of Neurological and Neurosurgical Psychiatry* 23: 56–62.

Hammen, C. 1988. Self-cognitions, stressful events, and the prediction of depression in children of depressed mothers. *Journal of Abnormal Child Psychology* 16: 347–60.

Hammen, C., Adrian, C., Gordon, D., Burge, D., Jaenicke, C., and Hiroto, D. 1987. Children of depressed mothers: Maternal strain and symptom predictors of dysfunction. *Journal of Abnormal Psychology* 96: 190–98.

Hammen, C., Adrian, C., and Hiroto, D. 1988. A longitudinal test of the attributional vulnerability model in children at risk for depression. *British Journal of Clinical Psychology* 27: 37–46.

Harrington, R., Fudge, H., Rutter, M., Pickles, A., and Hill, J. 1990. Adult outcomes of childhood and adolescent depression. *Archives of General Psychiatry* 47: 465–73.

Herjanic, B., Herjanic, M., Brown, F., and Wheatt, T. 1975. Are children reliable reporters? *Journal of Abnormal Psychology* 5: 41–48.

Herjanic, B. and Reich, W. 1982. Development of a structured psychiatric interview for children: Agreement between child and parent on individual symptoms. *Journal of Abnormal Child Psychology* 10: 307–24.

Hodges, K., Kline, J., Stern, L., Cytryn, L., and McKnew, D. 1982. The development of a child assessment interview for research and clinical use. *Journal of Abnormal Child Psychology* 10: 173–89.

Hoier, T.S., and Kerr, M.M. 1988. Extrafamilial information sources in the study of childhood depression. *Journal of the American Academy of Child and Adolescent Psychiatry* 27: 21–33.

Ivens, C., and Rehm, L.P. 1988. Assessment of childhood depression: Correspondence between reports by child, mother and father. *Journal of the American Academy of Child and Adolescent Psychiatry* 27: 738–41.

Jaenicke, C., Hammen, C., Zupan, B., Hiroto, D., Gordon, D., Adrian, C., and Burge, D. 1987. Cognitive vulnerability in children at risk for depression. *Journal of Abnormal Child Psychology* 15: 559–72.

Jefferson, J.W. 1982. The use of lithium in childhood and adolescence: An overview. *Journal of Clinical Psychiatry* 43: 174–77.

Jensen, J.B., Burke, N., and Garfinkel, B.D. 1988a. Depression and symptoms of attention deficit disorder with hyperactivity. *Journal of the American Academy of Child and Adolescent Psychiatry* 27: 742–47.

Jensen, J.B., and Garfinkel, B.D. 1990. Growth hormone dysregulation in children with major depressive disorder. *Journal of the American Academy of Child and Adolescent Psychiatry* 29: 295–301.

Jensen, P.S., Traylor, J., Xenakis, S.N., and Davis, H. 1986b. Child psychopathology rating scales and interrater agreement: I. Parents' gender and psychiatric symptoms. *Journal of the American Academy of Child and Adolescent Psychiatry* 27: 442–50.

Jensen, P.S. Xenakis, S.N., Davis, H., and DeGroot, J. 1988c. Child psychopathology rating scales and interrater agreement: II. Child and family characteristics. *Journal of the American Academy of Child and Adolescent Psychiatry* 27: 451–61.

Jorm, A.F. 1987. Sex and age differences in depression: A quantitative synthesis of published research. *Australian and New Zealand Journal of Psychiatry* 21: 46–53.

Joshi, P.T., Capozzoli, J.A., and Coyle, J.T. 1987. Children's depression rating scale: normative data, utility with child inpatients. Paper presented at the Annual Meeting of the American Academy of Child and Adolescent Psychiatry, Washington, D.C.

Kashani, J.H., McGee, R.O., Clarkson, S.E., Anderson, J.C., Walton, L.A., Williams, S., Silva, P.A., Robins, A.J., Cytryn, L., and McKnew, D.H. 1983. Depression in a sample of 9-year-old children. *Archives of General Psychiatry* 40: 1217–23.

Kashani, J.H., Orvaschel, H., Burk, J.P., and Reid, J.C. 1985. Informant variance: The issue of parent-child disagreement. *Journal of the American Academy of Child and Adolescent Psychiatry* 24: 437–41.

Kashani, J.H., Orvaschel, H., Rosenberg, T.K., and Reid, J.C. 1989. Psychopathology in a community sample of children and adolescents: A developmental perspective. *Journal of the American Academy of Child and Adolescent Psychiatry* 28: 701–06.

Kashani, J.H., Shekim, W.O., and Reid, J.C. 1984. Amitriptyline in children with major depressive disorder: a double-blind crossover pilot study. *Journal of the American Academy of Child Psychiatry* 23: 348–51.

Kashani, J.H., and Simonds, J.F. 1979. The incidence of depression in children. *American Journal of Psychiatry* 136: 1203–5.

Kashani, J.H., Vaidya, A.F., Soltys, S.M., Dandoy, A.C., and Reid, J.C. 1990. Life events and major depression in a sample of inpatient children. *Comprehensive Psychiatry* 31: 266–74.

Kaslow, N.J., Rehm, L.P., Pollack, S.L., and Siegel, A.W. 1988. Attributional style and self-control behavior in depressed and nondepressed children and their parents. *Journal of Abnormal Child Psychology* 16: 163–75.

Kaslow, N.J., Rehm, L.P., and Siegel, A.W. 1984. Social-cognitive and cognitive correlates of depression in children. *Journal of Abnormal Child Psychology* 12: 605–20.

Kazdin, A.E. 1981. Assessment techniques for childhood depression - a critical appraisal. *Journal of the American Academy of Child Psychiatry* 20: 358–75.

– 1987. Children's Depression Scale: Validation with child psychiatric inpatients. *Journal of Child Psychology and Psychiatry* 28: 29–41.

Kazdin, A.E., Esveldt-Dawson, K., Unis, A.S., and Rancurello, M.D. 1983a. Child and parent evaluations of depression and agression in psychiatric inpatient children. *Journal of Abnormal Child Psychology* 11: 401–13.

Kazdin, A.E., French, N.H., Unis, A.S., and Esveldt-Dawson, K. 1983b. Assessment of childhood depression: Correspondence of child and parent ratings. *Journal of the American Academy of Child Psychiatry* 22: 157–64.

Kazdin, A.E., and Petti, T.A. 1982. Self-report and interview measures of childhood and adolescent depression. *Journal of Child Psychology and Psychiatry* 23: 437–57.

Keller, M.B., Beardslee, W.R., Dorer, D.J., Lavori, P.W. Samuelson, H., and Klerman, G.R. 1986. Impact of severity and chronicity of parental affective illness on adaptive functioning and psychopathology in children. *Archives of General Psychiatry* 43: 930–37.

Kendall, P.C., Stark, D.D., and Adam, T. 1990. Cognitive deficit or cognitive distortion in childhood depression. *Journal of Abnormal Child Psychology* 18: 255–70.

Kendall, P.C., and Watson, D. 1989. *Anxiety and depression: distinctive and overlapping features.* San Diego: Academic Press.

Khandelwal, S.K., Varma, V.K., and Murthy, R.S. 1984. Renal function in children receiving long-term lithium prophylaxis. *American Journal of Psychiatry* 141: 278–79.

Knight, D., Hensley, V.R., and Waters, B. 1988. Validation of the Children's Depression Scale and the Children's Depression Inventory in a prepubertal sample. *Journal of Child Psychology and Psychiatry* 29: 853–63.

Kovacs, M. 1980–1981. Rating scales to assess depression in school-aged children. *Acta Paedopsychiatrica* 46: 305–15.

– 1982. *The longitudinal study of child and adolescent psychopathology: I. The semi-structured psychiatric interview schedule for children.* Pittsburgh: University of Pittsburgh. Manuscript.

– 1985a. The children's depression inventory. *Psychopharmacology Bulletin* 21: 995–98.

– 1985b. The natural history and course of depressive disorders in childhood. *Psychiatric Annals* 15: 387–89.

Kovacs, M., and Beck, A.T. 1977. An empirical clinical approach toward a definition of childhood depression. In *Depression in childhood,* edited by J.G. Schulterbrand, and A. Ruskin, 21–25. New York: Raven Press.

Kovacs, M., Feinberg, T.L., Crouse-Novak, M.A., Paulauskas, S.L., and Finkelstein, R. 1984a. Depressive disorders in childhood. I. A longitudinal prospective study of characteristics and recovery. *Archives of General Psychiatry* 41: 229–37.

Kovacs, M., Feinberg, T.L., Crouse-Novak, M., Paulauskas, S.L., Pollock, M., and Finkelstein, R. 1984b. Depressive disorders in childhood. II. A longitudinal study of the risk for a subsequent major depression. *Archives of General Psychiatry* 41: 643–49.

Kovacs, M., Gatsonis, C., Paulauskas, S.L., and Richards, C. 1989. Depressive disorders in childhood. IV. A longitudinal study of comorbidity with and risk for anxiety disorders. *Archives of General Psychiatry* 46: 776–82.

Kovacs, M., Paulauskas, S., Gatsonis, C., and Richards, C. 1988. Depressive disorder in childhood. III. A longitudinal study of comorbidity with and risk for conduct disorders. *Journal of Affective Disorders* 15: 205–17.

Kupfer, D.J., Coble, P., Kane, J., Petti, T., and Conners, C.K. 1979. Imipramine and EEG sleep in children with depressive symptoms. *Psychopharmacology* 60: 117–23.

Lang, M., and Tisher, M. 1978. *Children's Depression Scale.* Victoria, Australia: Australian Council for Educational Research.

Laroche, C., Cheifetz, P., Lester, E.P., Schibuk, L., Di Tommaso, E., and Engelsmann, F. 1985. Psychopathology in the offspring of parents with bipolar affective
disorders. *Canadian Journal of Psychiatry* 30: 337–43.

Laroche, C., Sheiner, R., Lester, E., Benierakis, C., Marrache, M., Engelsmann,
F., and Cheifetz, P. 1987. Children of parents with manic-depressive illness: A
follow-up study. *Canadian Journal of Psychiatry* 32: 563–69.

Lefkowitz, M.M., and Tesiny, E.P. 1980. Assessment of childhood depression. *Journal
of Consulting and Clinical Psychology* 48, 43–50.

Lefkowitz, M.M., Tesiny, E.P., and Gordon, N.H. 1980. Childhood depression, family
income and locus of control. *The Journal of Nervous and Mental Disease* 168:
732–35.

Lena, B. 1979. Lithium in childhood and adolescent psychiatry. *Archives of General
Psychiatry* 36: 854–55.

Leon, G.R., Kendal, P.C., and Garber, J. 1980. Depression in children: Parent, teacher
and child perspectives. *Journal of Abnormal Child Psychology* 8: 221–35.

Lewinsohn, P.M., Sullivan, J.M., and Grosscup, S.J. 1980. Changing reinforcing
events: An approach to the treatment of depression. *Psychotherapy: Theory, Research and Practice* 17: 322–34.

Livingston, R., Nugent, H., Rader, L.m and Smith, G.R. 1985. Family histories
of depressed and severely anxious children. *American Journal of Psychiatry* 142:
1497–99.

Livingston, R., Reis, C.J., and Ringdahl, I.C. 1984. Abnormal dexamethasone suppression test results in depressed and nondepressed children. *American Journal
of Psychiatry* 141: 106–8.

Loosen, P.T., and Prange, A.J. 1982. Serum thyrotropin response to thyrotropin
releasing hormone in psychiatric patients: A review. *American Journal of Psychiatry* 139: 405–16.

McCauley, E., Mitchell, J.R., Burke, P.m and Moss, S. 1988. Cognitive attributes
of depression in children and adolescents. *Journal of Consulting and Clinical
Psychology* 56: 903–8.

McCracken, J.T. 1987. Depressive disorders in rural nine-year-old children: Prevalence
and characteristics. Los Angeles: UCLA Neuropsychiatric Institute Manuscript.

McGee, R., and Williams, S. 1988. A longitudinal study of depression in nine-
year-old children. *Journal of the American Academy of Child and Adolescent
Psychiatry* 27: 342–48.

Marriage, K., Fine, S., Moretti, M., and Haley, G. 1986. Relationship between depression and conduct disorder in children and adolescents. *Journal of the American
Academy of Child Psychiatry* 25: 687–91.

Maser, J.D., and Cloninger, C.R. 1990. *Comorbidity of mood and anxiety disorders*
Washington, D.C.: American Psychiatric Press.

Merikangas, K.R., Prusoff, B.A., and Weissman, M.M. 1988. Parental concordance
for affective disorders: Psychopatholgy in offspring. *Journal of Affective Disorders*
15: 279–90.

Meyer, N.E., Dyck, D.G., and Petrinack, R.J. 1989. Cognitive appraisal and attributional correlates of depressive symptoms in children. *Journal of Abnormal Child Psychology* 17: 325–36.

Minuti, E., and Gallo, V. 1982. Use of antidepressants in childhood: Results of maprotiline treatment in 20 cases. In *Typical and atypical antidepressants: Clinical practice,* edited by E. Costa, and G. Racagni, New York: Raven Press.

Mitchell, J., McCauley, E., Burke, P., Calderon, R., and Schloredt, K. 1989. Psychopathology in parents of depressed children and adolescents. *Journal of the American Academy of Child and Adolescent Psychiatry* 28: 352–57.

Mitchell, J., McCauley, E., Burke, P.M., and Moss, S.J. 1988. Phenomenology of depression in children and adolescents. *Journal of the American Academy of Child and Adolescent Psychiatry* 27: 12–20.

Mokros, H.B., Poznanski, E., Grossman, J.A., and Freeman, L.N. 1987. A comparison of child and parent ratings of depression for normal and clinically referred children. *Journal of Child Psychology and Psychiatry* 28: 613–27.

Moretti, M.M., Fine, S., Haley, G., and Marriage, K. 1985. Childhood and adolescent depression: child-report versus parent-report information. *Journal of the American Academy of Child Psychiatry* 24: 298–302.

Mouren, M.C., Denis, H.P., and Dugas, M. 1983. Traitement de la depression chez l'enfant et l'adolescent par une nouvelle molecule non tricyclique: la mianserine. *Neuropsychiatrie de l'Enfance* 31: 485–90.

Mullins, L.L., Siegel, L.J., and Hodges, K. 1985. Cognitive problem-solving and life event correlates of depressive symptoms in children. *Journal of Abnormal Child Psychology* 13: 305–14.

Munir, K., Biederman, J., and Knee, D. 1987. Psychiatric comorbidity in patients with attention deficit disorder: A controlled study. *Journal of the American Academy of Child and Adolescent Psychiatry* 26: 844–48.

Offord, D.R. 1989. Conduct Disorder: Risk factors and prevention. In *Prevention of mental disorders, alcohol and other drug use,* edited by D. Shaffer, I. Philips, and N.B. Enzer. Rockville, Md.: U.S. Department of Health and Human Services.

Offord, D.R., Boyle, M.H., and Racine, Y. 1989. Ontario Child Health Study: Correlates of disorder. *Journal of the American Academy of Child and Adolescent Psychiatry* 28: 856–60.

Offord, D.R., Boyle, M.H. Szatmari, P., Rae-Grant, N.I., Links, P.S., Cadman, D.T., Byles, J.A., Crawford, J.W., Munroe Blum, H., Byrne, C., Thomas, H., and Woodward, C.A. 1987. Ontario Child Health Study II. Six-month prevalence of disorder and rates of service utilization. *Archives of General Psychiatry* 44: 832–36.

Orvaschel, H., Puig-Antich, J., Chambers, W., Tabrizi, M.A., and Johnson, R. 1982. Retrospective assessment of prepubertal major depression with the Kiddie-SADS-E. *Journal of the American Academy of Child Psychiatry* 21: 392–97.

Peet, M., and Coppen, A. 1980. Lithium treatment and prophylaxis in unipolar depression. *Psychosomatics* 21: 303–13.

Petti, T.A. 1978. Depression in hospitalized child psychiatry inpatients: Approaches to measuring depression. *Journal of the American Academy of Child Psychiatry* 17: 49–59.

Petti, T.A., and Law, W. 1982. Imipramine treatment of depressed children: A double-blind pilot study. *Journal of Clinical Psychopharmacology* 2: 107–10.

Petty, L.K., Asarnow, J.R., Carlson, G.A., and Lesser, L. 1985. The dexamethasone suppression test in depressed, dysthymic and nondepressed children. *American Journal of Psychiatry* 142: 631–33.

Pfeffer, C.R., Lipkins, R., Plutchik, R., and Mizruchi, M. 1988. Normal children at risk for suicidal behavior: A two-year follow-up study. *Journal of the American Academy of Child and Adolescent Psychiatry* 27: 34–41.

Pfeffer, C.R., Stokes, P., Weiner, A., Shindledecker, R., Faughnan, L., Mintz, M., Stoll, P.M., and Heiligenstein, E. 1989. Psychopathology and plasma cortisol responses to dexamethasone in prepubertal psychiatric inpatients. *Biological Psychiatry* 26: 677–89.

Poznanski, E.O., Carroll, B.J., Banegas, M.C., Cook, S.C., and Grossman, J.A. 1982. The dexamethasone suppression test in prepubertal depressed children. *American Journal of Psychiatry* 139: 321–24.

Poznanski, E.O., Cook, S.C., Carroll, B.J. 1979. A depression rating scale for children. *Pediatrics* 64: 442–50.

Poznanski, E.O., Freeman, L.N., and Mokros, H.B. 1985. Children's depression rating scale – revised. *Psychopharmacology Bulletin* 21: 979–89.

Poznanski, E.O., Krahenbuhl, V., and Zrull, J.P. 1976. Childhood depression: A longitudinal perspective. *Journal of the American Academy of Child Psychiatry* 15: 491–501.

Preskorn, S.H., Weller, E.B., Hughes, C.W., Weller, R.A., and Bolte, K. 1987. Depression in prepubertal children: Dexamethasone nonsupression predicts differential response to imipramine vs. placebo. *Psychopharmacology Bulletin* 23: 128–33.

Preskorn, S.H., Weller, E., Jerkovich, G., Hughes, C.W., and Weller, R. 1988. Depression in children: Concentration - dependent CNS toxicity of tricyclic antidepressants. *Psychopharmacology Bulletin* 24: 140–42.

Preskorn, S.H., Weller, E.B., Weller, R.A., and Glotzbach, E. 1983. Plasma levels of imipramine and adverse effects in children. *American Journal of Psychiatry* 140: 1332–35.

Prien, R.F. 1983. Long-term prophylactic pharmacologic treatment of bipolar illness. In *Psychiatry update: The American Psychiatric Association annual review.* Vol. 2, edited by L. Grinspoon, 303–318. Washington, D.C.: American Psychiatric Press Inc.

Prien, R.F., Kupfer, D.J., Mansky, P.A., Small J.G., Tuason, V.B., Voss, C.B., and Johnson, W.E. 1984. Drug therapy in the prevention of recurrences in unipolar and bipolar affective disorders. *Archives of General Psychiatry* 41: 1096–1104.

Puig-Antich, J. 1980. Affective disorders in childhood. *Psychiatric Clinics of North America* 3: 403–25.

– 1982a. Major depression and conduct disorder in prepuberty. *Journal of the Amer-*

68   Depression and the Social Environment

ican Academy of Child Psychiatry 21: 118-28.

- 1982b. The use of RDC criteria for major depressive disorder in children and adolescents. *Journal of the American Academy of Child Psychiatry* 21: 291-93.
- 1984. Clinical and treatment aspects of depression in childhood and adolescence. *Pediatric Annals* 13: 37-45.
- 1987. Affective disorders in children and adolescents: Diagnostic validity and psychobiology. In *Psychopharmacology: The third generation of progress*, edited by H.Y. Meltzer, 843-59. New York: Raven Press.
- 1988. Comments at the Annual Childhood Depression Consortium, Yale University, New Haven, Conn.
Puig-Antich, J., and Chambers. W. 1978. *The schedule for affective disorders and schizophrenia for school-aged children*. New York: New York State Psychiatric Institute.
Puig-Antich, J., Dahl, R., Ryan, N., Novacenko, H., Goetz, D., Goetz, R., Twomey, J., and Klepper, T. 1989b. Cortisol secretion in prepubertal children with major depressive disorder. *Archives of General Psychiatry* 46: 801-9.
Puig-Antich, J., Goetz, R., Davies, M, Fein, M., Hanlon, C., Chambers, W.J., Tabrizi, M.A., Sachar, E.J., and Wietzman, E.D. 1984b. Growth hormone secretion in prepubertal children with major depression II. Sleep-related plasma concentrations during a depressive episode. *Archives of General Psychiatry* 41: 463-66.
Puig-Antich, J., Goetz, D., Davies, M., Kaplan, T., Davies, S., Ostrow, L., Asnis, L., Twomey, J., Iyengar, S., and Ryan, N.D. 1989a. A controlled family history study of prepubertal major depressive disorder. *Archives of General Psychiatry* 46: 406-18.
Puig-Antich, J., Goetz, R., Davies, M., Tabrizi, M.A., Novacenko, H., Hanlon, C., Sachar, E.J., and Weitzman, E.D. 1984b. Growth hormone secretion in prepubertal children with major depression IV. Sleep-related plasma concentrations in a drug-free, fully recovered clinical state. *Archives of General Psychiatry* 41: 479-83.
Puig-Antich, J., Goetz, R., Hanlon, C., Davies, M., Thompson, J., Chambers, W.J., Tabrizi, M.A., and Weitzman, E.D. 1982. Sleep architecture and REM sleep measures in prepubertal children with major depression. *Archives of General Psychiatry* 39: 932-39.
Puig-Antich, J., Goetz, R., Hanlon, C., Tabrizi, M.A., Davies, M., and Weitzmann, E.D. 1983. Sleep architecture and REM sleep measures in prepubertal major depressives: Studies during recovery from the depressive episode in a drug-free state. *Archives of General Psychiatry* 40: 187-92.
Puig-Antich, J., Novacenko, H., Davies, M., Chambers, W.J., Tabrizi, M.A., Krawiec, V., Ambrosini, P.J., and Sachar, E.J. 1984c. Growth hormone secretion in prepubertal children with major depression I. Final report on response to insulin-induced hypoglycemia during a depressive episode. *Archives of General Psychiatry* 41: 455-60.
Puig-Antich, J., Novacenko, H., Davies, M., Tabrizi, M.A., Ambrosini, P., Goetz, R., Bianca, J., Goetz, D., and Sachar, E.J. 1984d. Growth hormone secretion

in prepubertal children with major depression III. Response to insulin-induced hypoglycemia after recovery from a depressive episode and in a drug-free state. *Archives of General Psychiatry* 41: 471–75.

Puig-Antich, J., Orvaschel, H., Tabrizi, M.A., and Chambers, W. 1980. *The schedule for affective disorders and schizophrenia for school-age children - epidemiologic version (Kiddie-SADS-E).* 3d ed. New York: New York State Psychiatric Institute and Yale University School of Medicine.

Puig-Antich, J., Perel, J.M., Lupatkin, W., Chambers, W.J., Tabrizi, M.A., King, J., Goetz, R., Davies, M., and Stiller, R.L. 1987. Imipramine in prepubertal major depressive disorders. *Archives of General Psychiatry* 44: 81–9.

Puig-Antich, J., and Rabinovich, J. 1986. Relationship between affective and anxiety disorders in childhood. In *Anxiety disorders of childhood*, edited by R. Gittleman, 136–56. New York: The Guilford Press.

Rehm, L.P., Kaslow, N.J., and Rabin, A.S. 1987. Cognitive and behavioral targets in a self-control therapy program for depression. *Journal of Consulting and Clinical Psychology* 55: 60–67.

Reich, W., Herjanic, B., Welner, Z., and Gandhy, P.R. 1982. Development of a structured interview for children: Agreement on diagnosis comparing child and parent interviews. *Journal of Abnormal Child Psychology* 10: 325–36.

Reynolds, W.M., Anderson, G., and Bartell, N. 1985. Measuring depression in children: A multimethod assessment investigation. *Journal of Abnormal Child Psychology* 13: 513–26.

Robins, L.N. 1979. Longitudinal methods in the study of normal and pathological development. In *Grundlagen und Methoden der Psychiatrie* Vol. 1, edited by K.P. Kisker, J.E. Meye, C. Muller and E. Stromgren, 627–684. Heidelberg: Springer-Verlag.

Rolf, J.E., Johnson, J.L., Israel, E., Baldwin, J.m and Chandra, A. 1988. Depressive affect in school-aged children of alcoholics. *British Journal of Addiction* 83: 841–48.

Rosenthal, N.E., Carpenter, C.J., James, S.P., Parry, B.L., Rogers, S.L.B., and Wehr, T.A. 1986. Seasonal affective disorder in children and adolescents. *American Journal of Psychiatry* 143: 356–58.

Rosenthal, N.E., Sack, D.A., Gillin, C., Lewy, A.J., Goodwin, F.K., Davenport, Y., Mueller, P.S., Newsome, D.A., and Wehr, T.A. 1984. Seasonal affective disorder: A description of the syndrome and preliminary findings with light therapy. *Archives of General Psychiatry* 41: 72–80.

Rotundo, N.m and Hensley, V.R. 1985. The children's depression scale: A study of its validity. *Journal of Child Psychology and Psychiatry* 26: 917–27.

Rutter, M. 1986. Depressive feelings, cognitions, and disorders: A research postscript. In *Depression in Young People*, edited by M. Rutter, C.E. Izard and P.B. Read, 491–519. New York: The Guilford Press.

Rutter, M., and Quinton, D. 1984. Parental psychiatric disorder: Effects on children. *Psychological Medicine* 14: 853–80.

Ryan, N.D., Puig-Antich, J., Ambrosini, P., Rabinovich, H., Robinson, D., Nelson, B., Iyengar, S., and Twomey, J. 1987. The clinical picture of major depression in children and adolescents. *Archives of General Psychiatry* 44: 854–61.

Sacco, W.P., and Graves, D.J. 1984. Childhood depression, interpersonal problem-solving, and self-ratings of performance. *Journal of Clinical Child Psychology* 13: 10–15.

– 1985. Correspondence between teacher ratings of childhood depression and child self-ratings. *Journal of Clinical Child Psychology* 14: 353–55.

Sallee, F., Stiller, R., Perel, J., and Rancurello, M. 1986. Targetting imipramine dose in children with depression. *Clinical Pharmacology Therapy* 40: 8–13.

Saylor, C.F., Finch, A.J., Baskin, C.H., Furey, W., and Kelly, M.M. 1984. Construct validity for measures of childhood depression: Application of multitrait-multimethod methodology. *Journal of Consulting and Clinical Psychology* 52: 977–85.

Seligman, M.E.P., Peterson, C., Kaslow, N.J., Tanenbaum, R.L., Alloy, L.B., and Abramson, L.Y. 1984. Attributional style and depressive symptoms among children. *Journal of Abnormal Psychology* 93: 235–38.

Shaffer, D., Campbell, M., Cantwell, D., Bradley, S., Carlson, G., Cohen, D., Denckla, M., Frances, A., Garfinkel, B., Klein, R., Pincus, H., Spitzer, R.L., Volkmar, F., and Widiger, T. 1989. Child and adolescent psychiatric disorders in DSM-IV: Issues facing the work group. *Journal of the American Academy of Child and Adolescent Psychiatry* 28: 830–35.

Shaffer, D., Schwab-Stone, M., Fisher, P., and Cohen, P. 1987. A modified version of the diagnostic interview schedule for children (DISC 2). I. Revision of the instrument. Paper presented at the Annual Meeting of the American Academy of Child and Adolescent Psychiatry, Washington, D.C.

Sonis, W.A., Yellin, A.M., Garfinkel, B.D., and Hoberman, H.H. 1987. The antidepressant effect of light in seasonal affective disorder of childhood and adolescence. *Psychopharmacology Bulletin* 23: 360–63.

Spitzer, R.L., Endicott, J., and Robins, E. 1978. Research diagnostic criteria. *Archives of General Psychiatry* 35: 773–82.

Stark, K.D., Reynolds, W.M., and Kaslow, N.J. 1987. A comparison of the relative efficacy of self-control therapy and a behavioral problem-solving therapy for depression in children. *Journal of Abnormal Child Psychology* 15: 91–113.

Stavrakaki, C., Vargo, B., Boodoosingh, L., and Roberts, N. 1987a. The relationship between anxiety and depression in children: Rating scales and clinical variables. *Canadian Journal of Psychiatry* 32: 433–39.

Stavrakaki, C., Vargo, B., Roberts, N., and Boodoosingh, L. 1987b. Concordance among sources of information for ratings of anxiety and depression in children. *Journal of the American Academy of Child and Adolescent Psychiatry* 26: 733–37.

Stavrakaki, C., Vargo, B., and Williams, E. 1987c. Anxiety and depression in prepubertal children. Paper presented at the Annual Meeting of the Canadian Academy of Child Psychiatry, London, Ontario.

Strauss, C.C., Last, C.G., Hersen, M., and Kazdin, A.E. 1988. Association between anxiety and depression in children and adolescents with anxiety disorders. *Journal of Abnormal Child Psychology* 16: 57-68.

Sylvester, C.E., Hyde, T.S., and Reichler, R.J. 1987. The diagnostic interview for children and personality inventory for children in studies of children at risk for anxiety disorders or depression. *Journal of the American Academy of Child and Adolescent Psychiatry* 26: 668-75.

Velez, C.N., Johnson, J., and Cohen, P. 1989. A longitudinal analysis of selected risk factors for childhood psychopathology. *Journal of the American Academy of Child and Adolescent Psychiatry* 28: 861-64.

Weinberg, W.A., Rutman, J., Sullivan, L., Penick, E.C., and Dietz, S.G. Depression in children referred to an educational diagnostic center: Diagnoses and treatment. *Behavioral Pediatrics* 83: 1065-72.

Weiss, B., and Weisz, J.R. 1988. Factor structure of self-reported depression: Clinic-referred children versus adolescents. *Journal of Abnormal Psychology* 97: 492-95.

Weissman, M.M. 1987. Advances in psychiatric epidemiology: Rates and risks for major depression. *American Journal of Public Health* 77: 445-51.

Weissman, M.M., Gammon, G.D., John, K., Merikangas, K.R., Warner, V., Prusoff, B.A., and Sholomskas, D. 1987a. Children of depressed parents - increased psychopathology and early onset of major depression. *Archives of General Psychiatry* 44: 847-53.

Weissman, M.M., and Klerman, G.L. 1977. Sex differences and the epidemiology of depression. *Archives of General Psychiatry* 34: 98-111.

Weissman, M.M., Leaf, P.J., Holzer, C.E., Myers, J.K., and Tischler, G.L. 1984. The epidemiology of depression: An update on sex differences in rates. *Journal of Affective Disorders* 7: 179-88.

Weissman, M.M., Orvaschel, H., and Padian, N. 1980. Children's symptom and social functioning self-report scales. *The Journal of Nervous and Mental Disease* 168: 736-40.

Weissman, M.M., Warner, V., Wickramaratne, P., and Prusoff, B.A. 1988. Early-onset major depression in parents and their children. *Journal of Affective Disorders* 15: 269-77.

Weissman, M.M., Wickramaratne, P., Warner, V., John, K., Prusoff, B.S., Merikangas, K.R., and Gammon, G.D. 1987b. Assessing psychiatric disorders in children. *Archives of General Psychiatry* 44: 747-53.

Weisz, J.R., Stevens, J.S., Curry, J.F., Cohen, R., Craighead, W.E., Burlingame, W.V., Smith, A., Weiss, B., and Parmelee, D.X. 1989. Control-related cognitions and depression among inpatient children and adolescents. *Journal of the American Academy of Child and Adolescent Psychiatry* 28: 358-63.

Weisz, J.R. Weiss, B., Wasserman, A.A., and Rintoul, B. 1987. Control-related beliefs and depression among clinic-referred children and adolescents. *Journal of Abnormal Psychology* 96: 58-63.

Weller, E.B., Weller, R.A., Fristad, M.A., and Preskorn, S.H. 1984. The dexamethasone suppression test in hospitalized prepubertal depressed children. *American Journal of Psychiatry* 141: 290–91.

Weller, E.B., Weller, R.A., Fristad, M.A., Cantwell, M.L., and Preskorn, S.H. 1986. Dexamethasone suppression test and clinical outcome in prepubertal depressed children. *American Journal of Psychiatry* 143: 1469–70.

Weller, R.A., and Weller, E.B. 1986. Tricyclic antidepressants in prepubertal depressed children: review of the literature. *Hillside Journal of Clinical Psychiatry* 8: 46–55.

Welner, Z., and Rice, J. 1988. School-aged children of depressed parents: A blind and controlled study. *Journal of Affective Disorders* 15: 291–302.

Welner, Z., Reich, W., Herjanic, B., Jung, K., and Amado, H. 1987. Reliability, validity, and parent-child agreement studies of the Diagnostic Interview for Children and Adolescents (DICA). *Journal of the American Academy of Child and Adolescent Psychiatry* 26: 649–53.

Wierzbicki, M. 1987. A parent form of the children's depression inventory: Reliability and validity in nonclinical populations. *Journal of Clinical Psychology* 43: 390–97.

Wilkes, T.C.R. 1987. Management of affective disorders in children. *Update* March 15: 617–26.

Wilkes, T.C.R., and Rush, A.J. 1988. Adaptations of cognitive therapy for depressed adolescents. *Journal of the American Academy of Child and Adolescent Psychiatry* 27: 381–86.

Williams, J.M.G. 1984. *The psychological treatment of depression: A guide to the theory and practice of cognitive-behavior therapy.* New York: Free Press.

Wirt, R.D. Lachar, D., Klinedinst, J.K., and Seat, P.D. 1977. *Multidimensional description of child personality: A manual for the personality inventory for children.* Los Angeles: Western Psychological Services.

Yaylayan, S.A., Weller, E.B., Weller, R.A., Fristad, M.A., and Preskorn, S.H. 1989. DST status and blood chemistries in prepubertal children. *Psychiatry Research* 29: 215–19.

Young, W., Knowles, J.B., MacLean, A.W., Boag, L., and McConville, B.J. 1982. The sleep of childhood depressives: Comparison with age-matched controls. *Biological Psychiatry* 17: 1163–68.

Zeitlin, H. 1986. *The natural history of psychiatric disorders in children.* New York: Oxford University Press.

CHAPTER THREE

Adolescent Depression

STAN KUTCHER, PETER MARTON,
AND CAROLYN BOULOS

The syndrome of depression in adolescents has recently gained recognition as a serious psychiatric disturbance (Cantwell and Carlson 1983; Puig-Antich and Gittleman 1982; Rutter et al. 1986; Ryan and Puig-Antich 1986). Indeed this view has supplanted previously held constructs, which included denial of the existence of the disorder or conceived of adolescent-depressive disturbance as a normative developmental phenomenon (Baker 1978; Freud 1958; Geleerd 1961; Sugar, 1968). Studies of nonclinical samples of teenagers have led to a revision of earlier concepts, which held that mood disorder in adolescence was inevitablly attributable to universal adolescent turmoil. A clearer identification has also emerged of the boundaries between normative development and the syndrome of depression (Offer and Offer 1975; Offer and Sabshin 1984; Rutter et al. 1976).

THEORETICAL PERSPECTIVES

Clinical understanding of adolescent depression has been directed to a great degree by theoretical postulates that have rarely been empirically tested, thus limiting their scientific value (Caws 1965; Hempel 1966; Nazel 1961; Popper 1959). Indeed, until recently, many authors used the case-report method to support their view of, and interventions into, adolescent depression, although often that was done for the mistaken purpose of hypothesis verification – something a case report can never do – rather than hypothesis generation (Anthony 1970; Baker 1978; Blos 1967; Ladame 1987; McCartney 1987). The vague writing in this area has caused unnecessary confusion as well. Witness, for example, the interchangeable use of "depression" to mean a "symptom" (which is ubiquitous and nonspecific) or "syndrome" (as defined, for instance, in *the Diagnostic and Statistical Manual of Mental Disorder-Third Edition* [DSM-III] or *the Diagnostic and Statistical Manual of Mental Disorders-Third Edition-revised* [DSM-III-R]) (Anthony 1970; Baker 1978; Blos 1967; Freud 1958; Geleerd 1961; Ladame 1987; McCartney 1987; Sugar 1968). In addition, many writers (Anthony 1970; Baker 1978; Ladame 1987; McCartney 1987) have seemingly not grasped that hypotheses generated to explain the development of depressed feelings may be inappropriate to explain the development of a depressive syndrome and, following from this, that treatment designed to improve depressed feelings may be inappropriate for ameliorating the depressive syndrome.

In addition, certain theoretical frameworks have tended toward more of a "truth by faith" approach (classical psychoanalysis), while others have been subjected to empirical testing (cognitive/behavioural, neurobiological). Although this chapter cannot hope to describe and critique, adequately, the many and varied theories of adolescent depression, it will briefly review several of the more commonly held perspectives, thereby serving as an introduction to current knowledge about adolescent depression as it has developed from the scientific study of its phenomenology, epidemiology, comorbidity, outcome, and treatment.

Analytic-Developmental Theories

In Sigmund Freud's classic conceptualization of depression (Freud 1917) the loss of an ambivalently held love object is introjected into the unconscious, resulting in an unleashing of hostile impulses against the self. A tremendous decrement in self-respect – depression – results. This "anger turned inwards" model was based on the simplistic concept of energy transfer and entropy acting within a hypothetical structure of the self. The difficulties with this unproven model are many; nonetheless, it has profoundly influenced the "understanding" of adolescent depression, in that adolescent depression is now often viewed as resulting from significant loss.

But not only has it not been shown that this "anger turned inwards" is an invariable feature of adolescent depression, it is also clear that most adolescent depressives do not demonstrate significant losses that predate the onset of their depression. Nevertheless, some authors have expanded this loss concept to the untested hypothesis that depression in teens is ubiquitous because it arises from the mourning of the loss of childhood (Baker 1978; Freud 1958; Sugar 1968).

Others (Anthony 1970; Baker 1978; Ladame 1987; McCartney 1987) invoking a developmental recapitulation hypothesis, have postulated that breakdown of parental idealization inevitably leads to aggression against the self in which, as one author overdramatically puts it, "both self and [the] hated incorporate objects are annihilated and death is the punishment for the wish to kill" (Anthony 1970). In addition, theorists of both persuasions, although lacking concrete evidence, have invoked the sexual maturation of adolescence as a causal factor (never explained) in these processes (Anthony 1970; Baker 1978; Blos 1967; Freud 1958; Geleerd 1961; Ladame 1987; McCartney 1987; Sugar 1968).

Influential writings by Klein and others (Segal 1975) postulated that depression arises from early infantile conflicts between inner drives and denial of external gratification, as the child interacts with a "part-object" (for example the breast). These concepts, although they are based mostly on untested assumptions plus the later work of Mahler (Mahler 1971; Mahler et al. 1975), have led, in turn, to another type of developmental recapitulation hypothesis, one in which the adolescent task of separation-individuation is seen to rekindle unresolved infantile conflicts, thus leading to depression (Anthony 1970; Baker 1978; Bowlby 1969, 1980; Freud 1917; Klerman 1980; Ladame 1987; Mahler 1961, 1971; Mahler et al. 1975; McCartney 1987; Rutter 1986; Segal 1975). Unfortunately, neither the concepts of developmental arrest nor those of separation-individuation conflict demonstrate that these phenomena lead to depression *per se*.

Attachment theory (Bowlby 1969, 1980), in which early loss of close relationships operates as a vulnerability factor leading to adolescent depression, although heuristically appealing, awaits careful scrutiny as well (Klerman 1980). Teens who are insecurely attached may, indeed, be more vulnerable to depression. This hypothesis, however, still needs proper testing. Preliminary data from our ongoing research project on adolescent depression suggests that loss of close peer, or parental, relationships, as a precipitating factor, is rather rare in teens with major depression. Indeed, less than 18 per cent of adolescents meeting DSM-III-R criteria for major depressive disorder reported such a loss in the six months preceding their illness onset – a finding not significantly different from age- and sex-matched, nondepressed, psychiatric controls. Similarly, the depressed and psychiatric control groups did not differ significantly in frequency of either lifetime parental losses or major separations from a parent. Much further study of these issues, however, is necessary before any clear conclusions can be drawn.

Analytic-developmental theories, those noted above and others, need to explain not only why depression begins but also why it emerges specifically during adolescence. Rutter (1986) has outlined possible causal associations between early developmental events and illness onset, all of which are testable hypotheses and all of which may be operating in specific subgroups. To date, however, they await empirical validation.

Cognitive-Behavioural Theories

Theories postulating that external events are translated through specific cognitive schemata into meaningful internalizations have been advanced to explain the etiology of depression (Beck 1967, 1974). Inasmuch as maladaptive cognitive mechanisms have been thought both to lead to and perpetuate depression, methods of restructuring these maladaptive mechanisms (cognitive therapy) have been developed to treat the ensuing depression. Indeed, some evidence as to the explanatory power of this model, perhaps best advanced through the work of Beck (Beck 1974; Rutter 1986), in the area of etiology and utility in treatment already exists (Beck 1967, 1974; Beck et al. 1979). But why this phenomenon should occur specifically in the adolescent years has not yet been clearly elucidated; often it is even unclear which actually comes first – the depression leading to the classic "negative triad," or vice versa.

The developmental model described above may help explain family or environmental factors acting as a spur to the development of a vulnerable cognitive set. For example, children who are constantly criticized by their parents may learn to attach negative attitudes to their own personal attributes. During the teen years, under the stress of peer scrutiny and high social expectations, the negative self-view may lead to despondency and feelings of worthlessness, to social withdrawal and a loss of regular social reinforcers, and, thus, to a depression. Such a pattern would also explain some of the possible familial factors in depression which, regrettably, have never been studied properly. Again, however, this appealing theory awaits validation, as does its specific applicability to teen depression rather than to a host of other disorders marked by low self-esteem (personality disorders, eating disorders, substance abuse).

The learned helplessness theory of depression, based on work by Seligman and others (Overmier and Seligman 1967; Seligman 1975) suggests that an individual's inability to control traumatic events can lead to a depressive state. But why depression and not anxiety should ensue is not clear. Nevertheless, and although both the specific and general applicability of this theory have been critically questioned (Blaney 1977; Costello 1984), it remains valuable for generating testable hypotheses, such as apropos the neurobiologic effects of inescapable trauma that may be relevant to adolescent depression.

Biological Theories

Biological theories stress the effect of genetic and neurochemical factors on the development of adolescent depression. Studies of adult depressives, for example, have identified high degrees of depressive-disorder-loading in pedigrees of depressed probands (Weissman et al. 1984a; Weissman et al. 1984b).

And recent work by our own group has found the rate of unipolar depression in first-degree relatives of depressed teens to be 20 per cent, compared to a rate of 4 per cent in age- and sex-matched controls ($p = .006$), suggesting a heritable component to this disorder (Kutcher and Marton, 1991).

The theories of neurotransmitter disturbances of the central nervous system either at the synaptic or second-messenger levels in serotonin, norepinephrine, and acetylcholine, have been well described in adults; recent work (see Biological Aspects) has identified abnormalities of these systems in adolescent depressives. Developmentally, however, major biological changes occur in brain growth and function over the adolescent years; thus deviant brain organization may underlie the development of a depressive disorder. Much work must be done in this area before firm conclusions can be drawn.

The above theoretical perspectives are not mutually exclusive and attempts should be made to link psychodynamic, cognitive-behavioural, and neurologic models. For example, severe childhood trauma could lead to aberrant brain development that then becomes manifest in mood-control difficulties as brain synaptic reorganization occurs during adolescent years. Many other possible models, however, also exist and the prudent approach is to accept the strengths and weaknesses of each theory, while putting hypotheses to the empirical test gathering further knowledge about the phenomenology, course, comorbidity, biology, and social/family parameters of the disorder.

CURRENT KNOWLEDGE

Phenomenology

The symptom complex of adolescent depression has repeatedly been shown to be similar to that of adults (Carlson 1981; Ryan et al. 1987; Strober et al. 1981a). When DSM-III-R criteria are applied to the adolescent population both vegetative and negative cognitive features commonly appear in the adolescent-depressive syndrome. However, adolescents also show some developmentally specific symptomatology. Hypersomnia is probably their most characteristic sleep disturbance, while vegetative symptoms are generally less prevalent than the negative cognitive symptoms of hopelessness, helplessness, self-reproach, and low self-esteem/self-evaluation. In fact, adolescent depressives will often identify their mood not as depressed, but as irritable or bored. The younger the adolescent, the more likely the disorder is to be associated with significant degrees of anxiety.

The time course of adolescent depression may differ slightly from that of adults. The younger adolescent's depression may be characterized by periods of depressed mood lasting twenty to forty days. As the adolescent matures, the length of the depressive period tends to increase, such that those of late adolescents are characterized by a more commonly recognized adult pattern of low moods persisting for three to six months at a time.

Some clinicians have difficulty in making the diagnosis of this disorder in adolescents. In some cases, this difficulty is due to the physicians' reluctance to label an adolescent with an affective-disorder diagnosis (Ryan and Puig-Antich 1986). In others, the depression may not be diagnosed because of a clinician's failure either to apply diagnostic criteria systematically or to inquire thoroughly into the signs and symptoms of depression. Friedman et al. (1982) reported that the use of systematic diagnostic criteria resulted in a two- to fourfold increase in the clinical diagnosis of depressive disorders in an adolescent inpatient population. Similarly, Kutcher et al. (1985) found that one third of the adolescent patients diagnosed as depressed using a structured interview were not so diagnosed by the clinical interviewer. A review of the clinical material collected in the charts suggests that the reason for this oversight may be that the appropriate questions had never been asked.

Variability in diagnostic practice because of criterion variance (the criteria used to define a disorder) and information variance (the information collected) can be reduced by incorporating structured interviews into the assessment protocol. Several interviews already exist that are appropriate for children and adolescents: the Schedule for Affective Disorders and Schizophrenia in School-aged Children (Kiddie-SADS); the Diagnostic Interview for Children and Adolescents (DICA); the Child Assessment Schedule (CAS); and the Interview Schedule for Children (ISC). As well, structured interviews will ensure that clinicians ask the most relevant questions regarding depressive disorders in adolescence and that the diagnostic criteria are applied systematically.

Help-seeking behaviour in adolescents may also differ from that of adults. Clinically, it is common to see depressed adolescents many weeks, or even months, after the onset of a disturbance. Many depressed teenagers do not seek mental health help for a number of reasons: the unavailability of such help, their negative view of mental health professionals in general and psychiatrists in particular, an acceptance of the widely held myth of the "normality" of depression in teenagers, or a feeling that the depression is simply "a phase" that they will grow out of. Often, the reason for psychiatric intervention is not the low mood itself but a suicide attempt, frequent absences from school, failure at school, conflict with family, or some other type of behavioural disturbance. This help-seeking behaviour may underlie the described co-occurrence of conduct disorder and depressed mood, previously reported in adolescent psychiatric clinical populations (Marriage 1986). It is thus recommended that clinicians inquire about a depressive syndrome whenever adolescents present with such behaviours.

Self-Report Scales

The use of self-report scales for the assessment of symptoms of depression in adolescents is increasing. Such scales have been used to determine the prevalence of depressive symptoms, to select depressed research subjects, to determine prevalence of depressive disorders, and to evaluate treatment outcome (Albert and Beck 1975; Barrera and Garrison-Jones, in press; Marton et al. 1991; Strober et al. 1981b; Teri 1984). Although such scales are useful in clinically depressed populations for evaluating the severity of depression, their diagnostic specificity has been questioned (Myers and Weissman 1980). Furthermore, although self-report scales are useful screening tools, they are inadequate as diagnostic instruments by themselves.

The Beck Depression Inventory (BDI), a self-report measure, has been applied as a diagnostic instrument with adult and adolescent patients. It is easily administered, has good test-retest reliability, is a good measure of severity of depression, and has been recommended for use in general adolescent clinical populations (Albert and Beck 1975; Teri 1984). Moreover, scores on the BDI agree well with ratings on the Hamilton Depression Rating Scale for adolescents who are depressed (Albert and Beck 1975). In addition, the BDI differentiates between adolescents with a diagnosis of major depression and dysthymic disorder (Marton et al. 1991).

Not all investigators, however, have found the BDI to be a valid *diagnostic* instrument in the teenage group. Strober et al. (1981b) noted a 20-per-cent discrepancy between the BDI and clinical diagnoses of depressive syndromes. In a similar study, Barrera and Garrison-Jones (in press) found a 25-percent discrepancy rate. In a large sample of adolescent outpatients and inpatients, Marton et al. (1989) found that 75 per cent was the optimum diagnostic accuracy obtained with the BDI. Gotlib (1984) suggests that the BDI is a measure of general dysphoria rather than depression and has reported significant correlations between the BDI measures of anxiety, hostility and other categories of psychological distress. Kutcher and Marton (1989a) found, in a sample of thirty-seven adolescent psychiatric outpatients, that the BDI tended to overdiagnose the presence of depressive disorder. Furthermore, the BDI scores tended to be higher in personality disordered patients than in those with a primary diagnosis of depression or dysthymia. Thus, the Beck Depression Inventory can be useful as a screening tool to identify adolescents who may be depressed. However, it is inadequate as a diagnostic tool and should not be used as a substitute for a comprehensive diagnostic assessment.

Epidemiology

Depressive symptoms occur commonly in adolescents and need to be differentiated from the depressive syndrome. Also, symptoms of transient low mood are ubiquitous and often associated with losses, external stressors, or difficulties in interpersonal relationships. Various epidemiologic studies have reported that 35 to 50 per cent of the teenage population report depressive symptoms at a given point in time (Frederichs et al. 1981; Kandel and Davies 1982; Kashani et al. 1987; Kutcher and Marton 1989b; Offord et al. 1987; Schoenbach et al. 1983). Rutter et al. (1986) found that 40 per cent of eleven- to fifteen-year-olds on the Isle of Wight complained of depressive feelings at clinical interview. In the Ontario Child Health Study, Offord et al. (1987) noted that 35 per cent of boys and 55 per cent of girls aged twelve to sixteen complained of depressive symptoms. Similarly, Kandel and Davies (1982) reported depressive symptoms in over 50 per cent of students in American high schools.

The depressive syndrome, however, is less common. Although studies using self-report questionnaires report prevalence rates ranging from 22 to 60 per cent (Kutcher and Marton 1989b; Schoenbach et al. 1983), the use of self-report scales as diagnostic instruments is invalid, inasmuch as their diagnostic specificity is generally low and they tend to measure generalized distress and dysphoria (Gotlib 1984; Schoenbach et al. 1983). Indeed, epidemiological surveys using more clearly defined sampling strategies and rigorous diagnostic criteria have identified the prevalence of the depressive syndrome in teenagers at about 4 to 8 per cent. In terms of sex, girls outnumber boys about two to one (Frederichs et al. 1981; Kashani et al. 1987; Kutcher and Marton, 1989b; Offord et al. 1987).

During adolescent years, the increase in prevalence of depressive symptoms as well as the depressive syndrome itself, is most marked in females. It seems that boys report more depressive symptomatology before puberty, while girls report more after. Although prevalence rates vary from study to study, general findings suggest that the incidence of depressive disorders increases with age, and appears to peak in the late teens and early twenties (Frederichs et al. 1981; Kandel and Davies 1982; Kashani et al. 1987; Kutcher and Marton 1989b; Offord et al. 1987; Rutter, et al. 1986; Schoenbach et al. 1983). In fact, recent data from the National Institute of Mental Health's (NIMH) collaborative program on the psychobiology of depression has suggested that the increase in the prevalence of the disease since World War II may be linked to this decreasing age of onset (Klerman 1988).

Adolescent depression is commonly found in clinical populations and, in general, the adolescent depressive syndrome is found in both inpatients and outpatients. Studies of inpatient units, although coloured by population biases and unique sample characteristics, tend to report prevalence rates of around 40 per cent (Friedman et al. 1982; Kutcher et al. 1985; Welner et al. 1970). Outpatient clinic studies report a somewhat lower rate: approximately 30 per cent. Some authors note even higher rates, arguing that reports of lower prevalence rates reflect either a clinician's reluctance to make the diagnosis or a lack of rigour in the application of diagnostic criteria (Friedman et al. 1982; Kutcher et al. 1985).

Comorbidity

Depression in teenagers, which rarely occurs in a "pure" form, is commonly found in association with a variety of other disorders, including attention deficit disorders (Biederman et al. 1987), conduct disorders (Marriage et al. 1986), eating disorders (Blaney 1977), and anxiety disorders (Costello 1984). This high rate of comorbidity is found in both clinical and nonclinical populations. In a study of high-school students, Kashani et al. (1987) noted the presence of a coexisting disorder in each case of depression identified. Of their sample of depressed adolescents, 75 per cent had anxiety disorders, 50 per cent had an oppositional disorder, and 33 per cent had a conduct disorder. In the Ontario Child Health Study (Offord et al. 1987), about half of the adolescents with depressive disorders were found to have a concurrent psychiatric disturbance.

The nature of the relationship between depression and other psychiatric disorders in the adolescent age group is unclear. Depression may arise during the course of another illness, reflecting adaptive failure, or the presence of other disorders may reflect different subtypes of a depressive syndrome. Alternatively, the disorders may be unrelated, with each arising from specific interactions between the individuals' biological makeup and their social and familial environments. Kovacs et al. (1988) recently suggested that conduct disorders that are comorbid with adolescent depression arise from the depressive disturbance but persist after the primary depression has remitted. However, before any conclusions as to the relationship between the syndrome of adolescent depression and other psychiatric illnesses in this age group can be made, further longitudinal study of adolescent depressive probands, both with and without specific types of comorbidity, are necessary.

Adolescent depression exerts a profound effect on social, vocational, academic, and personality functioning. Earlier work has suggested that adolescent depressives may exhibit specific personality disorders, such as a borderline personality disorder (Clarkin et al. 1984). It has also been shown that the co-occurrence of borderline personality disorder and depression in teenagers is associated with suicidal lethality (Clarkin et al. 1984). However, the specificity of the relationship between adolescent depression and a borderline personality disorder is unproven. Other investigators, for example Robbins et al. (1983), have observed heterogeneity in personality disorder among depressed teenagers.

More recently, Marton et al. (1989) compared the personality characteristics of depressed adolescents with those of non-psychotic psychiatric controls. Although they found that while more teenagers during their depression were meeting diagnostic criteria for personality disorders than were adolescents with psychiatric disorders of the non-depressive, non-psychotic variety, no one specific personality disorder was associated with the depressive syndrome. The personality presentation of adolescents, however, was influenced by their depressed mood. At a six- to twelve-month follow-up, when the depressed group was euthymic (mood not depressed or manic), only half the adolescents who initially had met criteria for personality disorders while in the depressive episode continued to meet those same criteria when no longer depressed (Korenblum et al. 1988). Nevertheless, they continued to demonstrate greater interpersonal dysfunction and emotional reactivity than members of the control group, suggesting that while a single depressive episode may not predispose to enduring personality disorder, some persistent deficits in personality functioning can result that may be either a reflection of the effect of the depression itself or an exacerbation of pre-existing personality difficulties secondary to the depressive episode.

Clinicians dealing with depressed adolescents must keep several things in mind regarding personality disorder diagnosis. First, it is premature to diagnose a personality disorder when adolescents are in the middle of a depression. Second, it is important to clarify the presence or absence of personality disorder when adolescents are euthymic. Third, it is important to be aware that depressed adolescents, even when they are euthymic, may have some deficits in personality functioning that may be addressed using psychotherapeutic means.

Course and Outcome

Follow-up studies of depressed adolescents show that significant numbers experience recurrent episodes of depression (Garber et al. 1988; Keller et al. 1988; McCauley et al. 1988; Strober and Carlson 1982). McCauley et al. (1988), in a sample of fifty-nine depressed children and teenagers, reported that 61 per cent had a recurrence of the illness within three years. This rate is similar to that reported by Garber et al. (1988) in an eight-year follow-up study of adolescents initially hospitalized for major depression. Strober and Carlson (1982) reported that 80 per cent of their adolescent inpatients hospitalized for depressed mood experienced a recurrence of major depression.

Similar findings are reported in nonclinical samples. Keller et al. (1988), for example, found that 21 per cent of thirty-eight nonreferred, depressed young adolescents, identified in a high-risk population study, continued to be depressed at one year follow-up. Kandel and Davies (1982) noted that depressive symptoms during adolescence significantly predicted depressive symptoms in adulthood. Further, adolescent depression was associated with psychiatric hospitalization, vocational problems, and difficulties with interpersonal relationships in adulthood.

Adolescent-onset major depression may also be associated with the development of bipolar disorders. Strober and Carlson (1982) found that 20 per cent of adolescents hospitalized for a major depression developed a bipolar disorder within four years. Features predictive of a future bipolar course included: a cluster of symptoms indicating rapid onset of depression; psychomotor retardation and mood congruent psychosis, affective disorder in the family; and pharmacologically induced hypomania. Recently, Kutcher et al. (1985) noted that over 40 per cent of adolescents with bipolar disorders also meet the criteria for conduct disorders; they suggested that the co-occurrence of conduct disorder with depression that begins in the earlier years of adolescence (ages 13 to 15) may be predictive of a future bipolar course.

Suicide

The most unfortunate outcome of adolescent depression is suicide, with the rise in the last decade's suicide rate being associated with the already noted increase in prevalence of depression. Although suicidal behaviour is a complex multi-determined behaviour, depressed mood is consistently associated with suicidality. Various studies have reported rates of up to 60 per cent of adolescents who attempt suicide having concurrent depressive disorders (Brent 1987; Crumley 1979; Hawton 1986; Shaffer 1982; Shaffer et al. 1988). Suicide risk is increased when depressed adolescents suffer from personality disturbance, substance abuse, and impulsivity (Barrera and Garrison-Jones, in press; Myers and Weissman 1980). At this time, it is unclear whether unrecognized clinical depressions contribute significantly to successful suicide. Certainly, administrators of suicide-prevention programs (Shaffer et al. 1988) should be aware of the relationship between adolescent depression and adolescent suicide. Clinicians evaluating an adolescent who has made a suicide attempt should make a concerted effort to determine the presence or absence of an underlying depressive disorder and not merely deal with the behavioural disturbance that may have precipitated the event.

Biological Aspects

Although the phenomenological, developmental, personality, and social aspects of adolescent depression are currently undergoing detailed study, interest in the biological aspect of this disorder is really just beginning (Gotlib 1984). Electrophysiographic and neuroendocrine features of adolescent depression cannot be inferred from adult data, for the central nervous system and hormonal milieu of the teenager are significantly different from that of the adult (Puig-Antich 1986; Seifert et al. 1980). Biological studies that can contribute to the understanding of the etiology of the disorder, identify depressive subgroups, or predict clinical course and treatment outcome need to be developed.

Electroencephalographic studies of sleep in adolescent depression have shown a variety of different findings, including increased sleep latency, decreased sleep efficiency, hypersomnia, normal rapid eye movement (REM) latency, increased length of the first REM period, and shortened REM latency (Enslie et al. 1987; Goetz et al. 1987; Lahmeyer et al. 1983). Age differences in the population studied and the central nervous system (CNS) maturational effect on the sleep electroencephalograph (EEG) may explain the sometimes contradictory findings (Ulrich et al. 1980). Taken as a group, the studies suggest that whereas a shortened REM latency may be a robust biological marker of depression in older teenagers, it probably does not apply in younger adolescents. Whether a shortened REM latency is predictive of treatment response or whether it is a state marker that normalizes with successful treatment is not yet clear in the adolescent population. However, work by Kutcher and Marton (1989b) suggests that the short REM latency found in depressed adolescents reverts to normal with successful pharmacological treatment.

Neuroendocrine studies have identified hypersecretion of nocturnal growth hormone in depressed adolescents (Kutcher et al. 1988) and a blunted growth hormone response to desipramine infusion (Ryan et al. 1988a). These findings are suggestive of a primary serotonergic dysfunction in adolescent depression, but much further work needs to be done in this area before any firm conclusions can be drawn.

Although abnormalities of cortisol secretion are well recognized in adult depressives (Pepper and Krieger 1985), detailed studies of 24-hour cortisol secretion profiles have yet to be reported in teenagers. Some depressed teenagers exhibit nocturnal hypersecretion and an early rise in nocturnal cortisol levels (Kutcher and Marton 1989b); when compared to normal controls, however, adolescent depressives as a group do not show a significantly different nocturnal cortisol pattern. Nonsuppression has been reported with the dexamethasone suppression test in some depressed adolescents (Klee and Garfinkel 1984; Targum and Capodamo 1983); the specificity (low false-positive rate) of this finding, however, has not been established and its sensitivity (true positive rate) is less than that reported for depressed adults. Studies that evaluate the dexamethasone suppression test's use in predicting clinical recovery, relapse, or response to specific somatic treatments have not yet been reported in the adolescent population.

Preliminary studies of the hypothalamic pituitary-thyroid axis show that although the thyroid-stimulating hormone response to throtropin-releasing hormone is abnormal in some depressed adolescents, that abnormality occurs less frequently than in adults (Khan 1987). At this time, none of the neuroendocrine parameters noted above can be said to have diagnostic utility in the adolescent age group, even though the multiple abnormalities described above would suggest that altered central neurotransmission provides the "final common pathway" for expression of the depressive syndrome in teenagers.

Treatment

Relatively few treatment procedures have been specifically designed for the treatment of adolescent depression. Depressed adolescents receive whatever treatment is available. Furthermore, little empirical study of treatment outcome has been done (Kutcher and Marton 1989b; Shaffer 1984). So far, in fact, only two controlled evaluative studies of psychotherapy have been conducted, and these suggest that 40 to 50 per cent of depressed adolescents respond to cognitive behavioural techniques. First, Reynolds and Coates (1986) reported that both cognitive behaviour therapy and progressive muscle relaxation led to improvement in a nonclinical sample of older adolescents who endorsed depressive symptoms on the Beck Depression Inventory. Second, Lewinsohn et al. (1987) demonstrated that both individual cognitive behavioural therapy and a cognitive behavioural psychoeducation group produced significantly more improvement in depressed teens than in members of a waiting-list control group. Treatment gains were achieved independently of parental involvement and were maintained over a two-year follow-up. Individual and family psychotherapy is often prescribed as well, although there is no evidence that either alone, or in combination, these treatments are effective in alleviating the symptoms of adolescent depression (Kutcher and Marton 1989b; Shaffer 1984). Unfortunately, many of the psychological treatments of adolescents are based on psychodynamic theories of depression that still need validation. So far, the efficacy of expensive and time-consuming, long-term psychotherapy has not been demonstrated, nor have the possible harmful effects of this treatment been fully considered. Furthermore, although as in most disorders supportive therapy is probably indicated, the specificity of the various psychotherapies for treating adolescent depression remains to be clarified (Kutcher and Marton 1989b; Shaffer 1984).

Somatic treatments have also not been sufficiently studied. Indeed, only the efficacy of some tricyclic antidepressants has been evaluated (Rifkin et al. 1986; Ryan and Puig-Antich 1987). Kramer and Feiguine (1981) found no differences between drug and placebo treatments in a group of twenty adolescent inpatients treated with amitryptiline, and Ryan et al. (1986) found a disappointing response rate to an open trial of imipramine in thirty-four younger adolescents. Nevertheless, conclusions from these latter studies can only be considered tentative, for both suffered from methodological deficiencies. Our own studies evaluating desipramine treatment of adolescent depression are still ongoing; early results, however, indicate that differences between drug and placebo treatments may be insignificant. Controlled studies of monoamine oxidase inhibitors have not been reported in this population, although their use in augmenting tricyclic treatment has met with some success (Ryan et al. 1988). The difficulties associated with antidepressant use in teens, particularly their potential lethality in overdose and their ability to precipitate mania in susceptible individuals (Mattesson and Seltzer 1981), caution against their overenthusiastic prescription to depressed adolescents. Perhaps they should be used only in controlled conditions in which patients are carefully monitored; this can best be done either through an inpatient assessment or in specialized psychopharmacology clinics. In any case, antidepressants should not be prescribed apart from a comprehensive treatment program in which a multi-modal approach is offered.

Clearly, evaluative studies of psychological and somatic treatments are urgently needed in the area of adolescent depression. These studies should focus on the uniqueness of the treatment modality, specific capabilities for alleviating the depression itself, as well as the particular aspects of the treatment that might be useful for improving general functioning. Interpersonal skills and social relationships, in addition to mood control, are suitable treatment targets as well. The identification of treatment-sensitive subgroups is important too, inasmuch as different types of adolescent depression may have differing responses to treatments. Further, the effect of treatment on the longitudinal course of the illness and on the expression of personality and social difficulties, either in the acute or the "euthymic" state, needs to be carefully assessed. Thus, treatment outcome studies in adolescent depression should have a research priority in this area.

FUTURE DIRECTIONS

Adolescent depression is now a relatively well-defined disorder that can be appropriately diagnosed by experienced clinicians. It is associated with significant morbidity and mortality in this age group and great advances have been made in its definition and description. Much further systematic work is needed, however, to more fully define etiologies, clinical course, and effective treatment.

Studies of pharmacologic and psychotherapeutic modalities are urgently needed as well. Biological studies to elucidate etiological factors, identify diagnostic tests, and define treatment predictors should be undertaken too, as should longitudinal research to clarify issues of natural course, intervention outcome, and the effect of adolescent depression on long-term interpersonal and vocational functioning. It is hoped that education of mental health professionals, educators, parents, and teens, themselves, in the signs and symptoms of adolescent depression will lead to earlier case identification, more effective treatment, and a decrease in the psychological, social, and economic toll of this depressive disorder.

Acknowledgment: The authors wish to thank Jean Stewart and Jill Green for their help in preparing this manuscript.

BIBLIOGRAPHY

Albert, N. and Beck, A. 1975. Incidence of depression in early adolescence: A preliminary study. *Journal of Youth and Adolescence* 4: 301–6.

Alessi, N., Robbins, D., and Dilsaver, S. 1987. Panic and depressive disorder among psychiatrically hospitalized adolescents. *Psychiatric Research* 20: 175–283.

Anthony, E.J. 1970. Two contrasting types of adolescent depression and their treatment. *Journal of the American Psychoanalytical Association* 18: 841–59.

Baker, R. 1978. Adolescent depression: An illness or developmental task? *Journal of Adolescence* 1: 309–17.

Barrera, M., and Garrison-Jones, C. N.d. Properties of the BDI as a screening instrument for adolescent depression. *Journal of Abnormal Child Psychology*. In press.

Beck, A. 1967. *Depression: Clinical experimental and theoretical aspects.* New York: Harper and Row.

– 1974. The development of depression. In *The psychology of depression: Contemporary theory and research*, edited by R. Friedman and M. Katz. New York: Winston-Wiley.

Beck, A., Rush, A., Shaw, B. and Emery, G. 1979. *Cognitive therapy of depression.* New York: Guilford Press.

Biederman, J., Munir, K., Knee, D., Armentano, M., Autor, S., Waternaux, C., and Tsuang, M. 1987. High rate of affective disorders in probands with attention deficit disorder and in their relatives: A controlled family study. *American Journal of Psychiatry* 144: 330–33.

Blackburn, I., and Bonham, K. 1980. Experimental effects of cognitive therapy technique in depressed patients. *British Journal of Social Consulting in Psychology*, 19: 353–63.

Blaney, P. 1977. Contemporary theories of depression: Critique and comparison. *Journal of Abnormal Psychology* 86: 203–23.

Blos, P. 1967. The second individuation process of adolescence. *Psychoanalytical Studies on Children*, 22: 162–86.

Bowlby, J. 1969. *Attachment and loss I. Attachment.* London: Hogarth Press.

– 1980. *Attachment and loss III. Loss, sadness and depression.* New York: Basic Books.

Brent, D. 1987. Correlates of the medical lethality of suicide attempts in children and adolescents. *Journal of the American Academic Child and Adolescent Psychology* 26: 87–89.

Cantell, D., and Carlson, G. 1983. *Affective disorders in childhood and adolescence.* New York: Spectrum.

Carlson, G. 1981. The phenomenology of adolescent depression. *Adolescent Psychiatry* 9: 411–21.

Caws, P. 1965. *The philosophy of science.* Princeton: D. Van Nostrand Co.

Clarkin, J., Friedman, R., Hurt, S., Corn, R., and Aronoff, M. 1984. Affective and character pathology of suicidal adolescents and young adult inpatients. *Journal of Clinical Psychiatry* 45: 19–22.

Costello, C. 1984. A critical review of Seligman's laboratory experiments on learned helplessness and depression in humans. *Journal of Abnormal Psychology* 87: 21–31.

Crumley, F. 1979. Adolescent suicide attempts. *Journal of the American Medical Association* 241: 2404–07.

Enslie, G., Roffwarg, H., Rush, J., Weinberg, W., and Parkin-Feigenbaum, L. 1987. Sleep EEG findings in depressed children and adolescents. *American Journal of Psychiatry* 144: 668–70.

Frederichs, R., Aneheusel, C. and Clark, B. 1981. Prevalence of depression in Los Angeles County. *American Journal of Epidemiology* 113: 691–99.

Freud, A. 1958. Adolescence. *Psychoanalytic Study of the Child* 13: 255–78.

Freud, S. 1917. *Mourning and melancholia. Completed Psychological Works. Vol.* 14 edited by J. Strachey . (standard ed.), New York: Hogarth Press.

Friedman, R., Clarkin, J., Corn, R., Aronoff, M., Hurt, S., and Murphy, M. 1982. DSM III and affective pathology in hospitalized adolescents. *Journal of Nervous Mental Disorders* 170: 511–21.

Garber, J., Kriss, M., Koch, M., and Lindholm, L. 1988. Recurrent depression in adolescents: A follow-up study. *Journal of the American Academy of Child and Adolescent Psychiatry* 27: 49–54.

Geleerd, E. 1961. Some aspects of ego vicissitude in adolescence. *Journal of American Psychoanalytic Assocation,* 9: 394–405.

Goetz, R., Puig-Antich, J., Ryan, N., Rabinovich, H., Ambrosini, P., Nelson, B., and Krawiec, V. 1987. Electroencephalographic sleep of adolescents with major depression and normal controls. *Archives General Psychiatry* 44: 61–68.

Gotlib, I. 1984. Depression and general psychopathology in university students. *Journal of Abnormal Psychology* 93: 19–30.

Hawton, K. 1986. *Suicide and attempted suicide among children and adolescents* Beverley Hills: Sage Publications.

Hempel, C. 1966. *Philosophy of natural science.* Englewood Cliffs: Prentice-Hall Inc.

Kandel, D. and Davies, M. 1982. Epidemiology of depressive mood in adolescents. *Archives of General Psychiatry,* 39: 1205–12.

Kashani, J., Carlson, G., Beck, N., Hoeper, E., Corcoran, C., McAllister, J., Fallahi, C., Rosenberg, T., and Reid, J. 1987. Depression, depressive symptoms and de-pressed mood among a community sample of adolescents. *American Journal of Psychiatry* 144: 931–34.

Keller, M., Beardslee, W., Lavori, P., Wunder, J., Drs, D., and Samuelson, H. 1988. Course of major depression in non-referred adolescents: A retrospective study. *Journal of Affective Disorders* 15: 235–43.

Khan, A. 1987. Biochemical profile of depressed adolescents. *Journal of the American*

Academy of Child Psychiatry, 26: 873–78.

Klee, S., and Garfinkel, B. 1984. Identification of depression in children and adolescents: The role of the dexamethasone suppression test. *Journal of the American Academy of Child Psychiatry* 23: 410–15.

Klerman, G. 1980. Adaptation, depression and transitional life events. In *Adolescent Psychiatry*, edited by S. Feinstein. Chicago: University of Chicago Press.

– 1988. The current age of youthful melancholia. *British Journal of Psychology* 152: 4–14.

Korenblum, M., et al. (1988). *Personality dysfunction in depressed adolescents: State or trait?* Poster presented at the annual meeting of the American Academy of Child and Adolescent Psychiatry, Seattle.

Kovacs, M., Paulauskas, S., Gatsonis, C., and Richards, C. 1988. Depressive disorders in childhood disorders III: A longitudinal study of co-morbidity with and risk for conduct disorders. *Journal of Affective Disorders* 15: 205–17.

Kramer, A. and Feiguine, R. 1981. Clinical effect of amitriptyline in adolescent depression: A pilot study. *Journal of the American Academy of Child Psychiatry* 20: 636–44.

Kutcher, S., and Marton, P. 1989a. Utility of the Beck Depression Iinventory with psychiatrically disturbed adolescent outpatients. *Canadian Journal of Psychiatry* 34: 107–9.

– 1989b. Parameters of adolescent depression. *Psychiatric Clinics of North America*, 4: 845–918.

– 1991. Affective disorders in first degree relatives of adolescent onset bipolars, unipolars and normal controls. *Journal of the American Academy of Child and Adolescent Psychiatry* 30: 75–78.

Kutcher, S., Marton, P. and Korenblum, M. 1989. Relationship between psychiatric illness and conduct disorder in adolescents. *Canadian Journal of Psychiatry*, 34: 526–29.

Kutcher, S., Williamson, P., Silverberg, J., Marton, P., Malkin, D., and Malkin, A. 1988. Nocturnal growth hormone secretion in depressed adolescents: A preliminary study. *Journal of the American Academy of Child and Adolescent Psychiatry* 27: 751–54.

Kutcher, S., Yanchyshyn, G., and Cohen, C. 1985. Diagnosing affective disorder in adolescents: The use of the schedule for affective disorders and schizophrenia. *Canadian Journal of Psychiatry* 30: 605–08.

Ladame, F. 1987. Depressive adolescents, pathological narcissism, and therapeutic failures. In *Adolescent psychiatry Vol. 14*, edited by Chicago: University of Chicago Press.

Lahmeyer, H., Poznanski, E. and Bellar, S. 1983. EEG sleep in depressed adolescents. *American Journal of Psychiatry* 140: 1150–53.

Lewinsohn, P. Clarke, G., and Hops, H. 1987. Treatment of depression in adolescents. Paper presented at the annual meeting of the Association for the Advancement of Behaviour Therapy, Boston.

Marton, P., Churchard, M., Kutcher, S.P., and Korenblum, M. 1991. Diagnostic utility of the Beck Depression Inventory with adolescent outpatients and inpatients. *Canadian Journal of Psychiatry* 36: 428–31.

McCauley, E., et al. 1988. Clinical course of depression in young people. a 3-year prospective study. Poster presented at the American Academy of Child and Adolescent Psychiatry, Seattle.

Mahler, M. 1961. On sadness and grief in infancy and childhood: Loss and restoration of the symbiotic love object. *The Psychoanalytical Study of the Child* 16: 332–54.

– 1971. A study of the separation-individuation process and its possible application to borderline phenomena in the psychoanalytic situation. *The Psychoanalytic Study of the Child* 26: 403–24.

Mahler, M., Pine, F., and Bergman, A. 1975. *The Psychological birth of the human infant: Symbiosis and Individuation.* New York: Basic Books.

Marriage, K., Fine, S., Moretti, M., and Haley, G. 1986. Relationship between depression and conduct disorder in children and adolescents. *Journal of the American Academy of Child Psychiatry* 25: 687–91.

McCartney, J. 1987. Adolescent depression: A growth and developmental perspective. In *Adolescent psychiatry Vol.* 14, edited by S. Feinstein Chicago: University of Chicago Press.

Marton, P., Korenblum, M., Kutcher S.P., Stein, B., Kennedy, B., and Pakes, J. 1989. Personality dysfunction in depressed adolescents. *Canadian Journal of Psychiatry* 24: 810–13.

Mattesson, A. and Seltzer, R. 1981. MAOI-induced rapid cycling bipolar affective disorder in an adolescent. *American Journal of Psychiatry* 138: 677–79.

Myers, J. and Weissman, M. 1980. Use of self-report symptoms scale to detect depression in a community sample. *American Journal of Psychiatry* 137: 1081–84.

Nazel, E. 1961. *The structure of science.* New York: Harcourt, Bruce and World.

Offer, D., and Offer, J. 1975. *From teenage to young manhood.* New York: Basic Books.

Offer, D., and Sabshin, M., 1984. *Normality and the life cycle.* New York: Basic Books.

Offord, D., Boyle, M., Szatmari, P., Rae-Grant, N., Links, P., Cadman, D., Byles, J., Crawford, J., Blum, H., Byrne, C., Thomas, H., and Woodward, C. 1987. Ontario Child Health Study II. Six month prevalence of disorder and rates of service utilization. *Archives of General Psychiatry* 44: 832–36.

Overmier, J., and Seligman, M. 1967. Effects of inescapable shock upon subsequent escape and avoidance learning. *Journal of Comparative and Physiological Psychology* 63: 28–33.

Pepper, G., and Krieger, D. 1985. Hypothalamic-pituitary-adrenal abnormalities in depression: Their possible relation to central mechanisms regulating ACTH release. In *Neurobiology of mood disorders* edited by R.M. Post, and J.C. Ballander, 245–70. Baltimore: Williams and Wilkins.

Popper, K. 1959. *The logic of scientific discovery.* London: Hutchinson and Co.

Puig-Antich, J. 1986. Psychobiological markers: Effects of age and puberty. In *Depression in young people*, edited by M. Rutter, C. Izard, and P. Read. New York: Guilford Press.

Puig-Antich, J., and Gittleman, R. 1982. Depression in childhood and adolescence. In *Handbook of affective disorders*, edited by E. Paykel. New York: Basic Books.

Reynolds, W., and Coates, K. 1986. A comparison of cognitive behavioural therapy and relaxation training for the treatment of depression in adolescents. *Journal of Consulting in Clinical Psychology* 54: 653–60.

Rifkin, A., Wartman, R., Reardon, G., and Siris, S. 1986. Psychotropic medication in adolescents: A review. *Journal of Clinical Psychiatry* 47: 400–8.

Robbins, D., Alessi, N., Yanchyshyn, G., and Colfer, M. 1983. Psychodynamic and characterlogical heterogeneity among adolescents with major depressive disorders. *Journal of the American Academy of Child Psychiatry* 22: 487–91.

Rutter, M. 1986. The developmental psychopathology of depression: Issues and perspectives. In *Depression in Young People*, edited by M. Rutter, C. Izard, and P. Read New York: Guilford Press.

Rutter, M., Izard, C. and Read, P., 1986. *Depression in young people*. New York: Guilford Press.

Rutter, M., Graham, P., Chadwick, O., and Yule, W. 1976. Adolescent turmoil: Fact or fiction? *Journal of Child Psychology and Psychiatry* 17: 35–56.

Ryan, N., and Puig-Antich, K. 1986. Affective illness in adolescence. In *American Psychiatric Association Annual Review Vol. 5*, edited by A. Francis and R. Hales. Washington: American Psychiatric Press Inc.

– 1987. Pharmacological treatment of adolescent psychiatric disorders. *Journal of Adolescent Health Care* 8: 137–42.

Ryan, N., Puig-Antich, K., Ambrosini, P., Rabinovich, H., Robinson, D., Nelson, B., Tyengar, S., and Twomey, J. 1987. The clinical picture of major depression in children and adolescents. *Archives of General Psychiatry* 44: 854–61.

Ryan, N., Puig-Antich, K., Cooper, T, Rabinovich, H., Ambrosini, P., Davies, M., King, J., Torres, D., and Fried, J. 1986. Imipramine in adolescent major depression: Plasma level and clinical response. *Acta Psychiatrica Scandinavica* 73: 275–288.

Ryan, N., Puig-Antich, K., Rabinovich, H., Ambrosini, P., Robinson, D., Nelson, B., and Novacenko, H. 1988. Growth hormone response to desmethylimipramine in depressed and suicidal adolescents. *Journal of Affective Disorders* 15: 323–37.

Ryan, N., Puig-Antich, K., Rabinovich, H., Fried, J., Ambrosini, P., Meyer, V., Torres, D., Dachille, S., and Mazzie, D. 1988. MAOIs in adolescent major depression unresponsive to tricyclic antidepressants. *Journal of the American Academy of Child Adolescent and Psychiatry* 27: 755–58.

Schoenbach, V., Kaplan, B., Wagner, E., Grimson, G., and Miller, F. 1983. Prevalence of self-reported depressive symptoms in young adolescents. *American Journal of Public Health* 73: 1281–87.

Segal, H. 1975. *Introduction to the work of Melanie Klein*. London: Hogarth Press.

Seifert, W., Foxx, J., and Butler, I. 1980. Age effect on dopamine and serotonin metabolite levels in CSF. *Annals of Neurology* 8: 38–42.

Seligman, M. 1975. *Helplessness: On depression development and death.* San Francisco: Freeman and Co.

Shaffer, D. 1982. Diagnostic considerations in suicidal behaviour in children and adolescents. *Journal of the American Academy of Child Psychiatry* 21: 414–16.

– 1984. Notes on psychotherapy research among children and adolescents. *Journal of the American Academy of Child Psychiatry* 23: 552–61.

Shaffer, D., Garland, A., Gould, M., Fisher, P., and Trautman, P. 1988. Preventing teenage suicide: A critical review. *Journal of the American Academy of Child and Adolescent Psychiatry* 27: 675–87.

Strober, M., and Carlson, G. 1982. Bipolar illness in adolescents with major depression: Clinical, genetic and psychopharmacologic predictors in a 3- to 4-year prospective follow-up investigation. *Archives of General Psychiatry* 39: 549–53.

Strober, M., Green, J. and Carlson, G. 1981a. Phenomenology and subtypes of major depressive disorder in adolescence. *Journal of Affective Disorders* 3: 281–90.

– (1981b). Utility of the Beck Depression Inventory with psychiatrically hospitalized adolescents. *Journal of Consulting and Clinical Psychology* 49: 482–83.

Sugar, M. 1968. Normal adolescent mourning. *American Journal of Psychotherapy* 22: 258–69.

Swift, W., Andrews, D., and Barklage, N. 1986. The relationship between affective disorders and eating disorders: A review of the literature. *American Journal of Psychiatry* 143: 290–99.

Targum, S., and Capodamo, A. 1983. The dexamethasone suppression test in adolescent psychiatric inpatients. *American Journal of Psychiatry* 140: 589–92.

Teri, L. 1984. The use of the Beck Depression Inventory with adolescents. *Journal of Abnormal Child Psychology* 10: 277–84.

Ulrich, R., Shaw, D., and Kupfer, D. 1980. Effects of aging on EEG sleep in depression, *Sleep* 3: 31–40.

Weissman, M., Gershon, E., Kidd, K., Prusoff, B., Leckman, J., Dibble, E., Hamovit, J., Thompson, D., Pauls, D., and Guroff, J. 1984. Psychiatric disorders in the relatives of probands with affective disorders: The Yale University-National Institute of Mental Health collaborative study. *Archives of General Psychiatry* 41: 13–21.

Weissman, M., Wickramaratne, P., Merikangas, K., Leckman, J., Prusoff, B., Caruso, K., Kidd, K., and Gammon, G. (1984). Onset of major depression in early adulthood: Increased familial loading and specificity. *Archives of General Psychiatry* 41: 1136–43.

Welner, A., Welner, Z., and Fishman, R. 1970. Psychiatric adolescent inpatients. *Archives of General Psychiatry* 35: 698–700.

CHAPTER FOUR

Suicidal Behaviour and Depression in Young Adults

MICHEL TOUSIGNANT AND DORIS HANIGAN

In young adults, suicidal behaviour and suicide, itself, share many similarities with depression. Both suicidal gestures and depression are a form of despair. They share such etiological factors as negligence and abuse in the family, as well as life events characterized by a loss; often, too, they are associated with a history of alcohol and drug abuse. In the last twenty-five years, suicide and depression in young adults have increased dramatically. Although not too long ago a diagnosis of depression was rare for young persons, clinicians today are increasingly seeing this phenomenon. Despite the increase in the standard of living, the suicide rate climbed sharply in Canada, especially during the '60s and '70s.

In this chapter, we will stress the elements common to suicidal behaviour and depression in young people. We attempt to summarize the specific etiological factors of suicidal behaviour, with an emphasis on Canadian research. We devote a large section to our own research. For our present purposes, we have defined young adulthood as a period spanning the ages of fifteen to twenty-four; however, some studies whose subjects only partially overlap this age range are included in our discussion.

INTRODUCTION

The Difficult Challenge of Intervention

Many practitioners feel helpless when treating suicidal behaviour. Nevertheless, a high percentage of young adults with psychological problems are likely to show suicidal tendencies. A suicide attempt, especially in the case of a young person, induces a state of shock and horror in those trying to help – be it a family member, friend, or therapist. The malaise originates from the implicit message: "I have decided to do away with myself because I do not believe that anyone can help me." Not only are such situations a blow to the self-esteem of helpers. For the professionals involved, there is always the threat of a lawsuit for malpractice. Sometimes, too, the helping relationship is made more difficult by the presence of a drug problem, a factor that interferes with the development of a good emotional rapport with the suicidal young adult.

In the field of prevention, still greater efforts are necessary. As yet, public awareness programs, although they communicate information, have not yet fully reached their intended target audience. For instance, many high school and college administrators still deny the importance of suicidal behaviour within their institutions. A dramatic case is needed – to open their eyes and to obtain their collaboration for prevention programs. Even when the phenomenon is acknowledged, however, the fear is often expressed that discussing suicide with students, teachers, and parents will provoke suicide attempts, thereby further tarnishing the name of the institution.

Despite some hesitation, prevention efforts have increased significantly over the last ten years. Conferences, scientific projects, task forces, committees, films and television specials – all have indicated the thirst for more knowledge. Even as suicide prevention centers sprout, they are being inundated by requests from health practitioners for help with suicide crises.

The Relevance of Research

The editorial in the November 1987 issue of the *Canadian Journal of Psychiatry* sounded an alarm, rallying psychiatrists around a working group designed to promote the research needed to guide intervention. The wide recognition accorded the social relevance of youth suicide is not new. Indeed, suicide has been a major interest of sociologists since Durkheim (1897), when it was perceived as the reflection, at the individual level, of social processes. The suicide of young adults, in fact, raises serious questions about our social organization. Research both at the macrosocial and individual levels is needed to understand the complex etiology of this phenomenon.

THE ETIOLOGY OF SUICIDAL BEHAVIOUR

The following section describes the major conclusions of recent research. First, we examine the difficult question of the role of depression in suicidal manifestations. We then look at several risk factors of youth suicide, before concluding with a discussion of culture.

Depression and Suicide in Young Adults

Is suicide the product of mental illness, especially depression, or is it the consequence of finding life's difficulties too hard to cope with? In other words, do people want to kill themselves because they are pushed toward it by depression, or do their problems really have no solution? We may think of suicide as an irreversible process that takes place when depression reaches a certain threshold of severity. Yet, we must contend with the fact that it is sometimes the most lucid part of individuals that decides to die in order to avoid the intense pain of a desperate situation.

The relationship between suicide and depression is further complicated by alcohol or substance abuse. This abuse induces depression and, consequently, the risk of suicide.

Some authors believe that the symptoms of hopelessness and suicidal behaviour lie at the end of a "severity continuum" of depressive states (Newmann 1984). The *Diagnostic and Statistical Manual of Mental Disorders-Third Edition-Revised* (DSM-III-R) lists suicidal ideation as a symptom of major depression. This clinical observation is complicated, however, by another paradox: the fact that a suicidal attempt, especially in young adults, sometimes reflects an inner vitality, freeing the victim from depression. Take, for example, the study that showed that none of the people who had jumped from the Golden Gate Bridge with a clear suicidal intent – only to be saved by a security net – made a second attempt during the follow-up period (Tousignant and Mishara 1981). Is it because all their remaining energy had been consumed in this attempt? Or perhaps the very fact of being saved gave the victim a second chance?

As we can see, more empirical research is needed to answer the complex question of the relationship between suicide and depression. Theoretical clarification of the debate is also needed. Clearly, if we are to advance the debate, we must better distinguish between the concepts of depression, depressive state, absence of coping strategies, and helplessness.

Most suicidal youths present at least some of the clinical symptoms of depression. In one sample of 149 rural students in Mississippi, investigators found a high level of depressive symptoms. In fact, the scores on the Center for Epidemiological Studies – Depression (CES-D) Scale were twice as high as those in the population used for standardization (Sherer 1985). In another study, which included eighty-two subjects aged twelve to eighteen years hospitalized for self-destructive behaviour, scores on the Children's Depression Rating Scale correlated at .50 with a scale of suicidal risk (Gispert et al. 1985). The young patients were described as moderately depressed. In general, the most depressed had intended more strongly to kill themselves, had had accurate knowledge of the lethality of the means they had used, were more agitated, and had more difficulty expressing their anger in a socially acceptable manner.

Many studies using instruments such as the Minnesota Multiphasic Personality Interview (MMPI), the Beck and Hamilton Depression Inventories, and the Levine-Pilowsky scales (Goldney and Pilowsky 1980) suggest that the diagnosis of depression is present in anywhere from 35 to 79 per cent of youths who have made a suicide attempt. However, Goldney (1981), in a sample of youths who had attempted suicide, found no relation between depression and either a suicide-intention scale or the degree of lethality of the means employed. Friedrich et al. (1982) even concluded that the phenomena of suicidal ideation and depression are quite different. Other authors (Slater and Depue 1981), while recognizing the substantial association between suicide and depression, believe that it is impulsivity that determines the act of suicide. Similarly, Friedman et al. (1984) found a high frequency of diagnoses of depression in a suicidal group (that is, in fifty of seventy-six cases); more than a third, however, also had very high scores on axis II of the DSM-III for personality disorders. In fact, the investigators found that if this second diagnosis was present, suicide attempts were both more frequent and more serious. In general, then, higher rates of depression are found among suicide "attempters" in psychiatric units, with the lowest rates identified among those in medical units (Spirito et al. 1989).

Another series of studies shows that traits linked with depression, such as external locus of control and despair, are closely associated with suicidal behaviour (Allen 1987). Also, studies based on cases of so-called successful suicides clearly show the presence of depressive traits. According to an analysis of the archives of the city of Chicago, the young people who committed suicide appeared to be at least as depressed and desperate as the older people who committed suicide (Maris 1985).

The best comparison of successful suicides among youth and older people was conducted in San Diego between 1981 and 1983 (Rich et al. 1986). In all, 283 cases were studied; people acquainted with the victims and, in a few cases, their clinicians were questioned with a specific set of interview questions, including a list of symptoms that allowed for a DSM-III diagnosis. Toxicology reports were also available. The analysis compared 133 subjects less than thirty years of age with 150 subjects over thirty years of age. Over 92 per cent of those under thirty had received a psychiatric diagnosis. Of these, more than a third had received a diagnosis of affective disorder; of the 137 people who had committed suicide, however, only nine (6.6%) met the criteria of major depression, most of the others (32 of 137) being classified as having "atypical depression" accompanied by the use of psychotropic substances. Particularly characteristic of this group of young suicides, as compared with those over thirty, was the linking of their disorders with drug abuse. Indeed, almost two-thirds of the youths who had committed suicide had a diagnosis of drug or alcohol abuse (88 of 137), compared with only a quarter of those over thirty. Difficulties related to alcohol were present in about half of the youths who had committed suicide (72 of 137), about the same proportion as found in older victims. These data support the opinion that drug abuse may be the most important factor behind the increase in youth suicide during recent decades (Miles 1977).

A comparative study based on diagnostic criteria has shown that youths hospitalized in psychiatry after repeated suicide attempts were no more depressed than those who had been hospitalized without having attempted suicide (Robbins and Alessi 1985). However, of the six persons who had made a serious attempt from a medical point of view, five had received a diagnosis of major depression on the Schedule for Affective Disorders and Schizophrenia (SADS). Once again, no one knows whether the symptoms of depression appeared before or after the alcohol abuse so strongly associated with suicide in this study. In a recent study of college students, investigators showed that, among those who reported a suicide attempt, diagnoses of major depression and substance abuse were related but independent factors (Levy and Deykin 1989), while major depression was less prevalent than in clinical samples.

The high rates of psychiatric consultation and DSM-III-type diagnoses in young adults who have committed suicide raise the question of mental illness as a primary factor in suicide. Clearly, for anyone who sees evidence of mental illness in any psychiatric diagnosis, most young adults who commit suicide suffer from mental illness. But if one restricts the semantic field of this concept to cases of psychosis or to those interfering with the accomplishment of major roles, one must rally behind the conclusion of Jilek-Aall (1988), who states that there is no evidence of mental disorder among most young adults committing or attempting suicide.

While the relationship between alcohol or drug abuse and suicide is well established in North America, the link between these abuses and suicide has not been established in many countries. For example, Ireland, with its high rate of alcoholism, has a low youth suicide rate. In some Middle-Eastern countries where drugs are tolerated, low suicide rates prevail as well. It may be that episodic rather than chronic use of drugs and alcohol, or use linked with cultural practices, reduces the negative effects.

In summary, the high frequency of depressive symptoms among youths who commit suicide must be recognized; at the same time, it should be underlined that it is primarily the impulsive aspects of personality that are at the origin of numerous suicide attempts. Depressive symptoms, moreover, are frequently associated with drug and alcohol use.

VULNERABILITY FACTORS

Social Integration

The major etiological factors linked to depression are found in varying degrees among young people who commit suicide. These factors include a lack of social support, certain kinds of life events, the presence of a physical illness, and a negative family history.

Young people who commit suicide often have problems of social integration, despite the presence of many people in their social network. While adults who commit suicide often live alone, the San Diego study showed that only 3 per cent of young people who commit suicide lived alone (Rich et al. 1986). Is it possible, then, that young suicidal adults lack a circle of friends to give them support when needed? Or do the youths simply feel socially alienated, without necessarily being isolated?

Some authors have suggested that one of the main obstacles to socialization at the beginning of young adulthood is the youths' *investment* in an exclusive love relationship, together with a distancing from a group of peers. Jacobs and Teicher (1967) observed that a lack of parental love often pushes suicidal young people to invest seriously and at an early age in a love relationship, only later to face a state of hopelessness and loneliness when the relationship ends. As well, Fisher and Ladame (1979) found that suicidal youths were precociously involved in exclusive relationships, even before they had had time to develop a circle of friends.

A series of studies with samples of hospitalized suicidal youths concluded that the youths had had serious problems with social integration. The youths reported more problems with their peers than nonsuicidal youths hospitalized in psychiatry, more difficulty in confiding their problems (Topol and Reznicoff 1982), and fewer adequate relationships (Stanley and Barter 1970). Suicidal youths have sometimes been described as more ambivalent and dependent than nonsuicidal youngsters (Lester 1969), more solitary (Peck and Schrut 1971; Marks and Heller 1977), or as having problems with solitude (Crumley 1979). A nonclinical study demonstrated, moreover, that suicidal youths obtained high scores on measures of solitude and social-emotional alienation, and low scores on interpersonal problem solving (Bonner and Rich 1987).

Major difficulties of integration are reported in school as well. Suicidal youths have fewer friends at school than their nonsuicidal peers; they report more conflicts with their friends and teachers; and they change schools more often. Also, they are more often absent and drop school more often because of personal problems (Hanigan 1987).

In general, these conclusions would reflect the finding that suicidal youths are not as well integrated socially as their nonsuicidal peers. Most of the studies, however, involve hospitalized clinical samples, where control groups are not always paired on basic variables.

Life Events

Suicidal youths report a high number of stressful events, especially losses (Bonner and Rich 1987). In one study, they experienced four times more stressful life events in the six months preceding their attempt than members of a control group (Paykel et al. 1975). Such a large difference is rarely found with other pathological conditions. Jacobs (1967) reported that 58 per cent of those who had carried out a suicide attempt had experienced a broken relationship during the same period. Another study (Wenz 1979) found that 33 per cent of youths who were experiencing a loss had suicidal thoughts.

Bad health or a serious physical disability can be related to the suicidal behaviour of youths as well. In France, between 30 and 40 per cent of a suicidal sample reported poor physical health (Davidson and Choquet 1981). Half of the youths who had made a suicide attempt had visited their physician during the month preceding their attempt, and a quarter did so during the week before (Hawton et al. 1982). It is not known, unfortunately, how many of these medical visits were related to psychogenic illnesses rather than somatic states, or whether they were made to secure psychotropic drugs. The illnesses most frequently associated with suicidal states among youths are diabetes, kidney transplants, and multiple sclerosis (Petzel and Kline 1978; Bryan and Herjanic 1980).

Family Situation

The loss of a parent through death (Crook and Raskin 1975) or separation (Kosky 1983) is sometimes associated with suicidal behaviour. In the latter study, 80 per cent of the suicidal youths seen in psychiatry had suffered the loss of a parent, compared to only 20 per cent in a nonsuicidal psychiatric group. In many cases, the loss had occurred within the twelve months preceding the suicide attempt. Several other studies have reported an association with the loss of a parent (Goldney 1981; Shrutt 1968; Ross et al. 1983; Pettifor et al. 1983). On the other hand, a number of studies have been unable to find such a relationship; the control groups in these studies were drawn from both clinical and community groups (Stanley and Barter 1970; Shafii et al. 1985; Dorpat 1965; Jacobs 1967; Kienhorst et al. 1989). A bad family climate is often found in the genesis of suicidal behaviour among youth (Jacobs 1967). Several factors are involved, according to a study covering ten countries (Farberow 1985): chaotic relationships, violence and physical abuse, parental alcoholism, marital conflict, and suicidal behaviour on the part of one of the parents. A French researcher concluded that disappointments in love or school failure did not lead to suicide when not accompanied by a disturbed or chaotic family climate (Chabrol 1984). Many situations of neglect and abuse have been associated with youth suicidal tendencies as well. Physical abuse (Brooksbank 1985; Hawton et al. 1982), maternal immaturity and incompetence, as well as paternal indifference or abuse (Margolin and Teicher 1968), have been reported. One high-school study showed that a number of family problems are associated with suicidal behaviour (Smith and Crawford 1986). The same finding was obtained in a large university sample, where fourteen of the fifteen family variables could distinguish between suicidal and nonsuicidal youths. The most discriminant variables were parental angry behaviour, physical abuse, and parent-child conflicts (Wright et al. 1984). Similarly, a study of fifteen youths who had attempted suicide in Lauzanne, Switzerland – four of whom came from immigrant families – found that all the families showed signs of chronic dysfunction (Masson and Collard 1987).

Other studies that have examined the quality of the parent-child relationship confirm these conclusions. Similar observations have been made in a variety of settings: university (Ross et al. 1983), college, high school (Kashani et al. 1989; Wright 1985), and clinic (McHenry et al. 1982).

On the theoretical level, Brown (1985) has suggested that disturbances in the family system prevent emotional exchanges between parents and child and, as a consequence, the validation of self-image in the child. Hendin (1963) argued that such family situations lead to a numbing of emotional life and a feeling of depersonalization, symptoms characteristic of personality disorders; these flaws in the socialization process lead to negative self-esteem and a sense of lack of control over one's life. Paradoxically, the suicidal act can be a last effort to exercise control over one's destiny (Farberow 1985). This behaviour has also been viewed as an individual's effort to find meaning in life by engaging in a deviant act (Kaplan 1980). According to this model, the suicidal youth, after feeling rejected, does not attach value to the social norms of his or her group of origin; this nonvaluing leads, in turn, to deviant acts, such as a suicide attempt, as a means of recreating an identity. In many suicidal youths, this process may be a reaction against depression: rather than letting themselves be carried along by a tendency towards passivity and helplessness, they try to compensate for their lack of power and control.

Canadian research generally supports the findings of the international literature. A study by Garfinkel et al. (1982) compared the records of 550 suicidal youths at the Hospital for Sick Children in Toronto, aged fourteen years and over, with a control group of children admitted for other diagnoses. Less than half of the suicidal group had been living in an intact family, compared with 84 per cent of the control group. In one-quarter of the suicidal cases, the father was absent; in a second quarter, the child lived in a group or foster home. A good deal of this family disruption was probably due to the psychiatric status of the parents, half of whom had had a history of mental illness. More than two-thirds of the suicidal group, however, had had contact with psychosocial services, which may partially reflect a clinical sample bias. Moreover, two-thirds of the suicidal group had received a psychiatric diagnosis, and more than 37 per cent reported having abused drugs. Very few of the cases had used highly lethal means (1.2%) in their attempt, the degree of lethality being medium in only one case in five. The presence of psychiatric symptoms was associated with a high risk of death.

One of the best studies of family climate among suicidal youths was done with students aged seventeen to twenty-seven at McGill University's mental health clinic. The investigators found that suicide attempts and serious ideations were related to family structure and climate (Adam et al. 1982). Only 15 per cent of students coming from intact families had serious ideas of suicide, compared with 43 per cent of those who had lost a parent because of marital discord and 51 per cent of those who had lost a parent through death. Only 5 per cent of the students from an intact family had attempted suicide, compared with 18 per cent of the students from a broken home. As well, the results showed that if the home climate had reached an acceptable level of comfort several months after the separation of the parents, it was sufficient to protect the students against suicidal behaviour (see Adam et al. 1982a, for similar results in New Zealand).

There is no doubt that suicidal youths come from families that are often very disturbed, mainly because of parental mental illness or alcohol dependence. Unfortunately, little is known about the other factors that lead such families to produce suicidal youths. Is it because these families are isolated, whether from the social network of a neighbourhood or an extended family? Is it because the school or other institutions are unsuccessful, even inadequate, in replacing incompetent parents? Is it because the suicidal child has fewer brothers and sisters to share his or her fate? Or is it because parents have invested too much in their work or professional activities? None of these factors, independently, would be sufficient to explain the genesis of suicidal behaviour. But their cumulative effect can make a disturbed family life impossible, rather than merely difficult, to cope with.

The Role of Culture

The literature on risk factors does not tell us much about the macrosociological level of suicidal behaviour in youth. Intercultural comparisons can fill the void and lead to original hypotheses, as long as they rely on an intimate knowledge of the culture. Thus, Jilek-Aall (1988), who compared the situations of Denmark and Norway – the former having had a much higher rate of youth suicide than the latter up until the beginning of the 1970s – suggests that Norwegian society remained strongly traditional as it underwent modernization without any external interference. The tradition of community help among villagers to survive the assaults of the seasons, the egalitarianism of the society, the relative absence of competition, the custom of never putting one's sick members in institutions – all these practices contributed to the maintenance of strong family ties and a deep involvement in the socialization of children. Denmark, on the other hand, was a society in which the family was more fragmented, more competitive, and one which placed an emphasis on upward social mobility. Parental control strategies relied heavily on guilt, and parents and children were emotionally distant. These conclusions are obviously no longer valid because, since the mid 70's, the Norwegian suicide rate for youths has equaled that of the Danes.

In Japan, where the incidence of youth suicide is also high, one sees both similarities and differences *vis-à-vis* the Danish society. For example, in Japan, parents push their children strongly toward social mobility, although the number of places at the top is small. A lack of success on the part of children, whether in the form of school failure or premarital pregnancy, reflects badly on their parents. The subsequent shame that overcomes the children often leads them to despair, even to attempted suicide.

Suicide among youth is also present in rural societies of the Third World (Tousignant and Mishara 1981). For example, the Truk Islands in the South Pacific underwent an epidemic after the arrival of the Americans following the Second World War. Adolescents were sent to high schools far from home and became alienated from their parents. Finding themselves overwhelmed by these changes and no longer able to assume moral control over their children, the parents started nagging their offspring constantly. Thus, it became common for children to take their own lives for motives that seemed trivial. An increase in youth suicide is also evident in the Arab countries of North Africa, a region where suicide has traditionally been absent, after migration and rapid acculturation upset family structures. In the West, several countries besides Canada have high suicide rates, such as Finland, Austria, Hungary, and West Germany. Unfortunately, good comparative data is lacking on the life histories of youths in these countries. For example, it would be interesting to investigate why some countries such as Italy (which, like Canada, has a high divorce rate, low birth rate, and high average consumption of alcohol) have low rates of youth suicide.

The Canadian Scene

The period 1960-80 was marked by a sudden increase in youth suicide rates in Canada and the industrialized countries. In fact, World Health Organization statistics for 1985 show that few countries have a higher rate than

Canada. What characterizes Canada, compared to most other countries, is its relatively flat suicide-rate curve as a function of age. In fact, for each five-year age category above twenty years of age, no group has a rate lower than 15.5 per 100,000 or higher than 18.2. The rates for fifteen- to nineteen- and twenty- to twenty-four- year-olds are, respectively, 11.2 and 17.7. Clearly, it is wrong to think that suicide is higher among youth than among elderly or middle-aged persons. As well, the gap between the sexes is relatively high: six times as many men as women commit suicide between the ages of fifteen and twenty-four; after thirty, the ratio of men to women drops to about 3.5:1.

In Canada, the increase in youth suicide was steady between 1961 and 1980: whereas for youths fifteen to nineteen years of age, the rate increased by more than five times; for those aged twenty to twenty-four it has more than tripled. Yet the phenomenon is particularly disturbing because the suicide rate is increasing as each cohort gets older. Take, for example, Solomon and Hellon's (1980) finding of the progressive increase in rates in Alberta as early as 1951. Even if youth suicide decreases in the future, these rates may still continue to increase for a certain period of time among the older cohorts.

Between 1980 and 1985, trends showed the beginning of a rate decrease in both sexes, particularly for that last year. In fact, the rate of 11.2 among fifteen- to nineteen-year-olds has not been so low since 1976, and the rate of 17.7 among the twenty- to twenty-four-year-olds has not been so low since 1973. What is the reason for this decrease? Can it be attributed to a higher public awareness and better preventive efforts? Although we would like to agree with this hypothesis, there is little evidence of its veracity. It is also difficult to verify whether depression rates have decreased in the same proportion. Statistics on drug and alcohol consumption would lead one to believe that the recent decreases in illicit drugs, for example, in the high schools of Ontario (Smart et al. 1983) or even for the consumption of alcohol in the Santé-Québec survey (Ministère de la santé et des services sociaux du Québec 1988), might have contributed to this decrease.

Among the provinces, Quebec and the three Prairie provinces had the highest youth suicide rates for 1984-85. (The Yukon and the Northwest Territories, however, had much higher rates.) With the exception of Quebec, it is the Native population that contributes to the elevated rates. This hypothesis is confirmed for Alberta, where suicide among young Natives is five times the Canadian average (Jarvis and Boldt 1982). In Manitoba, Thompson (1987) analyzed coroners' records on all suicides between 1971 and 1982 among youths under twenty. During this period there were fifty-eight suicides among young Natives within the fifteen- to twenty-year-old age group, compared to 105 among the Caucasian population (and that latter group was much larger). The suicide rate of the first group was eleven times higher than that of the Caucasian group of the same age. The same observation was made in British Columbia (Tonkins 1983): among those younger than twenty years of age, Natives accounted for 33 per cent of the suicides but represented only 3.5 per cent of the total population. As in Manitoba, alcohol abuse occurred more frequently among Native youths (60% of cases) than among Caucasians (38%) and more often in a rural (53%) than an urban (38%) or a metropolitan setting (30%). The latest data for Quebec (1988) indicate a rate of 14.1 for the fifteen- to nineteen-year-old group, and a rate of 24.8 for the twenty- to twenty-four-year-old group.

If Native suicides are subtracted from the totals of the Prairie provinces, Quebec would have by far the highest rate of any Canadian province. (Subtracting Native suicides in Quebec would have little effect, because of the small Native population.) Furthermore, if one were to include the Métis with the Indians, the suicide rate for young Québécois of Caucasian origin would probably be even more distant from those of young non-Natives in other provinces.

The Manitoba study revealed that alcohol abuse among the Caucasian group had been observed in nearly 40 per cent of suicide youth cases (nearly 60% among Natives) and drug abuse in a little less than 20 per cent (40% among Natives). This type of abuse was twice as frequent among men who had committed suicide as among women. Moreover, alcohol abuse was less frequent among urban Caucasians who had committed suicide, than for those in rural regions. It is noteworthy that, of the eight native women who committed suicide, three did so after losing custody of a child.

A number of authors have tried to explain the higher suicide rate among young Natives. One theorist suggests that social disorganization, produced by a loss of traditional values and without any genuine parallel integration into the dominant society, has transformed these persons into internal immigrants despite the absence or near-absence of geographic mobility (Berry 1985). Jilek-Aall (1988), in her description of the Indian communities where she worked for many years, states that, although many communities chose modernity in order to benefit from technological progress, few of their members have been successful in the process; most, in fact, have found themselves dependent on social welfare. She attributes the high suicide rates among youth to a lack of confidence in the wider group, the negative effects of alcohol, and the wish to relive the status of a brave through very risky acts, including suicide. She notes, however, that in those villages where alcohol is banned by the local elite and where movements of cultural renaissance have taken off, there is room for cautious optimism.

Only regional data of suicide attempts and ideation are available. A survey of parasuicide carried out in London, Ontario, between 1969 and 1971, included all files of hospitals, psychiatric institutions, and prisons, as well as more than 85 per cent of physicians' files (Jarvis et al. 1976). The results showed that 1 per cent of young women had attempted suicide or had self-inflicted bodily injuries – a rate twice that of men. From these data, the estimated ratio of suicide attempts to successful suicide would be 30:1 among men aged fifteen to twenty-four, and 200:1 among women of the same age. Of course, these figures are only a conservative estimate; a certain percentage of suicide attempts are not followed by a medical visit – only one in four according to a Montreal high-school survey (Tousignant et al. 1988). These gender differences in ratios are also observed in the international literature. The usual explanation is that women use less violent methods, even if they are more depressed and have more suicidal ideation. The fact that more men than women abuse alcohol and drugs may also contribute to the surplus of successful attempts among men.

In a very different domain, the grimness of certain seasons, which makes such a profound mark on the cycle of activities and moods of Canadians, does not seem to have any influence on youth suicide, according to an analysis of the records of 129 adolescents aged ten to nineteen who committed suicide in Montreal between 1978 and 1982 (Cheifetz et al. 1987).

In conclusion, it is difficult to offer as elaborate reasons for the higher suicide rate in Quebec as those given for the Natives. The most immediate question is whether risk factors are more prevalent in Quebec, such as, for example, family conflicts, substance abuse, or small social networks. Only in-depth surveys with large samples will yield satisfactory answers. Even if, on the cultural level, one hypothesizes that the modernization of Quebec society was simply too fast at the beginning of the 1960s, it is difficult to use such an explanation for the last decade. It is possible, however, that today's parents, after witnessing the dramatic collapse of their parents' values, now lack guidelines to instruct their own children. For example, although the church used to be the basis of family authority, currently only 20 per cent of the population in many regions, even in rural areas, is engaged in regular religious practice. The values that parents now favour – and this is even more evident in disturbed families – are those connected with success; such an approach creates the feeling in children that their success is, in the long run, useful only to buttress the narcissism of their parents.

AUTHORS' RESEARCH PROGRAM

We will now describe some of the results from our own research program. These data, we feel, add some information to the issues raised in the literature review. In these studies, we have concerned ourselves primarily with the social ecology of young suicidal persons.

Theoretical Framework

At the turn of the century, Durkheim (1897) had already observed that suicide was not simply determined by individual psychological characteristics. Rather, it reflected certain weaknesses in European society, particularly with regard to the liberal and individualistic attitudes that did not allow adequate containment of a person's instinctual forces, nor offer the individual a framework of norms suitable for monitoring his or her own behaviour. Durkheim's argument showed that suicide was more frequent among people living alone, especially those widowed, separated, or divorced; and in households with fewer children, in which egotistic forces (in its psychological, rather than moralistic, sense) were stronger than the integrative forces. According to this theory, in religious groups where the choice of norms is left to a person's free will, there is a threat that the individual may feel less supported by the social structure and, therefore, be more frequently tempted by suicide as a solution. Durkheim showed that suicide rates were lowest among Jews, where centripetal forces were strong in the nineteenth century, a little higher among Catholics, and much higher among Protestants, with Anglicans being halfway between the last two groups. A long series of observations subsequently showed that a high frequency of suicides, or attempted suicides, occurred in urban zones with a higher density of solitary persons. Such studies could not, however, demonstrate that it was the mere fact of living alone that brought people to despair and suicide. In fact, Hughes and Gove (1981) suggested that it was not so much the lack of social support among those living alone that increased the probability of suicide as it was the lack of control and supervision.

Unfortunately, ecological correlations cannot confirm conclusions concerning the social networks of suicidal persons. Researchers must instead describe the processes that occur between suicidal people and their networks. But the data from the files of individuals who have tried or almost completed a suicide are often incomplete in that respect. Moreover, loneliness and lack of social integration, if present, might be merely the result of the last stage of a series of unfortunate events. As well, the last months of life might not be representative of the whole suicidal career.

We thus became interested in investigating the period when a suicidal career begins to take shape among young adults. Doing a retrospective qualitative analysis of relationships with the network appeared to be the best way of developing a dynamic profile of the social ecology of young suicidal persons. A second series of studies, the results of which are preliminary, was done on a number of ecological dimensions related to the family. These studies analyze the social stability of the families of suicidal youths. The key question was whether parental negligence or abuse was sufficient for a young person to become suicidal, or whether a certain social disruption or isolation between the family and its environment was also necessary. These latter characteristics were measured by such indices as lack of contact between the parents and the extended family; geographic mobility, especially residential moves preventing the social integration of the child; and, finally, school changes related to such moves. Our second goal was to provide baseline epidemiological data on suicide attempts, as well as serious suicidal ideation and their sociodemographic correlates.

Our research program is thus made up of two series of studies, carried out by means of interviews, for which large-scale surveys were necessary in order to locate samples of suicidal youths. Whereas part one covers epidemiological results, part two describes the more qualitative ecological analyses.

Frequency of Suicide

METHOD. The first survey included 667 students (average age: 18.2 years) enrolled in four public, French-language colleges (CEGEPS) of Greater Montreal. The return rate for the questionnaire (filled out at home) was 63.9 per cent. Because the aim of this study was to determine the prevalence of serious suicidal thoughts and suicide attempts, we asked the following questions: "Have you ever seriously thought of committing suicide?" and "Have you ever attempted to commit suicide?" A follow-up interview with an experimental group of twenty-five suicidal youths demonstrated that all those who had answered one of these questions positively had experienced a serious suicidal crisis (Hanigan et al. 1986).

The second survey included 2,327 students (average age: 16.2 years) enrolled in secondaire III to V in six high schools on the island of Montreal (Tousignant et al. 1988). More restrictive criteria were used to define the category "serious suicidal ideation." Inasmuch as having suicide plans was deemed one of the critical elements, two of the following three criteria were necessary for inclusion in that category: to have thought of committing suicide at least three times (frequency); to have thought of committing suicide during at least two weeks (duration); and to have believed that there was some possibility of being successful (intensity). The same questionnaire was subsequently administered by telephone to 700 young adults age eighteen to twenty-four in the Montreal area.

RESULTS. The frequency of serious suicidal ideation was relatively high in the sample of college students. More than one-fifth of college students (21.2%) admitted having had thoughts of suicide, and the ratio of girls to boys was 1.5: 1. One in eight students reported an ideation during the last year. Also, one student in eight reported having carried out at least one attempt on his or her life, the ratio of girls to boys being 2.4: 1. Our comparison of the rate of attempted suicide within the last year (3.6%) with the overall suicide rate for this age group produced a ratio of 200: 1.

Our findings regarding the risk factors echoed other North American results. We found that young people from broken homes had almost twice the rate of ideation of those from intact families. Respondents with a health problem had a rate two-and-a-half times higher than healthy respondents. On the other hand, no relationship was found with the fathers' educational level (usually a good index of socioeconomic status) or with the death of the father.

The high-school survey and college samples had similar rates of attempted suicide and suicidal ideation. The high-school students had a lifetime rate of suicide attempts of 6.6 per cent and, for the last twelve months, 4.1 per cent; the respective rates for the college sample were 8.1 and 3.6 per cent. The rate for serious suicidal ideation was 13.2 per cent in the high-school sample and for a borderline category – that is, all respondents who only partially met the criteria mentioned above – it was 5.3 per cent. The total of the two rates, 18.5 per cent, was only slightly lower than the rate of 21.5 per cent obtained for the college sample, using only one question concerning the presence of serious suicidal ideation. A study by Pronovost (1986), conducted in the second, third, and fourth years of a high school in the area of Trois Rivières (Quebec) (n=518) produced similar results.

There, the rate of serious ideation was 20.7 per cent (the ratio of girls to boys was 1.3:1) and there were no real differences between the three grade levels. The rate of suicide attempts was 3.9 per cent (ratio of the girls to boys of 2:1). On the other hand, subtracting those not reporting any plan lowers the rate to 14.7 per cent, a rate very close to that of the 13.2 per cent obtained in Montreal with similar criteria. The combined rate of attempts and serious ideation was a little lower at 10.9 per cent in a sample of 706 students from the Université de Montréal (Morval and Bouchard 1987). In our telephone survey, 14.0 per cent of respondents aged eighteen to twenty-four years met the criteria of the suicidal category. Nearly half of this group, or 6.1 per cent, had made a suicide attempt during the last three years. Contrary to the results of the high-school data, there were no sex differences: men had a suicidal rate of 14.6 per cent and women 13.4 per cent. These results show not only that the rate of serious suicidal ideation is roughly the same in young adult and high-school populations, but also that the rates are similar in the Montreal area and in a city of 100,000.

An analysis of the effects of parental separation and quality of the parent-child relationship in the high-school survey clearly showed that both factors contributed independently to an increase in the suicidal rate, although the quality of the relationship emerged as slightly more important than the separation factor. In the group where the relationship with parents was good, separation raised the rates; if the relationship was bad, separation played a much less important role. There was also an interaction between the educational level of the father and the family structure: in the case of intact (but not separate) families, the suicidal rate was lower when the father had more education.

The college survey included the CES-D Scale. The mean for the CES-D of nonsuicidal students (36.6) was much lower than that for the suicidal students (51.8; $p < .0001$). On the other hand, those who seriously believed their plans could have been carried out were no more depressed than those who did not believe their plans were serious. Also, although the suicidal youths had experienced more stressful life events during the last twelve months than those who were not suicidal, both sexes reported approximately the same number of events ($X^2 = .2$; $p < 0.70$). We could not establish any cause-effect relationship, however, because data concerning the dates of both events and suicidal behaviour were missing.

The suicidal youths reported eleven of the twenty-eight events more often than the nonsuicidal youths (see Table 1). Many of these events were associated with personal problems or predispositions; they included: running away from home, dropping out of school, "doing" a bad drug trip, being rejected from a group, or being the victim of a physical attack. As well, suicidal young women reported more events such as abortions and pregnancies (or the fear of pregnancy) than did nonsuicidals. Breakups with boyfriends, girlfriends, or friends, as well as changes of residence were also associated with suicidal tendencies. Events experienced by the suicidal group's parents, however, were not significantly more frequent.

Ecological Factors

METHOD. The research program also compared twenty-five suicidal and twenty-five nonsuicidal college youths with regard to the quality of social support in stressful situations (Hanigan et al. 1986). All the subjects had experienced either the breakup of a love relationship or of a friendship during the previous year. Subjects were interviewed regarding the composition and size of their social network, the presence of conflicts, and their confidence with significant members of that network following the loss experienced. Coefficients of interjudge agreement varied between .54 and .94, a satisfactory result given the nature of the task required from the judges.

In another ecological analysis, we compared the changes of residence among suicidal and nonsuicidal high-school students.

RESULTS. Contrary to the hypothesis, the suicidal youths' network of important persons among their peers was almost as large as that of the nonsuicidal youths. The nonsuicidal youths, however, reported 50 per cent more so-called important people among their relatives, including parents, than the

Table 1
Reported life events and suicidal behaviour

Life events	Suicidal group n	%	Nonsuicidal group n	%	χ^2	p
(Total sample)	(75)		(525)			
Failed a course	36	4	191	36	1.6	n.s.
Dropped out of school	8	11	12	2	12.6	.001
Fell in love	47	63	245	47	2.2	n.s.
Broke up with lover/friend	51	68	189	36	10.3	.01
Started new friendship	39	52	242	46	0.3	n.s
Rejected by group	18	24	33	6	19.9	.001
Began living together	9	12	27	5	4.6	.05
Personal illness	4	5	11	2	2.6	n.s.
Attacked	6	8	1	-	32.1	.001
Bad trip (drugs)	14	19	28	5	14.3	.001
Ran away from home	10	13	5	1	36.0	.001
Moved	22	29	90	17	4.1	.05
Lost job	11	15	56	11	0.8	n.s.
Death of parent	2	3	3	1	3.4	n.s.
Other death	14	19	54	10	3.4	n.s.
Separation (parents)	3	4	17	3	0.1	n.s.
Threat of separation (parents)	7	9	36	7	0.5	n.s.
Remarriage (parents)	3	4	13	2	0.6	n.s.
Illness (parents)	6	8	27	5	0.9	n.s.
Illness (other person)	3	4	30	6	0.3	n.s.
Suicide attempt (by parents)	1	1	5	1	0.1	n.s.
Suicide attempt (by others)	6	8	18	3	3.2	n.s.
Accident	9	12	32	6	3.0	n.s.
Pregnancy	2	3	2	-	5.0	.05
Fear of pregnancy	20	27	52	10	12.4	.001
Had an abortion	2	3	2	-	5.0	.05
Raped or sexually assaulted	3	4	7	1	2.7	n.s.

nonsuicidal youths ($p < .008$). Moreover, the suicidal students had twice as many conflicts with their relatives as the nonsuicidal students ($p < .01$), although no significant difference was observed among nonrelatives. The suicidal youths did not generally correspond to the image of lonely people on the margins of social life; if their contacts were more restricted, it was only with their kin. We later analyzed all the excerpts in the interview during which the subject mentioned his family (Tousignant et al. 1986). Among the suicidal youths, eleven subjects had experienced a separation of their parents and ten of these had had difficult family situations: a second separation of the mother, mental illness, a suicide attempt, alcoholism of a parent, or pressure on the child to move out. Four other subjects had a deceased parent (three mothers and one father) and the situation with the other living parent was so poor that none of the children lived with this parent. In the ten cases of intact families, the relationship with one or both parents was poor in at least eight cases. A brief extract is quoted to depict the state of these relationships: "When I will commit suicide, my father will be happy because he will have one less mouth to feed."

Concerning the experience of loss, it should be noted that the stressful event reported by the suicidal group was, on average, more serious than that of the control group. On a four-point scale of seriousness, fifteen of the nonsuicidal youths were classified in the least serious category, compared with only three of the suicidal youths. The criteria of evaluation here were largely objective: longer duration of the relationship or a dramatic rupture caused by an external cause such as death.

In both groups, an approximately equal number of people within the social network had been informed of the stressful event. However, the suicidal students had informed people personally less frequently. Reactions were described as negative or partly negative for both groups in half the cases, the major complaint being a lack of understanding. When it was a question of confiding rather than simply transmitting information, the reactions were much more positive, probably because one chooses a confidant carefully and expects a positive reaction. A surprising result was that the suicidal group did not report fewer confidants than the control group. Perhaps if the stressful event had been more serious, the need for a confidant would have been stronger in the nonsuicidal group.

Although both groups were equally satisfied by the reactions to their sharing of confidences, their interpretations of the situations were different. The nonsuicidal youths had not considered the loss as major and their expectations with regard to the confidant were therefore not very high. They considered disappointments in love as part of normal development and expected the suffering would disappear with time. The suicidal youths, on the other hand, were not ready to allow others to take care of their problems. Often, their self-esteem was threatened by the available help. They stated that they wanted to work through their difficulties alone, in order to prove that they could rely on their own resources. A few suicidal students also refused to accept the reality of the truth of the breakup and continued to long for a reunion without seeking assistance.

In conclusion, we offer the following interpretation. Suicidal youths were rarely socially isolated, although they often felt a strong sense of alienation from others. Whereas they were generally surrounded by people who could have helped, they were reluctant to take advantage of this assistance. The suicidal youths had probably learned from their families not to rely on others to get along in life.

The preliminary results concerning social stability in the families of suicidal youths showed a number of differences. When comparing thirty suicidal and nonsuicidal cases, we found no significant difference in terms of number of moves during childhood. However, we did find that two-thirds of the suicidal youths had experienced at least one move involving a change of city, province, country, or continent, compared with only a third of the control group (X^2 analysis: $p < .05$). A further analysis, however, showed no difference between a suicidal group and a nonsuicidal group reporting a bad family environment. In the suicidal group, long-distance moves were rarely associated with the upward social mobility or professional advancement of their parents. The motives were rather atypical: the moving of depressed parents, dissatisfied with urban life, to the countryside; a father who wanted to disappear to avoid debts; a youth going back and forth between countries to live with the separated father or mother; a mother who wished to become a missionary in a developing country; a mother who married a stranger whom she had met on vacation and who later decided to emigrate. In such circumstances, the youths often found themselves far from their social network. Not only did it usually take several months, even years, to build a similar network, the parents, because of their personal problems, usually did not have much energy to devote to the social integration of their children.

SUGGESTIONS AND PRIORITIES

Professional Intervention

Suicidal youths are not always easy people with whom to establish a relationship: the simple fact of their wanting to end their life reflects a lack of trust in other people. The day-to-day experience of listening to these young people in preventive counselling has shown the difficulties of dealing with chronic cases, particularly those with no visible progress, who constantly go back to square one. Although these youths may become dependent, they are still fundamentally distrustful, which impedes any therapeutic or helping relationship. Moreover, suicidal youths are often not willing to be helped.

Our review of the literature established that many suicidal youths abuse alcohol and drugs. We already know that therapists and physicians do not like dealing with such individuals and will try to refer them to specialized professionals and nonprofessionals. In our opinion, we need ways of intervening differently, apart from simply listening or doing traditional therapy, if we are to transform the lives of the many people who present a high risk of suicide and who have not yet reached a point of no return. The fact that would-be suicidal youngsters are often impulsive, or in rebellion against the world, makes the application of cognitive approaches still more difficult. Another paradox is that these youths find more value in helping others than in being helped. A strategy that would make them more active and engage them in projects with other people would probably bear more fruit than an approach centred on introspection; indeed, the latter strategy is likely only to increase their anxiety. Today, certain prevention centres are aware of these personal resources and require the youths to carry out plans of action for which they themselves must bear responsibility.

Physicians are often consulted in the days preceding a suicide attempt, but without the suicidal intention necessarily being manifested. When there are signs of despair, they should perhaps probe for suicidal ideas and give the needed assistance or suggest appropriate referral. Some of these patients report vague complaints in order to obtain medication for their intended attempt. Physicians should be aware of such tactics so as not to become partners in these strategies. As for the parents, leaving drugs which could be used for attempting suicide within easy reach is often a question of carelessness. Also, pharmacists should be offering more advice about potentially dangerous drugs.

Concerning prevention, we need to increase the public's awareness of suicidal young adults and the helping strategies available. Very often, people being told about suicidal ideations either freeze or panic; they feel unable to offer solutions and find it hard to accept the difficult reality. To talk about death is never easy, but confidants should learn to discuss life situations leading to despair.

Institutions such as schools and colleges have a role to play in early intervention as well. Visible places are needed where desperate and needy young people can go with trust. In high schools, the nurse is often the person able to listen to personal problems without endangering the self-esteem of the young adult. But we also need clearly identifiable refuges to assist young persons during stressful periods, such as during runaways or pregnancies.

Government Action

Government officials understand the nature of youth suicide very well. The numerous task forces both at the national and provincial levels, in Canada as well as the United States, are evidence of good will. The policies being articulated, however, often lag behind.

In the health area, the providers of emergency services are overwhelmed; they resent the arrival of voluntary injuries when so many accident victims need care. Such services could hire consultants to train emergency-team employees to meet the needs of suicidal persons. The period of crisis immediately after an attempt is a period crucial to restoring self-confidence.

Given that emergency services can only do so much because of their situation and that psychiatry services are booked for months in advance, governments should support community services with an adequate long-term financing policy. Also research is needed to evaluate such services. What prevention strategies are the most valuable for the different types of suicidal persons? What is their short- and long-term impact?

At the level of primary prevention, a family policy protecting children against the abuses of parents and foster families is essential. Parents who are incompetent and unable to recognize the basic needs of their children require adequate help. Herein lies a fundamental cultural problem, for it is the very system of the transmission of values from one generation to the next that is being called into question. Because parents often reject values learned in a society undergoing a rapid transition, or perceive their own upbringing as a failure, we need programs for disoriented parents to meet one another and find solutions to raising their children. It may also be necessary to intervene with parents being treated for mental illness, suicide attempts, or alcoholism; they should be provided with coping skills for family problems.

We have seen that drug and alcohol abuse is closely associated with suicidal behaviour in young adults. It is time to publicize this information on a wider scale. As is done in highway-safety campaigns, young adults and their parents must be made aware of the many dangers.

Finally, we have seen that certain Native groups have very high suicide rates because of cultural disorganization, alcohol abuse, and family violence. Governments are generally uneasy. On the one hand, they are partly responsible for the modernization causing social turmoils; on the other hand, too much interference in local affairs runs the danger of alienating these populations even more. Schools and media have been at the root of the social breakdown, teaching tools of adaptation to the modern world but, at the same time, invalidating the traditional values. Suicide prevention must therefore include efforts to revitalize the culture and cope with the integration to modern life. This can take place only if Native adults participate in the process of socializing the children and young adults.

Professional Training

Everyone wishes to include his or her own preoccupations in curriculum revisions. But if everyone was heard, training programs would soon double in size. The most difficult problems to treat in clinical settings, substance abuse and suicidal behaviour, unfortunately receive little curricular attention. Yet to be able to provide the public with information about youth suicide, we must first teach our professionals. If not properly trained, clinicians will face severe anxiety with their suicidal clients and try to keep them as far away as possible. In fact, a number are currently being trained as volunteers in prevention centers. It is necessary to change the curriculum of other professionals in contact with youth as well, such as community-health nurses in schools, physicians, counsellors, not to mention the police officers and lawyers working with delinquent youths likely to turn their aggression against themselves when under high stress.

These training programs must not be limited to the transmission of information. They should include role-playing so that intervention skills are enhanced. People from the helping professions should also confront their own suicidal tendencies, before attempting to help others. It is not unusual to meet trainees with such problems. Because people without the appropriate motivation or the basic skills run the risk of professional burnout, service workers should not be pressured to work with suicidal cases if they are uncomfortable with the problem.

Research

As shown by the literature and conference proceedings, youth suicide is becoming an increasingly legitimate object of study. But there is room for much more to be done. The family domain has been well analyzed; we now need studies that will give additional clues on the specific problems most likely to make a young person vulnerable. Why are some more protected than others from planning suicide? Our own work is heading in this direction, as we analyze how the relationship of the family with the immediate environment and the community can help ensure the children some stability.

There is much to be done in the field of alcohol and drug abuse, especially in the form of longitudinal studies. For example, we need to know whether young adults lack coping strategies before abusing alcohol or other substances, and whether these substances weaken their psychological resources and coping mechanisms.

Although we now have an accurate portrait of the psychiatric status of young adults who kill themselves, we still know little about the social pathways leading to this decision. International conferences must be convened to compare the social situation of countries with high and low youth-suicide rates.

Our concluding plea is for better liaison between research and intervention. We urgently need to translate knowledge of research into programs. Such research could be stimulated by grant agencies if a certain portion of the funds were allocated to spreading findings among practitioners. Meetings between researchers and practitioners are also needed, to complement their respective efforts.

BIBLIOGRAPHY

Adam, K.S. 1973. Childhood parental loss, suicidal ideation, and suicidal behaviour. *The child in his family: The impact of disease and death*, edited by E.J. Anthony, and C. Koupernik, 275–97. New York: John Wiley.

Adam, K.S., Bouckoms, A., and Streiner, D. 1982. Parental loss and family stability in attempted suicide. *Archives of General Psychiatry* 39:1081–85.

Adam, K.S., Lohrenz, J.G., Harper, D., and Streiner, D. 1982. Early parental loss and suicidal ideation in university students. *Canadian Journal of Psychiatry* 27:275–81.

Allen, B.P. 1987. Youth suicide. *Adolescence* 22:271–90.

Berry, J.W. 1985. Acculturation and mental health. In *Cross-cultural psychology and health: Towards applications*, edited by P.R. Dasen, J.W. Berry, and N. Sartorius. London: Sage.

Bonner, R.L., and Rich, A.R. 1987. Toward a predictive model of suicidal ideation and behaviour: Some preliminary data in college students. *Suicide and Life-Threatening Behaviour* 17:50–63.

Brooksbank, D. 1985. Suicide and parasuicide in childhood and early adolescence. *British Journal of Psychiatry* 146:459–63.

Brown, G., and Harris, T. 1978. *The social origins of depression*. London: Tavistock.

Brown, S. 1985. Adolescent and family systems. In *Youth Suicide*, edited by M.L. Peck, N.L. Farberow, and R.E. Litman. New York: Springer.

Bryan, D.P., and Herjanic, B. 1980. Depression and suicide among adolescents and young adults with selective handicapping conditions. *Exceptional Education Quarterly*, 1:57–65.

Chabrol, H. 1984. *Les comportements suicidaires de l'adolescent*. Paris: Presses Universitaires de France.

Cheifetz, P.N., Posener, J.A., LaHaye, A., Zajdman, M., and Benierakis, C.E. 1987. An epidemiologic study of adolescent suicide. *Canadian Journal of Psychiatry* 32:656–59.

Crook, T., and Raskin, A. 1975. Association of childhood parental loss with attempted suicide and depression. *Journal of Consulting and Clinical Psychology* 43:277.

Crumley, F.E. 1979. Adolescent suicide attempts. *Journal of the American Medical Association* 241:2404–07.

Davidson, M., Choquet, M. 1981. *Le suicide de l'adolescent*. Paris: ESF.

Dorpat, T.L. 1965. Broken homes and attempted and completed suicides. *Archives of General Psychiatry* 12:213.

Durkheim, E. 1897. *Le suicide*. Paris: Alcan.

Farberow, N.L. 1985. Youth suicide: a summary. In *Youth Suicide*, edited by M.L. Peck, N.L. Farberow, and R.E. Litman. New York: Springer.

Fisher, W., and Ladame, F.G. 1979. Premiers résultats de recherche sur les tentatives de suicide des adolescents: Itinéraires pré-suicidaires. *Médecine Sociale et Préventive* 24:49–52.

Friedman, R.C., Corn, R., Aronoff, M.S., Hurt, S.W., Fibel, B. and Clarkin, J.F. 1984. The seriously suicidal adolescent: Affective and character pathology. In *Suicide in the young*, edited by H.S. Sudak, A.B. Ford, and N.B. Rushforth, 209–26. Boston: John Wright PSG, Inc.

Friedrich, W., Reams, R., and Jacobs, J. 1982. Suicide attempts in children and adolescents. *American Journal of Psychiatry* 138:35–40.

Garfinkel, B.D., Froese, A., and Hood, J. 1982. Suicide attempts in children and adolescents. *American Journal of Psychiatry* 138:35–40.

Gispert, M., Wheeler, K., Marsh, L., Davis, M.S. 1985. Suicidal adolescents: Factors in evaluation. *Adolescence* 20:753–62.

Goldney, R.D. 1981. Parental loss and reported childhood stress in young women who attempted suicide. *Acta Psychiatrica Scandinavia* 64:34–49.

Goldney, R.D., and Pilowsky, I. 1980. Depression in young women who have attempted suicide. *Australian and New Zealand Journal of Psychology* 14:203–11.

Hanigan, D. 1987. *Le suicide chez les jeunes adultes et les personnes âgées.* Québec: Les Publications du Québec.

Hanigan, D., Tousignant, M., Bastien, M.F., and Hamel, S. 1986. Le soutien social suite à un événement critique chez un groupe de cégépiens suicidaires. *Revue Québécoise de Psychologie* 7:63–81.

Harris, T., Brown, G.W., and Bifulco, A. 1986. Loss of parent in childhood and adult psychiatric disorder: The role of lack of adequate parental care. *Psychological Medicine* 16:641–59.

Hawton, K., Cole, D., O'Grady, J., and Osborn, M. 1982. Motivational aspects of deliberate self-poisoning in adolescents. *British Journal of Psychiatry* 141:286–91.

Hendin, H. 1963. The psychodynamics of suicide. *Journal of Nervous and Mental Diseases* 136:236–244.

Hughes, M., and Gove, W.R. 1981. Living alone, social integration, and mental health. *American Journal of Sociology* 87:48–75.

Jacobs, G.K., and Teicher, J.D. 1967. Attempted suicide of adolescents. *International Journal of Social Psychiatry* 13:139–149.

Jacobs, J. 1967. Adolescents suicide attempts: The culmination of a progressive social isolation. Ph.D. thesis. University of California, Los Angeles.

Jarvis, G.K., and Boldt, M. 1982. Death styles among Canada's Indians. *Social Science and Medicine* 16:1345–1352.

Jarvis, G.K., Ferrence, R.G., and Johnson, E.G. 1976. Sex and age patterns in self-injury. *Journal of Health and Social Behaviour* 17:146–55.

Jilek-Aall, L. 1988. Youth and Suicide. *Transcultural Psychiatric Research Review* 25:87–105.

Kaplan, H.B. 1980. *Deviant behaviour in defense of self.* London: Academic Press.

Kashani, J.H., Goddard, P., and Reid, J.C. 1989. Correlates of suicidal ideation in a community sample of children and adolescents. *Journal of the American Academy of Child and Adolescent Psychiatry* 28:912–17.

Kienhorst, C.W.M., DeWilde, E.J., Van den Bout, J., Diekstra, R.F.W., and Wolters, W.H.G. 1989. Characteristics of suicide attempters in a population-based sample of Dutch adolescents. *British Journal of Psychiatry* 156:243–58.

Kosky, R. 1983. Childhood suicidal behaviour. *Journal of Child Psychology and Applied Disciplines* 24:457–68.

Lester, D. 1969. Resentment and dependency in the suicidal individual. *Journal of*

General Psychology 81:137-45.

Levy, J.C., and Deykin, E.Y. 1989. Suicidality, depression, and substance abuse in adolescents. *American Journal of Psychiatry* 146:1462-67.

McHenry, P.C., Tishler, C.L., and Kelley, C. 1982. Adolescent suicide: A comparison of attempters and nonattempters in an emergency room population. *Child Pediatrics* 21:266-70.

Margolin, N.L., and Teicher, J.D. 1968. Thirteen adolescent male suicide attempts. *Journal of the American Academy of Child Psychiatry* 7:296-315.

Maris, R. 1985. The adolescent suicide problem. *Suicide and Life-Threatening Behaviour* 15:91-109.

Marks, P.A., and Heller, D.L. 1977. Now I lay down for keeps: A study of adolescent suicide attempts. *Journal of Clinical Psychology* 33:390-400.

Masson, D., and Collard, M. 1987. Jeunes suicidants et leur famille. *Social Psychiatry* 22:85-92.

Miles, C.P. 1977. Conditions predisposing to suicide: A review. *Journal of Nervous and Mental Diseases* 164:231-46.

Ministère de la santé et des services sociaux du Québec. 1988. *Et la santé, ça va?* (Tome 1). Rapport de l'enquête Santé Québec 1987. Québec: Les Publications du Québec.

Morval, M., and Bouchard, L. 1987. *Enquête sur le vécu des étudiants et les comportements suicidaires à l'Université de Montréal.* Montréal: Table de Prévention du Suicide de l'Université de Montréal.

Newmann, J.P. 1984. Sex differences in symptoms of depression: Clinical disorder or normal distress? *Journal of Health and Social Behaviour* 25:136-59.

Paykel, E.S., Prusoff, B., and Myers, J.K. 1975. Suicide attempts and recent life events. *Archives of General Psychiatry* 32:327-33.

Peck, M.L, and Schrut, A. 1971. Suicidal behaviour among colleges students. *HSMHA Health Reports* 86:343-98.

Pettifor, J., Perry, D., Plowman, B., and Pitcher, S. 1983. Risk factors predicting childhood and adolescent suicides. *Journal of Child Care* 1:17-49.

Petzel, S.V., and Cline, D.W. 1978. Adolescent suicide: Epidemiological and biological aspects. *Adolescent Psychiatry* 9:343-98.

Pronovost, J. 1986. *Dépistage des adolescents à tendances suicidaires en milieu scolaire secondaire.* Rapport de recherche inédit. Trois-Rivières: Université du Québec à Trois-Rivières.

Radloff, L.S. 1977. The CES-D Scale: A self-report depression scale for research in the general population. *Applied Psychological Measurement* 1:385-401.

Rich, C.L., Young, D., and Fowler, R.C. 1986. San Diego suicide study. *Archives of General Psychiatry* 43:577-82.

Robins, D.R., and Alessi, N.E. 1985. Depressive symptoms and suicidal behaviour in adolescents. *American Journal of Psychiatry* 142:588-92.

Ross, M.W., Clayer, J.R., and Campbell, R.L. 1983. Parental rearing patterns and suicidal thoughts. *Acta Psychiatrica Scandinavia* 67:429-33.

Schrut, A. 1968. Some typical patterns in the behaviour and background of adolescent girls who attempt suicide. *American Journal of Psychiatry* 125:69–74.

Shafii, M., Carrigan, S., Whittinghill, A.C., and Derrick, A. 1985. Psychological autopsy of completed suicide in children and adolescents. *American Journal of Psychiatry* 142:1061–64.

Sherer, M. 1985. Depression and suicidal ideation in college students. *Psychological Reports* 57:1061–62.

Slater, J, and Depue, R.A. 1981. The contribution of environmental events and social support to serious suicide attempts in primary depressive order. *Journal of Abnormal Psychology* 90:275–85.

Smart, R.G., Goodstadt, M.S., Sheppard, M.A., Shan, G.C., Adlaf, E.M., and Lieban, C.B. 1983. *Preliminary report on alcohol and other drug use among Ontario students in 1983,* and trends since 1977. Toronto: Alcoholism and Drug Addiction Research Foundation, substudy no. 1203.

Smith, K., and Crawford, S. 1986. Suicidal behaviour among "normal" high school students. *Suicide and Life-Threatening Behaviour* 16:313–25.

Solomon, M.I., and Hellon, C.P. 1980. Suicide and age in Alberta, Canada, 1951 to 1977: A cohort analysis. *Archives of General Psychiatry* 37:511–21.

Spirito, A., Brown, L., Overholser, J., and Fritz, G. 1989. Attempted suicide in adolescence: A review and critique of the literature. *Clinical Psychology Review* 9:335–63.

Stanley, E.J., and Barter, J.T. 1970. Adolescent suicidal behaviour. *American Journal of Orthopsychiatry* 40:87–95.

Thompson, T.R. 1987. Childhood and adolescent suicide in Manitoba: A demographic study. *Canadian Journal of Psychiatry* 32:264–69.

Tonkins, R.S. 1984. Suicide methods in British Columbian adolescents. *Journal of Adolescent Health Care* 5:172–77.

Topol, P., and Reznikoff, M. 1982. Perceived peer and family relationships, hopelessness and locus of control as factors in adolescent suicide attempts. *Suicide and Life-Threatening Behaviour* 12:141–50.

Tousignant, M., Bastien, M.-F., and Hamel, S. 1988. Comportements et idéations suicidaires chez les cégépiens de Montréal: La part familiale. *Apprentissage et Socialisation* 9:17–25.

Tousignant, M., Bastien, M.-F., Hamel, S. and Hanigan, D. 1986. Comportements et idéations suicidaires chez les cégépiens de Montréal: la part familiale. *Apprentissage et Socialisation* 9(1):17–25.

Tousignant, M., Hanigan, D., and Bergeron, L. (1984). Le mal de vivre: comportements et idéations suicidaires chez les cégépiens de Montréal. *Santé Mentale au Québec* 9:122–33.

Tousignant, M., and Mishara, B.L. 1981. Suicide et culture: A review of the literature (1969–1980). *Transcultural Psychiatric Research Review* 18:5–31.

Wenz, F.V. 1979. Self-injury behaviour, economic status and the family anomie syndrome among adolescents. *Adolescence* 14:387–98.

Wright, L.S. 1985. Suicidal thoughts and their relationship to family stress and personal problems among high school seniors and college undergraduates. *Adolescence* 20:575–80.

Wright, L.S., Snodgrass, G., and Emmons, J. 1984. Variables related to serious suicidal thoughts among college students. *Naspa Journal*, 22 (1): 57–65.

CHAPTER FIVE

Gender, Psychosocial Factors, and Depression

JANET M. STOPPARD

Although there has been considerable research into the etiology and treatment of depression in adult men and women, the importance of gender issues in understanding depression has been overlooked until fairly recently. Greater awareness of the salience of gender-related factors in understanding depression has arisen, in part, because of the now well-documented finding of a sex difference in rates of depression. Indeed, prevalence rates of depression generally are found to be higher among women than men (Nolen-Hoeksema 1987; Weissman et al. 1988). One important implication of this finding is that models of depression must be able to account for the predominance of women among those who become depressed (Lewinsohn et al. 1985). Although explanations for sex differences in the prevalence of depression reflect a wide spectrum of theoretical orientations, a broad distinction can be drawn between approaches that emphasize biological factors and those that focus on psychosocial factors. The terms *sex* and *gender* are still another distinction underlying the difference between the biological and psychosocial approaches. Whereas "sex" refers to the biological aspects of maleness and femaleness (for example, the differences in reproductive physiology), "gender" is a more encompassing term that includes the array of attributes, behaviours, roles, and experiences that characterize and differentiate women and men in the sociocultural sense (Lips 1988). Thus, psychosocial approaches are more likely to be compatible with the gender perspective on differences between men and women, than with the more limited focus on sex differences.

Although attempts have been made to explain higher rates of depression among women on the basis of genetic factors, or on the hormonal changes associated with menstruation, pregnancy, and menopause, the available evidence is not compelling (Gotlib et al. 1989; Kaufert and Gilbert 1986; McKinlay et al. 1987; Merikangas et al. 1985b; Nolen-Hoeksema 1987). This is not to rule out the possibility that depression (in both sexes) may eventually be best accounted for in terms of an interaction between a biological predisposition and psychosocial factors (that is, a form of diathesis-stress model). The aim of this chapter, however, is to review research relevant to psychosocial explanations for differences in rates of depression between men and women.

Given the distinction already made between sex and gender, it is useful at this point to clarify the way in which these terms will be used in the remainder of the chapter. When a comparison between men and women is based primarily on their membership in the biological category of male or female, the term "sex" will be used (for example, sex differences in rates of depression). The term "gender" will be used in all other cases in which references to the categories male and female extend beyond a biological distinction to include sociocultural influences.

OVERVIEW OF CHAPTER

After discussing the importance of knowledge concerning gender-related factors in depression for practitioners and researchers, I will briefly review the findings regarding sex differences in rates of depression. In general, the findings of Canadian studies resemble those of studies carried out in other Western countries.

The main part of this chapter will focus on psychosocial explanations for sex differences in depression. One of the central questions is whether epidemiological findings reflect a "true" difference between men's and women's rates of depression. Consideration of this question requires discussion of the supposition that men and women are equally likely to become depressed, the observed difference in rates being an artifact of other gender-related differences. Here, the two most commonly proposed artifact explanations – that of response bias and masked depression – will be considered. Proponents of artifact explanations claim that depression rates are either overestimated among women, or underestimated among men, or both. Based on findings in Canada and elsewhere, I conclude that the available evidence is inconsistent with artifact explanations for sex differences in depression rates. Following this, psychosocial explanations for differences in rates of depression between women and men are reviewed. For the purpose of discussion, these explanations are grouped according to whether psychological, gender-role, or social factors are emphasized.

From a psychological perspective, the assumption has been made that, because of the differing socialization experiences of men and women, women are more likely than men to develop some of the psychological characteristics and behaviour patterns thought to increase vulnerability to depression. Within this perspective, attempts to account for sex differences in depression have followed two main directions. The first focuses on the psychological aspects of gender, in terms of whether an individual's personality is predominantly characterized by "masculine" or "feminine" traits. Development of a "sex role orientation" in which feminine traits predominate is assumed to be a factor in women's greater vulnerability to depression. The second approach draws on cognitive-behavioural theories of depression. Essentially, these theories identify individual differences in ways of interpreting personal and social reality (for example, beliefs, attitudes, attributional style), and in typical patterns of behaviour (for instance, social skills and problem-solving abilities) as vulnerability factors for depression (see Beckham and Leber 1985, for an overview of cognitive-behavioural theories). Cognitive-behavioural theories imply that the greater prevalence of depression among women occurs because the vulnerabilities posited by the theories are more characteristic of women than men. Among the cognitive-behavioural theories, the learned helplessness theory (Abramson et al. 1978) has been applied most often to the problem of explaining sex differences in depression.

Gender-role explanations focus on the different ways men and women experience apparently similar social roles. The underlying assumption is that gender shapes both the nature and experience of specific role activities, and thus the psychological consequences of involvement in various social roles (for example, as parent or paid employee) are different for women and men. The finding that women are more depressed than men, even when involved in the same social roles, would therefore offer support for gender-role explanations of sex differences in depression.

Social explanations for sex differences in depression also consider the effects of role involvement; their focus, however, is on differences in the distribution of various roles and statuses between men and women. Proponents of this approach argue that sex differences in rates of depression arise because men and women tend to occupy different social roles (for example, men are more likely to have full-time employment) as well as different statuses within roles (for instance, men are more likely to be employed in occupations with higher prestige). Finding no difference between men and women in rates of depression, when they are comparable in role involvement and social status, would be consistent with social explanations of sex differences in depression.

The final section of the chapter will address the implications of current knowledge with regard to the links between gender, psychosocial factors, and depression for practice and research within the Canadian context.

IMPORTANCE OF A GENDER PERSPECTIVE IN UNDERSTANDING DEPRESSION

Importance for Practice

In Western countries, the higher rates of depression found among women compared to men means that mental health professionals are likely to encounter many women among their clients. Indeed, the available Canadian information on utilization of inpatient and outpatient services (Berger 1985; D'Arcy and Schmitz 1979; Statistics Canada 1987) indicates that a substantial portion of the work of various health professionals involves treatment of depressed individuals, the majority of whom are women. These data imply that health and mental health professionals need to be aware of the potential role of gender-related factors in depression.

Lack of attention to gender issues when treating depressed clients, or even inaccurate assumptions about gender-related factors in depression, will likely render interventions less effective than they might otherwise be. For instance, clinicians who hold traditional beliefs about women (for example, that women should gain primary fulfilment in marital and family roles) are likely to overlook sources of stress in women's lives that arise within the context of these roles (for instance, that women bear the burden of responsibility for housework and childcare). Similarly, beliefs that women are psychologically or biologically (or both) predisposed to depression may lead to an overemphasis on intrapsychic and organismic factors in clinical formulations, to the relative neglect of social-contextual factors, such as economic dependency. More accurate knowledge about the ways in which the lives of women can increase their vulnerability to depression should enhance the ability of clinicians to understand and respond to depressed women clients.

An understanding of depression that takes gender into account would also allow for the development of intervention approaches that are more responsive to the needs of depressed women (and men). Such interventions could include approaches developed by therapists working within a feminist perspective, approaches in which clients are helped to recognize and change stressful situations in their lives, rather than merely adjust to circumstances (Greenspan 1983). Better understanding of gender-related factors in depression might also suggest strategies for relapse prevention, as well as for primary prevention if high risk groups can be identified. For instance, evidence, to be reviewed later in this chapter, suggests that women with young children at home may constitute a high-risk group. These findings imply that strategies designed to relieve the social and emotional burdens experienced by women caring for young children could serve to reduce the overall rate of depression among women. Evidence of links between sex differences in rates of de pression and gender-related inequalities on socioeconomic indices (income, occupational status) could also have implications for the development of social policy for promotion of mental health (Rootman 1988).

Importance for Research

Diagnoses in which depression is a major feature are among the leading psychiatric reasons for hospitalization among women in Canada (Statistics Canada 1987), as well as in other Western countries (Belle and Goldman 1980; Cochrane and Stopes-Roe 1981; Zerssen and Weyerer 1982). Although a variety of hypotheses has been proposed to account for the preponderance of women among depressed patients, none has yet received consistent support. In this era of escalating health-care costs, it is imperative to gain a better understanding of why depressed women are overrepresented in treatment populations.

In the last decade, there has been considerable debate among researchers concerning the validity of epidemiological findings of a sex difference in rates of depression (for example, Hammen 1982; Nolen-Hoeksema 1987). For the time being, this debate appears to have been settled by recent findings in the United States of greater prevalence of depression among women than men when depression is diagnosed according to the *Diagnostic and Statistical Manual of Mental Disorders-Third Edition* (DSM-III) criteria, currently endorsed by the psychiatric profession in North America (Weissman et al. 1988).

Despite the growing consensus that sex differences exist regarding prevalence of depression, explanations for the observed higher rates of depression among women continue to be debated. As mentioned already, much of the research relevant to this debate has been carried out within the framework provided by psychosocial theories. One limitation of this body of research, however, has been the diverse ways in which depression has been defined and measured, thereby precluding the emergence of consistent empirical generalizations. For instance, a broad distinction can be made between using self-report symptom measures and using diagnostic criteria to assess depression. The findings that result from these two types of measures need to be evaluated separately, however; they do not necessarily have similar implications for understanding the role of pychosocial factors in depression.

A more serious problem, however, is the lack of attention given to gender influences in research on depression. For example, research on the impact of unemployment on psychological distress has been carried out primarily with men, although women's participation in the paid labour force has increased rapidly in recent years, making them vulnerable to loss of employment as well. Similarly, although the effects of systemic discrimination in employment on women's earnings and opportunities for advancement have been documented, investigation of the implications for women's mental health posed by the disadvantages they face in earning capacity, fringe benefits (pensions, and so on), and working conditions has been limited.

Furthermore, although there has been considerable research exploring the influence of family roles on depression in women, relatively little research has been carried out on the effects of family roles on the mental health of men (Barnett and Baruch 1987). For instance, although research to be reviewed later indicates that married men report lower levels of depressive symptoms than do other men, the mental health advantages derived by men from marriage and family roles have not been a focus of research on depression.

The foregoing discussion implies that an important criterion for evaluating the adequacy of depression theories is whether they can account for depression in men *and* women and, in particular, whether they can account for sex differences in rates of depression. It is clear that, unless research takes gender into account, progress in understanding depression is unlikely to occur as rapidly as might be hoped.

SEX DIFFERENCES IN DEPRESSION: EPIDEMIOLOGICAL FINDINGS

Summary of International Findings

Recent reviews conclude that rates of depression are consistently higher among women than men (Cleary 1987; Nolen-Hoeksema 1987). Whether depression is assessed by self-report symptom questionnaires or diagnostic criteria, the female-to-male ratio is found to be in the region of 2:1 or higher. In her review of twenty-three studies carried out in nine countries, Nolen-Hoeksema (1987) reported that the few exceptions to the pattern of higher depression rates in women occurred in studies involving college students, the elderly, or residents in nonmodern, rural communities.

Canadian Findings

Studies with representative community samples have yielded a consistent pattern of higher rates of diagnosable depression among women than men. Kovess et al. (1987) reported point prevalence rates of Major Depressive Episode (MDE) (defined according to DSM-III criteria) for urban and rural communities in Quebec. The overall rate of MDE was significantly higher among women (3.7%) than men (1.7%). Bland et al. (1988) also found a significantly higher rate of MDE (six-month prevalence) among women (3.9%)

than men (2.5%) in a randomly selected sample of adults in Edmonton, Alberta. The lifetime rate of MDE was also significantly higher for women (11.4%) than men (5.2%). Turner and Beiser (1987) reported six-month and lifetime prevalence rates of MDE for a representative sample of disabled adults and a matched, nondisabled group living in southwestern Ontario. In each group, the rate of MDE among women was at least twice that among men.

In addition to these more recent studies, Murphy et al. (1984) reported rates of aggregated depression and anxiety disorders based on a re-analysis of data collected in a 1970 survey of adults residing in a rural area of Nova Scotia (the Stirling County Study). Point prevalence of combined depression and anxiety disorders, defined within a DSM-III framework, was found to be higher among women (15.5%) than men (10.4%). A comparison with the earlier (1952) findings revealed little change in overall prevalence, although the rates of disorder in 1970 were higher for younger women and older men than at the earlier assessment time.

Several studies have been conducted in which self-report questionnaires were used to assess depressive symptoms in representative community samples. Typically, however, the questionnaires assessed a range of symptoms, including depression. For instance, data collected in the 1978-79 Canada Health Survey (Health and Welfare Canada and Statistics Canada 1981) indicated that more than twice as many women as men reported "frequent" symptoms of depression and anxiety. In a further analysis of these data, D'Arcy and Siddique (1985) found that, within each marital status category, women reported significantly more symptoms than did men. Consistent with these national data, in a representative sample of Saskatchewan residents, D'Arcy (1982) found that the level of depression and anxiety symptoms reported on the General Health Questionnaire was significantly higher for women than men. Turner and Noh (1988) used the Centre for Epidemiologic Studies-Depression (CES-D) Scale to assess depressive symptoms in their study of physically disabled and nondisabled adults in southwestern Ontario. In each group, a significantly higher proportion of women than men had CES-D scores above a cutoff score of sixteen used to identify high-risk groups (disabled: 41% vs. 33%; nondisabled: 15% vs. 8%).

Interestingly, no consistent evidence of a sex difference in self-reported depressive symptoms has been found among students attending Canadian universities, a finding that parallels those reported for American students (Nolen-Hoeksema 1987). It seems that even though a few studies have reported higher levels of depressive symptoms among women than men students (Dobson and Breiter 1983; Lips and Ng 1986), it is more common to find no differences (Bryson and Pilon 1984; Gotlib 1984; O'Neil et al. 1985; Stoppard and Paisley 1987).

EXPLAINING SEX DIFFERENCES IN DEPRESSION

Artifact Explanations

The hypothesis that sex differences in rates of depression are artifactual, rather than a valid index of the preponderance of women among the depressed, is based on the assumption that depressive symptoms are more compatible with cultural notions of "femininity" than with conceptions of "masculinity." As indicated previously, the response-bias and masked depression forms of artifact explanation will be evaluated in this section.

Proponents of the response-bias explanation argue that, because depression is more consistent with femininity than masculinity, women are more willing than men to acknowledge their depressive experiences and to disclose their symptoms to others. According to proponents of the masked depression hypothesis, the higher depression rate in women is an artifact of sex differences in symptom formation and expression. Thus, while women tend to express their psychological distress as depressive symptoms, men are more likely to manifest their distress by different symptoms, such as alcohol abuse or dependence. Unless artifact explanations for sex differences in depression can be ruled out, a more reasonable assumption is that there is no overall difference between men and women with regard to their likelihood of becoming depressed.

The response-bias explanation is rooted in the assumption that differences exist between men and women in their capacity to recognize, and willingness to disclose, depressive experiences. These differences are presumed to arise from socialization practices that permit (if not encourage) emotional expressiveness in females, while proscribing such behaviour in males (Hammen 1982; Warren 1983). Specific hypotheses derived from the response-bias position have focused on the content of depressive symptoms, the influence of disclosure conditions, and the response of others to depressed individuals.

Because some of the experiences associated with depression (for instance, crying, sadness, self-blame) are gender-typed as feminine, their expression is more compatible with behaviour expected of women than men (Hammen 1982). For example, if the content of self-report questionnaires or diagnostic criteria were biased so that more feminine depressive symptoms were included, this might account for the higher levels of depression found among women. The primarily subjective nature of the mood and cognitive symptoms of depression also makes these symptoms particularly susceptible to response bias. Moreover, if response-bias were to occur in the direction of underreporting by men, it could be a factor in the lower rates of depression observed among men.

Rothblum (1983) addressed the issue of gender bias in depressive symptoms by examining the degree to which the content of items pooled from widely used, self-report measures of depression overlapped with the content of gender stereotypes. She found the overall degree of overlap between the two sets of items to be rather small, with slightly more feminine than masculine characteristics (nine vs. four) corresponding to specific depressive symptoms. In fact, the majority of symptoms did not correspond to characteristics contained in either the male or female stereotype. Moreover, Rothblum found no overlap between gender stereotypes and the symptoms included in the DSM-III criteria for depressive disorders.

Although sex differences have been reported in responses to specific items on depression measures, the findings have been inconsistent. For instance, studies have shown the symptom "difficulty making decisions" as being endorsed more by women (Hammen and Padesky 1977; Byrne 1981), more by men (Vredenburg et al. 1986), and equally by men and women (Byrne et al. 1977; Lips and Ng 1986; O'Neil et al. 1985). Thus, even though "indecisiveness" may be gender-typed as feminine, the tendency for women to endorse this symptom more frequently than do men is inconsistent.

Although the available evidence does not entirely rule out the possibility that sex differences in depressive symptom levels found in general community surveys are the result of gender bias in the content of self-report measures, other findings are more difficult to reconcile with this type of artifact explanation. First, among depressed patients, no sex differences have been found for "core" symptoms considered diagnostic of depression (Byrne et al. 1977; Hamilton 1989; Vredenberg et al. 1986). Second, in Amenson and Lewinsohn's (1981) study involving a general community sample of adults, women diagnosed as depressed were less likely than similarly diagnosed men to label themselves as depressed. This latter finding is contrary to the hypothesized greater willingness of women to acknowledge feelings of depression. Finally, Byrne (1981) hypothesized that sex differences would be more apparent for mood and cognitive symptoms than for somatic symptoms, the latter being less susceptible to response bias because they are more readily corroborated by independent observation. As well, somatic symptoms are considered less likely to be underreported by men, because such symptoms are more congruent with masculinity (Warren 1983). Byrne's analysis of depressive symptoms reported by community residents revealed, contrary to his hypothesis, that somatic symptoms were reported more frequently by women but that the sexes did not differ in their reports of mood and cognitive symptoms. Overall, then, the available findings do not appear to be in accord with the hypothesis that sex differences in depression are an artifact of gender bias in the symptom content of depression measures.

Another suggestion has been that male unwillingness to express depressive feelings will be most marked at mild levels of depression and that disclosure will occur only under conditions of anonymity or when confidentiality is assured (Warren 1983). However, studies with college students, a group in which mild levels of depressive symptoms are typical, have failed to identify any effects of disclosure conditions on men's depression-questionnaire scores (Bryson and Pilon 1984; King and Buchwald 1982). When given the opportunity to respond to depression measures anonymously and privately, men do not report more symptoms than when measures are completed under conditions involving more public disclosure.

On the assumption that gender-inappropriate behaviour is likely to result in negative social sanctions, lower depression rates in men have also been hypothesized to arise from men's unwillingness to disclose depressive feelings to others in order to avoid rejection (Warren 1983). Although the evidence is fairly consistent that depressed individuals are more often rejected by others than are nondepressed individuals (Gurtman 1986), findings with respect to the gender of depressed persons have been contradictory. In some studies, for example, mildly depressed males were more often rejected than depressed women (for example, Dow and Craighead 1987; Hammen and Peters 1977); other studies, however, found a greater rejection of females (Frank et al. 1987; Sommers 1984). Two Canadian studies actually showed no difference in rejection as a function of a depressed person's gender (Gotlib and Beatty 1985; Ulch and Stoppard 1985). It would appear that additional research is required to clarify the conditions under which the gender of depressed individuals will influence other people's responses.

Higher depression rates in women have also been explained as an artifact of sex differences in symptom formation and expression. More specifically, researchers have proposed that depression in men may be "masked" by other symptoms, so that an underlying depression goes unrecognized. In the strong form of the masked depression hypothesis, alcohol abuse and dependence are considered male counterparts to depression in women (Dohrenwend and Dohrenwend 1976). Alcohol abuse and dependence disorders have been identified as potential forms of masked depression in men, because these disorders are much more prevalent among men than women (Bland et al. 1988; Regier et al. 1988). A weaker form of the masked depression hypothesis is that depressive symptoms in men may be overlooked (or "masked") when another disorder, such as alcohol abuse, is also present.

The available evidence is inconsistent, however, with either form of the masked depression hypothesis. A recent investigation of familial transmission of alcohol abuse/dependence and depression found that the diagnosis of a depressive disorder in members of one generation did not predict an increased risk of alcohol abuse/dependence in the next generation (Merikangas et al. 1985a). Depression in one generation, however, was associated with an increased risk of depression in the next generation of family members.

The findings by Merikangas et al. are more consistent with the proposition that depression and alcohol abuse/dependence are independent disorders (Weissman and Klerman 1987).

Further support for the position that alcohol abuse/dependence is not an alternative form of depression is provided by the results of a study by Deykin et al. (1987), who examined prevalence of major depressive disorder and alcohol abuse (defined according to DSM-III criteria) in a sample of college students in the United States. Deykin et al. found that depression almost always preceded the onset of alcohol abuse and that, contrary to the masked depression hypothesis, a history of depression was a stronger predictor of alcohol abuse in females than in males. Other research on the link between alcohol abuse and depression has identified a greater tendency for depression to follow onset of alcohol abuse, especially in men, than the reverse. Thus, in some men, depression may be a consequence of the toxic effects of chronic alcohol abuse (Nolen-Hoeksema 1987).

If some men manifest depression symptomatically in a masked form, such symptoms should be detectable in married men, a group generally reporting very low levels of depressive symptoms (Aneshensel et al. 1981). There is no evidence, however, that the relative absence of depressive symptoms among married men is offset by an elevated level of alcohol-related problems (Radloff 1975).

In summary, research to date has failed to yield support for the hypothesis that alcohol abuse is the male equivalent of depression in women. At the same time, the possibility that depression may be missed or overlooked in some men when alcohol abuse is also present cannot entirely be ruled out. Nevertheless, modern diagnostic methods used in epidemiological studies allow for a person having more than one disorder; thus, the likelihood of depression being overlooked when another disorder, such as alcohol abuse, is present is considerably reduced.

As indicated by this evaluation of research bearing on the response-bias and masked depression explanations for sex differences in depression prevalence, findings have failed to support these "artifact" hypotheses. It appears warranted, then, to interpret epidemiological findings as providing evidence of a "true" difference between men and women in the prevalence of depression.

Psychological Explanations

As outlined, attempts to use a psychological perspective when explaining sex differences in depression have followed two main directions. The first focuses on the sex-role orientation of an individual's personality, in terms of whether masculine or feminine traits predominate. The second approach draws on cognitive-behavioural theories of depression, with the learned helplessness theory having been applied most directly to the problem of explaining sex differences in depression.

Clinical descriptions of depression-prone individuals have highlighted the characteristics of interpersonal dependency and passivity. People who are overdependent on a relationship for self-esteem and identity are considered particularly at risk for depression when faced with relationship disruption or loss. Because self-esteem is derived primarily from external sources, such people lack the resources to cope with loss and react passively rather than acting autonomously. The parallel between the depression-prone personality and the constellation of traits thought to characterize women in the normal course of female development has led to the hypothesis that a feminine personality style may be a factor in women's predisposition to depression. (See chapter 8 in Penfold and Walker [1983] for an overview of this theoretical position.)

Most research on the link between feminine personality characteristics and depression has employed self-report symptom measures. Femininity has been assessed, along with masculinity, using a variety of questionnaire measures of sex-role orientation. Based on a meta-analysis of findings in this area, Whitley (1985) concluded that the available evidence did not support the hypothesized link between femininity and depression. Instead, there was consistent evidence of a relationship between masculinity and depression, with lower masculinity predicting higher depression. Studies reported since Whitley's review have yielded similar findings (Morgan et al. 1986; Stoppard and Paisley 1987).

Because a sex-role orientation characterized by low masculinity is more typical of women than men, the suggestion has been made that a relative lack of masculine personality traits may underlie vulnerability to depression in some women. A problem with this interpretation, however, is that the correlational nature of the findings does not permit a causal inference to be drawn. The possibility that low masculinity is causally related to depression was explored by Flett et al. (1985), using a "cross-lagged panel" design. Flett et al. found that level of depressive symptoms was a better predictor of masculinity than the reverse, which suggests that low masculinity is a consequence, rather than an antecedent, of depression.

In a further extension of this approach, Feather (1985) found that both depressive symptoms and low masculinity were consequences of low self-esteem. According to Feather, low self-esteem, rather than low masculinity, may underlie women's vulnerability to depression. Other evidence of the role of self-esteem in depression has been inconsistent, however. Amenson and Lewinsohn (1981) found no overall difference in self-esteem between men and women in a general community sample, and a sex difference in depression (self-reported symptoms and diagnosed disorder) was essentially unchanged after controlling for self-esteem. Lewinsohn et al. (1988) found that low self-esteem was a risk factor for depression assessed prospectively. In contrast, Hirschfeld et al. (1989) found that premorbid "social self-confidence" did not predict first onset of major depression in a longitudinal study of first-degree relatives and spouses of patients with affective disorders. Based on these findings, the role of low self-esteem in the greater prevalence of depression among women remains unclear. A complicating issue in findings on self-esteem is the wide variety of measures in current use, reflecting the lack of consensus on how this construct is best defined and measured (Carson 1989).

The learned helplessness theory identifies, as a depression vulnerability factor, the belief that one is helpless to control the outcome of events, particularly when the consequences of events are likely to be adverse. Helplessness beliefs are thought to be especially likely in individuals who typically attribute the causes of negative events to factors that are stable, pervasive, and located within the person (Peterson and Seligman 1984). People with this type of attributional style tend to blame themselves when things go wrong in their lives.

According to some theorists, the socialization experiences of girls are particularly likely to foster the feelings of helplessness and lack of control that, according to the learned helplessness theory, underlie vulnerability to depression (Abramson and Andrews 1982; Radloff and Rae 1979). Thus, if women were found to be more likely than men to endorse helplessness beliefs and to have a self-blaming attributional style, this would be consistent with the learned helplessness explanation for sex differences in depression. Similarly, the other cognitive-behavioural theories could account for sex differences in depression if the specific form of vulnerability posited by each was found to be more prevalent among women than men.

Based on an extensive review of research on cognitive-behavioural vulnerability factors, Stoppard (1989) concluded that evidence of greater depression vulnerability among women is entirely lacking. Instead, in the few cases where differences in vulnerability between women and men have been reported, they are in the direction of men, rather than women, being more "vulnerable" to depression. This conclusion held for studies with community residents as well as students. A recent review of research on cognitive strategies for coping with stress reached a similar conclusion. After evaluating findings in this area, Miller and Kirsch (1987) concluded that "available evidence shows that females are more prone to psychological distress than males are, yet do not consistently demonstrate any underlying cognitive characteristics that would account for this difference" (p 298). A more fundamental problem of this approach to explaining sex differences in depression is the lack of evidence that the hypothesized cognitive-behavioural vulnerabilities are causally related to depression (Barnett and Gotlib 1988; Lewinsohn et al. 1988).

In conclusion, psychological explanations for women's higher rates of depression, whether in terms of sex-role orientation or vulnerability factors posited by cognitive-behavioural theories, appear to lack empirical support. Although the explanations reviewed here are those that have received most attention, they do not exhaust the range of psychological factors that potentially could play a role in sex differences in depression. For instance, Feather's (1985) work indicates that low self-esteem may be a factor in women's greater vulnerability to depression. Feather suggests that diminished self-regard in women is a consequence of women's relative lack of opportunity for involvement in the socially valued activities that, in Western culture, are associated with men and masculinity. Socially based explanations for sex differences in depression are discussed in the next two sections.

Gender-Role Explanations

Gender-role explanations focus on men's and women's differing experiences in similar life roles (for example, parents, spouses, workers) in accounting for sex differences in depression. First proposed by Gove and Tudor (1973) to explain the overrepresentation of married women among psychiatric inpatients in the United States, the gender-role approach has more recently been applied to the problem of explaining the predominance of women among the depressed. According to this formulation, more women than men become depressed because women's roles are potentially more stressful than men's roles. Given that the roles of women and men diverge most in the area of family responsibilities, differences in depression between women and men are expected to be most pronounced among the married.

For married women not involved in paid employment outside the home (housewives), sources of stress are thought to be social isolation, lack of structure, and low social value of housework, coupled with financial dependence on the husband. Although paid employment, by providing an alternative source of self-esteem, may offset the stress associated with the housewife role, married women with paid employment face the additional burden of combining family responsibilities with work outside the home. Gove's (1980) gender-role hypothesis predicts an interaction between sex and marital status, such that women are more depressed than men in the married but not in the other marital status categories. Women caring for dependent children and those combining family roles with work outside the home are expected to be most at risk for depression.

Gove's claim that marriage is particularly detrimental to women's mental health has not received much support. Married or not, women report higher levels of depressive symptoms than do men. Such findings have emerged from studies with representative samples of adults in the United States (Amenson and Lewinsohn 1981; Aneshensel et al. 1981), as well as England

(Cochrane and Stopes-Roe 1981), and Canada (D'Arcy and Siddique 1985). Moreover, U.S. studies have repeatedly found lower levels of depressive symptoms among married than nonmarried persons (Aneshensel et al. 1981; Cleary and Mechanic 1983; Ensel 1982), especially when the married are compared to those formerly married (Barnett and Baruch 1987). Similar findings have emerged from studies using diagnostic criteria to assess depression in community residents. Lower rates of major depression have been found among married than nonmarried individuals, both in the United States (Weissman and Klerman 1987) and Canada (Bland et al. 1988; Kovess et al. 1987). Thus, there appears to be little support for the view that being married is uniquely a source of depression among women. Instead, marriage seems to offer some measure of protection against depression in both sexes.

Stress associated with the housewife role has been implicated as a factor in the higher levels of depression among married women than married men (Gove 1980). In the absence of a "househusband" group, most research in this area has compared housewives with married women employed outside the home. Studies of this kind in the United States have revealed that although employed women may report higher levels of stress (Kandel et al. 1985; Stewart and Salt 1981), they are no more depressed (Ensel 1982; Shehan 1984; Stewart and Salt 1981) or less depressed (Aneshensel et al. 1981) than housewives. In line with these findings, Turner and Avison's (1989) study with physically disabled adults in Ontario found higher levels of stress but similar levels of depressive symptoms among employed married women as compared to housewives. Other Canadian studies have also reported a tendency for employed women to report lower levels of depressive symptoms than housewives (Burke and Weir 1976; Health and Welfare Canada and Statistics Canada 1981; Welch and Booth 1977). Thus, although the housewife role may not be more stressful, there is some evidence, albeit mixed, that housewives experience higher levels of depressive symptoms than do other married women. One interpretation of these findings is that absence of paid employment serves to increase the housewives' vulnerability to stress (Kandel et al. 1985; Turner and Avison 1989).

Gove (1980) also pointed to the added burden of stress for married women of combining work outside the home with family roles, suggesting that married women experience more demands and conflicts than do married men when they combine family responsibilities with paid employment. According to Gove, this is a factor in the increased risk of depression among women. The available findings, however, are more in keeping with the conclusion that paid employment has beneficial effects in protecting women against depression, similar to those observed in men (Barnett and Baruch 1987). As well, depressive symptom levels generally are found to be higher in the unemployed than the employed in each sex (Amenson and Lewinsohn 1981; Aneshensel et al. 1981; Cochrane and Stopes-Roe 1981; Turner and Avison

1989). At the same time, findings in the United States (Aneshensel et al. 1981; Radloff 1975) as well as Canada (Health and Welfare Canada and Statistics Canada 1981; Turner and Avison 1989) have indicated that married women employed outside the home tend to report higher levels of depressive symptoms than do their male counterparts, although this is not always the case. In several U.S. studies, the lowest levels of depressive symptoms were found among women employed part-time (Ensel 1982; Rosenfield 1989). These findings indicate the importance of considering employment status (that is, part-time vs. full-time) in any investigation of the effects of combining family roles with paid employment on depression in women.

Other research has explored the links between involvement in the parental role and depression. The evidence that women bear the burden of child care responsibilities, whether or not they work outside the home (Scarr et al. 1989), implies that the parental role may be an important source of stress for women. Studies in this area have indicated that the presence of children in the home is associated with an increased risk of depression among women. Married women with children at home report higher levels of depressive symptoms than do either married women without children or those whose children are no longer living at home (Ensel 1982; Radloff 1975; Ross and Mirowsky 1988). Levels of depressive symptoms are also higher among married women with children than among their male counterparts (Aneshensel et al. 1981; Ensel 1982; Ross and Mirowsky 1988). Among men, depressive symptom levels are found to be lowest of all among those who are married, employed, and parents of dependent children (Aneshensel et al. 1981; Ensel 1982; Ross and Mirowsky 1988). In contrast to the findings with women, the combination of parental and employment roles appears to have particularly beneficial consequences for the mental health of men.

Additional findings regarding child care responsibilities and depression in women are provided by Ross and Mirowsky (1988), based on the results of a survey involving a national probability sample of husbands and wives in the United States. The highest levels of depressive symptoms were reported by employed women who encountered difficulties in arranging child care and/or whose husbands shared few of the child care responsibilities. When child care was not difficult to arrange and husbands shared the responsibility, employed women had low depression levels, comparable to employed women without children and to husbands. In their study with women in Saskatchewan, D'Arcy and Siddique (1984) also found that lack of spousal support was a significant predictor of depressive symptoms among women with at least one child at home.

Studies in which depression was assessed according to diagnostic criteria also have yielded evidence that child care is a risk factor for depression in women. In a study in England, Bebbington et al. (1981) found the rate of depression among women with dependent children at home to be particularly high (23.4%), although there was no case of depression among men who were parents. In the United States, based on data from a representative sample of North Carolina residents, Crowell et al. (1986) reported that being a mother of a preschool child was a significant predictor of major depression and that this effect remained significant after controlling for other demographic and psychosocial variables. In their longitudinal study with Oregon residents, Lewinsohn et al. (1988) found that presence of preschool children in the home was a predictor of major depression in both sexes. In contrast to the findings by Crowell et al. (1986), however, the effect of presence of children was no longer significant after controlling for parental age. This latter finding suggests that child care is more stressful for younger parents.

Attempts to specify more precisely the processes underlying the observed effects of marital, employment, and parental roles on depression, as a function of gender, have pointed to the strains and conflicts experienced by women in coping with demands in each domain (Barnett and Baruch 1987). For instance, Radloff (1975) found that controlling for the amount of time spent on housework and child care reduced, but did not entirely eliminate, a sex difference in depressive symptoms. In addition, Rosenfield (1989) reported survey findings from three U.S. communities consistent with the hypothesis that higher levels of depressive symptoms in women are the result of high demands coupled with relative powerlessness in their everyday lives.

An alternative hypothesis is that exposure to life-stress events is mediated by gender role, such that women are more likely than men to experience certain kinds of stressful events, with a concomitant increase in risk of depression among women. Specifically, because women are expected to provide social support and care to others, they are more likely than men to be affected by stressful events involving others in their kinship and social networks (Kessler and McLeod 1984).

Thoits (1987) has reported findings in support of this "cost-of-caring" hypothesis. She found that while married men and women were equally likely to be exposed to stressful events involving significant others in the family network, exposure to such events was associated with greater vulnerability to depression among women than men. Turner and Avison (1989), in their investigation of gender differences in exposure and vulnerability to stressful events in disabled adults in southwestern Ontario, found that while married women and men were equally exposed and vulnerable to stressful events happening to themselves, women were both more exposed and more vulnerable to events happening to their spouse. These findings are consistent with those of U.S. studies (Kessler and McLeod 1984; Thoits 1987) in suggesting a specific vulnerability in women to stressful events occurring to significant others.

In summary, research has yielded some findings consistent with the position that the relationship between role occupancy and depression differs as a function of gender. Evidence does exist of an increased risk of depressive symptoms and diagnosed depression among women combining marital and parental roles, but not among married men who are parents. Although employment outside the home appears to moderate the risk of depression in women, married women who are employed full-time may still be more vulnerable to depression than their male counterparts, especially if employment is combined with child care responsibilities.

Further conclusions with respect to gender-role explanations are limited by the fact that research has focused on family and employment roles primarily in women, rather than on both sexes (Barnett and Baruch 1987). A particular problem for research in this area lies with the lack of an appropriate comparison group for housewives. Although there has been some evidence, albeit inconsistent, that risk of depression is greater among housewives than married women in paid employment, such findings cannot be attributed directly to characteristics (isolation, lack of power) imputed to the housewife role in the absence of comparison with an equivalent male group. Because the role of "househusband" is not sanctioned for men, in large part because of the stigma associated with male unemployment, a suitable comparison group is unavailable.

Another limitation of the existing research is the lack of attention paid to the interpersonal and social-structural factors that shape the context of women's everyday lives. A woman with young children might decide to forego employment for a variety of reasons, including personal and spousal preference, lack of alternative child care or suitable employment, and so on. The way in which women's "choices" are structured by factors both inside and outside the family has yet to receive investigation.

As a final point, very little research relevant to gender-role explanations for sex differences in depression appears to have been conducted in Canada. Given the differences between Canada and other Western countries with respect to social policies in such areas as income assistance and child care services, the generalizability of findings from other jurisdictions to the Canadian context cannot be assumed.

Social Explanations

Instead of focusing on the differential effects of social roles as a function of gender, social explanations focus on the effects of differences in the distribution of social roles and status between men and women. Sex differences in depression are hypothesized to arise because of differences between men and women on various social indicators, such as income, which are also associated with depression (Nolen-Hoeksema 1987). A corollary of this approach is that the more similar men and women are in their social circumstances, the more equal will be the risk of depression in each sex (Hammen 1982). For instance, higher levels of depressive symptoms in women could be the result of fewer women than men being in the paid workforce, because employment status itself is a predictor of depression.

Two main kinds of evidence are available to test social explanations for sex differences in depression. First, in surveys with general community samples, sex differences in depression can be examined before and after controlling statistically for social status indicators. Thus, if a sex difference in depression were reduced or eliminated after controlling for social indicators, a social explanation would be supported. The second strategy involves comparing depression levels of groups of men and women who are homogeneous with respect to socioeconomic status. Finding that homogeneous groups of men and women do not differ in level or rate of depression would also be consistent with a social explanation for sex differences in depression.

In six studies using the first strategy, a sex difference in depressive symptom level was either eliminated (Aneshensel et al. 1981; Golding 1988; Gore and Mangione 1983) or considerably reduced (Amenson and Lewinsohn 1981; Newmann 1986; Radloff and Rae 1979) after controlling for various sociodemographic variables. Two other studies found that a sex difference in depressive symptoms was unaltered after controlling for sociodemographic variables (Eaton and Kessler 1981; Ensel 1982). With these two exceptions, the available evidence suggests that much of the difference in men's and women's depressive symptom levels in general community samples may be explained by gender-related differences on background social characteristics.

Findings with homogeneous groups are also consistent with this interpretation. A sex difference in level of depressive symptoms is generally not found in college students (Bryson and Pilon 1984; O'Neil et al. 1985; Stoppard and Paisley 1987). Similarly, Jenkins (1985) found no sex difference in depressive symptoms among young, primarily unmarried adults selected from the same job category in the British civil service. A study in the United States by Repetti and Crosby (1984) also found no difference in depressive symptom levels between men and women matched for occupational prestige, although those in high-prestige professions were less depressed than those in low-prestige, sales or service occupations.

The relationship between occupational prestige and depression reported by Repetti and Crosby has particular relevance for understanding sex differences in depression, because women are less likely than men to enter high-prestige occupations and are overrepresented in the low-prestige, sales and clerical occupations. In addition, the traditionally female professions (such as, nursing, elementary teaching) are lower in prestige than the traditionally male professions (for instance, engineering, dentistry). Thus, differences between men and women in occupational status may be a factor contributing to sex differences in depressive symptoms.

The findings reviewed so far are consistent with a social status explanation for sex differences in depressive symptoms. One implication of these findings is that if social status inequalities between the sexes were eradicated, sex differences in depressive symptoms would also be considerably reduced. A plausible interpretation of the findings of higher levels of depressive symptoms among women is that they are a manifestation of the more general pattern of "demoralization" (Link and Dohrenwend 1980) characteristic of socially and economically disadvantaged groups in society.

Rather different findings have emerged, however, from studies in which depression was assessed according to diagnostic criteria. In the United States, Amenson and Lewinsohn (1981) and Crowell et al. (1986) found that sex remained a significant predictor of depression once sociodemographic variables were controlled for. A study in England by Bebbington et al. (1981) found a relationship between social class and diagnosed disorder in men, but not in women. In Canada, Costello (1982) found no relationship between social class or employment status and diagnosed depression among women in Calgary. Thus, to date, no evidence exists to support a social explanation for sex differences in prevalence of depressive disorder. Overall, the findings indicate that sex differences in depressive symptoms can be explained, in part, by social status factors.

Drawing on Lewinsohn et al.'s conclusion (1988) that depressive symptoms are a necessary but insufficient condition for the onset of a depressive episode, findings for the social and gender-role explanations can be integrated in the following way. First, the evidence that sex differences in depressive symptoms, but not diagnosed depression, may be accounted for, in part, by socioeconomic inequalities between the sexes suggests that such inequalities act as "vulnerability" factors that increase the risk of depressive symptoms among women. Second, if depressive symptoms are present, the risk of a depressive disorder developing in women who experience stress arising from gender-role influences (for example, child care responsibilities) is likely to be exacerbated.

The possibility that social factors and gender-role influences may operate as part of a more complex, two-stage process that results in greater vulnerability to depressive disorder among women is consistent with the findings of Brown and Harris (1978) in their study of depression among women in London, England. They found that presence of children was associated with an increased risk of depressive disorder among working-class, but not middle-class, women. The risk, moreover, was highest among working-class mothers who did not work outside the home. Bebbington et al. (1981) also found that rate of depressive disorder was highest among housewives with children at home.

IMPLICATIONS FOR PRACTICE AND
RESEARCH IN CANADA

Available data indicate that depressed women are likely to form a significant proportion of the individuals seen by mental health professionals in community and hospital settings. This observation implies that professional training programs must provide a thorough grounding in current knowledge about gender and depression, including coverage of explanatory models for sex differences in depression. Practitioners should also become familiar with the range of treatments for depression, including therapeutic approaches developed specifically for depressed women (Corob 1987). While antidepressant drugs are widely used, they too often represent the sole form of treatment. As Penfold (1987a) has pointed out, because women are the major users of antidepressant drugs, they are also more exposed to their adverse effects. Strategies for encouraging medically trained practitioners to consider psychosocial interventions as alternatives to drug treatment need to be pursued, especially in light of indications that prescription rates for antidepressant drugs may be increasing in Canada (Penfold 1987a).

In addition to knowledge about therapeutic approaches, training programs must promote awareness of community services and resources, with particular relevance to depressed women clients. Job-training and re-entry programs, as well as services providing support and relief to women caring for handicapped children or infirm family members, or raising children alone, are examples of such resources.

The evidence of a link between depression in women and gender-role influences underscores the need to incorporate material on gender issues in the curricula of healthcare professionals' training programs. Lack of a gender perspective in understanding the experiences of depressed clients implies limitations in professional practice. These limitations also characterize the prevailing etiological theories of depression, which foster decontextualized conceptions of mental health problems. Because people's lived experience is largely ignored by these theoretical models, the gender-specific character of everyday life experiences is taken for granted. For instance, the expectation is that married women are responsible for housework and child care. That expectation goes unquestioned and is seen as a normal, and largely unproblematic, part of women's lives, rather than as a potential source of stress. In order to prepare practitioners to respond more effectively to the needs of depressed women clients, the curricula of training programs must incorporate topics that address gender issues. Although efforts had been made to include coverage of gender issues in course content in Canadian medical schools and psychiatry-training programs (Penfold 1987b), such subject matter is not yet required in Canadian clinical psychology programs.

At the policy level, the evidence of a link between higher rates of depressive symptoms in women and their disadvantaged social and economic status underlines the importance of federal and provincial initiatives, directed toward employment and pay equity, in redressing systemic discrimination in the workplace. Public policy also needs to be formulated to give appropriate recognition and support to women's work in the home, especially that of caring for dependent children. Important in this regard, too, are efforts to improve availability of good quality child-care services for mothers who work outside the home, whether by choice or in support of themselves and their families.

Evidence linking the higher rates of depression in women to the particular nature of their family responsibilities, as well as to their disadvantaged social and economic status, points to the need for additional research – both to elaborate more precisely the processes underlying the observed relationships and to resolve conflicting findings. For instance, the discrepancies noted between findings based on diagnostic criteria and those based on self-report measures for depression assessment clearly warrant further study. As a preliminary strategy toward exploring reasons for the discrepant findings, future research should include both methods of assessment.

Although epidemiological studies are useful in identifying potential risk factors for depression, the scope of such studies usually necessitates a reliance on demographic factors (for example, marital status) to index complex social processes. In addition, the relative inflexibility and static character of epidemiological research methods (for instance, large samples, quantitative analyses) precludes a more fine-grained analysis of individual experiences in relation to depression. Smaller-scale, more intensive studies using qualitative methods offer an alternative set of research strategies; such studies could complement epidemiological findings by uncovering processes with potential importance for understanding the role of gender-related factors in depression. For instance, women's and men's accounts of their experiences with depression could be analyzed for commonalities, as well as differences, in the way such experiences arise in the context of their everyday lives.

If further progress is to be made in understanding the role of gender-related factors in depression, interdisciplinary research is clearly required. Now that available findings on depression no longer can be accommodated by any single factor explanation, interest has shifted to the development of multifactorial models that incorporate more interactive, transactional processes (Lewinsohn et al. 1985). Although the conditions facilitating interdisciplinary research are still not fully understood, a number of elements appear to mitigate against the development of a more coordinated effort. Clearly, the structure of health-related disciplines in Canada (and elsewhere) limits the ready interchange of ideas across disciplinary boundaries. Mechanisms need to be developed for the dissemination of findings among researchers working in related areas but different disciplines. Another barrier to interdisciplinary research is the organization of the present funding mechanisms along disciplinary lines. For instance, research that spans both the social sciences and health disciplines does not clearly fall within the guidelines of any one major funding agency in Canada. Moreoever, although more emphasis in recent years has been placed on funding social science research relevant to gender issues, the guidelines of the main Canadian agency providing support for research in this area exclude support of research with a clinical focus on depression. To stimulate the kind of research on sex differences in depression that appears to be required, the mechanisms for funding interdisciplinary research must be improved.

CONCLUSION

This review has yielded a number of conclusions regarding the status of findings on sex differences in depression and the part played by psychosocial factors in explaining these findings. In line with other Western studies, the research conducted in Canada indicates that depressive symptom levels and rates of depressive disorder are higher among women than men. Consistent with the conclusions reached by other reviewers (for example, Nolen-Hoeksema 1987), support for artifact explanations for sex differences in depression was found to be lacking. Evidence was presented that cannot easily be reconciled with either the response-bias or masked depression form of artifact explanation. Attempts to account for sex differences in depression in terms of psychological differences between men and women also were found to lack empirical support.

With regard to the gender-role and social explanations, the strategy of evaluating findings with self-report symptom measures separately from those based on diagnostic criteria revealed an interesting pattern of findings. It seems that while available evidence is consistent with both gender-role and social explanations for sex differences in depressive symptoms, findings are more in line with gender-role explanations for higher rates of diagnosed depression among women. This pattern of findings not only indicates the importance of maintaining a distinction between different methods of assessing depression when reviewing research, but also underscores the need to include both types of measures in investigations of gender and depression.

Although further research is required before more definitive conclusions can be drawn, it was suggested that women's greater vulnerability to depressive disorder may be explained in terms of a two-stage process that involves both social factors and gender-role influences. In general, the findings of this review are consistent with the position that researchers, practitioners, and policymakers would benefit from including a gender perspective in efforts to understand, alleviate, and prevent depression.

BIBLIOGRAPHY

Abramson, L., and Andrews, D. 1982. Cognitive models of depression: Implications for sex differences in vulnerability to depression. *International Journal of Mental Health* 11: 77–94

Abramson, L., Seligman, M., and Teasdale, J. 1978. Learned helplessness in humans: Critique and reformulation. *Journal of Abnormal Psychology* 87: 49–74.

Amenson, C., and Lewinsohn, P. 1981. An investigation into the observed sex difference in prevalence of unipolar depression. *Journal of Abnormal Psychology* 90: 1–13.

Aneshensel, C., Frerichs, R., and Clark, V. 1981. Family roles and sex differences in depression. *Journal of Health and Social Behavior* 22: 379–93.

Barnett, P.A., and Gotlib, I.H. 1988. Psychosocial functioning and depression: Distinguishing among antecedents, concomitants, and consequences. *Psychological Bulletin* 104: 97–126.

Barnett, R.C., and Baruch, G.K. 1987. Social roles, gender, and psychological distress. In *Gender and stress*, edited by R.C. Barnett, L. Biener, and G.K. Baruch, 122–43. New York: Free Press.

Bebbington, P., Hurry, J., Tennant, C., Sturt, E., and Wing, J.K. 1981. Epidemiology of mental disorders in Camberwell. *Psychological Medicine* 11: 561–79.

Beckham, E.E., and Leber, W.R., 1985. *Handbook of depression: Treatment, assessment, and research*. Homewood, Ill.: Dorsey.

Belle, D., and Goldman, N. 1980. Patterns of diagnosis received by men and women. In *The mental health of women* edited by M. Guttentag, S. Salasin, and D. Belle, 21–30. New York: Academic Press.

Berger, J. 1985. Private practice: The first five years. *Canadian Journal of Psychiatry* 30: 566–72.

Bland, R.C., Newman, S.C., and Orn, H. 1988. Period prevalence of psychiatric disorders in Edmonton. *Acta Psychiatrica Scandinavica* 77(suppl. 338): 33–42.

Brown, G., and Harris, T. 1978. *Social origins of depression: A study of psychiatric disorder in women*. New York: Free Press.

Bryson, S., and Pilon, D. 1984. Sex differences in depression and the method of administering the Beck Depression Inventory. *Journal of Clinical Psychology* 40: 529–34.

Burke, R.J., and Weir, T. 1976. Relationship of wives' employment status to husband, wife and pair satisfaction and performance. *Journal of Marriage and the Family* 38: 279–87.

Byrne, D.G. 1981. Sex differences in the reporting of symptoms of depression in the general population. *British Journal of Clinical Psychology* 20: 83–92.

Byrne, D.G., Boyle, D., and Pritchard, D.W. 1977. Sex differences in response to a self-rating depression scale. *British Journal of Social and Clinical Psychology* 16: 269–73.

Carson, R.C. 1989. Personality. *Annual Review of Psychology* 40:227–48.

Cleary, P. 1987. Gender differences in stress-related disorders. In *Gender and stress* edited by R.C. Barnett, L. Biener, and G.K. Baruch, 39–72. New York: Free Press.

Cleary, P., and Mechanic, D. 1983. Sex differences in psychological distress among married people. *Journal of Health and Social Behavior* 24: 111–21.

Cochrane, R., and Stopes-Roe, M. 1981. Women, marriage, employment and mental health. *British Journal of Psychiatry* 139: 373–81.

Corob, A. 1987. *Working with depressed women.* Aldershot, England: Gower.

Costello, C. 1982. Social factors associated with depression: A retrospective community study. *Psychological Medicine* 12: 329–39.

Crowell, B.A., George, L.K., Blazer, D., and Landerman, R. 1986. Psychosocial risk factors and urban/rural differences in prevalence of major depression. *British Journal of Psychiatry* 149: 307–14.

D'Arcy, C. 1982. Prevalence and correlates of nonpsychotic psychiatric symptoms in the general population. *Canadian Journal of Psychiatry* 27; 316–24.

D'Arcy, C., and Schmitz, J. A. 1979. Sex differences in the utilization of health services for psychiatric problems in Saskatchewan. *Canadian Journal of Psychiatry* 24: 19–27.

D'Arcy, C., and Siddique, C.M. 1984. Social support and mental health among mothers of preschool and school age children. *Social Psychiatry* 19: 155–62.

D'Arcy, C., and Siddique, C.M. 1985. Marital status and psychological well-being. A cross national comparative analysis. *International Journal of Comparative Sociology* 26(3–4): 149–66.

Deykin, E.Y., Levy, J.C., Wells, V. 1987. Adolescent depression, alcohol and drug abuse. *American Journal of Public Health* 77: 178–82.

Dobson, K.S., and Breiter, H.J. 1983. Cognitive assessment of depression: Reliability and validity of three measures. *Journal of Abnormal Psychology* 92: 107–09.

Dohrenwend, B.P., and Dohrenwend, B.S. 1976. Sex differences in psychiatric disorders. *American Journal of Sociology* 81: 1447–54.

Dow, M.G., and Craighead, W.E. 1987. Social inadequacy and depression: Overt behavior and self-evaluation processes. *Journal of Social and Clinical Psychology* 5: 99–113.

Eaton, W.W., and Kessler, L.G. 1981. Rates of symptoms of depression in a national sample. *American Journal of Epidemiology* 114: 528–38.

Ensel, W.M. 1982. The role of age in the relationship of gender and marital status to depression. *Journal of Nervous and Mental Disease* 170: 536–43.

Feather, N.T. 1985. Masculinity, femininity, self-esteem, and subclinical depression. *Sex Roles* 12: 491–500.

Flett, G., Vredenburg, K., Pliner, P., and Krames, L. 1985. Sex roles and depression: A preliminary investigation of the direction of causality. *Journal of Research in Personality* 19: 429–35.

Frank, R.G., Elliot, T.R., Wonderlich, S.A., Corcoran, J.R., Umlauf, R.L., and Ashkanazi, G.S. 1987. Gender differences in the interpersonal response to depression and spinal cord injury. *Cognitive Therapy and Research* 11: 437–48.

Golding, J.M. 1988. Gender differences in depressive symptoms: Statistical considerations. *Psychology of Women Quarterly* 12: 61–74.

Gore, S., and Mangione, T. 1983. Social roles, sex roles and psychological distress: Additive and interactive models of sex differences. *Journal of Health and Social Behavior* 24: 300–12.

Gotlib, I.H. 1984. Depression and general psychopathology in university students. *Journal of Abnormal Psychology* 93: 19–30.

Gotlib, I.H., and Beatty, M.E. 1985. Negative responses to depression: The role of attributional style. *Cognitive Therapy and Research* 9: 91–103.

Gotlib, I.H., Whiffen, V.E., Mount, J.H., Milne, K., and Cordy, N.I. 1989. Prevalence rates and demographic characteristics associated with depression in pregnancy and the postpartum. *Journal of Consulting and Clinical Psychology* 57: 269–74.

Gove, W.R. 1980. Mental illness and psychiatric treatment among women. *Psychology of Women Quarterly* 4: 345–62.

Gove, W. R., and Tudor, J. 1973. Adult sex roles and mental illness. *American Journal of Sociology* 78: 812–35.

Greenspan, M. 1983. *A new approach to women and therapy.* New York: McGraw-Hill.

Gurtman, M. B. 1986. Depression and the response of others: Reevaluating the reevaluation. *Journal of Abnormal Psychology* 95: 99–101.

Hamilton, M. 1989. Frequency of symptoms in melancholia (depressive illness). *British Journal of Psychiatry* 154: 201–06.

Hammen, C.L. 1982. Gender and depression. In *Gender and psychopathology* edited by I. Al-Issa, 133–52. New York: Academic Press.

Hammen, C., and Padesky, C.A. 1977. Sex differences in the expression of depressive responses on the Beck Depression Inventory. *Journal of Abnormal Psychology* 86: 609–14

Hammen, C., and Peters, S.D. 1977. Differential responses to male and female depressive reactions. *Journal of Consulting and Clinical Psychology* 45: 994–1001.

Health and Welfare Canada and Statistics Canada. 1981. *The health of Canadians: Report of the Canada Health Survey.* Ottawa: Government of Canada.

Hirschfeld, R.M.A., Klerman, G.L., Lavori, P., Keller, M.B., Griffith, P., and Coryell, W. 1989. Premorbid personality assessments of first onset of major depression. *Archives of General Psychiatry* 46: 345–50.

Jenkins, R. 1985. Sex differences in minor psychiatric morbidity. *Psychological Medicine* (monograph suppl.) 7: 1–53.

Kandel, D., Davies, M., and Raveis, V. 1985. The stressfulness of daily social roles for women: Marital, occupational, and household roles. *Journal of Health and Social Behavior* 26: 64–78.

Kaufert, P.A., and Gilbert, P. 1986. The context of menopause: Psychotropic drug use and menopausal status. *Social Science and Medicine* 23: 747–55.

Kessler, R.C., and McLeod, J.D. 1984. Sex differences in vulnerability to undesirable life events. *American Sociological Review* 49: 620–31.

King, D., and Buchwald, A. 1982. Sex differences in subclinical depression: Administration of the Beck Depression Inventory in public and private disclosure situations. *Journal of Personality and Social Psychology* 42: 963–69.

Kovess, V., Murphy, H.B.M., and Tousignant, M. 1987. Urban-rural comparisons of depressive disorder in French Canada. *Journal of Nervous and Mental Disease* 175: 457–66.

Lewinsohn, P.M., Hoberman, H.H., and Rosenbaum, M. 1988. A prospective study of risk factors in unipolar depression. *Journal of Abnormal Psychology* 97: 251–64.

Lewinsohn, P.M., Hoberman, H.H., Teri, L., and Hautzinger, M. 1985. An integrative theory of depression. In *Theoretical issues in behavior therapy*, edited by S. Riess, and R.R. Bootzin, 331–59. Orlando, Florida: Academic Press.

Link, B., and Dohrenwend, B.P. 1980. Formulation of hypotheses about the true prevalence of demoralization in the United States. In *Mental illness in the United States: Epidemiological estimates*, edited by B.P. Dohrenwend, B.S. Dohrenwend, M.S. Gould, B. Link, R. Neugebauer, and R. Wunsch-Hitzig, 114–32. New York: Praeger.

Lips, H.M. (1988). *Sex and gender: An introduction*. Mountain View, Calif.: Mayfield.

Lips, H.M., and Ng, M. 1986. Use of the Beck Depression Inventory with three non-clinical populations. *Canadian Journal of Behavioural Science* 18: 62–74.

McKinlay, J.B., McKinlay, S.M., and Brambilla, D. 1987. The relative contributions of endocrine changes and social circumstance to depression in mid-aged women. *Journal of Health and Social Behavior* 28: 345–63.

Merikangas, K.R., Leckman, J.F., Prusoff, B.A., Pauls, D.L., and Weissman, M.M. 1985a. Familial transmission of depression and alcoholism. *Archives of General Psychiatry* 42: 367–72.

Merikangas, K.R., Weissman, M.M., and Pauls, D.L. 1985b. Genetic factors in the sex ratio of major depression. *Psychological Medicine* 15: 63–69.

Miller, S.M., and Kirsch, N. 1987. Sex differences in cognitive coping with stress. In *Gender and stress*, edited by R.C. Barnett, L. Biener, and G.K. Baruch, 278–307. New York: Free Press.

Morgan, C.S., Affleck, M., and Riggs, L.R. 1986. Gender, personality traits, and depression. *Social Science Quarterly* 67: 69–83.

Murphy, J.M., Sobol, A.M., Neff, R.K., Olivier, D.C., and Leighton, A.H. 1984. Stability of prevalence: Depression and anxiety disorders. *Archives of General Psychiatry* 41: 990–97.

Newmann, J.P. 1986. Gender, life strains, and depression. *Journal of Health and Social Behavior* 27: 161–78.

Nolen-Hoeksema, S. 1987. Sex differences in unipolar depression: Evidence and theory. *Psychological Bulletin* 101: 259–82.

O'Neil, M.K., Lancee, W.J., and Freeman, S.J. 1985. Sex differences in depressed university students. *Social Psychiatry* 20: 186–90.

Penfold, P.S. 1987a. Antidepressants. *Depending on Ourselves: Proceedings of a National Consultation on Women and Drugs*, 14–15. Ottawa: Health and Welfare Canada.

– 1987b. Women in academic psychiatry in Canada. *Canadian Journal of Psychiatry* 32: 660–65.

Penfold, P.S., and Walker, G.A. 1983. *Women and the psychiatric paradox*. Montreal: Eden Press.

Peterson, C., and Seligman, M.E.P. 1984. Causal explanations as a risk factor for depression: Theory and evidence. *Psychological Review* 91: 347–74.

Radloff, L. 1975. Sex differences in depression: The effects of occupation and marital status. *Sex Roles* 1: 249–65.

Radloff, L., and Rae, D. 1979. Susceptibility and precipitating factors in depression: Sex differences and similarities. *Journal of Abnormal Psychology* 88: 174–81.

Regier, D.A., Boyd, J.H., Burke, J.D., Rae, D.S., Myers, J.K., Kramer, M., Robins, L.N., George, L.K., Karno, M., and Locke, B.Z. 1988. One-month prevalence of mental disorders in the United States: Based on five epidemiologic catchment area sites. *Archives of General Psychiatry* 45: 977–86.

Repetti, R., and Crosby, F. 1984. Gender and depression: Exploring the adult-role explanation. *Journal of Social and Clinical Psychology* 2: 57–70.

Rootman, I. 1988. Inequities in health: Sources and solutions. *Health Promotion* 26(3): 2–8.

Rosenfield, S. 1989. The effects of women's employment: Personal control and sex differences in mental health. *Journal of Health and Social Behavior* 30: 77–91.

Ross, C.E., and Mirowsky, J. 1988. Child care and emotional adjustment to wives' employment. *Journal of Health and Social Behavior* 29: 127–38.

Rothblum, E.D. 1983. Sex-role stereotypes and depression in women. In *The stereotyping of women: Its effects on mental health*, edited by V. Franks, and E.D. Rothblum, 83–111. New York: Springer.

Scarr, S., Phillips, D., and McCartney, K. 1989. Working mothers and their families. *American Psychologist* 44: 1402–9.

Shehan, C.L. 1984. Wives' work and psychological well-being: An extension of Gove's social role theory of depression. *Sex Roles* 11: 881–99.

Sommers, S. 1984. Reported emotions and conventions of emotionality among college students. *Journal of Personality and Social Psychology* 46: 207–15.

Statistics Canada. 1987. *Mental health statistics: 1982–83, 1983–84*. Ottawa: Government of Canada.

Stewart, A., and Salt, P. 1981. Life stress, life-styles, depression, and illness in adult women. *Journal of Personality and Social Psychology* 40: 1063–69.

Stoppard, J.M. 1989. An evaluation of the adequacy of cognitive/behavioural theories for understanding depression in women. *Canadian Psychology* 30: 39–47.

Stoppard, J.M., and Paisley, K.J. 1987. Masculinity, femininity, life stress, and depression. *Sex Roles* 16: 489–96.

Thoits, P.A. 1987. Gender and marital status differences in control and distress: Common stress versus unique stress explanations. *Journal of Health and Social Behavior* 28: 7–22.

Turner, R.J., and Avison, W.R. 1989. Gender and depression: Assessing exposure and vulnerability to life events in a chronically strained population. *Journal of Nervous and Mental Disease* 177: 443–55.

Turner, R.J., and Beiser, M. 1987. Major depression and depressive symptomatology among the physically disabled: Assessing the role of chronic stress. Paper presented at the meeting of the American Public Health Association, New Orleans.

Turner, R.J., and Noh, S. 1988. Physical disability and depression: A longitudinal analysis. *Journal of Health and Social Behavior* 29: 23–37.

Ulch, S.E., and Stoppard, J.M. 1985. Social perception of depression in men and women as a function of sex role style and situational context. Paper presented at the meeting of the Canadian Psychological Association, Halifax, Nova Scotia, Canada.

Vredenburg, K., Krames, L., and Flett, G.L. 1986. Sex differences in the clinical expression of depression. *Sex Roles* 14: 37–49.

Warren, L. 1983. Male intolerance of depression: A review with implications for psychotherapy. *Clinical Psychology Review* 3: 147–56.

Weissman, M.M., and Klerman, G. 1987. Gender and depression. In *Women and depression: A lifespan perspective*, edited by R. Formanek, and A. Gurian, 3–15. New York: Springer.

Weissman, M.M., Leaf, P.J., Tischler, G.L., Blazer, D.G., Karno, M., Bruce, M.L., and Florio, L.P. 1988. Affective disorders in five United States communities. *Psychological Medicine* 18: 141–53.

Welch, S., and Booth, A. 1977. Employment and health among married women with children. *Sex Roles* 3: 385–97.

Whitley, B. 1985. Sex-role orientation and psychological well-being: Two meta-analyses. *Sex Roles* 12: 207–25.

Zerssen, D. von, and Weyerer, S. 1982. Sex differences in rates of mental disorders. *International Journal of Mental Health* 11: 9–45.

CHAPTER SIX

Depression in General Practice Attenders

GORDON E. BARNES

PREVALENCE OF PSYCHIATRIC DISORDERS
IN THE GENERAL POPULATION AND
TREATMENT UTILIZATION PATTERNS

In the classic epidemiological surveys (Bland et al. 1988; Myers et al. 1984; Murphy 1980; Weissman and Myers 1978), the six-month prevalence for psychiatric disorders of any kind in the general population has generally ranged between 15 and 25 per cent. The one-month prevalence rates generally run a bit lower, with around 15 per cent of the population eighteen years of age and over in the five National Institute of Mental Health (NIMH) catchment areas exhibiting signs of at least one psychiatric disorder (Regier et al. 1988). These rates are comparable to those reported in Australian and European studies (Regier et al. 1988).

In the most recently conducted epidemiological studies (Bland et al. 1988), the most commonly reported types of psychiatric disorder have been: (1) phobias, (2) substance abuse, and (3) affective disorders. In that Bland et al. (1988) Edmonton study, 5.7 per cent of the sample were diagnosed as suffering from an affective disorder according to *Diagnostic and Statistical Manual of Mental Disorders–Third Edition* (DSM-III) criteria. These results are comparable to the results observed in the three NIMH catchment areas (Myers et al. 1984), where the six-month prevalence rate for depression ranged between 4.6 per cent in Baltimore and 6.5 per cent in New Haven.

Although the prevalence of psychiatric disorders in the general population is quite high, the percentage of people actually receiving treatment for their mental health problems in the specialty mental health sector is generally thought to be much lower. Regier et al. (1978) have estimated that less than 20 per cent of the persons suffering from mental disorders were receiving treatment in the specialty mental health sector, while 60 per cent were being treated in the general health sector. These results have been confirmed by the recent NIMH catchment area studies (Hough et al. 1987) in which Hough et al. reported that over 80 per cent of Los Angeles respondents with psychiatric diagnoses had not made a health-care visit for mental problems. This pattern seems to hold up in a number of different countries. Tansella et al. (1986), who conducted research in an Italian community, estimated that for every one hundred contacts at the primary-care level, only ten would be seen at the extramural specialist level and only one admission would be made to a psychiatric hospital bed. Canadian data furnished by D'Arcy (1976) on the delivery of psychiatric care in Saskatchewan shows similar results. Of the Saskatchewan patients receiving medical treatment for psychiatric diagnoses, 78 per cent were seen solely by general practitioners; only 12 per cent were seen by psychiatrists.

If the majority of psychiatric cases are being treated within the general health rather than the specialty mental health sector, the manner in which these problems are being recognized and dealt with by general practitioners is extremely important. This holds particularly true for depressive patients. Depression, one of the most common forms of psychiatric morbidity encountered by general practitioners, is a serious disorder that, if not recognized and treated, can lead to impairment in quality of life and, possibly, to suicide. When recognized and dealt with properly, however, it can in many cases be treated effectively by general practitioners. In fact, general population studies have shown that 70 to 90 per cent of people who eventually develop depressive disorders consult their general practitioner for help (Blacker and Clare 1988).

In this chapter, we examine the problem of depression for clients of general practictioners (referred to as "general practice attenders" or "GP attenders"). The review will focus on the prevalence and severity of depression, as well as the risk factors for depression among general practice attenders. The treatment patterns and outcomes for this disorder in general practice are discussed as well.

DEPRESSION IN GENERAL PRACTICE

Prevalence

CASES.   To date, studies examining the prevalence of depression in general practice attenders have been of two types. In the first, psychiatric diagnostic procedures are employed to determine the percentage of GP attenders that would qualify as cases of depression. These studies sometimes employ screening tests, such as the Beck Depression Inventory (BDI), the Zung Self-Rating Depression Scale (SDS) or the Center for Epidemiologic Studies–Depression (CES-D) Scale to give a preliminary indication of depression and to identify subjects requiring a psychiatric interview. Other studies examine a percentage of the low scoring subjects so as to identify the percentage of false negatives that may have been missed by the screening instrument. The second type of study looks at symptoms of depression using symptom scales only.

A summary of seven recent studies of the first type is presented in Table 1. A number of generalizations can be made. First, although these studies have used fairly different screening and diagnostic procedures, the sampling is nonrandom, and the rates of participation are sometimes low, there is a remarkable similarity in the studies' results. Second, the percentage of depressed patients in the seven studies ranges between 5.5 per cent and 10 per cent with a median of 9.2 per cent. Although these rates seem to be somewhat higher than the rates reported earlier for the general population, it should be remembered that samples of patients from general practice are neither random nor representative; furthermore they always reflect a much higher percentage of females than the general population. Third, all these studies, except the study conducted by Blacker and Clare (1988), were conducted in the United States. Blacker and Clare's findings suggest a similar prevalence for depression in the United Kingdom's general practice attenders (10%) to that reported in the U.S. studies.

SYMPTOMS. In recent years, numerous studies using a variety of screening instruments have examined the prevalence of symptoms of depression in general practice attenders. The measure of depression most commonly used in these studies has been the Zung (1965) Self-Rating Depression Scale. A summary of the ten studies using this scale is provided in Table 2. Again, most of these studies were conducted in the United States.

Comparing results in the different studies is unfortunately complicated, because most did not use a common cut-point. For example, Zung et al. (1988) suggest a cut-point of fifty be used to identify minimal levels of depression and a cut-point of sixty-plus be used to indicate moderate to severe depression. According to these criteria, the range for minimal levels of depression in the studies reported in Table 2 would be wide (21% to 57%), with most of the studies clustered around the median of 37 per cent. In the Bradshaw and Parker (1983) study, the only study conducted outside the United States, an idiosyncratic cut-point (40) was used, thus making cross-national comparisons difficult. At the upper end of the severity spectrum, two studies reported on the prevalence of Zung-scale scores of seventy-plus: Linn and Yager (1984), who reported a prevalence of 7 per cent for severe depression; and Davis et al. (1987a) who reported a prevalence of

Table 1
Prevalence of psychiatric cases of depression in general practice

Study	Sample	Measures used	Percentage depressed
Nielsen and Williams (1980)	526 ambulatory medical patients ≥ 21 years Washington, D.C.	Beck screening (BDI >10) and psychiatric diagnoses (Feighner Criteria)	9.0
Zung and King (1983)	499 North California general practice patients	Zung screening & DSM-III	9.8 major depressive disorder
Schulberg et al. (1985)	294 Pittsburgh primary care patients with continuing appointments	DIS	9.2
Parker et al. (1986)	564 attenders from Sydney, Australia, general practice 35 with Beck scores ≥ 10 interviewed	Beck and PSE DSM-III	17.7* depressed according to PSE 5.5 met DSM-III criteria for major depression or dysthymia
Von Korff et al. (1987)	809 primary-care patients, Baltimore group practice	DSI	5.0 major depression 3.7 dysthymia 8.7 depressive disorders
Barret et al. (1988)	1,055 patients visiting Hanover primary care physicians	Self-report screen and RDC	10.0 depressive disorders
Blacker and Clare (1988)	2,308 persons attending British general practice	GHQ and SADS	5.7 RDC minor depression 4.3 RDC major depression 10.0 depressive disorder
Coulehan et al. (1988)	294 primary-medical care	DIS	7.1 major depression

*Rates were computed by: (1) computing percentage of screened and interviewed patients depressed; (2) assuming that same rate of depression applied in those positive screens not interviewed: and (3) assuming no depression in negative screens.

DSM-III = Diagnostic and Statistical Manual of Mental Disorders - Third edition; DIS = Diagnostic Interview Schedule; PSE = Present State Examination; RDC = Research Diagnostic Criteria; GHQ = General Health Questionnaire; SADS = Schedule for Affective Disorders and Schizophrenia.

Table 2
Prevalence of symptoms of depression in general practice: Zung scale

Study	Sample	Cutoff scores	Percentage depressed
Raft et al. (1975)	100 American outpatients	Unspecified	56
Moore et al. (1978)	212 patients, 20-60 seen at North Medical Centre (North California)	≥ 50	45
Wright et al. (1980)	199 family practice patients (Louisville, Ky.)	≥ 50 ≥ 60	41 17
Bradshaw and Parker (1983)	251 Australian general practice attenders	≥ 40	21
Zung et al. (1983)	1,086 family medicine outpatients, Duke-Watts Family Medicine Program	≥ 55	13.2
Zung and King (1983)	499 North Carolina general practice patients	55+	12
Linn and Yager (1984)	95 UCLA department of medicine patients	50+ minimal 60+ moderate 70+ severe	51 32 7
Rosenthal et al. (1987)	123 patients (U.S. urban teaching-hospital)	50+ 55+	37 21
Davis et al. (1987)	488 family practice urban patients (southern USA)	50 70	41 4
Zung et al. (1988)	764 black and 773 white adult, North Carolina outpatients in primary care	50+ ≥ 60	Black 23 White 21 Black 6 White 6

4 per cent for scores that high. Although it is not easy to convert symptom-prevalence rates to prevalence rates for DSM-III diagnoses, Zung and King (1983) noted that forty-nine of the sixty (82%) patients with Zung scores of fifty-five or more met the DSM-III criteria for cases of depression.

The Beck Depression Inventory (Beck et al. 1961; Beck 1978) has been used in eight studies of depression in GP attenders conducted in the United States, Britain, and Australia. The results of these studies are summarized in Table 3. The lack of consensus regarding cut-points employed with the BDI makes any comparison of results across these studies difficult. Research by Nielson and Williams (1980) has nevertheless provided four possible guidelines for determining which BDI-scale cut-points to use in general practice research. First, they note that a cut-point of thirteen provides the best balance of sensitivity (.79) and specificity (.77). Second, they recommend a cut-point of ten if sensitivity is more important than specificity. Third, they recommend a cut-point of seventeen if it is important to exclude mild

Table 3
Prevalence of symptoms of depression in general practice: Beck scale

Study	Sample	Cutoff scores	Percentage depressed	
Schwab et al. (1967)	153 Florida inpatients (73% of admissions) ≥ 15 yrs.	≥ 13 ≥ 43	22 23	
Salkind (1969)	80 patients, British general practice	≥ 11 ≥ 17	48 25	
Raft et al. (1975)	100 American outpatients	Unspecified	56	
Nielson and Williams (1980)	526 ambulatory medical patients ≥ 21 years (Washington, D.C.)	≥ 13 ≥ 17	12.2 5.5	
Seller et al. (1981)	222 family practice patients (Buffalo, N.Y.)	> 10 > 20	M* F** M F	29.7 36.7 13.9 14.7
Parker et al. (1986)	564 general practice attenders (Sydney, Australia)	≥ 10	21	
Rosenthal et al. (1987)	123 patients, U.S. urban teaching-hospital	8+ 13+	57 28	
Williamson (1987)	484 University of Missouri family care patients	≥ 13	M F	15.3 15.7
Davis et al. (1987)	64 children 57 adults	11 5 16	50 39 11	

  * M = Male
** F = Female

cases of depression. Fourth, they identify thirteen-plus as the most commonly employed cut-point for the BDI. For the four studies in Table 3 employing this last cut-point, the percentages for depression in GP attenders ranged between 12.2 per cent and 28 per cent. Interestingly, all of the studies using this cut-point were conducted in the United States. Unfortunately, the use of small and often unrepresentative samples and different cut-points makes any attempt at cross-national comparisons a dubious enterprise.

The four studies that used depression scales other than those of the Beck or Zung tests to measure symptoms of depression in GP attenders are summarized in Table 4. Two studies employed the CES-D Scale (Barnes and Prosen 1984; Schulberg et al. 1985); a third used a combination of Hopkins' check-list items and CES-D items (Barrett et al. 1987); the fourth (Davis et al. 1987b) reported prevalence rates using the Depression Adjective Check List (DACL) (Lubin 1965). More specifically, in the Schulberg et al. (1985)

Table 4
Prevalence of symptoms of depression in general practice: CES-D and other measures

Study	Sample	Measures used	Cutoff scores	Percentage depressed
Barnes and Prosen (1984)	1,250 general practice attenders (Winnipeg, Brandon and Virden; Manitoba, Canada)	CES-D	≥ 16 ≥ 30	32 Winnipeg 8.7 Brandon 5.7
Schulberg et al. (1985)	1,554 Pittsburgh primary-care patients	CES-D	≥ 16	47
Davis et al. (1987)	488 family practice urban patients (Southern USA)	DACL	13 16	37 15
Barret et al. (1987)	1,010 unselected New England primary-care patients	16 items from Hopkins 4 items from CES-D	9+ (equiv. to CES-D 12) 12+ (equiv. to CES-D 16) 17+ (equiv. to CES-D 23)	28.3 18.3 8.8

CES-D = Center for Epidemiologic Studies-Depression Scale; DACL = Depression Adjective Check List

study, 47 per cent of the subjects scored above the CES-D cut-point of sixteen. In the Barrett et al. (1987) study, 18.3 per cent of the sample scored above twelve on the scale used (which the authors judged to be equivalent to a score of 16-plus on the CES-D Scale). In the Davis et al (1987b) report, 37 per cent scored above the cut-point of thirteen on the DACL. Incidentally, none of these studies employed random or representative samples of GP attenders. In our own research (Barnes and Prosen 1984, 1985), described below, attempts were made to obtain random samples of general practitioners so as to test all patients visiting each general practitioner over a short period of time.

In our own research (Barnes and Prosen 1984; 1985), for which we used the CES-D Scale (Radloff 1977), we attempted to obtain as representative a sample as possible of the GP attenders. We began with a list of physicians registered to practise in Manitoba, selecting all general practitioners in Brandon and Virden and a random sample of Winnipeg general practitioners. Physicians were sent letters requesting their participation in the study. (Participation meant that a research assistant spent one week in each doctor's office, asking patients to complete a short five-minute questionnaire that measured depression. The overall participation rate of the general practi-

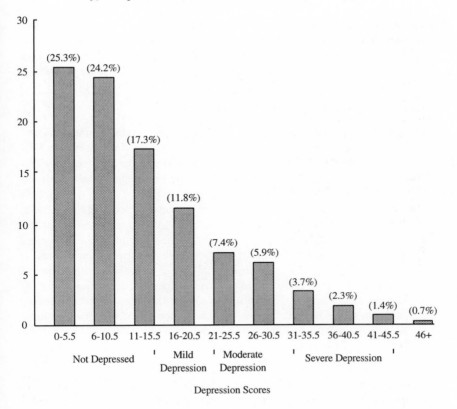

Figure 1
Frequency Distribution of Depression Scores

tioners approached (and who had practices suitable for this project) was 44 per cent.

Once the general practitioners had agreed to participate in this project, they were contacted and a suitable week was scheduled. All patients eighteen years of age and over were approached and asked to complete the short questionnaire. Anonymity of response was guaranteed. The overall participation rate for patients reached 70 per cent. The total sample for this study numbered 1,250 patients (932 patients tested in twenty-six Winnipeg offices; 279 patients tested in eight Brandon offices; and 39 patients in three Virden offices). Of the overall patient sample tested, 34 per cent were male and 66 per cent female. The mean age of the overall sample was 37.7 years, and the majority (60.1%) were married. Overall, about two-thirds of the sample had completed high school. All types of occupational status were represented.

The frequency distribution for the depression scores in the overall sample is summarized in Figure 1. Although cutoff scores of sixteen or more are generally regarded as indicating depression on the CES-D Scale (Boyd and Weissman 1981), the present distribution shows the lack of a sharp distinction between depressed and nondepressed patients. In our sample, 33.2 per cent obtained scores of sixteen or more. A cutoff score of sixteen may seem a bit low for classification as a case of depression, for scores in clinically depressed groups have traditionally been much higher (for example, Weissman et al. [1977] reported a mean of 38.1, and standard deviation (SD) of 9.0, in a sample of 148 depressed patients). Based on the frequency distribution, an examination of the CES-D items, and knowledge of how clinically depressed groups score on this scale, Barnes and Prosen (1984) suggested the following classifications: (1) 0 to 15.5 = not depressed; (2) 16 to 20.5 = mild depression (scores in this range fall outside two standard deviations of scores obtained in depressed patients and, hence, are unlikely to represent true clinical depression); (3) 21 to 30.5 = moderate depression (scores in this range fall within two standard deviations of depressed patient means and, hence, are more likely to indicate true or clinical depression); and (4) 31 and above = severe depression (to obtain this high a score, patients must obtain scores of three, indicating that symptoms are experienced most or all of the time on half the CES-D items, or lesser scores on more than half the items [this score also puts them within one standard deviation of scores among depressed patients]). Using these criteria, the overall prevalence of depression in our sample was as follows: (1) no depression = 66.8 per cent; (2) mild depression = 11.8 per cent; (3) moderate depression = 13.3 per cent; and (4) severe depression = 8.1 per cent.

Although the rates for depressive symptomatology presented in Tables 2 to 4 seem high, it is difficult to know how many of these cases would actually meet more stringent clinical criteria as cases of depression. For instance, prevalence rates for depression in studies using DSM-III or related criteria (Table 1) indicate a much lower prevalence rate than studies employing symptom scales. Research by Parker et al. (1986) is particularly pertinent to this question, inasmuch as 83 per cent of their subjects classified as cases with the Beck Depression Inventory also met the criteria for cases as specified by the Present State Exam. As for the CES-D Scale, Myers and Weissman (1980) have indicated that it has a fairly low false-positive rate of about 6 per cent (that is, 6% of those scoring above 16 on the CES-D Scale would not meet Research Diagnostic Criteria [RDC] for depression). As well, Amenson and Lewinsohn (1981) reported quite a high correlation between CES-D Scale scores and clinical diagnoses ($r=.7$). These results are for the general population, however. Different cut-points may be required for general practice attenders. For instance, Schulberg et al. (1985) examined the issue of sensitivity and specificity of diagnoses in GP attenders with differing cut-

Table 5
Symptoms of depression in the general population and in general
practice attenders.

Sample	Male		Female	
	% CES-D ≥ 16	Mean	% CES-D ≥ 16	Mean
GENERAL POPULATION (WINNIPEG) (Barnes et al. 1988) n=230 males n=285 females	15.1	8.6	18.8	9.8
MANITOBA GENERAL PRACTICE* (Barnes and Prosen 1984) n=390 males n=740 females	29.8	12.1	35.4	13.9

*Virden patients excluded

points on the CES-D Scale. Their results showed that although the cut-point
of sixteen provided good sensitivity (96.3%) in general practice attenders,
the specificity of diagnoses at this cut-point was quite poor (38.6%). They
found that the best balance between sensitivity and specificity seemed to
occur at the cut-point of thirty, with a sensitivity of 74.1 per cent and specificity of 77.5 per cent. When the cut-point of thirty is applied in the Barnes
and Prosen (1984) study, the prevalence for depression (8%) comes very
close to the rate reported in studies employing DSM-III criteria.

It is hard to know how much higher the depression rates observed in
GP attenders are than the rates observed in the general population. Usually,
studies of depression in GP attenders do not include general population comparison groups. In my own research (Barnes et al. 1988), we also administered
the CES-D Scale to a large Winnipeg general population random sample
(n=525). Depression scores in the general practitioner and general population
samples are compared in Table 5. These results show that depression scores
are much higher for the GP attenders and that rates of depression (that
is, scores of 16 and higher) are about twice as common in the GP attender
sample.

Severity of Depression

Several studies have examined the issue of severity of depression in general
practice attenders. In at least two studies (Blashki 1972; Fahy 1974), comparisons have been made between depressed patients seen in general practice
and patients hospitalized for depression. In Blashki's (1972) study (83 GP-

identified depressives compared with 92 hospitalized depressives), the hospitalized group scored "more depressed" on the Hamilton scale but not significantly higher on the Zung scale. Blashki noted that while depressive episodes in the GP attender group were characterized by "occurrence of apathy, anxiety, irritability, and social withdrawal" (319), the "hospital patients more commonly had a history of cyclical mood variation, previous suicidal attempt, and attempted suicide just prior to their presentation" (319).

In a similar study, Fahy (1974) compared forty-nine depressives identified in general practice with fifty-one hospitalized patients. Fahy observed, however, that the depression of the hospitalized group seemed to be more severe than that of the general practice cohort, with higher scores on the Hamilton and Beck depression scales. Suicide attempts were also much more common among hospitalized depressives. The chief qualitative difference in the two groups was the rarity of psychomotor retardation among the GP-identified depressives.

In two other studies, general practice depressives were compared with depressed outpatients (Coulehan et al. 1988; Sireling et al. 1985). In Sireling et al.'s research (1985), ninety-five depressed GP patients who were receiving anti-depressant treatment and forty-eight patients who were receiving other treatment were compared with eighty-nine depressed outpatients. The symptoms of the outpatients were rated as more severe than the general-practice patients on the Hamilton rating scale. Comparing the GP patients and outpatients, Sireling et al. (1985) concluded "The differences were considerable: the GP depressives were less severely ill, had shorter illnesses, a lower incidence of primary, endogenous or retarded major depression, and milder symptoms of depressed mood, biological and psychomotor changes" (123).

Results of Coulehan et al.'s (1988) research were not nearly as dramatic. They compared twenty-one depressed patients from primary medical care with sixty-six depressives from community mental health centres. Although the PMC patients reported loss of libido less frequently than the CMHC depressives, they did not seem to be more depressed overall than the PMC patients. The two groups' CES-D Scale scores were similar and their suicidal tendencies comparable. Somatic symptoms, however, were more commonly reported in the PMC than the CMHC group. As noted by Coulehan et al. (1988), the small and unrepresentative samples employed in this study may have mitigated against differences appearing between the two groups. Symptoms of depression may, in fact, have been more severe in CMHC patients, but this difference may have been obscured by the small and unrepresentative samples employed.

In a slightly different type of study, Johnson and Mellor (1977) studied the severity of depression in two samples of depressives identified via general practice, and reported that 18 per cent of one sample and 12 per cent of the other were bothered by troublesome or persistent thoughts of suicide. On the basis of these results, Johnson and Mellor concluded that it would be wrong to dismiss the forms of depression observed in GP attenders as trivial. In a similar vein, Davis et al. (1987a) noted that of the sixty-four patients age six to twelve years tested in a family practice clinic, twenty-eight reported suicidal ideation. The scores of the children reporting suicidal ideation were much higher on the Kovacs Childhood Depression Inventory, than the scores of the children not reporting suicidal ideation.

In the research conducted to date comparing general GP and depressed inpatients and outpatients, there is some indication that the severity and symptom patterns in the two groups may differ. More research seems to be required, and with larger and more representative samples, before definitive conclusions can be reached. Of particular interest would be an examination of possible differences in somatic symptoms in the different types of depressed patients. Even if the symptom patterns of depressed GP patients were ultimately shown to be less severe than depressed inpatients or outpatients, the need to address the problem of depression in general practice attenders would still be present. Suicide seems to be a concern, particularly among depressed children.

Patient Visits

Research suggests that patients with psychiatric disorders may in fact make more visits to their general practitioners than patients without psychiatric disorders (Cummings and Follette 1968; Houpt et al. 1980; Locke and Gardner 1969; Locke et al. 1966; Tessler et al. 1976). Houpt et al. (1980), for instance, estimated that patients with psychiatric disorders make about twice as many visits to their physicians, require more time per visit, and use more general services such as X-rays and laboratory tests than patients without psychiatric disorders. Canadian data also supports the relationship between psychiatric symptomatology and the use of nonpsychiatric medical services. Cassell et al. (1972) found significant correlations between psychiatric symptoms and number of visits to the doctor in both male and female samples.

Research has also shown that depressed patients visit nonpsychiatric physicians (Weissman and Myers 1978) frequently and that the frequency of visits increases in the period prior to their diagnosis of depression (Widmer and Cadoret 1978, 1979). In the Barnes and Prosen (1984) study, a low but significant ($r=.14$, $p<.001$) positive correlation between depression and number of visits to the doctor in the previous year was observed.

Further clarification on the relationship between patient visits and depression is provided in the research conducted by Widmer and Cadoret (1978, 1979). In their first study (1978), (Widmer and Cadoret) examined the patient-visit patterns of 154 depressed patients and 154 controls during two time intervals: (1) the seven-month period just prior to the diagnosis of depression in the experimental group; and (2) the seven-month period beginning nineteen months before diagnosis of depression in the experimental group. Study results showed an increase in patient visits and hospitalizations among depressed patients in the period prior to diagnosis. Three main types of presenting complaints were seen for the depressed patients in the period prior to diagnosis: ill-defined functional complaints; pain of undetermined etiology; and nervous complaints.

In their second (1979) study, Widmer and Cadoret followed up on forty-three of the depressed patients who had had later depressive episodes and a suitably matched control group. Once again, the depressed patients showed increased visits to the doctor, increased hospitalization, and an increase in functional complaints, pain, and tension. Widmer and Cadoret concluded that the increased office visits and the types of presenting complaints could be important harbingers of subsequent depressive episodes.

In more recent research by the Widmer and Cadoret group, Wilson et al. (1983) compared patient visits and symptom patterns for 101 depressed general practice patients and 101 age- and sex-matched controls. Patients' records were examined for the eighteen-month period leading up to diagnosis and for a similar period after diagnosis. Results showed that visits to the doctor by the depressed patients were more numerous during all the study periods. The depressed patients had more pain and functional complaints than the controls in the period immediately before diagnosis. It is interesting to note that, after treatment, the number of these complaints fell to the same level as that reported for the control group.

In an extension of the research described above, Wilson et al. (1987) added a group of fifty-eight patients with anxiety to the study, comparing their symptom patterns in the period leading up to diagnosis with those of the depressives and controls. Results of this analysis showed that the depressives had a much longer period of somatic and functional complaints leading up to diagnosis than did the anxiety patients. These studies are important in that they draw attention to the importance of considering a diagnosis of depression when patients visit their doctor frequently, reporting pain and functional complaints in the absence of any known physical problems.

Physical Illness

If patients who visit the doctor often also suffer more from symptoms of depression than patients who visit the doctor less often, the question arises as to whether the symptoms of depression are primary symptoms indicative of depressive disorder, or are secondary to the physical ailments. Locke and

Gardner (1969) studied this problem and found that 35 per cent of patients with a psychiatric problem reported it to their physician as a primary complaint. In another article, Locke et al. (1966) noted that two-thirds of the patients with psychiatric problems had no physical ailments.

In research that is more specific to the relationship between depression and physical illness, Schwab et al. (1967a) compared the physical-illness patterns of depressed and nondepressed GP attenders. Their results showed that, as a group, the depressed patients had less severe medical illnesses than the nondepressed. Schwab et al. (1967a) reported that depression occurred in patients with all levels of severity of physical illness: (1) as an isolated entity (20%); (2) in association with minor illnesses (25%); and (3) in association with major illness (55%). Johnson (1973), who tested ninety-one depressed patients identified in British general practices, found that, in 60 per cent of cases, the depression was not associated with organic illness. A similar result was reported in the more recent research by Sireling et al. (1985), who reported that 65 per cent of the treated depressives in general practice had no associated physical illnesses.

Risk Factors and Depression

SOCIAL AND DEMOGRAPHIC CHARACTERISTICS. Several of the studies reported in Tables 1 to 4 have examined the relationship between demographic characteristics and depression in general practice attenders and term the research results as somewhat inconsistent. One reason for this inconsistency may be the small and unrepresentative samples used in many of the studies. Where larger and more representative samples have been used (for example, in Barnes and Prosen 1984), the findings with respect to demographic differences seem to resemble the results reported in general population surveys. Another possible reason for the inconsistent findings may be the different measures used to assess depression in these studies. Both Schwab et al. (1967a) and Schwab et al. (1967b), for example, found inconsistent results within the same study depending on which method of assessing depression was used. When the Beck inventory of depression was used as a measure of depression, Schwab et al. (1967a) reported no significant associations between demographic characteristics and depression. However, when data were analyzed using the Hamilton scale (Schwab et al. 1967b), higher depression scores were reported for blacks, young patients, and patients with lower incomes. Marital status and sex remained unrelated to depression.

Sex. One of the most frequently reported findings in research on the epidemiology of depression in the general population has been the sex difference in depression (Boyd and Weissman 1981). For example, in studies where psychiatric diagnoses were conducted on GP attenders (see Table 1), there is some indication that female patients have a greater prevalence of depression than do male patients. In the recent research by Blacker and Clare (1988), the sample contained four times as many depressed women as men. Barrett et al. (1988) also reported a higher prevalence for depression in women than men, but with some variation according to the type of depression involved. In the research using self-report symptom inventories to measure depression (Tables 2 to 4), sex differences have been commonly reported. On the Zung scale, for example, results reported by Zung et al. (1983) indicated that twice as many males as females score a higher than fifty-five plus. Significantly higher scores for females than males were also reported by Bradshaw and Parker (1983). Wright et al. (1980), however, did not find any sex difference in Zung scale scores in their Kentucky sample.

Results in the studies using the Beck scale have been inconsistent. Although a sex difference was reported in the largest study (Nielson and Williams 1980), no significant sex differences were reported in two other studies (Seller et al. 1981; Williamson 1987). These results suggest that the sex difference may be rather weak, only showing up when large samples are employed. Alternatively, it could be that the sex difference in depression diminishes both with time and the changes in sex-role-related behaviours. Williamson (1987) noted that the factor structure for the Beck scale differed for men and women: the first two test factors were identical, but a third factor emerged for males that was interpreted as an interpersonal behavioural change. The lack of sex differences on the Beck scale might well be related to this finding, for the Beck scale contains an extra dimension of depression for males.

Most of the general population research conducted to date using the CES-D Scale shows a significant sex difference (for a review, see Barnes et al. 1988). A sex difference has also been reported in the two GP attender studies employing the CES-D Scale (Barnes and Prosen 1984; Schulberg et al. 1985).

Table 5 presents the sex differences in depression scores on the CES-D Scale observed in the Barnes and Prosen (1984) general practice attender study and the Barnes et al. (1988) general population study. In the general practice sample (Barnes and Prosen 1984), a significant sex difference was reported. When the results were further analyzed, Barnes and Prosen (1984) showed that this significant sex difference also applied at the most severe end of the depression spectrum (scores of 31+), with 9.7 per cent of women being severely depressed and 5.1 per cent of men scoring in this range. These results support the epidemiological literature suggesting that depression is twice as common in women as in men (see Boyd and Weissman 1981; Regier et al. 1988). It is also interesting to note that further analyses of our data did not reveal any significant interactions between sex and marital status, age, education, or occupational status. In other words, the sex difference in depression was fairly robust and did not depend on a particular occupational or marital status group. Also, although the results in the general population sample were in the anticipated direction, the sex difference was not significant.

Age. In the general population research on the prevalence of depressive disorders, depressive disorders have been found most commonly in the twenty-five- to forty-four-year age range, the lowest rates for depression being in the sixty-five and over age group (see Regier et al. 1988). On the symptom scales, the highest scores have been reported for the youngest age groups, particularly in studies where the CES-D Scale has been employed (for a review, see Barnes et al. 1988). In the research on GP attenders, a similar pattern emerges for studies in which clinical diagnoses have been employed. For example Blacker and Clare (1988) reported that a high percentage of depressed patients seen in general practice are under thirty-five years of age. Both Barrett et al. (1988) and Barrett et al. (1987) also reported a low prevalence of depression among elderly patients. Both groups reported that, in their studies the highest rate of severe depression occurred in the youngest age group, while the lowest prevalence of depression occurred in the oldest age group.

Not many of the studies using self-report scales seem to have focused on the issue of age-related differences in depression scores. Rosenthal et al. (1987) noted that there was little association between age and depression in their study employing the Zung and Beck scales. As well, Nielson and Williams (1980) reported no association between Beck scale scores and age. In one interesting study conducted by Davis et al. (1987a) of children and their parents attending a family practice, the children were given the child's version of the BDI called the Children's Depression Inventory (CDI) (Kovacs 1982). Results showed that 50 per cent of the children age six to twelve years scored in the depressed range, a higher percentage than that of their parents, who scored in the depressed range on the BDI (37%). Using the CES-D Scale, the Barnes and Prosen (1984) study reported a significant contribution for age in a multivariate analysis predicting depression: younger patients scored as less depressed than older patients.

Taken as a whole, the above results suggest that cases of depression in general practice are most common in the under thirty-five age group and least common in the over sixty-five age group. Patterns with regard to symptoms of depression, however, are less clear cut. Results would likely be more consistent with the clinical diagnoses studies if patterns of high levels of symptomatology (perhaps over 30 on the CES-D Scale) were examined by age. The high rates of symptomatology observed in children (Davis et al. 1987a) suggest that this is an important area for future research. Of course, age differences in depression can be interpreted as either cohort effects or differences related to aging. Current thinking in the field of psychiatric epidemiology regarding age differences in depression seems to be that such differences pertain to cohorts (Klerman 1976; Klerman et al. 1985; Weissman et al. 1984). This perspective is bolstered by longitudinal research on depression (Hagnell et al. 1982), and the birth-cohort research being conducted in the suicide field (Hellon and Solomon 1980; Murphy and Wetzel 1981). If it is true that, as suggested by Klerman (1976), we are entering an age of melancholy, general practitioners will be experiencing a growing influx of depressed patients in the years ahead.

Race. Although some reports from general population research have suggested that whites may score lower than blacks (Craig and Van Natta 1978) or Mexican Americans (Frerichs et al. 1981; Vernon and Roberts 1982) on symptoms of depression, most research seems to suggest that these differences can be explained on the basis of socioeconomic differences (Husaini et al. 1980; Vega et al. 1984). In the one large study that examined racial differences in symptoms of depression among GP attenders, Zung et al. (1988) found no significant differences in symptom patterns between whites and blacks.

Social class. In studies examining the relationship between social class and symptoms of depression in GP attenders, higher depression scores have been linked to a variety of social class indicators. Nielson and Williams (1980), for one, reported higher Beck scale scores for patients with lower socioeconomic status. In Wright et al.'s (1980) and Bradshaw and Parker's (1983) research, the Zung scale was employed and similar results were observed, with higher depression scores reported for lower socioeconomic (SES) patients. In the Barnes and Prosen (1984) research, which employed the CES-D Scale, higher depression scores have been found to be associated with lower SES factors, such as education, occupational, status, and number of children (see Table 6).

Marital status. Recent general population research (see Bland et al. 1988) suggests that depression is more common among separated, divorced, or widowed people than among the married or never married. Similar findings have been found in the research on depression among GP attenders. Nielson and Williams (1980), for example, reported higher depression scores on the Beck scale for patients who were separated as opposed to married. Higher Zung scale scores were reported for those who were separated or divorced in the research conducted by Wright et al. (1980).

In the Barnes and Prosen (1984) study, a significant relationship between marital status and depression was also found (see Table 6). Divorced or separated patients had higher scores than married or single patients ($p < .005$, Duncan's Multiple Range Test). Widows had intermediate scores. Because

Table 6
Demographic variables and depression one-way ANOVA

Variable	Classification	N	Mean	F
City	Winnipeg	902	13.7	3.0*
	Brandon	275	11.9	
	Virden	39	13.4	
Sex	Male	413	12.1	8.0†
	Female	802	13.9	
Marital status	Single	325	13.2	4.7†
	Widowed	75	15.3	
	Married or equivalent	731	12.7	
	Divorced or separated	84	16.7	
Education	6 grades or less	32	20.0	5.9‡
	9 grades or less	142	15.8	
	Some high school	217	14.4	
	High school completed	395	12.1	
	Some college or technical diploma	219	12.7	
	University graduate	98	11.7	
	Some postgraduate work	51	10.6	
Occupational status	Employed full-time	656	12.7	8.5‡
	Employed part-time	106	12.6	
	Housewife	212	13.4	
	Retired	115	13.0	
	Student	50	11.8	
	Unemployed	57	21.8	
Number of children	None	496	13.3	2.6*
	1	187	12.2	
	2-3	371	13.0	
	4+	146	15.4	

* $= p < .05$
† $= p < .01$
‡ $= p < .001$

writers such as Durkheim (1951) have proposed that marriage is more protective of men than women, we also examined the interaction between sex and marital status. No significant sex by marital status interaction was found, however. In other words, divorce and separation are risk factors for depression in both men and women.

Urban vs. rural. In the Barnes and Prosen (1984) study, general practice attenders were tested in three different settings (large urban: Winnipeg; small urban: Brandon; and town: Virden). Although the Virden sample was rather small to allow for comparisons, the differences between Winnipeg and Brandon were based on fairly large samples. Results reported in Table 6 show that depression scores were higher in Winnipeg than in Brandon. The differences remained significant when demographic characteristics were controlled (Barnes and Prosen 1984). The differences between Winnipeg and Brandon are interesting, particularly as Brown and Harris's (1978) research has shown that the prevalence of symptoms of depression in a large urban centre (London) was higher than the prevalence figures in a less populated area (outer Hebrides).

In a recent Canadian general population study on the prevalence of depression, Kovess et al. (1987) studied rural-urban differences *vis-à-vis* the prevalence of depression. Their results showed a rural-urban difference, with higher depression scores reported in the urban sample. The authors also reported that this result seemed to be accounted for primarily by the urban sample's unemployed males and unmarried females.

OTHER RISK FACTORS. Not much attention has been paid to other risk factors in the research on depression of GP attenders. Sireling et al. (1985) compared symptom patterns for depression in GP patients and depressed outpatients. They found that depressed outpatients showed more evidence of endogenous depression than the GP patients, suggesting perhaps that the heritable form of depression may be less common in GP attenders. On the other hand, Davis et al. (1987a) have found that all the children who scored in the depressed range in their sample also had parents who were depressed. More research seems to be required on family history and the prevalence and nature of the depression in GP attenders.

Blacker and Clare (1988) have examined time of year in general practice as yet another possible risk factor for depression. They identified the winter months as associated with the onset of depression in their sample of GP patients. Although this finding seems to contradict the hospital-admission patterns for depression and suicide, which seem to peak in spring, Blacker and Clare (1988) reported that this, in fact, is not the case. They argue that there is usually a lapse between the time of symptom onset and help-seeking behaviour, and that their study is merely picking up subjects earlier in the course of their illness. This argument highlights an important distinction between general practice studies and other clinical research on depression. Indeed, this consideration may help to explain certain other observed differences between general practice depressives and depressed patients. The finding that depressed patients in general practice seem to have more symptoms of anxiety (Barrett et al. 1988; Blazer et al. 1988) and more somatic complaints (Coulehan et al. 1988; Widmer and Cadoret 1983; Wilson et al. 1983; Wilson et al. 1987) than patients seen by psychiatrists could perhaps be explained by the fact that more of these patients are in an earlier phase of their disorder.

Writers since Freud (1917) have commented on the possible significance of losses in predicting depression. In my own research (Barnes and Prosen 1985), parental loss was included as a predictor of depression. Analyses of the relationship between parental loss and depression revealed a significant effect on depression after the loss of a father, but no significant effect after the loss of a mother. Highest depression scores were reported for patients who had lost a father when they were in the zero to six, and ten to fourteen age ranges. The "father-loss" effect remained significant when other possible confounding demographic characteristics such as age, sex, and education were controlled.

The effect of father loss on depression is intriguing. In a review article on this topic, Heinicke (1973) concluded that loss effects were important, particularly a father loss that occurred in the zero to five and ten to fourteen age groups. Subsequent reviews on this topic have been more mixed, with some reviewers (for example, Lloyd 1980; Nelson 1982) concluding that a relationship exists, and others (for example, Crook and Eliot 1980; Tennant et al. 1980) concluding that no relationship exists or that the relationship is an artifact. In my own review of this literature (Barnes and Krenn 1988), in which the technique of meta-analysis (Rosenthal 1986) was employed, I concluded that there does seem to be a relationship between parental loss and depression, and that this relationship is unlikely to be an artifact.

Parker et al. (1986) interviewed thirty-five subjects, identified as depressed in the general practice sample, in their research. Subjects were asked questions concerning social support and life events. Unfortunately, the absence of data on nondepressed comparison groups weakens the utility of this data. With respect to social support, Parker et al. (1986) stated that 83 per cent of the subjects reported having a key attachment, but only six of these identified their spouse as that figure. Seven subjects reported the termination of a relationship in the previous twelve months. When asked about life events precipitating their depression, the most commonly reported stressors were difficulty with intimate relationships (71%), health problems (51%), financial problems (43%), and work problems (31%).

A recent general practice study in psychiatric morbidity (including depression) among earthquake victims (Maj et al. 1989) reported that the prevalence of psychiatric disorder was greatest in communities forced to relocate because of seismic activity or forced to accommodate victims of seismic activity. Neurotic depression, the most common psychiatric symptom reported, occurred more frequently in the high-stress communities. Psychiatric symptoms were much more common among subjects reporting one or more social problems.

More research is required into the possible causal factors involved in predicting depression in GP attenders. Social variables of the kind suggested by Brown and Harris (1978) seem to be promising variables for inclusion in future studies. People with low levels of social support might be even more likely to visit their general practitioner when they are depressed than other depressed patients. The higher prevalence in GP patients of somatic complaints as well as mixed anxiety/depression suggests that personality factors may also be worth examining in this population. Perhaps depressives tend to be stimulus augmenters, as described by Petrie (1967). Perhaps too, they score higher on trait anxiety than other depressives seen in the specialty mental health sector.

Recognition and Treatment of Depression

RECOGNITION OF DEPRESSION BY GENERAL PRACTITIONERS. With the prevalence of symptoms of depression being so high in GP attenders, an obvious question arises: To what extent are these symptoms recognized and treated by physicians? Goldberg and Blackwell (1970) estimated that about one-third of the psychiatric morbidity evident in general practices was hidden (that is, that the patient presents with a physical complaint). More recently, Parker et al. (1986) reported that only one of thirty-five depressed patients had specifically gone to the general practitioner for depression treatment. When questioned further regarding the depression, however, 83 per cent were able to define when their depression began. The mean duration reported for the symptoms of depression was 9.4 months. Only two subjects reported that they were unable to identify the precipitating event leading to their depression. A high percentage of subjects (86%) reported that they had experienced at least one previous episode of depression.

There are two ways of examining the relationship between the true prevalence of depression in GP attenders and the treated prevalence of depression. One technique involves direct comparisons of depression scores or diagnoses and physician assessments and response. The second method involves comparing the prevalence of depression as determined by psychiatric diagnoses on symptom scales with the public records that are available regarding the treatment in question. Research using both of these techniques is reviewed in the following sections.

Several studies have attempted to examine the relationship between physician diagnoses for depression and rates of depression as determined by psychiatric diagnoses or scores on self-report symptom scales. In the research in which physician diagnoses were compared with psychiatric diagnoses, the results seemed to show that physicians are generally quite competent at recognizing what has been called "conspicuous psychiatric morbidity." Blacker and Clare (1988) reported that the physicians in their study were generally aware of their major depressed patients and were providing some form of counselling and support. It was also noted, however, that 22 per cent of the patients were receiving treatment more appropriate for anxiety, and that the dosages of antidepressants were subtherapeutic in many cases. In a similar vein, Von Korff et al. (1987) noted that 72.8 per cent of the Diagnostic Interview Schedule (DIS)-diagnosed cases of anxiety or depression were assessed as such by practitioners.

The agreement between physician diagnoses and depression seems to be much lower when symptom scales are employed or when residents are studied rather than fully qualified physicians. Seller et al. (1981) reported that residents' diagnoses were unrelated to patient scores on the Beck Depression Inventory. Resident diagnoses also seemed to be biased by sex, with six times as many females as males diagnosed as being depressed. These results were in contrast with the Beck scores, which showed no significant sex difference. Researchers using the Zung scale have reported similar findings (Davis et al. 1987b). Davis et al. (1987b) noted that residents had failed to diagnose depression in 85 per cent of those patients who were mildly depressed on the Zung scale and in 70 per cent of those who were severely depressed. Rosenthal et al. (1987) examined the correlations between physician assessments and self-report scores for both the Beck and Zung scales. Results were not much better than those described above, with the correlations being $r=.45$ with the Zung scale, and $r=.34$ with the Beck scale. More positive results were reported by Linn and Yager (1984), who noted that physicians seemed to be identifying depression in their patients at appropriate levels as determined by the Zung scale. However, they also noted that physicians seemed to be much less accurate in detecting anxiety and were likely to treat a patient for depression if that depression occurred in conjunction with anxiety.

Much more research needs to be done on the issue of recognition and management of depression in general practice. In particular, general practitioners seem to need more information on how to distinguish anxious from depressed patients in their clientele, and how to provide the most effective treatment. As Von Korff et al. (1987) noted, it would be desirable to have more clinical trials using careful diagnoses, as well as experimental procedures employing different treatment options with general practice patients. Enlisting the cooperation of general practitioners and patients for this type of research might prove difficult, however. In my own research (Barnes and Prosen 1984), which required minimal assistance from doctors and patients, only 44 per cent of doctors and 70 per cent of patients agreed to participate. In more demanding research projects, lower participation rates are common. Parker et al. (1986), for instance, found that only 29 per cent of his potential depressives (as identified by questionnaire) agreed to be interviewed.

There is one other technique that can be employed to obtain an approximation of the treated prevalence for depression. In provinces such as Manitoba and Saskatchewan, certain pharmacare plans cover pharmaceutical expenses. At one time, the Saskatchewan plan was comprehensive, covering all prescription drug use. The Manitoba plan, in contrast, only covers expenditures on prescription drugs in households when expenditures exceed $75.

Harding's research (1978) into the Saskatchewan file revealed that some 3 per cent of the population was receiving anti-depressant medication. Because this figure is fairly close to the estimated prevalence of major depression in the general population (estimated at around 4% by Murphy [1980] in Sterling County and 3.2% by Bland et al. [1988] in Edmonton), the pharmacare files seem to provide a good potential source as to the prevalence of treated depression.

There are at least two other studies of this kind: one was conducted in Italy (Tansella et al. 1986); the other in Great Britain (Royal College of General Practitioners – Birmingham Research Group 1978). In these two studies, the prevalence of antidepressant medications has been reported to be quite a bit higher than that reported in the Saskatchewan study — with a rate of 150 antidepressant prescriptions per 1,000 inhabitants reported in South Verona, Italy; and a comparable rate of 154 per 1,000 reported in Birmingham (Royal College of General Practitioners – Birmingham Research Group 1978). In the Italian research, the availability of a psychiatric case register allowed the investigators to compare the prescribing patterns with the figures for psychiatric treatment for depression in the same region. Results showed that the number of patients receiving outpatient treatment for depression was only about one-tenth the number receiving antidepressant medication. The number of patients receiving inpatient treatment was only one-tenth the number receiving outpatient treatment.

In order to pursue the treated prevalence of depression in the province of Manitoba still further and compare the results with the actual prevalence of depression symptoms as reported by Barnes and Prosen (1984), we decided to examine pharmacare claims in the Brandon and Winnipeg areas for the same period in which the general practitioner survey was conducted (1981). First, the Manitoba Health Service Commission identified a random sample of Brandon (n=1,000) and Winnipeg registrants (n=2,000). Files for each registrant were then searched to identify whether any persons listed in the registrants' households had received antidepressant medication that year. Data concerning the use of antidepressant medication was available with respect to 4,606 people (18 years and over), along with basic information as to their age, sex, and city of domicile. In this sample, 8.7 per cent had received a prescription for an antidepressant medication. The prescribing patterns by age and sex are summarized in Table 7. In order to compare the prescribing patterns for antidepressant medication with the symptom patterns for depression reported in our general practitioner (Barnes and Prosen 1984) and general population (Barnes et al. 1988) samples, we then compared the prevalence rates for antidepressant medication with the prevalence rates for severe depression (that is, CES-D Scale scores of 31 and over). The results of this comparison (see Table 7) show the remarkable similarity between estimated prevalence of severe depression among GP attenders and the

Table 7
Depression rates by demographics in three samples*

Variable	General practice study (Barnes and Prosen 1984) (%)	Pharmacare files (Barnes 1984) (%)	Winnipeg area survey (Barnes et al. 1988) (%)
CITY			
Winnipeg	8.7	8.7	4.2
Brandon	5.7	8.6	
SEX			
Male	5.1	5.0	4.3
Female	9.7	11.5	4.1
AGE GROUP			
18-30	6.7	4.5	5.1
31-45	10.3	11.9	4.4
46-64	10.2	10.6	2.3
65+	5.5	9.2	4.2

*For general practice study, severe depression = score of 31 or higher on CES-D Scale;
For Pharmacare study, severe depression = percentage of patients on anti-depressants;
For Winnipeg area survey, severe depression = score of 31 or higher on CES-D Scale.

percentage of subjects in the pharmacare file receiving antidepressant medication. For example, in the pharmacare file, 8.7 per cent of the subjects
on the Winnipeg claims were receiving antidepressant medication, the exact
same figure as the percentage of Winnipeg general practitioner subjects who
scored thirty-one or over on the CES-D scale. Prescribing patterns by age
and sex were also found to be quite similar to the actual patterns of symptoms
reported in the survey of general practice attenders. Although the percentage
of females receiving prescriptions for antidepressants was a little over twice
as high as the percentage of males receiving antidepressants, the percentage
of female GP attenders with severely elevated depression scores was twice
as high as that observed for males. As well, the pharmacare and general
practitioner studies showed fairly similar distributions by age.

When the results of the general practitioner survey are compared with
those of the Winnipeg area general population sample (see Table 7), it becomes clear that symptoms of depression are much more common among
people visiting general practitioners than in the general population. The ratio
is slightly over two to one in favour of more depression in GP attenders.
It is also interesting to note that this difference occurs only in the female
sample. One of the possible explanations for this large difference in the prevalence of depression among female, as opposed to male, GP attenders could

lie in a sex difference in help-seeking behaviour. Whereas females may be more likely to go to the doctor when they feel depressed, males may simply stay home from work (Selzer et al. 1978). Although doctors have sometimes been accused of overprescribing mood-modifying drugs to women (Cooperstock 1981), our results seem to suggest that doctors' prescribing patterns are following fairly closely the symptom patterns reported by GP attenders.

Although the comparisons described above are interesting and seem to show a fairly good correspondence between the actual prevalence of symptoms of depression and the treated prevalence for this disorder, certain limitations on the data need to be considered. Although attempts were made to make the general practice sample as representative as possible by selecting general practices at random and so on, the low participation rate among doctors indicates some caution may be warranted in generalizing from this sample to all GP attenders. The pharmacare sample was also chosen at random from all registrants in the file, but not all families are registered. Only families who spend over seventy-five dollars per year on drugs and file a claim are included. In Winnipeg, therefore, there were 46,770 registrants out of a total of 305,105 eligible families, a figure that results in a registration percentage of only about 15 per cent. However, even given these limitations, it is likely that the same people who visit doctors frequently would show up in the pharmacare file as having received prescriptions. It is also likely that most people who receive antidepressant medication might show up in the pharmacare file because of the cost of these prescriptions and the length of time that these prescriptions must be taken.

It should also be noted that although the prevalence figures for antidepressant medication in the pharmacare file are very similar to the prevalence patterns for symptoms of depression, the doctors may be giving the prescriptions to the "wrong" people. Remember that we know only that prescriptions are being given out in a manner that is consistent with the symptom patterns expressed by patients attending general practitioners.

TREATMENT OUTCOME. Most of the people with psychiatric problems who are seen by general practitioners are not referred to psychiatrists but are treated by these general practitioners. Locke et al (1966) reported that only 17 per cent of patients with psychiatric problems were referred to psychiatrists by their general practitioner.

Several studies have examined the course of depression among GP attenders. Johnson and Mellor (1977) did a sixteen- to eighteen-week follow-up on nineteen patients treated by general practitioners and found that 51 per cent were fully recovered, 10 per cent were much improved, and 21 per cent were unchanged or worse. Widmer and Cadoret (1978) also conducted a follow-up study of 154 depressed GP patients for six years after the original diagnoses. Of the 154 patients, most had a recurrence of symptoms, with one hundred having one episode, forty-one having two episodes, nine having three episodes, and four having four or more episodes. In a subsequent follow-up study, Widmer and Cadoret (1979) also noted the tendency for repeated depressions to occur among females rather than males.

In a study on depression in GP attenders, Zung et al. (1983) examined the effect of physicians' awareness of their patients' Zung scale scores on treatment outcome. In a sample 143 depressed patients, 102 were assigned to the identified group and doctors were given Zung-screening test scores for this sample. A control sample (n=41) was included for which doctors did not receive any additional information. In the control sample of depressed patients, doctors identified only 15 per cent as depressed. In a four-week follow-up component of the study, depression scores were compared in a group of identified and treated patients (n=25), a group of identified and untreated patients (n=25), and a control group (n=22). Results showed that the identified group, which was treated with antidepressant medication, showed the greatest improvement. Results from this study are important in that they confirm the finding that general practitioners do not generally recognize depression. Results also show that, when depression is recognized and treated by general practitioners, improvements are observed in the patient's condition.

The most common method of dealing with depression in general practice is to prescribe antidepressants. Widmer and Cadoret (1978) noted that of 227 depressive episodes in their sample, 198 were treated with tricyclic antidepressants. Johnson (1974) reported that 61 per cent of a sample of depressed GP attenders in Britain received tricyclics. Johnson (1973, 1974) also observed that general practitioners tend to prescribe rather low, often subtherapeutic, doses of medication, and that patient compliance with drug regimens is rather poor. Patient noncompliance seemed to be most strongly associated with poor communication between patients and doctors (Johnson 1973, 1974).

Recent clinical trials have generally supported the effectiveness of antidepressants in reducing symptoms of depression in GP attenders (Hamilton et al. 1989; Laws et al. 1990). These trials have also attempted to address some of the problems associated with the administration of antidepressants, in particular the problematic side-effects associated with some antidepressant medications. In one clinical trial (Laws et al. 1990), nausea and vomiting occurred in 21 per cent of patients taking fluvoxamine; all patients encountered this side-effect when discontinuing the treatment. In another clinical trial, Hamilton et al. (1989), reported that flupenthixol was just as effective as fluvoxamine in reducing symptoms of depression in GP attenders, and produced fewer side-effects.

Another problem that occurs in general practice concerns the most effective treatment for patients with mixed symptoms of anxiety and depression.

Laws et al. (1990) have reported that fluvoxamine was as effective as lorazepam in reducing symptoms for this group of patients. Antidepressants may be preferable to benzodiazepines, because they are less addictive.

An important consideration in prescribing medication to depressed patients is the toxicity of the medication (Beaumont 1989). The high risk of suicide in this patient group makes drug-prescribing precautions particularly important. Beaumont (1989), after examining the toxicity records of the antidepressant medications, concluded that drugs developed before 1970 were more toxic than antidepressants developed after 1970.

Given some of the problems described above regarding drug therapy for depression in GP attenders, it is important to know how other forms of treatment, such as cognitive-behaviour therapy, might fare with this sample. A recent study by Teasdale et al. (1984) examined the effectiveness of cognitive therapy in a primary-care depressed sample (n=17), with a control group (n=17) receiving treatment as usual. This study was well designed in that the subjects were randomly assigned to treatment groups. The cognitive-therapy treatment included up to twenty one-hour sessions of cognitive therapy along the lines suggested by Beck et al. (1979). The treatment was conducted by experienced therapists and the appropriateness of the therapy sessions was verified by having tape-recorded sessions coded for their appropriateness. In the treatment-as-usual control group, ten patients received antidepressant medications. Results showed that while both groups improved on their depression scores, the group receiving cognitive therapy improved significantly more than the treatment-as-usual comparison group on all three outcome measures of depression. The results of this study suggest that a purely psychological intervention can be effective in reducing symptoms of depression in GP attenders.

SUMMARY AND CONCLUSIONS

Psychiatric disorders affect between 15 and 25 per cent of the general population, with depression being one of the most common psychiatric disturbances. Studies show that only a small fraction (20%) of the people suffering from psychiatric disorders are treated in the specialty mental health sector (Hough et al. 1987). General population studies have also shown that 70 to 90 per cent of depressed patients consult their general practitioner for help (Blacker and Clare 1988). Obviously, general practitioners have an important role to play in the diagnosis and management of depression.

Research on the prevalence of depression has been of two kinds. In the first, psychiatric diagnoses are employed to derive DSM-III diagnoses for depression. In these studies, results have consistently shown that between 7 and 10 per cent of GP attenders meet the criteria for a depression diagnosis. The second type of research has looked at the prevalence of symptoms of depression. Results from this research have been much less consistent, because of the different measures employed, the different cut-points used, and the small and unrepresentative samples employed. When an empirically verified cut-point is used, such as occurred in the Barnes and Prosen (1984) research project, the estimated prevalence of severe symptoms of depression in GP attenders (8%) is very similar to the estimated prevalence of psychiatric cases of depression (7 to 10%), and about twice as high as the prevalence reported in the general population.

Although symptoms of depression among GP attenders may be less severe than those reported in hospitalized depressed patients, with fewer suicide attempts and less psychomotor retardation, the depression experienced by GP attenders is still very debilitating. The presenting symptoms of depressed patients in general practice often include more anxiety and somatic complaints, suggesting perhaps that patients are at an earlier stage in their illness. General practitioners should be aware of these symptom patterns and be prepared to deal with them effectively.

Symptoms of depression among GP attenders are most commonly found in those that are female and of a lower socioeconomic status. Subjects who are divorced or separated are also at greater risk. Depression among GP attenders, although associated with more frequent visits to the doctor, is not necessarily associated with major physical illnesses. Not much research on other risk factors has been conducted in this population. Losses seem to be one other risk factor possibly associated with depression in GP attenders. More research is required on risk factors associated with depression in the general practice population.

With respect to the recognition and treatment of depression in this population, only a fraction of the depressed patients who visit their general practitioner are identified as depressed. Follow-up studies, however, suggest that depression is a recurring phenomenon among GP attenders. Research on the treatment outcome for depressed patients also indicates that when depression is identified and treated by general practitioners, patients often show improvement. The most common form of treatment is antidepressant medication. One possible problem with using this mode of treatment has been the general practitioners' tendency to employ subtherapeutic dosages of medication. Recent research (Teasdale et al. 1984) has demonstrated that cognitive therapy can be used effectively, as well, to treat depression in this population. More research is required, however, to determine the most cost-effective way of delivering this type of treatment.

More research is also needed into the prevalence of depression among GP attenders, the risk factors associated with depression in this sample, and the treatment prospects for this population. In future research, comparisons between studies would be facilitated by the use of common measures of depression and common cut-points. When investigators use a different cut-point than that used previously, results of both should be reported so as to facilitate comparisons between studies. The use of random samples wherever possible would also facilitate such comparisons. More research on risk factors associated with depression in GP attenders is also required. It is interesting that although female GP attenders reported higher levels of depression in the Manitoba research (Barnes and Prosen 1984) than male GP attenders, no differences were found between males and females in the general population (Barnes et al. 1988). It appears that depressed females may be more inclined to visit their general practitioner than depressed males.

Treatment practices and outcomes constitute two additional areas requiring further research. The pharmacare files provide an interesting data source for examining the prevalence of treated depression and the physician's drug-treatment practices. The pharmacare file could also act as a useful social indicator of the shifts in depression in the population. Indeed, the prevalence among pharmacare registrants of prescriptions for antidepressant medication may be a more sensitive indicator of mental health in the general population than other social indicators, such as hospitalizations or suicide rates. People are more likely to be prescribed an antidepressant by their general practitioner, before being hospitalized or committing suicide.

Clearly, given the current high prevalence of depression in general practice and particularly the fact that it is unlikely to decline in the near future, we need some method of dealing effectively with this problem. In the general practice literature, some practitioners argue that screening for mental health problems should be routinely conducted (Kamerow 1987). The short screening instruments of the type developed by Goldberg et al. (1988) might, they say, be effectively used to screen for anxiety and depression in general practice patients. Others (Campbell 1987) have argued that such widespread screening should not be employed, mainly because the rates of false-positives on measures such as the Beck scale would be too high, and the costs for treating cases with minimal levels of depression would overburden the already pressured mental health system. These arguments should be examined in empirical research. As well, efforts should be made to enlist the cooperation of the medical profession in conducting more research into the management of mental health problems by general practitioners.

BIBLIOGRAPHY

Amenson, C.S., and Lewinsohn, P.M. 1981. An investigation into the observed sex difference in prevalence of unipolar depression. *Journal of Abnormal Psychology* 90(1): 1–13.
Barnes, G.E. 1984. Depression and aging: Relevant research. Paper presented

at Second Annual Spring Research Symposium, Centre on Aging, University of Manitoba, Winnipeg, Manitoba.

Barnes, G.E., Currie, R.F., and Segall, A. 1988. Symptoms of depression in a Canadian urban sample. *Canadian Journal of Psychiatry* 33: 386–93.

Barnes, G.E., and Krenn, M.J. 1988. Parental loss during childhood and subsequent adult depression: A meta-analysis. Paper presented at XXIV International Congress of Psychology, August 28 – September 2, Sydney, Australia.

Barnes, G.E., and Prosen, H. 1984. Depression in Canadian general practice attenders. *Canadian Journal of Psychiatry* 29: 2–10.

– 1985. Parental death and depression. *Journal of Abnormal Psychology* 94(1): 64–69.

Barrett, J.E., Barrett, J.A., Oxman, T.E., and Gerber, P.D. 1988. The prevalence of psychiatric disorders in a primary care practice. *Archives of General Psychiatry* 45: 1100–6.

Barrett, J.E., Oxman, T., and Gerber, P. 1987. Prevalence of depression and its correlates in a general medical practice. *Journal of Affective Disorders* 12: 167–74.

Beaumont, G. 1989. Suicide and antidepressant overdosage in general practice. *British Journal of Psychiatry* 155(suppl. 6): 27–31.

Beck, A.T. 1978. *Beck Depression Inventory.* Philadelphia: Center for Cognitive Therapy.

Beck, A.T., Rush, A.J. Shaw, B.F., and Emery, G. 1979. *Cognitive therapy of de pression.* Chichester: J. Wiley.

Beck, A.T., Ward, C.H., Mendelson, M.M., Mock, J. and Erbaugh, J. 1961. An inventory for measuring depression. *Archives General Psychiatry* 4:, 53–63.

Blacker, C.V.R., and Clare, A.W. 1988. The prevalence and treatment of depression in general practice. *Psychopharmacology* 95: S14–17.

Bland, R.C., Newman, S.C., and Orn, H. 1988. Period prevalence of psychiatric disorders in Edmonton. *Acta psychiatrica Scandinavica* 77(suppl 338): 33–42.

Blashki, T.G. 1972. Depressive disorders in hospital and general practice. In *Depressive illness some research studies,* edited by B. Davies, B.J. Carrol, and R.M. Mowbray, 311–22. Springfield, Ill.: Charles C. Thomas.

Blazer, D., Swartz, M., Woodbury, M., Manton, K.G., Hughes, D., and George, L.K. 1988. Depressive symptoms and depression diagnoses in a community population. *Archives of General Psychiatry* 45: 1078–84.

Boyd, J.H., and Weissman, M.M. 1981. Epidemiology of affective disorders. *Archives of General Psychiatry* 38: 1039–46.

Bradshaw, G., and Parker, G. 1983. Depression in general practice attenders. *Australian and New Zealand Journal of Psychiatry* 17: 361–65.

Brown, G.W., and Harris, T. 1978. *Social origins of depression.* London: Tavistock Publications.

Campbell, T.L. 1987. An opposing view. *The Journal of Family Practice* 25(2): 184–87.

Cassell, W.A., Fraser, H.N., and Spellman, A. 1972. Psychiatric morbidity and utilization of insured health services. *Canadian Psychiatric Association Journal* 17: 417–21.

Cooperstock, R. 1981. A review of women's psychotropic drug use. In *Women and mental health*, edited by E. Howell, and M. Bayes. New York: Basic Books.

Coulehan, J.L., Schulberg, H.C., Block, M.R., and Zettler-Segal, M. 1988. Symptom patterns of depression in ambulatory medical and psychiatric patients. *The Journal of Nervous and Mental Disease* 176(5): 284–88.

Craig, T.J., and Van Natta, P.A. 1978. Current medication use and symptoms of depression in a general population. *American Journal of Psychiatry* 124: 1036–39.

Crook, T., and Eliot, J. 1980. Parental death during childhood and adult depression: A critical review of the literature. *Psychological Bulletin* 87: 252–59.

Cummings, N.A., and Follette, W.T. 1968. Psychiatric services and medical utilization in a prepaid health plan setting: Part II. *Medical Care* 6(1): 31–41.

D'Arcy, C. 1976. Patterns in the delivery of psychiatric care in Saskatchewan 1971–1972: An overview of service sectors and patient volumes. *Canadian Psychiatric Association Journal* 21: 91–100.

Davis, T.C., Hunter, R.J., Nathan, M.M., and Bairnsfather, L.E. 1987. Childhood depression: An overlooked problem in family practice. *The Journal of Family Practice* 25(5): 451–57.

Davis, T.C., Nathan, R.G., Crouch, M.A., and Bairnsfather, L.E. 1987. Screening Depression in primary care: Back to the basics with a new tool. *Family Medicine* 19: 200–2.

Durkheim, E. 1951. *Suicide.* Trans. by John Spaulding, and George Simpson. Glencoe, Illinois: The Free Press.

Fahy, T.J. 1974. Depression in hospital and in general practice: A direct clinical comparison. *British Journal of Psychiatry* 124: 240–42.

Frerichs, R.R., Aneshensel, C.S., and Clark, V.A. 1981. Prevalence of depression in Los Angeles County. *American Journal of Epidemiology* 113(6): 691–99.

Freud, S. 1917. Mourning and melancholia. In *Collected papers* 4: 152–72. London: Hogarth Press, 1950.

Goldberg, D.P. and Blackwell, B. 1970. Psychiatric illness in general practice: A detailed study using a new method of case identification. *British Medical Journal* 2: 439–43.

Goldberg, D.P., Bridges, K., Duncan-Jones, P., and Grayson, D. 1988. Detecting anxiety and depression in general medical settings. *British Medical Journal* 297: 897–99.

Hagnell, O., Lanke, J., Rorsman, B., and Ojesio, L. 1982. Are we entering an age of melancholy? Depressive illness in a prospective epidemiological study over 25 years: The Lundby Study, Sweden. *Psychological Medicine* 12: 279–89.

Hamilton, B.A., Jones, P.G., Hoda, A.N., Keane, P.M., Majid, I., and Zaidi, S.I.A. 1989. Flupenthixol and fluvoxamine in mild to moderate depression: A comparison in general practice. *Pharmatherapeutica* 5: 292–97.

Harding, J. 1978. *A socio-demographic profile of people prescribed mood-modifiers in Saskatchewan.* Regina, Sask.: The Alcoholism Commission of Saskatchewan.

Heinicke, C.M. 1973. Parental deprivation in early childhood. In *Separation and depression - clinical and research aspects,* edited by J.P. Scott, and E.C. Senay. Washington, D.C.: Association for the Advancement of Science.

Hellon, C.P., and Solomon, M.I. 1980. Suicide and age in Alberta, Canada, 1951-1977. *Archives of General Psychiatry* 37: 505-10.

Hough, R.L., Landsverk, J.A., Karno, M., Burnam, M.A., Timbers, D.M., Escobar, J.I., and Regier, D.A. 1987. Utilization of health and mental health services by Los Angeles Mexican Americans and non-hispanic whites. *Archives of General Psychiatry* 44: 702-09.

Hough, R.L., Landsverk, J., Stone, J., Jacobsen, G., and McGranahan, C. 1982. *Comparison of psychiatric screening questionnaires for primary care patients: Final report.* National Institute of Mental Health contract no. 278-81-0036 (DB). Rockville, Md: National Institute of Mental Health.

Houpt, J.L., Orleans, C.S., George, L.K., and Brodie, H.K.H. 1980. The role of psychiatric and behavioural factors in the practice of medicine. *American Journal of Psychiatry* 137(1): 37-47.

Husaini, B.A., Neff, J.A., and Stone, R.H. 1980. Psychiatric impairment in rural communities. *Journal of Community Psychology* 7: 137-46.

Johnson, D.A.W. 1973. Treatment of depression in general practice. *British Medical Journal* 2: 18-20.

- 1974. A study of the use of antidepressant medication in general practice. *British Journal of Psychiatry* 125: 186-92.

Johnson, D.A.W., and Mellor, V. 1977. The severity of depression in patients treated in general practice. *Journal of the Royal College of General Practitioners* 27: 419-22.

Kamerow, D.B. 1987. Is screening for mental health problems worthwhile in family practice? *The Journal of Family Practice* 25(2): 181-83.

Klerman, G.L. 1976. Age and clinical depression: Today's youth in the 21st century. *Journal of Gerontology* 31: 318-23.

Klerman, G.L., Lavori, P.W., Rice, J., Reich, T., Endicott, J., Andreason, N.C., Keller, M.B., and Hirschfield, R.M.A. 1985. Birth cohort trends in rates of major depressive disorder among relatives of patients with affective disorder. *Archives General Psychiatry* 42: 689-93.

Kovacs, M. 1982. The Children's Depression Inventory: A self-rated depression scale for school-aged youngsters. Manuscript.

Kovess, V., Murphy, H.B.M., and Tousignant, M. 1987. Urban-rural comparisons of depressive disorders in French Canada. *The Journal of Nervous and Mental Disease* 175(8): 457-66.

Laws, D., Ashford, J.J., and Anstee J.A. 1990. A multicentre double-blind comparative trial of fluvoxamine versus lorazepam in mixed anxiety and depression treated in general practice. *Acta Psychiatrica Scandinavica* 81: 185-89.

Linn, L.S., and Yager, J. 1984. Recognition of depression and anxiety by primary physicians. *Psychosomatics* 25(8): 593–600.

Lloyd, C. 1980. Life events and depressive disorder reviewed. I. Events as predisposing factors. *Archives of General Psychiatry* 37: 529–35.

Locke, B.Z., and Gardner, E.A. 1969. Psychiatric disorders among the patients of general practitioners and internists. *Public Health Reports* 84(2): 167–73.

Locke, B.Z., Krantz, G., and Kramer, M. (1966). Psychiatric need and demand in a prepaid group practice program. *American Journal of Public Health* 56: 895–904.

Lubin, B. 1965. Adjective checklist for measurement of depression. *Archives of General Psychiatry* 12: 57–62.

Maj, M., Starace, F., Crepet, P., Lobrace, S., Veltro, F., De Marco, F., and Kemali, D. 1989. Prevalence of psychiatric disorders among subjects exposed to a natural disaster. *Acta Psychiatrica Scandinavica* 79: 544–49.

Murphy, G.E., and Wetzel, R.D. 1981. Suicide risk by birth cohort in the United States, 1949–1974. *Archives of General Psychiatry* 37: 519–23.

Murphy, J.M. 1980. Continuities in community-based psychiatric epidemiology. *Archives of General Psychiatry* 37: 1215–23.

Myers, J.K., and Weissman, M.M. 1980. Use of a self-report symptom scale to detect depression in a community sample. *American Journal of Psychiatry* 137: 1081–84.

Myers, J.K., Weissman, M.M., Tischler, G.L., Holzer, C.E., Leaf, P.J., Orvaschel H., Anthony J.C., Boyd, J.H., Burke, J.D., Kramer M., and Stoltzman, R. 1984. Six-month prevalence of psychiatric disorders in three communities. *Archives of General Psychiatry* 41: 959–67.

Nelson, G. 1982. Parental death during childhood and adult depression: Some additional data. *Social Psychiatry* 17: 37–42.

Nielson, A.C., and Williams, T.A. 1980. Depression in ambulatory medical patients prevalence by self-report questionnaire and recognition by nonpsychiatric physicians. *Archives of General Psychiatry* 37(9): 999–1004.

Parker, G. Holmes, S., and Manicavasagar, V. 1986. Depression in general practice attenders: caseness, natural history and predictors of outcome. *Journal of Affective Disorders* 10(1): 27–35.

Petrie, A. 1967. *Individuality in pain and suffering.* Chicago, Ill: University of Chicago Press.

Radloff, L.S. 1977. The CES-D scale: A self-report depression scale for research in the general population. *Applied Psychological Measurement* 1: 385–401.

Raft, D., Davidson, J., Toomey, T.C., Spencer, R.F., and Lewis, B.F. 1975. Inpatient and outpatient patterns of psychotropic drug prescribing by nonpsychiatrist physicians. *American Journal of Psychiatry* 132(2): 1309–12.

Regier, D.A., Boyd, J.H., Burke, Jr., J.D., Rae, D.S., Myers, J.K., Kramer, M., Robins, L.N., George, L.K., Karno, M., and Locke, B.Z. 1988. One-month prevalence of mental disorders in the United States. *Archives of General Psychiatry* 45: 977–86.

Regier, D.A., Goldberg, I.D., and Taube, C.A. 1978. The de facto U.S. mental health service system. *Archives of General Psychiatry* 35: 685–93.

Rosenthal, M.P., Goldfarb, N.I., Carlson, B.L., Sagi, P.C., and Balaban, D.J. 1987. Assessment of depression in a family practice center. *The Journal of Family Practice* 25(2): 143–49.

Rosenthal, R. 1986. *Meta-analytic procedures for social research*. Beverly Hills: Sage.

Royal College of General Practitioners – Birmingham Research Group 1978. Practice activity analysis: Psychotropic drugs. *Journal of the Royal College of General Practitioners*. 28: 122–24.

Salkind, M.R. 1969. Beck Depression Inventory in general practice. *Journal of the Royal College of General Practitioners* 18: 267–71.

Schulberg, H.C., Saul, M., McCelland, M., Ganguli, M., Christy, W., and Frank, R. 1985. Assessing depression in primary medical and psychiatric practices. *Archives of General Psychiatry* 42: 1164–70.

Schwab, J.J., Bialow, M., Brown, J.M., and Holzer, C.E. (1967). Diagnosing depression in medical inpatients. *Annals of Internal Medicine* 4: 695–707.

Schwab, J.J., Bialow, M., Clemmons, R.S., and Holzer, C.E. 1967. Hamilton rating scale for depression with medical inpatients. *British Journal of Psychiatry* 113: 83–88.

Seller, R.H., Blascovich, J., and Lenkei, E. 1981. Influence of stereotypes in the diagnosis of depression by family practice residents. *The Journal of Family Practice* 12(5): 849–54.

Selzer, M.L., Paluszny, M., and Carroll, R. 1978. A comparison of depression and physical illness in men and women. *American Journal of Psychiatry* 135(11): 1368–70.

Sireling, L.I., Freeling, P., Paykel, E.S., and Rao, B.M. 1985. Depression in general practice: Clinical features and comparison with out-patients. *British Journal of Psychiatry* 147: 119–26.

Tansella, M., Williams, P., Balestrieri, M., Bellantuono, C., and Martini, N. 1986. The management of affective disorders in the community. *Journal of Affective Disorders* 11: 73–79.

Teasdale, J.D., Fennell, M.J.V., Hibbert, G.A., and Amies, P.L. 1984. Cognitive therapy for major depressive disorder in primary care. *British Journal of Psychiatry* 144: 400–06.

Tennant, C., Bebbington, P., and Hurry, J. 1980. Parental death in childhood and risk of adult depressive disorder: A review. *Psychological Medicine* 10: 289–99.

Tessler, R., Mechanic, D., and Diamond, M. 1976. The effect of psychological distress on physician utilization: a prospective study. *Journal of Health and Social Behavior* 17: 353–64.

Vega, W., Warheit, G., Buhl-Auth, J., and Meinhardt, K. 1984. The prevalence of depressive symptoms among Mexican Americans and Anglos. *American Journal of Epidemiology* 120(4): 592–607.

Vernon, S.W., and Roberts, R.E. 1982. Prevalence of treated and untreated psychiatric disorders in three ethnic groups. *Social Science and Medicine* 16: 1575–82.

Von Korff, M., Shapiro, S., Burke, J.D., Teitlebaum, M., Skinner, E.A., German, P., Turner, R.W., Klein, L., and Burns, B. 1987. Anxiety and depression in a primary care clinic. *Arch Gen Psychiatry* 44: 152–56.

Weissman, M.M., Leaf, P.J., Holzer, C.E., Myers, J.K., and Tischler, G.L. 1984. The epidemiology of depression: An update on sex differences in rates. *Journal of Affective Disorders* 7: 179–88.

Weissman, M.M., and Myers, J.K. 1978. Rates and risks of depressive symptoms in a United States urban community. *Acta Psychiatrica Scandinavica* 57: 219–31.

Weissman, M.M., Sholomskas, D., Pottenger, M., Prusoff, B.A., and Locke, B.Z. 1977. Assessing depressive symptoms in five psychiatric populations: A validation study. *American Journal of Epidemiology* 106: 203–14.

Widmer, R.B., and Cadoret, R.J. 1978. Depression in primary care: Changes in pattern of patient visits and complaints during a developing depression. *The Journal of Family Practice* 7(2): 293–302.

– 1979. Depression in family practice: Changes in patterns of patient visits and complaints during subsequent developing depressions. *The Journal of Family Practice* 9(6): 1017–21.

– 1983. Depression: The great imitator in family practice. *The Journal of Family Practice* 17(3): 485–505.

Williamson, M.T. 1987. Sex differences in depression symptoms among adult family medicine patients. *The Journal of Family Practice* 25(6): 591–94.

Wilson, D.R., Cadoret, R.J., Widmer, R., and Judiesch, K.J. 1987. Anxiety in family practice. *Journal of Affective Disorders* 12: 179–83.

Wilson, D.R., Widmer, R.B., Cadoret, R.J. & Judiesch, K. (1983). Somatic Symptoms: A major feature of depression in a family practice. Journal of Affective Disorders, 5, 199–207.

Wright, J.H., Bell, R.A., Kohn, C.C., et al. 1980. Depression in family practice patients. *Southern Medical Journal* 73(8): 1031–34.

Zung, W.W.K. 1965. A self-rating depression scale. *Archives of General Psychiatry* 12: 63–70.

Zung, W.W.K., and King, R.E. 1983. Identification and treatment of masked depression in a general medical practice. *Journal of Clinical Psychiatry* 44: 365–68.

Zung, W.W.K., MacDonald, J., and Zung, E.M. 1988. Prevalence of clinically significant depressive symptoms in black and white patients in family practice settings. *American Journal of Psychiatry* 145(7): 882–83.

Zung, W.W.K., Magill, M., Moore, J.T., and George, D.T. 1983. *Journal of Clinical Psychiatry* 44: 3–6.

CHAPTER SEVEN

Effect of Unemployment on Depressive Affect

ROBERT J. FLYNN

This chapter reviews recent empirical studies dealing with the impact of unemployment on depressive affect. The first of the five sections, a description of the historical influences on unemployment-related psychological research, discusses some of the major theoretical perspectives from which the unemployment-depression relationship has been approached. In the second section, cross-sectional studies are reviewed to determine whether unemployment is associated with depressive affect. The third section examines longitudinal investigations, to establish whether the association may be causal in nature. In the fourth section, data are presented from the author's own research on re-employment as a "treatment" for alleviating depression in the unemployed. The final section advances suggestions for improving theory, research, policy, and practice. The chapter is intended to be thorough, but not exhaustive, in its coverage.*

Many of the studies reviewed herein assessed a range of the psychological ill effects of unemployment, including depressive affect. In this chapter, however, we are concerned exclusively with the latter. We will also limit our attention to research pitched at the individual, rather than the population-aggregate, level of analysis, for consensus on the appropriateness of analytic methods, as well as on the implications of findings for intervention and policy, is greater in individual than in aggregate-level studies (Dooley and

*The author is grateful for the support provided by Health and Welfare Canada, National Welfare Grants Program (project no. 4555-74-2), and Employment and Immigration Canada for the writing of this chapter. The author bears sole responsibility for the contents of this chapter.

Catalano 1988). One final word: in this chapter, "unemployment" refers to the state of wanting but not having a paid job, while "depressive affect" refers to the dysphoria characteristic of people who are low on pleasure and arousal – the two main dimensions of affective well-being (Warr 1987).

HISTORICAL AND THEORETICAL CONTEXT

Historical Influences on Unemployment Research

The *focus* of psychological research on unemployment in Western countries appears to be directly influenced by the absolute level of unemployment that prevails at a particular time (Kelvin and Jarrett 1985). When the absolute level is high, researchers focus mainly on the psychological effects of unemployment, especially among ordinary people. When the absolute level is low, investigators concern themselves primarily with the psychological causes of unemployment, particularly among persons with special problems. The *amount* of research during a given period, on the other hand, seems to be affected more by the relative rate of unemployment. In other words, when rapid increases in the rate of unemployment occur, psychologists and other social scientists conduct more unemployment-related research than when rates are stable or declining.

Large increases in unemployment rates in North America and Europe during 1929-31 triggered an outpouring of research during the 1930s concerning the effects of being out of work. These studies constituted the first wave of modern psychological research on the topic. During the postwar period, from 1950 to 1970, when levels of unemployment were low and stable, a period of relative quiet was observed, except for research looking at causes of joblessness among the "hard-core" unemployed. More recently, in 1970-71, 1974-76, and 1981-82, major economic recessions occurred in North America and Europe. Marked by sudden and significant increases in unemployment levels, they triggered a second wave of psychological studies that were published mainly during the 1980s. That second wave of research, reviewed here, concerns itself largely with the effects of unemployment on broad sectors of the working population.

Western countries are likely to experience relatively high levels of unemployment in the future, with even higher levels occurring during recessionary periods. Such expectations ensure that governments, workers, and researchers alike will remain interested in the causes and effects of unemployment. The United States, for example, has experienced a long-term rise in unemployment rates: from 4.5 per cent in the 1950s, through 4.8 per cent in the 1960s, 6.2 per cent in the 1970s, and 8.0 per cent or more in the first half of the 1980s (Baily 1987). In Canada, the unemployment rate averaged 9.3 per cent during the 1980s, 37 per cent higher than the average of 6.8 per cent in the 1970s (*The Globe and Mail* 1990a). In selected years, the Canadian unemployment rate rose – from 3.4 per cent in 1966, to 8.1 per cent in 1977, and 11.9 per cent in 1983 (Fortin 1987) – before declining to 7.2 per cent in April 1990 (*The Globe and Mail* 1990b). It increased again, however, during the current recession to 10.6 per cent in August 1991, and to an eight-year high of 11.6 per cent in June 1992 (*The Globe and Mail* 1991, 1992).

The national level of unemployment may hide very different rates of joblessness in different parts, or population subgroups, of a country. In June 1992, for example, Canada had an overall unemployment rate of 11.6 per cent, with the rate in Newfoundland (20.3%) more than two and a half times that of Saskatchewan (7.6%) (*The Globe and Mail* 1992). Similarly, demographic changes during the first half of the 1990s seem likely to improve the job prospects of Canadians aged fifteen to twenty-four, while those in the thirty-five to fifty-four age group may experience unemployment rates that, by 1996, reach more than four times the national average (Foot and Li 1987).

Theoretical Models of the Depressive Impact of Unemployment

Employment status (that is, being competitively employed vs. unemployed) accounts for 10 to 16 per cent of the variance in a person's psychological health (Fryer and Payne 1986). Research on the depressive impact of unemployment has been conducted from both "broadband" and "narrowband" perspectives. Broadband studies typically investigate a number of negative effects, only one of which is depression, and include mediating variables of a relatively general nature. Narrowband studies, on the other hand, concentrate on the single dependent variable of depressive affect, incorporating specific mediators as suggested by the particular theory of depression being tested.

BROADBAND THEORETICAL PERSPECTIVES. Several broadband versions of a basic "psychological deprivation" model have been influential since the 1930s. The model attempts to explain why unemployment usually leads to a decline in many aspects of psychological adjustment (Fryer and Payne 1986; O'Brien 1985). The origins of the model can be traced to two classic works from the 1930s; the first, a review of the psychological effects of unemployment (Eisenberg and Lazarsfeld 1938); the second, a field study of the effects of widespread unemployment in Marianthal, Austria (Jahoda et al. 1933/1972). Both sources provide a historical perspective with which to grasp more easily the second wave of research reviewed later in the chapter.

Eisenberg and Lazarsfeld's (1938) review, often cited even today, synthesized the findings from 112, mainly qualitative, studies, all but two of which were published during the 1930s. Sixty per cent were American, with smaller proportions being of British, German, Polish, and Czech origin. Eisenberg and Lazarsfeld (1938) clearly articulated the basic tenets of the psychological deprivation model, affirming not only that practically all workers in the field concluded that "unemployment tends to make people more emotionally unstable than they were previous to unemployment," (359) but that "there is a general lowering of morale with unemployment" (361). Anticipating some current writers, Eisenberg and Lazarsfeld (1938) also asserted that the psychological deprivation engendered by unemployment unfolds in several distinct stages: the first being a period of shock, followed by optimistic job search efforts; the second a stage of anxiety, pessimism, and active distress that sets in when employment is not found; and the third a period of fatalistic and "broken" adaptation to long-term unemployment.

The second classic study (Jahoda et al. 1933/1972) was an ethnographic investigation of Marienthal, a village in Austria devastated by the closure in 1929 of its only industry, a flax factory. Jahoda and her colleagues took up residence in the village in 1931, collecting data on the effects of unemployment on many aspects of personal and social life (Fryer and Payne 1986). According to a summary of the research that Jahoda (1982) provided many years later, unemployment in Marienthal brought widespread poverty. Indeed, anticipating several more recent studies, Jahoda et al. showed a direct relationship between the amount of financial strain and the severity of the negative psychological effects suffered by the unemployed. Jahoda and her colleagues found that they could classify the four types of family responses to unemployment that they observed – the *unbroken, resigned, despairing*, and *apathetic* (Jahoda, 1982) – according to a scale of decreasing family economic resources. Compared with the unbroken families, resigned families had (on average) 88 per cent as much money at their disposal, despairing families had 74 per cent as much, and apathetic families had only 56 per cent as much.

People in Marienthal appeared to react to unemployment according to well-defined stages. A stage of immediate shock and panic was followed by a period of coping, adaptation, and some measure of recovery; after that, as economic hardship increased, a gradual deterioration in psychological mood frequently took place. Moreover, unemployed men tended to lose their sense of time, and their wives (less affected by the absence of time structure) often complained that they were late for meals. Sleeping increased greatly, such that the waking day was reduced for the average unemployed man to a mere 13.5 hours. In virtually all cases, the destruction of habitual time structures was perceived as a heavy psychological burden (Jahoda 1982).

A sense of purposelessness became widespread, and private activities dropped off considerably. For example, the number of people borrowing library books declined as the length of unemployment increased, despite the abolition of borrowing charges. Subscriptions to daily newspapers, though offered at a greatly reduced price to the unemployed, dropped by 60 per cent. Political organizations and clubs lost between a third and two-thirds of their members. Workers between the prime working ages of twenty-one and fifty came to define themselves occupationally as "unemployed," evidence of the psychological deterioration that accompanies long-term unemployment. When Hitler, with his soup kitchens and promises of work, invaded Austria in 1938, the people of Marienthal welcomed him. Ideology meant little in the face of their life circumstances; they would have supported anyone who gave them employment (Jahoda 1982).

Jahoda (1981, 1982) proposed a broadband functional theory of the effects of work that attempts to account, simultaneously, for the psychological benefits of employment and the deprivations of unemployment. Her theory asserts that work has a single manifest function, that of permitting people to earn a living. She notes four important latent functions of work as well: the imposition of time-structure and activities; the widening and sharing of social experience outside the nuclear family; the linking of the individual to wider collective objectives; and the conferring of personal identity and status. According to Jahoda, these five functions meet central and enduring psychological needs. Thus, when unemployment disrupts the functions, people almost inevitably suffer psychological distress, including depressed mood.

Warr's (1987) environmentally oriented "vitamin" theory is a new, comprehensive broadband model of the links between work, unemployment, and mental health. (Brief accounts are available in Warr 1983, and Warr et al. 1988). Warr explains people's responses to employment and unemployment in terms of nine key, "nutritive" elements ("vitamins") present in their environments, as well as their baseline mental health, coping strategies, and level of commitment to employment. Specifically, he accounts for the finding that unemployment usually decreases mental health, whereas re-employment improves it, by the fact that persons with paid work, relative to those who are unemployed, typically have higher and psychologically more beneficial levels of nine environmental resources: opportunity for control; opportunity to use skills; externally generated goals; variety; environmental clarity; availability of money; physical security; opportunity for interpersonal contact; and valued social position.

NARROWBAND THEORETICAL PERSPECTIVES. Recently, relatively specific theories of depression derived from mainstream social and clinical psychology have begun to inform pychological research on unemployment (O'Brien 1986). Fineman (1983), for example, has conceptualized unemployment as a significant life stressor, whose depressing effects may be alleviated by adaptive coping and social support. Oatley and Bolton (1985) have proposed that job loss may lead to depression when a role that has been primary in providing the basis for a person's sense of identity is disrupted and the person has no alternatives that allow the sense of self to be maintained. Later, Bolton and Oatley (1987) pointed out that their model is but a specific variant of Jahoda's (1982) general approach, according to which work serves important social and psychological needs.

Feather and Davenport (1981) found support for the expectancy-valence theory with their observation that depressive affect following failure to find a job was greater among unemployed youth who were strongly motivated to find employment than among those who were less motivated. Feather and Barber (1983) found additional support for this same hypothesis (and thus for expectancy-valence theory), although their evidence for the learned helplessness account of depression was weak. More recently, Feather (1990) has provided an excellent overview of theoretical approaches to research on the psychological effects of unemployment, in addition to a detailed synthesis of his own programmatic research on the topic.

Furnham (1984) interpreted the results of the British literature as more supportive of the expectancy-valence than the learned helplessness theory, but added that both models may be true under different conditions. Perhaps the expectancy-valence theory is more valid in explaining depression among highly motivated, skilled, and educated unemployed persons, whereas the learned helplessness theory is more valid with individuals who are less motivated, skilled, and educated.

The increasing use of narrowband models is likely to clarify the specific mechanisms linking unemployment and depressive affect. On the other hand, in the absence of an integrative theory, additional narrowband studies will only add to the difficulty noted by Lewinsohn et al. (1985): that there are, indeed, findings consistent with many different theories of depression, but that each theory accounts for only a small portion of the variance. All in all, Warr's (1987) situationally oriented model is the best available broadband perspective for integrating specific findings on unemployment and depression. It is also highly congruent with the cognitive-environmental view advocated in chapter 1 of this volume.

IS UNEMPLOYMENT RELATED TO DEPRESSIVE AFFECT?

To judge whether unemployment is linked to depressive affect, we must first review the relevant cross-sectional studies. Warr et al. (1988) identified two types of cross-sectional studies: CS1 and CS2. The CS1 investigations (the category to which most of the studies reviewed in this section belong) compare the mental health of employed and unemployed people, provide benchmark information, and allow for the examination of possible mediating factors. However, causal interpretation is usually impossible in CS1 studies. For example, is it employment status that affects mental health, mental health that affects employment status, a third variable that affects both, or some combination thereof? Cross-sectional comparisons also usually do not distinguish the potential causal impact of *becoming* unemployed from that of *remaining* unemployed.

The CS_2 studies use a particular form of cross-sectional design, one that compares specific groups of unemployed people at one point in time. Such studies permit inferences about the relationship with mental health of factors within unemployment itself, rather than inferences about unemployment versus employment. They are limited, however, because (by definition) they involve only a single wave of measurement.

Because the psychological effects of unemployment may be quite different in young and adult groups (Donovan and Oddy 1982), we will review the cross-sectional (and longitudinal) studies of youth and adults separately. For example, unemployed youths often have little or no occupational identity; their personal identity is too incompletely developed to help them cope with the stress of joblessness. On the more positive side, they frequently have the option of living with their parents and may not suffer as much financial strain as unemployed adults.

Cross-Sectional Studies of Youth

Four cross-sectional investigations, two British and two Australian, have been carried out regarding the impact of unemployment on depressive affect among adolescents and young adults. No cross-sectional (or longitudinal) studies of Canadian youth appear to have been conducted.

Donovan and Oddy (1982 [CS_1]) were particularly interested in young unemployed persons, most previous research having been done on adults alone. They selected twelve male and twelve female unemployed school-leavers, all sixteen years of age, through the British Careers Service. None had imminent job prospects, a known psychiatric history, or a criminal record. These unemployed subjects were matched with twelve male and twelve female employed school-leavers, also sixteen years of age. Besides being well-matched in terms of gender, age, and educational attainment, the unemployed and employed groups were comparable in terms of racial background, social class, family structure, parental employment, and the number of potentially stressful life events to which they had been exposed in the two years preceding the study.

Depressive affect was measured with the Leeds Depression and Anxiety Scale (Snaith et al. 1976). Analysis of variance (ANOVA) showed a significant effect of employment status, with the unemployed school-leavers manifesting a higher level of depressive affect than their employed peers. As well, females had a higher level of depressed mood than males. Within the unemployed group (collapsing across gender), but not in the employed sample, poorer social/leisure and family adjustment was associated with a higher level of depression and may have mediated the impact of unemployment.

Although the cross-sectional nature of their design rendered a firm conclusion about causal direction impossible, Donovan and Oddy (1982) suggested that unemployment was causing the depressive affect rather than the reverse. First, two-thirds of the unemployed sixteen-year-olds had worked since leaving school; of these, most had been laid off rather than leaving voluntarily. Second, the matching process had produced groups that were equivalent on a number of potential confounds.

Doherty and Davies (1984 [csi]) focused on a question that Donovan and Oddy (1982) had raised but could not answer; that is, whether even a short period of employment, such as that provided by government youth-opportunities programs, "innoculates" school-leavers against the worst psychological effects of unemployment. Doherty and Davies (1984) compared an unemployed group of British adolescents with two other groups, one in a Youth Opportunities Programme (YOP), the other in full employment. The unemployed sample consisted of twenty-five male and twenty-five female youths who had been unemployed for at least nine months. The YOP sample was composed of twenty-five male and twenty-five female youths. Whereas the young men were unemployed but attending a ten-week, government-sponsored training course at a college of further education in such areas as welding and electrical fitting, the young women were participants in a government-sponsored Work Experience on Employer's Premises project. The women were, in fact, on short-term employment (lasting six months), but were attending the college of further education one day per week for courses in office skills. The employed group consisted of twenty-five employed males and twenty-five employed females, between the ages of sixteen and eighteen, who had been working for over nine months; they attended day-release courses at a college of further education (engineering courses for the males, commercial courses for the females).

Depression was assessed with the Rosenberg (1965) Depressive Affect scale. A three-way (sex x employment status x educational level) ANOVA revealed a significant main effect for employment status, with the unemployed group displaying a significantly higher level of depressive affect than the employed or YOP groups. The investigators found that the YOP youths were more depressed than their employed age peers, and that the sex, educational level, and interaction effects were not significant. The unemployed youths also had lower self-esteem, which may have mediated the impact of unemployment on depressive affect. While acknowledging the equivocality inherent in their cross-sectional design, Doherty and Davies (1984) stated that a plausible interpretation of their findings was that unemployment leads to depressed mood.

In his (1982 [CS1]) study, Feather compared seventy-eight employed, and sixty-nine unemployed, Australian young men and women. He predicted that the unemployed youths would display more depressive symptoms than their employed age peers and would also be more likely to attribute both good and bad events to external, less stable, and more specific causes. The employed sample was made up of thirty-nine males and thirty-nine females, the unemployed group of thirty-seven females and thirty-two males. None were students and all lived in metropolitan Adelaide. The employed sample was slightly older (mean = 21.4 years) than the unemployed sample (mean = 19.9). Both groups had left school at about the same age (16.8 vs. 16.7 years). The unemployed youths had been unemployed for an average of thirty-one weeks (median = 18 weeks). Both samples came from families of similar socioeconomic status.

Depression was measured with the twenty-one-item Beck Depression Inventory (BDI: Beck 1967). A sex x employment status ANOVA showed that the unemployed sample had a significantly higher depression score (mean BDI score = 11.25) than that of the employed sample (mean = 5.78). Neither the main effect for sex, nor the employment status x sex interaction, was significant. The unemployed youths had lower self-esteem and higher apathy and, among those with more depressive symptoms, looked for work less frequently. While acknowledging that the higher level of depressive symptoms among the unemployed youths may have been the outcome of repeated negative experiences in attempting to obtain work, Feather felt it was more likely that unemployment had produced the more depressed mood.

In 1983, Feather and Bond (CS1) tested the hypothesis that unemployed persons would have more problems in their use of time, and therefore suffer more depressive symptoms, than the employed. Subjects were respondents who had answered a mailed survey sent to recent graduates of Flinders University in Australia. Whereas the unemployed group consisted of 13 males and 30 females who had been jobless for an average of thirty weeks, the employed sample consisted of 156 males and 99 females who had been in their current full-time jobs for an average of 19.6 months. The mean age of both groups was 26.5 years.

Depression was assessed with a thirteen-item short form of the Beck Depression Inventory (Beck and Beck 1972). A sex x employment status ANOVA showed that the unemployed group had a significantly higher level of depression (mean = 5.44) than that of the employed group (mean = 2.57). Neither the main effect for sex nor the sex x employment status interaction was significant. The mean levels of depression were in the minimal range for the employed group and in the mild range for the unemployed sample, according to the cutoff scores provided by Beck and Beck (1972). As predicted, a more structured and purposeful use of time and a higher self-esteem were negatively related to, and may have mediated, depression in the unemployed and employed groups alike.

CROSS-SECTIONAL STUDIES OF YOUTH: SUMMARY. Several conclusions emerge from the four cross-sectional studies of youth. First, in each case, depressive affect was higher in the unemployed than employed subjects. Second, the average level of depressed mood in the unemployed youths tended to be in the mild range, although the group means reported may have masked more severe levels of depressive symptoms in a minority of the unemployed youth. Third, possible mediators of the unemployment-depressive affect relationship were identified as: gender (females were more depressed in one study but not in two others), social/leisure adjustment, family adjustment, self-esteem (in two studies), apathy, frequency of job search, and time structuring and purposeful activity.

Cross-Sectional Studies of Adults

With regard to adults, Radloff (1975 [CS1]) investigated the effects of social role factors on depression with survey data from the Community Mental Health Epidemiology Program of the Center for Epidemiologic Studies (CES) at the National Institute of Mental Health (NIMH). Interviews with respondents aged eighteen years and over were carried out in representative households in Kansas City (KC), Missouri, in 1971-72 and in Washington County (WC), Maryland, in 1971-73. Radloff's (1975) analyses were based on data from 876 KC and 1639 WC white subjects.

The twenty-item Center for Epidemiology Studies – Depression (CES-D) Scale (Radloff 1977), a gauge of depressive symptoms, was used to measure depression. The unemployed respondents had higher mean depression scores (11.84 for the unemployed KC subjects, 11.34 for the unemployed WC subjects) than either the employed or retired persons (unreported means). A third of the unemployed KC sample and a quarter of the unemployed WC sample had CES-D scores above sixteen, the cutoff above which the possibility of clinical depression should be considered.

A significant interaction was found among the married respondents (excluding housewives), using an employment status (working, retired, unemployed) x sex ANOVA. Women were more depressed than men if working (means $= 9.01$ vs. 7.05, respectively) or retired (means $= 9.86$ vs. 7.59), but less depressed if unemployed (means $= 9.40$ vs. 12.79). Radloff suggested that traditional social norms, according to which married men are expected to support their families, may have made unemployment a more depressing matter for married men than for married women. Such an interpretation is consistent with a frustrated-motivation explanation that is derivable from expectancy-valence theory.

Writing in a special issue of the *International Journal of Mental Health* on unemployment, mental health, and social policy, Margolis and Farran (1984 [CS1]) assessed the consequences of parental job loss on children. They estimated that in 1982, at the height of the 1981-82 recession, 22 per cent of the U.S. work force experienced at least one week of unemployment and that over 13 million children were in families in which the primary wage-earner experienced some loss of work.

With the onset of the recession, Margolis and Farran initiated a study of families affected by parental joblessness. They studied 121 families satisfying the following criteria: presence of a child aged eighteen months to thirteen years, presence of two parents in the home, and experience by the father of either a recent indefinite layoff (experimental group) or the anticipation of continuous employment (comparison group). At the time of the first interview, sixty-six fathers were experiencing a lay-off and fifty-five were employed. The participants were or had been employed in skilled or semi-skilled manufacturing jobs in the private sector in a northeastern U.S. metropolitan area.

Margolis and Farran (1984) used the same measure of depressive affect that Cobb and Kasl (1977) had employed in their influential study concerning the effects of plant closure on adult men. According to Kasl (1979), the measure was a brief scale developed through factor analysis of a large pool of mental health items taken mainly from existing measures. Margolis and Farran (1984) found that unemployed fathers were significantly more likely than employed fathers to feel depressed. The families of the unemployed fathers had lower incomes as well and scored higher on an index of economic deprivation than those in which the father was employed – all of which suggests that the effects of unemployment on depressive affect were mediated by financial strain.

Melville et al. (1985 [CS1]) studied ninety-eight unemployed and ninety-eight employed men in Southampton, England, to assess the effect of unemployment on clinically meaningful depression. The unemployed subjects, recruited at a local unemployment benefit office, were unemployed due to involuntary redundancy. They had been jobless for two to eighteen months (mean = 38 weeks), were twenty-five to fifty years of age and white, and had no illness or disability preventing work. With no part-time work, they had suffered an average estimated reduction in income of 44 per cent. They were matched for sex, age, and social class with ninety-eight full-time employees of a large utility in Southampton.

Depression was measured with the Beck Depression Inventory (BDI). Melville et al. (1985) found that BDI scores were significantly higher in the unemployed, than the employed, group (means = 11.1 and 5.6, respectively). Comparing the unemployed and employed men, 26 versus 9 per cent had BDI scores in the mildly depressed range, 11 versus 3 per cent in the moderately depressed range, and 7 versus 3 per cent in the severely depressed range. Overall, three times as many unemployed men (18%) as their employed peers (6%) scored eighteen or more on the BDI, a score characteristic of clinical depression (Beck et al. 1961). The relationship between unemployment and depressive affect appeared to be a direct one, with no relationship found between the BDI scores and the potential mediators of age, duration of unemployment, social class, marital status, or decrease in income. Although aware of their cross-sectional design's interpretive limitations, Melville et al. (1985) argued that because involuntary redundancy is likely caused by labour market factors rather than pre-existing psychiatric morbidity, much of the depressive affect observed in their subjects was most plausibly interpreted as an effect of being laid off.

In what appears to be easily the most methodologically sophisticated cross-sectional investigation carried out to date, Kessler et al. (1988 [CSI]) reported on the results of a survey conducted in a high-unemployment area in Michigan. They used stratified samples of currently unemployed, previously unemployed, and stably employed persons to estimate the negative effects of unemployment and the positive effects of re-employment. Their cross-sectional study had four desiderata that are often absent in such research: problems of selection bias were taken into account in estimating the impact of unemployment; close attention was paid to social support, self-concept, and coping as potential modifiers of the negative effects of unemployment; possible pathways through which unemployment engenders its ill effects were investigated; and the design of the study was linked to a future intervention program intended to alleviate mental health problems among unemployed persons.

Kessler et al. (1988) interviewed 146 currently unemployed, 162 previously unemployed, and 184 stably employed, respondents. (Detailed information on sampling and other procedures is available in Kessler et al. 1987a.) Overall, respondents had an average age of thirty-five and a mean educational level of twelve years; 60 per cent were male, 20 per cent black, and 50 per cent married. The measure of depressive affect used was the depression subscale of the Symptom Checklist-90 (SCL-90; Derogatis 1977).

Kessler et al. (1988) found that subjects who had experienced one or more episodes of unemployment during the recession of the early 1980s (that is, those who had been previously unemployed but were now either re-employed or unemployed) had higher depressive affect than those who had been stably employed during the same period. Moreover, unemployment had health-damaging effects severe enough to be considered clinically significant. With age, sex, race, education, and marital status statistically controlled, subjects who had experienced one or more episodes of unemployment during the recession had an average depression score that was .27 standard deviation (SD) units above the average score for the sample as a whole, while those currently unemployed had an average level of depression that was .50 SD units higher. Subjects who had experienced one or more episodes of unemployment during the recession had a 55 per cent greater chance of scoring in the highly depressed range (defined as at, or above, the 80th percentile on the SCL-90 depression scale) than stably employed respondents. Selection bias analyses indicated that poor pre-unemployment emotional or physical health was not a confounding variable in these results.

Modifying factors capable of buffering the impact of job loss were also discovered. Social support (integration into an affiliative social network) and a positive self-concept (high self-esteem and low self-denigration) were helpful as resources in reducing the depressive impact of unemployment among currently unemployed subjects. The cross-sectional nature of the design made these findings tentative, however, because depressive affect could have influenced the resources or the respondents' reports about them.

Of several mediating mechanisms studied (financial strain, marital strain, low social integration, and stressful life events), only financial strain emerged as important. It mediated 51 per cent of the total effect of current unemployment on depression and 48 per cent of the total impact of past unemployment during the recession (Kessler et al. 1987b). Unemployment also appeared to create a heightened vulnerability to the negative effects of other, nonfinancial, stressful events; in other words, depressive affect was especially high in unemployed people who were already contending with other undesirable life events.

An encouraging finding relevant to intervention was that re-employment appeared to reverse the negative impact of unemployment. Few differences were found in depressive symptoms between subjects who had been previously unemployed but were now re-employed and those who had been stably employed. Kessler et al. (1988) recommended that interventions should include resources that reduce financial strain, facilitate effective job search, and promote re-employment.

Four cross-sectional Canadian studies bear on the question at hand. The first, conducted by Joshi and de Grâce (1985 [CS2]) evaluated the impact of the length of unemployment (rather than unemployment status itself) on depressed mood and other mental health measures. Subjects recruited at a Canada Employment Centre in Sainte-Foy, Quebec, were divided into three categories comparable with regard to gender, age, occupation, education, marital status, and number of children: forty persons unemployed for one month or less, forty unemployed for six to seven months, and forty unemployed for eleven to twelve months. The subjects included seventy-seven men and forty-three women, with an average age of 29.6 years and an average educational level of 12.3 years. No subjects had attended university.

Depressive affect was assessed with a French-language version of the Beck Depression Inventory (Gauthier et al. 1982). Joshi and de Grâce (1985) found that length of unemployment was unrelated to BDI depression (the mean

BDI scores for the three groups being 5.62, 8.02, and 8.25, respectively). They speculated that high unemployment rates in the Quebec City region at the time of the study encouraged subjects to make external, nondepressogenic attributions about responsibility for their joblessness. The investigators also suggested that the considerable socioeconomic supports typically available to unemployed people may have helped account for the lack of a relationship between length of unemployment and depressed mood.

In a companion study, de Grâce and Joshi (1986 [cs2]) hypothesized that differences in depressive affect among the three length- of-unemployment categories previously defined (1 month or less, 6 to 7 months, and 11 to 12 months) would occur among unemployed university graduates. They also anticipated differences between unemployed subjects with and without university degrees. Their university-educated sample included forty-seven men and thirty-four women; thirty were recently unemployed, thirty had been unemployed for six to seven months, and twenty-one had been unemployed for eleven to twelve months. These subjects had a mean age of 28.3 years. The comparison group, composed of persons without a university degree, was the one used in their previous study (Joshi and de Grâce 1985).

The measure of depression was again the French version of the Beck Depression Inventory (Gauthier et al. 1982). Among the university graduates, the average BDI scores for the two groups that had been unemployed for either eleven to twelve months (mean = 13.4) or six to seven months (mean = 9.3) were higher (p < .01) than the mean for the recently unemployed group (4.78); they did not differ from each other, however. When the 81 university graduates and 120 nongraduates were compared, within each of the three duration-defined classes, the only significant difference in mean BDI scores was found in those unemployed for eleven to twelve months: university graduates (mean = 13.4) had a higher level of depressive affect than the nongraduates (mean = 8.3, p < .01).

De Grâce and Joshi (1986) interpreted their results as evidence that duration of unemployment mediates the impact of joblessness among university graduates. Moreover, as seen among those unemployed for eleven to twelve months, the significant difference in average BDI scores suggested that commitment to employment also mediated the effect of unemployment. This finding is consistent with the frustrated-motivation hypothesis mentioned earlier and provides further support for the expectancy-valence theory.

D'Arcy and Siddique (1987 [cs1]), in a revised version of a paper originally published in 1985, analyzed data from a nationally representative survey of 32,000 Canadians interviewed for the Canada Health Survey (CHS) during 1978-79 (Statistics Canada 1981). Their CHS-derived "depression" measures were, unfortunately, only approximate indices of the construct: a "global unhappiness" index based on Bradburn's (1969) Affect-Balance

Scale, a "psychological distress" summary score based on Bradburn's Affect-Balance Scale, and a sixteen-item "anxiety and depressive symptoms" scale derived from MacMillan's (1957) Health Opinion Survey.

D'Arcy and Siddique (1987) restricted their analyses to all respondents aged fifteen and over who were in the labour force. Of these 14,313 subjects, 87 per cent were employed and 12 per cent unemployed (the latter included both unemployed and discouraged workers). Examining the hypothesis that regions in Canada with higher unemployment rates would report higher levels of depressive affect, D'Arcy and Siddique found no clear pattern of results. Interregional differences were small, and regions with the highest levels of unemployment (the Atlantic provinces and Quebec) did not have higher symptom levels than other regions (Ontario, the Prairies, and British Columbia). On the other hand, within each region, unemployed respondents had consistently higher levels of depressive affect than their employed counterparts, on all three measures. Compared with respondents who were working, those who were unemployed also had higher levels of short- and long-term disability, more health problems, more hospitalizations, and more visits to physicians during the past year, suggesting that physical ill health may have mediated the impact of unemployment on depressive affect. Unemployed subjects who were female, under forty, or had low incomes were especially likely to report high levels of distress.

Acknowledging the ambiguity inherent in any cross-sectional design, D'Arcy and Siddique (1987) interpreted their results as supportive of the hypothesis that unemployment is a stressful event that produces depressive affect. The national, representative sampling frame of the CHS minimized the possibility that depressed unemployed, or nondepressed employed, persons would self-select themselves into the CHS sample. Also, the relationship between depressive affect and unemployment remained even after potential confounds had been controlled statistically: physical illness, disability days, major activity limitations, health problems, and alcohol and drug consumption.

Soderstrom (1988) provided a more disaggregated analysis of the Quebec portion of the CHS data base by conducting separate analyses for married men aged twenty-five to sixty-four, married women aged twenty-five to sixty-four, and youths aged fifteen to twenty-four. Appropriately, Soderstrom considered the CHS measures to be measures of "mental health" rather than "depression." He limited his analyses to 2,493 Quebec respondents who were employed or unemployed and between the ages of fifteen and sixty-four. Soderstrom found that unemployment had important, negative effects on the mental health of most women who experienced it. He also found that the negative mental health effects among unemployed men were significant, even though only a minority were as severely affected as most unemployed women. Negative physical health, especially new health problems experienced after the onset of unemployment, may have been an important mediator of mental ill health in subgroups of unemployed men and women. Finally, among unemployed youths, widespread negative mental health effects were observed. These effects were of lower severity than among the adult subjects, however, and physical ill health did not appear to mediate the unemployment-mental ill health relationship among youths.

CROSS-SECTIONAL STUDIES OF ADULTS: SUMMARY. The results of the eight studies of adults were generally similar to those of youths, except that a somewhat different group of possible mediators was identified. First, as with the youths, unemployed adults in each study had higher levels of depressive affect than their employed counterparts. Second, and again as had been the case for the youths, the average level of depressive affect tended to be in the mild range. This time, however, the investigators occasionally provided percentage breakdowns regarding the dependent variable, depressive affect, which showed that a minority of the adults had moderate and severe (that is, probably clinically significant) levels of depression. Third, a number of possible mediators and moderators of the unemployment-depression link emerged, only some of which had been identified in the studies of youths: gender (in one study, unemployed women were less depressed than unemployed men, whereas the reverse was true in another); financial strain (present in three studies, but not in a fourth); physical health problems (present in two studies); age (observed in two studies, but not in a third); social support (present in one study, but not in a second); length of unemployment (found in one study, but not in another); self-esteem; self-denigration; and commitment to the labour market.

DOES UNEMPLOYMENT CAUSE DEPRESSIVE AFFECT?

Having established that unemployment is indeed consistently related to depressive affect, we now review longitudinal studies to determine whether the association appears to be causal in nature. Warr et al. (1988) distinguished two kinds of longitudinal investigations: L_1 and L_2 studies. The L_1 studies – most of the studies reviewed here are examples of this category – investigate the movement into unemployment as, by and large, a negative event. Data gathered before and after subjects experience joblessness permit longitudinal comparisons within groups of employed and unemployed people as well as cross-sectional comparisons of the CS_1 type at each time point. Such investigations enable several effects to be estimated: the main effect of employment status (employed versus unemployed), the main effect of time (pre-test versus post-test), and, most crucially, the effect due to the employment status x time interaction. It is this last – the interaction effect – that provides the most convincing evidence of a causal relationship between unemployment and depressive affect (Feather and O'Brien 1986; Nunnally 1975; Tiggemann and Winefield 1984).

The L2 studies examine the process and consequences of periods of unemployment. Repeated data-gathering takes place within the jobless situation itself. In addition, L2 studies often involve subjects who have become re-employed by a second interview. This permits auxiliary analyses: CS1-type comparisons between re-employed subjects and their still-unemployed counterparts at follow-up; analysis of the crucial employment status x time interaction term; comparisons of employed subjects' responses with those made when they were unemployed; and CS2-type comparisons at a single time point between subgroups of unemployed persons.

Longitudinal Studies of Youth

Four longitudinal studies, all Australian, have been conducted vis-à-vis youth. In each case, the youths were school-leavers making the transition from formal schooling into the labour market. In what was essentially a pilot study for a later large-scale investigation (reviewed next), Tiggemann and Winefield (1980 [L1]) used a pre-test/post-test design to assess the psychological effects of unemployment on school-leavers in South Australia. In November, 1978, data were gathered on 118 secondary-school students who intended to leave school at the end of the 1978-79 academic year. Seven months later, in June 1979, follow-up data were collected on 102 (86%) of the original respondents. Sixty-one per cent of the follow-up sample were males, 53 per cent were employed (almost all full-time), 25 per cent were unemployed, and 22 per cent were full-time students (the latter were excluded from all analyses).

The main measure of depressive affect consisted of a scale made up of six items applicable to normal groups from the Zung Self-Rating Depression Scale (Zung 1965). The auxiliary measure was a single item that had respondents rating how often they felt "depressed." The employed and unemployed groups (defined in terms of post-test employment status) did not differ significantly on either measure of depressed mood, whether at pre-test or post-test. The unemployed group did become significantly more depressed, however, between the pre-test and the post-test, whereas the employed group did not change. One weakness of this study was the investigators' failure to test for the statistical significance of the employment status x time interaction term.

Tiggemann and Winefield (1984 [L1]) conducted a large-scale test of the hypothesis that unemployed school-leavers report higher levels of depressive affect than those employed. Subjects were 761 youths drawn from twelve randomly selected schools in Adelaide, Australia; they were initially assessed during the school year in 1980 and again a year later. At the post-test, comparisons were made between those who were employed (310 males, 307 females) and unemployed (58 males, 86 females). Depression was assessed by means of Rosenberg's (1965) Depressive Affect Scale as well as by a one-item measure of depressed mood.

Measured by the one-item mood measure, depression was greater among the unemployed than the employed. However, because this difference appeared to have been present while the youths were still in school, depression may have been a predisposing factor rather than a consequence of unemployment. On the Rosenberg scale, on the other hand, a significant interaction occurred between employment status and time: whereas the employed group declined in depressive affect between the pre- and post-tests, the unemployed group did not change. Tiggemann and Winefield (1984) interpreted the significant employment status x time interaction as strong evidence that it was the experience of unemployment (versus employment) that had produced the difference on the Rosenberg depressive affect measure. Possible mediators included gender (females were more depressed than males), self-esteem, boredom, and feelings of helplessness.

Patton and Noller (1984 [L1]) studied fifty-seven males and fifty-six females in their final year of compulsory schooling at an Australian high school. The mean age of the subjects was fifteen. Three groups were studied at a pre-test (when subjects were still in school, or "time 1") and at a post-test five months later ("time 2"): twenty-one employed school-leavers (defined as of the post-test), twenty-one unemployed school-leavers, and sixty-eight school-returners. The Beck Depression Inventory was used as the measure of depressed mood.

Results were strong and consistent. No differences among groups were found at the pre-test. At the post-test, the unemployed school-leavers had higher BDI depression scores (mean = 17.7) than the employed school-leavers (mean = 5.6) or the school-returners (mean = 3.4). There was also a significant interaction between employment status and time, with only the unemployed group becoming more depressed between the pre-test and the post-test. Females in all three groups had higher levels of depression at time 2. Between times 1 and 2, the unemployed group experienced lower self-esteem and higher external control, factors that may have mediated the impact of unemployment. Patton and Noller suggested that the increase in depression in their relatively affluent unemployed group, compared with the lack of change in Tiggemann and Winefield's (1984) less affluent unemployed group, may have reflected a higher motivation to find work. When it went unfulfilled, this greater attachment to working may have contributed to the greater change observed in depressive affect. Such an interpretation is supportive of the expectancy-valence account of depression.

In a large-scale study of Australian secondary-school leavers, Feather and

O'Brien (1986 [L1]) conducted what appears to be the only longitudinal investigation to date to use quasi-experimental controls for testing effects (practice and/or reactivity effects) or historical effects (cohort and/or period effects). Four groups of subjects were studied. Group A was composed of 2,976 students in the last three years of high school in Adelaide, aged fifteen to eighteen, who were tested in 1980 (when they were still in school) and again in 1981 and 1982 (when they were either unemployed, employed, or still secondary or post-secondary students). Group B was made up of 480 subjects who were selected in 1980 but tested only in 1981 and 1982. Group C was composed of 545 subjects who had been selected in 1980 but tested only in 1982. Group D was made up of 930 students from the last three years of high school who were selected and tested only in 1982. All analyses were restricted to subjects who, at a given period, were either students, employed full-time, or unemployed. The measure of depressive affect was a four-item scale derived by factor analysis from a group of twenty-five bipolar adjective scales. The adjective scales were "happy-sad," "elated-depressed," "tense-relaxed," and "satisfied-dissatisfied." Given the large-scale and unusually well-controlled nature of the study, it is unfortunate that a well-standardized measure of depressive affect was not used.

Feather and O'Brien (1986) found no evidence of important testing or historical effects that might have confounded their findings. In two of the three analyses that varied in the time comparisons made and the subjects involved, they found a significant main effect for employed versus unemployed status. This result indicated that not only had group differences existed before the subjects left school but that they had been subsequently maintained. In the same two analyses, they also found a significant employment status x time interaction, with depressive affect increasing for unemployed, but not employed, school-leavers. According to Feather and O'Brien, pre-existing differences between the groups in depressive affect became more pronounced because of the experience of employment versus unemployment. Unemployed youths also rated themselves as less competent, active, and satisfied with life than they had been previously, which was also plausibly attributable to the unemployment experience. They became more likely to blame youth unemployment on external labour-market forces and less likely to attribute it to lack of motivation – a finding more consistent with the expectancy-valence than the learned helplessness theory (Furnham 1984).

LONGITUDINAL STUDIES OF YOUTH: SUMMARY. As before, the yield from these longitudinal studies can be stated succinctly. First, in three of the four investigations, unemployed youths at post-test had higher levels of depressive affect than their employed counterparts. Second, in the same three longitudinal studies, a statistically significant employment status x time interaction was found, a finding that provides convincing evidence that it was the unemployment experience itself rather than pre-existing vulnerabilities that caused (at least partially) the greater depressive affect observed in the unemployed. Third, in the single study (Patton and Noller 1984) using a clinically relevant measure of depressive affect (the Beck Depression Inventory), unemployed subjects had a level of depressed mood (mean BDI score = 17.7) characteristic of clinical depression (Beck et al. 1961). Fourth, several previously encountered, as well as some new, variables emerged as possible mediators of the unemployment-depression relationship: gender (females were more depressed in two of the four studies), self-esteem (three studies), external locus of control, boredom, helplessness, activity level, self-rated competence, life satisfaction, and attributions of responsibility for unemployment directed toward the external labour market rather than internal motivation.

Longitudinal Studies of Adults

In 1979, Kasl (L1) updated his classic 1965-68 prospective study of 100 blue-collar workers who had lost their jobs because of a permanent plant closing (Cobb and Kasl 1977). He and Cobb also examined a control group of stably employed men in comparable blue-collar jobs. Data were gathered during the four to seven weeks before the plant was closed and at six weeks, six months, one year, and two years after it was shut down. Depressive affect was assessed with a brief scale derived, by factor analysis, from a large pool of items borrowed from existing mental health scales (for example, "things seem hopeless"). The depression measure was converted to a standard score (mean = 0, standard deviation [SD] = 1), with the data on the control subjects serving as the basis of standardization.

Before the plant was shut down, subjects who were soon to become unemployed were .35 SD units more depressed than the stably employed controls. Across all occasions during their unemployment, the unemployed subjects were, on average, .55 SD units more depressed than their employed counterparts. Longitudinal comparisons showed that between time 1 (anticipation of the plant closing) and time 2 (6 weeks after the closing), the men who became unemployed showed an average increase in depressive affect of .30 SD units. Those who became re-employed had an average decline in depression of .43 SD units. Between time 2 and time 3 (4 to 6 months after the plant closing), those who remained unemployed experienced an average decline in depression of .39 units, evidence of an adaptational response. The unemployed workers also suffered relatively severe economic and work-role deprivation (that is, loss of the work-related satisfactions of physical activity, keeping busy, doing interesting things, using valued skills, socializing with friends, and so on), which may have mediated the impact of unemployment on depression.

Kasl's (1979) interpretation of his findings was that many blue-collar workers do not experience severe depressive or other negative mental health effects from loss of the work role, because they have abandoned any expectation that work will be meaningful. Other investigators, however, have challenged this interpretation. Frese and Mohr (1987), for example, pointed out that Cobb and Kasl's (1977) study differed from many others in that it was carried out during an economically prosperous period (1965-68). Their unemployed blue-collar workers found new jobs relatively quickly, such that only twelve of their ninety-six unemployed subjects were still without work six months after the plant closing. According to Frese and Mohr, Cobb and Kasl's rather optimistic findings about the depressive consequences of unemployment do not apply to conditions of prolonged unemployment. Payne and Jones (1987) also commented that enduring unemployment was not a strong threat in the region studied by Cobb and Kasl, a situation that precludes their results being generalizable to areas of more chronic joblessness.

Linn et al. (1985 [L1]) investigated the effects of job loss on psychological and physical functioning. Subjects were drawn from a pool of 300 men enrolled in a prospective study examining the impact of stress on health among armed service veterans, aged thirty-five to sixty, at the Veterans Administration Medical Center in Miami, Florida. The unemployed subjects were thirty men who had lost their jobs because of inadequate performance or lay-offs between any two of the interviews repeated every six months. These unemployed subjects were matched for age and race with thirty men from the pool of 300 who continued to work during the study. Depressive affect was assessed at the six-month interview following job loss, using the Hopkins symptom checklist (Derogatis et al. 1974).

Multivariate analysis of variance showed that those who lost their jobs had worse psychological adjustment, including a higher level of depressive symptoms, than those continuing to work. Unemployed subjects who perceived their job loss as relatively stressful, or experienced a decline in physical health, also had higher levels of depressive symptoms. Overall, Linn et al. (1985) suggested that job loss, rather than pre-existing symptoms, was responsible for the higher level of depressive affect in these unemployed subjects.

In a West German study of prolonged unemployment, Frese and Mohr (1987 [L2]) tested two hypotheses: that prolonged unemployment produces depression, rather than the reverse, and that financial difficulties and disappointed hope for control mediate the unemployment-depression relationship. Subjects were fifty-one German, male, blue-collar workers, all unemployed at the initial assessment in 1975. At follow-up, in 1977, twenty-six were unemployed, fifteen were employed, and ten had retired.

A German translation of Zung's (1965) self-rating scale was used to measure depressive affect. Analysis of covariance on the 1977 depression scores, with 1975 depression scores serving as the covariate, showed a significant difference between unemployed and non-unemployed (employed/retired) subjects. Over the two-year period, depression increased among the unemployed but declined in the employed/retired group. Unemployed subjects thus showed no adaptational response to unemployment. Besides their increased depression, they also experienced more financial problems and less hope for control than the employed/retired group. As hypothesized, these variables appeared to intervene between unemployment and depressive affect. Competing mediators – internal versus external locus of control, general activity level, age, and physical illness – were ruled out. Frese and Mohr (1987) suggested that it was the long-term daily hassles that accompany prolonged unemployment (especially financial problems and dashed hopes of control) rather than the one-time event of job loss that had led to depression. They noted that re-employment or retirement appeared to reverse the depressive effect of unemployment.

In their work and unemployment project, Liem and Liem (1988 [LI]) conducted interviews two, four, seven, and twelve months after job loss. The unemployed group consisted of eighty-two families in which husbands had recently lost their blue- or white-collar jobs. All these men had experienced relatively stable employment for at least a year before job loss. The median length of unemployment was four months over the one-year period. Control families with stably employed husbands were matched with the experimental families in terms of family size, husband's age and occupation, age of youngest child, and wife's work status. Liem and Liem (1988) used a measure of depression from Derogatis's (1977) Brief Symptom Inventory (BSI).

Among unemployed husbands, depressed mood was significantly higher two months after job loss than it had been before the event. Four months after job loss, depressive symptoms were even higher. By mid-year, seven months after job loss, depressed mood had stabilized. At the one-year interview, the greatest increase in depressive affect among the unemployed husbands was seen. On the other hand, among initially unemployed husbands who were re-employed at two months, a dramatic decline in depressive symptoms occurred. At seven months, those who were re-employed showed little further reduction in depressed mood. By year's end, however, they exhibited a significant decline in symptoms.

According to Liem and Liem (1988), even though the seven-month data did not indicate an increase in depressed mood among the unemployed, the latter still had a significantly higher level of depression than the employed control husbands. As for the wives of the unemployed men, Liem and Liem found that their depressive affect was not elevated (compared with that of the control wives) two months after job loss. However, by four months, the wives' depression had increased significantly. Overall, Liem and Liem interpreted their data as consistent with the hypothesis that involuntary unemployment generates a good deal of emotional strain, including a rise in depressive affect. This seemed especially true over the short term, and perhaps also over the long term. Both husbands and wives were affected, indicating that unemployment is more than just the unemployed individual's problem. Indeed, the husbands' emotional reactions to their job loss appeared to have an important impact on their wives' emotional reactions. In this study, an increase in husbands' level of depressive affect weakened overall family cohesion, with the result that separations and divorces were 3.5 times more frequent in the families with an unemployed husband.

Liem and Liem found that, one to two months after unemployment had begun, a number of factors – financial strain, interesting and challenging work prior to job loss, previous treatment for emotional problems, and negative life events during the past year – were significantly correlated with depressive symptoms among the unemployed husbands. By the fourth month, however, only financial strain and the degree of interest and challenge in the lost job were correlated with depression. By the eighth month, only intrinsic job satisfaction (in the lost job) was associated with depression. Liem and Liem interpreted the continuing association between work-related variables and depressive affect as consistent with other evidence (for example, that of Feather 1990; Warr 1987) indicating that employment commitment is an important mediator of the depressive impact of unemployment.

LONGITUDINAL STUDIES OF ADULTS: SUMMARY. Several summarizing observations are in order. First, all four longitudinal studies of adults found that unemployed persons had greater depressive affect at follow-up than their employed counterparts. Second, in three of the four studies, re-employment was associated with a reduction in depressive symptoms – a development that strengthens the case for a causal interpretation of the unemployment-depressed mood relationship. Third, a number of familiar variables were acting as possible mediators in these studies: economic deprivation (three studies); work-role deprivation and employment commitment (two studies); stressfulness of job loss; physical health (in one study, but not in another); disappointed hopes for control; negative life events; and prior treatment for emotional problems.

CONCLUDING COMMENT ON THE EMPIRICAL LITERATURE: Feather (1990) has remarked, much as Jahoda (1982) did, that research findings apropos unemployment are a joint product of generic factors common to all unemployed people, group factors applying only to particular categories of people (for example, school-leavers, women, or middle-aged men), and unique factors specific to particular individuals. It would thus be unrealistic to expect a very high level of consistency in the findings from the four sets of studies reviewed. On the other hand, the results do provide general support for Warr's (1987) "vitamin" model, with its emphasis on the key environmental factors necessary for good mental health and the interaction of these factors with individuals' personal characteristics, baseline mental health, and coping strategies. The cross-sectional studies of youth indicated that the unemployed had higher levels of depressive affect than the employed and suggested that deficiencies in the purposeful use of time, in social/leisure and family adjustment, and in self-esteem and sense of control were related to this heightened depressed mood. The cross-sectional investigations of adults also found higher levels of depressive affect in the unemployed, while implicating certain deficits in personal finances, physical health, social support and self-esteem. The longitudinal studies of youth provided evidence that it is unemployment itself that causes depressed mood, implicating such factors as deficits in activity level and feelings of low self-esteem, external locus of control, boredom, helplessness, low personal competence, and dissatisfaction. The longitudinal investigations of adults also supported the causal role of unemployment in depression, implicating financial strain, work-role deprivation, frustrated employment commitment, dashed hopes for control, negative life events, and pre-existing emotional difficulties. All these variables can be related to the environmental or personal characteristics that Warr (1987) has identified as producing good or bad psychological health.

DOES RE-EMPLOYMENT REVERSE THE DEPRESSIVE EFFECT OF UNEMPLOYMENT?

One of the cross-sectional (Kessler et al. 1988) and three of the longitudinal studies (Kasl 1979; Frese and Mohr 1987; Liem and Liem 1988) reviewed here indicate that re-employment alleviates the depressive impact of unemployment. At this point, I shall present findings from my own research that bear directly on this hypothesis. These data are, to my knowledge, the first Canadian data of a prospective, longitudinal nature related to this question – a question that is central from the point of view of intervention.

Study Method

SUBJECTS. Of the 314 disabled or socially disadvantaged participants in a large study examining the effects of self-directed job-search training (Flynn 1991), we studied 238 who were unemployed and looking for work at the point of pre-test, and who had completed the Brief Symptom Inventory (Derogatis and Spencer 1982) at both the pre-test and post-test. Of these 238 individuals, 60 per cent were men, 38 per cent were physically disabled, 33 per cent were psychiatrically disabled, 25 per cent were socially disadvantaged (for example, they received social assistance, were ex-prisoners, and so on), and 4 per cent were learning disabled. Their mean age was 35.6 years (range 20 to 62) and their mean educational level was 12.6 years. Forty-six per cent were single, 27 per cent were married, and 24 per cent were divorced or separated. At the pre-test, subjects had been unemployed for an average of seventeen months (median = 9 months). At the post-test, which occurred about fifteen months after the pre-test, 137 subjects (58%) were competitively employed. Of these, ninety-nine (72%) were employed full-time (35 or more hours per week); eighteen (13%) were employed part-time (20 to 34 hours per week), and twenty (15%) were employed part-time (4 to 19 hours per week). The other 101 subjects (42%) were unemployed. Of these, seventy-eight (77%) were still looking for work, while the other twenty-three (23%) were no longer doing so.

MEASURE OF DEPRESSIVE AFFECT. The depression scale of the Brief Symptom Inventory (BSI: Derogatis and Spencer 1982) was used to assess depressed mood. The BSI scores are normalized T-scores (with a mean of 50 and a standard deviation of 10). Male and female subjects were scored with the appropriate gender norms in order to control for gender differences. At the pre-test, the 137 employed and 101 unemployed subjects (whose employed/unemployed status was defined as of the post-test) had virtually identical means (61.9 and 62.0, respectively; t [236] $= -.02, p = .99$). Of the combined sample, 35 per cent had BSI depression scores of sixty-five or above, and 24 per cent had scores of seventy or above. Hence, at the pre-test, when all subjects were unemployed, they displayed a relatively high level of depressive symptoms.

DATA ANALYSIS. A split-plot factorial ANOVA, with a least-squares solution (Kirk 1968) for unequal n's, was used to analyse the data. Employment status was a between-subjects factor, time of assessment a within-subjects factor. The employment status x time interaction term was of primary interest, given the longitudinal design used (Feather and O'Brien 1986; Nunnally 1975).

Study Results and Discussion

Figure 1 displays the group means and interaction. The ANOVA revealed that the effect due to the employment status x time interaction was significant (F [1, 236] $= 4.68, p < .05$), the main effect due to employment status was not significant (F [1, 236] $= 1.61, p > .21$), and the main effect for time was significant (F [1, 236] $= 18.08, p < .001$).

Tests of simple main effects showed that, at the post-test, subjects who were re-employed had a significantly lower level of depressive affect than those who remained unemployed (t [236] $= -2.14, p < .05$). Only the re-

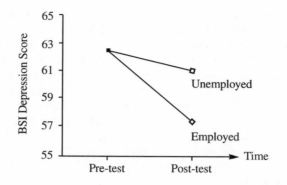

Figure 1
Pre-test and post-test means for the Brief Symptom Inventory (BSI) depression scale (subjects unemployed at pre-test, but employed [n = 137] or unemployed [n = 101] at post-test).

employed group experienced a significant reduction in depressive symptoms over the fifteen-month period separating the pre- and post-test (t [136] = 4.97, $p < .001$). The unemployed group showed no such change (t [100] = 1.36, $p > .18$).

These findings are consistent with those of several other studies reviewed earlier and indicate that becoming re-employed has a beneficial impact on depressive symptoms. The implications are encouraging for interventions such as job-search training and job placement.

SUGGESTIONS FOR THEORY, RESEARCH, POLICY, AND PRACTICE

It remains for us, in this concluding section, to identify and discuss briefly some of the main implications of the reviewed work for improvements in theoretical understanding, research and evaluation, social policy, and clinical practice.

Theory

Warr's (1987) model of the relationship between work, unemployment, and mental health is particularly promising in terms of its ability to integrate the numerous specific findings that diverse theoretical perspectives have generated regarding the unemployment/re-employment/depressive affect relationship. The model has a useful balance between environmental and personal-cognitive features. On the personal-cognitive side, Warr (1987) affirms the importance of baseline mental health (for example, neuroticism, self-esteem, a belief in control over what happens in life) and personal coping strategies as either predisposing or protecting factors in the face of negative features of the unemployment environment. Other personal-cognitive elements include demographic features (age, gender, ethnic group membership), abilities (intellectual, interpersonal, and psychomotor skills), and general values and specific attitudes.

On the environmental side, the usually negative effect of unemployment and the typically beneficial effect of employment are accounted for in terms of nine situational elements with which the personal-cognitive variables may interact: opportunity for control, opportunity for skill use, externally generated goals, variety, environmental clarity, availability of money, physical security, opportunity for interpersonal contact, and valued social position. Warr (1987) explains, for example, the psychological deterioration that takes place during the early months of unemployment in terms of a decline in the availability of money, increasing worry that important skills are being lost, a growing inability to plan, and decreasing social contacts through entertainment activities that require money. These environmental elements interact with a particular individual's baseline mental health, demographic characteristics, abilities, and attitudes and values to produce a given level of depressive and other symptoms. Similarly, the frequently observed low-level stabilization (rather than continued decline) in an unemployed person's mental health after three to six months is explained mainly in terms of environmental clarity: the uncertainty of the early period of joblessness is replaced by the certainty of now familiar daily activities and routines.

The rapid improvement usually seen in unemployed people who find suitable jobs is explainable in the same terms. With the transition back to employment, the person's opportunities for interpersonal contact, availability of money, and valued social position all improve. Opportunities for use of skills, externally generated goals, and environmental clarity also become more favourable. The interaction of people's personal characteristics with these environmental features determines the extent to which their affective well-being will improve (Warr 1987). In his positive evaluation of Warr's model, Feather (1990) observed that his own research has pointed to two especially influential environmental conditions in unemployed individuals' negative reactions to their joblessness: lack of money and lack of structure and purpose in life.

Research

In an area that has tended to be overly practical in orientation, there is clearly room for new theoretically oriented studies (see Feather 1990, and Warr 1987, for a wide range of suggestions). Such studies should employ large samples and be longitudinal in design. In some, instruments such as the Diagnostic Interview Schedule should be used along with more traditional symptom measures, in order to permit an evaluation of the impact of unemployment and re-employment on both clinical depression and depressive affect. To date, such studies are almost entirely absent from the literature (Kates et al. 1990).

Second, programmatic research would be greatly facilitated if government departments such as Employment and Immigration Canada (EIC) were to invest in investigator-initiated studies of unemployment and re-employment issues. Given the billions of dollars spent by EIC each year on job training and job placement, the allocation of a few million dollars for field-initiated research would be both cost-effective and informative for program design. Even the routine inclusion of selected personal, environmental, and mental health variables of the type suggested by Warr's (1987) model would be a great improvement to the current, fiscally oriented evaluations.

Third, research should go beyond identifying the "main effects" of unemployment. The studies reviewed in this chapter consistently show that such main effects exist. What is needed now is research into the specific mechanisms involved and the interventions that take these mechanisms into account. The guidance that only good theory can provide will become all the more necessary.

Policy

For policymakers, the major lessons of this chapter are twofold: unemployment indeed causes depressive affect, and re-employment is an effective way of treating the problem. Policies that foster employment and reduce demand-deficient, structural, and frictional unemployment are, thus, the indispensable first line of defence.

A second line of defence is also needed, however, for the many individuals who want paid work but cannot seem to obtain it. Warr (1987) suggests a number of helpful environmental modifications: the provision of adequate income support; development of attractive and effective job-training and job-search programs; creation of centres for unemployed workers (Forrester and Ward 1986); development of resource networks and skill exchanges (Senior and Naylor 1984); creation of unpaid work roles within voluntary agencies; and development of subsidized adult education and leisure options.

Practice

Vocational counsellors and other practitioners should expect to find mild or moderate levels of depressive affect in many of their unemployed clients and clinical depression in a minority. They should thus be familiar with psychometric and diagnostic instruments designed to assess depressive affect and clinical depression, in order to make informed referral decisions. They also need to be acutely aware of the psychological ill effects of unemployment and of the major mental health benefits of re-employment. The research reviewed in this chapter should help practitioners better understand why work-related problems, along with marital distress and interpersonal losses, have a particularly strong relationship to the subsequent development of depression (Lewinsohn et al. 1985).

As well, mental health practitioners need to recognize that both effective vocational assessment and career counselling are important strategies for reducing depressive symptoms and improving other aspects of mental health (Bluestein 1987; Brown and Brooks 1985). The need for practitioners with well-developed skills in this area will continue to grow as rapid labour-market transformations render the experience of unemployment and career change increasingly commonplace.

BIBLIOGRAPHY

Baily, M.N. 1987. Rising unemployment in the United States. In *Unemployment: International perspectives*, edited by M. Gunderson, N.M. Meltz, and S. Ostry, (63–73). Toronto: University of Toronto Press.

Beck, A.T. 1967. *Depression: Clinical, experimental and theoretical aspects*. New York: Harper & Row.

Beck, A.T., and Beck, R.W. 1972. Screening depressed patients in family practice: A rapid technic. *Postgraduate Medicine* 52: 81–85.

Beck, A.T., Ward, C.H., Mendelson, M., Mock, J., and Erbaugh, J. 1961. An inventory for measuring depression. *Archives of General Psychiatry* 4: 561–71.

Bluestein, D.L. 1987. Integrating career counseling and psychotherapy: A comprehensive treatment strategy. *Psychotherapy* 24: 794–99.

Bolton, W., and Oatley, K. 1987. A longitudinal study of social support and depression in unemployed men. *Psychological Medicine* 17: 453–60.

Bradburn, N.M. 1969. *The structure of psychological well-being*. Chicago: Aldine.

Brown, D., and Brooks, L. 1985. Career counseling as a mental health intervention. *Professional Psychology* 16: 860–67.

Cobb, S., and Kasl, S.V. 1977. *Termination: The consequences of job loss*. Cincinnati: Department of Health, Education, and Welfare, National Institute of Occupational Safety and Health, Publication no. 77-224.

D'Arcy, C.M., and Siddique, C.M. 1985. Unemployment and health: An analysis of Canadian Health Survey data. *International Journal of Health Services* 15: 609–35.

– 1987. Health and unemployment: Findings from a national survey. In *Health and Canadian society: Sociological perspectives* 2d ed., edited by D. Coburn, C. D'Arcy, G. M. Torrance, & P. New, 239–61. Markham, ON: Fitzhenry & Whiteside.

De Grâce, G.R., and Joshi, P. 1986. Estime de soi, solitude et dépression chez les chômeurs diplômés d'université selon la durée du chômage: Une comparaison avec les non diplômés. *Revue Canadienne de Sante Mentale Communautaire* 5: 99-109.

Derogatis, L.R. 1977. *SCL-90*: Administration, scoring and procedures manual for the revised version. Baltimore, Md: Johns Hopkins University School of Medicine, Clinical Psychometrics Research Unit.

Derogatis, L.R., Lipman, R.S., Rickels, D., Uhlenhuth, E.H., and Covi, L. 1974. The Hopkins symptom checklist: A self-report inventory. *Behavioral Science* 19: 1-15.

Derogatis, L.R., and Spencer, P.M. 1982. *The Brief Symptom Inventory: Administration, scoring and procedures manual*. Baltimore: Clinical Psychometric Research.

Doherty, J., and Davies, C. 1984. The psychological effects of unemployment on a group of adolescents. *Educational Review* 36: 218-28.

Donovan, A., and Oddy, M. 1982. Psychological aspects of unemployment: An investigation into the emotional and social adjustment of school leavers. *Journal of Adolescence* 5: 15-30.

Dooley, D., and Catalano, R. 1988. Recent research on the psychological effects of unemployment. *Journal of Social Issues* 44(4): 1-12.

Eisenberg, P., and Lazarsfeld, P.F. 1938. The psychological effects of unemployment. *Psychological Bulletin* 35: 358-90.

Feather, N.T. 1982. Unemployment and its psychological correlates: A study of depressive symptoms, self-esteem, Protestant ethic values, attributional style, and apathy. *Australian Journal of Psychology* 34: 309-23.

– 1990. *The psychological impact of unemployment*. New York: Springer-Verlag.

Feather, N.T., and Barber, J.G. 1983. Depressive reactions and unemployment. *Journal of Abnormal Psychology* 92: 185-95.

Feather, N.T., and Bond, M.J. 1983. Time structure and purposeful activity among employed and unemployed university graduates. *Journal of Occupational Psychology* 56: 241-54.

Feather, N.T., and Davenport, P.R. 1981. Unemployment and depressive affect: A motivational and attributional analysis. *Journal of Personality and Social Psychology* 41: 422-36.

Feather, N.T., and O'Brien, G.E. 1986. A longitudinal study of the effects of employment and unemployment on school-leavers. *Journal of Occupational Psychology* 59: 121-44.

Fineman, S. 1983. *White collar unemployment*. Chichester, U.K.: Wiley.

Flynn, R.J. 1991. Matching job-search training interventions with client characteristics: Employment outcomes. *Canadian Journal of Rehabilitation* 4: 133-43.

Foot, D.K., and Li, J.C. 1987. Demographic determinants of unemployment. In *Unemployment: International perspectives*, edited by M. Gunderson, N.M. Meltz, and S. Ostry, 140-51. Toronto: University of Toronto Press.

Forrester, K., and Ward, K. 1986. Organising the unemployed? The TUC and the unemployed workers centres. *Industrial Relations Journal* 17: 46-56.

Fortin, P. 1987. Unemployment in Canada: Macroeconomic disease, macroeconomic cure. In *Unemployment: International perspectives*, edited by M. Gunderson, N.M. Meltz, and S. Ostry, 74–83. Toronto: University of Toronto Press.

Frese, M., and Mohr, G. 1987. Prolonged unemployment and depression in older workers: A longitudinal study of intervening variables. *Social Science and Medicine* 25: 173–78.

Fryer, D., and Payne, R. 1986. Being unemployed: A review of the literature on the psychological experience of unemployment. In *International review of industrial and organizational psychology* 1986, edited by C.L. Cooper and I. Robertson, 235–78. Chichester, U.K.: John Wiley.

Furnham, A. 1984. Unemployment, attribution theory, and mental health: A review of the British literature. *International Journal of Mental Health* 13(1–2): 51–67.

Gauthier, J., Theriault, F., and Morin, C. 1982. Adaptation française d'une mesure d'auto-évaluation de l'intensité de la dépression (Beck). *Revue Québécoise de Psychologie* 3(2): 13–27.

Globe and Mail (The) 1990a. Jobless rate 9.3% in 1980s: Statscan, 20 March, p. B8.

Globe and Mail (The) 1990b. Jobless rate edges lower in June, 7 July, p. B3.

Globe and Mail (The) 1991. August jobless rate hits six-year high, 7 September, p. B3.

Globe and Mail (The) 1992. Jobless rate rises to eight-year high, 11 July, p. B1

Glyptis, S. 1983. Business as usual? Leisure provisions for the unemployed. *Leisure Studies* 2: 287–300.

Jahoda, M. 1981. Work, employment, and unemployment: Values, theories, and approaches in social research. *American Psychologist* 36: 184–91.

– 1982. *Employment and unemployment: A social-psychological analysis.* Cambridge, U.K.: Cambridge University Press.

Jahoda, M., Lazarsfeld, P.F., and Zeisel, H. 1933/1972. *Marienthal: The sociography of an unemployed community.* London: Tavistock Publications.

Joshi, P., and de Grâce, G.R. 1985. Estime de soi, dépression, solitude et communication émotive selon la durée du chômage. *Revue Québécoise de Psychologie* 6(3): 3–21.

Kasl, S.V. 1979. Changes in mental health status associated with job loss and retirement. In *Stress and mental disorder*, edited by J.E. Barrett, R.M. Rose, and G.L. Klerman, 179–200. New York: Raven.

Kates, N., Grieff, B.S., and Hagen, D.Q. 1990. *The psychosocial impact of job loss.* Washington, D.C.: American Psychiatric Press.

Kelvin, P., and Jarrett, J.E. 1985. *Unemployment: Its social psychological effects.* Cambridge: Cambridge University Press.

Kessler, R.C., House, J.S., and Turner, J.B. 1987a. Unemployment and health in a community sample. *Journal of Health and Social Behavior* 28: 51–59.

Kessler, R.C., Turner, J.B., and House, J.S. 1987b. Intervening processes in the relationship between unemployment and health. *Psychological Medicine* 17: 949–61.

Kessler, R.C., Turner, J.B., and House, J.S. 1988. Effects of unemployment on health in a community survey: Main, modifying, and mediating effects. *Journal of Social Issues* 44(4): 69–85.

Kirk, R.E. 1968. *Experimental design: Procedures for the behavioral sciences.* Belmont, Calif.: Brooks/Cole.

Lewinsohn, P.M., Hoberman, H., Teri, L., and Hautzinger, M. 1985. An integrative theory of depression. In *Theoretical issues in behavior theory*, edited by S. Reiss and R. Bootzin, 331–59. New York: Academic.

Liem, R., and Liem, J.H. 1988. Psychological effects of unemployment on workers and their families. *Journal of Social Issues* 44(4): 87–105.

Linn, M.W., Sandifer, R., and Stein, S. 1985. Effects of unemployment on mental and physical health. *American Journal of Public Health* 75: 502–506.

MacMillan, A.M. 1957. The Health Opinion Survey: Techniques for estimating prevalence of psychoneurotic and related types of disorders in communities. *Psychological Reports* 3: 325–39.

Margolis, L.H., and Farran, D.C. 1984. Unemployment and children. *International Journal of Mental Health* 13: 107–24.

Melville, D.I., Hope, D., Bennison, D., and Barraclough, B. 1985. Depression among men made involuntarily redundant. *Psychological Medicine* 15: 789–93.

Nunnally, J.C. 1975. The study of change in evaluation research: Principles concerning measurement, experimental design, and analysis. In *Handbook of evaluation research*, edited by E.L. Struening & M. Guttentag, Vol. 1, 101–37. Beverly Hills, Calif.: Sage.

Oatley, K., and Bolton, W. 1985. A social-cognitive theory of depression in reaction to life events. *Psychological Review* 92: 372–88.

O'Brien, G.E. 1985. Distortion in unemployment research: The early studies of Bakke and their implications for current research on employment and unemployment. *Human Relations* 38: 877–94.

– 1986. *Psychology of work and unemployment.* Chichester: Wiley.

Patton, W., and Noller, P. 1984. Unemployment and youth: A longitudinal study. *Australian Journal of Psychology* 36: 399–413.

Payne, R., and Jones, J.G. 1987. Social class and re-employment: Changes in health and perceived financial circumstances. *Journal of Occupational Behaviour* 8: 175–84.

Radloff, L. 1975. Sex differences in depression: The effects of occupation and marital status. *Sex Roles* 1: 249–65.

Radloff, L.S. 1977. The CES-D scale: A self-report depression scale for research in the general population. *Applied Psychological Measurement* 1: 385–401.

Rosenberg, M. 1965. *Society and the adolescent self-image.* Princeton, N.J.: Princeton University Press.

Senior, B., and Naylor, J.B. 1984. A skills exchange for unemployed people. *Human Relations* 37: 589–602.

Snaith, R.P., Bridge, W.K., and Hamilton, M. 1976. The Leeds scale for the self assessment of anxiety and depression. *British Journal of Psychiatry* 128: 156–165.

Soderstrom, L. 1988. Some effects of unemployment on the health of unemployed Quebec workers. *Relations Industrielles* 43: 341–77.

Statistics Canada 1981. *The health of Canadians: Report of the Canada Health Survey.* Catalogue no. 82–538. Ottawa: Supply and Services Canada.

Tiggemann, M., and Winefield, A.H. 1980. Some psychological effects of unemployment in school-leavers. *Australian Journal of Social Issues* 15: 269–76.

– 1984. The effects of unemployment on the mood, self-esteem, locus of control, and depressive affect of school-leavers. *Journal of Occupational Psychology* 57: 33–42.

Warr, P. 1983. Work, jobs, and unemployment. *Bulletin of the British Psychological Association* 36: 305–11.

– 1987. *Work, unemployment, and mental health.* Oxford: Clarendon.

Warr, P., Jackson, P., and Banks, M. 1988. Unemployment and mental health: Some British studies. *Journal of Social Issues* 44(4): 47–68.

Zung, W.W.K. 1965. A self-rating depression scale. *Archives of General Psychiatry* 12: 63–70.

CHAPTER EIGHT

Depression in Canadian Native Indians

HARVEY ARMSTRONG

To understand the problem of depression among Native Indians in Canada, it is essential to begin with some basic information concerning their history, culture, and current socioeconomic situation.*

A BRIEF INTRODUCTION TO THE NATIVE INDIANS OF CANADA

Cultural and Socioeconomic Diversity

The geographic, cultural, and economic context in which Canada's Native Indians live is often very different from that of other Canadians. Canadian Indians comprise ten distinct language groups and speak more than fifty-eight dialects (Department of Indian and Northern Affairs 1980a; Jenness 1977; Maclean 1982). Cultural differences among Indian peoples are great, often exceeding those between Italians and Russians.

Certain similarities hide these differences from non-Native eyes. For example, the Indian's skin is light brown and their hair straight and black. Their traditions are oral, their capital is social and spiritual rather than ma-

*Although a non-Native, the author has worked with Native Indians for nearly twenty years as a psychiatrist with the University of Toronto-Sioux Lookout (Ontario) mental health program. During this period he served as a member and past chairperson of the section on Native mental health of the Canadian Psychiatric Association. He is also the current director of the Native Mental Health Association of Canada.

terial, and their tolerance for other cultures very great. Unfortunately, from their first contacts with Europeans, they were taught that their ways of being are inferior – a message reinforced by their material poverty and limited ability to manufacture goods (Adams 1975; Bailey 1969; Department of Indian and Northern Affairs 1980a; Haycock 1971; Jennings 1976; LaRoque 1975). The exercise of substantial control over their lives by a federal government department and media depictions that were often sensationalized and paternalistic made them even less self-confident.

The 2,300 reserves on which Canadian Indians live are very diverse (Department of Indian and Northern Affairs 1980b). Some are located in mountain, prairie, boreal, or sub-arctic settings; others are on rich farm land; still others are situated in metropolitan downtown areas. Many of Canada's 580 Indian bands, particularly those in British Columbia, have more than one reserve. A few bands are extremely rich because of enormous oil reserves, while others are extremely poor with no economic base other than welfare. Some Indian reserves have thousands of inhabitants, while others have only twenty to thirty. In some of the smaller tribes, few or no members still speak the original language. Few of the original languages are expected in fact, to survive, because they lack support in government or academia.

Post-contact historical developments magnified pre-existing differences among Indian groups. For example, English would not be spoken in Canada today had the Iroquois not fought to contain the French in Quebec, nor would Canada be separate from the United States had the Iroquois not sided with the British. A grateful Canada gave the Iroquois special advantages, including productive farmland as reserves and a long history of educational support (McMillan 1988; Patterson 1972). Since the War of 1812, there have been many highly educated and successful Iroquois and Micmac. In contrast, until recently, some northern reserves have had few English-speaking residents, and many have yet to produce a high-school graduate.

The Cree and the Chippaweyan and their allies, initially trading out of Hudson's Bay and then adapting to the North West Company, helped to create a pattern of trade that supported the development of a separate Canadian nation. There is evidence that Cree trappers took considerable pains to keep Yankee traders and their Indian allies south of the current Canada-U.S. border by overtrapping the border area.

Confusion exists as to who is, or is not, an Indian. People of Canadian Native ancestry number well over one million and include Métis, Inuit, and Indians with and without official status. Although many Indians once had Indian status, they, according to the fashion of the time, gave it up by leaving the reserve or, in the case of female Indians, by marrying a non-Native (Department of Indian and Northern Affairs 1980b; Patterson 1972).

Currently, about 350,000 Indians have band numbers (Department of Indian and Northern Affairs 1980b). Some of these numbers were assigned through treaties. In other cases, however, particularly in western Canada, treaties were never forthcoming. The Crown simply assigned traditional hunting and fishing lands to new owners without the conquests or purchases that had occurred in the older parts of Canada. This situation is currently being addressed as the dominant culture faces the illegality of these acquisitions.

Members of Indian groups that signed treaties were called "treaty Indians." These groups gave up their hunting and fishing lands to the federal government in exchange for federal financial support, services, and goods. Adult group members and their children received band numbers, entitling them to basic government services; these services increased as government programs expanded. Although certain of the Indians' rights were guaranteed in treaties, some were later abrogated (for example, Native Indians have sometimes been prosecuted for hunting migratory birds under laws passed after the treaties guaranteeing their hunting rights). Overall, the Indians of Canada obtained very little in exchange for their land; the services they now receive are minimal compared to what they gave up (McMillan 1988).

The province of Ontario has the greatest number of treaty Indians, about 70,000. These are Indians whose names are on band lists and who belong to bands toward which the government of Canada has certain recognized obligations. Many treaty Indians in Ontario live in remote areas where they are not visible to the dominant culture. About a third, however, live away from their reserves, in cities, including some 35,000 in Toronto. They are becoming less and less visible, resembling poorly dressed Orientals in the eyes of many members of the dominant culture. Even Indians with band numbers cease to receive special services when they live in the city. Not only are they abandoned by the federal government but also by their band councils, who no longer feel responsible for members' welfare once they have left the reserves.

In provinces with much smaller non-Native populations than Ontario, Natives are sometimes still highly visible. In Saskatchewan and Manitoba, in particular, there seem to be many Indians in the cities. Native people migrate to the urban areas in hopes of a better life but, because of deficits in formal education and job skills, they frequently end up on the urban welfare rolls. Their numbers in urban areas are increasing as they seek environments in which employment, running water, and electricity are available.

Indian Values

DISCREDITATION. The Indians' medicines and religions, even their familial values, were initially discredited by the white man. Indian medicine, able to cope with pre-contact but not post-contact diseases, offered no resistance when faced with smallpox, tuberculosis, typhus, tularemia Type B, influenza, measles and chicken pox. Some 90 per cent of the Native population was accordingly swept into the grave. These losses discredited Indian medicine and the accompanying spiritual values (Bishop 1974; Martin 1978).

The Potlatch laws of 1885 in British Columbia legalized the suppression of native religions, with the result that the Indian religion was deemed illegal until the revision of the federal Indian Act in 1951. Between 1885 and 1951, Native Indians were threatened and even jailed for practising their religions, although these religions emphasized unity and harmony with nature rather than dominance over it. Despite threats from the police, civil servants, and missionaries, a few elders continued to practise their religions.

Two or three generations of Indians were forcibly taken from their families and placed in church-operated residential schools between the ages of six and sixteen. They often lost their language, religion, culture, values, links with their family and village, even the ability to parent. Many adopted the values of the residential schools, which were more like prisons than homes. Later, many of these schools' inmates seemed to be more comfortable in prisons than in any other social institution. Virtually all were abused psychologically and physically, and recent evidence indicates that many were abused sexually.

IN TRANSITION. It is difficult to generalize about Indian values as they used to exist, for, today, they are either idealized by those promoting Indian values and identity or else demeaned by certain intolerant historians. It appears, however, that spiritual values were paramount in the Indian culture. Social and ecological values were also important, permeating Natives' every thought and action. Cooperation, so essential for survival in a harsh environment, was a dominant tribal and family value, as was tolerance, inasmuch as all adult males and some other individuals had lethal weapons and potent guardian spirits (Landes 1971). These values contrasted sharply with the materialism, open aggressiveness, competitiveness, and acquisitiveness of the new arrivals.

Although current Native values are in transition, the sharing of confined living quarters, material support, and a fairly homogeneous gene pool within the clan has tended to create a nurturing atmosphere, a tolerance of deviance, and an avoidance of confrontation that is difficult for many Europeans to understand. Other strongly advocated values include solving problems from a collective and traditional perspective and maintaining a sense of obligation toward one's extended family and clan. Overall, the values of tolerance and cooperation have produced a broad ethic of non-interference. The latter fostered an environment in which behavioural shaping was unacceptable and modeling the only avenue to behavioural change (Brant 1983; Bryde 1971; Morey 1974).

Indian Child-Rearing and Education

Indian and European child-rearing practices have differed greatly and on many levels, including such notions as parenting figures, parenting styles, and adult expectations of children. In Indian families, behavioural shaping was avoided and adolescence did not exist. As a result, Native Indian psychology has differed profoundly and those differences are at the root of some of the people's depression (Brant 1986; Bryde 1971; Morey 1974). Take, for example, the swaddling ethos of the cradle-board in both Indian and European cultures (Stein 1978), which may conceivably have had a strong impact on later personality development.

In hunting and gathering societies, especially in a land that was plentiful only in summer and fall, human energy was precious. If a group were to survive, the energies of adult men and women in their prime could not be consumed in child-rearing. Grandparents thus became the most important caregivers for many Indian children, followed by older uncles and aunts who were less physically able than the children's parents. Each child had a large extended family, whose members shared a small living space and were available to provide for the child's needs. There was none of the separation from caregivers that existed in European families. As a result, Native Indians raised in traditional families did not experience the separation-anxiety types of disorders so common in the dominant society. Unfortunately, however, when Natives move off reserves and the extended family is no longer present, parenting patterns do not always change.

Because of the dangers inherent in harsh environmental conditions, Native children were swaddled for protection and warmth. According to Piaget's theories, this custom may have created difficulties for the children's functioning during the stage of concrete operations; in times of stress, it may also have encouraged a watchful passivity rather than the active protest and mastery seen in non-Native children. In addition, this passivity may have reinforced the Native model of learning based on passive observation until tasks are mastered.

In the case of eight- to ten-year-old boys preparing for the guardian spirit quest – that quest involved a solo vigil that might last several days – the indulgent family structure had to be withdrawn. In a premature although supportive manner, the boys were told that they were now young men and no longer needed their parents in the same way. When their quest was complete, it was the guardian spirit – with which parents were not to compete – who became the source of personal and spiritual power and guidance (Salerno and Vanderburgh 1980). Today, the tradition of the guardian spirit quest is gone but, unfortunately, parental withdrawal still continues. A bad situation is compounded by the fact that many of today's parents and grandparents attended residential schools and internalized the prisonlike style of child-rearing encountered there (Johnston 1988; Willis 1973). In sum, although Indian children may experience a caring and indulgent early childhood, they are then cast adrift and expected to fend for themselves, emotionally, at too young an age. Such treatment creates a feeling of great vulnerability in the children.

It is the educational system that delivers the *coup de grâce* to the psyches of many Indian children. Because elementary schools on many remote reserves have been about two years behind non-Native schools in the south (Netley and Hawke 1973), the Native children beginning their secondary or post-secondary education in urban centres – as is common – are often already two years behind their southern peers academically. They are also deprived of the support of their families and communities. Already homesick, many must cope as well with prejudice at the hands of non-Natives. Not surprisingly, many flee back to their reserves as failures (Johnston 1988). If they remain, many of the boys suffer the assaults of racial strife and many of the girls are raped. The problem, moreover, is compounded by parents on remote reserves giving their children the double message: "Get an education to serve your people better, but do not succeed because you will be lost to your tribe and village."

Economic and Social Conditions

On reserves, there are typically few jobs and 50 to 70 per cent of the inhabitants are on social assistance. Native people live in houses that usually lack running water and are half the size of non-Native houses; they also have incomes that are less than half those of non-Natives (Department of Northern and Indian Affairs 1980b). However, the problems facing Native Indians because of their social and economic conditions go far beyond poor housing and low incomes. They include high rates of alcoholism, drug abuse, divorce, out-of-wedlock children, wife assault, sexual abuse of children, and intervention by child-welfare agencies (Department of Northern and Indian Affairs 1980b). Even life expectancy at birth is 8.4 years lower for Native Indian males than for non-Native males and 7.3 years lower for females (Health and Welfare Canada 1988). And if the rate of infant mortality among Native Indians is two to three times higher than the Canadian average, the youth-mortality rate is about four times as high. Perhaps the most difficult realization is that approximately 30 per cent of the Indian deaths due to accidents or violence – compared to the 9 per cent in the rest of the population – occur among young people and are related to alcohol use (Department of Indian and Northern Affairs 1980b).

DEPRESSION: PREVALENCE AND ENVIRONMENTAL CONTRIBUTORS

Prevalence

In a recent survey of leaders of fifty-seven reserves in Manitoba, Rodgers and Abas (1986) found that 47 per cent of the respondents perceived depression as a serious community problem. Hard data regarding mental health among Natives are difficult to come by. Nevertheless, if one uses information relative to end-stage outcomes (for example, wife assault, poverty, child-welfare interventions, suicide, incarceration, and homicide) as rough proxies for mental and emotional status, it soon becomes clear that Native people are much worse off than other Canadians.

Reliable and valid measures of Native mental disorders have never been constructed. The Ontario Child Health Study investigators, for example, were unable to locate instruments suitable for assessing the mental health of Native children. Thus they were initially excluded (Offord, personal communication). Even in the United States, the measurement of mental disorders among Indians is in its infancy (Neligh 1988).

Nevertheless, a few studies using survey methods to assess the prevalence of mental health problems have been attempted. Rodgers and Abas (1986), for example, reported a very high rate of mental health problems in many Native communities. Two years later, Fiddler (1988) found that 100 per cent of the children attending school during one target week in an Indian village in northern Ontario were as clinically depressed as children in an inpatient unit. Researchers have also shown that on several reserves in Canada and the United States, children above the age of nine consistently show more emotional disturbance than their non-Native age peers.

Even in the area of formal psychiatric disorder, little firm information exists concerning prevalence. I believe, however, that the chronic stresses of daily life, rather than diagnosable psychiatric disorders, account for Native Indians' high rates of arrest, homicide, suicide, incarceration, wife and child abuse, and violent death. Indeed, it seems safe to assume that hard data regarding mental health in Native communities – if indeed such a thing existed – would reveal a much more serious problem than members of the federal government, or the Native people themselves, have yet grasped. Yet instances of primary mood disorder (bipolar) appear to occur rarely except in those of mixed ancestry, and unipolar depression seems to be mainly reactive. Most depressive symptoms appear to be related to the difficulty of coping with an environment that is extremely stressful (Dinges and Joos 1988), one that provides little opportunity for change or escape, and in which the negative emotions of members of the ghettoized community are turned against themselves, their families, and other community members, particularly when chemical releasers are involved. Under these conditions, the women and children tend to become depressed and frightened while the men often end up in jail. Overall, the women seem to function better, because they maintain their roles as mothers and family caretakers. Their husbands, in contrast, because the lack of fish and game and the absence of an economic base have undercut most employment possibilities on the reserve, typically lose their provider role.

Depression in Native communities often seems to be community-wide, characterized by a sense of hopelessness about the future for oneself, one's family, and one's community (Brant 1986; Rodgers and Abas 1986). Investigators, in a study of depression among Indians from three U.S. reserves the used research diagnostic criteria (Shore et al. 1987), suggested that the depression seems to come in three forms: uncomplicated; associated with a past history of alcohol abuse; or superimposed on an underlying chronic depression or personality disorder. The primary symptoms were quite similar to those usually described for a non-Native population, except that there were more frequent hallucinatory experiences (especially ones involving the figure or voice of a deceased loved one).

Environmental Factors Contributing to Depression and Suicide

GENERAL PHYSICAL AND SOCIAL CONDITIONS ON RESERVES. In the northern winter, short days and long nights reduce exposure to light, a scenario that has been shown to be associated with an increased incidence of depression. Winter is especially inhospitable, with extremely cold temperatures that may reach −50° C. Going outside to visit or shop in such conditions is almost painful. Outdoor recreation becomes virtually impossible and may even be dangerous.

Indian villages are extremely prone to gossip. Everyone knows everything about everyone else, and the moccasin telegraph carries fresh gossip at high speeds throughout the community. Once in difficulty, a person is often branded and socially isolated. Thus, although reserves can be very nurturing, once one falls into the bad graces of the community, social rehabilitation can be almost impossible.

Indians live in an environment in which there is a need to fish, hunt, carry water to the house, chop and split wood for the stove, and manage farm animals. Such an environment includes many potentially dangerous items, including knives, axes, ropes, and firearms – all of which can be used to injure oneself or others.

ALCOHOLISM AND SOLVENT ABUSE. In their survey of opinion leaders on Manitoba reserves, Rodgers and Abas (1986) discovered that alcoholism was perceived as a serious problem on 58 per cent of the reserves. In another study, Merskey et al. (1988) found that about 15 per cent of Native adults and 44 per cent of clinic populations are affected by alcoholism. Excessive use of alcohol is often involved in youth suicides, violent and accidental deaths, wife abuse, child abuse, and family separation. It also increases the poverty of people who are already living on marginal welfare incomes.

Solvent (usually gas) sniffing occurs on many Indian reserves (Barnes 1985), especially among children. The effects of tetraethyl lead and the demyelinating impact of organic solvents combine to produce lead neurotoxicity, via lead encephalopathy. The resulting impairment of the brain is an important cause of failure at school, as well as many accidents. If adults sniff gas in childhood and adolescence, many will have very short-term memory and will be unable to benefit from adult education courses. Unfortunately, it is almost impossible to control the misuse of gas, because it is needed for outboard motors in the summer and skidoos in the winter. The only feasible approach to prevention lies in the development of appropriate educational programs on reserves. Specifically, parenting programs for adults would promote an intimacy and adaptive rolemodeling that is now often absent. For youths, recreational programs would furnish interesting alternatives to solvent sniffing.

The Medical Services Branch (MSB) of Health and Welfare Canada is the branch of the federal government that sees the casualties of alcohol, solvent, and drug abuse. Unfortunately, the mandate of MSB strongly emphasizes aiding people *after* impairment or injury has occurred. Thus, although MSB may spend tens of thousands of dollars on rehabilitating a brain-damaged victim of an unsuccessful suicide attempt, it has no mandate to support, on reserves, the community-development process that might prevent many suicide attempts, accidents, and violence.

DEPRESSION AND SUICIDE IN THE YOUNG. The suicide rate in Native children and adolescents aged ten to fourteen is ten times the national average for females and 2.7 times that for males (Health and Welfare Canada 1988). Among Native youths aged fifteen to nineteen, the rate rises, to 7.8 times the national average for females and 5.3 times that for males. In the fifteen to twenty-four year-old age group, the rate rises still higher – to 120 per 100,000 versus less than 20 per 100,000 for non-Natives in the same age group.

The causes of depression in young Indians centre around sexual abuse, poverty, lack of opportunity, identity confusion, and a lack of acceptable role models in either culture. Set-backs in their own lives, such as the death of highly valued elders and family, difficulties in peer or love relationships, and educational and job failures result in suicidal behaviour as well, much of it being alcohol related. In Indian groups, suicide is most likely to occur when cohesion and support are low and standards and expectations high

(May 1987). In a Canadian study of an epidemic of suicides that took the typical cluster form, Ward and Fox (1977) found that most involved the use of firearms and hanging, both common methods of suicide for men (Termansen and Peters 1979).

Among the young, male suicide attempts are more lethal than those of females, with the ratio of such male to female suicides being 5:1. Yet attempted suicides are far more likely to involve females, with medication being the most frequent agent and the likelihood of resuscitation far greater. It is the long distance between many Indian homes and hospital facilities that makes the numbers of Native female fatalities higher than among non-Natives. Also, in general, Indian women and girls appear to use more violent means of attempting suicide than non-Natives, perhaps because of the availability of firearms, the presence of dangerous instruments, the excessive use of alcohol, and gas sniffing.

Suicides among young people in villages tend to occur in clusters. In one study of the phenomenon in a village of 7,000 (Ward and Fox 1977), the suicide rate reached a high of four per hundred. Isolated and unsupported, the young people usually killed themselves in a violent fashion. In an American study of a like epidemic (Bechtold 1988), the suicides had similar characteristics, and all those who took their own lives were closely related by ties of blood or friendship.

DEPRESSION AND SUICIDE IN WOMEN. Although the suicide rate is higher for Native than non-Native women up to the age of sixty-nine (Health and Welfare Canada 1988), it declines among older Native women. The adult female role, including the nurturing of children, seems to sustain Native women. As well, women's roles are more flexible than men's and have been less altered by the advent of new technologies and belief systems. In effect, depression among women is often related to physical and psychological abuse by spouses or boy friends, or to disasters that happen to their children, family, or friends. Also, parents are sometimes abused by youths living in the home who have many privileges but few responsibilities or limits. Such abuse causes parents to become depressed. Members of the family and village are reluctant to interfere because of the ethic of non-intervention. In fact, because there are few alternative living situations, intervention is likely to remove the young person only temporarily from the parents' home.

The usual causes of depression among women include poverty; demanding duties, including cooking, cleaning, and getting wood and water; subservience to males in the family; submission to mothers-in-law early in the marriage; and physical, psychological, and sexual abuse. Indian women, moreover, are often trapped. Because the scarce housing is controlled by the usually all-male band council, separated women are unlikely to find housing. The band council, threatened by wive's attempting to escape from abusive husbands, often will simply moralize about the evils of marital separation. In addition, the welfare cheque is usually given to husbands; they spend it as they wish, even to the point of leaving their wives with no food for the children. Moreover, both the church and Indian traditions hold that women should stay with their husbands, no matter what the cost to them or the children. Thus, most Indian women, feeling ill-equipped to cope in a non-Native community, hold no hope of escaping to the white community without enormous cost. Clearly, unless the women have relatives willing to allow them and the children to stay, separation – frequently used by non-Native women to bring men into treatment – is not an available option. Moreover, most Indian men are resistant to treatment: they will not participate unless forced to do so by their wives' leaving. Shelters for battered Indian women are needed to change this situation. Ideally, such shelters would be located near reserves and easily accessible. In fact, however, not only are they not close to reserves, but it is impossible for many battered and abused Indian women to gather enough money to flee with their children to a shelter.

I have worked with many Indian women whose courage and strength were almost beyond belief. Some women were non-clinically depressed, despite experiencing four or five deaths among their first- and second-degree relatives in the previous few months and many more such losses before that. Others had been shot in the leg or foot by their husbands as a tactic of intimidation, yet at the hospital pretended that they had been cleaning their husband's gun when it discharged accidentally. I have also known many Indian women who have been able to raise children, manage a home without electricity or plumbing, function as role models for the community, and still maintain a good-humoured optimism.

DEPRESSION AND SUICIDE IN MEN. For men over forty, the Native Indian suicide rate is less than the Canadian average (Health and Welfare Canada 1988). Young Indian men, however, are very often depressed. In childhood, passivity has been fostered by child-rearing practices, including the swaddling- or cradle board. Later, the joint traditions of a guardian spirit quest (even though the rite itself is no longer practised) and a residential school encourage parents to cast the young men off at a premature age. The youth often respond to such parental severance by employing massive denial tactics and acting in a macho fashion. In addition, as they become more fluent in English or French, a language barrier often grows up between them and their extended family. In effect, they become caught between identities and models of living that are unrealistic and incompatible. A return to ancestral identities and ways is impractical – not only because of today's lack of fish and game, but also because such practices would result in an unacceptably low standard of living. The identities and models provided by the young men's elders are simply not functional, whether now or in the future. Native youths may try to emulate models from the non-Native world, but these are usually beyond their means. As a result, many never develop clear identities or else strive for the unreachable. Many seethe with rage, becoming depressed at the inaccessibility of positive identities, opportunities, and success.

If young Indian men leave the reserve, they lose contact with their extended families and lifelong friends, give up housing and other social benefits, and face prejudice, discrimination, and probable failure. On the other hand, if they stay on the reserve, they have little hope of a better life, unless their families are politically powerful and can obtain for them one of the guaranteed jobs controlled by the band. Frequently, with nothing constructive to do with their time, many revert to gas sniffing and alcohol use, as the more exotic drugs – now available on virtually all reserves – become too expensive.

Young Indian men's anger is expressed in vandalism, fire setting, antisocial behaviour, fighting, sexual abuse of females, social withdrawal, and theft. When combined with disinhibiting intoxicants, this anger becomes even more lethal. Depending on whether that anger is directed against the self or others, suicide or homocide may be the result.

DEPRESSION AND SUICIDE IN THE ELDERLY. Traditionally, respect for elders has been an important Indian value. Indeed, in many Native religions, "grandfather" is also used as a term for God. In well-functioning families, grandparents have always had a secure place. Unfortunately, this value has now deteriorated. Today, grandparents have become less important: because of smaller houses, the language barrier, and the adoption by native families of a European family model, they have less contact than ever with their families. Clearly, dysfunctional families are unable to take care of *anyone* well, grandparents included. On the other hand, elders often do not understand the forces and values that younger people must struggle with. Their advice, once valued, is not sought; nor are they accorded the respect they once received. Combined with this loss of status comes physical illness, confinement to the home because of disability, and lack of services. Depression results. The elder's depressive symptoms are frequently somaticized, appearing as aches and pains (often abdominal) for which no organic cause can be found. As well, older women find themselves widowed — many men die prematurely and violently — or bereaved because of their adult children's violent deaths. In a recent instance known to me personally, the fifteenth and last surviving child of an older Indian woman was raped, tortured, murdered, and then buried in her own front yard. Despite the fact that this was her last surviving child, the older woman was still able to cope effectively with the tragedy.

Little has appeared in the literature about depression among elderly Indians. One reason is that elders are a relatively small proportion of the

Indian population, because of the relatively high rate of premature death from accidents, disease, and the difficult environment. Another reason is that Indian elderly people have usually survived many traumas and seem to have a toughness and stoicism that make it difficult for them to make their needs known.

As children move off the reserve and families become smaller, having many children is no longer an effective form of social insurance. Nevertheless, elderly Indians, who are usually more spiritually than psychologically minded and often take the Christian doctrine seriously, tend to be generous, undemanding, and stoical; no longer do they expect the kind of care that elders once received.

IMPLICATIONS FOR INTERVENTION AND PREVENTION

The federal government, which for years has had responsibility for Native people's health care, has never had a policy on Native mental health. Only in the past year has even the possibility existed of developing a policy for mental health services for Natives. Getting adequate funding for such services has always proved difficult, however. With one exception (Department of Psychiatry, University of Toronto 1978; Timpson 1984), Indian mental health services have never been integrated with primary care, such as general medical and nursing services, even though such a separation of services is contrary to the recommendations of the Institute of Medicine (Hamburg et al. 1982). As a result, mental health services have encountered nothing but disinterest and neglect on the part of the government. Frequently, the nurses' first line of defence was to send Natives out to provincial mental hospitals when counselling at nursing stations on the reserves had failed. Natives' mental health problems have typically been dealt with in other ineffective ways as well, such as the use of avoidance, the hiring of unskilled nurses and physicians, and the evacuation of Natives as corpses or prisoners of the police.

Many models of service have been developed in recent years, but most seem to have had serious weaknesses. For example, mental health and child-welfare services were placed in the hands of professionals who neither spoke the language nor understood the culture; services for women never really existed; and Natives were either not invited to participate in mental health services or were reluctant to do so because mental health and correctional services partly overlapped.

Canadian Natives often live in small villages in remote areas, each with its own politics and priorities. This virtual isolation makes it difficult to provide cost-effective services that meet the needs of the community in question. There is rapidly increasing awareness that mental health treatment and prevention services for Natives must be delivered by Natives, that preventive programs must be administered and staffed mainly by Native personnel, and that services must be located on or near reserves. Indeed, many papers and monographs have been written about the often remarkable results achieved through a return to traditional ways of healing (Jelik 1981; Nagel 1989). In addition, across Canada, Native traditions and professional health expertise are being combined, and links are being formed between Native organizations and mental health professionals (Department of Psychiatry, University of Toronto 1978; Timpson 1984).

Natives are increasingly operating their own child-welfare services.* Mental health services, formerly independent of medical services, are now being encouraged. At the request of Indian leaders, who are seeing increasing levels of emotional and mental strain in their people, the federal government is beginning to develop a national policy for Native mental health. As services are developed, however, care must be taken to avoid extremes. That is, whereas too much professional and too little Native (both cultural and spiritual) influence on service delivery will only reproduce the culturally insensitive services of the past, too much Native and insufficient professional input will only lead to a divorce between mental health services and other health services.

As natives become more responsible and aware of the casualties among their people, models of prevention are developing across the country. A preventive program on the Brokenhead Reserve in Manitoba, focusing on the nurturing and emotional education of children, and prevention programs such as the Ma-Ma-Wichita program in Winnipeg, constitute examples of this type of preventive service.

A number of blended services are in place, programs in which Native front-line and administrative staff support non-Native professionals. The University of Toronto has one such mental health program that serves the eastern Arctic; another serves Natives in the northwestern region of Ontario. As well, the Northern Medical Unit of the University of Manitoba provides services and support to people of northern Manitoba, while the University of Western Ontario supports services to the Cree and Ojibwa of northeastern Ontario.

It is hoped that similar primary care and preventive programs will be encouraged by Indian leaders and the federal government in the future. Two fundamental principles must be respected in any such efforts. First, the planning and development of the programs should be under the control of Indian people who have an interest and experience in mental health, with civil serv-

*The Brokenhead Reserve has collaborated with the Canadian Mental Health Association to provide a remarkable prevention program for Native children on the reserve. Information on the program may be obtained by writing to Harvey Olson, Brokenhead Band, Mental Health Steering Committee, Scanterbury, Manitoba ROE 1 WO.

ants and non-Native professionals providing the necessary support and skills to achieve the requisite blend of Native and non-Native strengths for successful programs. Second, no matter how effective mental health treatment and prevention services become, the alleviation of depression among Native people will emerge only through a major improvement in their own social and economic status, such that they benefit fully from the riches of a country that was once theirs.

BIBLIOGRAPHY

Adams, H. 1975. *The basis of racism.* Toronto: New Press.

Bailey, A.G. 1969. *The conflict of European and Eastern Algonkian cultures 1504-1700.* Toronto: University of Toronto Press.

Barnes, G.E. 1985. Gasoline sniffing. *Revue Canadienne d'Economie Familiale* 5: 144-46.

Bechtold, D.W. 1988. Cluster suicide in American Indian adolescents. *American Indian and Alaska Native Mental Health Research* 1(3): 26-35.

Bishop, C.A. 1974. *The northern Ojibwa and the fur trade.* Toronto: Holt, Rinehart and Winston of Canada.

Brant, C.C. 1983. Native child-rearing practices. In *The native family: Traditions and adaptations.* Proceedings of the annual meeting of the Canadian Psychiatric Association, Section on Native Mental Health, Ottawa, Ontario, 30-37.

- 1986. Mechanisms of depression. In *Depression in the North American Indian: Causes and treatment.* Proceedings of the annual meeting of the Canadian Psychiatric Association, Section on Native Mental Health, Nechi Institute/Pound Maker's Lodge, 32-43.

Bryde, J.F. 1971. Modern Indian psychology. Vermillion, S. Dak.: Institute of Indian Studies. Department of Indian and Northern Affairs. 1980a. *The linguistic and cultural affiliations of Canadian Indian bands.* Ottawa: Department of Indian and Northern Affairs.

Department of Indian and Northern Affairs. 1980a. *The linguistic and cultural affiliations of Canadian Indian bands.* Ottawa: Department of Indian and Northern Affairs.

- 1980b. *Indian conditions: A survey,* catalogue no. R32-45/1980E. Ottawa: Department of Indian and Northern Affairs.

Department of Psychiatry, University of Toronto. 1978. Providing psychiatric care and consultation in remote Indian villages. *Hospital and Community Psychiatry* 29: 678-80.

Dinges, N.G. and Joos, S.K. 1988. Coping and health: Models of interaction for Indian and Native populations. Behavioural health issues among American Indians and Alaska Natives. *American Indian and Alaska Mental Health Research* (monograph no. 1), 8-64.

Fiddler, B. 1988. *Childhood depression in New Osnaberg.* Manuscript, Sioux Lookout, University University of Toronto.

Hamburg, D.A., Elliot, G.R. and Parron, D.L. 1982. *Health and behaviour: Frontiers of research in the biobehavioural sciences.* Washington, D.C.: National Academy Press. Haycock, R.G. 1971. *The image of the Indian.* Waterloo, ON: Waterloo Lutheran University Press.

Health and Welfare Canada. 1988. *Health indicators derived from vital statistics for Indian and Canadian populations.* Ottawa: Health and Welfare Canada.

Jelik, W.G. 1981. *Indian healing.* Surrey, B.C.: Hancock House.

Jenness, D. 1977. *The Indians of Canada.* 7th ed. Toronto: University of Toronto Press.

Jennings, F. 1976. *The invasion of America.* New York: Norton.

Johnston, B.H. 1988. *Indian school days.* Toronto: Key-Porter Books.

Landes, R. 1971. *The Ojibwa woman.* New York: Norton.

LaRoque, E. 1975. *Defeathering the Indian.* Toronto: Book Society of Canada.

Maclean, H. 1982. *Indians, Inuit, and Métis of Canada.* Toronto: Gage.

McMillan, A.D. 1988. *Native peoples and cultures of Canada.* Vancouver/Toronto: Douglas & McIntyre.

Martin, C. 1978. *Keepers of the game.* Berkeley: University of California Press.

May, P.A. 1987. Suicide and self-destruction among American Indian youths. *American Indian and Alaska Mental Health Research* 1: 52–69.

Merskey, H., Brant, C.C., Malla, A., Helmes, E., and Mohr, V. 1988. Symptom patterns of alcoholism in a northern Ontario population. *The Canadian Journal of Psychiatry* 33: 46–50.

Morey, S.M. 1974. *Respect for life: The traditional upbringing of American Indian children.* Garden City, N.Y.: Waldorf Press.

Nagel, J.K. 1989. Unresolved grief and mourning in Navejo women. *American Indian and Alaska Native Mental Health Research* 2: 32–40.

Neligh, G. 1988. Major mental disorders and behaviour among American Indians and Alaska Natives. *American and Alaska Native Mental Health Research* (monograph no. 1): 116- 59.

Netley, C., and Hawke, W.A. 1973. Educational and behavioral characteristics of Indian children in northern Ontario. Manuscript, Sioux Lookout, University of Toronto.

Patterson, E.P. 1972. *The Canadian Indian: A history since 1500.* Toronto: Collier MacMillan Canada.

Rodgers, D.D., and Abas, N. 1986. A survey of native mental health needs in Manitoba. In *Depression in the North American Indian: Causes and treatment.* Proceedings of the 1986 annual meeting of the Canadian Psychiatric Association, Section on Native Mental Health, 9–31. Ottawa.

Salerno, N.F., and Vanderburgh, R.S. 1980. *Shamans' daughter.* New York: Dell Books.

Shore, J.H., Manson, S.M., Bloom, J.D., Keepers, G., and Neligh, G. 1987. A pilot study of depression among American Indian patients with research diagnostic criteria. *American Indian and Alaska Mental Health Research* 1: 4–15.

Stein, H.F. 1978. The Slovak-American "swaddling ethos": Homeostat for family dynamics and cultural continuity. *Family Process* 17: 31–44.

Termansen, P.E., and Peters, R.W. 1979. *Suicide and attempted suicide among status Indians in British Columbia*. Paper presented at the meeting of the World Federation of Mental Health, Salzburg, Austria.

Timpson, J.B. 1984. Indian mental health: Changes in the delivery of care in northwestern Ontario. *Canadian Journal of Psychiatry* 29: 234–41.

Ward, J.A., and Fox, J. 1977. A suicide epidemic on an Indian reserve. *Canadian Psychiatric Association Journal* 22: .

Willis, J. 1973. *An Indian girlhood*. Toronto: New Press.

CHAPTER NINE

Depression among Immigrants and Refugees

GRANVILLE A. daCOSTA

It has long been speculated that international migration predisposes to, and may even cause, depression in immigrants and refugees; that is, in migrants (Eitenger 1959; Murphy 1952; Pedersen 1949; Tyhurst 1951). The present review is an attempt to synthesize what is known, or at least widely accepted, about the development, nature, and course of depression in migrants. No assumption is made that migration is of any greater etiological significance for the development of depression than the genetic, personality, familial, general health, or life-event factors. A number of recommendations are included in this chapter, recommendations geared to improving interventions, service delivery, and research.

PREVALENCE OF DEPRESSION AMONG IMMIGRANTS AND REFUGEES

The "Ubiquitous Depression" Assumption

Largely on the basis of anecdotal evidence, it is assumed that depressive states are an almost inevitable part of the migrant's adjustment during re-settlement and acculturation. This assumption gains some credibility from evidence that social disruptions increase the risk of depression (Brown and Harris 1978; Brown and Prudo 1981). There is a dearth of supportive clinical and epidemiological data, for the "ubiquity of depression" assumption. Instead, the present literature review suggests that the nature and prevalence of depression or depressive symptoms in migrants have yet to be properly investigated. In addition, the relatively few clinical and research findings that deal with the impact of migration *per se* on mental health do not constitute a compelling case for migration-specific effects (Canadian Task Force on Mental Health Issues Affecting Immigrants and Refugees 1988a). In fact, in most studies, comparisons of the rates of major affective disorders between migrant groups and their host societies have tended to show no appreciable difference (Bagley 1971; Cochrane and Stopes-Roe 1977; Dean et al. 1980). Some research, however, has suggested the opposite: Cochrane and Bal (1987), for example, concluded that immigrants collectively referred to as "Caribbean" had lower rates of depression, based on hospital admissions, than the "English-born." Others have suggested that individuals with bipolar (Pope et al. 1983) or cyclothymic (London 1986) affective disorders may be more likely to migrate because of the particular symptomatology of those disorders.

Comparisons of the rates of psychopathology in native-born British citizens as well as Indian, Pakistani, and Irish immigrants, showed that these rates were either about the same or lower among the immigrants (Cochrane & Stopes-Roe 1977, 1979). In a study of illness behaviour in a sample of Asian immigrants and British-born citizens (Murray and Williams 1986), although the male Asian immigrants had poorer self-assessments of their health and more physician contacts than the British-born males, they had fewer psychiatric symptoms and spent less time being ill. No differences between the two groups of females were observed.

Problems in Determining Prevalence

CONCEPTUAL AND OPERATIONAL ISSUES. The problems of defining and measuring depression, already noted in chapter 1, will not be repeated here. Instead, I will examine the issues directly related to the study of depression in immigrants and refugees, including the challenges inherent to conducting research on the topic.

Cross-culturally comparable ways of describing the nature and experience of well-being and illness are obviously needed to study mental disorders in different ethnocultural groups. In part, the language used by a specific group to talk about disordered states depends on what group members consider salient about their feelings, experience, and symptoms (Aday et al. 1980; Jones and Korchin 1982; Westermeyer 1985). These cultural selectivities in talking about mental states include beliefs about illness and the symbolic meanings attached to mental disorders. Certain researchers have taken several of these nuances into account when designing scales for the measurement of mental disorders in different ethnocultural populations (for example, Kinzie et al. 1982; Westermeyer 1988). Others have translated English-language scales into other languages, with or without such validity checks as back translation or bilingual restandardization (Beiser and Fleming 1986; Chan

1985; Cochrane et al. 1977; Fava 1983; Hurh and Kim 1982; Karno et al. 1983; Westermeyer 1988). Still others have proposed that a detailed understanding of the nature of mental disorders in specific ethnocultural groups is a prerequisite for the design of valid measurement scales (Sue 1983; Eyton and Neuwirth 1984).

Uncertainty about the meaning of questionnaire-based research findings arises from the ethnocultural groups' differing usages of terms denoting feeling states, as well as the relation these states are felt to have with depression. In a survey of mental health problems in a refugee population, for example (Rahe et al. 1978), subjects' ratings of a questionnaire item "worst possible world," as well as levels of pessimism, were not readily translatable into categories of depression. In part, this is because symptoms do not necessarily constitute a diagnosable mood disorder (Rabkin 1982). Also, the language in many reports on mental health problems of immigrants and refugees is heavily descriptive and often imprecise with regard to the presence or absence of depression. One frequently finds such general terms as "stress," "emotional disorder," "mental disorder," "suicide," "role and status change," "family dysfunction," "psychological distress," "alienation," "neurosis," and so on in these reports. From a clinical perspective, virtually any of these conditions could include depression as a component, with some (such as suicide, and alienation) being more suggestive of the presence of a depressive state than others.

Health status self-assessments and self-reports by immigrants and refugees can often be problematic and lead to the underreporting and underdetection of mental disorders such as depression. Indeed, self-reporting of illness is related to one's evaluation of the nature and perceived threat of a symptom. In ethnocultural groups, such evaluations are likely to be based on culture-specific concepts of illness and health (Zola 1966). The migrant may perceive the disclosure of certain symptoms or illnesses to others as inadmissible (Brewin 1980) or at least as a breach of cultural decorum (Aday et al. 1980; Jones and Korchin 1982). This underreporting may lead, in turn, to health care professionals' failure to recognize symptoms of disorders in migrant patients (Brewin 1980). On the other hand, low levels of symptomatology or mental disorder in migrants in a specific ethnocultural group may reflect self-selection (that is, those ethnocultural group members who migrate may have better mental health) or above-average levels of mental well-being in the particular group in question (Canadian Task Force 1988a).

A model of depression that has broad cross-cultural applicability remains an elusive goal. Difficult as it is in North America to reach consensus about the concept of depression, it is even more so in a cross-cultural context, because depression is likely to be experienced, understood, manifested, or remedied differently in the various ethnocultural populations (Marsella 1978; Rabkin 1982). In some cultures, there are no linguistic or conceptual correspondences to the Western term "depression" (Resner and Hartog 1970;

Tseng and Hsu 1969). Consequently, there is no broadly accepted, standardized instrument for the cross-cultural measurement of depressive disorders (Zung et al. 1988).

Finally, because the etiology, clinical presentation, and course of depressive disorders are heterogeneous, any difficulties in differentiating between types of depression will result in heterogeneous study populations, all of which tends to make findings non-comparable and inconsistent across studies (Hirschfeld and Cross 1983).

OTHER POTENTIAL BIASES. Investigations of rates of depression in immigrant and refugee groups should use standardization techniques to control statistically for between-group differences on such variables as age. Such techniques are necessary because migrants may constitute quite different proportions of the population of the host country, depending on the age category in question. Cochrane and Bal (1987) found, for example, that in England, in 1981, 41 per cent of English males were in the sixteen- to forty-four-year-old age group, compared to 52 per cent of Caribbean immigrants, 56 per cent of Indian immigrants, and 57 per cent of Pakistani/Bangladeshi immigrants. The data for females were even more divergent: 37 per cent of English-born women were aged sixteen to forty-four; versus 63, 59, and 66 per cent, respectively, for women from the other countries or regions.

Statistical control also needs to be exercised for the variable "length of residence in the host country." It is widely believed that length of residence is related to the expression of symptoms in migrants prone to develop mental disorders (Canadian Task Force 1988a). Studies of service utilization or of symptom occurrence, for example, may be biased if length of residence is not taken into account. Similarly, the point at which outcomes are measured, in relationship to length of residence with or without a specific intervention for depression, needs to be controlled as well.

Data on rates of depression in specific ethnocultural, immigrant, and refugee populations have come mainly from clinical samples; that is, from patients attending assessment and treatment facilities (Harvey and Chung 1980; London 1986; Neff 1984; Zung et al. 1988). However, there have also been studies of migrant populations (Chan and Lam 1983; Kuo and Tsai 1986; Mirowsky and Ross 1984; Vega et al. 1984). It is difficult to disentangle the incidence or prevalence of a mental disorder from patterns of service utilization, particularly as these patterns often differ between migrants and members of the host society (Allodi and Fantini 1985; Boxer and Garvey 1985; Cochrane and Bal 1987; Littlewood and Lipsedge 1981; Lopez 1981; Morgan and Andrushko 1977; Rwegellera 1980). A further problem in many of these studies is that sample sizes are often small, further compromising the accuracy of the estimates of prevalence of mental disorders, including depression (London 1986).

Most epidemiological studies of mental disorders in migrant populations have been observational and retrospective. They have tended to focus on certain characteristics of specific ethnocultural groups and/or the relationship between these characteristics and the experience of mental disorders. In attempting to understand the process whereby depression and other mental disorders develop and manifest themselves, these studies have often failed to control for factors other than subjects' status as migrants. Moreover, the use of patient samples in many studies has meant that many distressed individuals have probably been missed; that is, those experiencing dysfunction but whose symptoms did not meet current criteria for a formal diagnosis of depression.

The fact that most research on migrants has studied patients admitted to or attending hospitals and affiliated facilities has possibly given rise to a confounding of differential rates of admission (Lilienfeld and Lilienfeld 1980). There may, for example, be a disproportionate rate of diagnosis of major psychoses in migrant patients (Zung et al. 1988; Marsella 1978; London 1986). This inadvertent weighting may occur because of migrants' difficulties in gaining access to treatment at, or shortly after, the onset of depression or other disorders, making hospitalization more difficult to avoid. Also, hospitals and other services may show a predisposition, even in the absence of predetermined selection or admission criteria, to favour certain diagnoses or to admit particular types of patients. In a study of the psychiatric management of migrant inpatients from three ethnocultural groups, for example, Italian-born immigrants were more likely than other groups to be given a diagnosis of affective disorder at admission (daCosta and Persad 1987). On the other hand, certain types of depression may have a greater likelihood of detection because of easier accessibility to treatment or because certain individuals or members of certain ethnocultural groups are differentially motivated to seek treatment (Marsella 1978).

Another difficulty stems from the fact that studies on mental disorders in immigrants and refugees rarely include data on subjects' attributes or situations in their countries of origin (London 1986). Pre-migration data on pre-morbid personality, coping skills, and personal and social support systems have all been deficient. This lack of knowledge of baseline conditions has obscured the natural history of depression in immigrants and refugees. This lack has also made it difficult to isolate the impact of migration, resettlement, and acculturation on depression; to distinguish between first episodes of depression and recurrences; and to assess precisely the onset, end, or duration of episodes of depression. The relationship in specific ethnocultural populations between migration/acculturation and depression might be better understood if one were to compare rates of treated and untreated depression in migrants with those of comparable groups in their countries of origin.

There has also been a lack of data (or perhaps inaccurate data) on the racial and cultural origins of individuals (Baskin et al. 1981). For example, researchers have sometimes failed to distinguish between patients from the same ethnic group but born in different places, or those from the same birthplace but from different ethnocultural groups. These errors have introduced unreliability into intergroup comparisons on demographic variables (London 1986). Reliable and accurate classification of patients and control subjects has also been marred by treating migrants and citizens of the host society as if they were ethnoculturally and racially homogeneous, as is implied by the use of loose terms such as "blacks," "whites," "British," "South East Asians," "West Indians," "Third World," and so on.

PREDISPOSING AND CAUSATIVE FACTORS OF DEPRESSION

The migrant's measure of the voluntariness or coerciveness in mobility and contact with another culture, the vicissitudes of displacement, and the nature of receptivity of the host society all contribute to changes in mental health during migration and resettlement.

Types of Immigration

There are generally three types of immigrants: voluntary, involuntary, and illegal.

Voluntary immigration implies an element of individual choice. In fact, most immigration is voluntary, although personality characteristics, combined with intrafamilial dynamics, may weaken or even remove the voluntariness of the decision to resettle, as happens, for example, in the case of the young or elderly. *Involuntary* immigration frequently characterizes refugees, whose freedom of choice is curtailed by local, coercive social forces. *Illegal* immigration describes migrants who bypass official channels for residency. There is little reliable information on the number of illegal immigrants, and demographic characteristics of illegal immigrants, or on the prevalence of psychopathology among them. It is often thought that they suffer an increased risk of mental disorders, including depression, because of the unique stresses of avoiding detection and the generic stresses that accompany acculturation.

Canada has three official categories of admission to the country: *family class* (persons older than eighteen, who may sponsor close relatives); *independent class* (assisted relatives and others arriving on their own initiative); and *refugees*. During 1978-87, 43 per cent of the total number of admissions to Canada were labelled "family class," 40 per cent "independent class," and 17 per cent "refugee class" (Canadian Task Force 1988b). At present, patterns of family immigration include the traditional set-up, wherein one spouse precedes the other spouse and their children; as well as the reverse pattern, wherein children arrive first and then, under a policy of reunification, sponsor older relatives. Under the Immigration Act of 1976, sponsors must assume responsibility, for a period of ten years, of the housing, care, and maintenance of those they have sponsored.

A number of factors that accompany migration, rather than migration itself, may predispose immigrants to develop depression or other mental disorders: drop in socioeconomic status; lack of skill in the language of the host country; separation from family; prejudice or discrimination at the hands of citizens of the host country; isolation from people of similar ethnocultural heritage; unusual pre-migration stresses; and developmental level at the time of migration (Canadian Task Force 1988a). Beyond these factors, however, and although there has been little research on the topic in Canada, it is plausible that the occurrence, nature, and outcome of depression may vary according to the pattern and type of migration. In the 1960s, after the introduction of the immigration point system, persons allowed entry to Canada from West Indian countries were mostly women. Many had left behind their partners and children. Among children born in these West Indian countries and then reunited with their parents after being in the care of others, almost 80 per cent were found to be depressed, even years after the reunion had taken place (daCosta 1974). Burke (1982) found the same pattern among West Indian delinquent females who had experienced a similar pattern of migration and resettlement: over 65 per cent had depressive symptoms.

In the absence of research data, the organizations serving immigrants and refugees, and migrants themselves, share a broad concern that the current conceptual framework in Canada for fostering migrant adaptation and family reunification may not be working well. Immigration policies lead to family conflicts and, in older migrants, to inadequate housing, reduced control over their lives, and depression. Previous patterns of immigration are also believed to be involved. In the past, more single males than females immigrated to Canada, with the gender differential varying by ethnocultural group. As a result, in some groups, such as the Chinese populations of Toronto and Vancouver, there are a preponderance of single and possibly vulnerable elderly men (Driedger and Chappell 1987). Depression in such a group is a likely outcome.

International Migration as a Stressor

Studies of the effects of stressful life events on the development of psychological distress and symptomatology have been conducted mainly apropos non-migrant populations. Viewing international migration as a stressful life event may help in understanding the development of depression in immigrants and refugees. The stressors that the general literature identifies as most strongly related to the emergence of symptomatology include the number and desirability of changes in the lives of individuals and the actual or perceived loss involved in these changes (Cadoret et al. 1972; Dohrenwend and Dohrenwend 1969, 1974; Infeld 1977; Paykel et al. 1969; Ross and Mirowsky 1979; Vadher and Ndetei 1981). Whether or not individuals feel that change is controllable also appears to be important (Grant et al. 1981; Johnson and Sarason 1978; Mirowsky and Ross 1983). The beneficial effects of social relationships and family ties on stress and depression related to life changes and loss have also received considerable attention (Aneshensel and Stone 1982; Brown and Harris 1978; Cobb 1976; Dean et al. 1980; Eaton 1978; Husaini et al. 1982; Parker and Brown 1982; Tolsdorf 1978; Warheit 1979).

Perhaps the central characteristic of international migration is the fact of sudden change in many areas of the migrant's life, within a very short time period. Changes typically affect living conditions, occupation, socioeconomic status, education, language use, family structure and function, social networks, and political attitudes. The combination of rapid change and disorganization of the psychosocial milieu and family system appears to increase susceptibility to depression and other disorders among migrants (Cassel 1976 [cited in Galanter 1988]; McGoldrick 1982; Shuval 1982; Tseng and McDermott 1981). Clearly, short- term and long-term reactions to a change of environment are almost certainly affected by the migrant's developmental level (Marcos 1982) and current mental status. Among younger and often healthier individuals, for example, there may be less risk of significant psychiatric disorder (Murray and Williams 1986). The labelling question is also important. Should, for example, the reactions of frustration or disappointment to the migration experience be classified as symptoms of affective disorder (Shuval 1982), or simply understood as part of a successful adaptation to migration that often involves some anxiety, suspiciousness, or moodiness (Westermeyer 1988)?

The stresses of migration and resettlement appear to be related to psychiatric symptomatology, including depressive states, in the middle years of childhood, in adolescence, and among seniors (daCosta 1974; Canadian Task Force 1988a). Migration in the middle years of childhood may be followed some years later by psychiatric disorders; among adolescents and young adults, there have been reported depression and depressive equivalents, such as substance abuse. Among seniors, role changes, feelings of isolation, and other sequelae of the stresses of adaptation have been related to depression (Canadian Task Force 1988a).

The assumption that refugees are more prone to higher rates and more severe changes in mental health than other migrants, would be in keeping, theoretically and clinically, with the former's markedly different pattern of migration, involving such life-events as coercive uprooting, in-transit trauma, and catastrophic loss. Refugee status is also associated both with depressive symptoms (Baskauskas 1981; Cook and Timberlake 1984; Eitinger 1959; Murphy 1955; Pedersen 1949; Westermeyer 1988) and with high rates and severity of affective disorder (Pfister-Ammende 1955; Westermeyer et al. 1983a, 1983b). Factors that seemed to allow Hmong refugees to function, even with high levels of depressive symptoms, include continuity with past activities, control over their lives, and stability in sponsorship and living arrangements (Westermeyer 1988). Interestingly, language training, vocational training, or a social network composed of fellow refugees did not appear to contribute to coping well (Westermeyer 1988). A similar phenomenon was observed among Hmong migrants who settled in Hawaii: their close social network apparently had both supportive and detrimental effects on their adaptation (Tack 1981).

An intriguing, albeit unsettled, issue concerns the relationship of stressors to disturbances of psychophysiological processes, which are expressed as complaints about bodily dysfunctions. The expression of depressive states in terms of psychophysiological symptoms is thought not only to be more common in non-Western cultures (Marsella 1980) but also prevalent in certain ethnocultural groups (Chakrabarti and Sandel 1984; Goldstein 1979; Kohn et al. 1989; Teja et al. 1971). Although culture-specific syndromes (Yap 1969) have no counterpart in current psychiatric nosology (Kohn et al. 1989; Weller and Ameen 1982), it is plausible that some may be expressions of depression.

Prejudice and Discrimination

Because of a lack of empirical data on the topic in different ethnocultural groups, it is difficult to estimate what part racial and ethnic prejudice (attitudes) and discrimination (behaviour) play in the development of depression in immigrants and refugees (Driedger and Clifton 1984; Driedger and Mezoff 1981). When, as is commonly done, migrants are lumped together as "visible minorities" or as coming from "Third World" countries, useful data are not generated because reactions to actual or perceived racism probably differ by ethnocultural group.

This having been said, more informal data sources provide a glimpse of the prejudice that exists beneath the national veneer of tolerance in Canada. In 1986, "visible minorities" constituted 14 per cent of Metro Toronto's population and 8.2 per cent of the combined populations of Canada's three largest cities: Toronto, Montreal, and Vancouver. Demographers predict that, by 2010, Third World migrants will compose 17.7 per cent of the population of Metro Toronto and 10.7 per cent of the combined populations of the three cities just mentioned (Harper 1989). In a national poll of attitudes toward "minorities" (who were not identified any more precisely), 60 per cent of Canadians responded positively to the ideal of generosity toward minorities. When issues were made more specific, however, 59 per cent of

Canadians preferred that minorities abandon their ethnocultural customs and language and become more like most Canadians (Beltrame 1990). Also, in gatherings convened to discuss ethnic and migrant issues, individuals and groups frequently attest to the pervasiveness of racism in Canada. That such conditions foster depression is hardly surprising. Clearly, information about the extent, manifestations, and mechanisms of the impact of racism on different ethnocultural groups, including its relationship to depressive reactions, would be very useful in developing prevention and intervention strategies.

PRIORITIES FOR RESEARCH AND INTERVENTION

Researchers must try to understand the processes and mechanisms involved in the paths negotiated by migrants into the host society, and to assess the generality of principles derived from empirical data in different ethnocultural groups. Interventions should address the recognition and amelioration of present problems and their prevention in the future.

Research Priorities

Although existing epidemiological data provide some evidence linking migration to depression, the empirical data are not yet convincing. In order to clarify this basic issue, certain investigations are needed. Such a range of studies must (1) examine different immigrant and refugee populations, taking into account patterns of migration; (2) establish temporal relationships that clarify cause-effect links between emigration, resettlement, and depression; (3) link the breaking and making, and the quality, of social relationships to the development of depression in migrants; (4) undertake interventions in diverse migrant groups that lower the prevalence of depression or significantly alter its course; and (5) develop an explanatory model knitting together biological, psychological, and social mechanisms that convincingly explain associations between migration and depression. Because of the insufficiency of current knowledge about depression in migrants, clinical case reports, naturalistic studies, and follow-up studies would likely be informative, even if they were not to satisfy the criteria just listed.

The study of migrants as potentially at high-risk for depression, using longitudinal and prospective methods, should attempt not only to assess psychosocial factors before the onset of depression, but also to disentangle individual and environmental effects. This allows a clearer appreciation of the relationship of psychosocial variables to depression (Hirschfeld and Cross, 1983). Psychosocial stresses are often identifiable before the first episode of depression, although the latter can occur without identifiable stresses (Gold et al. 1988).

Given that the major depressions appear to have a heritable and recurrent component (Gold et al. 1988), constitutional and genetic issues could be better understood by controlled family studies in which psychopathology, personality, and psychosocial variables are evaluated independently (Hirschfeld and Cross 1983). When people from different ethnic and racial groups are collected into heterogeneous categories and given broad labels such as "Asians," "Orientals," "English," "Blacks," "Caucasians," or "Occidentals," it seems that any specificity as to their genetic characteristics and lineage of individuals is lost.

Falk and Feingold (1987), in their proposed model that uses differential responses to drugs to examine ethnic and racial factors, mention certain desiderata that are pertinent well beyond the domain of drug-related research. For example, they suggest that ethnic and racial factors relevant to drug usage be identified, that populations be compared in terms of numbers of variables, and that a theoretical explanation be constructed to encompass the findings. Other relevant considerations when conducting such studies include the use of sample sizes large enough to demonstrate statistically significant differences between ethnocultural groups; the measurement of appropriate environmental factors (for example, dietary habits and exposure to other chemical agents); and the relevance of psychosocial factors to the giving and taking of drugs. Attention should also be paid to genetic predispositions, for example, autonomic nervous system sensitivities (Pi et al. 1986), as well as to the racial and ethnic homogeneity of experimental and comparison subjects, to be drawn, ideally, from non-depressed and depressed populations with comparable depressive disorders.

In addition, differences in cultural attitudes may influence self-assessments of health and the reporting of illness in various ethnocultural groups and gender subgroups. Research needs to address the impact of such factors so that the presentation of symptoms by migrants who do not complain of long-standing psychiatric disorders, yet seek professional help more often than their counterparts in the host society, can be understood (Murray and Williams 1986).

Finally, information is needed about the effects of societal trends vis-à-vis immigration, income, family structure, and disability. Such knowledge would encourage service innovations tailored to particular ethnocultural groups, innovations respectful of cultural preferences apropos caring for ill or disabled family or group members.

Intervention Priorities

OBSTACLES TO REFORM. One might assume from the many reports on immigrants and refugees made by various governmental and non-governmental bodies over the past two decades, and from the current interest of politicians and the public-at-large in immigration matters, that much thought and energy would be going into reforming mental health services to better address the needs of migrants. Unfortunately, much of what is being done is ritualistic and overly focused as seen, for example, on the organization of short-term language and job-training programs. The reality that mental disorders, including depression, may be evident not at the time of immigration but only some years down the road is simply not being addressed. Even in the academic and scientific community, few researchers attempt to understand the adaptational problems that immigrants and refugees face. The public, for its part, seems to believe that migrants should be self-directed and self-sufficient. Unfortunately, too, the gaps in our knowledge are currently being addressed mainly by narrowly published and, at times, alarmist literature emanating from ethnocultural organizations. A number of salient themes recur therein: the denial or postponement of treatment due to inadequate resources or restricted access, which leads to avoidable illness and suffering; the depletion of personal resources; the increase in health and social service costs; and the loss of economic productivity.

The philosophy and structure of the formal health-care system, rather than financial issues, have been targeted as the principal factors behind the difficulties encountered by migrants in gaining ready access to health care (Social Planning Council of Metropolitan Toronto 1987). There is considerable merit in such an analysis, particularly in its identification of where changes need to take place. Solutions that depend only on the resources of the formal system will never constructively address the needs of immigrants and refugees. The design of a comprehensive system of services must be based, instead, on a recognition of the steady retreat of governments at all levels from expenditures on health care.

PREVENTION. Principles of management do exist that may be useful for migrants who are clinically depressed, have another type of psychiatric disorder, or have less serious symptomatology. For example, early enrollment by the migrant in language training is generally thought to foster positive adaptation, as is physical proximity to others of the same ethnocultural group (Canadian Task Force 1988b). Other preventive interventions include maintaining or restructuring social support systems, preserving sociocultural activities, and introducing activities similar to culturally familiar ones in such areas as sport or religious ritual. Work that taps pre-migration skills, as well as other activities that maintain aspects of former social roles, is also likely to be useful.

Scarcely recognized, however, are the migrant's restorative practices based on ethnocultural beliefs about illness. Research in prevention and intervention could be informed as to the various ethnocultural groups' strategies that enhance, protect and restore individual and group health.

CROSS-CULTURAL AWARENESS TRAINING. Formal in-service training programs dealing with the nature and management of mental health disorders in ethnocultural populations are still rare in Canadian health and social service agencies. Attempts at providing such training have met with limited success, despite their broad appeal and vitality. Such programs, moreover, are rarely mandatory or evaluated, and there is little shared sense or data regarding their effectiveness and durability, which certainly clouds their appeal to health care institutions. One program, however, was developed in a large children's welfare agency in Toronto (Children's Aid Society of Metropolitan Toronto 1982), based on an extensive review of the accessibility, quantity, and quality of the services provided by the agency to ethnocultural clients. Mandatory cross-cultural awareness training for all agency staff and volunteers was implemented with evaluation of the effects of the training.

One constant refrain in writings on ethnoculturally sensitive services is that cross-cultural awareness training is a key strategy for enhancing service providers' skills in recognizing, understanding, and managing mental disorders. The fact that this suggestion is rarely heeded may be due less to a lack of empirical support than to institutional resistance (Children's Aid Society 1982). In fact, cultural awareness training would enable mental health professionals to view mental disorders from more diverse perspectives. Topics to be covered should include the question of how cultural factors influence the meaning of mental disorder in different ethnocultural populations; the variety of ways in which symptoms are expressed; the major helping resources tapped and the pathways taken during the process by which an individual becomes a client; sociocultural factors that affect symptom occurrence in different ethnic populations; the impact of cultural differences on the process of client-therapist interaction; the client's adherence to treatment and its effect on treatment response; factors that affect the prognosis of symptomatology; and the outcomes of depression in migrants.

The care of relatives at home is likely influenced by culturally rooted beliefs about familial roles and obligations. It has sometimes been asserted, though without good empirical evidence, that migrant families are more likely than those of the host society to take care of ill, handicapped, or mentally disordered family members at home. To the extent that such practices do, in fact, exist, they may contribute to depression in some migrants. For instance, if access to appropriate public services is restricted or lacking, the purchasing of private care may be prohibitively expensive. Several societal trends today that affect all segments of the population render this whole issue more complex, including the economic recession, the increasing proportion of women who work outside the home, high rates of divorce, the high cost of housing, forced retirement, and decreasing mortality rates.

UNDERUTILIZATION OF MENTAL HEALTH SERVICES. The underuse of mental health services by immigrants and refugees has been a recurrent theme in the clinical and research literature (Canadian Task Force 1988b). Although 20 to 25 per cent of people with broadly defined depressions in Western nations contact physicians, the proportion of depressed migrants receiving medical care is probably lower, due to cultural and social factors (Canadian Task Force 1988b). On the other hand, despite the gaps in our knowledge mentioned earlier, the proportion of immigrants and refugees who are depressed probably equals, and perhaps exceeds, the proportion of members in the host society who are depressed.

Even when migrants gain access to a mental health facility, they will tend to obtain treatment at a lower rate than expected. Indeed, it seems that ethnocultural group members are less likely than members of the majority culture to continue in treatment (Hough et al. 1987; Liu and Yu 1985; Sue 1977). In fact, users of mental health facilities from ethnocultural groups other than the majority have been shown to have a drop-out rate of up to 50 per cent after the first interview, compared to 30 per cent for majority culture members (Sue 1977).

REFORM OF SERVICE SYSTEMS AND SERVICE DELIVERY. Mental health services in Canada constitute a two-tiered structure, composed of a formal system mandated to deliver specific mental health services (public hospitals, affiliated health care organizations, and licensed health care professionals) and a relatively independent system. The latter itself has two tiers. The first consists of institutional services, structurally unrelated to mental health services, that are used as a first or continuing contact by migrants with mental disorders (for example, remedial educational programs; public health services; child protection services; and probation services). The staff of these services are pressed to respond to the mental health problems of migrants without the education or training to do so, because migrants are either reluctant to enter the formal system or the system is unable to accommodate them. The second tier of the independent system is composed of ethnocultural community organizations, created to address specific needs of migrants. A central characteristic of these two systems is their disconnectedness from each other in the management of migrants. The result is a potpourri of interventions for the variety of problems presented by immigrants and refugees: modern medical services; traditional cultural practices; innovative supportive initiatives; ad hoc help; and band-aid ministrations.

A comprehensive survey by a federal task force on the nature of services available to immigrants and refugees resulted in recommendations for improving service delivery (Canadian Task Force 1988b). These proposals recognized the significant contribution of indigenous ethnocultural organizations in promoting better services and facilitating migrant adaptation. They also recognized the need for generic community programs (for example, in rehabilitative services) to hire staff who are sensitive to cultural issues and who can, ideally, communicate with migrants in their own language. The report stressed, as well, the necessity of coordinating federal, provincial, and municipal governments' efforts to support effective services by adequate funding and systematic program evaluation.

The task force also formulated suggestions for national and provincial strategies in two main areas: public education and service delivery. Over half the recommendations addressed education and training issues: the education received by migrants in their country of origin; their access to different kinds of information about the host society before and after their arrival; language training; educational programs about migrants at all levels of the education system; and training programs for future mental health professionals. The host society's attitudes toward migrants were seen as contributing as much to mental health as the factors inherent in the processes of migration and adaptation.

An alternative proposal would be to redesign formal health care systems to include both preventive and primary-care services, with designated urban hospitals providing sophisticated secondary and tertiary services, along with training, education, and research. Those parts of the system providing prevention and primary care for migrants would be integrated into a network of formal and ethnocultural (or non-governmental) agencies. Such a structure would provide a linked system of community-based primary care programs. Decentralized facilities of the formal system, together with a number of ethnocultural agencies, could form local joint ventures, each serving a particular ethnic population. These community-based primary-care programs should be easily accessible, eliminating barriers such as high transportation costs, shortages of child care services for parents using the programs, and inflexible hours of operation. Volunteers and interpreters would be integrated into professional consultative, inpatient, outpatient, and public health services. Similarly, demographic, medical, and other pertinent information about clients would be integrated within a central data-base. Such a system would avoid repetitious data-gathering as well as the creation of separate files on the same person in different locations.

Finally, underuse of health services by migrants will not be resolved unless restructuring of the formal system is linked to more efficient service delivery. The design of interventions will be more comprehensive and effective if the key target is the individual client rather than programs, agencies, or systems. All in all, reform of the current system, with the new alliances proposed here, could likely be achieved by a careful reallocation of resources.

BIBLIOGRAPHY

Aday, L.A., Chiu, G.Y., and Andersen, R. 1980. Methodological issues in health care surveys of the Spanish heritage population. *American Journal of Public Health* 70: 374–76.

Allodi, F., and Fantini, N. 1985. The Italians in Toronto: A data system for psychiatric services to an immigrant community. *American Journal of Psychotherapy and Psychopathology* 2: 49–58.

Aneshensel, C.S., and Stone, J.D. 1982. Stress and depression: A test of the buffering model of social support. *Archives of General Psychiatry* 39: 1392–96.

Bagley, C. 1971. Mental illness in immigrant minorities in London. *Journal of Biosocial Science* 3: 449–59.

Baskauskas, L. 1981. The Lithuanian refugee experience and grief. *International Migration Review* 15: 276–91.

Baskin, D., Bluestone, H., and Nelson, M. 1981. Ethnicity and psychiatric diagnosis. *Journal of Clinical Psychology* 37: 529–37.

Beiser, M., and Fleming, J.A.E. 1986. Measuring psychiatric disorder among South East Asian refugees. *Psychological Medicine* 16: 627–39.

Beltrame, J. 1990. Intolerance on rise, 54% say. *Toronto Star*, 23 February.

Boxer, P.A. and Garvey, J.T. 1985. Psychiatric diagnoses of Cuban refugees in the United States: Findings of medical review boards. *American Journal of Psychiatry* 142: 86–9.

Brewin, C. 1980. Explaining the lower rates of psychiatric treatment among Asian immigrants to the United Kingdom: A preliminary study. *Social Psychiatry* 15: 17–19.

Brown, G.W., and Harris, T. 1978. *Social origins of depression: A study of psychiatric disorder in women.* New York: Free Press.

Brown, G.W., and Prudo, R. 1981. Psychiatric disorder in a rural and urban population: Aetiology of depression. *Psychological Medicine* 11: 581–99.

Burke, A.W. 1982. Determinants of delinquency in female West Indian immigrants. *International Journal of Social Psychiatry* 28: 28–34.

Cadoret, R.J., Winokur, G., Dorzab, J., and Baker, M. 1972. Depressive disease: Life events and onset of illness. *Archives of General Psychiatry* 16: 133–36.

Canadian Task Force on Mental Health Issues Affecting Immigrants and Refugees. 1988a. *Review of the literature on migrant mental health.* Ottawa: Health and Welfare Canada.

Canadian Task Force on Mental Health Issues Affecting Immigrants and Refugees. 1988b. *After the door has been opened.* Ottawa: Health and Welfare Canada.

Cassel, J. 1976. The contribution of the social environment to host resistance: The fourth Wade Hampton Frost lecture. *American Journal of Epidemiology* 104: 107–23.

Chakrabarti, A., and Sandel, B. 1984. Somatic complaint syndrome in India. *Transcultural Psychiatry Research Review* 21: 212–16.

Chan, D.W. 1985. The Chinese version of the General Health Questionnaire: Does language make a difference? *Psychological Medicine* 15: 147–55.

Chan, K.B., and Lam, L. 1983. Resettlement of Vietnamese-Chinese refugees in Montreal, Canada: Some socio-psychological problems and dilemmas. *Canadian Ethnic Studies* 15: 1–17.

Children's Aid Society of Metropolitan Toronto. 1982. *Task force on multicultural programmes. Final report.* Toronto: Children's Aid Society of Metropolitan Toronto.

Cobb, S. 1976. Social support as a moderator of life stress. *Psychosomatic Medicine* 38: 300–14.

Cochrane, R., and Bal, S.S. 1987. Migration and schizophrenia: An examination of five hypotheses. *Social Psychiatry* 22: 181–91.

Cochrane, R., Hashmi, F., and Stopes-Roe, M. 1977. Measuring psychological disturbance in Asian immigrants to Britain. *Social Science and Medicine* 11: 157–64.

Cochrane, R., and Stopes-Row, M. 1977. Psychological and social adjustment of Asian immigrants to Britain: A community survey. *Social Psychiatry* 12: 195–206.

– 1979. Psychological disturbance in Ireland, in England, and in Irish emigrants to England: A comparative study. *Economics and Sociology Review* 10: 301–20.

Cook, K.O., and Timberlake, E.M. 1984. Cross cultural counselling with Vietnamese refugees. *Social Work* 29: 108–14.

daCosta, G.A. 1974. *Parent-child separation among West Indian immigrants.* Paper presented at the annual meeting of the Canadian Psychiatric Association, Ottawa.

daCosta, G.A., and Persad, E. 1987. *A study of the impact of race and culture on the inpatient experience of the foreign-born psychiatric patient.* Paper presented at the annual meeting of the Canadian Psychiatric Association, London.

Dean, A., Lin, H., and Ensel, N.M. 1980. The epidemiological significance of support systems in depression. *Research in Community Mental Health* 2: 77–109.

Dohrenwend, B.P., and Dohrenwend, B.S. 1969. *Social status and psychological disorder.* New York: Wiley.

Dohrenwend, B.S., and Dohrenwend, B.P. 1974. *Stressful life events: Their nature and effects.* New York: Wiley.

Driedger, L., and Chappell, N. 1987. *Ageing and ethnicity: Toward an interface.* Toronto: Butterworth.

Driedger, L., and Clifton, R.A. 1984. Ethnic stereotypes: Images of ethnocentrism, reciprocity, or dissimilarity? *Canadian Review of Sociology and Anthropology* 21: 287–301.

Driedger, L., and Mezoff, R.A. 1981. Ethnic prejudice and discrimination in Winnipeg high schools. *Canadian Journal of Sociology* 6: 1–17.

Eaton, W.W. 1978. Life events, social support and psychiatric symptoms: A re-analysis of the New Haven data. *Journal of Health and Social Behaviour* 19:, 230–34.

Eitinger, L. 1959. The incidence of mental disease among refugees in Norway. *Journal of Mental Science* 105: 326-38.

Eyton, J., and Neuwirth, G. 1984. Cross-cultural validity: ethnocentrism in health studies with special reference to the Vietnamese. *Social Science and Medicine* 18: 447-53.

Falk, J.L., and Feingold, D.A. 1987. Environmental and cultural factors in the behavioural action of drugs. In *Psychopharmacology, the third generation of progress*, edited by H. Y. Meltzer, 1503-10. New York: Raven Press.

Fava, G.A. 1983. Assessing depressive symptoms across cultures: Italian validation of the CES-D self-rating scale. *Journal of Clinical Psychology* 39: 249-51.

Galanter, M. 1988. Research on social supports and mental illness. *American Journal of Psychiatry* 145: 1270-73.

Gold, P.W., Goodwin, F.K., and Chrousos, G.P. 1988. Clinical and biochemical manifestations of depression. *New England Journal of Medicine* 319: 348-53.

Goldstein, E. 1979. Psychological adaptation of Soviet immigrants. *The American Journal of Psychoanalysis* 39: 257-63.

Grant, I., Sweetwood, H.L., Yaker, J., and Gerst, M. 1981. Quality of life events in relation to psychiatric symptoms. *Archives of General Psychiatry* 38: 335-39.

Harper, T. 1989. French, English urged as priority for immigration. *Toronto Star* 4 April.

Harvey, Y.S.K., and Chung, S.H. 1980. The Koreans. In *People and cultures of Hawaii: A psychocultural profile*, edited by J. F. McDermott, Jr., W.S. Tseng, and T.W. Maretzki, 135-154. Honolulu: University Press of Hawaii.

Hirschfeld, R.M.A., and Cross, C.K. 1983. Personality, life events, and social factors in depression. In *Psychiatry Update* Vol. 2, edited by L. Grinspoon. Washington, DC: American Psychiatric Press.

Hough, R., Landsverk, J., Karno, M., Burnam, A., Timbers, D., Escobar, J., and Regier, D. 1987. Utilization of health and mental health services by Los Angeles Mexican Americans and non-Hispanic Whites. *Archives of General Psychiatry* 44: 702-9.

Hurh, W.M., and Kim, K.C. 1982. Methodological problems in the study of Korean immigrants: Conceptual, interactional, sampling and interviewer training difficulties. In *Methodological problems in minority research*, edited by W.T. Liu, 61-80. Chicago, IL: Asian American Mental Health Research Center.

Husaini, B.A., Neff, J.A., Newbrough, J.R., and Seymour, M. 1982. The stress-buffering role of social support and personal competence among the rural married. *Journal of Community Psychology* 10: 409-26.

Infeld, F.W. 1977. Current social stressors and symptoms of depression. *American Journal of Psychiatry* 134: 161-66.

Johnson, J.H., and Sarason, I.G. 1978. Life stress, depression and anxiety: Internal-external locus of control as a moderator variable. *Journal of Psychosomatic Research* 22: 205- 8.

Jones, E.E., and Korchin, S.J. 1982. Minority mental health: Perspectives. In E.E.

Jones and S.J. Korchin *Minority mental health.* New York: Praeger.

Karno, M., Burnam, M.A., Escobar, J.I., Hough, R.L., and Eaton, W.W. 1983. Development of the Spanish language version of the National Institute of Mental Health Diagnostic Interview Schedule. *Archives of General Psychiatry* 40: 1183–88.

Kinzie, J.D., Manson, S.M., Vinh, D.T., Tolan, N.T., Anh, B., and Pho, T.N. 1982. Development and validation of a Vietnamese-Language depression rating scale. *American Journal of Psychiatry* 139: 1276–81.

Kohn, R., Flaherty, J.A., and Levav, I. 1989. Somatic symptoms among older Soviet immigrants: An exploratory study. *The International Journal of Social Psychiatry* 35: 350–60.

Kuo, W.H., and Tsai, Y.M. 1986. Social networking, hardiness, and immigrants' mental health. *Journal of Health and Social Behaviour* 27: 133–49.

Lilienfeld, A.M., and Lilienfeld, D.E. 1980. *Foundations of epidemiology.* New York: Oxford University Press.

Littlewood, R., and Lipsedge, M. 1981. Some social and phenomenological characteristics of psychotic immigrants. *Psychological Medicine* 11: 289–301.

Liu, W., and Yu, E. 1985. Ethnicity, mental health, and the urban delivery system. In *Urban ethnicity in the United States: New immigrants and old minorities,* edited by L. Maldonado and J. Moore, 211–248. Beverley Hills: Sage.

London, M. 1986. Mental illness among immigrant minorities in the United Kingdom. *British Journal of Psychiatry* 149:, 265–73.

Lopez, S. 1981. Mexican-American usage of mental health facilities: Under-utilization considered. In *Exploration in Chicano psychology,* edited by A. Baron, Jr. New York: Praeger.

McGoldrick, M. 1982. Ethnicity and family therapy: An overview. In *Ethnicity and family therapy,* edited by M. McGoldrick, J. K. Pearce, and J. Giordano, 3–30. New York: Guilford.

Marcos, L.R. 1982. Adults' recollection of their language deprivation as immigrant children. *American Journal of Psychiatry* 139: 607–10.

Marsella, A.J. 1978. Thoughts on cross-cultural studies on the epidemiology of depression. *Culture, Medicine and Psychiatry* 2: 343–57.

– 1980. Depressive experience and disorder across cultures. In *Handbook of cross-cultural psychology: Psychopathology* Vol. 6, edited by H. C. Triandis and J. G. Draguns, 237–289. Boston: Allyn and Bacon.

Mirowsky, J., and Ross, C.E. 1983. Paranoia and the structure of powerlessness. *American Sociological Review* 48: 228–39.

– 1984. Mexican culture and its emotional contradictions. *Journal of Health and Social Behaviour* 25: 2–13.

Morgan, P., and Andrushko, E. 1977. The use of diagnostic-specific rates of mental hospitalization to estimate underutilization by immigrants. *Social Science and Medicine* 11: 611–18.

Murphy, H.B.M. 1952. Practical methods for refugee mental health in Britain. *World*

Mental Health 4: 198–203.

– 1955. Refugee psychoses in Great Britain: Admissions to mental hospitals. In *Flight and resettlement*, edited by H. B. M. Murphy 173–194. Paris: United Nations Educational Scientific and Cultural Organization.

Murray, J., & Williams, P. 1986. Self-reported illness and general practice consultations in Asian-born and British-born residents of West London. *Social Psychiatry* 21: 139–45.

Neff, J.A. 1984. Race differences in psychological distress: The effects of sex, urbanicity, and measurement strategy. *American Journal of Community Psychology* 12: 337–51.

Parker, G.B., and Brown, L.B. 1982. Coping behaviours that mediate between life events and depression. *Archives of General Psychiatry* 39: 1386–91.

Paykel, E.S., Myers, J.K., Dienelt, M.N., Klerman, G.L., Lindenthal, J.J., and Pepper, M.P. 1969. Life events and depression: A controlled study. *Archives of General Psychiatry* 22:, 753–60.

Pedersen, S. 1949. Psychopathological reactions to extreme social displacements (refugee neurosis). *Psychoanalytical Review* 36: 344–54.

Pfister-Ammende, M. 1955. The symptomatology, treatment, and prognosis in mentally ill refugees and repatriates in Switzerland. In *Flight and Resettlement*, edited by H. B. M. Murphy (pp. 147–172). Paris: United Nations Educational Scientific and Cultural Organization.

Pi, E.H., Simpson, G.H., and Cooper, T.B. 1986. Pharmacokinetics of desipramine in Caucasian and Asian volunteers. *American Journal of Psychiatry* 143: 1174–76.

Pope, H.G. Jr., Ionescu-Proggia, M., and Yurgelun-Todd, D. 1983. Migration and manic depressive illness. *Comprehensive Psychiatry* 24, 158–165.

Rabkin, J.G. 1982. Stress and psychiatric disorders. In *Handbook of stress: Theoretical and clinical aspects*, edited by L. Goldberger and S. Breznitz, 566–84. New York: Free Press.

Rahe, R.H., Looney, J.G., Ward, H.W., Tung, T.M., and Liu, W.T. 1978. Psychiatric consultation in a Vietnamese refugee camp. *American Journal of Psychiatry* 135: 185–90.

Resner, J., and Hartog, J. 1970. Concepts and terminology of mental disorder among Malays. *Journal of Cross-Cultural Psychology* 1: 369–81.

Ross, C.E., and Mirowsky, J. 1979. A comparison of life-event weighting schemes: Change, undesirability and effect-proportional indices. *Journal of Health and Social Behaviour* 20: 166–77.

Rwegellera, G.G. 1980. Differential use of psychiatric services by West Indians, West Africans and English in London. *British Journal of Psychiatry* 137: 428–32.

Shuval, J.T. 1982. Migration and stress. In *Handbook of stress: Theoretical and clinical aspects*, edited by L. Goldberger and S. Breznitz, 677–91). New York: Free Press.

Social Planning Council of Metropolitan Toronto 1987. *Access to health and social* services for members of diverse cultural and racial groups in Metropolitan Toronto. Report no. 2. Toronto: Social Planning Council of Metropolitan Toronto.

Sue, S. 1977. Community mental health services to minority groups: Some optimism, some pessimism. *American Psychologist* 32: 616–24.

– 1983. Ethnic minority issues in psychology: A re-examination. *American Psychologist* 38: 583–92.

Tack, C. 1981. The people of Indochina. In *People and cultures of Hawaii: A psychocultural profile*, edited J.F. McDermott, Jr., W.S. Tseng, and T.W. Maretzki, 201–24. Honolulu: University of Hawaii Press.

Tanaka-Matsumi, J., and Marsella, A.J. 1976. Ethnocultural variations in the subjective experience of depression: Word Association. *Journal of Cross-cultural Psychology* 7: 379–97.

Teja, J.S., Narang, R.L., and Aggarwal, A.K. 1971. Depression across cultures. *British Journal of Psychiatry* 119: 253–60.

Tolsdorf, C.C. 1978. Social networks, support, and coping: An exploratory study. *Family Process* 13: 11–17.

Tseng, W.S., and Hsu, J. 1969. Chinese culture, personality formation, and mental illness. *International Journal of Social Psychiatry* 16: 5–14.

– 1972. The Chinese attitude toward parental authority as expressed in Chinese children's stories. *Archives of General Psychiatry* 26(11): 28–34.

Tseng, W.S., and McDermott, J.F., Jr. 1981. *Culture, mind and therapy: An introduction to cultural psychiatry*. New York: Brunner-Mazel.

Tyhurst, L. 1951. Displacement and migration: A study in social psychiatry. *American Journal of Psychiatry* 107: 561–68.

Vadher, A., and Ndetei, D.M. 1981. Life events and depression in a Kenyan setting. *British Journal of Psychiatry* 139: 134–37.

Vega, W., Warheit, G., Buhl-Auth, J., and Meinhardt, K. 1984. The prevalence of depressive symptoms among Mexican Americans and Anglos. *American Journal of Epidemiology* 120: 592–607.

Warheit, G.J. 1979. Life events, coping, stress and depressive symptomatology. *American Journal of Psychiatry* 136: 502–7.

Weller, M.P.I., and Ameen, N. 1982. Elvis Presley, reactive hypomania, and Koro. *American Journal of Psychiatry* 139: 970. (letter).

Westermeyer, J. 1985. Psychiatric diagnosis across cultural boundaries. *American Journal of Psychiatry* 142: 798–805.

– 1988. DSM-III psychiatric disorders among refugees in the United States: A point prevalence study. *American Journal of Psychiatry* 145: 197–202.

– 1988. A matched pairs study of depression among Hmong refugees with particular reference to predisposing factors and treatment outcome. *Social Psychiatry and Psychiatric Epidemiology* 23: 64–71.

Westermeyer, J., Vang, T.F., and Neider, J. 1983a. Refugees who do and do not seek psychiatric care: An analysis of premigratory and postmigratory characteristics. *Journal of Nervous and Mental Disease* 171: 86–91.

– 1983b. A comparison of refugees using and not using a psychiatric service: An analysis of DSM-III criteria and self-rating scales in cross-cultural context. *Journal of Operational Psychiatry* 14: 36–41.

Yap, P.M. 1969. The culture bound reactive syndromes. In *Mental health research in Asia and the Pacific*, edited by W. Candill and T.Y. Lin. Honolulu: East-West Centre Press.

Zola, I.K. 1966. Culture and symptoms: An analysis of patients' presenting complaints. *American Sociological Review* 31: 615–30.

Zung, W.W.K., MacDonald, M.S., and Zung, E.M. 1988. Prevalence of clinically significant depressive symptoms in black and white patients in family practice settings. *American Journal of Psychiatry* 145: 882–3.

CHAPTER TEN

Depression among People with Physical Disabilities

MARY ANN McCOLL AND
JUDITH FRIEDLAND

The visibility of people with physical disabilities has increased dramatically in the past ten to fifteen years. No longer is it uncommon in Canadian communities to see men and women using wheelchairs, canes, or other mobility aids. Canadian society has begun to deal with the physical reality of accommodating people with disabilities. However, even as the public moves toward a greater awareness of the challenges faced by disabled people, attention to the psychological and social aspects of disability lags far behind. In this chapter, we examine why the prevalence of depression is higher among those who are disabled than in the general population. An intuitive response would be that people who are disabled have suffered something out of the ordinary, something that is clearly unpleasant; as a result, they are more likely to be unhappy. Some degree of sadness is to be expected after the onset of a serious physical disability; in fact, there would be concern if this were not the case. Sadness, however, should be differentiated from depressive disorder. Our concern here is to discover why some people are able to overcome sadness and adjust to disability, while others go on to suffer depression. We suggest that the precipitants of depression may be different both in kind and degree for the disabled population, thus making them even more vulnerable.

DEFINITIONS AND EPIDEMIOLOGY

Definition of Disability

To begin, we look at the notion of disability as used throughout this chapter. Historically, physical disabilities were defined in the context of a particular disease, or diagnostic category, and classified according to the International Classification of Diseases (ICD). Although useful, this method of classification failed to incorporate many important dimensions of disability, such as severity, functional limitation, or the impact of the person's social and physical environment. Individuals who had suffered a stroke, for example, were all classified together, regardless of whether they had recovered completely (to their former level of functioning), or had sustained permanent losses in the areas of communication, mobility, self-care, perception, cognition, or role performance.

In 1980, in response to both the International Year of Disabled Persons and the inadequacy of the ICD classification system, the World Health Organization (WHO) developed the International Classification of Impairments, Disabilities, and Handicaps. According to that system, *disability* is defined as "any restriction or lack of ability to perform an activity in the manner or within the range considered normal for a human being." The WHO document identified nine categories of disability, including disabilities of behaviour, communication, personal care, locomotion, body disposition, dexterity, and other specific activity areas.

In the WHO system, disability is contrasted with notions of *impairment*, a term that refers to the structural or functional abnormality itself, and *handicap*, a term that refers to a disadvantage that prevents or inhibits performance or functional fulfillment. Together, the concepts form a progression. That is, impairments may or may not result in a disability depending on their severity; and a disability may or may not result in a handicap, depending on the social and environmental context of the individual with the disability, as well as the demands of a particular situation (Wright 1983). Thus, for example, a disability may prove to be a social handicap, as well as a physical handicap. It is important to note that the term "disability" carries with it the possibility of successful role performance, but with modifications of time, method, or equipment that make the task possible.

As an example, let us look at two individuals. Both are of the same age, gender, and educational and social status. One is a concert pianist, the other an accountant. Both have primarily skeletal impairments, in that they have had their middle finger on the dominant hand amputated. While both are clearly disabled (that is, restricted in their ability to undertake specific behaviours), the concert pianist is handicapped in his vocational role, whereas the accountant is not. Although certain tasks will have to be modified for the accountant, successful performance of the vocational role is not threatened by the disability.

In this chapter, we restrict our discussion to physical disability and its many manifestations. We do not deal with disabilities that are primarily mental or emotional in origin. Our focus, rather, is on the relationship of depression to disability, or to the inability to perform usual activities in the customary way. To the extent that a disability results in a handicap, the effects on a depressive outlook are expected to be all the more severe. But before discussing depression and disability, let us attempt to ascertain the extent to which disability affects Canadians.

Prevalence of Disability

Estimates of the prevalence of disability in Canadian society arise out of a number of recent surveys. Josie (1973) found that eighty-seven per thousand of the noninstitutionalized Canadian population were limited in terms of activity and function. Walker and McWhinnie (1980) reported that 85 per thousand Canadians under sixty-five were disabled and 206 per thousand over sixty-five. The Canada Health Survey (1981) estimated the prevalence of disability at 116 per thousand of all Canadians, with an increase to 300 per thousand for those over sixty-five (Statistics Canada 1981). The Canada Health and Disability Survey (Statistics Canada 1983-84) reported 128 per thousand disabled Canadians, based on the who definition of disability. (As noted above, this definition includes mental, emotional and behavioural disabilities, as well as those with a primarily physical origin). Finally, Wood and Turner (1985) estimated the prevalence of disability in southwestern Ontario at sixty-seven per thousand. Their prevalence estimates varied by gender, with overall prevalence for women in excess of that for men (71 and 63 per thousand, respectively).

Estimates of the prevalence of disability in Canada can be compared to those in Britain and the United States. One of the earliest population-based estimates of the prevalence of physical disability comes from Great Britain: seventy-eight per thousand (Bennett et al. 1970). American estimates in 1976 (Nagi) and 1981 (U.S. Department of Health, Education and Welfare) are considerably higher: 230 and 146 per thousand, respectively. Much of the discrepancy between these estimates and the former is accounted for by the inclusion of mental handicaps in the definition of disability. Age differences also contribute to the discrepancies. For example, whereas Nagi (1976) surveyed noninstitutionalized people eighteen years of age and older, the National Health Survey estimate (U.S. Department of Health, Education and Welfare 1981) was based only on those between fifteen and sixty-four years of age. Given what we know about the positive relationship between age and disability, the older sample was expected to produce a higher estimate.

The variability among estimates of disability makes it difficult to generate a coherent perception of the proportion of the population actually disabled (as defined herein). Much of this variability, however, is due to differences in the definition of disability. Whereas some authors exclude disabilities of psychiatric or emotional origin, others include them. Furthermore, although most studies define disability as the presence of a chronic condition with activity limitation, the extent of the limitation varies from study to study.

Perhaps the most useful estimates for our purposes are those recent figures that deal with Canadians of all ages in terms of the WHO definition of disability (Statistics Canada 1988). According to the Health and Activity Limitations Survey, it appears that somewhere around 13 per cent of Canadians consider themselves disabled; this number includes more women than men, and the estimated number increases dramatically with age, particularly over the age of sixty-five. It is difficult to ascertain from the data available whether or not a temporal trend is present, because of inconsistencies in the methods of estimation. However, most authors would agree that the increase in "survivorship" with most disabling conditions has contributed to an overall increase in prevalence over the past few decades.

Heterogeneity of Disability

No matter how clearly the term "disability" is defined, its meaning becomes amorphous as soon as it is used to describe the people who have the disability. A host of parameters must be applied to the definition, each contributing to the heterogeneity of the population. For example, *age of onset* is a particularly notable variable. One must ask whether the disorder affected a child born with a disability who knows no other state of existence, a teenager just beginning to come to terms with body image and self concept, a young adult ready to begin a new stage of life for which there has been lengthy preparation, a person at mid-life questioning both the past and the future, or an elderly individual with few reserves to face the added burden of the disability?

In the same way that disability itself is a heterogeneous concept, depression among disabled people must also be considered within a multidimensional context. In this section, we discuss the heterogeneity of disability, as well as the variety of factors that can exert different effects on the depression of disabled people.

Conventional wisdom dictates that nature, severity, and type of disability all influence estimates of depression in various disability groups. But the type of onset of the disabling condition also affects the meaning of the term "disability." A slow and insidious onset, as is typical with Parkinson's disease, sets in train a very different notion of disability than does an acute and sudden onset, such as occurs with a spinal cord injury. The onset of both of these conditions may be further contrasted with impairments such as rheumatoid arthritis, where attacks are episodic and recovery is usually incomplete following each episode or exacerbation.

Prognosis is another major factor in the heterogeneity of the concept of disability. Relatively few chronic diseases or conditions have a favourable prognosis or offer much hope of complete recovery. Some conditions, like spinal cord injury, have a finite outcome with residual disability that is life-long, while others, like multiple sclerosis, are progressively degenerative or recurring. Each of these scenarios has a differential effect on prognosis and perceptions about the future. The risk of recurrence that accompanies a stroke, for example, may result in a more fearful view of the future than that resulting from a traffic accident. Similarly, levels of pain and discomfort and degrees of dysfunction are all influential factors.

The meaning of disability may also vary according to socioeconomic and cultural factors. Financial constraints may result in an inability to minimize handicap, whether because expensive aids are needed to improve accessibility in the home or workplace, or because vocational retraining is required. One's culture attaches its own meaning to the concept of disability. We know from ethnographic research, for instance, that the meaning of disability varies among cultures – from intolerance, through shame and pity, to relative acceptance and even honour (Wright 1983).

In addition to age, type of onset, prognosis, and socioeconomic and cultural factors, gender and role also influence response to disability. All these factors provide filters, through which the concept of disability must pass before its meaning can be appreciated. In reality, however the true meaning of disability can only be understood when that disability is placed within the context of an individual's existence. This subjective meaning takes precedence over all other factors. The ultimate question, then, is how the individual perceives the disability at this moment, within the context of his or her own life experience.

Prevalence of Depression with Disability

Prevalence is defined by Last (1983) as the number of cases of a disease or disorder found in a population at a given point (or period) in time. Unlike *incidence*, which is an estimate of the number of new cases, prevalence measures the burden of a particular disorder on a population. Most investigators prefer to use prevalence as their index for depression, because of the chronic nature of depression and its ambiguous time of onset (Murphy et al. 1984; Turner and Wood 1985).

Estimates of the prevalence of depression among disabled persons vary from very low (for example, Cook 1976: 2 per cent among spinal-cord-injured individuals) to very high (for example, Robinson and Szetela 1981: 61 per cent among stroke survivors; Gotham et al. 1985: 46 per cent of Parkinson's disease patients.) If the presence or absence of an *excess* risk for depression among disabled people (that is, a risk beyond that expected for the general population), is to be determined, these estimates must be compared with reliable estimates from the general population. The best estimates come from community surveys of the 1960s and '70s (Stirling County, Nova Scotia: Hughes et al. 1960; midtown Manhattan: Srole 1962; New Haven: Weissman and Myers 1978) as well as the recent American Epidemiological Catchment Area Surveys (Myers et al. 1984). These estimates place the risk for affective disorder in the general population between 5 and 9 per cent. Estimates such as Cook's (1976) for spinal cord injured individuals (2%) are thus clearly below the expected value, whereas those for people with strokes (61%) are much in excess of population-based expectations.

Because of the heterogeneity of the concept of disability discussed earlier, this notion of variability in depression according to disability is not unexpected. If we combine what we know about the effect of demographic variables *vis-à-vis* the risk of depression with the effect of those same variables on the risk of specific disabilities, some notable differences are bound to occur. For instance, when we combine the fact that depression is more common with increasing age and among women (Radloff and Rae 1979) with the fact that most spinal cord injuries occur to young men, it is not surprising that the risk for depression in this particular population is very low. Conversely, those disabilities that affect older individuals, and particularly women, would be expected to be accompanied by a larger risk for depression.

To establish the presence of an excess risk for disabled people, we therefore need an approach to estimating depression that overcomes the inherent confounding and methodological problems (Rodin and Voshart 1986; Turner and Noh 1988). Two sets of factors influence the accuracy of prevalence estimates of depression among disabled people: those that influence indicators in the general population, and those that are peculiar to depression among people with a disability.

Perhaps the most important issue with regard to the latter factors is the definition of depression itself. A number of authors have suggested that ambiguous definitions cause depression to be overdiagnosed in those with disabilities (Cushman and Dijkers 1990; Bodenhamer et al. 1983; Ernst 1987; Lawson 1978). Cushman and Dijkers (1990) further suggest that this labeling may actually have a detrimental effect on the process of rehabilitation and on independent living outcomes for people with disabilities. Wright (1983) explains that professionals impose a "requirement of mourning" on people with a disability; that is, that professionals expect a pathological response because of the very suddenness and severity of the circumstances surrounding the trauma or illness. Within this context, any negative affect or demonstration of emotion is subject to interpretation as depression. In this way, the normal grief reactions of people with a disability become medicalized and marginalized and, in many cases, the complexity and idiosyncrasy of the reaction to disability is lost.

When defining depression, it is also important to distinguish between the colloquial and clinical uses of the word. Turner and Beiser (1990) use the Center for Epidemiological Studies-Depression (CES-D) Scale and the Diagnostic Interview Schedule (DIS) from the *Diagnostic and Statistical Manual of Mental Disorders – Third Edition* (DSM-III) to distinguish between the clusters of depressive symptomatology that may be a normal part of the process of adjustment, and true depression, as described in the DSM-III. Turner and Beiser found 37 per cent of their sample of 727 disabled individuals with CES-D scores in the so-called depressed range (>16), whereas only 11.3 per cent had a lifetime prevalence for depression, and only 5.6 per cent had a six-month prevalence for depression, as classified by the DSM-III. Two groups of researchers have provided further evidence for this distinction between intermittent depressive symptomatology and clinical depression in the spinal cord injured population. In their study of seventy-one newly spinal cord injured individuals during the inpatient phase of their recovery, Judd et al. (1989) found that 62 per cent of their sample were consistently not depressed (using three common measures of clinical depression), 18 per cent were intermittently depressed, usually with readily attributable social causation, and the remaining 20 per cent were persistently depressed throughout the period. McDonald et al. (1987), in their study of fifty-three spinal cord injured individuals living in the community, found (again using three common indices of depression) that 13 per cent of their sample were definitely depressed, consistent with DSM-III definitions; 2 per cent could not be reliably classified; and the remaining 85 per cent were not depressed, although 45 per cent had experienced mild depression or distress intermittently. In both these studies, the truly depressed proportion was larger than general population estimates, and the depression was of a severity and magnitude consistent with psychiatric and pharmacological treatment. However, in all three studies, the majority of the sample was not depressed, even though a certain proportion (between 11 and 20%), although clinically not depressed, were clearly in the midst of emotional turmoil associated with adjustment. These studies emphasize the need for awareness of both the pathological and the nonpathological levels of adjustment to disability, and for specificity in definition and measurement. Recent work by McColl and Skinner (1992a, 1992b) supports this distinction between two levels of psychological-emotional reaction by providing a two-dimensional model for adjustment to disability. One dimension represents depressive symptomatology; the other represents normative adjustment reactions to disability.

Pursuant to differences in definition are differences in the measurement of depression. Although a number of psychometrically sound measures exist for depression (for example, The Beck Depression Inventory: Beck et al. 1961; the CES-D Scale: Radloff 1977; the General Health Questionnaire: Goldberg and Hillier 1979), consensus as to their application in research remains limited. There is often disagreement, moreover, regarding the use of cutoff scores to classify people as depressed or not. Time of measurement is an important consideration, as well, when generating a consistent estimate of depression (Cassileth et al. 1984; Richards 1986), particularly if we assume that depression is a dynamic rather than a static state.

These same problems – inconsistencies in definition, measurement, cutoff scores, and time of measurement – also arise when estimating depression in the disabled person. For example, time-since-onset and time-since-discharge from hospital are both temporal factors that can influence the presence or absence of depression. Take, for instance, the findings of Sjogren (1982), who noted depression among stroke survivors to be relatively low in the first six months post-stroke, high between seven and twelve months, and low again after one year.

Rodin and Voshart (1986) have suggested a further problem in using the usual measures of depression for disabled people; namely, that somatic symptoms of the disorder or disability may become confounded with somatic indicators of depression, thereby biasing the estimates of depression. Using the Beck Depression Inventory, Peck et al. (1989) showed that depression scores are particularly contaminated by the inclusion of somatic items in an arthritic sample; in addition, they advocated using only the dysphoria subscale for research involving disabled subjects. Noh and Posthuma (1990), on the other hand, found that the (CES-D) Scale produced consistent results across both somatic and nonsomatic items in a disabled sample. Hence, they recommend the use of the CES-D Scale for both clinical and research applications in disabled populations.

Design elements may also be important when estimating depression. The approach of Turner and Noh (1988) – they used a multivariate model to allow for control of demographic and treatment factors – is one way of minimizing the extent to which extraneous factors, or factors other than the disability itself, influence the risk of depression. The use of a comparison group is another useful approach to controlling confounding in estimates of depression among people with disabilities (Strayhorn 1982). For example, Westbrook and Viney (1982) – who compared a number of psychological variables, including depression, in a disabled population and a sample of mature and undergraduate students – found that, although comparability of the two groups was less than ideal, the notion of a control sample was useful.

Sampling strategy is also an important consideration in obtaining an unbiased estimate of depression. Researchers have found that sampling done within a clinical population is far more likely to result in an overestimate of depression than is sampling done within a community-based population. Indeed, depression has such pervasive effects that it is likely to be associated with hospitalization for a variety of complaints, thus ensuring an overrepresentation of the prevalence of depression in clinical populations.

Table 1
Prevalence studies of depression following stroke, according to
sampling: A summary

Study	Prevalence (%)	Sample size	Sample source
Feibel and Springer 1982	26	91	Population
Folstein et al. 1977	50	20	Hospital
Friedland and McColl 1987	27	85	Outpatient
Labi et al. 1980	50	121	Population
Reding et al. 1985	49	78	Hospital
Robinson and Benson 1981	44	25	Hospital
Robinson and Szetela 1981	61	18	Hospital
Robinson et al. 1983	27	103	Hospital
Robinson and Price 1981	30	103	Outpatient

Sample size is still another factor that influences prevalence estimates.
A crude rule of thumb suggests that the larger the sample size, the more
precise the parameter estimate. An example of the influence of some of
these sampling issues is shown in Table 1, where estimates of depression
within the stroke population are compared in terms of sample size and source
(McColl and Friedland 1988).

Recent studies confronting these methodological problems provide consistent and compelling evidence of an *excess* risk of depression among disabled people. For example, Cassileth et al. (1984) found rates for depression
among disabled people to be significantly different from those of the general
population, after controlling for age and sex. Turner and Noh (1988) found
a significant relationship between depression and disability in a community
sample, with demographic factors controlled. Rosenbaum and Raz (1977)
found a significant main effect for both brain-injured and non-brain-injured
disability on depression. Westbrook and Viney (1982) found chronically ill
patients significantly more depressed, more anxious, and more angry than
a comparison sample. Evidence such as this has prompted Turner and Wood
(1985) to assert that the presence of a relationship between disability and
depression is irrefutable.

ETIOLOGY OF DEPRESSION AMONG DISABLED
PERSONS

The etiological factors related to depression for the general population (Kaplan and Sadock 1988) are, of course, factors for the physically disabled
population as well. A physical disorder offers no immunity from a mental
disorder. In fact, as already discussed, a physical disability is seen to increase
the likelihood of depression.

If we wish to improve our understanding of these precipitants and develop effective means to counteract them, we must closely examine the known etiological factors in depression and how they may be influenced by disability. These factors can be divided into two broad categories: biological and psychosocial.

Biological Factors

Biological factors that influence depression include those that are genetic and predispose a person to depression, those that are manifest in structural changes or neurochemical imbalance and are part of the disease process itself, and those that are related to the use of prescribed medication.

GENETIC FACTORS. Twin studies suggest that, for the most part, the risk of all forms of affective disorder for first-degree relatives of unipolar probands falls within the range of 11 to 16 per cent (Strayhorn 1982). For monozygotic twins the concordance rate is reported to be between 50 and 60 per cent; for dizygotic twins it is between 15 and 20 per cent. Adoption studies also show evidence of a purely genetic component to the disorder (Andreason 1984). Obviously, people with a disability are at least as likely to have this hereditary component in their constitution as anyone else in the general population. Moreover, for someone who is genetically predisposed to psychiatric illness, a serious medical illness may act as a precipitant for depression. Thus, it would seem wise to ensure that careful histories are taken of all who become physically disabled, to see whether they or their family members show evidence of previous psychiatric illness. Such information would signal the possibility of an increased risk of depression.

STRUCTURAL CHANGE AND NEUROCHEMICAL IMBALANCE. There has been a strong focus on biological factors that predispose to depression, both in the psychiatric and rehabilitation literatures. Whereas depression was previously thought of as an understandable reaction to many disorders, it is now seen in some cases as a biologically influenced outcome. We examine briefly the neurochemical correlates of depression that can be expected to accompany some physical disabilities.

When looking for direct influences on the emotions, the most obvious may well be those disorders that directly affect the physical structure of the brain. The search for structural sites of behaviours, which began in earnest with Gall and the phrenologists and continued in the work of the localizationists, remains a focus today (Kolb and Wishaw 1985). Although the limbic system has long been considered an essential component of the emotional system (Papez 1937), the role of the hypothalamus and the function of neocortical connections are currently of special interest. Research into emotional disturbances following brain injury presents contrasting views of the role played by the two hemispheres. For example, in their comparison of outcomes in a mixed sample of left- and right-hemisphere stroke patients and orthopaedic cases, Folstein et al. (1977) found that mood disorder was a specific complication of right-hemisphere stroke. Research by Ross and Rush (1984) reiterated the possibility that the emotions may be regulated by the right hemisphere, inasmuch as the lesions there result in the blunting of affect commonly seen in depression. However, Robinson and associates, in an extensive series examining patients with strokes, have demonstrated that lesions in the left hemisphere and those nearest the frontal pole are actually more likely to result in depression (Robinson and Szetela 1981; Robinson et al. 1983; Robinson et al. 1984).

The catecholamine hypothesis of depression proposes that decreased levels of norepinephrine or serotonin, or both, may be responsible for depression. Researchers have also suggested that a decreased ratio of catecholamines to acetylcholine may be responsible for the disorder. This dysfunction in neurotransmitter substances is of particular interest, because such an imbalance may result from a variety of disorders in which there is physical insult to the brain (for example, with stroke, head injury, tumours, Parkinsonism, multi-infarct dementia, and multiple sclerosis).

Researchers have also suggested that disorders with primary focuses located outside the brain may actually affect the brain's neurochemical balance. This is especially true if the disorder acts on the central nervous system itself in some way. For example, in a spinal cord injury, it has been suggested that hypersecretion of cortisol may be affecting the depressive outcome. According to Frank et al. (1985), traumatic damage to the spinal cord permanently alters the normal rhythm of catecholamine secretion. When combined with the stressful daily problems encountered by spinal cord injured persons, a fertile environment for depressive episodes is created. In their study of thirty-two spinal cord injured patients, Frank et al. found that 44 per cent have some form of depression. Risk for depression in the spinal cord injured population is thus not only a factor in the months immediately following the injury, but, because of the injury's lasting effect on the central nervous system (CNS), it may also be a consideration over the long-term.

Autoimmune diseases, such as multiple sclerosis (MS), appear to have a special propensity for disturbing emotional equilibrium. In their sample of sixty-one subjects with MS, Dalos et al. (1983) found abnormally high depression scores during exacerbations of the disease. An actual change in depression was noted as MS subjects moved from remission to exacerbation. Investigators have suggested that the plaques that typically are seen throughout the CNS with MS may be occurring in brain areas associated with mood, affect, and cognition.

Rheumatoid arthritis offers another example of the immune response's effect on psychological outcome. In a recent study of eight-six adults with a confirmed diagnosis of rheumatoid arthritis, 31.8 per cent of the sample was found to be depressed (Chandarana et al. 1978). Historically, an etiological link was hypothesized between what was previously called the "arthritic personality" (encompassing a depressive element) and the occurrence of the disease (for a review, see Anderson et al. 1985). This theory suggested that the emotional condition preceded the physical one, predisposing the individual to the disease. However, more recent work suggests that the etiology of rheumatoid arthritis lies within the immune system itself. With this interpretation, concomitant depression may be seen as a reaction to aberrations of immune system functioning, as well as an emotional reaction to physical variables such as stiffness and pain.

Acquired Immune Deficiency Syndrome (AIDS) is another autoimmune disease that appears to provide a biological predisposition to depression. Although the prognosis for the AIDS population is currently poor and the condition known to become rapidly terminal, it is likely that improved treatment will result in a somewhat longer period of illness and disability within the near future. As the disease progresses, 30 to 40 per cent of AIDS patients present signs and symptoms of CNS dysfunction, most notably nonfocal encephalopathy (Faulstich 1987). Both depression and dementia are concomitants of AIDS, and careful testing will be required to separate the two.

MEDICATION. Many of the medications necessary in the treatment of a physical disorder must also be considered as potential contributors to depression. For example, L-dopa in the treatment of parkinsonism, steroids in the treatment of arthritis, digitalis in the treatment of heart disease, methyldopa in the treatment of hypertension, and anti-convulsant medication after cerebral vascular accidents and head injuries may all be implicated in depression. The potential for increasing depressive outcome is also attributed to the drug diazepam, frequently prescribed for the generalized anxiety that accompanies many disorders (Strayhorn 1982). Clearly, medication must be carefully monitored for these populations, given the potential side-effect of depression.

Psychosocial Factors

The distinction between biological and psychological determinants of depression has not always been altogether clear. For example, in a review article on depression in Parkinson's disease, Gotham et al. (1985) suggested a mean estimate for depression of 46 per cent. This high rate of depression is thought to be reactive in nature as well as endogenous, the latter resulting from disturbances in brain amine levels. As Bowlby (1980) points out, attributing a major role in the etiology of depressive disorders to neurophysiological processes does not preclude also attributing a significant role to psychosocial events, such as loss. He reminds us, further, that the causal relatedness between abnormal neurochemical levels and the affective states and disorders are by no means clear.

The difficulty in distinguishing between biologically and psychologically mediated depression was highlighted in a recent study by Winokur et al. (1988). They compared patients with depressions secondary to medical diseases to those with depressions secondary to other psychiatric disorders. They suggested that depression secondary to medical illness may be a true reactive depression, appropriate to the life situation. In an attempt to separate biological depressions from those considered reactive to a disturbing life event, Winoker et al. recommended that biological etiology should only be assumed when no precipitating life event is evident. Unfortunately, this approach is not particularly helpful when dealing with people with a disability, for all have already had a significant predisposing event. Indeed, if we were to follow this logic, we would be obliged to conclude that all depression in disability is reactive, or psychological, in nature. Given the preceding discussion, we know this is not the case. However, the problem remains as to how to differentiate etiologically between these two situations.

In this section, four etiological theories of depression will be considered, all of which are psychological in nature. They include the traditional psychodynamic understanding of depression as a response to loss, the learned helplessness model, the cognitive approach, and the stress-outcome approach.

RESPONSE TO LOSS. The work by many investigators (Bowlby 1980; Brown and Harris 1977; Lindemann 1944; Parkes 1964; Paykel 1974) to establish the link between loss and depression is of particular interest in the context of depression among disabled people. First, people with a disability are as likely as anyone else to suffer depression from the recent loss of a significant other (for example, loss of a spouse, parent, or friend). Similarly, they are as likely as anyone else to have suffered the loss of a parent in early childhood, making them especially vulnerable to depression (Bowlby 1980). However, people with a disability must inevitably encounter additional losses of a different kind – whether that be the loss of function, role, body image, or "the self that was."

Wright (1960) suggested that such losses require the same mourning process as that necessary for the loss of a loved one. If this process is not completed, she says, the same response as when a loved one is not properly mourned – that is, depression – can be expected. Wright explains that people mourning the loss of a loved one do not give up the past; instead, they bring the past into the present, thus enabling themselves to withdraw their emotional investment from the lost person and to prepare to establish a relationship with someone new. Similarly, by mourning the losses that result from disability, people gradually give up the loss intrapsychically. As Simon (1971) puts it, anger is resolved and psychic energy is freed for new activity. Only then can people begin to develop a new self-image. Wright (1983) suggests that a loss must be truly mourned before people can begin to enlarge their scope of values and thus start the process of adjustment.

The concept of loss and depression may also be examined within the context of existential anxiety. For most people, having to come to terms with a disability brings them face to face with their own mortality; it acts as a catalyst for examining the meaning of life. Those who have tended toward introspection may find themselves confronted with major questions about their existence. As the inevitability of death and the sense of aloneness come sharply into focus, these people may be overcome with anxiety. The phenomenological context in which this is placed makes it difficult for others to intervene; they must accept that the experience is unique to the individual, that it is subjective and exists at that moment. Such an experience may, of course, lead such individuals to find meaning in suffering and, hence, new meaning in life. On the other hand, it may lead to emptiness, a pervasive feeling of sadness that life has been robbed of the meaning so carefully fashioned before the arrival of the disability.

Kubler-Ross (1969) did much to popularize the notion of adjustment to loss. In her work on death and dying, she conceptualized adjustment as a process. That process includes predictable stages through which the individual must pass on his or her way toward the end point of adjustment. *Stage models*, based more or less strictly on this conceptualization, are frequently called upon to explain depression in disability. Although the various models are slightly inconsistent in terms of number, order, and names of the stages (for example, shock, denial, depression, acceptance, adjustment), each contains a significant depressive stage. They suggest that depression is a natural response to the loss of physical function, and that it will be remediated by the passage of time (Bishop 1981; Hohmann 1975; Kreuger 1981; Sakinofsky 1980; Salmon 1981; Stewart 1978).

These stage models of adjustment to disability have recently been criticized by a number of authors (Wortman and Silver 1987). For instance, Judd et al. (1986) criticized the stage models for overgeneralizing the definition of depression to include any sadness, despondency, or withdrawal that may be observed following disability. These investigators emphasized the importance of distinguishing between normal adjustment responses and depression. Richards (1986) challenged the notion that, in stage models, progress through the stages is predictable and orderly, and once depression is overcome, it is unlikely to recur. Clinical observations suggest that this is not the case, that the process of adjustment is dynamic and idiosyncratic. Richards

(1986) further challenged the idea that adjustment is a fixed end-point that can be achieved with some finality. He suggests that people do not ultimately achieve adjustment, but rather fluctuate constantly between stages as new challenges to the status quo are presented. Furthermore, Trieschmann (1981) questioned the stage models' implication that depression is universally associated with a disability. She noted that clinical observations suggest that not everyone who suffers a disability will inevitably suffer depression at some point. Finally, the stage models must be challenged on the basis that they lack empirical support in the literature on adjustment to disability (Frank and Elliott 1987). Clearly, although these models have dominated our thinking about adjustment over the past two decades, little evidence exists to support them.

The stage models, as we understand them, are only one application of the theory of loss as an etiological precursor to depression. Indeed, criticisms of the stage models apply not to the notion that loss, in one form or another, has the potential to elicit a depressive reaction, but rather to the notion of an orderly and fixed sequence of response. The theory of loss continues to contribute much to our attempts to understand depression associated with a disability.

The implications of the work on loss and depression for an individual with a disability are clear. First, the individual must be helped through the mourning process to ensure that it is adequately attended to. In addition, the normal losses that exist aside from the disability must be kept in mind, for they also contribute to the vulnerability for depression.

LEARNED HELPLESSNESS. Another traditional framework for understanding depression is Seligman's (1975) notion of learned helplessness. To look at contingencies of behavious, Seligman and colleagues began their inquiries into the etiology of depression using animal models (Seligman and Maier 1967; Seligman et al. 1968). They studied the animals in a variety of circumstances in which they had no control over reinforcement contingencies and in which their actions did not produce predictable results. They found that, under such circumstances, the animals became withdrawn and passive, making no attempt to extricate themselves from unpleasant situations. The animals also undertook no proactive behaviour and exhibited a cluster of symptoms consistent with clinical depression.

The extension of this research to human subjects revealed the influence of an additional dimension; that is, cognition or causal attribution (Abramson et al. 1978). Depending on the perceived duration and cause of this uncertainty (or lack of control of reinforcement), subjects developed different levels of chronicity in their passive or depressed behaviour. Furthermore, depending on the pervasiveness of the attributed cause, the subjects generalized their helplessness to more or less unrelated situations (Abramson et al. 1978).

At about the same time as Seligman and colleagues were beginning work in this field, Rotter (1966) described a similar construct, which he referred to as "locus of control." According to Rotter, individuals could be evaluated in terms of the extent to which they viewed reinforcement from the environment as resulting from their own initiatives (that is, internal control), or from the influence of fate, chance, or powerful others (that is, external control). Once a tendency toward an external locus of control was linked with depression, the relationship became analogous to Seligman's notion of learned helplessness (Seligman 1975). In terms of mechanisms, Rotter viewed the adoption of an external locus of control, or a belief that control of reinforcement was external to the self, as a means of preserving self-esteem in the presence of repeated failure.

With regard to depression among disabled people, the disability itself could be construed as the source, or origin, of frustrated relationships with one's environment and one's sources of reinforcement. Thus depression might be interpreted as a learned response to attempts to interact with a hostile or unreceptive environment. Turner and Wood (1985) suggest that the environment encountered by people with disabilities may be full of situations that are not amenable to problem-solving efforts, thereby promoting a sense of helplessness. The fact that rewards are not necessarily contingent upon the duly directed efforts of disabled people might result in a learned response of passive withdrawal. In addition, Nicassio and colleagues (1985) identify the unpredictable nature of remissions and exacerbations from some disabling conditions as a source of uncertainty and, thus, a possible contributor to a sense of helplessness.

The evidence for a relationship between depression among the disabled and a sense of helplessness is largely theoretical or anecdotal. However, Viney and Westbrook (1981) found sufficient numbers of both inpatients and outpatients with disabilities who reported a sense of helplessness. Westbrook and Viney (1982) reported that significantly fewer controls than disabled individuals experienced the phenomenon of helplessness. Turner and Noh (1988), who looked at mastery in their community-based sample of disabled individuals, found that a sense of mastery was inversely related to depression across all age groups. Based on this finding, they targeted mastery as a promising area for intervention. Albrecht and Higgins (1977) had earlier underlined the importance of the sense of mastery or control for success in rehabilitation, thus supporting its identification as a possible intervention against depression and poor adjustment following disability.

COGNITIVE APPROACH. The cognitive theory of depression put forth by Beck (1976) states that people who are depressed hold a negative view of themselves, their future, and the world. This trio of negative beliefs referred to by Beck as the *cognitive triad of depression*, is thought to develop not from events themselves but from the way people perceive the events. Whether the events are objectively good or bad, depressed individuals will see them negatively: if something good happens, it is interpreted as luck and not of their own doing; when something bad happens, it is used to prove that they are inadequate and that nothing ever turns out right. Individuals who have tended to interpret events in this light may use the same attributional set for the disability itself. The disability may be seen as proof that their negative view of themselves, their future and the world is, in fact, warranted. This negative view of the self is often evidenced by statements in which people characterize themselves as worthless or culpable. For instance, Wright (1983) notes that someone who has suffered a disability does not ask, "Why did this happen?", but rather, "Why did this happen to me?" She suggests that this common expression reflects the individual's search for a personal offence to justify the situation.

Society's traditional view of disability may also be seen as supporting disabled people's views of themselves as unworthy. Historically, the notion of disability has been closely tied to the concept of evil and the notion of punishment. For example, in one Biblical Psalm, the affliction of a stroke is interpreted as punishment for wrongdoing: "If I forget thee, O Jerusalem, let my right hand lose her cunning. If I do not remember thee, let my tongue cleave to the roof of my mouth." Similarly, our views of physical disability have been influenced by Platonic notions that deviations from the related virtues of goodness, truth and beauty must be seen as errors and, therefore, related to evil. To be disabled is to be different, or deviant. But the word "deviant" carries with it connotations beyond the simple fact of a difference. As Wolfensberger (1972) suggested, a whole constellation of attributes are thrust upon deviant persons; they are often seen as less than human, as immature, or as objects of dread or pity. It is not surprising, then, to find that some people with disabilities hold a view of themselves that mirrors society's view. They see themselves as bad and deserving of what has happened, and have low expectations of themselves. These negative feelings form the basis of the cognitive attribution of the disability and are taken as evidence of one's essential unworthiness for a normal, happy life. It is but a short step, then, to complete the cognitive triad of depression and to see the world and one's future in it as hopeless.

STRESS-OUTCOME APPROACH. Another useful way of understanding depression following physical disability is the stress-outcome model (Frank and Elliott 1987; Friedland and McColl 1992a; Patrick et al. 1986). This approach evolved out of the now classic work by Holmes and Rahe (1967) on the effect of stressful life events on health outcomes. Research showed that stressful events could be counted and evaluated in terms of their impact on the individual, and then used to predict future health. Further, it showed that the accumulation of life changes, particularly those that are unexpected, undesirable, or uncontrollable placed the individual at risk of subsequent illness (Streiner et al. 1981).

However, the observation that these stressful events did not have an entirely predictable effect on all people led some authors to explore the presence and nature of certain modifying effects of the relationship between stress and outcome. A model produced by Cobb (1976) shows these hypothesized modifiers as filters of the effects of stress. Modifiers fit broadly into the categories of personal vulnerability factors, coping ability, and social resources. Major disabling illness is seen as a source of stress in two major respects. First, undesirable changes resulting from the illness may be interpreted as stressful life events (Counte et al. 1983). Caplan et al. (1984), in their attempts to estimate actual numbers of stressful life events experienced by those with disabling illness, found a preponderance of stressful events in the post-illness/injury phase, placing subjects at elevated risk of illness outcomes, particularly depression. Second, alterations in functional status that require constant and ongoing readjustment may be interpreted as chronic strains (Avison and Turner 1988; Pearlin et al. 1981). Within the stress-outcome framework, this clustering of stressful events and chronic strains predisposes disabled persons to further illness, especially depression and poor adjustment. Empirically, Counte et al. (1983) supported this approach with their finding that poor adjustment among people with multiple sclerosis was related to the number of stressors experienced. Further, Turner and Noh (1988) confirmed that stress had a major effect on depression among physically disabled individuals.

The utility of this model lies in its identification of buffers, or modifiers, of the relationship between stress and outcome. These buffers (that is, personal factors, coping, and social resources) are suggestive of intervention approaches that might modify depressive outcomes following disability. Of particular interest are those buffers, or modifiers, that appear amenable to therapeutic manipulation, such as social support.

Our own empirical work is aimed at the development of remedial strategies for depression and poor adjustment among disabled people, based on the stress-outcome model. (Friedland and McColl 1987, 1989, 1992b) Our current research program looks at social support for its utility in buffering or moderating depressive outcomes following disability. The matrix in Table 2 outlines our program of research, using both a methodological and a disability axis. Along the disability axis, stroke survivors were the first group to be considered (Friedland and McColl 1987). Descriptive work on both depression (McColl and Friedland 1988) and social support (McColl and

Friedland 1987) led to the development of a measurement model (McColl and Friedland 1987). With that measurement model, we have attempted to overcome problems previously encountered in social support measurement by: (a) explicitly stating the definition and theoretical conceptualization of social support on which the measure is based; (b) considering social support as a multidimensional construct; and (c) addressing the unique support needs and issues of the disabled population, such as types and sources of support, reciprocity, dependability and flexibility.

Based on five sources (personal contacts, family, close friends, community groups and professionals) and three dimensions of support (quality, quantity and satisfaction), the Social Support Inventory for Stroke Survivors was shown to posess acceptable psychometric properties (McColl and Friedland 1989). Next, we developed and evaluated a predictive model, in an attempt to ascertain the most influential dimensions of support for predicting favourable psychological outcomes after stroke (Friedland and McColl 1987). In a cross-sectional study of eighty-five stroke survivors, we found overall satisfaction with support to be the most important factor for predicting outcomes. This finding underscored the phenomenological nature of the construct and the need for support to be perceived in order to be effective (House 1981). We also found that support from an intimate personal source and from individuals in one's community (such as friends, neighbours, and colleagues) was significantly influential. Perhaps surprisingly, the support of professionals and groups was found to have little impact on psychosocial outcome (Friedland and McColl 1987).

Based on these findings, we developed a social support-intervention program that incorporated our own empirical findings with theoretical perspectives from the literature, placing them within a health-promotion framework (Friedland and McColl 1989). The program is client-directed, with the therapist acting not in a traditional clinical-therapeutic role, but rather as the client's agent or advocate in rebuilding, reinforcing and, where necessary, extending the social support system (Friedland and McColl 1988). Evaluation of this program helped to determine the extent to which it is possible to modify one's support system and, by extension, to augment the likelihood of favourable psychosocial adjustment. (Friedland and McColl 1992)

Similar programs of research are also underway with spinal cord injured, brain injured and AIDS populations (see Table 2). Descriptive work suggested the need for an adapted measurement model and a new predictive model. Multivariate linear modelling and covariate structural modelling have been used in a longitudinal study to determine which parameters of support are most important for adjustment in this population (McColl and Skinner 1988, 1992a, 1992b). Follow-up with an intervention study is part of future plans.

Table 2
Social support and depression in disability: A matrix model of author's current research

	Methodological Axis			
Clinical axis	*Descriptive*	*Measurement*	*Explanatory*	*Intervention*
Stroke survivors Spinal cord injured people People with AIDS People with brain injuries				

Finally, in collaboration with colleagues from a variety of clinical interests, we are beginning to explore the utility of this model with other populations.

DISCUSSION

Thus far, we have discussed the prevalence of depression among people with a variety of disabilities. To the extent that evidence is available, we have asserted that people with disabilities have an increased risk of becoming depressed. We also examined several etiological models for depression and presented evidence in favour of each. Although we do not pretend that these are the only theoretical models for explaining depression with disability, they are among the more prevalent in the literature and, as such, greatly enhance our understanding of the phenomenon.

The realization that people with disabilities are at an increased risk for depression demands a response from both the health care system and society at large. Let us turn our attention, then, to a discussion of the implications of these findings for practitioners, policymakers and researchers.

Clinical Implications

Efforts should be intensified so that people who are depressed can be identified at the earliest stages and appropriate care provided. During hospitalization, routine treatment should include the careful monitoring of mental status and the use of depression indices. Careful family history-taking will provide information regarding genetic predisposition to depression. Members of the treatment team should be aware of the increased risk of depression that can accompany certain disorders, particularly those involving the central nervous system, as well as the depressive side-effects of various medications used in the treatment of the disorder. Keeping abreast of the quickly growing body of research dealing with biological relationships between physical disorders and depression will also be important. In addition to antidepressant medication, which may be indicated in some cases, psychiatric consultation will often be required for those who are more seriously depressed.

For many people, adjustment to physical disability does not really begin until they return home. Once back in the community, they come face to face with their losses and the changes that must be made. In individuals already predisposed to depression, this realization may provide the precipitating event that results in clinical depression. Similarly, the neurochemical factors inherent in the physical disorder may appear at this stage, increasing the risk of depression, for these factors are by no means limited to the period of hospitalization. General practitioners, public health nurses, and other community health professionals must thus be educated as to the biological correlates of depression. They, too, must learn to routinely monitor mental status, and to remain alert to signs of depression in this population.

Clinical interventions aimed at the psychosocial factors influencing depression should also be put in place. For example, during hospitalization, opportunities can be provided for the formation of a therapeutic relationship between a member of the rehabilitation team and the patient, in an effort to provide support both during the early phases of adjustment and at times of recurrence. Ideally, such a relationship should be ongoing and not limited to the period of hospitalization. Case-management or peer-counselling approaches may be useful strategies for helping the individual deal with the losses that disability brings over time. Personnel skilled in dealing with the spiritual dimension of health may be an important resource as well, particularly for those who are dealing with existential issues. In some cases, more of an ecumenical than a religious approach may be appropriate.

The sense of helplessness and loss of control that accompanies so many disabilities can be countered through better education of hospital personnel. All must be taught to appreciate the importance of working *with* the person who has suffered a disability, of working as a *partner* in the problem-solving process, so as to allow ample opportunity for decision making. Furthermore, environments must be flexible enough to allow patients to see the impact of their decisions and to experience a sense of control. Mastery over the physical environment can be encouraged through the use of aids and adaptations, including computer-based technology. It is important to understand that the issue is not so much independence as autonomy and control. Thus it may, for example, be more important to allow individuals to plan and carry out the day's activities, than to promote independence in dressing (which may take up an inordinate amount of their time and energy). Activities that result in a sense of mastery and provide a feeling of pleasure can be used to help restructure the patient's negative cognitions.

By viewing depression as a negative outcome of the stressful events that accompany physical disabilities, much can be learned from the research on mediating factors. In particular, social support appears to be an especially viable intervention. Members of the individual's support system may require education and support themselves, if they are to be effective. They must understand the importance of their support in terms of outcome, as well as the types of support that may be needed. They also need to understand the necessity to coordinate their efforts in order to ensure that the system works. To be most effective, support personnel may need the backup of a health professional to guide them in their efforts and, at times, to provide them with support. Similarly, the disabled person must be educated to understand the mechanism of social support and the potential of this important source of help.

Policy Implications

As a general statement, increased risk of depression for disabled people would seem a worthy focus of attention for policymakers. In this population, as in others, depression often results in increased hospitalization, decreased productivity, and increased demands on community-health and social welfare resources. To the extent that this is true, spending to prevent depression among people with disabilities can be seen as a positive, health-promoting measure.

A useful framework for the examination of policy implications may be found in the federal document *Achieving health for all: A framework for health promotion* (Health and Welfare Canada 1986). That policy statement outlines three challenges that must be addressed by the health care system: how to increase the prevention effort; enhance people's ability to cope; and reduce inequities in health care delivery. All of these are seen as applicable when considering the health and adjustment of people with disabilities. Moreover, the proposed responses to these challenges, outlined in the document, reflect a health-promotion approach; that is, an approach directed toward the attainment of wellness, rather than the alleviation of illness. They include the development of self-care, mutual aid, and healthy environments.

In the area of self-care, one of the principal policy issues for people with disabilities relates to compensation for attendant care. Although legislated guidelines for eligibility and classification of levels of attendant care are available in many instances, they are extremely complex and poorly coordinated. An integrated policy approach to this basic necessity of life for many severely disabled persons is essential – both as a means of promoting a sense of control for these individuals, and reducting depressive outcomes.

In terms of mutual aid or social support, the framework recommends that policymakers become more aware of the potential of individual support systems to promoting adjustment. Perhaps support from the informal network in the form of information, practical help, and encouragement could be better used to prevent depression if policymakers and professionals were more attentive to this inexpensive, yet invaluable, resource.

In terms of healthy environments, social, economic, and physical surroundings can have a huge impact on adjustment among disabled people. Such stresses as inadequate housing, vocational and financial insecurity, inaccessibility, and the lack of available services may all be amenable to alleviation through social policy. In turn, a positive impact on adjustment can be expected. For example, accessible housing for people with disabilities will alleviate a major environmental stressor associated with independent living. Legislation to ensure that a proportion of all new units are physically accessible and competitively priced only begins to address this concern.

As a further example, many provinces now have programs in place that remove financial barriers to the purchase of assistive devices and services for people with disabilities. Such programs are seen as a distinctly positive response to the many financial stresses incurred in independent living with a disability. Additional examples of issues requiring the prompt attention of policymakers include benefits and compensation for people with disabilities, as well as transportation and vocational rehabilitation.

Aside from physical barriers, certain ideological and attitudinal barriers may be seen as contributing to a depressive outlook among disabled people. Many of these barriers can be dealt with at a structural level, through education of families, employers, colleagues, and the community at large. Some of these barriers, however, require the adaptation of attitudes within the health care system. Health professionals must be continually reminded that a paternalistic or patronizing attitude has a negative psychosocial impact, while an empowering attitude has a potentially positive impact.

Whatever strategies are invoked to deal with depression after it has occurred, none will be as effective as preventive efforts. Social policy should be directed toward educating society regarding the changing role of those with disabilities. Perceptions of illness behaviour and the sick role need to be altered as well. Such changes are best accomplished through the education of all members of our society, perhaps most importantly its youngest members. If children are given the opportunity to accept those who are different among them, to learn how to support one another, and to allow others the opportunity to control their own destiny, they will do so as adults. Furthermore, should any of them become disabled, their approach to their own adjustment will be vastly improved. With this in mind, society must do its share to accommodate the needs of those who are disabled, to provide a physical and social environment that is receptive to persons with physical disability. This approach is most effectively achieved when legislated change and public-attitude modification go hand in hand, thereby providing a structural and environmental context within which progressive measures can truly flourish.

Research Implications

Perhaps the most compelling theme in the preceding discussion of depression among disabled people is the paucity of empirical evidence supporting various assertions. Although clinical observations suggest that the problem is pervasive and far-reaching, systematic study of these phenomena is at a preliminary stage. The questions facing researchers in this area are numerous and complex. They can, however, be conveniently classified into two main subsets: distribution and etiology.

In the area of distribution, questions arise about the actual occurrence of depression among disabled people, as well as about the accuracy of currently available estimates concerning the nature and extent of the problem. Descriptive studies are required to better define the manifestations of depression among people with a variety of disabilities. Although it may be a reasonable assumption that depression will be qualitatively different for those who are disabled, this assumption needs to be tested empirically before it can be either validated or dismissed.

Measurement studies are also needed to ensure the appropriateness of available measures of depression being used with disabled people. In particular, conventional measures must be examined to ascertain whether a confounding influence of the disability is present in the measurement of depression. As an example, work cited earlier by Rodin and Voshart (1986) suggests that somatic manifestations of the disability may coincide with those signalling depression, thereby confounding the accuracy of measurement. As a further example, the accuracy of the Dexamethasone Suppression Test (DST), a common biological marker for depression, has been shown to be compromised in the presence of central nervous system disorders (Kaplan and Sadock 1988). Carefully controlled measurement studies are essential to the development of psychometrically sound indicators of depression accompanying disability.

Finally, survey work is required to produce stable, population-based estimates of depression among disabled people in the community. In order to overcome problems encountered in previous surveys, several methodological provisions are required. First, a consistent definition of disability is essential. We suggest using the WHO classification scheme (1980) to define disability in future research since it has already attained some consensus. We further recommend that, within the broad category of disability, specific types of disability be differentiated in terms of their impact on depression. The importance of this approach is underlined by previous work in which distinctions between physical and mental/emotional disabilities were not made. Second, an appropriate denominator is needed for the estimate of prevalence. This methodological issue requires comprehensive community sampling to determine the magnitude not only of the population of disabled people with depression, but of the population of disabled people as a whole. Third, such possible intervening variables as age, gender, urbanicity, social class, and other factors known to have an impact on depression need to be controlled through sampling or analysis.

The second broad group of research questions relates to the etiology of depression with disability. These questions are of a primarily hypothesis-testing nature and should be aimed at providing evidence to either support or refute hypotheses derived from the theoretical models discussed earlier, as well as other models not discussed herein. Achieving a fuller understanding of etiology is a preliminary step to the appropriate direction of initiatives in the clinical and policy areas. For example, within the psychodynamic models, what is the qualitative impact of loss on people with disabilities? Is losing a limb different from losing the use of a limb? Is losing some roles different from losing others? Is there any commonality to the natural history of the experience of loss and the response to loss among disabled people? Perhaps such information would coincidentally challenge the stage models of adjustment as we now understand them, thereby providing an alternative conceptualization of the response to losses accompanying disability. In terms of therapeutics, do conventional psychodynamic therapies offer anything to people whose depression arises out of a disability-related loss?

Within each of the other psychosocial models, a myriad of questions arise as to how to conceptualize these models to understand depression with disability more effectively, and how to intervene in a meaningful way. For example, within the learned helplessness approach, to what extent do disabled people experience a sense of helplessness in their interactions with others and their environment? Is the extent or nature of this feeling of helplessness different in kind, or in amount, from that experienced by able-bodied persons? Does a sense of mastery, as Turner and Noh (1988) suggest, facilitate successful dealing with the environment (both human and non-human) for people with disabilities? And if it does, what promotes this feeling of internal control? Can we do anything in a clinical or community health setting to foster its development?

Within the cognitive framework, what types of cognitions do disabled people use to explain to themselves their own situation, their future prospects, and the world around them? Does the phenomenon of self-blame contribute significantly to the experience of depression for people with disabilities? And if society is perceived as unreceptive by people with disabilities, to what extent is this perception accurate? What are the manifestations of this perception? And can these perceptions be changed to alter the cognitive triad that reinforces depressive feelings?

Within the stress-outcome approach, more work is needed regarding both the enumeration and description of the stresses experienced by disabled people, and the quantitative relationship of these stressors to negative psycho-social outcomes. Can we identify those individuals who are most likely to become depressed on the basis of the number of changes they have experienced as a result of their disability? What of those factors hypothesized to mediate between stress and outcome; that is, social support, coping, and personal factors? Can these resources be manipulated within a therapeutic context to alter the probability that depression will result?

Finally, the area of biological determination of depression after disability offers a wide scope for research and development. As knowledge accrues about the relationship of biological factors, such as neurochemical agents, to depression in the general population, these findings must to be examined expressly for their impact on people with disabilities. Increasing sophistication in the technology, isolation, and measurement of biological factors, should open the door to many possibilities for understanding the etiology and treatment of depression.

SUMMARY

We stated at the outset of this chapter that the integration of people with physical disabilities in Canadian society has shown promising development in the past decade. The availability of level entrances, ramped stairways, and accessible washrooms is no small accomplishment. It certainly must not be undervalued. However, we suspect that these developments may, in some instances, represent only a superficial understanding of the variety of challenges faced by disabled people in our communities. Physical provisions form only a part of the consideration that will permit disabled persons not only to establish a meaningful role in society, but also to adjust to the alterations in lifestyle and life plans required after a disabling illness or injury. For those who suffer depression following disability, these physical accommodations do little to enhance adjustment and reintegration. Of primary importance to this portion of the disabled population is a means of overcoming depression, of marshalling their resources, so they can once again begin to interact with society in a meaningful way.

BIBLIOGRAPHY

Abramson, L.Y., Seligman, M.E.P., and Teasdale, J.D. 1978. Learned helplessness in humans: Critique and reformulation. *Journal of Abnormal Psychology* 87: 49–74.

Albrecht, G.L., and Higgins, P.C. 1977. Rehabilitation success: The interrelationship of multiple criteria. *Journal of Health and Social Behavior* 18: 36–45.

Anderson, K.O., Bradley, L.A., Young, L.D., McDaniel, L.K., and Wise, C.M. 1985.

Rheumatoid arthritis: Review of psychological factors related to etiology, effects and treatment. *Psychological Bulletin* 98: 358–87.

Andreason, N.C. 1984. *The broken brain*. New York: Harper & Row.

Avison. W.R., and Turner, R.J. 1988 Stressful life events and depressive symptoms: Disaggregating the effects of acute stressors and chronic strains. *Journal of Health and Social Behaviour* 29: 253–64.

Beck, A.T. 1976. *Cognitive therapy and the emotional disorders*. New York: New American Library.

Beck, A.T., Ward, C.H., Mendelson, M., Mock, J., and Erbaugh, J. 1961. An inventory for measuring depression. *Archives of General Psychiatry* 4: 561–70.

Bennett, A.E., Garrad, J., and Halil, T. 1970. Chronic disease and disability in the community. *British Medical Journal* 3: 762–64.

Bishop, D.S. 1981. Behaviour and disability. In *Behavioural problems and the disabled* edited by D.S. Bishop 1–16. Baltimore: Williams and Wilkins.

Bodenhamer, E., Achterberg-Lawlis, J., Kevorkian, G., Belanus, A., and Cofer, J. 1983. Staff and patient perceptions of the psychosocial concerns of spinal cord injured persons. *American Journal of Physical Medicine* 62: 182–93.

Bowlby, J. 1980. *Loss: Sadness and depression*. Middlesex: Penguin.

Brown, G.W., and Harris, T. 1977. *Social origins of depression*. London: Tavistock Press.

Caplan, B., Gibson, C.J., and Weiss, R. 1984. Stressful sequelae of disabling illness. *International Rehabilitation Medicine* 6: 58–62.

Cassileth, B.R., Lusk, E.J., Strouse, T.B., Miller, D.S., Brown, L.L., Cross, P.A., and Tenaglia, A.N. 1984. Psychosocial status in chronic illness. *New England Journal of Medicine* 311: 506–11.

Chandarana, P.C., Eals, M., Steingart, A.B., Bellamy, N., and Allen, S. 1978. The detection of psychiatric morbidity and associated factors in patients with rheumatoid arthritis. *Canadian Journal of Psychiatry* 32: 356–61.

Cobb, S. 1974. A model for life events and their consequences. In *Stressful life events: Their nature and consequences*, edited by B.S. and B.P. Dohrenwend. New York: John Wiley and Sons.

– 1976. Social support as a moderator of life stress. *Psychosomatic Medicine* 38: 300–7.

Cook, D.W. 1976. Psychological aspects of spinal cord injury. *Rehabilitation Counselling Bulletin* 19: 535–43.

Counte, M.A., Bieliauskas, L.A., and Pavlou, M. 1983. Stress and personal attitudes in chronic illness. *Archives of Physical Medicine and Rehabilitation* 64: 272–75.

Cushman, L.A., and Dijkers, M.P. 1990. Depressed mood in spinal cord injured patients: Staff perception and patient realities. *Archives of Physical Medicine and Rehabilitation* 71: 191–96.

Dalos, N.P., Rabins, P.V., Brooks, B.R., and O'Donnell, P. 1983. Disease activity and emotional state in multiple sclerosis. *Annals of Neurolology* 13: 573–77.

Ernst, F.A. 1987. Contrasting perceptions of distress by research personnel and their spinal cord injured subjects. *American Journal of Physical Medicine* 66: 12–15.

Faulstich, M.E. 1987. Psychiatric aspects of AIDS. *American Journal of Psychiatry* 144: 551-56.

Feibel, J.H. and Springer, C.J. 1982. Depression and failure to resume social activities after stroke. *Archives of Physical Medicine and Rehabilitation* 63: 276-78.

Feighner, J., Robins, E., Guze, S., Woodruff, R.A., Winokur, A., and Munoz, R. 1972. Diagnostic criteria for use in psychiatric research. *Archives of General Psychiatry* 26: 57-63.

Folstein, M.F., Maiberger, R., and McHugh, P.R. 1977. Mood disorder as a specific complication of stroke. *Journal of Neurology, Neurosurgery & Psychiatry* 40: 1018-20.

Frank, R.G., and Elliott, T. 1987. Life stress and psychological adjustment following spinal cord injury. *Archives of Physical Medicine and Rehabilitation* 68: 344-47.

Frank, R.G., Kashani, J.H., Wonderlich, M.A., Lising, A., and Visot, L.R. 1985. Depression and adrenal function in spinal cord injury. *American Journal of Psychiatry* 144: 252-53.

Friedland, J., and McColl, M.A. 1987. Social support and psychosocial dysfunction following stroke: Buffering effects in a community sample. *Archives of Physical Medicine & Rehabilitation* 68: 475-80.

- 1989. Social support for stroke survivors: Development and evaluation of an intervention program. *Physical and Occupational Therapy in Geriatrics* 7: 55-69.

- 1992a. Depression with physical disability: Etiology and Implications. *Social Science and Medicine* 34: 395-403.

- 1992b. Social support intervention after stroke: Results of a randomized trial. *Archives of Physical Medicine and Rehabilitation* 73: 573-81.

Goldberg, D.P., and Hillier, V.F. 1979. A scaled version of the General Health Questionnaire. *Psychological Medicine* 9: 139-45.

Gotham, A.M., Brown, R.G., and Marsden, C.D. 1985. Depression in Parkinson's disease: A quantitative and qualitative analysis. *Journal of Neurology, Neurosurgery & Psychiatry* 40: 381-89.

Health and Welfare Canada 1986. *Achieving health for all: A framework for health promotion.* Ottawa: Supply and Services Canada.

Hohmann, G.W. 1975. Psychological aspects of treatment and rehabilitation of spinal cord injured individuals. *Clinical Orthopaedics* 112: 81-88.

Holmes, T.J., and Rahe, R. 1966. The social readjustment rating scale. *Journal of Psychosomatic Research* 11: 213-18.

House, J.S. 1981. *Work stress and social support* Reading, MA: Addison-Wesley.

Hughes, C.C., Tremblay, M., Rapoport, R.N., and Leighton, A.H. 1960. *People of the cove and woodlot.* New York: Basic Books.

Josie, G.H. 1973. *Medical care utilization in Canada.* Saskatoon: University of Saskatchewan, Department of Social and Preventive Medicine.

Judd, F.K., Burrows, G.D., and Brown, D.J. 1986. Depression following acute spinal cord injury. *Paraplegia* 24: 358-63.

Judd, F.K., Stone, J., Webber, J.E., Brown,D., and Burrows,G.D. 1989 Depression following spinal cord injury: A prospective in-patient study. *British Journal of Psychiatry* 154: 668–71.

Kaplan, H.I., and Sadock, B.J. 1988. *Modern synopsis of the comprehensive textbook of psychiatry*, 5th ed. Baltimore: Williams & Wilkins.

Kennedy, G.J., Kelman H.R., and Thomas C. 1990 The emergence of depressive symptoms in late life: The importance of declining health and increasing disability. *Journal of Community Health* 15: 93–104.

Kolb, B., and Whishaw, I.Q. 1980. *Fundamentals of human neuropsychology.* New York: WH Freeman.

Kreuger, D.W. 1981. Emotional rehabilitation of the physical rehabilitation patient. *International Journal of Psychiatry in Medicine* 11: 183–91.

Kubler-Ross, E. 1969. *On death and dying.* New York: Macmillan.

Labi, M.L.C., Philips, T.F., and Gresham, G.E. 1980. Psychological disability in physically restored long-term stroke survivors. *Archives of Physical Medicine and Rehabilitation* 61: 561–65.

Last, J. 1983. *A dictionary of epidemiology.* Toronto: Oxford University Press.

Lawson, N.C. 1978. Significant events in the rehabilitation process: The spinal cord patient's point of view. *Archives of Physical Medicine and Rehabilitation* 59: 573–79.

Lindemann, E. 1944. Symptomatology and management of acute grief. *American Journal of Psychiatry* 101: 141–49.

McColl, M.A. and Freidland, J. 1988. Epidemiology of post-stroke depression: Implications for rehabilitation. *Rehabilitation Research Canada* 1: 21–28.

– 1989. Development of a multidimensional index for assessing social support in rehabilitation. *Occupational Therapy Journal of Research* 9: 218–34.

McColl, M.A. and Skinner, H.A. 1989. Concepts and measurement of social support in rehabilitation. *Canadian Journal of Rehabilitation* 2: 93–108

– 1992a. Measuring psychological outcomes following rehabilitation. *Canadian Journal of Public Health* 83: 512–518.

– 1992b. Measuring social support and coping among disabled adults: Applying the stress-outcome model in rehabilitation. Manuscript.

McDonald, M.R., Nelson, W.R., and Cameron M.G.P. 1987. Depression and activity patterns of spinal cord injured persons living in the community. *Archives of Physical Medicine and Rehabilitation* 68: 339–43.

Murphy, J.M., Sobol, A.M., Neff, R.K., Oliver, D.C., and Leighton, A.H. 1984. Stability of prevalence: Depression and anxiety disorders. *Archives of General Psychiatry* 41: 990–97.

Myers, J.M., Weissman, M.M., Tischler, G.L., Holzer, C.E., Leaf P.J., Orvaschel, H., Anthony, J.C., Boyd, J.H., Burke, J.D., Kramer, M., and Stoltzman, R. 1984. Six-month prevalence of psychiatric disorders in three communities. *Archives of General Psychiatry* 41: 959–67.

Nagi, M. 1976. An epidemiology of disability among adults in the U.S. *Millbank Memorial Fund Quarterly* 54: 439–67.

Nicassio, P.M., Wallston, K.A., Callaghan, L.F., Herbert, M., and Pincus, T. 1985. The measurement of helplessness in rheumatoid arthritis: The development of the AHI. *Journal of Rheumatology* 12: 462–67.

Noh, S., and Posthuma, B. 1990 Physical disability and depression: A methodological consideration. *Canadian Journal of Occupational Therapy* 87: 9–15.

Papez, J.W. 1937. A proposed mechanism of emotion. *Archives of Neurology Neurosurgery and Psychiatry* 38, 724–44.

Parkes, C.M. 1964. Recent bereavement as a cause of mental illness. *British Journal of Psychiatry* 110: 198–204.

Patrick, D.L., Morgan, M., and Charlton, J.R.H. 1986. Psychosocial status and change in the health status of physically disabled people. *Social Science and Medicine* 12: 1347–54.

Paykel, E. 1974. Life stress and psychiatric disorder. In *Stressful life events: Their nature and consequences*, edited by B.S. and B.P. Dohrenwend 135–49. New York: John Wiley and Sons.

Pearlin, L.I., Menaghan, E.G., Lieberman, M.A., and Mullan, J.T. 1981. The stress process. *Journal of Health and Social Behavior* 22: 337–56.

Peck, J.R., Smith T.W., Ward, J.R., and Milano, R. 1989. Disability and depression in rheumatoid arthritis. *Arthritis and Rheumatism* 32: 1100–6.

Radloff, L.S. 1977. The CES-D Scale: A self-report depression scale for research in the general population. *Applied Psychological Measurement* 1: 385–401.

Radloff, L.S., and Rae, D.S. 1979. Susceptibility and precipitating factors in depression: Sex differences and similarities. *Journal of Abnormal Psychology* 88: 174–81.

Reding, M., Orto L., Willensky P., Fortuna I., DAy N., Steiner, S., Gehr L., and McDowell F. 1985. The dexamethasone suppression test: An indication of depression following stroke, but not a predictor of rehabilitation outcome. *Archives of Neurology* 42: 209–12.

Richards, J.S. 1986. Psychological adjustment to spinal cord injury during the first post-discharge year. *Archives of Physical Medicine & Rehabilitation* 67: 362–65.

Robinson, R.G., and Benson, D.F. 1981. Depression in aphasic patients: Frequency, severity and clinical-pathological correlates. *Brain and Language* 14: 282–90.

Robinson, R.G., and Price, T.R. 1982. Post stroke depressive disorders: A follow-up study of 103 patients. *Stroke* 13: 635–41.

Robinson, R.G., Starr, L.B., Kubos, K.L., and Price, T.R. 1983. A two-year longitudinal study of post-stroke mood disorders: Findings during the initial evaluation. *Stroke* 14: 736–41.

Robinson, R.G., Starr, L.B., Lipsey, J.R., Rao, R., and Price, T.R. 1984. A two-year longitudinal study of post-stroke mood disorders: Dynamic changes in association of variables over the first six months of follow-up. *Stroke* 15: 510–17.

Robinson, R.G., and Szetela, B. 1981. Mood changes following left hemispheric brain injury. *Annals of Neurology* 9: 447–53.

Rodin, G., and Voshart, K. 1986. Depression in the medically ill: An overview.

American Journal of Psychiatry 143: 696–705.

Rosenbaum, M., and Raz, D. 1977. Denial, locus of control and depression among physically disabled and non-disabled men. *Journal of Clinical Psychology* 33: 672–76.

Ross, E.D., and Rush, A.J. 1984. Diagnosis and neuroanatomical correlates of depression in brain damaged patients. *Archives of General Psychiatry* 38: 1344–54.

Rotter, J.A. 1966. Generalized expectancies of internal versus external control of reinforcement. *Psychological Monographs* 80: 1–28.

Sakinofsky, I. 1980. Depression and suicide in the disabled. In *Behaviour problems and the disabled*, edited by D.S. Bishop 17–51. Baltimore: Williams & Wilkins.

Salmon, H.E. 1981. Theories of aging, disability and loss. *Journal of Rehabilitation* 47: 44–50.

Seligman, M.E.P. 1975. *Helplessness: On depression, development and death.* San Francisco: Freeman.

Seligman, M.E.P., and Maier, S.F. 1967. Failure to escape traumatic shock. *Journal of Experimental Psychology* 74: 1–9.

Seligman, M.E.P., Maier, S.F., and Geer, J. 1968. The alleviation of learned helplessness in the dog. *Journal of Abnormal & Social Psychology* 73: 256–62.

Simon, J.I. 1971. Emotional aspects of physical disability. *American Journal of Occupational Therapy* 25: 408–10.

Sjogren, K. 1982. Leisure after stroke. *International Rehabilitation Medicine* 4: 80–88.

Srole, L. 1962. *Mental health in the metropolis: The Midtown Manhattan study.* New York: McGraw-Hill.

Statistics Canada 1981. *The health of Canadians: Report of the Canada health survey.* Ottawa: Supply and Services Canada.

– 1983–84. *Report of the Canada health and disability survey.* Ottawa: Supply and Services Canada.

– 1988. *The Health & Activity Limitations Survey.* Ottawa: Supply and Services Canada.

Stewart, T.D. 1978. Coping behaviour and moratorium following spinal cord injury. *Paraplegia* 15: 338–42.

Strayhorn, J.M. 1982. *Foundations of clinical psychiatry.* Chicago: Year Book Medical.

Streiner, D.L., Norman, G.R., McFarlane, A.H., and Roy, R.G. 1981. Quality of life events and their relationship to strain. *Schizophrenia Bulletin* 7: 34–42.

Trieschmann, R. 1981. *Spinal cord injury: Social, psychological and vocational adjustment.* New York: Demos Publications.

Turner, R.J., and Beiser, M. 1990 Major depression and depressive symptomatology among physically disabled: Assessing the role of chronic strains. *Journal of Nervous and Mental Disease* 178: 343–50.

Turner, R.J., and Noh, S. 1988. Physical disability and depression: A longitudinal analysis. *Journal of Health & Social Behavior* 29: 23–37.

Turner, R.J., and Wood, D.W. (1985). Depression and disability: The stress process in a chronically strained population. *Research in Community Mental Health* 5: 77–109.

U.S. Department of Health, Education and Welfare. 1981. *Current estimates from the Health Interview Survey.* Washington, D.C.: Vital and Health Statistics, 10–136.

Viney, L.L., and Westbrook, M.T. 1981. Coping and chronic illness: The mediating role of biologic and illness-related factors. *Journal of Psychosomatic Research* 26: 595–605.

Walker, C., and McWhinnie, J. 1980. *A composite picture of the disabled in Canada.* Ottawa, Canada: Health and Welfare Canada; Supply and Services Canada.

Weissman, M.M., and Myers, J.K. 1978. Affective disorders in a U.S. urban community. *Archives of General Psychiatry* 35: 1304–11.

Westbrook, M.T., and Viney, L.L. 1982. Psychological reactions to the onset of chronic illness. *Social Science and Medicine* 16: 899–905.

Winokur, G., Black, D.W., and Nassrallah, A. 1988. Depression secondary to other psychiatric disorders and medical illnesses. *American Journal of Psychiatry* 145: 233–37.

Wolfensberger, W. 1972. *The principles of normalization in human services.* Toronto: National Institute of Mental Retardation.

Wood, D.W., and Turner, R.J. 1985. The prevalence of disability in Southwestern Ontario. *Canadian Journal of Public Health* 76: 262–65.

World Health Organization. 1980. *International classification of impairments, disabilities and handicaps: A manual of classification relating to the consequences of disease.* Geneva: World Health Organization.

Wortman, C.B., and Silver, R.C. 1987 Coping with irrevocable loss. In *Cataclysms, crises and catastrophes: Psychology in action* edited by G.R. VandenBos, and B.K. Bryant, (189–235). Washington D.C.: American Psychological Association.

Wright, B.A. 1960. *Physical disability: A psychological approach.* New York: Harper & Row.

CHAPTER ELEVEN

Depression in Caregivers of Impaired Elderly Family Members

E. ANN MOHIDE AND
DAVID L. STREINER

Most supportive services and care for chronically ill, elderly people living in the community are provided by families (Stone et al. 1987). For some family members, the experience of providing the principal care to frail elderly relatives is associated with hardships and problems. Over the past two decades, the body of knowledge identifying the burden on primary family caregivers has been developing. As the absolute number of elderly people increases, the issue of caregiving by family members continues to gain importance in our society. Failure to attend to family caregivers' needs and problems may lead to the development of "hidden patients," a term coined by Fengler and Goodrich (1979, 175).

In this chapter, we address the question of whether family caregivers of the chronically ill elderly residing in the community experience depressive symptomatology or clinical depression. We review descriptive and explanatory investigations of caregiving, as well as intervention studies designed to reduce caregiver burden. We examine some intervention research and discuss a recent intervention study, with its implications for clinical practice and research. On the basis of this literature review, we conclude that a substantial number of family caregivers experience depressive symptomatology, with the strongest evidence emerging from the investigation of caregivers of demented relatives. As yet, the research is inconclusive regarding the precise phenomenology for this, a situation that may partly explain why intervention studies to date have not been shown to be effective.

The impact of caring for a chronically ill relative on the principal family caregiver did not emerge as a research theme until the 1960s. Initially, the research concentrated on the impact of caring for psychiatric patients living with one or more family members (Grad and Sainsbury 1963; Hoenig and Hamilton 1965). However, in the 1970s and '80s, this research broadened to include family caregivers of the frail elderly and, more specifically in the 1980s, family caregivers of elderly persons suffering from progressive irreversible dementias.

Over the years, several terms have been used to describe the negative aspects associated with the provision of ongoing supportive care to a dependent relative. "Caregiver burden," "stress," and "strain" have all appeared, with "burden" being the most commonly used term. Since the 1960s, many researchers have attempted to define the multidimensionality of the concept of caregiver burden; to date, however, empirical testing has not yet established an overall, well-validated model of caregiver burden. Since the conceptualization of burden is not clear, its assessment is not straightforward. A number of caregiver burden instruments have been developed; none, however, meet important measurement criteria such as reliability, validity, and responsiveness to change over time. One of the primary reasons is the difficulty of validating an instrument in the absence of a gold standard.

In response to these measurement issues, many investigators have chosen to focus on discrete aspects of burden, such as depressed mood or anxiety. However, even within these more restricted domains, there is no agreement regarding the ideal measurement instrument. Various studies have used self-reports, item-specific content in structured interviews, subscales of indices, and affect-specific scales.

As preparation for this review, we searched the Medline, PsychINFO and Cumulative Index to Nursing and Allied Health Literature (CINAHL) data bases. Based on our knowledge of this area, we decided to search back to 1980, using key terms such as aged, frail dementia, cerebrovascular disorder, and caregiver(s). Reference lists and personal libraries were used to augment the search process.

This chapter considers studies using validated depressive symptomatology scales, indices, or standardized diagnostic criteria to assess whether caregivers of chronically ill, elderly relatives are depressed as a group. Only investigations that specifically studied the principal individual responsible for providing care to the relative on a day-to-day basis were reviewed. Studies solely examining caregivers of institutionalized relatives were excluded, as were those with very small sample sizes (<20 subjects). Studies that did not report mean depression values or proportions of clinically depressed subjects were also not included. Finally, if the investigators had published several articles using an identical or similar data set, only one was considered. Despite these attempts to examine only the highest quality studies, we found that the quality of the studies varied.

REVIEW OF THE LITERATURE

Empirical work was categorized as being descriptive, explanatory, or inter-vention in nature. A *descriptive* study examined sample characteristics, whereas an *explanatory* study examined relationships among variables. An *intervention* trial tested the treatment effects or management techniques to determine their impact on the outcome of interest.

Descriptive and Explanatory Studies

Table 1 depicts aspects of the descriptive and explanatory studies that ex-amined depression in the caregiver. As can be seen from the table, most of the studies have focused on family caregivers of dementia victims. Unless stated in the text, the caregivers' mean age for the studies in the review was >60 years of age. Similarly, in studies examining both male and female caregivers, the proportion of females was ≥65 per cent, unless otherwise stated. Further to this last point, spouses were the predominant caregivers (≥50 per cent), unless otherwise stated.

It should be kept in mind while reading Table 1 that reliance on non-random cross-sectional designs may result in biased findings concerning de-pressive symptomatology levels, or the proportion of clinical depression among caregivers. For instance, those who were unwilling to become care-givers or those who were most vulnerable to the rigours of caregiving, and therefore relinquished the role, were not included in the cross-sectional stud-ies. One can only postulate regarding the degree and direction of this bias.

Table 2 provides some information with regard to scoring for the depression measures considered in this chapter.

STUDIES OF CAREGIVERS AMONG FRAIL ELDERLY PERSONS. We identified several studies examining depression among family caregivers of frail elderly persons (Poulshock and Deimling 1984; Sheehan and Nuttall 1988; Baillie et al. 1988; Stommel et al. 1990; Rivera et al. 1991). Of these, only Poulshock and Deimling (1984) and Stommel et al. (1990) included the mean depression score for the subjects. Rivera et al. (1991) determined the proportion of the sample currently experiencing depression, using categories defined by the Research Diagnostic Criteria (Spitzer et al. 1978).

In a study of 614 primary caregivers recruited from the 120 health-related sources in the Greater Cleveland metropolitan area and 10 adjacent non-metropolitan counties, Poulshock and Deimling (1984) used the Depression Status Inventory (Zung 1972) to test a model of burden for caregivers pro-viding care for elderly relatives in residence. In order to qualify for the study, the relatives had to demonstrate dependency in at least three of six areas.

Table 1
Descriptive or explanatory caregiver studies examining depression

Reference	Study purpose	Sample size	Study setting	Depression measure	Mean scores* (SD)
FAMILY CAREGIVERS OF FRAIL ELDERLY					
Poulshock and Deimling (1984)	To test a model of caregiver burden	614 family caregivers living with and caring for impaired elderly relatives	Greater Cleveland Metropolitan area and 10 nonmetropolitan counties Recruited from 120 health-related sources	Depression Status Inventory Standardized score	44.4 (11.30)
Stommel et al. (1990)	To test the assertion that caregiver depression rather than variations in caregiving conditions or specific patient characteristics explains most of the variation in perceived burden	307 family caregivers living with and caring for frail elderly relatives	Lower Michigan Recruited from 145 community agencies and groups	Center for Epidemiologic Studies - Depression Scale	15.78 (8.70)
Rivera et al. (1991)	To study the relationship between depression and social support	165 female caregivers of frail relatives	Volunteers from several respite programs in Palo Alto, California	Schedule for Affective Disorders and Schizophrenia Research Diagnostic Criteria	87 (53%) currently depressed

FAMILY CAREGIVERS OF ELDERLY STROKE VICTIMS

	Purpose	Sample	Setting	Measure	% Scoring > 15
Wade et al. (1986)	To determine the effects of the stroke on the mood of the chief carer at home	224 family caregivers at 6 months post-stroke 134 family caregivers at 2 years post-stroke	Bristol, England Recruited acute stroke patients with families discharged home in one health district	Wakefield Self-Assessment Depression Inventory	6 months: 45/224 = 20% 1 year: 57/235 = 24% 2 years: 31/134 = 23%
Schulz et al. (1988)	To investigate the longitudinal effects of a stroke on the social support system and caregiver well-being	162 family caregivers interviewed at Time 1- 3 to 10 wks after the stroke 140 interviewed 6 months later	Portland, Oregon and Pittsburgh, Pennsylvania Recruited from nine hospitals using admission diagnoses or referral from specialists	Center for Epidemiologic Studies - Depression Scale; modified 28-item version	Time 1: 18.15 (12.58) Time 2: 18.55 (13.50)
Thompson et al. (1989)	To examine factors related to patient depression and motivation following a stroke	40 family caregivers: 13 males† 27 females	Claremont, California Recruited from outpatient therapy at Casa Colina Rehabilitation Hospital	Geriatric Depression Scale	5.3 (4.2)

Reference	Study purpose	Sample size	Study setting	Depression measure	Mean scores* (SD)
FAMILY CAREGIVERS OF DEMENTIA PATIENTS					
Pagel et al. (1985)	To test several predictions derived from a depression model in a study of spouse caregivers	68 spouses with patients at home (n = 47) or in institutions: 25 males 43 females 38 interviewed 10 months later	Seattle, Washington Recruited from physicians, nursing homes and health organizations	Schedule for Affective Disorders and Schizophrenia Research Diagnostic Criteria Beck Depression Inventory	Current depression 28–41% Depression an earlier stage in the patient's illness 27–40% Currently depressed BDI - 13.3 (6.2) Previously depressed BDI - 9.0 (4.9) Time 1 (n = 68) BDI - 10.3 (5.7) Time 2 (n = 38) BDI - 10.3 (5.5)
Fitting et al. (1986)	To compare female and male spousal caregivers	54 spouses: 28 males 27 females	Within 125 miles of Baltimore, Maryland Recruited from two clinics at the Johns Hopkins Hospital	Minnesota Multiphasic Personality Inventory Depression Subscale	Females: 25.12** Males: 21.33**

Study	Purpose	Sample	Location	Measure	Results
Eagles et al. (1987)	To examine the psychological well-being of spouses with a cognitively impaired relative	28 spouses of demented and non-demented relatives selected from 274 couples. Non-demented controls were matched to demented subjects on age and sex; a couple was selected, in which the spouse was most closely matched in age to the caregiving spouse	Aberdeenshire area of Scotland. Recruited from a general practice of 14,000	Leeds Scales Self-Assessment of Anxiety and Depression-Depression Scale	28 spouses of demented subjects 2.29 (2.62); 28 spouses of non-demented subjects 2.04 (2.30)
Haley et al. (1987b)	To assess the effects of caregiving on a broad range of measures of caregiver functioning	44 caregivers. 44 comparison subjects matched as closely as possible on age, sex, race, and marital status	Birmingham, Alabama. Recruited from health and social agencies	Beck Depression Inventory	Caregivers 9.39 (5.45)‡; Comparison subjects 5.14 (4.27)

Reference	Study purpose	Sample size	Study setting	Depression measure	Mean scores* (SD)
Kiecolt-Glaser et al. (1987)	To determine whether caregivers would be more depressed and have poorer immune status than comparison subjects	34 caregivers with patients at home (n = 24) or in institutions 34 age-, sex-, and medication-(beta blockers and estrogen) matched comparison subjects	Columbus, Ohio Recruited from neurologists, internists and a local caregiver support group Controls recruited from newspaper and bulletin board advertisements, and personal contacts	Beck Depression Inventory - short form (1972)	Caregivers 4.88 (6.18)§ Comparison subjects 2.48 (2.58)
Anthony-Bergstone et al. (1988)	To compare emotional distress of caregivers with data from a normative sample of similar age and gender	184 caregivers 47 older males 13 younger males 77 older females 47 younger females	U.S.A.; site not specified	Brief Symptom Inventory-Depression Subscale Comparisons made to norms - an elderly noncaregiving sample, Hale et al. (1984)	RAW SCORES** Older males (≥ 60 years) Sample 0.44 Norm 0.43 Younger males (≤ 59 years) Sample 0.53 Norm 0.28 Older females (≥ 60 years) Sample 0.92‡ Norm 0.53 Younger females (≤ 59 years) 0.61

Study	Aim	Sample	Site	Measures	Results
Cohen and Eisdorfer (1988)	To test the attributional reformulation of the learned helplessness model of depression and to understand how cognitions about coping with the stress of caring relate to depressive symptoms	46 family caregivers of 27 patients. 22 of the 46 caregivers living with their relatives	Site not specified. Recruited from a geriatric diagnostic and treatment service	DSM-III. Beck Depression Inventory	Of the 22 living with their relative 12 (or 55%) met DSM-III criteria for unipolar depression or adjustment disorder with depressive symptoms. Clinically depressed BDI - 9.7 (5.2). Not depressed BDI - 2.3 (1.2)
Morris et al. (1988)	To explore the quality of marital relationship between dementia sufferers and their spouse caregivers	20 spouses	Close to or living in Newcastle-Upon-Tyne, England. Recruited from day centres and the local Alzheimer Society	Beck Depression Inventory	7.5 (6.9)

Reference	Study purpose	Sample size	Study setting	Depression measure	Mean scores* (SD)
Baumgarten et al. (1989)	To quantify and characterize the association between caregiving and health	103 caregivers 113 comparison subjects	Montreal, Quebec Caregivers recruited from a geriatric clinic Comparison subjects recruited from cataract surgery patients with a close non-caregiving relative	Center for Epidemiologic Studies - Depression Scale	Caregivers median = 11‡ Comparison subjects median = 5
Gallagher et al. (1989a)	To delineate the extent of clinical depression in several subgroups of family caregivers	Subgroup of interest: 58 non-help seeking spouses 23 male 35 female	Palo Alto, California Recruited as volunteers for a longitudinal study focusing on biological and psychological changes occurring during the course of Alzheimer's Disease	Schedule for Affective Disorders and Schizophrenia Research Diagnostic Criteria Beck Depression Inventory	18 of 51 (36%) had a probable or major depressive disorder (5), minor disorder (4), or depressive features (9) Males BDI - 4.2 (2.4)§ Females BDI - 7.8 (5.1)

| Gallagher et al. (1989b) | To systematically study the frequency and intensity of some of the negative emotions associated with being a caregiver | 112 family caregivers 78 family caregivers of relatives with non-cognitive health problems, e.g., heart disease | Palo Alto, California Recruited a volunteer sample of those who sought treatment in a psychoeducational program for distress related to their caregiving situation | Schedule for Affective Disorders and Schizophrenia Research Diagnostic Criteria Beck Depression Inventory | Caregivers of demented relatives: SADS Major depressive episode - 24 (23.5%) Minor depressive episode - 21 (20.6%) Intermittent depressive disorder - 2 (2.0%)

BDI Mild (11-16) - 27 (25.2%) Moderate to severe (>16) - 25 (23.4%)

Caregivers of relatives with noncognitive health problems: SADS Major depressive episode - 19 (26.4%) Minor depressive episode - 11 (15.3%) Intermittent depressive disorder - 4 (5.6%)

BDI Mild (11-16) - 14 (18.4%) Moderate to severe (>16) - 13 (17.1%) |

Reference	Study purpose	Sample size	Study setting	Depression measure	Mean scores* (SD)
Pruchno and Resch (1989)	To compare the mental health of husband and wife caregivers providing community care	315 spouses	Philadelphia, Pennsylvania Recruited through public service announcements, health and social agencies	Center for Epidemiologic Studies - Depression Scale	Males 12.96‡,** Females 18.89‡,**
Robinson (1989)	To investigate health of the caregiver, past marital adjustment and received social support as they relate to depression	78 female spousal caregivers	Louisville, Kentucky Recruited from health and social agencies and support groups	Center for Epidemiologic Studies - Depression Scale	21.90 (11.90)
Dura et al. (1990)	To determine if the stress of caregiving for a spouse gives rise to a greater cumulative incidence of depressive disorders during the caregiving period than for matched controls during the same time period	86 spousal caregivers with patients at home (n=67) or in institutions 86 comparison subjects matched on age, sex, and education	Columbus, Ohio Recruited from three hospital clinics, neurologists, support groups, newsletters, and caregiver programs Comparison subjects recruited through newspaper advertisements, church groups, notices posted in senior citizen centres	Structured Clinical Interview for DSM-III-R (non-patient version) Beck Depression Inventory - short form (1972)	Caregivers of demented relatives: DSM-III-R current depressive disorders Major depressive disorders (5) Dysthymic disorders (7)§ Other depressive disorders (8)§ DSM-III-R cumulative depressive disorders during caregiving

Major depressive disorders (8)§

Dysthymic disorder (10)‖

Other depressive disorders (8)‖

BDI

6.94 (6.30)#

Comparison subjects:
DSM-III-R current depressive disorders

Major depressive disorders (0)

Dysthymic disorders (0)

Other depressive disorders (0)

DSM-III-R cumulative depressive disorders during comparable time to caregiving

Major depressive disorders (1)

Dysthymic disorders (0)

Other depressive disorders (0)

BDI

3.45 (3.80)

Reference	Study purpose	Sample size	Study setting	Depression measure	Mean scores* (SD)
Cattanach and Tebes (1991)	To assess the relative impact of cognitive and functional impairments on the health and psychosocial functioning of adult daughters (79%) and daughters-in-law (21%) in the role of the primary family caregivers	39 caregivers of cognitively impaired elderly 30 caregivers of functionally impaired, but cognitively intact elderly 33 caregivers of elderly family members without significant cognitive and functional impairment	Connecticut, particularly the New Haven and Hartford areas Recruited through service organizations, senior centres, media advertisements	Center for Epidemiologic Studies - Depression Scale	Total sample (n = 102) 14.53 (11.05) Caregivers of cognitively impaired elderly (n = 39) 14.90 (12.19) Caregivers of functionally impaired, but cognitively intact elderly (n = 30) 16.13 (11.41) Caregivers of elderly without significant cognitive or functional impairment (n = 33) 12.64 (9.19)
Dura et al. (1991)	To determine if the stress of caregiving for a parent gives rise to a greater cumulative incidence of depressive disorders during the caregiving period than for matched controls during the same time period	78 adult children caring for a parent with progressive dementia 78 age-, sex- and education-matched control subjects	Columbus, Ohio Recruited from three hospital clinics, neurologists, support groups, newsletters, and caregiver programs	Structured Clinical Interview for DSM-III-R (non-patient version) Beck Depression Inventory - short form (1972)	Caregivers of demented relatives: DSM-III-R current depressive disorders‖ Major depressive disorders (8) Dysthymic disorders (4) Other depressive disorders (2)

Comparison subjects recruited through newspaper advertisements, church groups, notices posted in senior citizen centres

DSM-III-R cumulative depressive disorders during caregiving||
Major depressive disorders (13)
Dysthymic disorder (4)
Other depressive disorders (2)

BDI
6.02‡ (6.34)

Comparison subjects:
DSM-III-R current depressive disorders
Major depressive disorders (0)
Dysthymic disorders (0)
Other depressive disorders (0)

DSM-III-R cumulative depressive disorders during comparable time to caregiving
Major depressive disorders (3)
Dysthymic disorders (0)
Other depressive disorders (0)

BDI
2.78 (3.77)

Reference	Study purpose	Sample size	Study setting	Depression measure	Mean scores* (SD)
Neundorfer (1991)	To examine the effects of the demented patients' problems; caregivers' appraisals of the stressfulness of problems and the options for managing the caregiving situation, and coping efforts on the caregivers' physical health, depression and anxiety	60 spousal family caregivers living with demented patients at home 38 female 22 male	Recruited primarily from a research registry of an Alzheimer Center of a major midwestern University hospital in the U.S.A. Others recruited from service agencies	Brief Symptom Inventory-Depression Subscale Comparison made to norm, an elderly non-caregiving sample, Hale et al. (1984)	Sample 0.64 (0.67) Norm 0.48 (0.55) 15 (25%) reported some symptoms of depression
Schulz et al. (1991)	To prospectively determine the effect of caregiving over a two-year period on the level of depressive symptomatology	174 family caregivers of mildly to moderately impaired dementia patients Followed up at 6 months, 18 months and 24 months post-enrollment	Pittsburg and Cleveland metropolitan areas Recruited from diagnostic centres	Center for Epidemiologic Studies - Depression Scale	Of the 73 subjects contributing data at each measurement point, 14% consistently scored ≥ 16 and 41% had at least one score ≥ 16 during the two-year period

| Vitaliano et al. (1991) | To determine predictors of burden in spousal caregivers | 86 spousal caregivers of Alzheimer patients Followed up 15-18 months post-enrollment | Recruited from the general population of western Washington State | Beck Depression Inventory | At baseline, 34% experienced mild depressive symptoms, and at follow-up, of the 79 remaining caregivers, 30% experienced mild symptomatology |

* mean score unless otherwise stated

† sex of caregiver subjects

‡ $p < .001$

§ $p < .05$

‖ $p < .01$

# $p < .0001$

** = SD not reported

Table 2
Scoring information for depression measures

Scale	Reference	Score Min	Score Max	Cut-points for "caseness"
Beck Depression Inventory (BDI)	Beck et al. (1961)	0	63	0-9 normal range 10-15 mild depression 16-19 mild-moderate 20-29 moderate-severe 30-63 severe
Beck Depression Inventory (BDI) - short form	Beck and Beck (1972)	0	39	0-4 none or minimal 5-7 mild 8-15 moderate 16+ severe
Center for Epidemiologic Studies - Depression Scale (CES-D)	Radloff (1977)	0	60	0-15 not depressed 16-20 mild depression 21-30 moderate depression 31+ severe depression
Geriatric Depression Scale	Brink et al. (1982)	0	30	0-10 non-depressed 11-20 moderate depression
Leeds Scales for Self-Assessment of Anxiety and Depression - Depression Scale	Snaith et al. (1976)	0	36	6
Minnesota Multiphasic Personality Inventory (MMPI)	Hathaway and McKinley (1951)	0	54	30 for females (raw score) 25 for males (raw score) 70 (standardized score)
Wakefield Self-Assessment of Depression Inventory	Snaith et al. (1971)	0	36	15-18 probably depressed 19-36 depressed

Although the age of caregivers was not given, at least 50 per cent were spouses; it is therefore likely that the mean caregiver age was well above fifty years. The mean standardized depression score indicated that, as a group, the caregivers did not experience depressive symptomatology. In fact, the mean was well below that reported by Zung (1972) for a group of patients with depressive disorders (mean standardized score = 61).

Stommel et al. (1990) reported on the first wave of a large longitudinal study of 307 caregivers in lower Michigan who managed frail elderly relatives at home; the frail relatives depended on help for at least two activities of daily living. The mean caregiver age, kinship, and proportion of female caregivers were not described. As with the Poulshock and Deimling (1984) study, the caregivers were recruited from a large number of community-health agencies and groups. Similarly, as a group, the caregivers experienced mild depressive symptomatology just at the clinical cutoff point.

Rivera et al. (1991) recruited subjects from respite programs. These programs tended to be used by family caregivers who feel burdened. Both the possibility that burdened caregivers were overrepresented in this sample, and the grouping of minor and serious depressive disorders as one, may together account for the high proportion of subjects (53%) classified as "depressed."

DISEASE- OR CONDITION-SPECIFIC STUDIES. Looking at disease- or condition-specific studies, we identified two types of caregivers: family caregivers of patients who had survived an acute stroke, and those caring for relatives with progressive irreversible dementias.

STUDIES OF CAREGIVERS OF STROKE SURVIVORS. We found only three stroke studies that met the eligibility criteria for this review (Wade et al. 1986; Schulz and Tompkins 1988; Thompson et al. 1989) The first two included a follow-up component. Wade et al. (1986) found that the scores on the Wakefield Self-Assessment Depression Inventory (1971) indicated probable (score of 15 to 18) or actual (score of 19 to 36) depressed mood in approximately 20 per cent of the caregivers interviewed at any given assessment point. The patients' functional status and level of depressive mood were both associated with the caregivers' depression score over the first year, but not beyond. Unfortunately, Wade et al. did not give the caregivers' age and sex. This study had the lowest proportion of spousal caregivers (25% at 6 month follow-up) of all the studies reviewed.

Schulz and Tompkins (1988), who studied 162 caregivers ranging in age from sixteen to eighty-nine years (mean 56 years), did not find the group of patients and caregivers as a whole to be at or above the cutoff point for clinically depressed mood. (It should be noted that the authors used the Center for Epidemiologic Studies–Depression (CES-D) Scale version that contains twenty-eight items and has a higher potential maximum score [maximum = 84] than the original twenty-item CES-D Scale. Unfortunately, a conversion table was not provided.) However, the authors did note that three to ten weeks after the stroke, 34 per cent of caregivers were above the modified cutoff point of twenty-three. (No rationale was given for selecting this value as the cutoff point). Six months later, the same proportion of caregivers, although not necessarily the same caregivers, were at risk for depression.

Both the Wade et al. (1986) and the Schulz and Thompkins (1988) studies indicate that a substantial proportion of caregivers experienced depressive symptoms. On the contrary, in a smaller study, Thompson et al. (1989) found that caregivers of stroke survivors receiving outpatient therapy did not experience depressive symptomatology.

STUDIES OF CAREGIVERS OF PERSONS WITH DEMENTIA. With respect to caregivers of relatives with dementia, we identified nineteen studies in the literature that met the eligibility criteria for this review. Some consistency across findings was found.

Six studies including a concurrent non-caregiving control group were located (Eagles et al. 1987; Haley et al. 1987b; Kiecolt-Glaser et al. 1987; Baumgarten et al. 1989; Dura et al. 1990; Dura et al. 1991; and two studies comparing the norms of caregivers to those of elderly non-caregivers were found (Anthony-Bergstone 1988; Neundorfer 1991). Finally, two studies comparing different types of caregivers were identified. In one, Gallagher et al. (1989b) compared two types of caregivers: caregivers of demented relatives and caregivers of non-cognitively impaired relatives. In the other, Cattanach and Tebes (1991) compared caregivers of cognitively impaired elderly, caregivers of functionally impaired (but cognitively intact) elderly, and caregivers of elderly without significant cognitive and functional impairment. The remainder of the studies did not compare groups. Only two studies that published data from unique data sets actually followed caregivers prospectively (Schulz and Williamson 1991; Vitaliano et al. 1991). All others were cross-sectional.

Although Eagles et al. (1987) did not find a difference between spousal caregivers and the matched comparison group of spouses, and neither group experienced a depressive mood, their results may simply be due to inadequacies in the depression measure (Snaith et al. 1976), a relatively small sample, failure to identify a group of caregivers whose relatives were moderately to severely impaired, or a combination of these factors. Sex, age, or kinship were not described in this study.

Haley et al. (1987b) found a statistically higher Beck Depression Inventory (1961) score for their forty-one caregivers (mean 57 years, spouses 34%) than for matched controls (mean 53 years). However, this study may have included caregivers of relatives with early degenerative changes, inasmuch as caregivers of relatives with only a six-month history of dementia and scores from the Mini-Mental State Examination (Folstein et al. 1975) of as high as twenty-three were eligible for the study. Despite this, the caregiver group's mean was only slightly short of the clinical cutoff point, and nineteen (43 per cent) of the caregivers in their sample were at or above a score of eleven on the inventory.

In a study to determine whether thirty-four caregivers would be more depressed and have poorer immune status than matched controls, Kiecolt-Glaser et al. (1987) found that caregivers were at the cutoff point for mild symptomatology on the short form of the Beck Depression Inventory (Beck and Beck 1972). They also had a statistically higher mean score than the matched comparison group.

Similarly, in a large Canadian study, updated data received from Baumgarten et al. (1989) indicated that 39 per cent of the caregivers were at
or above the cut-point of sixteen for the CES-D Scale. Only 16 per cent
of the non-caregiving control subjects with a close relative undergoing cataract
surgery had scores at, or above the cutoff point.

Using a cross-sectional design, Dura et al. (1990) compared spousal caregivers and eighty-six non-caregiving spousal subjects (matched on age, sex,
and education) to see if the stress of caregiving had given rise to a greater
cumulative incidence of depressive disorders during the caregiving period
than during the same time period in well-matched controls. Apart from
its concurrent non-caregiving group, the study had a number of other methodological strengths. First, it used the Structured Clinical Interview for
the *Diagnostic and Statistical Manual of Mental Disorders–Third Edition-
revised* (DSM-III-R), the non-patient version (Riskind et al. 1987), as opposed
to relying on a depressive symptomatology scale alone. Second, it examined
possible psychopathology in first-degree relatives. Third, it included a comprehensive survey of the lifetime history of psychiatric diagnoses, not just
affective disorders. Fourth, it assigned symptoms of depression only when
the presence or intensity (or both) of the symptoms could not be explained
simply on the basis of the nature of the caregiving situation or normal aging;
for example, changes in sleeping patterns that occur with aging. Fifth, the
subjects reflected relative homogeneity in the stage of deterioration, with
over 80 per cent falling into stages 5 through 7 on the Global Deterioration
Scale (Reisberg et al. 1982). Lastly, subjects in both groups were recruited
from a variety of community agencies and organizations.

Despite the fact that only sixty-seven caregivers were managing their demented relatives at home, while the remainder of demented relatives were
living in institutions, Dura et al. (1990) found no significant difference in
the caregivers' depressive symptomatology scores on the basis of community
versus institutional care. Nor does it appear that the heterogeneity of the
dementia diagnoses (for example, Parkinson's disease as well as primary
degenerative dementia) affected the results.

The results of this study were striking. Before caregiving commenced,
eight caregivers and twelve comparison subjects had experienced a depressive
disorder, almost all of which constituted major depression. However, during
the caregiving period, twenty-six (30%) of the caregivers reported a major
depressive disorder, compared to only one (1%) non-caregiver during the
matched time period ($p < .001$). Moreover, only two of the depressed caregivers had reported a depressive episode in the pre-caregiving period. No
other group differences on axis I disorders were seen before or during the
caregiving, and a family history of mental disorders was not related to affective disorders during caregiving. Only one-third of the caregivers diag-

nosed according to the DSM-III-R had sought treatment for depression. Caregivers developing depressive disorders during the caregiving period had lower current incomes; nor were they quite as well educated as those who did not report depression.

In 1991, Kiecolt-Glaser et al. reported prospective follow-up data on the sample published by Dura et al. (1990). Seventeen (25%) of the sixty-nine caregivers available at follow-up had suffered from a diagnosable depressive disorder at intake; this number increased to twenty during the follow-up period. None of the sixty-nine control subjects experienced a depressive disorder at intake, and only four had disorders during the follow-up period. Differences between the two groups were statistically significant. Although loss to follow-up may have biased the proportion of caregivers found to be depressed and bias may have been introduced with non-comparable periods of follow-up, it is not possible to estimate the direction of the bias. As with any study of caregivers using a non-random method of subject selection for caregivers and controls, the differences between the groups may be inflated by systematically selecting more distressed caregivers, on the one hand, and better adjusted controls, on the other, than might be found in the general population.

Using a large sample from which the Dura et al. (1990) study data was generated, Dura et al. (1991) reported on the depressive illnesses experienced by adults (mean age 48.74 years, SD = 10.11) acting as caregivers for a parent with progressive dementia. The age, sex, and education of these subjects and their matched-control subject were compared. As with the study of spousal caregivers (Dura et al. 1990), a statistically significant higher proportion of caregivers experienced depressive disorders for the current and caregiving periods, compared to control subjects. As with the spousal caregivers (Dura et al. 1990), no statistical differences were found between the caregivers and controls prior to the caregiving period, or during the comparable time frame in the case of the controls.

Anthony-Bergstone et al. (1988) compared four subgroups of caregivers (young men, older men, young women, and older women) to an historical sample of elderly non-caregiving subjects (Hale et al. 1984); the latter group served as the norm. With the exception of the comparison between older caregiving and non-caregiving men (>60 years), the other three caregiving subgroups had higher mean scores on the Brief Symptom Inventory Depression Subscale than the non-caregiving comparison subgroups; however, the only statistical difference was found between older caregiving and non-caregiving women. Unfortunately, the kinship composition of the caregivers was not stated. Similarly, Neundorfer (1991) found a slightly higher mean score with the Brief Symptom Inventory Depression Subscale for elderly caregivers, when compared to the mean score for an elderly non-caregiving sample (Hale et al. 1984); this difference, however, was not statistically significant. Neundorfer (1991) did find that fifteen (25%) of the spousal care-givers' sample had some symptoms of depression, but further specification about numbers with a diagnosable depressive disorder was not given.

Gallagher et al. (1989b) compared 112 family caregivers of demented relatives with 78 caregivers of relatives with non-cognitive health problems; for example, heart disease. (The latter patients can be classified as "frail elderly".) Caregivers in both groups were recruited as volunteers for a psychoeducational program offered to caregivers experiencing distress related to their caregiving situation. Two gold standards for clinical diagnoses were applied – the Schedule for Affective Disorders and Schizophrenia (SADS) (Endicott and Spitzer 1978) and the Research Diagnostic Criteria (RDC) (Spitzer et al. 1978). Reviewing the findings from the SADS and RDC data, Gallagher et al. decided that 47 per cent of the caregivers with demented relatives, and 46 per cent of those caring for relatives with non-cognitive health problems, were suffering from a depressive episode or disorder. These data suggest that caregiving, irrespective of the type of care recipient, is associated with depression among caregivers. Further to this, Cattanach and Tebes (1991) expected to differentiate caregiver groups according to elderly relatives' impairments. However, no statistically significant differences in the CES-D scores were shown between caregivers of cognitively impaired relatives, caregivers of functionally but not cognitively impaired relatives, and caregivers of relatives without significant cognitive and functional impairment. The mean CES-D scores for the three groups of caregivers were at or below the cutoff point.

A number of descriptive or explanatory subjects that were without comparison groups, but met the criteria for inclusion in this review, were retrieved. Among these, Pagel et al. (1985) found that a large proportion of their sixty-eight caregiving subjects had experienced depressive moods either at the time of the study (41%) or at an earlier time during the dementing illness (40%). Fitting et al. (1986) found depressive symptomatology on the Minnesota Multiphasic Personality Inventory (MMPI) depression scale slightly below the male and female cutoff points for probable caseness. Although Fitting et al. (1986) reported statistically significant differences by sex, these calculations were made using raw data rather than the sex-adjusted T-scores.

In an examination of twenty-two caregivers living with their demented relatives, Cohen and Eisdorfer (1988) found that while twelve (55%) met the DSM-III criteria for unipolar depression or adjustment disorder with depressive symptoms, while also sitting at the cutoff point for mild depression on the Beck Depression Inventory (Beck et al. 1961), the non-depressed caregivers' score fell far below the cutoff point. Similarly, in an examination of a non-help-seeking sample of caregivers enrolled in a longitudinal observational study (Gallagher et al. 1989a), eighteen of fifty-one (36%) had a probable or major depressive disorder: major disorder (5), minor disorder (4), depressive features (9). The lower, but still substantial, percentage of depressed caregivers noted in this study compared to the Cohen and Eisdorfer (1988) study may be due, in part, to the more stringent diagnostic criteria required by the SADS (Endicott and Spitzer 1978) and the RDS (Spitzer et al. 1978) tests.

In a study of twenty spousal caregivers, Morris et al. (1988) found the mean Beck Depression Inventory (Beck et al. 1961) scores to be within the normal range. In a large comparative study of male and female caregiving spouses, Pruchno and Resch (1989) demonstrated that female spouses were in the mild depressive symptomatology range on the Center for Epidemiologic Studies - Depression Scale (mean = 18.89), while the mean for male spousal caregivers was well below the cutoff point. As with the female spousal caregivers in the Pruchno and Resch (1989) study, Robinson (1989) found the mean for the seventy-eight female spousal caregivers to be within the moderate depressive symptomatology range.

Schulz and Williamson (1991) prospectively studied 174 family caregivers with a mean age of 57.8 years over a two-year period. Two years after enrollment, only seventy-nine subjects remained. They found higher levels of depressive symptomatology among those lost to follow-up than among those who remained in the study. Of the seventy-three subjects contributing data at each measurement point during the two years, 14 per cent consistently scored $\geq$ 16 on the CES-D Scale, and 41 per cent had at least one score $\geq$ 16 during the two-year period. Females experienced a statistically higher mean level of symptomatology than males at each data point, although the former group's scores remained fairly stable while the latter's increased consistently over time. Even though the two-year scores approached the cutpoint, neither males nor females had mean scores at or above the cut-point.

In a prospective study of spousal caregivers, Vitaliano et al. (1991) found that a high proportion had experienced depressive symptoms at baseline, as well as at follow-up fifteen to eighteen months later. In this study, a higher retention rate was achieved than in the Schulz and Williamson (1991) study and the sample was restricted to spouses. These two factors may have contributed to Vitaliano et al.'s finding of a higher proportion of depressive symptomatology at follow-up than that of Schulz and Williamson (1991). Unfortunately, Vitaliano et al. (1991) did not present data in a way that permits examination of change or stability in symptomatology over time.

In summary, some differences in these findings are likely due to variations in sample characteristics, depression measures, and other methodological considerations. Despite these differences, however, substantial numbers of caregivers of chronically ill elderly relatives seem to experience some degree of depressed mood. Unfortunately, the data are insufficient to permit conclusions concerning the relationship between sex, age, and depression among caregivers. Nor is it possible to examine the stability of depressive symptomatology or clinical depression over time, for only four studies were prospective in nature – two examining caregivers of stroke patients (Wade et al. 1986; Schulz and Tompkins 1988), and two examining caregivers of demented relatives (Schulz and Williamson 1991; Vitaliano et al. 1991). Only one study presented data that would allow us to assess the proportion of caregivers above symptomatology cut-points upon re-examination of the subjects (Schulz and Williamson 1991). Furthermore, although Pagel et al. (1985), Dura et al. (1990), and Dura et al. (1991) used cross-sectional designs to examine clinical depression over time – they asked respondents to recall symptoms occurring in the past – no studies prospectively examining diagnosable depression among caregivers were found.

Intervention Studies

In general, most studies examining the caregiver burden are explanatory in nature. It is not surprising therefore, that we found very few published intervention studies using validated depression measures. Furthermore, we only examined intervention studies in which the type of impaired relative was homogeneous; for example, interventions for caregivers of relatives with dementia.

Zarit et al. (1982) evaluated two types of memory training for severe memory loss among demented patients, using the Zung Depression Scale to assess the impact on the family caregivers. Although the caregivers were slightly below the cut-point at the outset, their scores increased somewhat after the intervention period in the two training groups ($p = 0.05$); the scores of the control group, on the other hand, comprised of those on a waiting list, remained stable. The investigators hypothesized that the classes may have heightened the caregivers' awareness of the relatives' level of impairment, and that they may have been viewed as one of the last avenues of treatment available to them.

Using a waiting-list comparison group (n = 18), Kahan et al. (1985) tested a group support program specifically designed for relatives (n = 22) of Alzheimer patients. Although the study included subjects who were not the primary caregivers for their relatives, it has been included in this review because of the paucity of intervention studies in this area. Measuring depressive symptomatology using the Zung Depression Scale, Kahan et al. found eighteen (45%) caregivers who scored above fifty. The investigators showed a statistically significant reduction in the Zung score following intervention (preintervention = 50.2, SD = 11.4; postintervention = 48.3, SD = 10.4, $p < .05$). However, the clinical importance of this two-point change is questionable. In fact, the authors stated that the program did not seem as helpful to those with more clinical symptoms.

The only Canadian intervention study reported in the literature (Gendron et al. 1986), aside from the randomized trial reported later in this chapter (Mohide 1990), examined the effects of Supporter Endurance Training, a cognitive-behavioural, skills-acquisition program designed to augment the caregiver's coping repertoire. Single-case methodology was used. Eight caregivers received the eight, weekly training sessions, while four others received no intervention. Using the Beck Depression Inventory, "minimal levels of depression and somatic complaints" (878) were found for all caregivers before, during, and one year after the intervention period. Numerical values, however, were not provided.

In another study, two types of group support were tested for caregivers of demented relatives living at home (Haley et al. 1987a). Those on a waiting list were used as a control group. Approximately 20 per cent of the subjects dropped out after randomization to one of the two groups, leaving fourteen in the support group and seventeen in the support/skills group. Although the investigators did not present the Beck Depression Inventory scores, they stated that the pretreatment mean scores among caregivers were higher than for non-caregiving controls, and that there was no statistically significant improvement between pre- and post-treatments (Haley et al. 1987b).

Lawton et al. (1989) conducted a randomized trial of respite services for 632 caregivers of demented relatives managed at home. Institutional, day program, and inhome services were provided to the experimental group in the year-long trial. The investigators used the twenty-item CES-D Scale with a modified scoring schema (possible range of scores 23 to 80, with higher scores indicating less depressive symptomatology). A conversion table indicated that a score of sixty-four was equivalent to the clinical cutoff of sixteen (Lawton, personal communication, 1989). The subjects experienced a somewhat depressive mood at baseline, and no statistically significant improvements were found at the end of the trial.

Brodaty and Gresham (1989) conducted a non-randomized trial comparing two groups receiving different interventions with a "wait list" group for caregivers of mildly to moderately demented relatives. In the experimental group, thirty-six caregivers and their relatives were admitted to a Sydney teaching hospital for a two-week program including didactic education, group therapy, extended family therapy, training in management skills, assertiveness training, and basic principles of behaviour. The goal of the program was to alleviate difficulties associated with caring for a demented relative. During the two-week period, demented patients attended concurrent sessions in memory training, reminiscence therapy, environmental reality orientation, and general ward activities. They were thoroughly assessed, and appropriate treatment was offered. In the other intervention group, thirty-two caregivers received two weeks of respite, while the relatives were admitted for the patients' component of the program. Depressive symptomatology was measured using the Zung Depression Scale. The initial scores were found to be in the normal range, and there was no change over the one-year follow-up.

In summary, the intervention studies show levels of depressive symptomatology similar to those found in the nonintervention studies. Irrespective of the management strategies employed, clinically important improvements were not realized. Certainly, small sample sizes, failure to randomize or incomplete randomization, loss to follow-up, and other methodological problems contributed to the negative or inconclusive findings. Nevertheless, one must consider the possibility that the depressive symptomatology experienced by caregivers, particularly those with demented relatives, is actually resistant to management strategies.

CURRENT EMPIRICAL RESEARCH: A RANDOMIZED TRIAL OF FAMILY CAREGIVER SUPPORT

The authors conducted a randomized trial of family caregiver support for the home management of demented elderly between 1986 and 1989 in a southern Ontario urban centre (Mohide et al. 1990). At the time this study was designed, there was abundant evidence in the literature showing the wide-ranging negative aspects of caring for relatives suffering from progressive irreversible dementia. The studies showed that caregivers of demented relatives experience multiple and diverse problems: the need for physical relief from caregiving (Robertson et al. 1977; Dunn et al. 1983); health problems (Gilhooly 1984; Gilleard et al. 1984; Rabins et al. 1982; Sanford 1975), deficits in caregiving knowledge, skills, and problem solving (Rabins 1981; Morycz 1980; Levine et al. 1983); and inadequate self-help support networks (Aronson et al. 1984; Archbold 1980; Sands and Suzuki 1983). However, these studies tended to be descriptive or explanatory in nature. Few were intervention trials, and none was randomized. As for the intervention studies of caregivers with demented elderly relatives, none addressed the above-noted problems using supportive community-based services.

The objective of our study was to determine the effectiveness of a set of supportive interventions, the Caregiver Support Program, in reducing the burden on family caregivers managing demented elderly at home. The findings pertaining to depression are reported as a major outcome measure.

Methods

DESIGN. The caregiver-care-recipient dyads were randomized to receive the experimental set of interventions (the Caregiver Support Program), or an alternative (conventional community nursing care) for a six-month period. We decided to offer a form of treatment to the control group because subjects would probably not have agreed to be assigned to a "no care" alternative, especially those who were receiving some form of community care at the time of recruitment. The length of the intervention period was based on geriatric clinicians' estimates of treatment time needed for achievement of an overall effect.

SUBJECTS AND ELIGIBILITY. In order to be eligible for enrolment in the trial, both the caregiver and the cognitively impaired relative had to satisfy a number of criteria. Caregivers were eligible if they: (1) lived with the demented relative; (2) identified themselves as the principal family member providing day-to-day care to the relative; (3) spoke English; (4) scored eight or more on a short mental-status questionnaire (Robertson et al. 1982); (5) did not suffer from a life-threatening illness that would prevent them from continuing in the caregiver role over the length of the trial; (6) agreed to have nursing services provided by a specific, visiting nursing agency; and (7) gave signed consent to participate.

Relatives were eligible if they: (1) had a medical diagnosis of primary, degenerative, multi-infarct or mixed dementia; (2) were assessed as moderately to severely impaired; (3) did not suffer from a serious concomitant illness that would likely result in acute-care hospitalization, long-term institutionalization, or death during the trial; and (4) and were not likely to be placed in a long-term setting during the course of the study. To participate, the elderly relatives required written consent from their next-of-kin; written consent was also required to access medical records.

All but two of the caregivers and their relatives were recruited from physicians' practices and community-health and social services (see Table 3). Physicians and other health professionals were asked to review their caseloads and identify potential subjects, using a list of eligibility criteria. It was expected that this method would identify those caregivers who were feeling burdened by caregiving.

Caregivers who agreed to be contacted were screened by telephone regarding certain eligibility criteria, such as kinship, joint living arrangements and fulfillment of the role as caregiver. If these criteria were satisfied, a home interview was conducted to confirm the caregiver's orientation to time, place, and person. The relatives were rated using the Dementia Rating Scale (Blessed et al. 1968) and the Mini-Mental State Examination (Folstein et al. 1975). Following this rating, a geriatric nurse-clinician, who was blind to the test scores, rated the relative using the Global Deterioration Scale (Reisberg et al. 1982). Those with eligible scores on at least two of the three scales (8 or more on the Dementia Rating Scale, 19 or less on the Mini-Mental State Examination, stage 5 or greater on the Reisberg Global Deterioration Scale) had their medical records reviewed by a nurse research-assistant to confirm the diagnosis of progressive irreversible dementia. A

Table 3
Referral source and eligibility status

| | Eligible | | Ineligible | | |
Referral source	No.	%	No.	%	Total
Physicians					
Family physicians	17	31	37	69	54
Geriatricians	8	27	22	73	30
Community-health services	27	59	19	41	46
Social services	6	43	8	57	14
Self-referrals	2	100	0	0	2
Total	60	41	86	59	146

diagnostic work-up followed (Larsen et al. 1984), including history-taking, physical and neurological examination, and biochemical investigations. A computerized axial tomography (CAT) scan was done only if clinical features inconsistent with the typical picture of a progressive, irreversible, dementing illness presented. When diagnostic information was lacking, the physician was asked to complete the work-up. An adjudicating committee, consisting of a geriatric psychiatrist, nurse practitioner with psychogeriatric training, and family physician, assessed all potential subjects for eligibility.

Subjects were stratified on the basis of the caregiver's gender and the relative's attendance at a day program. In the latter case, severely burdened caregivers might be more likely than the less burdened to have their relative referred to a day program.

Of the 146 dyads assessed, 86 were deemed ineligible (see Table 3). The major reasons for ineligibility included refusal of caregivers to participate (16%); nonconfirmation of progressive irreversible dementia using results of the three screening tests and the diagnostic work-up (38%); unstable health of the caregiver or relative (14%); expectation of elderly relative's imminent institutionalization (12%); and other (20%).

RECRUITMENT AND TRAINING OF NURSES AND RESPITE WORKERS. Community nursing services were provided by the Hamilton-Wentworth and Halton Branches of the VON Visiting Nursing Program, a voluntary nonprofit organization. Nurses who were not contemplating a job change and had at least one year of community nursing experience were invited to participate; eleven volunteered. Three nurses (caregiver support nurses) were randomly allocated to the experimental Caregiver Support Program; eight others were allocated to the conventional care group. With a larger number of nurses providing care to the control group, and thus relatively fewer persons with dementia per nurse, we thought it was less likely that the nurses would change their nursing practices because of an artificially inflated proportion of demented patients on their caseloads.

The three caregiver support nurses and the Caregiver Support Program's team supervisor received an intensive eighty-hour training program that covered such content as caregiver needs and problems, methods of enhancing caregiver control over the caregiving situation, and the community care of demented elderly. The training was provided by a multidisciplinary team, including a geriatric psychiatrist and a community psychogeriatric-nurse consultant. The caregiver support nurses met with the nursing supervisor weekly (more often if needed) to discuss management issues and to ensure that the Caregiver Support Program was being applied in a consistent manner. In addition, monthly consultations were provided by the community psychogeriatric nurse.

Respite workers were recruited from the Hamilton-Wentworth Visiting Homemakers Association. Over a six-week period, the respite workers received eighteen hours of training for their work with demented patients.

INTERVENTIONS. The experimental set of supportive interventions was geared to helping caregivers enhance their competence and achieve a sense of control in their role as caregivers. The caregiver support nurses were assigned to the caregivers and initially made at least one home visit per week, at a regularly scheduled time convenient to the caregivers. They completed health assessments for all caregivers, using forms designed to encourage the assessment of common caregivers' problems. Caregivers were encouraged to seek medical attention for neglected health problems, such as hypertension. Whenever the caregiver's health was judged to be unstable, the caregiver support nurse would consult with the caregiver's family physician. The caregivers received education apropos dementia and caregiving, with content and teaching methods tailored to their knowledge level, caregiving situation, and learning style. They also received a copy of *The 36-Hour Day* (Mace and Rabins 1981) for use as a ready reference. At the beginning of the intervention, the caregivers completed the Texas Research Institute of Medical Sciences Behavioral Problem Checklist (Niederehe and Fruge 1984), identifying the most troublesome of their relatives' problems. Using these checklists, the caregiver support nurses then helped the caregivers find solutions that would prevent excessive disability and enhance the patients' remaining functional capacity (Dawson et al. 1986).

The Caregiver Support Program's intervention included a free, four-hour block of scheduled weekly in-home respite. The weekly respite permitted the caregivers to anticipate relief from the rigours of caregiving on a consistent basis. As well, the on-demand respite provided relief between periods of scheduled respite. The respite workers were assigned to specific caregivers and encouraged to discuss the demented patients' plan of care with the assigned caregiver support nurse.

Finally, caregivers and other interested family members were encouraged to attend a monthly, two-hour, self-help support group for caregivers that had been specifically designed for families with demented relatives.

In the control group, the conventional community nursing focused on the identified patient's care, rather than the care of the family caregiver. Although some time might be spent discussing the patient's behavioural problems with the caregivers, this was not the main focus of the home visit. The control group nurses were assigned specific subjects based on geographic location; the frequency of visits was left to the nurses' discretion. The control group nurses had no concentrated training in this particular field and did not use the consultative services of psychogeriatric clinicians. Caregivers received no other health or social services in a standardized or systematic manner. The participants incurred no charges for the services provided by the trial.

MEASURES AND DATA COLLECTION. Ideally, the primary outcome variable for such a trial would measure caregiver burden directly. Accordingly, the psychometric properties of several measures of caregiver burden (Greene et al. 1982; Sanford 1975; Zarit et al. 1980) were examined; none, however, could be shown to be responsive to change. It was therefore necessary to select symptom-specific instruments. Because negative emotional affects of caregiving were reported in the literature and depressive symptomatology was frequently cited, the latter was used as a major outcome variable. The CES-D Scale (Radloff 1977) was selected because it has been well validated on nonpsychiatric community populations; it also minimizes the somatic symptomatology that might confound symptoms of chronic disease.

Descriptive data were collected regarding the health history of the caregivers and demented relatives, the use of health-care and supportive services, and the types and amount of caregiving activities. The caregivers' self-rated health was assessed using a single-item seven-point scale; and the Cantril Self-Anchoring Striving Scale (Cantril 1965) was used to measure life satisfaction. Finally, the demented relative's functional status was assessed using the modified Barthel Index (Granger et al. 1979).

A research assistant interviewed the subjects at entry, mid-point (3 months), and on completion of the trial (6 months). If withdrawal from the study was anticipated, an end-of-study interview was conducted prior to the withdrawal wherever possible. All those completing the trial were followed up at three- and six-month intervals.

Although blinding of caregivers and service providers was not possible, the research assistant instructed subjects not to divulge the intervention(s)

Table 4
Characteristics of caregivers and their relatives

Characteristics	Experimental group $n = 30$		Control group $n = 30$		
	No.	(% or SD)	No.	(% or SD)	P value
CAREGIVERS					
No. females	21	(70%)	22	(73%)	
No. spouses - wife	14	(47%)	17	(57%)	
- husband	7	(23%)	8	(27%)	
Mean age	66.10	(13.47)	69.40	(8.61)	
Mean months caregiving	39.80	(30.23)	72.40	(61.93)	.013
No. with some or all of high-school education	23	(77%)	18	(60%)	
Mean annual income	27,607	(19,708)	18,155	(11,930)	.035
No. with moderate to extremely well self-rated health	22	(73%)	20	(67%)	
No. using psychotropic drugs	3	(10%)	3	(10%)	
DEMENTED PATIENTS					
No. females	15	(50%)	14	(47%)	
Mean age	77.80	(9.19)	75.90	(7.70)	
Mean Dementia Rating Scale	8.75	(3.01)	10.75	(4.75)	.057
No. at stages 5 or 6 on the Reisburg Global Deterioration Scale	27	(90%)	26	(87%)	
Mean Mini-Mental State Examination	13.21	(6.83)	11.04	(6.17)	
No. with Alzheimers-type dementia	19	(63%)	21	(70%)	
Mean Barthel Index Score	68.67	(18.1)	62.50	(24.52)	

being received. In addition, the interviewer was not responsible for data management.

Just prior to completion of the trial, all subjects' service needs were reviewed by a multidisciplinary group. Subjects and their demented relatives were referred to community agencies as appropriate.

Results

A total of sixty caregivers were enrolled in the trial. Table 4 outlines the

Table 5
Study withdrawals and mean numbers of weeks

Reasons for withdrawals	Experimental group (n = 8)		Control group (n = 10)	
	No. in study	Mean no. weeks (SD)	No. in study	Mean no. weeks (SD)
Long-term placement of relative	5	17.20 (6.87)	5	10.40 (5.03)
Hospitalization of relative > 1 month	2	3.00 (4.24)	4	7.25 (3.30)
Death of caregiver	0	0	1	21.00
Relocation outside study catchment	1	11.00	0	0
Total	8		10	

characteristics of the thirty subjects allocated to each group. The groups were similar in most areas. A statistically significant difference in the caregivers' perception of the length of caregiving was apparent between the two groups. (Given the gradual decline in the early to moderate stages of progressive irreversible dementia, no clear cut-point, at which caregiving begins, could be established. We relied on the caregivers' perceived length of caregiving.) Three control-group subjects had extremely long periods of caregiving in comparison to other subjects; only two of the three completed the trial. Overall, the experimental group had a higher annual family income than the control group. In addition, there was a marginally significant difference in the mean Dementia Rating Scale score, although it did not appear to be clinically important.

Only forty-two (70%) caregivers completed the trial, twenty-two in the experimental and twenty in the control group. The reasons for withdrawal and the mean number of weeks in the study are listed in Table 5. Whereas those in the experimental group who were institutionalized in long-term facilities during the trial remained in the study for an average of 17.2 weeks, those in the control group were placed after an average of 10.4 weeks ($p > .05$).

Overall, no statistically significant differences were found in the characteristics of those who completed the trial and those who withdrew. The characteristics of withdrawals were compared across the two groups. In the control group, those who withdrew had a much longer period of perceived caregiving (85.2 months, SD = 59.9) than in the experimental group (28.1, SD = 18.8; $p < .016$). Although not statistically different, the mean annual income of those withdrawn in the experimental group ($25,428, SD = 13,233) was higher than in the control group ($15,444, SD = 6,583). In addition, the relatives in the experimental group had a slightly lower Dementia Rating

Table 6
CES-D scores* for subjects completing the trial

	Experimental group (n = 22)		Control group (n = 20)	
Assessment	Mean	SD	Mean	SD
Baseline	21.55	11.57	15.40	9.2
Midtrial (3 months)	18.36	11.78	15.35	7.45
Trial completion (6 months)	21.50	12.98	18.20	10.05

* Min = 0, max = 60
CES-D = Center for Epidemiologic Studies - Depression Scale

Scale score (8.0, SD = 1.93) than those withdrawn from the control group (11.45, SD = 4.52).

The effectiveness analyses were conducted on those who completed the trial. The mean CES-D Scale scores used in the effectiveness analyses are provided in Table 6. These data were analyzed using an ANCOVA with between-groups and within-groups independent variables (intervention and time, respectively) and the dependent variable. Covariates included the baseline CES-D Scale values and other variables that differed between groups, such as annual family income and perceived length of caregiving. No statistically significant difference in the CES-D Scale scores emerged.

The mean CES-D Scale scores at baseline showed a minor level of clinically important depressive symptoms, more so in the experimental than the control group. The depression scores remained relatively stable in the experimental group and increased slightly in the control group. For purposes of comparison, an intent-to-treat analysis was conducted that included those who completed at least eighteen weeks of the intervention. This inclusion did not alter the values to a clinically important extent, and there were no significant differences between the groups.

The correlation between the CES-D Scale scores and the demented relatives' level of dependency, as reflected in their Barthel scores, was low (r = .3 or less) at each assessment point.

Six months following the trial, only fourteen (64%) of the demented relatives in the experimental group who completed the trial and ten (50%) of the demented relatives in the control group were still at home. The remainder had been hospitalized or placed in long-term institutions.

Discussion

As has been shown with most of the other studies reviewed in this chapter, subjects in both the experimental and control groups experienced depressive symptomatology above the level expected for the general public, but not

Table 7
Mean CES-D subscale scores (and SD) by gender

CES-D subscales	Females (n = 43)	Males (n = 17)
Depressed affect	4.33	2.47
	(3.87)	(2.81)
Somatic and retarded activity	5.91	3.88*
	(3.49)	(2.99)
Positive affect	4.10	4.71
	(2.99)	(3.72)
Interpersonal	0.19	0.12
	(0.59)	(0.33)

* p = .04
CES-D = Center for Epidemiologic Studies - Depression Scale

in the moderate to high range. At the end of the trial, the group means were at, or slightly above, the cut-point for possible caseness. Of those completing the trial, twenty-three (55%) were at or above the clinical cut-point of sixteen at baseline and at study completion. Another five (12%) were at or above the cut-point at baseline or study completion. Even though a multidimensional set of interventions was provided to alleviate the wideranging problems experienced by caregivers, depressive symptomatology was not reduced. Indeed, even if there were sufficient power to detect group differences at six months, the magnitude of the change would not be considered clinically important.

Although the females had a higher mean total score (18.4, SD = 10.91) than the males (15.12, SD = 10.16), when the depression scores were examined at baseline by gender, this finding was not statistically significant. We then analyzed the CES-D Scale subscales reported by Radloff (1977). Table 7 identifies the subscales and the scores for males and females at baseline. As might be expected, given the fact that females often report higher scores than males on self-report symptom scales (Robins et al. 1984), a statistically higher score for the somatic and retarded activity subscale was found for females than for males. This difference persisted after controlling for age. The fairly homogeneous sample with respect to age and the small sample size did not permit us to identify differences in depression according to different age groupings.

SUMMARY

One finds some consistency in the answers to the question: "Do family caregivers of chronically ill elderly living in the community experience depressive symptomatology?" The articles reviewed in this chapter did not find that all caregivers, as a group, suffered from depressive symptomatology. However, the proportion of caregivers at or above the cut-point is clinically important given the fact that most family caregivers of chronically ill elderly are older adults or elderly themselves, and also that the prevalence of depressive symptomatology among elderly persons is the lowest of any age group (Meyers et al. 1984; Bland et al. 1988). Indeed, twenty-one of the twenty-five studies in this review included a substantial proportion of caregivers whose scores exceeded the cut-points for the various measures.* Exceptions to this were: Poulshock and Deimling (1984), Thompson et al. (1986), Eagles et al. (1987), Anthony-Bergstone et al. (1988), Fitting et al. (1986), and Morris et al. (1988). Unfortunately, most studies did not provide details concerning the number of subjects who scored well above the cut-point for caseness; nor was there any documentation concerning the number of individuals who had a history of depressive illnesses, with the exception of Dura et al. (1990 and 1991).

IMPLICATIONS

For Practice

Much remains to be learned about the etiology and treatment of depressive symptomatology among family caregivers. Because most of what is known has come from the literature examining family caregivers of dementia patients, one cannot generalize the little that is known to family caregivers whose elderly relatives have other types of problems and needs.

Despite this cautionary note, clinicians should probably assess patients known to be family caregivers for depressive symptomatology. Some caregivers may be clinically depressed (as stated earlier, the number of caregivers in the clinically depressed range is not yet known). Fitting et al. (1986) noted that most caregivers of dementia patients experience a dysphoric mood that may "reflect their demoralized state rather than a major depression" (250), in that the caregivers are unable to change the outcome of their relatives' condition. This may lead caregivers to feel a sense of despair. In fact, family caregivers commonly use such phrases as "no end in sight" and "no way out." Nygaard (1988) reported that 85 per cent of the forty-six caregivers in his sample felt a sense of despair. As Callahan (1988) has stated, "All things may be endurable if the demands are finite in depth and time. But a future that offers no exit at all, even if the burden on a daily basis is not utterly overwhelming, can be an obvious source of sadness and depression ... No burden can be greater than trying to imagine how one can cope with a future that promises no relief" (325).

*Pruchno and Resch (1989) found elevated scores for females only.

The differentiation of symptoms of clinical depression from hopelessness and despair is an important issue. On the one hand, caregivers suffering from diagnosable depressive disorders may require treatment, yet not respond to supportive interventions alone. On the other hand, caregivers experiencing despair, because of their inability to change the inevitable outcome of their relatives' condition, are more likely to require services that will improve the quality of *their* lives. At present, if clinicians act on the basis of the tentative findings of this literature, caregivers may be at risk of being inappropriately labelled and treated for depressive illnesses, thus putting them at risk of iatrogenic disorders and the sequelae of such labelling.

Beyond identifying caregivers experiencing depressive symptomatology, and because no statistically and clinically important improvements have been shown in the intervention literature, it is difficult to recommend specific treatment, or management, strategies to clinicians. At the very least, it would make clinical sense to help caregivers identify the most troublesome problems, with the goal of alleviating those problems, where possible.

For Research

Although it appears that most studies reviewed would have a substantial proportion of caregivers with scores exceeding the clinical cut-points, we cannot draw firm conclusions from these studies. None is without some methodological problems, whether that be lack of diagnostic rigour, relatively small sample sizes, non-random samples drawn largely from tertiary-care settings, lack of homogeneity among the caregivers (that is, joint vs. separate living arrangements, wide variation in kinship ties), lack of homogeneity of the care recipients (that is, in terms of types of diagnoses and stages of dementia), and failure to employ a design with one or more comparison groups and a prospective component.

With respect to future research agendas, a number of issues require investigation. First, it is not at all clear which, if any, psychological disorder these caregivers suffer from. All too often, depressive symptomatology is assumed to be synonymous with clinical depression. Yet simply receiving a high score on a depression inventory, such as the Beck Depression Inventory or the CES-D Scale, does not necessarily imply that the caregiver suffers from the diagnostic entity called depression. Furthermore, both depression, as a clinical state, and depressive symptomatology must be differentiated from another, closely related condition called demoralization (Becker and Morrisey 1988). Clinical depression is defined using DSM-III-R (American Psychiatric Association 1987) or RDC (Spitzer et al. 1977), whereas depressive symptomatology includes several components of depression without necessarily meeting the essential DSM-III-R or RDC criteria. Although demoralization or despair is one component of depression, by itself it does not constitute either clinical depression or depressive symptomatology.

Compounding this problem is the fact that most depression inventories are inappropriate for older people. The inventories assume that disturbed sleep, poor appetite, or decreased libido, for example, are manifestations of a biological depression. In fact, all these "symptoms" can reflect either the natural course of aging or the nature of the caregiving situation itself. It is possible, therefore, that studies using scales standardized on younger samples may overestimate the prevalence of depression or depressive symptoms.

Thus, it would appear that the first two items on the research agenda should be to differentiate depression, depressive symptomatology, and despair on a conceptual basis; and to measure each of these, validated on an older population. With these two steps completed, we would be in a better position to attempt the third item: to investigate the prevalence of these conditions with samples that reflect both the general population of elderly persons as closely as possible, and the caregivers managing elderly relatives with different types of problems. Finally, the interventions to date have not had a major impact on depressive symptomatology. We must therefore re-examine the model of caregiver burden and the relationships between the variables, test other interventions, or target interventions to more specific subgroups of caregivers at highest risk.

Acknowledgment: This work was assisted by a research grant from the Alzheimer Association of Ontario, administered by the Ontario Mental Health Foundation.

BIBLIOGRAPHY

American Psychiatric Association. 1987. *Diagnostic statistical manual of mental disorders*, 3d ed. rev., Washington: American Psychiatric Association.
Anthony-Bergstone, C.R., Zarit, S.H., and Gatz, M. 1988. Symptoms of psychological distress among caregivers of dementia patients. *Psychology and Aging* 3: 245–48.
Archbold, P. 1980. Impact of parent caring on middle-aged offspring. *Journal of Gerontological Nursing* 6: 78–85.
Aronson, M., Levin, G., and Lipkowitz, R. 1984. A community-based family/patient group program for Alzheimer's Disease. *The Gerontologist* 24: 339–42.
Baillie, V., Norbeck, J.S., and Barnes, L.E.A. 1988. Stress, social support, and psychological distress of family caregivers of the elderly. *Nursing Research* 37: 217–22.
Baumgarten, M., Battista, R., Infante-Rivard, C., Becker, R., Hanley, J.A., and Gauthier, S. 1989. *The health consequences of caring for demented elderly*. Paper

presented at the Annual Canadian Public Health Association Meeting, Winnipeg, Manitoba.

Beck, A.T., and Beck, R.W. 1972. Screening depressed patients in family practice. A rapid technic. *Postgraduate Medicine* 52(6): 81-85.

Beck, A.T., Ward, C.H., Mendelson, M., Mock, J., and Erbaugh, J. 1961. An inventory for measuring depression. *Archives of General Psychiatry* 4: 53-63.

Becker, J., and Morrisey, E. 1988. Difficulties in assessing depressive-like reactions to chronic severe external stress as exemplified by spouse caregivers of Alzheimer patients. *Psychology and Aging* 3: 300-6.

Bland, R.C., Newman, S.C., and Orn, H. 1988. Period prevalence of psychiatric disorders in Edmonton. *Acta Psychiatrica Scandinavica* Suppl. 338: 33-42.

Blessed, G., Tomlinson, B.E., and Roth, M. 1968. The association between quantitative measures of dementia and of senile change in the cerebral grey matter of elderly subjects. *British Journal of Psychiatry* 114: 797-811.

Brink, T.L., Yesavage, J.A., Lum, O., Heersema, P., Adey, M., and Rose, T.L. 1982. Screening tests for geriatric depression. *Clinical Gerontology* 1: 37-43.

Brodaty, H., and Gresham, M. 1989. Effect of training programme to reduce stress in carers of patients with dementia. *British Medical Journal* 299: 1375-79.

Callahan, D. 1988. Families as caregivers: The limits of morality. *Archives of Physical Medicine and Rehabilitation* 69: 323-28.

Cantril, H. 1965. *The pattern of human concerns*. New Brunswick, N.J.: Rutgers University Press.

Cattanach, L., and Tebes, J.K. 1991. The nature of elder impairment and its impact on family caregivers' health and psychosocial functioning. *The Gerontologist* 31(2): 246-55.

Cohen, D., and Eisdorfer, C. 1988. Depression in family members caring for a relative with Alzheimer's Disease. *Journal of the American Geriatrics Society* 36: 885-89.

Dawson, P., Kline, K., Crinklaw Wiancko, D., and Wells, D. 1986. Preventing excess disability in patients with Alzheimer's Disease. *Geriatric Nursing* 7: 299-301.

Derogatis, L.R., Melisaratos, N. 1983. The Brief Symptom Inventory: An introductory report. *Psychological Medicine* 13: 595-605.

Dunn, R., MacBeath, L., and Robertson, D. 1983. Respite admissions and the disabled elderly. *Journal of American Geriatrics Society* 31: 613-16.

Dura, J.R., Stukenberg, K.W., and Kiecolt-Glaser, J.K. 1990. Chronic stress and depressive disorders in older adults. *Journal of Abnormal Psychology* 99(3): 284-90.

- 1991. Anxiety and depressive disorders in adult children caring for demented parents. *Psychology and Aging* 6(3): 467-73.

Eagles, J.M., Beattie, J.A.G., Blackwood, G.W., Restall, D.B., and Ashcroft, G.W. 1987. The mental health of elderly couples. I. The effects of a cognitively impaired spouse. *British Journal of Psychiatry* 150: 299-303.

Endicott, J., and Spitzer, R.L. 1978. A diagnostic interview. *Archives of General Psychiatry* 35: 837-44.

Fengler, A., and Goodrich, N. 1979. Wives of elderly disabled men: The hidden patients. *The Gerontologist* 19: 175–83.

Fitting, M., Rabins, P., Lucas, M.J., and Eastham, J. 1986. Caregivers for dementia patients: A comparison of husbands and wives. *The Gerontologist* 26: 248–52.

Folstein, M F., Folstein, S.E., and McHugh, P.R. 1975. Mini-Mental State. A practical method for grading the cognitive state of patients for the clinician. *Journal of Psychiatric Research* 12: 189–98.

Gallagher, D., Rose, J., Rivera, P., Lovett, S., and Thompson, L.W. 1989a. Prevalence of depression in family caregivers. *The Gerontologist* 29(4): 449–56.

Gallagher, D., Wrabetz, A., Lovett, S., Del Maestro, S., and Rose, J. 1989b. Depression and other negative affects in family caregivers. In *Alzheimer's Disease Treatment and Family Stress: Directions for Research*, edited by Light, E. and Lebowitz, B.D., 218–44. Washington: U.S. Department of Health & Human Services.

Gendron, C.E., Poitras, L.R., Engels, M.L., Dastoor, D.P., Sirota, S.E., Barza, S.L., Davis, J.C., and Levine, N.B. 1986. Skills training with supporters of the demented. *Journal of the American Geriatrics Society* 34: 875–80.

Gilhooly, M. 1984. The impact of caregiving on caregivers: Factors associated with the psychological well-being of people supporting a dementing relative in the community. *British Journal of Medical Psychology* 57: 35–44.

Gilleard, C., Belford, H., Gilleard, J.E., Whittick, J.E., and Gledhill, K. 1984. Emotional distress amongst supporters of the elderly mentally infirm. *British Journal of Psychiatry* 145: 172–77.

Grad, J., and Sainsbury, P. 1963. Mental illness and the family. *Lancet* I: 544–47.

Granger, C.V., Albrecht, G., and Hamilton, B. 1979. Outcome of comprehensive medical rehabilitation: Measurement by PULSES Profile and the Barthel Index. *Archives of Physical Rehabilitation* 60: 145–54.

Greene, J.G., Smith, R., Gardiner, M., and Timburg, G.C. 1982. Measuring behavioral disturbance of elderly demented patients in the community and its effect on relatives: A factor analytic study. *Age and Ageing* 11: 121–26.

Hale, W.K., Chochran, C.K., and Hedgepeth, B.E. 1984. Norms for the elderly on the brief symptom inventory. *Journal of Consulting and Clinical Psychology* 52: 321–22.

Haley, W.E., Brown, S.L., and Levine, E.G. 1987a. Experimental evaluation of the effectiveness of group intervention for dementia caregivers. *The Gerontologist* 27: 376–82.

Haley, W.E., Levine, E.G., Brown, S.L., Berry, J.W., and Hughes, G.H. 1987b. Psychological, social, and health consequences of caring for a relative with senile dementia. *Journal of the American Geriatrics Society* 35: 405–11.

Hathaway, S.R., and McKinley, J.C. 1951. *The MMPI Manual*. N.Y.: Psychological Corporation.

Hoenig, J., and Hamilton, M. 1965. Extramural care of psychiatric patients. *Lancet* I: 1322–25.

Kahan, J., Kemp, B., Staples, F.R., and Brummel-Smith, K. 1985. Decreasing the burden in families caring for a relative with a dementing illness: A controlled study. *Journal of the American Geriatrics Society* 33: 664–70.

Kiecolt-Glaser, J.K., Dura, J.R., Speicher, C.E., Trask, O.J. and Glaser, R. 1991. Spousal caregivers of dementia victims: Longitudinal changes in immunity and health. *Psychosomatic Medicine* 53: 345–62.

Kiecolt-Glaser, J.K., Glaser, R., Shuttleworth, E.D., Dyer, C.S., Ogrocki, P., and Speicher, C.E. 1987. Chronic stress and immunity in family caregivers of Alzheimer's disease victims. *Psychosomatic Medicine* 49: 523–35.

Larson, E.B., Reifler, B.V., Featherstone, H.J., & English, D.R. 1984. Dementia in elderly outpatients: A prospective study. *Annals of Internal Medicine* 100: 417–23.

Lawton, M.P., Brody, E.M., and Saperstein, A.R. 1989. A controlled study of respite service for caregivers of Alzheimer's patients. *The Gerontologist* 29: 8–16.

Levine, N., Dastoor, D., and Gendron, C. 1983. Coping with dementia: A pilot study. *Journal of the American Geriatrics Society* 31: 12–18.

Mace, N., and Rabins, P. 1981. *The 36-hour day: A family guide to caring for persons with Alzheimer's Disease, related to dementing illnesses, and memory loss in later life.* New York: Warner Books.

Meyers, J.K., Weissman, M.M., Tischler, G.L., Holzer, C.E., Leaf, P.J., Orvaschel, H., Anthony, J.C., Boyd, J.H., Burke, J.D., Kramer, M., and Stoltzman, R. 1984. Six-month prevalence of psychiatric disorders in three communities. *Archives of General Psychiatry* 41: 959–67.

Mohide, E.A., Pringle, D.M., Streiner, D.L., Gilbert, J.R., Muir, G., and Tew, M. 1990. A randomized trial of family caregiver support in the home management of dementia. *Journal of the American Geriatrics Society* 38: 446–54.

Morris, L.W., Morris, R.G., and Britton, P.G. 1988. The relationship between marital intimacy, perceived strain and depression in spouse caregivers of dementia sufferers. *British Journal of Medical Psychology* 61: 231–36.

Morycz, R. 1980. An exploration of senile dementia and family burden. *Journal of Clinical Social Work* 8: 16–27.

Neundorfer, M.M. 1991. Coping and health outcomes in spouse caregivers of persons with dementia. *Nursing Research* 40(5): 260–65.

Niederehe, G., and Fruge, E. 1984. Dementia and family dynamics: Clinical research issues. *Journal of Geriatric Psychiatry* 17: 21–56.

Nygaard, H. A. 1988. Strain on caregivers of demented elderly people living at home. *Scandinavian Journal of Primary Health Care* 6: 33–37.

Pagel, M.D., Becker, J., and Coppel, D.B. 1985. Loss of control, self-blame, and depression: An investigation of spouse caregivers of Alzheimer's Disease patients. *Journal of Abnormal Psychology* 94: 169–82.

Poulshock, S.W., and Deimling, G.T. 1984. Families caring for elders in residence: Issues in the measurement of burden. *Journal of Gerontology* 39: 230–39.

Pruchno, R.A., and Resch, N.L. 1989. Husbands and wives as caregivers: Antecedents of depression and burden. *The Gerontologist* 29(2): 159–65.

Rabins, P. 1981. Management of irreversible dementia. *Psychosomatics* 22: 591–97.

Rabins, P., Mace, N., and Lucas, M. 1982. The impact of dementia on the family. *Journal of the American Medical Association* 248: 333–35.

Radloff, L.S. 1977. The CES-D Scale: A new self-report depression scale for research in the general population. *Applied Psychological Measurement* 1: 385–401.

Reisberg, B., Ferris, S., DeLeon, M., and Crook, T. 1982. The Global Deterioration Scale for assessment of primary degenerative dementia. *American Journal of Psychiatry* 139: 1136–39.

Riskind, J.H., Beck, A.T., Berchick, R.J., Brown, G. and Steer, R.A. 1987. Reliability of DSM-III diagnoses for major depression and generalized anxiety disorder using the structured clinical inerview for DSM-III. *Archives of General Psychiatry* 44: 817–20.

Rivera, P.A., Rose, J.M., Futterman, A., Lovett, S.B. and Gallagher-Thompson, D. 1991. Dimensions of perceived social support in clinically depressed and non-depressed female caregivers. *Psychology and Aging* 6(2): 232–37.

Robertson, D., Griffiths, R.A., and Cosin, L.Z. 1977. A community-based continuing care program for the elderly disabled: An evaluation of planned intermittent hospital readmission. *Journal of Gerontology* 32: 334–39.

Robertson, D., Rockwood, K., and Stolee, P. 1982. A short mental status questionnaire. *Canadian Journal on Aging* 1: 16–20.

Robins, L.N., Helzer, J.E., Weissman, M.M., Orvaschel, H., Gruenberg, E., Burke, Jr, J.D., and Regier, D.A. 1984. Lifetime prevalence of specific psychiatric disorders in three sites. *Archives of General Psychiatry* 41: 949–58.

Robinson, K.M. 1989. Predictors of depression among wife caregivers. *Nursing Research* 38(6): 359–63.

Sands, D., and Suzuki, T. 1983. Adult day care for Alzheimer's patients and their families. *The Gerontologist* 23: 21–23.

Sanford, J.R. 1975. Tolerance of disability in elderly dependents by supporters at home: Its significance for hospital practice. *British Medical Journal* 3: 471–73.

Schulz, R., and Tompkins, C.A. 1988. A longitudinal study of the psychosocial impact of stroke on primary support persons. *Psychology and Aging* 3: 131–41.

Schulz, R. and Williamson, G.M. 1991. A 2-year longitudinal study of depression among Alzheimer's caregivers. *Psychology and Aging* 6(4): 569–78.

Sheehan, N.W., and Nuttall, P. 1988. Conflict, emotion, and personal strain among family caregivers. *Family Relations* 37: 92–8.

Snaith, R.P., Ahmed, S.N., Mehta, S., and Hamilton, M. 1971. Assessment of the severity of primary depressive illness. Wakefield Self-Assessment Depression Inventory. *Psychological Medicine* 1: 143–49.

Snaith, R.P., Bridge, W.K., and Hamilton, M. 1976. The Leeds Scales for the Self-Assessment of Anxiety and Depression. *British Journal of Psychiatry* 128: 156–65.

Spitzer, R.L., Endicott, J., and Robins, E. 1978. Research diagnostic criteria: Rationale and reliability. *Archives of General Psychiatry* 35: 773–82.

Stone, R., Cafferata, G.L., and Sangl, J. 1987. Caregivers of the frail elderly: A national profile. *The Gerontologist* 27: 616–26.

Stommel, M., Given, C.W., and Given, B. 1990. Depression as an overriding variable explaining caregiver burdens. *Journal of Aging and Health* 2(1): 81–102.

Thompson, S.C., Sobolew-Shubin, A., Graham, M.A., and Janigian, A.S. 1989. Psychosocial adjustment following a stroke. *Social Science Medicine* 28(3): 239–47.

Vitaliano, P.P., Russo, J., Young, H.M., Teri, L. and Maiuro, R.D. 1991. Predictors of burden in spouse caregivers of individuals with Alzheimer's Disease. *Psychology and Aging* 6(3): 392–402.

Wade, D.T., Legh-Smith, J., and Hewer, R.L. 1986. Effects of living with and looking after survivors of a stroke. *British Medical Journal* 293: 418–20.

Zarit, S.H., Reever, K.E., and Bach-Peterson, J. 1980. Relatives of the impaired elderly: Correlates of feelings of burden. *The Gerontologist* 20: 649–55.

Zarit, S.H., Zarit, J.M., and Reever, K.E. 1982. Memory training for severe memory loss: Effects on senile dementia patients and their families. *The Gerontologist* 22: 373–77.

Zung, W.W.K. 1972. The depression status inventory: An adjunct to the Self-rating Depression Scale. *Journal of Clinical Psychology* 28: 539–42.

CHAPTER TWELVE

Depression in Elderly Persons: Prevalence, Predictors, and Psychological Intervention

PHILIPPE CAPPELIEZ

With the growing number of adults living to advanced ages in industrialized countries, concerns about emotional adaptation and well-being in the later portion of life have been amplified. In particular, many people worry that large numbers of older adults may experience psychological distress, as manifested in depression.

This chapter does not cover the various aspects of depression that occur in late adulthood. Instead, in line with the theme of this book, I have pursued three objectives. First, in view of the widespread, yet controversial, belief that depression is rampant among older adults, I examine the initial questions regarding the identification and evaluation of depression. Second, using an etiological model that adopts a psychosocial perspective and emphasizes the particular challenges and deficits of older adulthood, I analyze the occurrence of depression in late adulthood. Finally, I review the research that looks at the development and evaluation of psychotherapeutic modalities of change in the elderly.

PREVALENCE OF DEPRESSION

Late adulthood is commonly thought to be a time of pervasive mental distress and, therefore, a period characterized by a surge of depression. Such an outcome is regarded as an inevitable consequence of aging – itself a progression of disengagements, separations, and losses at numerous levels, from the physical to the social. One of the results of such a perspective may be that many older adults think of themselves as actual, or potential, victims of an unavoidable and uncontrollable process. The first objective of this chapter is to evaluate this rather pessimistic view in light of recent research on the prevalence of depressive conditions in older adults.

It is a surprise to most people to learn that mental health professionals find depression at times difficult to identify and hard to classify. The term "depression" is, in fact, used to describe several different conditions. Depending on the context, the term may describe a transitory mood fluctuation, a normal way of behaving given the circumstances, a symptom, a syndrome, an illness, or a biochemical disorder. These inconsistencies in the terminology and taxonomy of depressive conditions explain, in large part, the difficulty of interpreting incidence and prevalence data.

The prevalence of affective disorders varies with the method used to collect data and identify cases. To cite only a few possible sources of variation, such indices will vary depending on whether prevalence is based on psychiatric diagnoses obtained from hospital records, on psychiatric assessments of community samples, or on self-reports of subjects living within the community.

Two major approaches to assessing depressive conditions have been used to study the relationship between age and prevalence of depression. On the one hand, depression can be considered from the perspective of psychiatric diagnosis. Diagnostic criteria for affective disorders, initially proposed as a research tool (Research Diagnostic Criteria [RDC], [Spitzer et al. 1978]), and subsequently adopted in the *Diagnostic and Statistical Manual of Mental Disorders, Third Edition* (DSM-III). (American Psychiatric Association 1980) and *Diagnostic and Statistical Manual of Mental Disorders, Third Edition, revised* (DSM-III-R) (American Psychiatric Association 1987), represent notable progress in the diagnosis of clinical depression. The criteria of major depression proposed by DSM-III and DSM-III-R make it possible not only to isolate a syndrome of severe clinical depression (major depression), but to differentiate that syndrome both from transitory states of affliction and from other less severe, but chronic, conditions (dysthymic disorders). Many recent epidemiological studies with large samples have used these strict diagnostic criteria to quantify the prevalence of depression in the community.

On the other hand, it is possible to quantify the depressive state by means of scales, inventories, or questionnaires on which subjects report the intensity of their depressive symptomatology. These instruments, which originate in the psychometric tradition in psychology, have been designed for the purpose of quantifying the severity of depressive conditions. A frequently used screening instrument in community studies is the Center for Epidemiological Studies -Depression (CES-D) Scale (Radloff 1977). Another example of a widely used instrument for measuring the intensity of depressive symptomatology is the Beck Depression Inventory (BDI) (Beck et al. 1961; Beck et al. 1979).

It is worth remembering that these questionnaires were not intended to serve as instruments for the diagnosis of depression, but rather as tools for measuring the intensity of depressive symptoms. Diagnosis of depression is typically approximated by a score above a normative cutoff point on the particular questionnaire. The distinction between these two ways of evaluating the prevalence of depression is fundamental to understanding the divergence in the research findings and will be used for the organization of the empirical results.

Clinical Depressions

On the basis of recent major epidemiological studies, taken as a whole, it is possible to estimate that between 0.8 and 8 per cent of older adults (65 years and over) meet the criteria of major depression, as formulated in DSM-III (Blazer et al. 1987; Blazer and Williams 1980; Kivelä et al. (1988); Kovess et al. 1987; Myers et al. 1984; O'Hara et al. 1985; Robins et al. 1984; Weissman and Myers 1978; Weissman et al. 1988). The data reported by Myers et al. (1984), Robins et al. (1984), and Weissman et al. (1988) originate from a large epidemiological investigation, the National Institute of Mental Health – Epidemiological Catchment Area (ECA) project, which involved a sample of 18,000 adults eighteen years of age and over and represented five communities in the United States (Regier et al. 1984). These studies relied on structured diagnostic interviews, leading to diagnoses according to DSM-III criteria, with the assistance of the Diagnostic Interview Schedule (DIS). The DIS assesses the presence, severity, and duration of symptoms (Regier et al. 1984; Robins et al. 1981), focusing on the identification of major episodes of depression and excluding minor episodes, bereavement, and the various depressive symptoms associated with physical illness. Preliminary data from three of the five sites (Myers et al. 1984; Robins et al. 1984) have indicated that, for most psychological disorders, including the affective disorders, the twenty-five to forty-four-year-old group shows the highest prevalence, with a clearly reduced prevalence among the over-sixty-five group. This trend was particularly evident in the case of affective disorders, considered as a single entity, with six-month prevalence rates going down from 4.7 per cent (males) and 10.1 per cent (females) for the twenty-five to forty-four age group, to 1.3 per cent (males) and 3.7 per cent (females) for the sixty-five and over group. More recent and complete data have given us a comprehensive clinical picture (Weissman et al. 1988). With respect to both major depression and dysthymic disorders, this latter study again confirmed the generally higher rate among women, in every age group. Among women, those in the eighteen- to forty-four-year age range presented the highest risk for major depression, with an annual prevalence rate of 4.8 per cent, a rate significantly higher than the annual rate of 1.4 per cent for women aged sixty-five and over. With respect to lifetime rates of dysthymia, the highest rates were recorded in the forty-five- to sixty-four-year age group (4.8%), decreasing for women aged sixty-five and over (2.3%). Regier et al. (1988) reported the one-month prevalence rates of affective disorder for all five sites of the ECA project. Persons aged sixty-five years and over had a rate of 2.5 per cent, the lowest across all age groups. In contrast, persons aged twenty-four to forty-four years had a rate of 6.4 per cent. Additionally, the median age at onset for unipolar major depression has been reported as twenty-five years, on the basis of data collected in the NIMH–Epidemiologic Catchment Area study (Christie et al. 1988).

Bland et al. (1988) recently announced the findings of an epidemiological study, conducted in Edmonton, Alberta (Canada), that also indicated a lower rate of depression for older than younger adults. This study reported that, among older people living in the community, six-month prevalence rates for major depression were 0.9 per cent for males and 1.4 per cent for females, with rates for dysthymia of 1.8 per cent for males and 4.3 per cent for females. These data are in agreement with those gathered in the United States. In this Canadian study, lifetime prevalence rates showed similar trends in favour of the sixty-five-plus age group, both for major depressions (8.6% of adults in general, 4.1% of those aged 65 and over) and for mood disorders in general (10.2% of adults in general, 5.3% of those aged 65 and over).

However, in a recent study conducted in Quebec, Kovess et al. (1987) reported a finding at variance with other studies. They indicated that rates of major depression and dysthymia were not lower in the sixty-five years and over group compared to the younger group. At this point, it is difficult to evaluate properly the significance of this divergent finding.

More generally, the diversity of prevalence rates among studies requires a closer examination. The lack of uniformity in diagnostic practices from one study to another may account for some of this discrepancy. Typically, the lowest percentages are reported in studies adopting strict DSM-III criteria for the diagnosis of major depression. A recent analysis of the distribution of diagnoses of depression in a subsample (Epidemiologic Catchment Area – Duke) of the large epidemiological research mentioned above, composed of people aged sixty and over, sheds some light on this issue (Blazer et al. 1987). Apparently, while 0.8 per cent of this sample was diagnosed as suffering from major depression, the percentage of clinically significant depressions climbed to 8 per cent when dysthymia (according to DSM-III criteria) (2%), mixed anxio-depressive syndromes (1.2%), and "symptomatic" depressions (4%) were included. In this study, "Symptomatic depression" meant a mild to moderate depression that the authors likened to an adjustment disorder with depressed mood (in line with the DSM-III).

A recent British study (Copeland et al. 1987) reported a rate of 11.3 per cent of serious depressive disorders in a community-residing group of subjects aged sixty-five and over. This study differs from the others reviewed above, in that it used an assessment instrument known as the Geriatric Mental State Schedule (Copeland et al. 1976), which provides diagnoses not directly comparable to those obtained with DSM-III. According to the authors, this figure incorporates not only the DSM-III type of major depression but also dysthymic disorders and severe psychotic depressions. These inclusions would explain the comparatively higher percentage reported. A similar explanation can be advanced to explain the higher rate of depression reported among aged Finns living in a semi-industrialized municipality (Kivelä et al. 1988; Kivelä and Pahkala 1989). There, the authors reported prevalence rates of 20.6 per cent for dysthymic disorders and 3.7 per cent for major depression, assessed through semi-structured interviews. The authors noted, however, that although actual higher prevalence rates of depression in Finland cannot be ruled out, differences in diagnostic practices may also have led to the recording of these higher rates.

Kay et al. (1985), who studied depressive disorders in the elderly living in the Hobart community of Australia using a version of the Geriatric Mental State Schedule, found a prevalence rate of 12.7 per cent for mild depression and 13.9 per cent for moderate and severe depression for persons aged seventy to seventy-nine years. In those over eighty years of age, rates were higher at 20.9 per cent for mild depression and 14.8 per cent for moderate and severe depression. In sharp contrast to the this last study, Kua (1990), using the same assessment instrument, reported a much lower rate of 4.6 per cent for the prevalence of depressive disorders among elderly Chinese people living in the Singapore community. This last finding is difficult to interpret. The author points to social and cultural influences, emphasizing the respect, social status, and social support given to elderly parents in the Chinese culture.

Depressive Symptomatology

Several studies present data on the frequency of depressive symptoms among older adults based on answers to self-report questionnaires and inventories. A majority of community studies have used the CES-D to suggest that the rate of depression for adults over age sixty or sixty-five is in the 9- to 18-per-cent range (Comstock and Helsing 1976; Frerichs et al. 1981; Gatz et al. 1986; Goldberg et al. 1985; Hertzog et al. 1990; Kennedy et al. 1989; Murrell et al. 1983; O'Hara et al. 1985; Phifer and Murrell 1986). Gatz and Hurwicz (1990) recently reported prevalence of depressive symptomatology at 17 per cent for fifty-five- to sixty-nine-year-olds, and 24.4 per cent for those aged seventy to ninety-eight. These findings reflect the proportion of subjects with scores above a pre-established cutoff point, typically a score above sixteen in the case of the CES-D. Other studies relying on other instruments, such as the SCL-90-R (Derogatis et al. 1973), the Self-Rating Depression Scale (SDS) (Zung 1965), the Hamilton Depression Rating

Scale (HDRS) (Hamilton 1960), the Geriatric Depression Scale (GDS) (Ye-savage et al. 1983) or the Beck Depression Inventory (BDI) (Beck et al. 1979) have reported similar, or slightly higher percentages: 13 per cent (Griffiths et al. 1987); 15 per cent (Blazer and Williams 1980); 17 per cent (Carpiniello et al. 1989; Feinson and Thoits 1986); 19 per cent (Bourque et al. 1990); 20 per cent (Kukull et al. 1986; Smallegan 1989); 24 per cent (Borson et al. 1986); and 25 per cent (Vézina et al. 1991).

These results coincide with the rates reported in a comparative epidemiological study conducted in London and New York (Gurland et al. 1983; Copeland et al. 1987b) that used semi-structured interviews. Rates of 12.4 per cent (London) and 13 per cent (New York) were reported, reflecting the proportions of older adults manifesting depressive symptomatology sufficiently severe and persistent to interfere significantly with daily functioning. These results are similar to those reported by the same research team in an earlier study (Gurland et al. 1980) of older residents of New York, for whom clinical depression was found in 13 per cent of the sample. Recently, Livingston et al. (1990) who assessed prevalence rates of depression using the same type of instrument but among elderly residents of Inner London, reported a pervasive depression (that is, a depressed mood severe enough to warrant intervention) rate of 15.9 per cent. This rate, higher than that of other studies, was attributed to the relative socioeconomic deprivation of the study site from which the sample was drawn.

It appears that some reported percentages include cases of clinical depression as well as milder cases of depression. This client duality must be kept in mind when interpreting certain studies' reportedly higher proportions. Gurland et al. (1980) noted the presence of depressive symptomatology in the 22 per cent of their older subjects living in New York, having added the 9 per cent of subjects manifesting at least six depressive symptoms to the 13 per cent regarded as clinically depressed. More recently, the same group of researchers (Copeland et al. 1987a) reported an identical rate of 22 per cent of depressive symptomatology among older adults. Kemp et al. (1987), studying a sample of older Hispanic-Americans, also reported that a little over 25 per cent of their subjects suffered from one or another form of depression.

In line with the studies just mentioned, Blazer et al. (1987) reported a 27 per cent overall rate of depressive symptomatology. The details provided by the authors (1987) regarding their subjects support the points made here. Whereas 8 per cent of their subjects suffered from a depression meeting DSM-III criteria, 19 per cent suffered from what the authors labelled as dysphoria. This term, the etymology of which suggests bad feeling (in opposition to "eu-phoria") and the difficulty ("dys-") of bearing or enduring, corresponds to a less severe and more diffuse depressive symptomatology; that is, it is characterized by a sense of being overwhelmed, by a marked lack of satisfaction with life, by self-depreciation, and by a noticeable pessimism and hopelessness.

Studies that have directly compared scores obtained in various age groups have typically reported an inverse relationship between age and depressive symptomatology, with the highest rates found among the younger groups (Feinson 1985; Gatz et al. 1986; Jorm 1987). Recent epidemiological data have also shown that the highest rates of depressive symptomatology were in the eighteen to twenty-four-year-old age group (Amenson and Lewinsohn 1981; Comstock and Helsing 1976; Frerichs et al. 1981; Myers et al. 1984; Robins et al. 1984). In a review of prevalence studies conducted in the United States since 1980, Feinson (1989) concluded that the younger cohorts, rather than the older, reported more disorders for depressive symptoms, major depression, and clinical affective disorders.

Conclusions

Taken together, the research findings do not support the hypothesis that risk for depression inexorably increases with age. By incorporating the results of the various studies, I propose a simplified picture of depressive conditions for the group of adults aged sixty-five and over. First, between 20 and 25 per cent may manifest dysphoria. Signs of dysphoria may include global dissatisfaction, gloominess, loneliness, and various somatic complaints. As suggested by Newmann et al. (1990), these symptoms may exist as delimited forms of distress, related to the stresses and strains of daily life, but can be distinguished from clinical symptom patterns. Second, about half of these cases (some 10 to 15% of the overall population of older adults) present additional depressive symptoms that vary from moderate to severe. In comparison to the previous group, feelings of worthlessness and hopelessness and a lack of both motivation and interest are more pronounced. Approximately half of the cases (that is, 5 to 8% of the overall population of older adults) suffer from clinical depression; that is, a depression that meets the criteria of a psychiatric diagnosis of major depression or dysthymic disorder, according to the DSM-III or DSM-III-R formulations of diagnostic criteria.

This general conclusion must, however, be qualified at several levels. First, it is necessary to reassert the important distinction between an evaluation of diffuse depressive symptomatology and the diagnosis of depression, a distinction which allowed us to organize the above presentation of research data. Furthermore, from a review of the data, I realize that the arguments supporting the hypothesis that older adults do not present a higher risk for depression actually originate from studies that diagnose clinical depressions. As justifiably underlined by Newmann (1989), who critically reviewed this research literature, a detailed analysis of the studies bearing on the assessment on depressive symptomatology leads to the opposite conclusion:

that depressive risk increases in the last two decades of life, compared to the middle adult years. Similarly, based on data collected in Canada, D'Arcy (1987) has concluded that, whereas lower rates of depressive disorders were found in the older compared to the younger age groups, reports of more diffuse psychological distress were found more frequently among the elderly.

Furthermore, it should be noted that data were obtained, for most of the studies, from samples of relatively healthy subjects living in the community. One can still, however, reasonably conclude that other subgroups of older adults, such as the medically ill, very old, institutionalized, or socioeconomically deprived elderly persons, could manifest significantly higher rates of depression. The prevalence of major depression among elderly persons with acute and chronic medical problems has been reported to range from 12 to 45 per cent (Kitchell et al. 1982; Koenig et al. 1988a, 1988b; Okimoto et al. 1982; Sadavoy et al. 1990; Waxerman and Carner 1984). Even now, advances are underway regarding the proper use of self-rated depression scales for the screening of depression among elderly medical patients (Harper et al. 1990; Koenig et al. 1988a; Rapp et al. 1988). Parmelee et al. (1989) reported rates of 12.4 per cent of major depression and 30.5 per cent of serious depressive symptomatology among their sample of institutionalized older persons. Cohen and Eisdorfer (1988) recently reported that 55 per cent of their sample of major caregivers, primarily elderly spouses living with an older relative with dementia, experienced clinical depression. A few rare studies that have distinguished age subgroups within the larger group of over sixty-fivers have noted a higher prevalence of depressive symptomatology among the oldest group – that is, in persons over seventy-five – compared to younger subjects of this group (Gatz and Hurwicz 1990; Gurland et al. 1983; Murrell et al. 1983). Also, as suggested by the study of Livingston et al. (1990), higher rates of depression may be found among older adults living in socioeconomically deprived urban environments.

Other critical comments can be advanced concerning research methodology. Given that most of the existing data were collected through interviews and questionnaires, the subjects' answers may have been influenced by a series of factors. For example, it is possible that memory gaps, especially among older subjects, contributed to an underreporting of the frequency of depressive episodes, particularly regarding retrospective accounts of lifetime episodes. Nevertheless, some investigators (for example, Prusoff et al. 1988) have defended the reliability of older adults' reports on the basis of empirical data. It is possible, however, that other factors bias the results even more subtly. For example, a particular fragility regarding memories of depressive periods can be associated with the generalized tendency to "reconstruct" the personal past so as to make it compatible with present life conditions (Aneshensel et al. 1987). Also, ideas and attitudes about mental health in general, and depression in particular, may bias the results. Compared to younger and more educated individuals, older adults of contemporary cohorts tend to give less importance to emotions, to analyze them less, and to communicate them less openly to others. Generally, too, older adults of today tend not to communicate their psychological distress, unless it has reached an incapacitating level. Hasin and Link (1988) recently demonstrated that contemporary older adults think of depression less as a psychological or emotional problem than do younger adults. Again, it is possible that these factors contribute to an underreporting of depressive symptomatology on the part of older adults. The instruments used to assess depression constitute still another related methodological caveat. It is possible that the instruments currently in use do not properly capture the features of elderly depression, thus leading to lower prevalence rates.

Additional factors have been mentioned to explain the comparatively low rates of depression found among older groups in recent epidemiological studies (Feinson 1989; Kermis 1986; Klerman and Weissman 1989; Newmann 1989). These same criticisms also apply to other studies conducted in the community. They include a bias toward the identification of dementias to the detriment of depressions in older samples; the exclusion of cases of severe depression in community samples, due to earlier deaths or placements in an institution; a disproportionate participation of physically and mentally healthier subjects among research volunteers; a tendency for older adults to attribute depression to a physical illness; a tendency among younger adults to report more symptoms of a benign or transitory nature; and a genuine historical increase in depression and associated problems (alcohol and drug abuse) in the generations born since the Second World War (Klerman 1988; Klerman and Weissman 1989; Klerman et al. 1985). It is also possible that the prevalence of depressive symptomatology is underestimated among older adults of lower socioeconomic and educational levels. Such individuals appear particularly sensitive to the socially undesirable quality of some items used by self-reporting inventories to quantify depressive symptomatology (Cappeliez 1989), an attitude that may contribute to their underreporting of depressive symptoms.

Several fundamental questions remain concerning the prevalence of depressive conditions in older adulthood and the relationship between age and depression. Most importantly, our conceptualization and operationalization of depression in late adulthood need refining. It may be that older adults manifest clinically meaningful depressive disorders in ways that do not neatly correspond with present assessment and diagnostic practices, largely derived from research on general adult samples.

As noted by Newmann (1989), our understanding of depression in late adulthood would benefit from an extension of the research; needed are longitudinal naturalistic studies that probe the phenomenology of depression in community samples. Newmann et al. (1990) underlined the usefulness of distinguishing between depressive syndromes and more delimited forms of distress when addressing the depressive symptom experiences of older adults. These authors proposed that the depressive syndrome – a category more classic in form, that shows decreasing levels of depression with increasing age – be distinguished from the depletion syndrome – a category characterized by loss of interest and social withdrawal, the levels of which increase with advancing age (Newmann et al. 1991). In the same vein, Gatz and Hurwicz (1990) suggested that expressions of lack of well-being in old age be distinguished from "true" depression, so as to clarify the construct of late-life depression. Undoubtedly, the longitudinal identification of the variables that trigger and modulate the expression of depressive symptoms is one of the most important issues on the agenda of research on late-life depression.

A PSYCHOSOCIAL PERSPECTIVE ON THE ETIOLOGY OF DEPRESSIVE CONDITIONS

The psychosocial analysis of depression proposed by Billings and Moos (1982, 1985) is as a useful theoretical framework, not only for organizing the review of research findings but also for fostering the study of depression as it occurs during the course of the elderly person's life. In essence, this model assumes that depression results from the interplay of several types of variables, in particular the resources of people and their environment, their stressful life events, and the individuals' coping responses. The concept of personal resources must be understood in a broad sense (Billings and Moos 1982, 1985; Dohrenwend 1978; Murrell and Norris 1983), to include all the resources available to individuals for coping with life changes. The term thus includes such personal characteristics as level of education, health status, income, as well as social skills, problem-solving abilities, sense of control over environmental influences, and so on. When referring to environmental resources, we would include both the material and emotional support provided by friends, relatives, family members, and others within the individuals' social network.

It is within this context of resources that individuals produce coping responses to minimize the negative effects of stressful situations. The appraisal of stressors (perception and interpretation) is considered an integral part of the coping process. The result of this process influences both the quality of functioning and the adaptation of individuals.

The psychosocial model takes into consideration the relationship between these factors. Thus, the nature and efficacy of the individuals' appraisal of a stressor and their coping responses are said to determine the extent to which the stressor will lead to depression. These processes are essentially determined by the resources of the persons involved and those of their environment. For instance, such resources as self-confidence, or support from a friend, can buffer the depressive effect by reducing the frequency or intensity of stressful situations, or by facilitating the implementation of constructive coping strategies. In turn, depression itself and its consequences on the functioning of individuals can influence each of the aforementioned factors.

Following this model, three major categories of factors – sociodemographic variables, life events, and personal resources – are presented here. Each category independently and jointly contributes to the emergence and maintenance of depression. This selection is governed by the dual objectives of identifying the distinctive characteristics of depressive conditions in the elderly and of stimulating research. A similar perspective on depression in the elderly has been adopted by Fry in the study presented in detail in chapter 13 of this volume.

Sociodemographic Variables

Available data suggest that certain risk factors associated with adult depressive conditions are also risk factors for depressive conditions of late adulthood. Several authors have reviewed these factors (Akiskal 1985; Billings and Moos 1982; Brown and Harris 1978; Hirschfeld and Cross 1982; Lewinsohn et al. 1985; Phifer and Murrell 1986). As we saw earlier, the one well-documented risk factor is younger age. Other characteristics, however – being female, having a family history of depression, and belonging to a low socioeconomic level – have also been considered as risk factors for depression in adulthood (Lewinsohn et al. 1985).

These same sociodemographic characteristics can be considered as risk factors for the occurrence of depressions in late adulthood as well. Even if gender differences in prevalence tend to decrease from middle to late adulthood (Jorm 1987), it appears that prevalence rates of depressive symptomatology remain higher in women than men (Blazer et al. 1987; Freedman et al. 1982; Good et al. 1987; Griffiths et al. 1987; Gurland et al. 1983; Myers et al. 1984; O'Hara et al. 1985). Several studies (Blazer et al. 1987; Gurland et al. 1983; O'Hara et al. 1985) have documented that, among the elderly, depressive symptomatology is more frequent among unmarried individuals from lower socioeconomic levels. In addition, Frerichs et al. (1981), Goldberg et al. (1985), Murphy (1982), and Murrell et al. (1983) have indicated that older adults from lower socioeconomic levels present a higher incidence of depression.

A number of authors have reported data indicating higher rates of depression among elderly urban, as compared to rural, residents (for example, Carpiniello et al. 1989; Livingston et al. 1990; O'Hara et al. 1985). Given that older people in Canada tend to move from rural areas to urban centres as they age (Statistics Canada 1984), it may be critical for us to study how social support and integration, as well as socioeconomic conditions, influence depression.

A recent study by George et al. (1987) suggests that sociodemographic variables such as gender, marital status, and socioeconomic status may be more strongly related to depression in younger than older adults. They found a significant age-by-sex interaction in the determination of levels of depressive symptoms, such that younger women were more likely to manifest depressive symptoms than other subjects. Also, age interacted with marital status, with the young unmarried persons showing higher levels of depressive symptoms than older unmarried persons and the married of all ages. Additionally, a socioeconomic status-by-age interaction was found, indicating that low socioeconomic status is a significant determinant of depressive symptoms for younger, but not older, subjects. This study deserves mention as it indicates that antecedents of depression need to be examined in an age-specific way.

Life Events

A detailed review of the large and complex literature on life events that predispose to depression, or trigger a depressive episode, is beyond the intended scope of this chapter. It appears more relevant to delineate several fundamental differences between the life circumstances of younger and older adults and their relationship with depression.

The first set of remarks pertains to the nature of stressful events associated with depression. Research on the relationship between stressful life events and depression focuses mainly on major life events such as divorce, loss of employment, or the unexpected death of a loved one. The notion of loss is central to all these stressors. In most instances, these are events which occur quite suddenly and do not necessarily relate to anticipated life transitions. These life events are also closely linked with social roles central to young and middle adulthood: those pertaining to employment and career, the couple, economic survival, or the education of children. Without neglecting the impact of losses on morale, it should be recognized that older adults face fewer undesirable events of this type, compared to younger and middle-aged adults (Goldberg and Comstock 1980; Hughes et al. 1988; Lieberman 1983; McCrae 1984). The nature of the stressful events also changes. Compared to younger adults, older persons are more likely to report health events, retirement, and loss of family and friends (for example, Goldberg and Comstock 1980; Hughes et al. 1988). Linn et al. (1980) and Smallegan (1989) indicated that the death of a spouse or relative, personal illness, or the illness of a friend or relative were among the stressful events most frequently reported by older adults.

It seems that stressful life events have a less important contribution to the etiology of late adulthood depressions, than to the depressions of younger adulthood. Phifer and Murrell (1986) recently demonstrated that life events (in the sense of major life events of the type just described), as etiological factors, have a lesser influence on depressive conditions of the elderly than on those of younger adults.

The relationship between stressful events and depressive symptomatology is also weak and inconsistent (Linn et al. 1980; Smallegan 1989). In contrast, these two same studies demonstrated a significant association between two specific subject characteristics – lower levels of disability and the condition of living with a spouse – and lower levels of depressive symptomatology. It is interesting to note that the significant relationship was found with characteristics of the subjects and not with aspects of the life events confronting them.

If, on the one hand, the elderly do in fact experience fewer unpleasant events associated with major social roles than do younger adults, they nevertheless face an increase in chronic problems that could contribute to a rise in their overall stress level, and in a more undifferentiated way. Two domains that are potential sources of chronic difficulties – health and social relations – will be discussed later, in the section on personal resources.

It is important to mention the potential contribution of "micro-stressors" in the etiology of depression; that is, those sources of frustration associated with daily functioning, such as coping with memory difficulties, household management, personal finances, and so on. The importance of these hassles as predictors of stress in general, and of depressive conditions in particular, has been underlined (Kanner et al. 1981; Monroe 1983; Pearlin et al. 1981). Folkman et al. (1987) showed that, while younger adults reported significantly more hassles in household responsibilities, finances, and work, older adults reported more hassles in the domains of health, social and environmental issues, and home maintenance. These circumstances of frustration and helplessness could, in effect, represent the truly stressful consequences of adaptation to negative life events, such as the death of a spouse, for instance. Recently, Landreville and Vézina (1992) have suggested that the frequency of daily hassles is a stronger correlate of well-being in older adults than the frequency of major life events.

In brief, it is important to consider a shift in perspective when addressing the depressive conditions of older adults. Theories of depression in late adulthood must take into account the fact that life events typically associated with depressive conditions in late adulthood differ fundamentally from those in early adulthood. Adaptation to chronic stressors (for example, poor health, difficult financial situations, loss of spouse) seems to dominate the picture. The impact of these life circumstances on the morale of older individuals, as modulated by the social context and the resources of the person, should be considered as well.

Personal Resources

The concept of resources is used here in its broadest sense. Some of the factors involved, such as socioeconomic and educational levels, have already been mentioned in the discussion of sociodemographic risk factors. It is, nevertheless, important to underline once again the well-documented association between low socioeconomic level and depression. Krause (1986a, 1987) presented data that suggest that older adults facing chronic financial difficulties are particularly vulnerable to depressive feelings. Krause (1986b) noted that older women, in particular, are the victims of financial stress, a worry that often accompanies widowhood.

A discussion of the role of other resources in depression such as personality dispositions, cognitive styles, coping strategies, and social skills goes beyond the scope of the present review. That domain of inquiry, with its goal of understanding depressive conditions in the older adult, is in its infancy. We focus here on two specific types of resources that have received the scrutiny of contemporary researchers: health status and social support. Studies concerning the role of social support in the specific domain of depression are numerous and were recently critically assessed (Alloway and Bebbington 1987; Cohen and Wills 1985). Here, we will comment only on those studies that specifically address depressive conditions in the elderly.

HEALTH AND SOCIAL SUPPORT. Several studies have documented an association between physical health and depression in samples of older adults. McNeil and Harsany (1989) concluded that health is the main predictor of depression among older adults, a stronger predictor even than social support and stressful life events. Murphy (1982) and Goldberg et al. (1985) pointed out that the higher incidence of depression in their older subjects with lower incomes could largely be attributed to their poor health and serious financial difficulties. In addition to the stress rooted in difficult economic conditions, Krause (1986a) noted the importance of the association between depression and health-related chronic stress. Gurland et al. (1983) argued that physical illness and associated limitations are among the major determinants of depression in the elderly. Recently, Gurland et al. (1988) suggested that limitation in activities and capacities is more closely associated with the presence of depressive symptoms than events such as isolation, retirement, widowhood, financial difficulties, and cognitive deficits. In their study, Murrell et al. (1983) found that health status was the best predictor of depression. Kukull et al. (1986) underlined the contribution of physical illness as a risk factor for the emergence of depression in a sample of older outpatients of a general medical clinic. Blazer et al. (1987) demonstrated that older adults with depressive symptomatology were more likely to complain of poor health, to feel isolated and useless, and to have lost a loved one. According to Burvill et al. (1986), the presence of a serious and chronic physical illness can actually be related to a poorer prognosis for treatment of depression. And Turner and Noh (1988) found that measures of physical disability (pain and functional disabilities) represented significant predictors of depression for an elderly sample.

Findings reported by Kennedy and collaborators strongly suggest that poor health contributes substantially to the emergence and persistence of depressive symptoms in older adults. In a cross-sectional study with a large sample of individuals aged sixty-five years of age and older living in an urban community, Kennedy et al. (1989) reported that physical health and disability dominated the hierarchy of characteristics associated with substantial levels of depressive symptomatology. In this report, poor health and disability outranked demographic, social support, and life-event characteristics in their association with depressive symptoms. Longitudinal analyses of the same sample revealed that increased disability and worsening health preceded the onset of depressive symptoms in many subjects (Kennedy et al. 1990). Among the variables studied, availability of social support and recent undesirable life events contributed little to the distinguishing of individuals with emerging symptoms from those remaining free of symptoms. A subsequent study aimed at identifying variables influencing the course of depressive symptoms indicated that poor health and disability also contributed substantially to the remission or persistence of depressive symptoms (Kennedy et al. 1991).

In a prospective study on the etiological factors of depression in the elderly, Phifer and Murrell (1986) reported that social support and physical health were the two most influential predictors of depression. On the basis of these data, the authors concluded that health and social support have both direct and indirect effects on depressive symptomatology. The health factor, they say, contributes directly and independently to the depressive symptomatology and also interacts with the social support factor. The social support factor, they note, contributes both directly, to the extent that a person's integration within a social network promotes positive affect, a sense of stability, and the recognition of personal worth, and indirectly, by buffering the individual against stress. They suggest that this buffering effect may operate by either reducing the number or intensity of situations perceived as stressful, or simply by decreasing, or possibly eliminating, stress reactions. Social support, they add, seems to buffer the negative effects of bad health and material and interpersonal losses on mood. Finally, the authors found that older adults in poor health and with a weak social support network were most at risk for depression.

The importance of social support in reducing the negative impact of stress on older adults' mental health and mood has also been emphasized by Cutrona et al. (1986), Arling (1987), and Holahan and Holahan (1987). Krause (1987) recently added that, in the specific case of stress stemming from chronic financial difficulties, social support, especially as a source of information, acted as a buffer against the emergence of depressive feelings.

THE NATURE OF SOCIAL SUPPORT. Several authors have attempted to analyze the concept of social support in its complex relationship with adaptation and depression, among older adults. This research literature has recently been the topic of a critical review (Landreville and Cappeliez [in press]). Certain authors emphasized the lack of intimate and confiding relationships, and the affective and practical consequences of such a situation (Brown and Harris 1978; Goldberg et al. 1985; Murphy 1982, 1985). Other authors identified the reduction in the network of diffuse relationships as the determining factor that eventually leads to a lack of social stimulation (Henderson et al. 1986). One interesting research direction has been the attempt to clarify the interpersonal and intrapersonal mechanisms underlying the influence of social support on the adaptation process. In this regard, Krause (1986c) stressed the necessity of analysing the buffering role of social support on depressive symptomatology specifically in relation to the nature of the stress and the type of support (for example: emotional support, social integration, source of information, practical assistance).

THE INFLUENCE OF RESOURCES. The theoretical framework of the studies mentioned above is that the individual's resources (social support, health, self-esteem, education, income, and so on) have a doubly beneficial role in the face of depressive feelings. On the one hand, these resources reduce the simple risk associated with exposure to stress and promote a sense of self-worth, order, and stability in the individual's personal life. In this sense, these resources have a nonspecific and lasting protective effect against depressive feelings. On the other hand, these resources have more indirect effects, which are most evident in times of crisis. At such times, they promote a sense of self-efficacy (Bandura 1982) and, consequently, increase the probability of a positive adaptation to experienced stress, while decreasing the likelihood of distress and helplessness reactions. These views concerning the role of social support in depression in general have been critically discussed elsewhere (Alloway and Bebbington 1987; Cohen and Wills 1985). Fry, by adopting such a theoretical framework (see chapter 13), further clarifies the influence of social support in mediating depressive reactions in older adults.

These propositions are particularly interesting because they encourage researchers to address the issues of depression and the elderly from the larger context of adaptation to stress. Thus, we propose that resources as a whole play a protective role, not so much against depression *per se*, but rather against undifferentiated stress; that is, they reduce the probability of the individual's experiencing global stress and of stress leading to demoralization and hopelessness. The previously noted emphasis on the etiological contribution of "micro-stressors" becomes particularly meaningful in this context.

The etiological importance of medical and social factors has been discussed *vis-à-vis* its relationship to depressive symptomatology in general, without distinguishing between depressive conditions. However, it remains possible that the etiological importance of the psychosocial factors mentioned here will differ, depending on the nature of the depressive condition. Addressing primarily geriatric major depressions, some authors (Alexopoulos et al. 1988a; Alexopoulos et al. 1988b; Meyers and Alexopoulos 1988b) have underlined the usefulness of distinguishing depressions that occur with a first episode in late adulthood from those recurrent depressions with earlier onset. These authors claim that the etiological contribution of psychosocial factors would be more important in depressions with early onset in young adulthood. In contrast, they propose a biological hypothesis for explaining late-onset geriatric depressions, saying that these result from the acceleration of a deficit, associated with normal aging, in some neurotransmitters, particularly noradrenaline. It should be stressed, however, that firm statements regarding interactions between the neurobiological effects of aging and depression are premature. The effects of normal aging on neurotransmitter systems in the central nervous system, and their potential contribution to the etiology of depression in late adulthood, remain to be determined (for a review, see Veith and Raskind 1988).

Conclusions

The preceding analysis underscores the importance of addressing depressive states of the older adult within the context of the challenges and difficulties specific to that phase of life. In terms of situations triggering depression, the stress of life events related to the requirements of the adult social roles of young and middle years appears to be replaced by a more undifferentiated stress, caused by current life difficulties. As argued by Brink (1979), the most salient psychopathology in late adulthood does not appear to be the existential despair nourished by past failures and regrets, but rather the depressive reactions to experienced events and changes. The nature of the problems that precipitate or increase depressive reactions among older adults suggest some fruitful avenues for research and intervention. As far as research on predictors of depressive conditions is concerned, this perspective encourages the development of multifactorial and prospective studies such as the one presented by Fry in the present volume (chapter 13). At the level of practice, examples of interesting modalities to be pursued in intervention with older adults would include intervention in the social support network, training in behavioural and cognitive skills for managing stress and coping with depression, and psychological interventions for improving health status. Because the role of behaviours as causes of certain disease processes and of hindrances to healing is now largely recognized, an intervention focused on behaviours that promote the maintenance of health and facilitate its return would appear doubly beneficial, for both health and mood. McNeil and Harsany (1989) emphasized the potential benefits of a health-psychology perspective in intervention with depressed elderly. Older depressed adults can benefit from interventions that pay attention to the real problems they experience: worries, anxious ruminations, pessimistic perceptions and expectations (health is a case in point), negative attitudes toward aging and toward other people, and so on. All these targets for intervention can be integrated into the therapeutic modalities now used in the treatment of depression, particularly the cognitive-behavioural approach (Beck et al. 1979).

As far as the issue of prevalence of depressive conditions is concerned, both the relevance of the criteria and assessment instruments and the validity of the classification categories need to be re-evaluated. The tools now in use were largely elaborated and validated on younger adult populations. As mentioned earlier, their use for older adults may minimize the extent of the problems or bias the investigation in an as yet unknown fashion. Some efforts are being made to delineate the relevant components of older adults' depressive syndromes (for example, Gatz and Hurwicz 1990; Good et al. 1987, Newmann et al. 1990). So far, however, the detailed, prospective study of the phenomenology of depressive conditions in the elderly in the context of daily living remains an item for future research.

One rather neglected area is the prevention of depression in advanced adulthood. A better understanding of the coping strategies used by older adults who are depressed and by older adults who live happily would provide valuable data on which to base interventions (Cappeliez and Blanchet 1986; Foster and Gallagher 1986; Gerbaux et al. 1988; Vézina and Bourque 1984, 1985). The studies, taken as a whole, suggest that older adults in general cope with depressive feelings in much the same way as adults of various ages; that is, by taking a more specifically active and concerted problem-solving stance. Findings regarding the distinguishing characteristics of coping strategies of depressed individuals are not as straightforward, however. Vézina and Bourque (1985) reported that depressed and nondepressed subjects differed not so much in terms of the type of strategies used, as by the reduction in the frequency of their use and in their perceived benefit. Cappeliez and Blanchet (1986) suggested that the essential difference is that depressed persons make less use of problem-solving strategies than nondepressed persons. Foster and Gallagher (1986) underlined the higher frequency of emotional discharge, as a coping strategy, among depressed as opposed to nondepressed subjects. Recently, Gerbaux et al. (1988) found that, compared to nondepressed subjects, depressed subjects reported using the strategy of avoidance more often than the strategies of problem-solving, positive reappraisal, distancing, and self-control of emotions. In summary, beyond the divergent viewpoints of these studies, it seems that older adults suffering from depression are less inclined to use active coping strategies, both behavioural (problem-solving) and cognitive (positive reappraisal), than their nondepressed peers. The relevance of this proposition is highlighted by the efficacy of problem-solving as a moderator of the effects of stress (Fry, chapter 13).

Interesting though they may be, these initial studies do not entirely eliminate several problems of interpretation. First, coping mechanisms should be defined and measured so that the process of coping and its actual outcome are not confounded (Moos and Billings 1982). So far, the coping measures typically used in research have not allowed for this distinction. Second, it is often not possible to determine whether subjects are reporting their actual coping efforts or their ideal response in fighting against depressive feelings. Examination of the influence of systematic trends in answering study instruments' questions (for example, the tendency to answer in a socially desirable manner) has only just begun (Cappeliez 1989). In their present format, with the notable exception of the recent study of Gerbaux et al. (1988), these studies can be criticized on the grounds that the subjects report their coping strategies in general and in the long term, rather than specifically and in relation to particular, and actually experienced, depressing situations. Since physical health seems to play such a pivotal role in the etiology of depression in older adults, it is important to assess coping strategies within the specific context of coping with illness and its consequences. Third, the self-reporting inventory method used in these studies to assess coping strategies (subjects are asked to identify the strategies they use) is unduly limiting and static. These instruments are also vulnerable to the biases in responding mentioned above. A better method would entail inviting subjects to describe their adaptation efforts in a free-response format, responses that would later be categorized by independent raters. In addition, these studies do not necessarily take into account the variable of health. Thus, the differences noted earlier could well be attributable to reactions to a debilitated state of health rather than to depression as such.

Clearly, these methodological problems should be rectified in the future. Particular attention should be paid to the specific nature of the stressors facing the elderly in their attempts to maintain a positive mood. A dynamic analysis of these adaptation efforts is needed.

PSYCHOTHERAPEUTIC INTERVENTIONS

Except for some slight modifications, the interventions proposed for the treatment of depression in older adults do not differ from those adopted when treating younger depressed adults. The rate of success of somatic interventions such as antidepressant pharmacotherapy and electroconvulsive therapy, and psychotherapeutic interventions of varying types, in the treatment of geriatric depressions generally corresponds to that obtained when treating younger adults. It is not within the scope of the present chapter to review in detail the applications and efficacy of somatic treatments. This has been done elsewhere (Gaylord and Zung 1987; Gerner 1985; Martin 1987; Meyers and Alexopoulos 1988a, 1988b; Rockwell et al. 1988; Ruegg et al. 1988; Stoudemire and Blazer 1985). Typically, in controlled trials involving patients with various forms of depression, rates of improvement with antidepressant drugs have averaged about 60 to 80 per cent, with placebo responses in the range of 20 to 45 per cent. This next section will focus on the nature and efficacy of psychotherapies.

Whether combined with pharmacotherapy or used alone, psychotherapy is a useful modality for intervention with depressed individuals. In the case of older people, whose use of antidepressant medications is limited by a series of contraindications (cardiotoxicity, anticholinergic effects, adverse interactions with other medications), psychotherapy is a particularly relevant alternative. Moreover, some forms of psychotherapy such as the behavioural and cognitive approaches are especially well equipped to address the depressive problems of older individuals (Cappeliez 1986). Several factors related to aging may contribute to reduced involvement in reinforcing and pleasant activities; for example, decreased income, loss of spouse and friends, health problems, and so on. The behavioural approach, geared as it is to re-establishing better levels of reinforcement and social interaction by fostering an active problem-solving attitude, thus constitutes a useful intervention. At another level, the negative attitudes, beliefs, and thoughts that some older adults entertain towards themselves, their future, and the world may represent targets for cognitively based interventions.

Efficacy of Psychotherapies: Controlled Studies

Because research in this area of psychotherapy is very recent, the scientific literature is limited to a handful of studies. This review will address only those studies that used a control condition and samples of depressed elderly persons meeting the diagnostic criteria of major depression.

Thompson and Gallagher (1984) examined the efficacy of three treatment modalities – cognitive therapy, behavioural therapy, and psychodynamic therapy – with a total sample of sixty-one depressed older adults. The control condition was a five-week, delayed-treatment period. Interventions lasted three to four months, for a total of sixteen to twenty sessions of individual therapy. After six weeks, subjects in all three therapeutic groups showed an improvement in depression, in contrast to those in the wait-list condition. Globally, by the end of the interventions, 75 per cent of the subjects in the experimental groups were either in remission or had significantly improved, clinically, without any form of treatment performing better than another. At one-year follow-up, the positive results were maintained: only 9 per cent of the treated subjects had experienced a full relapse, while 15 per cent had had a partial relapse.

Steuer et al. (1984) evaluated the efficacy of cognitive-behavioural therapy and psychodynamic therapy with a sample of twenty-six and twenty-seven subjects. The therapies were administered in a group format for forty-six sessions spread over a period of nine months. By the end of treatment, the two interventions had engendered similar decreases in depression levels on all measures.

Thompson et al. (1987) reported the findings pertaining to ninety-one depressed older adults, who received sixteen to twenty individual sessions of behavioural, cognitive, or brief psychodynamic therapy. The control condition was a six-week, delayed-treatment period. By termination of treatment, 52 per cent of the subjects were no longer clinically depressed and 18 per cent were manifesting a significant improvement in depression. These positive results were obtained across all three modalities of intervention and on all measures. The dependent measures included a diagnostic assessment according to specific criteria (SADS-Change: Spitzer and Endicott 1977) and several evaluations, mainly through self-report of levels of depression, general symptomatology, global adjustment, and thought contents. It should be noted that this lack of difference between treatment modalities had previously been reported in a smaller study by the same group of researchers (Gallagher and Thompson 1982). Recently, Gallagher-Thompson et al. (1990) presented follow-up data from this outcome study: at one-year and two-year follow-ups, 58 and 70 per cent of the sample, respectively, were not depressed, and there was no difference among therapy modalities. This study extends prior research by showing that older adults are able to maintain therapeutic gains as well as younger patients.

With a total sample of fifty-six subjects suffering from major depression, Beutler et al. (1987) attempted to study the efficacy of group cognitive therapy and a medication, Alprazolam, administered separately and in combination for a period of twenty weeks. Assessments were performed at various points in the intervention (at 4 to 6, 9 to 12 and 17 to 19 weeks) and at a three-month follow-up. The authors concluded that the cognitive approach was useful when treating geriatric depressions. This study deserves a closer examination, however, because results were heterogeneous and generally less positive than those reported by Thompson et al. (1987). First, according to an external evaluation of depressive symptomatology by independent psychiatrists, all groups (including the support-only control group) showed a reduction in depressive symptomatology between weeks four and six; this improvement was maintained without change until the follow-up, three months after termination of the active-treatment phase. However, except for two subjects, all subjects still met the diagnostic criteria of major depression at the three-month follow-up. Self-report of depressive symptomatology and objective laboratory evaluation of sleep quality presented a more optimistic picture, and supported the cognitive intervention. Analysis of these results suggested that only the subjects receiving cognitive therapy experienced a continuing reduction of their depressive symptoms throughout the treatment phase, including the follow-up assessment. The quality of their sleep also improved throughout the intervention, whereas the sleep of other subjects deteriorated during the same period. The clinical significance of these results is limited, however, given that only 29 per cent of the subjects treated with cognitive therapy were free of depressive symptoms on the follow-up self-report. Another distinctive characteristic of this study was its high level of attrition. As many as 67 per cent of the subjects in the drug-only group, and 31 per cent of the subjects in the cognitive therapy groups (with or without medication), dropped out of treatment between weeks four and twenty. The authors attributed this attrition to the negative consequences of pharmacotherapy, either a lack of response to the drug treatment or the occurrence of undesirable side-effects, or both. Most cases of drop-out from cognitive therapy were in the combined (drug-cognitive) therapy condition, apparently motivated by the side-effects of the drug. This level of attrition contrasts sharply with the 17 per cent reported by Thompson et al. (1987) for their entire initial sample of 109 subjects. These authors did not report any difference in attrition between the three modalities studied. In this last study, psychotherapies were offered in an individual format, in contrast to the group format of Beutler et al. (1987). The possibility offered by tailoring the intervention to the particular needs of the patient might partially explain the differences between the two studies, including the variation in attrition rates.

Scogin et al. (1989) have documented the usefulness of self-paced bib-liotherapy – the use of literary work for treating emotional and physical problems – for the treatment of mildly and moderately depressed older adults. In their study, depressed older adults recruited from the community were told to read a self-help presentation dealing with either cognitive or behaviour therapy for depression (Burns 1980; Lewinsohn et al. 1986) to be completed in a period of four weeks; weekly phone calls checked compliance levels. The two experimental treatments were found to be superior to a delayed-treatment control condition. The outcome measures used in this study were the Hamilton Depression Rating Scale (HDRS) (Hamilton 1960) and the Geriatric Depression Scale (GDS) (Yesavage et al. 1983). The treatment gains, similar for the two bibliotherapies, were maintained at a six-month follow-up. At follow-up two years after intervention, Scogin et al. (1990) found that improvements were maintained, according to both clinician- and self-rated measures of depression. These studies demonstrate the potential of cognitive and behavioural bibliotherapy programs as alternatives or adjuncts to other interventions with mildly and moderately depressed older adults, provided the subjects are motivated to engage in, and comply with, a self-help program. Bibliotherapy programs of this sort may also constitute a cost-effective "booster" treatment.

Conclusions

In summary, the few available controlled studies suggest that psychological interventions are useful treatment modalities for geriatric major depression. Reported improvement rates, as well as the magnitude of improvement, compare favourably with those reported for younger adults treated with similar psychotherapeutic interventions (for reviews, see McLean and Carr 1989; Nietzel et al. 1987; Robinson et al. 1990). According to these studies, between 60 and 80 per cent of depressed subjects respond positively to psychotherapies, either in the form of complete remission, or as a statistically and clinically significant improvement in symptomatology.

So far three interventions have been studied systematically: behaviour therapy, modelled after the approach of Lewinsohn (Gallagher and Thompson 1981; Lewinsohn 1974); cognitive therapy, derived from Beck's theory (Beck et al. 1979; Yost et al. 1986); and psychodynamically oriented therapy (Horowitz and Kaltreider 1979). Up to now, these studies have agreed not only that these various modalities bring about similar positive results by the end of the active treatment phase, but that the changes typically exceed those obtained with minimal-treatment control conditions. One controlled study that compared the efficacy of psychotherapy and pharmacotherapy in the treatment of depression with older adults (Beutler et al. 1987) also supported the usefulness of psychotherapy.

Several basic questions, however, remain. So far, the efficacy of the interventions tested has not been proved to be truly superior to either the social support provided by contacts with clinicians and researchers, or the supportive relationships subjects develop with each other in group interventions (Krames et al. 1989). Also, the specific utility of the interventions has yet to be settled, given that the most consistent finding of existing research has been the absence of difference in efficacy among the various modalities tested. Furthermore, when positive changes do occur, they appear early in the treatment and globally on most measures, without any specific link between the type of intervention and the therapeutic process. Additionally, no study has yet been conducted comparing psychotherapy versus tricyclic pharmacotherapy in the treatment of depression with older patients. The study by Beutler et al. (1987) involved the use of a benzodiazepine, which is not a standard medication for depression.

These issues are not unique to interventions with older adults. They are the subject of much discussion in the research on the efficacy of psychological treatment of unipolar depression (McLean and Carr 1989). Several hypotheses can be presented to account for these results. One parsimonious explanation for the undifferentiated outcomes among the various approaches is that, despite the care taken in controlling the application of interventions and in preserving the integrity of the distinct modalities, the differences between the psychotherapies vanish in actual practice. It is certainly possible to identify several communalities in the practice of cognitive and behavioural interventions. Several areas of overlap between these two approaches and the practice of brief psychodynamic psychotherapy are also evident. These findings suggest that certain actions of psychotherapeutic processes may be common to the various interventions. The nature of these key processes in the context of psychotherapeutic interventions with older adults, however, is still unknown. Among the hypotheses being considered are the provision of social support and social reintegration, the development of a sense of control, the reduction of negative expectations and comparisons, the renewal of hope, and the development of active problem-solving strategies. It appears to be useful to maintain a distinction between the mechanisms responsible for the progress during the active phase of treatment and those involved in the maintenance of improvement and reduction of depressive relapses in the long term. Indeed, certain approaches may prove to be better than others – not for producing positive results initially, but rather for facilitating the maintenance of therapeutic gains over time.

Despite the contemporary emphasis on common active components within the various psychotherapeutic approaches, it is entirely possible that some older depressed adults, on the basis of as yet unknown characteristics, might benefit more from one form of therapy than another. So far, however, the choice of modality and its mode of application for a given client remain practical questions without answers. To date, only a few studies have systematically addressed the relationship between patient characteristics and psychotherapy outcomes. For instance, Gallagher and Thompson (1983) suggested that subjects presenting with endogenous symptoms (following the criteria of clinical manifestations of the DSM-III) showed worse outcomes in psychotherapy. More recently, however, Thompson et al. (1987) did not find that endogeneity signalled a differential response to psychotherapeutic intervention. In a subsequent study, Thompson et al. (1988) noted the poor results obtained with older depressed patients who also manifested personality disorders. Another influential variable may be the cooperation of the client. After a re-analysis of the data presented by Thompson et al. (1987), Zeiss et al. (in press) underlined that the cooperation of clients was a factor regularly associated with positive results of the intervention, irrespective of the particular psychotherapeutic modality offered.

The agenda of future research has two main items: the identification of subjects most likely to benefit from a given approach; and the development of interventions for the refractory cases (still between 20 to 40 per cent of the individuals who start therapy). It is rather unfortunate to note that, as yet, controlled research on the design and implementation of intervention strategies for depressed older adults has made little use of the growing research literature on factors contributing to the emergence, persistence, and recurrence of depressive symptoms. For example, the documented association between health problems and depression, reviewed in the first part of this chapter, suggests the usefulness of adding a health-psychology perspective to standard psychotherapies for depression (McNeil and Harsany 1989).

Efforts should also be directed at making psychotherapy services more available to elderly depressed outpatients. Many depressed older adults do not readily seek these services; being poorly informed about the nature and objective of psychotherapies, they entertain negative ideas about the nature of depression. It would therefore be useful to develop strategies that inform participants about the various interventions and constructively modify their expectations regarding both the intervention and their own participation (Cappeliez 1990; Cappeliez and Latour 1992).

CONCLUSIONS

Implications for Practice

Depression represents a major public health problem by virtue of the toll it extracts in personal suffering, incapacitation, and risk of suicide. Even if conservative estimates of prevalence for future cohorts of seniors are adopted, the simple arithmetic of population aging indicates an increase in the absolute number of older adults afflicted by depression in the coming decades.

It is at least reassuring to learn that depression is a condition with a reasonably good prognosis and that age, in and of itself, does not predict a poor outcome. But too few depressed older adults actually benefit from help. The National Advisory Council on Aging, an agency of the federal government of Canada, recently released the findings of a national consultation on the main barriers to seniors' autonomy and on the strategies used by seniors to cope with these barriers (National Advisory Council on Aging 1989, 1990). Mental and emotional well-being constituted the second most significant domain of problems (after physical health) reported by both seniors and service-providers. In this category, depression was identified as one of four specific difficulties impeding independent living, together with loneliness, anxiety, fear, and dementia. Many seniors, however, reported that they attempt to cope with these difficulties largely on their own, without the help of informal or professional resources.

Clearly, much more should be done to provide depressed older adults with appropriate help. First, mental health professionals should take a leadership role in informing older adults that depression can be successfully treated. As argued above in this chapter, there is no sure link between chronological age and depression. Second, when depression does occur, clients need to know that age *per se* is not a barrier to successful intervention.

Recent evidence indicates a very high level of use of primary-care facilities (that is, the family physician) by older adults suffering from mental and emotional difficulties (Kessler et al. 1987). Yet those older adults who do seek help for depression are often treated exclusively with drugs prescribed by physicians who have little or no specialty training in psychogeriatrics. Of course, medication is not the sole avenue of treatment for depression. Depressed clients treated exclusively with drugs do not have the opportunity to learn about better coping skills, those that could help in the longer term. As documented in the previous section of this chapter, the last decade has witnessed major developments in the field of psychotherapy for depression. A number of efficient psychotherapeutic alternatives, or adjuncts to antidepressant drug treatment, are available. Several of these interventions (for example, behavioural and cognitive therapies), with their time-limited and structured emphasis on gradual improvement in coping and personal control, offer much promise for the work with older adults.

The treatment of depression in an older adult is better addressed from a multidisciplinary perspective, with professionals providing collaborative expertise at the somatic, psychological, and social levels. The co-occurrence of health problems, the recognized contribution of psychological and social factors in the etiology of depression, and the adverse consequences of depression on health and on cognitive functioning make such an approach mandatory.

Implications for the Training of Professionals

The vast majority of the mental health practitioners now working with emotionally disturbed older adults have obtained their training on the job. As a case in point, many clinical psychologists working with this population received their training in either general-adult clinical psychology or neuropsychology, and learned on their own how to assess and treat elderly clients. There is an urgent need for concerted efforts directed toward the development of graduate training (courses and internships) in clinical gerontology in psychology. This applies equally to the other mental health disciplines. In addition, government bodies, universities, and health-service professional organizations should be called upon to provide impetus and financial support for the structured development of gerontological training of mental health professionals.

Implications for Research

The study of depression in the elderly – as is the case in the entire field of clinical geropsychology for that matter – is in its inception. This chapter reviewed a portion of the first generation of research regarding the prevalence and predictors of depression among older adults, and the promise of psychotherapeutic interventions. Discussions of a number of important research issues ended each chapter section. The priority now is to further clarify the construct of depression in older adulthood. Studies monitoring the development of depressive symptoms over time in a longitudinal design may help to identify the influence of the variables that trigger or aggravate depression, as well as of those that prevent or limit depression. This knowledge will help us devise more effective interventions. Now that a number of traditional psychotherapeutic interventions have shown their potential for helping depressed older adults, it is necessary to improve these modalities. Work could usefully be directed at developing and evaluating cost-efficient and accessible interventions that take into account the assets and vulnerabilities specific to the older adult population.

BIBLIOGRAPHY

Akiskal, H.H. 1985. Interaction of biologic and psychologic factors in the origin of depressive disorders. *Acta Psychiatrica Scandinavica* 71 (suppl. 319): 131–39.

Akiskal, H.S., and McKinney, W.T. 1975. Overview of recent research in depression: Integration of ten conceptual models into a comprehensive clinical frame. *Archives of General Psychiatry* 32: 285–305.

Alexopoulos, G.S., Meyers, B.S., Young, R.C., Abrams, R.C., and Shamoian, C.A. 1988a. Brain changes in geriatric depression. *International Journal of Geriatric Psychiatry* 3: 157–61.

Alexopoulos, G.S., Young, R.C., Meyers, B.S., Abrams, R.C., and Shamoian, C.A. 1988b. Late-onset depression. *Psychiatric Clinics of North America* 11: 101–15.

Alloway, R., and Bebbington, P. 1987. The buffer theory of social support. A review of the literature. *Psychological Medicine* 17: 91–108.

Amenson, C.S., and Lewinsohn, P.M. 1981. An investigation into the observed sex difference in prevalence of unipolar depression. *Journal of Abnormal Psychology* 90: 1–13.

American Psychiatric Association. 1980. *Diagnostic and statistical manual of mental disorders*, 3d ed. Washington, D.C.: American Psychiatric Association.

– 1987. *Diagnostic and statistical manual of mental disorders* 3d ed., rev. Washington, D.C.: American Psychiatric Association.

Aneshensel, C.S., Estrada, A.L., Hansell, M.J., and Clark, V.A. 1987. Social psychological aspects of reporting behavior: Lifetime depressive episode reports.

Journal of Health and Social Behavior 28: 232–46.

Arling, G. 1987. Strain, social support, and distress in old age. *Journal of Gerontology* 42: 107–13.

Bandura, A. 1982. Self-efficacy mechanisms in human agency. *American Psychologist* 37: 122–47.

Beck, A.T., Rush, J., Shaw, B., and Emery, G. 1979. *Cognitive therapy of depression.* New York: Guilford Press.

Beck, A.T., Ward, C.H., Mendelson, M., Mock, J.E., and Erbaugh, J. 1961. An inventory for measuring depression. *Archives of General Psychiatry* 4: 561–71.

Beutler, L.E., Scogin, F., Kirkish, P., Schretlen, D., Corbishley, A., Hamblin, D., Meredith, K., Potter, R., Bamford, C.R., and Levenson, A.I. 1987. Group cognitive therapy and Alprazolam in the treatment of depression in older adults. *Journal of Consulting and Clinical Psychology* 55: 550–56.

Billings, A.G., and Moos, R.H. 1982. Psychosocial theory and research on depression: An integrative framework and review. *Clinical Psychology Review* 2: 213–37.

– 1985. Psychosocial stressors, coping, and depression. In *Handbook of depression: Treatment, assessment, and research,* edited by E.E. Beckham and W.R. Leber, 940–74. Homewood, Ill.: Dorsey Press.

Bland, R.C., Newman, S.C., and Orn, H. 1988. Prevalence of psychiatric disorders in the elderly in Edmonton. *Acta Psychiatrica Scandinavica* 77 (suppl. 338): 57–63.

Blazer, D., Hughes, D.C., and George, L.K. 1987. The epidemiology of depression in an elderly community population. *The Gerontologist* 27: 281–87.

Blazer, D., and Williams, C.D. 1980. Epidemiology of dysphoria and depression in an elderly population. *American Journal of Psychiatry* 137: 439–44.

Borson, S., Barnes, R.A., Kukull, W.A., Okimoto, J.T., Veith, R.C., Inui, T.S., Carter, W., and Raskind, M.A. 1986. Symptomatic depression in elderly medical out-patients. I. Prevalence, demography, and health service utilization. *Journal of the American Geriatrics Society* 34: 341–47.

Bourque, P., Blanchard, L., and Vézina, J. 1990. Étude psychométrique de l'Échelle de dépression gériatrique. *Revue Canadienne du Vieillissement* 9: 348–55.

Brink, T.L. 1979. *Geriatric Psychotherapy.* New York: Human Sciences Press.

Brown, G.S., and Harris, T. 1978. *Social origins of depression.* London: Tavistock Publications.

Burke, K.C., Burke, J.D., Regier, D.A., Rae, D.S., Boyd, J.H., and Locke, B.Z. 1988. Epidemiologic evidence for early onset of mental disorders and higher risk of drug abuse in young adults. *American Journal of Psychiatry* 145: 971–75.

Burns, D. 1980. *Feeling good.* New York: Guilford Press.

Burvill, P.W., Stampfler, H., and Hall, W. 1986. Does depressive illness in the elderly have a poor prognosis? *Australian and New Zealand Journal of Psychiatry* 20: 422–27.

Cappeliez, P. 1986. Thérapies cognitives: Interventions auprès des personnes âgées déprimées. *Le Gérontophile* 8: 12–15.

– 1989. Social desirability response set and self-report depression inventories in the elderly. *Clinical Gerontologist* 9: 45-52.

– 1990. *Thérapie cognitive-comportementale en groupe pour personnes âgées souffrant de dépression*. Paper presented at the "4ᵉ congrès international francophone de gérontologie," Montreal, Quebec.

Cappeliez, P., and Blanchet, D. 1986. Les stratégies d'adaptation des personnes âgées aux prises avec des sentiments dépressifs. *Revue Canadienne du Vieillissement* 5: 125-34.

Cappeliez, P., and Latour, D. 1992. La préparation des participants dépressifs âgés à la thérapie cognitive en groupe. In *Psychologie de la personne âgée : Aspects neuropsychologiques, cognitifs et cliniques du vieillissement*. Paris: Presses Universitaires de France. In press.

Carpiniello, B., Carta, M.G., and Rudas, N. 1989. Depression in elderly people: A psychosocial study of urban and rural populations. *Acta Psychiatrica Scandinavica* 80: 445-50.

Christie, K.A., Burke, J.D., Regier, D.A., Rae, D.S., Boyd, J.H., and Locke, B.Z. 1988. Epidemiologic evidence for early onset of mental health disorders and higher risk of drug abuse in young adults. *American Journal of Psychiatry* 145: 971-75.

Cohen, D., and Eisdorfer, C. 1988. Depression in family members caring for a relative with Alzheimer's Disease. *Journal of the American Geriatrics Society* 36: 885-89.

Cohen, S., and Wills, T.A. 1985. Stress, social support, and the buffering hypothesis. *Psychological Bulletin* 98: 310-57.

Comstock, G.W., and Helsing, K.S. 1976. Symptoms of depression in two communities. *Psychological Medicine* 6: 551-63.

Copeland, J.R.M., Dewey, M.E., Wood, N., Searle, R., Davidson, I.A., and McWilliam, C. 1987a. Range of mental illness among the elderly in the community. Prevalence in Liverpool using the GMS-AGECAT package. *British Journal of Psychiatry* 150: 815-23.

Copeland, J.R.M., Gurland, B.J., Dewey, M.E., Kelleher, M.J., Smith, A.M.R., and Davidson, I.A. 1987b. Is there more dementia, depression and neurosis in New York? A comparative study of the elderly in New York and London using the computer diagnosis AGECAT. *British Journal of Psychiatry* 151: 466-73.

Copeland, J.R.M., Kelleher, M.J., Kellett, J.M., Gourlay, A.J., Gurland, B.J., Fleiss, J.L., and Sharpe, L. 1976. A semi-structured clinical interview for the assessment of diagnosis and mental state in the elderly. The Geriatric Mental State Schedule. 1. Development and Reliability. *Psychological Medicine* 6: 439-49.

Cutrona, C., Russell, D., and Rose, J. 1986. Social support and adaptation to stress by the elderly. *Psychology and Aging* 1: 47-54.

D'Arcy, C. 1987. Aging and mental health. In *Aging in Canada: Social perspectives*, edited by V.W. Marshall, 424-50. Markham, Ontario: Fitzhenry & Whiteside.

Derogatis, L.R., Lipman, R.S., Rickels, K., Uhlenhuth, E.H., and Covi, L. 1973. The Hopkins Symptom Checklist (HSCL): A self-report symptom inventory. *Behavioral Science* 19: 1-15.

Dohrenwend, B. 1978. Social stress and community psychology. *American Journal of Community Psychology* 6: 1–14.

Feinson, M.C. 1985. Aging and mental helath: Distinguishing myth from reality. *Research on Aging* 7: 155–74.

– 1989. Are psychological disorders most prevalent among older adults? Examining the evidence. *Social Science and Medicine* 29: 1175–81.

Feinson, M.C., and Thoits, P.A. 1986. The distribution of distress among elders. *Journal of Gerontology* 41: 225–33.

Folkman, S., Lazarus, R.S., Pimley, S., and Novacek, J. 1987. Age differences in stress and coping processes. *Psychology and Aging* 2: 171–84.

Foster, J.M., and Gallagher, D. 1986. An exploratory study comparing depressed and non-depressed elders coping strategies. *Journal of Gerontology* 41: 91–93.

Freedman, N., Bucci, W., and Elkowitz, E. 1982. Depression in a family practice elderly population. *Journal of the American Geriatrics Society* 3: 372–77.

Frerichs, R.R., Aneshensel, C.S., and Clark, V.A. 1981. Prevalence of depression in Los Angeles County. *American Journal of Epidemiology* 113: 691–99.

Gallagher, D.E., and Thompson, L.W. 1981. *Depression in the elderly: A behavioral treatment manual.* Los Angeles: University of Southern California Press.

– 1982. Treatment of major depressive disorder in older adults with brief psychotherapies. *Psychotherapy: Theory, Research, and Practice* 19: 482–90.

– 1983. Effectiveness of psychotherapy for both endogenous and nonendogenous depression in older adult outpatients. *Journal of Gerontology* 38: 707–12.

Gallagher-Thompson, D.E., Hanley-Peterson, P., and Thompson, L.W. 1990. Maintenance of gains versus relapse following brief psychotherapy for depression. *Journal of Consulting and Clinical Psychology* 58: 371–74.

Gatz, M., and Hurwicz, M.-L. 1990. Are old people more depressed? Cross-sectional data on Center for Epidemiological Studies Depression Scale Factors. *Psychology and Aging* 5: 284–90.

Gatz, M., Hurwicz, M.-L., and Weicker, W. 1986. Are old people more depressed. Cross-sectional data on CES-D factors. Paper presented at the meeting of the American Psychological Association, Washington, D.C.

Gaylord, S.A., and Zung, W.W.K. 1987. Affective disorders among the aging. In *Handbook of clinical gerontology*, edited by L.L. Carstensen and B.A. Edelstein, 76–95. New York: Pergamon Press.

George, L.K., Landerman, R., and Blazer, D.G. 1987. Age differences in the antecedents of depression and anxiety: Evidence from the Duke Epidemiologic Catchment Area Program. Paper presented at the annual meetings of the American Association for the Advancement of Science, Chicago, Ill.

Gerbaux, S., Vézina, J., Hardy, J., and Gendron, C. 1988. Appraisal, hassles, coping responses and depression: A model. Paper presented at the annual meeting of the Canadian Association on Gerontology, Halifax, Nova Scotia.

Gerner, R.H. 1985. Present status of drug therapy of depression in late life. *Journal of Affective Disorders* (suppl. 1): S23–31.

Goldberg, E.G., and Comstock, G.W. 1980. Epidemiology of life events: Frequency in general populations. *American Journal of Epidemiology* 111: 736–52.

Goldberg, E.G., Van Natta, P., and Comstock, G.W. 1985. Depressive symptoms, social networks and social support of elderly women. *American Journal of Epidemiology* 121: 448–56.

Good, W.R., Vlachonikolis, I., Griffiths, P., and Griffiths, R.A. 1987. The structure of depressive symptoms in the elderly. *British Journal of Psychiatry* 150: 463–70.

Griffiths, R.A., Good, W.R., Watson, N.P., O'Donnell, H.F., Fell, P.J., and Shakespeare, J.M. 1987. Depression, dementia and disability in the elderly. *British Journal of Psychiatry* 150: 482–93.

Gurland, B.J. 1976. The comparative frequency of depression in various adult age groups. *Journal of Gerontology* 31: 283–92.

Gurland, B.J., Copeland, J., Kuriansky, J., Kelleher, M., Sharpe, L., and Dean, L.L. 1983. *The mind and mood of aging: Mental health problems of the community elderly in New York and London.* New York: Haworth Press.

Gurland, B.J., Dean, L., Cross, P., and Golden, R. 1980. The epidemiology of depression and dementia in the elderly: The use of multiple indicators of these conditions. In *Psychopathology in the aged*, edited by J.O. Cole and J.E. Barrett, 37–62. New York: Raven Press.

Gurland, B.J., Wilder, D.E., Golden, R., Teresi, J.A., Gurland, R., and Copeland, J. 1988. The relationship between depression and disability in the elderly: Data from the Comprehensive Assessment and Referral Evaluation (CARE). In *Psychological assessment of the elderly*, edited by J.P. Wattis and I. Hindmarch, (114–37). Edinburgh: Churchill Livingstone.

Hamilton, M. 1960. A rating scale for depression. *Journal of Neurology, Neurosurgery and Psychiatry* 23: 56–62.

Hasin, D., and Link, B. 1988. Age and recognition of depression: Implications for a cohort effect in major depression. *Psychological Medicine* 18: 683–88.

Henderson, A.S., Grayson, D.A., Scott, R., Wilson, J., Rickwood, D., and Kay, D.W.K. 1986. Social support, dementia and depression among the elderly living in the Hobart community. *Psychological Medicine* 16: 379–90.

Hertzog, C., Van Alstine, J., Usala, P.D., Hultsch, D.F., and Dixon, R. 1990. Measurement properties of the Center for Epidemiological Studies Depression Scale (CES-D) in older populations. *Psychological Assessment* 2: 64–72.

Hirschfeld, R.M.A., and Cross, C.K. 1982. Epidemiology of affective disorders - Psychosocial risk factors. *Archives of General Psychiatry* 39: 35–46.

Holahan, C.K., Holahan, C.J. 1987. Self-efficacy, social support, and depression in aging: a longitudinal analysis. *Journal of Gerontology* 42: 65–68.

Horowitz, M., and Kaltreider, N. 1979. Brief therapy of the stress response syndrome. *Psychiatric Clinics of North America* 2: 365–77.

Hughes, D.C., Blazer, D.G., and George, L.K. 1988. Age differences in life events: A multivariate controlled analysis. *International Journal of Aging and Human Development* 27: 207–20.

Jorm, A.F. 1987. Sex and age differences in depression: A quantitative synthesis of published research. *Australian and New Zealand Journal of Psychiatry* 21: 46–53.

Kanner, A.D., Coyne, J.C., Schaefer, C., and Lazarus, R.S. 1981. Comparisons of two modes of stress measurement: Daily hassles and uplifts versus major life events. *Journal of Behavioral Medicine* 4: 1–39.

Kay, D.W.K., Henderson, A.S., Scott, R., Wilson, J., Rickwood, D., and Grayson, D.A. 1985. Dementia and depression among elderly living in the Hobart community: The effect of diagnostic criteria on the prevalence rates. *Psychological Medicine* 15: 777–88.

Kemp, B.J., Staples, F., and Lopez-Aqueres, W. 1987. Epidemiology of depression and dysphoria in an elderly hispanic population. Prevalence correlates. *Journal of the American Geriatrics Society*, 35: 920–26.

Kennedy, G.J., Kelman, H.R., and Thomas, C. 1990. The emergence of depressive symptoms in late life: The importance of declining health and increasing disability. *Journal of Community Health* 15: 93–104.

– 1991. Persistence and remission of depressive symptoms in late life. *American Journal of Psychiatry* 148: 174–78.

Kennedy, G.J., Kelman, H.R., Thomas, C., Wisniewski, W., Metz, H., and Bijur, P.E. 1989. Hierarchy of characteristics associated with depressive symptoms in an urban elderly sample. *American Journal of Psychiatry* 146: 220–25.

Kermis, M.D. 1986. The epidemiology of mental disorders in the elderly: A response to the Senate/AARP Report. *The Gerontologist* 26: 482–87.

Kessler, L.G., Burns, B.J., Shapiro, S., Tischler, G.L., George, L.K., Hough, R.L., Bodison, D., and Miller, T.H. 1987. Psychiatric diagnoses of medical service users: Evidence from the epidemiologic catchment area program. *American Journal of Public Health* 77:18–24.

Kitchell, M.A., Barnes, R.F., Veitch, R.C., Okimoto, J.T., and Raskind, M.A. 1982. Screening for depression in hospitalized geriatric medical patients. *Journal of American Geriatrics Society* 30: 174–77.

Kivelä, S.L., and Pahkala, K. 1989. Dysthymic disorder in the aged in the community. *Social Psychiatry and Psychiatric Epidemiology* 24: 77–83.

Kivelä, S.L., Pahkala, K., and Laippala, P. 1988. Prevalence of depression in an elderly population in Finland. *Acta Psychiatrica Scandinavica* 78: 401–13.

Klerman, G.L. 1988. The current age of youthful melancholia: Evidence for increase in depression among adolescents and young adults. *British Journal of Psychiatry* 152: 4–14.

Klerman, G.L., Lavori, P.W., Rice, J., Reich, T., Endicott, J., Andreasen, N.C., Keller, M.B., and Hirschfeld, R.M.A. 1985. Birth-cohort trends in rates of major depressive disorder among relatives of patients with affective disorder. *Archives of General Psychiatry* 42: 689–93.

Klerman, G.L., and Weissman, M.M. 1989. Increasing rates of depression. *Journal of the American Medical Association* 261: 2229–35.

Koenig, H.G., Meador, K.G., Cohen, H.J., and Blazer, D.G. 1988a. Self-rated depression scales and screening for major depression in the older hospitalized patient with medical illness. *Journal of the American Geriatrics Society* 36: 699–706.

- 1988b. Depression in elderly hospitalized patients with medical illness. *Archives of Internal Medicine* 148: 1929–36.

Kovess, V., Murphy, H.B.M., and Tousignant, M. 1987. Urban-rural comparisons of depressive disorders in French Canada. *Journal of Nervous and Mental Disease* 175: 457–66.

Krames, L., Cino, P., Huxley, G., Ryan, E.B., and Steiner, M. 1989. Group treatment benefits for depressed seniors. Paper presented at the annual meeting of the Canadian Association on Gerontology, Ottawa, Ontario.

Krause, N. 1986a. Life stress as a correlate of depression among older adults. *Psychiatry Research* 18: 227–37.

- 1986b. Stress and sex differences in depressive symptoms among older adults. *Journal of Gerontology* 41: 727–31.

- 1986c. Social support, stress, and well-being among older adults. *Journal of Gerontology* 41: 512–19.

- 1987. Chronic financial strain, social support, and depressive symptoms among older adults. *Psychology and Aging* 2: 185–92.

Kua, E.H. 1990. Depressive disorder in elderly Chinese people. *Acta Psychiatrica Scandinavica* 81: 386–88.

Kukull, W.A., Koepsell, T.D., Inui, T.S., Borson, S., Okimoto, J., Raskind, M.A., and Gale, J.L. 1986. Depression and physical illness among elderly general medical patients. *Journal of Affective Disorders* 10: 153–62.

Landreville, P., and Cappeliez, P. 1992. Soutien social et symptômes dépressifs au sein des personnes âgées. *Canadian Journal on Aging*. In press.

Landreville, P., and Vézina, J. 1992. A comparison between daily hassles and major life events as correlates of well-being in older adults. *Canadian Journal on Aging* 11: 137–49.

Lewinsohn, P.M. 1974. A behavioral approach to depression. In *The psychology of depression: Contemporary theory and research*, edited by R. Friedman and M. Katz, 157–76. New York: Wiley.

Lewinsohn, P.M., Antonuccio, D.O., Steinmetz, J.L., and Teri, L. 1984. *The coping with depression course*. Eugene, Oreg.: Castalia Publishing Company.

Lewinsohn, P.M., Hoberman, H.M., Teri, L., and Hautzinger, M. 1985. An integrative theory of depression. In *Theoretical issues in behavior therapy*, edited by S. Reiss and R.R. Bootzin. Orlando, Fla.: Academic Press.

Lewinsohn, P.M., Munoz, R., Youngren, M.A., and Zeiss, A. 1986. *Control your depression*. Englewood Cliffs, N.J.: Prentice-Hall.

Lieberman, M.A. 1983. Social contexts of depression. In *Depression and aging: Causes, care, and consequences*, edited by D. Breslau and M.R. Haug, 121–33. New York: Springer.

Linn, M.W., Hunter, K., and Harris, R. 1980. Symptoms of depression and recent life events in the community elderly. *Journal of Clinical Psychology* 36: 675–82.

Livingston, G., Hawkins, A., Graham, N., Blizard, B., and Mann, A. 1990. The Gospel Oak Study: Prevalence rates of dementia, depression and activity limitation among elderly residents in Inner London. *Psychological Medicine* 20: 137–46.

McCrae, R.R. 1984. Situational determinants of coping responses: Loss, threat, and challenge. *Journal of Personality and Social Psychology* 46: 919–28.

McLean, P.D., and Carr, S. 1989. The psychological treatment of unipolar depression: Progress and limitations. *Canadian Journal of Behavioural Science* 21: 452–69.

McNeil, J.K., and Harsany, M. 1989. An age difference view of depression. *Canadian Psychology* 30: 608–15.

Martin, B.A. 1987. Medication. In *Psychogeriatrics: A practical handbook*, edited by D.A. Wasylenki, B.A. Martin, D.M. Clark, E.A. Lennox, L.A. Perry, and M.K. Harrison, 149–72. Toronto: Gage Educational Publishing Company.

Meyers, B.S., and Alexopoulos, G.S. 1988a. Geriatric depression. *Medical Clinics of North America* 72: 847–65.

– 1988b. Age of onset and studies of late-life depression. *International Journal of Geriatric Psychiatry* 3: 219–28.

Monroe, S.M. 1983. Major and minor life events as predictors of psychological distress: Further issues and findings. *Journal of Behavioral Medicine* 6: 189–205.

Moos, R.H., and Billings, A.G. 1982. Conceptualizing and measuring coping resources and processes. In *Handbook of stress*, edited by L. Goldberger and S. Breznitz, 212–30. New York: MacMillan.

Morgan, K., Dallosso, H.M., Arie, T., Byrne, E.J., Jones, R., and Waite, J. 1987. Mental health and psychological well-being among the old and old living at home. *British Journal of Psychiatry* 150: 801–07.

Murphy, E. 1982. Social origins of depression in old age. *British Journal of Psychiatry* 141: 135–42.

Murphy, E. 1985. The impact of depression in old age on close social relationships. *American Journal of Psychiatry* 142: 323–27.

Murrell, S.A., Himmelfarb, S., and Wright, K. 1983. Prevalence of depression and its correlates in older adults. *American Journal of Epidemiology* 117: 173–85.

Murrell, S.A., and Norris, F.H. 1983. Resources, life events, and changes in psychological states: A prospective framework. *American Journal of Community Psychology* 11: 473–91.

Myers, J.K., Weissman, M.M., Tischler, G.L., Holzer, C.E., Leaf, P.J., Orvaschel, H., Anthony, J.C., Boyd, J.H., Burke, J.D., Kramer, M., and Stoltzman, R. 1984. Six-month prevalence of psychiatric disorders in three communities - 1980 to 1982. *Archives of General Psychiatry* 41: 959–67.

National Advisory Council on Aging. 1989. *Understanding seniors' independence. Report no. 1: The barriers and suggestions for action.* Cat. no. H71-3/11-1-1989E. Ottawa, Canada: Minister of Supply and Services.

– (1990). *Understanding seniors' independence. Report no. 2*: Coping strategies. Cat. No. H71-3/13-1990E. Ottawa, Canada: Minister of Supply and Services.

Newmann, J.P. 1989. Aging and depression. *Psychology and Aging* 4: 150–65.

Newmann, J.P., Engel, R.J., and Jensen, J. 1990. Depressive symptom patterns among older women. *Psychology and Aging* 5: 101-18.

- 1991. Changes in depressive-symptom experiences among older women. *Psychology and Aging* 6: 212-22.

Nietzel, M.T., Russell, R.L., Hemmings, K.A., and Gretter, M.L. 1987. Clinical significance of psychotherapy for unipolar depression: A meta-analytic approach to social comparison. *Journal of Consulting and Clinical Psychology* 55: 156-61.

Norris, F.H., and Murrell, S.A. 1984. Protective function of resources related to life events, global stress, and depression in older adults. *Journal of Health and Social Behavior* 25: 424-37.

O'Hara, M.W., Kohout, F.J., and Wallace, R.B. 1985. Depression among the rural elderly. A study of prevalence and correlates. *Journal of Nervous and Mental Diseases* 173: 582-89.

Parmelee, P.A., Katz, I.R., and Lawton, M.P. 1989. Depression among institutionalized aged: Assessment and prevalence estimation. *Journal of Gerontology* 44: 22-29.

Pearlin, L.I., Menaghan, E.G., Lieberman, M.A., and Mullins, J.T. 1981. The stress process. *Journal of Health and Social Behavior* 22: 337-56.

Phifer, J.F., and Murrell, S.A. 1986. Etiologic factors in the onset of depressive symptoms in older adults. *Journal of Abnormal Psychology* 95: 282-91.

Prusoff, B., Merikangas, K., and Weissman, M.M. 1988. Life-time prevalence and age of onset of psychiatric disorders: Recall four years later. *Journal of Psychiatric Research* 22: 107-17.

Radloff, L. 1977. The CES-D scale: A self-report depression scale for research in the general population. *Applied Psychological Measurement* 1: 385-406.

Rapp, S.R., Parisi, S.A., Walsh, D.A., and Wallace, C.E. 1988. Detecting depression in elderly medical inpatients. *Journal of Consulting and Clinical Psychology* 56: 509-13.

Regier, D.A., Boyd, J.H., Burke, J.D., Rae, D.S., Myers, J.K., Kramer, M., Robins, L.N., George, L.K., Karno, M., and Locke, B.Z. 1988. One-month prevalence of mental disorders in the U.S., based on five Epidemiological Catchment Area sites. *Archives of General Psychiatry* 45: 977-86.

Regier, D.A., Myers, J.K., Kramer, M., Robins, L.N., Blazer, D.G., Hough, R.L., Eaton, W.W., and Locke, B.Z. 1984. The NIMH epidemiologic catchment area program: Historical context, major objectives and study population characteristics. *Archives of General Psychiatry* 41: 934-41.

Robins, L.N., Helzer, J.E., Croughan, J., and Ratcliff, K.S. 1981. National Institute of Mental Health Diagnostic Interview Schedule: Its history, characteristics, and validity. *Archives of General Psychiatry* 38: 381-89.

Robins, L.N., Helzer, J.E., Weissman, M.M., Orvaschel, H., Gruenberg, E., Burke, J.D., and Regier, D.A. 1984. Lifetime prevalence of specific psychiatric disorders at three sites. *Archives of General Psychiatry* 41: 949-58.

Robinson, L.A., Berman, J.S., and Neimeyer, R.A. 1990. Psychotherapy for the treatment of depression: A comprehensive review of controlled outcome research. *Psychological Bulletin* 108: 30–49.

Rockwell, E., Lam, R.W., and Zisook, S. 1988. Antidepressant drug studies in the elderly. *Psychiatric Clinics of North America* 11: 215–33.

Ruegg, R.G., Zisook, S., and Swerdlow, N.R. 1988. Depression in the aged: An overview. *Psychiatric Clinics of North America* 11: 83–99.

Sadavoy, J., Smith, I., Conn, D.K., and Richards, B. 1990. Depression in geriatric patients with chronic medical illness. *International Journal of Geriatric Psychiatry* 5: 187–92.

Scogin, F., Jamison, C., and Davis, N. 1990. Two-year follow-up of bibliotherapy for depression in older adults. *Journal of Consulting and Clinical Psychology* 58: 665–67.

Scogin, F., Jamison, C., and Gochneaur, K. 1989. Comparative efficacy of cognitive and behavioral bibliotherapy for mildly and moderately depressed older adults. *Journal of Consulting and Clinical Psychology* 57: 403–7.

Smallegan, M. 1989. Level of depressive symptoms and life stresses for culturally diverse older adults. *The Gerontologist* 29: 45–50.

Spitzer, R., and Endicott, J. 1977. *The SADS-Change Interview*. New York: New York State Psychiatric Institute.

Spitzer, R., Endicott, J., and Robins, E. 1978. *Research diagnostic criteria (RDC)*, 3d ed. New York: New York State Psychiatric Institute.

Statistics Canada 1984. *The Elderly in Canada*. Cat. no. 99–932. Ottawa: Minister of Supply and Services.

Steuer, J.L., Mintz, J., Hamilton, C.L., Hill, M.A., Jarvik, L.F., McCarley, T., Motoike, P., and Rosen, R. 1984. Cognitive-behavioral and psychodynamic group psychotherapy in treatment of geriatric depression. *Journal of Consulting and Clinical Psychology* 52: 180–89.

Stoudemire, A., and Blazer, D.G. 1985. Depression in the elderly. In *Handbook of depression: Treatment, assessment, and research*, edited by E.E. Beckham and W.R. Leber, 556–86. Homewood, Ill.: Dorsey Press.

Thompson, L.W., and Gallagher, D.E. 1984. Efficacy of psychotherapy in treatment of later life depression. *Advances in Behaviour Research and Therapy* 6: 127–39.

Thompson, L.W., Gallagher, D., and Breckenridge, J.S. 1987. Comparative effectiveness of psychotherapies for depressed elders. *Journal of Consulting and Clinical Psychology* 55: 385–90.

Thompson, L.W., Gallagher, D., and Czirr, R. 1988. Personality disorder and outcome in the treatment of later-life depression. *Journal of Geriatric Psychiatry* 21: 133–46.

Turner, R.J., and Noh, S. 1988. Physical disability and depression: A longitudinal analysis. *Journal of Health and Social Behavior* 29: 23–37.

Veith, R.C., and Raskind, M.A. 1988. The neurobiology of aging: Does it predispose to depression? *Neurobiology of Aging* 9: 101–17.

Vézina, J., and Bourque, P. 1984. The relationship between cognitive structure and symptoms of depression in the elderly. *Cognitive Therapy and Research* 8: 29–36.

- 1985. Les stratégies comportementales adoptées par les personnes âgées devant les sentiments dépressifs. *Revue Canadienne du Vieillissement* 4: 161-69.

Vézina, J., Landreville, P., Bourque, P., and Blanchard, L. 1991. Questionnaire de Dépression de Beck: Étude psychométrique d'une population francophone. *Revue Canadienne du Vieillissement* 10: 29-39.

Waxman, H.M., and Carner, E.A. 1984. Physician's recognition, diagnosis and treatment of mental disorders in elderly medical patients. *The Gerontologist* 24: 593-97.

Weissman, M.M., Leaf, P.J., Tischler, G.L., Blazer, D.G., Karno, M., Bruce, M.L., and Florio, L.P. 1988. Affective disorders in five United States communities. *Psychological Medicine* 18: 141-53.

Weissman, M.M., and Myers, J.K. 1978. Affective disorders in a U.S. urban community: The use of the Research Diagnostic Criteria in an epidemiological survey. *Archives of General Psychiatry* 35: 1304-11.

Yesavage, J.A., Brink, T.L., Rose, T.L., Lum, O., Huang, V., Adey, M., and Leirer, V.O. 1983. Development and validation of a geriatric depression screening scale: A preliminary report. *Journal of Psychiatric Research* 17: 37-49.

Yost, E.B., Beutler, L.E., Corbishley, M.A., and Allender, J.R. 1986. *Group cognitive therapy: A treatment approach for depressed older adults*. New York: Pergamon Press.

Zeiss, A.M., Breckenridge, J.S., Thompson, L.W., Gallagher, D., Silven, D., and Schmit, T. N.d. Client cooperation and the outcome of psychotherapy for depression in older adults. *Journal of Consulting and Clinical Psychology*. In press.

Zung, W. 1965. A self-rating depression scale. *Archives of General Psychiatry* 12: 63-70.

CHAPTER THIRTEEN

Mediators of Depression in Community-Based Elders*†

PREM S. FRY

Although no age group in North American society is immune to depression, it is the elderly, those sixty-five years of age and over, who are more likely than some younger cohorts to experience this condition. The concern is that as numbers of elderly persons increase, the incidence and prevalence of depression could reach epidemic proportions. This concern mirrors recent confirmation that depressive disorders constitute a major health problem in older adults (Blazer 1982; Lin and Dean 1984; Fry 1986, 1989a, 1989b; Zarit 1980).

Present estimates place the point prevalence of clinically significant depression at approximately 10 to 15 per cent, with as much as 25 to 30 per cent of the community-based population of older persons reporting significant depressive symptomatology. Moreover, field research (for example,

*This research was supported by a grant (File No. 492-83-0020) received from the Social Sciences and Humanities Research Council of Canada. The assistance of Anne Humenuk, Cynthia Cordery, Evelyn Doyle, Diane Hussein, and Mark Kolodziej at various stages of data collection and analysis was invaluable. Guidance in statistical design was obtained from consultants at the Free University of Berlin, where the author was visiting prior to commencement of data analysis. The author would like to express gratitude to the many concerned older persons who voluntarily cooperated and participated in this research. Without their involvement, this study would not have been possible.

†This chapter was first submitted to the editors of this volume in 1988; it has been revised as per their suggestions and now includes references to work published since 1988.

Arling 1987; Feinson and Thoits 1986; Norris and Murrell 1984) indicates that the relationship between older adults' personal functioning and depressive symptomatology is much more complex than was once assumed. For one thing, assuming that depressive reactions are specifically age-related does not always explain the etiology of depression in late life. The feeling is that the complex relationship involving personal functioning and depressive reactions in late life needs to be examined within the context of mediating factors (Costa and McCrae 1982; Lawton 1983). To date, longitudinal research focusing on predictive or mediating factors in depressive symptomatology and distress in late life has been very limited (Arling 1987).

Factors associated with the onset or maintenance of depression in late life are problematic, with differences of opinion in definition and etiology leading to variations in conceptualizing the psychological and social variables directly and indirectly associated with depression. From a clinical perspective, depression in the elderly presents other problems. Owing to specific age-related psychosocial adaptations and biological developments, depression in aged individuals is mediated, exacerbated, or moderated by factors or syndromes that differ greatly from those in other age groups (Salzman and Shader 1978). These highly varied forms of development in depressive disorders in the later years tend to confound the primary antecedent, mediating, or consequent factors associated with depression in other age groups (Lehmann 1981). Furthermore, because of prevailing variations in clinical approaches to the causes of depression in the aged, previous research has provided contradictory data regarding the exacerbating or buffering capacity of a number of environmental and personal factors associated with depressive symptoms among a random community sample of older adults (see Lawton and Nahemow 1973; Snow and Gordon 1980). These inconclusive findings may be traced, in part, to problems in conceptualizing the role of such environmental factors as social support and social integration, and such personal factors as personal problem-solving capacity and personal perceptions of self-efficacy, all of which may be mediating depressive responses in older adults (see Bandura 1982; D'Zurilla and Nezu 1982; Holahan et al. 1984). Gore (1981) emphasized that much of the research in this area has been too narrow. She recommended that studies be more attentive to the buffer effects and processes involved. Collectively, these issues suggest the need to expand on the simple age-related depression paradigm and to develop more conceptually based models that attend to both environmental and personal factors mediating depression in aging (Haug et al. 1984; Luke et al. 1981; Romaniuk et al. 1983), as well as to explore the link between personal and environmental resources of older adults.

The research presented in this chapter addresses some of these issues by attempting to identify the role of certain personal and social factors, either as mediators or moderators, in the depression process. To do this, we examine a model, via path analysis, that incorporates some of the environmental and personal factors related to the observed increase in depressive symptomatology. The overall purpose of this chapter is threefold: (1) to review and integrate the literature on some of the mediating or moderating variables associated with depression in older adults; (2) to formulate and examine, via path analysis, a conceptual model of depression that focuses on certain psychosocial factors related to depression in the later years; and (3) to present preliminary data that tentatively evaluate the proposed conceptual framework, drawing attention to a few of the predictive and mediating factors associated with depressive symptomatology in the later years.

Overall, the goal is to develop a preliminary framework that will help clinical practitioners to understand and clarify the determinants of depressive symptomatology and their implications for intervention and treatment.

THE DEPRESSION MODEL: AN INTEGRATION OF PERSONAL AND ENVIRONMENTAL FACTORS

Diverse conceptual models and empirical methods have been used with younger populations to explore intrapsychic, cognitive-phenomenological, social, and behavioural aspects of depression. Each of these approaches, when used with older populations, has implications for the formulation of clinical interventions. However, no one conceptual approach has attempted to evaluate the links between older people's personal and environmental resources in terms of their contribution to significant depressive symptomatology.

Studies of depression in late life that take into account only the effects of age have yielded mixed results regarding the role of negative life experiences, personality factors, social support and psychological functioning. A conceptual model hypothesizing the interrelationship between these variables is presented in Figure 1. Like emotion, depression is best regarded as a complex rubric, consisting of many interrelated variables that not only mediate the older individuals' perceptions and appraisals of their life circumstances but subsequently contribute to depressive symptomatology. Specifically, the model suggests that negative life events may control depressive symptomatology directly as well as indirectly through their impact on the older adults' perceptions of their self-efficacy, their problem-solving skills, and the social support available to them. For instance, a negative life event associated with normal aging, such as forced retirement and widowhood, may remove specific sources of social support. In addition, loss of familiar roles through negative life events may lead to a reduction in feelings of self-efficacy and self-competency (Kuypers and Bengtson 1973). In this context, the level of perceived self-efficacy, as articulated by Bandura et al. (1977), is an especially relevant personal factor to understanding and pre-

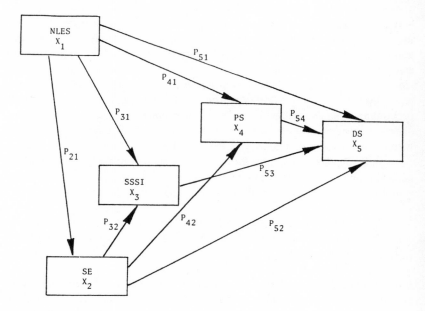

Figure 1
Conceptual model indicating direct and indirect relations between negative life experience
(NLE), self-efficacy (SE), social support and social integration (SSSI), problem solving (PS), and
depressive symptoms (DS) within a path-analytic framework.

dicting elderly persons' depressive states. Bandura (1982) notes that people's
sense of self-efficacy determines whether they will engage in problem-solving
behaviours, initiate new activity, participate in social relationships, and seek
social support networks, in order to overcome some of the deleterious effects
of negative life events assumed to cause depression in old age. Holohan
et al. (1984) note that individuals' feelings of self-efficacy have a spiralling
effect on adaptive functioning – with the rewards of positive functioning
increasing the level of self-efficacy, and the negative life experiences contributing to a decline in self-perceptions of competency. Negative life events
are therefore initially assumed to impact negatively on the self-efficacy perceptions of older individuals. But researchers have also postulated that individuals with initially enhanced perceptions of self-efficacy will feel the impact of negative life events less forcefully than others with lowered perceptions
of self-efficacy. Such individuals will resist depressive symptoms and distress
symptoms by participating in supportive networks and engaging in more
problem-solving activities.

    In our conceptual model, we suggest that experiencing major negative
life events is predictive of depression in late life. However, we postulate an
indirect association between negative life experiences and depression via per-

ceived self-efficacy, problem solving, and social support. With regard to depression, recent research (for example, Arling 1987; Holahan and Holahan 1987) has indicated that depressed elderly individuals show deficits in their ability to resolve problems or to obtain sufficient levels of social support. Other studies have found problem solving and adequate levels of social support and social activity, to be effective strategies for buffering the effects of negative life events from consequent depressive reactions and symptoms (Billings and Moos 1982; Holahan and Holahan 1987; Nezu 1985). Thus, in our model, we also propose a *direct* association between problem solving, social support networks, and depressive symptomatology, as well as an *indirect* association between perceived self-efficacy levels and depression, via these aforementioned mediating factors.

Review of the Related Literature

Before evaluating the conceptual framework proposed in Figure 1, we first review and integrate the existing research findings concerning negative life experiences, self-efficacy, social support, and problem solving. Our goal is to explore the influence of these variables as shown in previous research on depression, and to provide additional theoretical and empirical support for incorporating these factors into a preliminary integrative framework. We also draw a distinction between *depressive symptomatology* and *clinically significant depression.*

MEANING OF DEPRESSION. In our research, we use the terms "depression" and "depressive symptomatology" – denoting dysphoria, negative affectivity, general distress, and demoralization – interchangeably. Although it is assumed that some of these emotional states are accompanied by physiological symptoms such as nervousness and sleep and appetite disturbances, they are not intense and do not necessarily impair the daily functioning of the individual. In this way, we attempt to resolve the methodological problem of identifying clinically depressed individuals, or diagnostic groups as defined in the *Diagnostic and Statistical Manual of Mental Disorders-Third Edition* (DSM-III) (Uhlenhuth et al. 1983, 1168), within the community. Thus, too, we do not address primary dimensions of clinical depression, such as anxiety, somatization, paranoid ideation, and so on (Overall and Zisook 1980). Instead, we are more concerned with assessing overall observable dysphoric symptoms, such as dejected mood, loss of interest, worry, loneliness, impulse to cry, and decreased life satisfaction (Blazer 1982; Fry 1986; Lehmann 1981).

RESEARCH ON NEGATIVE LIFE EXPERIENCES. Much of the literature on stress and depression concerns itself with effects of major life events, such as death of a spouse, employment severance or retirement, and financial loss. But there is some evidence, however limited, which implicates environmental stressors and stressful events in the maintenance of depression (Fry 1989a; Paykel 1979). Previous empirical research examining the relationship between important life experiences and daily functioning has indicated that positive life events are not correlated with distress symptoms (Sarason et al. 1978). However, in the epidemiologic literature, the weight of evidence suggests that recent life changes have a significant, if modest, effect on the occurrence of depression in older adults (Lin and Dean 1984). Eckenrode and Gore (1981), for example, observed that negative life events contribute to depression in various ways by influencing the individual's resistance to stress. Also, much of the research conducted on the causes of depression has identified depression in terms of major negative life events (see Kanner et al. 1981; Nezu 1984; Nezu and Ronan 1985; Sarason et al. 1978). Indeed, most of the studies (for example, Billings and Moos 1981; Coyne et al. 1981) have demonstrated that an important source of depression for many individuals emanates from negative and dramatic life experiences (for example, death of a spouse, role loss, financial setback, serious illness, forced retirement, and so on) which impact, in turn, on psychological health. Surtees and Ingham (1980), referring to the depressive outcome of negative events in their application of a dissipation model to life events, identified certain depressogenic effects of undesirable life changes in the areas of health, finances, and interpersonal relationships, particularly those changes or events representing exits or losses in the social domain of older persons (see Pfeiffer 1980; Romaniuk et al. 1983). These events, which apparently have cumulative effects that may manifest themselves over several months, are three to six times more common among depressed individuals than among general population controls (Brown and Harris 1978). The comparability of findings regarding the effects of negative life events (examined primarily among community samples) and stressful events (typically explored among clinical samples) suggests an underlying commonality for the role of negative life events in both major and minor depressive outcomes (Billings and Moos 1982).

Despite some conceptual advances, negative life events still provide only a partial explanation for the development of serious depressive symptoms and reactions among so-called normal individuals. Among general community samples, typically less than 10 per cent of the variance in depressive symptoms can be accounted for by negative life experiences (Billings and Moos 1981; Warheit 1979). The recent methodological approaches concerning the effects of major negative life experiences must, therefore, be expanded to include the interplay of these experiences and other environmental and personal resources of individuals (Fry 1988, 1989a, 1989c; Norris and Murrell 1984). It is postulated that negative, or stressful, life experiences may either act "directly" on depression or elicit "indirect effects" by reducing social resources and engendering ineffective coping responses. Negative life experiences, defined in our study as "specific undesirable occurrences of changes," include both discrete life experiences and the less dramatic "hassles" and pressures.

SELF-EFFICACY RESEARCH. Self-efficacy may well be a factor that helps explain individual variability in depression in response to negative life events and experiences. With negative life events and daily hassles known to contribute in various ways to depression, it has been suggested that major losses in health, finances, and interpersonal relationships might well lead to feelings of loss in self-competency and self-control (Kuypers and Bengtson 1973). As well, a sense of self-efficacy, which also assumes high self-esteem and a sense of personal and environmental mastery, has been found to attenuate the depressive effects of negative life experiences among members of a community group (Pearlin and Schooler 1978). The development and maintenance of self-efficacy, or a sense of mastery, has been a focus in the work of several important theorists, including Bandura, Beck, and Seligman. Bandura (1977 1982) suggested that self-efficacious persons will typically persist in active efforts to overcome depression, while those who see themselves as less efficacious will use avoidance responses and succumb to depressive symptomatology. For these reasons, perceived self-efficacy, as articulated by Bandura (Bandura 1982; Bandura et al. 1977), is an especially relevant personal factor in understanding elderly persons' responses to some of the negative life experiences invariably associated with aging. In 1984, Holahan et al. found that self-efficacy was inversely associated with distress among elderly persons. More recently, Holahan and Holahan (1987) and Fry (1989a) provided data to show that self-efficacy levels of older persons function directly, as well as indirectly, via other personal and environmental resources in alleviating distress. These authors postulate that self-efficacy can affect depression in related ways. First, they may have "direct" effects on functioning, as supported by the finding that community-based individuals enjoying high self-efficacy and self-esteem are less likely to become depressed (Pearlin and Schooler 1978). In fact, some conceptual overlap will often occur in measures of self-efficacy as a personal resource as well as in measures of depression, since low self-efficacy is considered to be one aspect of a depressive syndrome (Bandura 1977, 1982; Billings and Moos 1982). Second, they claim that self-efficacy may have indirect effects on depression, whether by increasing coping or problem-solving responses or by fostering social support resources that attenuate the effects of stress emanating from negative life events (Ford 1984; Weinberg 1985).

We recognize, then, the importance of evaluating the interplay of initial self-efficacy with other influences in an integrative model of depression (Albee 1985). The concept of self-efficacy assumes that perceived competence in interpersonal skills and communications are important aspects of personal resources (Curran 1985). Depression-prone persons are thought to display low self-efficacy or competence in both communications and verbal activity (McLean 1981). But depression may also result when low self-efficacy individuals experience frequent negative life events. In our present study, we have assumed that high self-efficacy levels prevent depressive symptoms by fostering the use of social and personal resources. However, we also assumed that a sense of personal efficacy had to have developed in the early adulthood period, *prior* to the advent of late-life stresses and the negative life experiences that impact so strongly on the self-appraisals of aging individuals. The qualitative dimension of efficacy, which was achieved in the earlier adult years, is especially important to coping in old age.

SOCIAL SUPPORT AND SOCIAL INTEGRATION RESEARCH. The stress-mediating value of social support has been the most frequently noted of the environmental resources affecting personal resources and mental health functioning (Cassel 1976; Cobb 1976; Dean and Lin 1977). A direct relationship between lack of support and depression has been noted in several surveys of community samples (Andrews et al. 1978; Lin et al. 1979), especially in surveys of older persons (Fienson and Thoits 1986). The substantial contemporary interest in the epidemiologic functions of social support in depression and other disorders is rooted in a number of sources. According to Lin and Dean (1984), there is a growing scientific and clinical conviction that social support may actually reduce the risk of mental illness by buffering the effects of stress. Frerichs et al. (1981) have pointed out that social-network forces vie in importance with biological and psychological forces in maintaining the elderly individual's mental health status. Several earlier studies identified empirical evidence of the effect of social support on mental health (for example, Dean and Lin 1977; Nuckolls et al. 1972; Kaplan et al. 1977). Only recently, however, has the role of social support in the context of aging and depression been studied explicitly.

A number of recent research studies were undertaken (for example, Arling 1987; Norris and Murrell 1984) to model the life events, social support, and mental health of older persons; the goal was to demonstrate the causal sequence of undesirable life events, social support, and depression. Two types of joint effects of life events and social support were identified in the geriatric studies: the first shows that social support *mediates* the effect of life events, reducing the potential effect of negative events; the second shows that social support *counteracts* the effect of life events. In both these models, a significant relationship between undesirable life events and social support occurs. It seems that although there may be many different sources of support, studies of older adults have focused primarily on family, friends, and work settings as the primary sources of social-support resources. Thus, whereas in studies of a general community group, more symptoms of depression have been reported among individuals whose families were not cohesive, expressive, and supportive (Billings and Moos 1983), it is equally conceivable that depressive symptomatology will lead to an erosion of social support (McLean 1981). Still other researchers, however (Gore 1981; Lowenthal and Weiss 1976), have hypothesized that whether or not these resources are actually called on is less important than simply knowing they are available. In other words, when the social-support system is perceived to be strong, the effects of life events can be counteracted and the individual's degree of emotional vulnerability reduced. Conversely, when the social-support system is perceived to be weak or inaccessible, the individual's degree of emotional vulnerability is still not affected (Norris and Murrell 1984). This view holds, further, that the influence of social support on depressive symptoms is so, regardless of the individual's socioeconomic status, marital status, sex, or physical health, and that it accounts for a considerable degree of variance in depression among older individuals (Kahn 1979).

In discussing the protective function of social support resources for older persons, Norris and Murrell (1984) have argued that these resources may initially influence the degree to which older persons are exposed to negative or undesirable events. They go on to say that social-support resources may also influence the extent to which life events contribute to a more global appraisal of stress. Certainly, they reiterate, all older persons, including those with high levels of social resources, will inevitably go through a period of cognitive and behavioural decline and stress. They add, however, that older people's responses to negative life events may take many different forms (Dohrenwend 1978). For some, difficult and undesirable events may lead to more action and additional problem resolution, while others may feel hopelessness, despair, and depression. The hypothesis in most studies examining the relationship between depression and social support in old age is that depressive reactions are most likely for those with low social-support resources.

A number of field studies (for example, Fry 1989a; Holahan et al. 1984; Holahan and Holahan 1987) have examined the role of social-support and social-integration resources in mediating depression in aging. These studies provided partial support for the notion that social support is inversely related to psychological distress in older persons. For example, Arling (1987) confirmed that social support is related to psychological distress and has a moderating influence on the relationship between life stress and psychosomatic symptoms of distress in older persons. Several other studies reported that the absence of social support exacerbates the effect of negative life events, contributing directly to depression and other psychological symptoms (Luke et al. 1981; Pearlin 1980; Pearlin and Schooler 1978). Many of these same studies have suggested that the presence of social support buffers the impact of strain, thereby reducing depression. Billings and Moos (1982) explained that the inability to call upon others for social support heightens distress, leading to greater depression. Some studies (for example, Williams et al. 1981) have, nevertheless, failed to confirm a moderating or interactive effect of social support.

Our purpose in including the social-support factor in our integrative model was not only to demonstrate the direct, indirect, and overall relationships between the availability, or usage, of social resources and depressive symptoms in old age, but also to replicate the findings of earlier studies vis-à-vis social-support factors either as antecedents or moderators in the distress process of older adults. We thought that an examination of the relationships between social support, negative life experiences, and depressive symptoms might have implications for intervention and treatment programs for the distressed elderly (see Ward et al. 1984; Harel and Deimling 1984).

PROBLEM-SOLVING RESEARCH. Problem solving refers to the process by which people discover or identify effective means of coping with problematic situations encountered in daily living (D'Zurilla and Nezu 1982). Specifically with regard to depression, recent research (for example, Gotlib and Asarnow 1979; Nezu 1985, 1986) has indicated that depressed individuals show deficits in their ability to resolve interpersonal and social problems effectively. More importantly, relevant studies (for example, Nezu and Ronan 1985) have found that adequate levels of problem solving mediate the effects of negative life events, thereby moderating depressive outcomes. More specifically, a number of studies (for example, Nezu 1985; Nezu et al. 1984) have argued that depression stemming from negative experiences can often develop into a complex syndrome in individuals lacking problem-solving skills. Conversely, problem solving may be an effective coping strategy in buffering the effects of life stress regarding consequent depressive reactions. These findings are consistent with the idea that individuals with low levels of problem solving find it difficult to make decisions concerning their daily life events or to take action that puts them in control of their emotions (Beck et al. 1979). As with other domains, problem solving may attenuate the depressive effects of negative life experiences, or directly reduce or prevent the depressive symptomatology from emerging (Billings and Moos 1982). These views concerning the direct and indirect effects of problem solving on depressive states are supported in a few experimental studies (for example, Heppner et al. 1982; Gotlib and Asarnow 1979) conducted on younger adults. However, the potential avenue for assessing these hypotheses in older adults has remained relatively unexplored.

THE STUDY

The purpose of the data gathering was to explore in a preliminary manner the tenability of the conceptual framework of direct and indirect factors influencing depressive symptoms of old age (see Figure 1). Data concerning the variables were gathered from a sample of adults between the ages of sixty-five and eighty years. Basic and preliminary path-analytic techniques were used to evaluate the tenability of the model. The path-analysis procedure offers a rudimentary means of decomposing the effects of a given variable into its direct and indirect effects (Alwin and Hauser 1975), thus allowing for an exploratory examination of the proposed model.

Overall, the general purpose of the study was to provide a more general examination of a multidimensional personal and social resource model that has implications for intervention and treatment of depressed elders. More specifically, we postulated the following relationships between the selected variables: (1) experiencing negative life events influences self-efficacy levels of older adults; (2) the degree to which an individual copes with negative life experiences is related to current levels of self-efficacy; (3) initial self-efficacy related to obtaining social support and perceiving oneself as having basic problem-solving skills will be inversely related to depression in older adults.

Furthermore, we sought to explore the interrelationships among negative life experiences, self-efficacy, social support, problem solving, and depressive symptomatology in an integrative model. We hypothesized that, in addition to having mediating effects, the various levels of social support and problem solving function directly to influence the level of depressive symptoms in older adults.

Figure 1 illustrates the hypothesized relationships of these variables to depression in older adults. Negative life experiences are depicted in this model as having direct effects on depression. Although we recognized that specific individual resources may differ in their effects, we depicted negative life experiences as indirectly affecting depression through their effects on such resources as self-efficacy, social support, and problem solving.

STUDY METHOD

Time Frame for the Study

Data were collected over a period of six to eight months to study the factors that predict or mediate the emergence of depressive symptoms in older adults. Participants were followed prospectively over a twenty-four-month period. We assumed that persons with high levels of existing resources (that is, self-efficacy, social support, and problem-solving skills) might be less exposed to negative events than persons without such resources. However, as mentioned previously, our general objective was to study the relationship between negative life experiences and depressive symptomatology. Study data were collected by a variety of means, ranging from brief semi-structured interviews to questionnaires, and from telephone-administered check-lists, to informal reports provided by caregivers of older adults.

Study Group

The sample comprised eighty persons, drawn from a somewhat larger sample of older adults from three senior citizens' associations in three Alberta cities. Budgetary constraints dictated the use of volunteers from these associations for the primary sampling units. It was only after the recruitment of subjects was complete that we realized that at least 35 per cent of the subjects resided in semi-rural areas. Of the 100 persons who initially volunteered participation in the study, the attrition rate between the first and second assessment interviews was 10 per cent, caused mostly by participants' hospitalization or their move to other parts of the country. In another 10 per cent of the sample, the data collected at follow-up were incomplete in several respects and therefore had to be excluded from the analysis. Complete data on the two interviews' study variables were therefore available for eighty participants.

Participants

Eighty older adults (52 women and 28 men) between the ages of sixty-five and eighty years (mean age: 67 years) participated in the study. These were individuals who completed the initial assessment interview and the re-testing twenty-four months later.

The initial requirements for study participants were that they not be ill at the time of the study, nor be contemplating a major move to another part of the city. Subjects were predominantly white individuals who had been married at least once (95%) or were widowed (24%). Although exact income information was not volunteered, several participants estimated an annual income of $25,000 and above. Because precise income data were accessible for only 10 per cent of the sample, this variable was not included in the study design. At the time of the second interview, 60 per cent of the participants were married, 32 per cent were widowed, 5 per cent were single, and 3 per cent were divorced. Ninety-two per cent of the interviewees were not employed.

The testing conducted at time 1 and repeated approximately twenty-four to thirty months later involved a semi-structured interview of approximately one hour, followed by a test-administration session of about one hour and thirty minutes. Approximately 80 per cent of the subjects expressed a desire to complete the assessment in a single meeting. It was therefore agreed that they would be allowed short breaks whenever necessary. A trained interviewer typically conducted the semi-structured interview and testing in the participants' homes. However, there were many exceptions to this general rule of meeting at home. In all cases, the wishes of the participant were respected. The interview included administration of the following inventories.

Measures

Depressive symptomatology (DS). At the time of both the initial and follow-up testing, depressive symptomatology was measured using an index of five symptoms; these symptoms had to have been experienced fairly often during the previous twelve to sixteen weeks. Depression items on the check-list included such statements as "wondered if anything was worthwhile any more"; "felt that one just couldn't get going"; and "felt that nothing turned out right." Additionally, depressive symptoms were measured by means of a modified version of the General Malaise Scale (GMS) developed by Feinson and Thoits (1986) for use with older adults. These authors reported a reliability coefficient of .90 for this scale.

Whereas the five-item check-list examines specific clinical symptoms of depression, such as hopelessness and despair, the GMS taps into more general feeling states (sadness, fatigue, cheerfulness, nervousness, anxiety, "feeling blue"). The items ask respondents about their emotional responses over the past few weeks. For example, respondents are asked whether they feel sad, "blue," cheerful and light-hearted, refreshed, or tired after doing things they normally like to do; whether they feel refreshed after waking; and whether they look forward to things either most of the time or never.

Responses (ranging from 1 to 6) for the fifteen items of the GMS and five items of the check-list were summed. The scoring for the negative items was reversed so that all scale items were in the same direction, with low scores reflecting fewer depressive symptoms.

Negative life experiences (NLES) were measured via the *Negative Life Experiences Survey* (Sarason et al. 1978), which requires subjects to indicate both the incidence and stressful impact of various life-change events. Subjects were asked about events that had occurred during the past four to six months. This procedure was adopted because previous research, especially with elders (Norris and Murrell 1984), has suggested that recall of life events over long periods of time tends to be quite inaccurate (Monroe 1982). The negativity of events was assessed by means of a probe that required the respondent to indicate the incidence and severity of the negative impact on a three-point scale from slightly bad (1) to very bad (3). The total score was obtained by summing the item values across all events. Respondents with no negative impact to report received a score of zero.

Perceived self-efficacy (SE) was measured at the time of initial testing and at the subsequent follow-up testing by obtaining the respondents' judgment as to how competent or confident they felt in handling most of life's concerns. The items included in this measure were adapted from Holahan et al.'s (1984) scale, which assessed self-efficacy perceptions during encounters with a number of daily hassles, as well as life stresses having to do, for example, with family relationships, financial constraints, rejection by former friends and neighbours, fear of loneliness, fear of memory loss, fear of illness, social losses incurred through death, decline in physical energies, and isolation resulting from friends and family being too far away. The choice of items included in the perceived self-efficacy index was guided by previous accounts of concerns and problems encountered by middle-aged and elderly adults (Kanner et al. 1981) and from the personal competence measure adapted from Campbell et al.'s (1976) scale. Respondents' ratings of self-efficacy were obtained on a three-point scale as follows. First, respondents were asked to rate how well they had handled each of these concerns in the recent past and expected to handle them in the near future. Their responses were coded as follows: *very well* (3); *moderately well* (2); and *not too well* (1). The individual respondent's self-efficacy score indicated the average ratings for the fifteen areas of concern presented in the index. Because the mean ratings for handling concerns experienced in the past and similar concerns for the future were almost identical, the two types of ratings were combined in the analyses. Scores on the self-efficacy scale ranged from twelve to forty-five. Cronbach's alpha for the self-efficacy scale was .77.

The *problem-solving inventory* (PS) used in the study was adapted from the thirty-two-item inventory developed by Heppner and Petersen (1982) to assess personal problem-solving behaviours and attitudes; in the PS low scores reflect effective problem resolution. The inventory was *abbreviated considerably* so that elderly respondents' perceptions of their problem-solving behaviours and attitudes could be obtained within the eleven areas of living in which problems occur for the average adult (for example, leisure activities, religious pursuits, relationship with adult children or spouse, living conditions, legal problems, change in employment, competition on the job, financial difficulties, housing problems, and health problems) (Fry 1988). Problems were defined as "situations where no effective solution is immediately available to the individual confronted with the situation." Subjects were requested to indicate the frequency of problem situations recently encountered in each of the eleven areas. Low scores were reflective of effective problem resolution.

Social support and social integration (SSSI). Individuals' perceptions of the adequacy of their social support were measured through a summary index of largely instrumental forms of self-reported assistance (for example, advice about personal problems, shopping, transportation problems, and personal care; help with legal or financial problems; help in finding a new domicile and new employment; arrangements made for services; and checking out the recommendations made by adult children, relatives, friends, neighbours, and clergymen during the six months prior to the survey. Individuals responded to a list of twenty-six items and indicated whether they had received assistance from other individuals, either in person or over the phone, and the frequency of these contacts. The resulting index ranged from zero (no contacts, no persons to call on for help) to fifteen (high frequency of contacts with persons called upon to help). This procedure for measuring social-support contacts and feelings of social integration was adapted from Holahan and Moos (1981) and Liang et al. (1980). Scores for frequency of social-support contacts ranged between eighteen and sixty-seven.

Procedure

After completion of the semi-structured interview and test battery (which frequently took three hours with two or more short breaks), information was obtained about the participants' specific sociodemographic characteristics. In addition, we sought participants' written permission to approach them again some twenty-four months later. At that time, research assistants administered the same tests. A schedule of meeting times was set up in consultation with the elderly participant's primary caregiver. Thus two contacts were made with the participants: (1) at the initial meeting; and (2) approximately twenty-four to thirty months later. Participants were thanked for their cooperation.

STUDY RESULTS

Bearing in mind that the study is basically exploratory in nature, and also given the space constraints, the statistical results are presented here only in summary form. No details of the direction of various path coefficients are presented or discussed in this chapter, which is intended essentially to give the reader a conceptual understanding of various factors contributing directly or indirectly to depressive symptomatology in late life development.

Preliminary Regression Analysis

In order to provide estimates for the model illustrated in Figure 1, an initial series of regression analyses was performed. A single-path analysis was conducted on the combined data obtained at the two stages of assessment. The equations representing each of these analyses are as follows:

$$X_2 = P_{21}X_1 + e_2$$
$$X_3 = P_{31}X_1 + P_{32}X_2 + e_3$$
$$X_4 = P_{42}X_2 + P_{41}X_1 + e_4$$
$$X_5 = P_{51}X_1 + P_{52}X_2 + P_{53}X_3 + P_{54}X_4 + e_5$$

Table 1

Zero-order correlations between variables, means, and standard deviations for all measures

Measure	2 SE	3 SSSI	4 PS	5 DS	M	SD
NLES	.692*	.551*	.452*	.396*	11.20	6.91
SE		.548*	.198	.491*	29.10	8.20
SSSI			.188	.641*	42.80	18.91
PS				.172	12.10	4.81
DS					49.20	12.30

* $p < .05$

NLES = Negative Life Experiences Survey; SE = Self-efficacy scores; SSSI = Social support and social integration scores; PS = Problem-solving scores; DS = Depressive symptoms scores.

Table 2

Direct, indirect, and total effects on depression

Variable	Coefficients
NEGATIVE LIFE EXPERIENCES SURVEY	
Direct effect (P_{51})	.150
Indirect effects via	
Self-efficacy ($P_{52}P_{21}$)	.362*
Social support ($P_{53}P_{31}$)	.020
Problem solving ($P_{54}P_{41}$)	.005
Total effects (q_{51})	.537*
SELF-EFFICACY	
Direct effect (P_{52})	.384*
Indirect effects via	
Social support ($P_{53}P_{32}$)	.184
Problem solving ($P_{54}P_{42}$)	.018
Total effects (q_{52})	.586*
SOCIAL SUPPORT	
Direct effect (P_{53})	.429*
PROBLEM SOLVING	
Direct effect (P_{54})	.139

* $p < .05$

where X_1 = negative life experiences; X_2 = perceived self-efficacy; X_3 = social support and social integration; X_4 = perceived problem-solving capability; X_5 = depressive symptomatology; and e_2, e_3, e_4, and e_5 are random error terms.

The standardized path coefficients indicate the direct effects of that variable (for example, P_{21} in Figure 1 represents the direct effect of negative life experiences on perceived self-efficacy). Indirect effects represent the effect of one variable on a second as moderated by a third variable. For example, the indirect effects of negative life experiences (X_1) on depressive symptomatology (X_5), as mediated by social support, are represented as $P_{53}P_{31}$. Total effects, as represented by q_{ij}, are defined as the sum of the direct effect and any indirect effect via intervening variables (for example, $q_{52} = P_{52} + P_{53}P_{32} + P_{54}P_{42}$).

Table 1 contains the means, standard deviations, and zero order correlations for the various measures. These are self-explanatory to a large extent. Table 2 contains a summary of the direct, indirect, and total effects of negative life experiences, perceptions of self-efficacy, and perceived adequacy of social support and problem solving on depressive symptomatology.

Examination of the direct-effect path coefficients indicates that many of these variables are significantly related to depression. For example, with respect to the direct effects of negative life experiences on depressive symptomatology it was seen that these effects are not significant. However, the effects of negative life experiences are significantly moderated when we consider their indirect effects via self-efficacy levels perceptions. Further examination of Table 2 shows that the direct effects of self-efficacy perception on depression are also significant, suggesting that perceptions of inadequacy in self-efficacy are significantly associated with levels of depressive symptomatology. Similarly, the direct effects of perceived inadequacy of social support on depression are also significant, suggesting that perceptions of inadequacy of social support are closely associated with levels of depressive symptomatology. The total effects of negative life experiences (q_{51}) and perceptions of self-efficacy (q_5) on depression are significant, as are the direct effects of adequacy of social support on depression.

Subsequent examination of the regression analyses showed that the effects due to these three variables (negative life experiences, perceptions of self-efficacy and adequacy of social support) accounted for 51 per cent of the variance in predicting levels of depressive symptomatology over a 24- to 30-month period ($F_{3,76} = 46.51$, $p < .05$).

STUDY DISCUSSION

The study assumed that personal and social resources, such as problem solving and social support, negative life experiences, and existing levels of self-efficacy, all contribute in various ways to depressive symptoms in older adults.

We originally presented a conceptual model that expanded on a simple, negative life experiences–depressive symptoms paradigm and incorporated perceived levels of self-efficacy, problem solving, and social support as mediating factors impacting on the depression level of older adults. Specifically, we postulated the following relationship between these variables: (1) negative life events often impact on the existing self-efficacy levels of older adults; (2) the degree to which these individuals are able to protect themselves from the effects of negative life events is associated with perceived levels of self-efficacy; (3) the degree to which individuals can cope with negative life experiences is associated with perceptions of problem-solving capacities, social support, and social integration; and (4) the degree to which individuals can resolve problems and elicit social support via self-efficacy is associated with the likelihood of their experiencing fewer depressive symptoms. The exploratory results from the path analysis support this model. Indeed, the most general hypothesis of this study – that self-efficacy resources, personal problem-solving capacities, and social-support resources play a mediating and protective function in the relationship between negative life experiences and depressive symptomatology of older adults – has been supported by the results. These resources appear to have a direct and mediating effect, as well as interactive effects, in contributing to depressive symptoms, at least in this sample of older adults. In general, the overall findings of the direct and indirect results of the selected variables are considered to be theoretically sound and have been previously documented in reviews of the developmental and clinical literature on aging (see Feinson and Thoits 1986; Frerichs et al. 1981; Gurland et al. 1983; Norris and Murrell 1984). Although we recognized that the effects of the various resources were not mutually exclusive, we attempted to disaggregate the effects of each variable.

Overall, our findings led us to conclude, tentatively, that negative life experiences are associated with depressive symptoms in a direct and an indirect manner via levels of self-efficacy. Furthermore, we determined that an individual's level of self-efficacy has an impact on depressive symptoms via problem solving and social support. Finally, we decided that individuals' perceptions of adequacy of social support, by themselves, have a direct influence on level of depressive symptoms.

These findings suggest that the degree to which major negative life experiences contribute to depressive symptomatology depends upon a person's self-efficacy perceptions at the time of the negative events. In effect, high levels of perceived self-efficacy at the time of negative experiences are associated with low levels of depressive symptomatology and vice versa. Our findings are consistent with those of Holahan et al. (1984), who examined the role of life stress, hassles, and self-efficacy in the adjustment of older adults. However, self-efficacy levels are related to levels of problem solving and social support, which, in turn, may be related to levels of depressive symptomatology. A tentative conclusion, then, may be that perceptions of self-efficacy lead to greater problem-solving initiatives and integration of social support, thereby moderating the effects of negative experiences. The proposed model is thus able to identify the process by which negative life experiences ultimately influence the psychological health of older individuals. One of the possible interpretations of these findings is that negative life experiences may contribute greatly to depressive symptomatology in the case of older adults who have low self-efficacy perceptions, followed, in turn, by limited social-support contacts and limited problem-solving ability.

This discussion underlines the problem of attributing depression of older persons simply to negative life experiences without considering the mediating effects of personal and social resources. Future studies should recognize the complexity of these moderating factors. At the general level, the findings are consistent with those of previous studies of older people that indicate that depression and distress are associated with (1) the relative absence or presence of negative life events (Fry 1989a; Norris and Murrell 1984), (2) the relative absence or presence of social support (Coulton and Frost 1982; Harel and Deimling 1984; Norris and Murrell 1984; Holahan and Holahan 1987), and (3) the relative absence of problem solving (Fry 1989a). Further studies that examine the influence of older adults' problem solving on depression should be considered.

IMPLICATIONS FOR CLINICAL PRACTICE AND PREVENTION OF DEPRESSIVE SYMPTOMS IN OLD AGE

The results of this exploratory study support the importance of considering both the protective and preventive functions of such factors as self-efficacy, problem solving, and social support in intervention programs for depression. Almost two decades ago, Lowenthal and Haven (1968) suggested that depression during adulthood is significantly less frequent among people adequately supported within social networks. More recently, clinical practitioners (for example, Strain and Chappell 1982; Ward et al. 1984) provided further evidence that social support is protective with respect to depression in many ways. The present discussion emphasizes, initially, the growing importance of clinicians' work in strengthening older citizens' identity through ameliorating the social-support networks, both qualitatively and quantitatively (Fry 1992). Second, it is argued that social-support networks may provide a protective function in the face of negative events – including serious illnesses, economic losses, and role deprivations (Gore 1981) – by possibly reducing actual exposure to the stressful consequences. Third, it is suggested that strong social-support resources may reduce the level of global distress experienced by older adults, thereby reducing the level of depressive symptomatology associated with distress. With respect to prevention, therefore, the clinical practitioner must bear in mind that helping older people to consolidate the available social support has twofold implications: not only does it moderate the potentially negative effects of life events on the self-efficacy of older adults; it also provides assurance that troublesome situations can be handled via problem solving. Both these functions, in turn, may help to ease the actual depression process. But to maximize positive treatment outcome, therapists must also consider the depressed persons' social and personal resources and their coping responses. Direct intervention programs aimed at improving older adults' personal skills, competencies, and problem solving may contribute, simultaneously, to the enhancement of personal resources and the subsequent alleviation of depressive symptoms (Fry 1992).

Further implications for clinical practice with older adults derive from the fact that feelings of self-efficacy are often inversely related to feelings of old-age depression. Educational programs aimed at improving and enhancing self-esteem and positive self-appraisal can therefore play an important part in avoiding depression and in maintaining healthy functioning during the aging years. Maluccio (1981) proposes that the emphasis of intervention should be on the development of (1) competence through facilitating the natural adaptive capacities of persons; and (2) patterns for seeking and using social support. Teaching older adults how to take full advantage of whatever the community and environmental resources have to offer is no simple matter, inasmuch as resources for older adults are usually scarce and poorly coordinated. Indeed, incredible amounts of persistence and savvy are needed to wind one's way through the maze of unidentified social-support networks (Hatfield 1985). It is the clinical practitioner's obligation not only to inform the depressed client about what is available in terms of problem solving and social-support resources, and how to consolidate these in order to maximize their effectiveness for the person, but also to actively promote these programs. The initial feelings of self-efficacy are thought to be central to initiating and maintaining social integration and social networks. Thus, although negative life experiences cannot be eliminated or easily avoided, it is hoped that geriatric practitioners will emphasize anew the value of problem solving and encourage adults approaching old age to rediscover areas of competent functioning. Maluccio (1981) prefers the term "efficacy" or "competence" for that repertoire of skills, knowledge, and qualities that enable people to interact favourably with their environment. Fleming (1981) and Maluccio (1981), who both favour an ecological approach to efficacy development, suggest that clinical practitioners use an educational model to provide information and problem-solving skills and to avoid a fragmentation of self-identity (Hirschowitz 1976).

Although all age groups resist terms such as "depression" and "stress" because of the associated stigma, plans are afoot for the development of an educational and ecological model of self-efficacy that would meet with greater public acceptance. Indeed, interventions designed within an ecological, as opposed to a clinical, framework may prove fruitful in reducing the vulnerability to depression that negative life events can create for older adults.

SUMMARY

Today, theoretical and empirical concerns about the etiology and treatment of depression in older adults have increasingly come to the fore. We have presented an integrative conceptual framework in which negative life experiences, and other personal and social factors that may mediate depressive outcomes, are considered as contributors to depression. This framework suggests that there are a number of pathways to depression in old age. Just as negative life experiences may indeed predispose to depression, the presence of self-efficacy, social-support resources, and problem-solving ability may mediate the adverse effects of negative life experiences and indirectly influence depressive outcomes. Although negative life experiences cannot be eliminated, the presence of social resources and problem-solving coping may be pivotal factors in any treatment and prevention programs for older adults.

BIBLIOGRAPHY

Albee, G. 1985. Competency models. In *Competence development: Theory and practice in special populations*, edited by H.A. Marlowe, and R.B. Weinberg, 101–17. Springfield, Ill.: Charles C. Thomas Publisher.

Alwin, D.F., and Hauser, R.M. 1975. The decomposition of effects in path analysis. *American Sociological Review* 40: 37–47.

Andrews, G., Tennant, D., Hewson, D., and Vaillant, G. 1978. Life event stress, social support, coping style, and risk of psychological impairment. *Journal of Nervous and Mental Disease* 166: 307–16.

Arling, G. 1987. Strain, social support, and distress in old age. *Journal of Gerontology* 42: 107–13.

Bandura, A. 1977. Self-efficacy: Toward a unifying theory of behavioral change. *Psychological Review* 84: 191–215.

– 1982. Self-efficacy mechanism in human agency. *American Psychologist* 37: 122–47.

Bandura, A., Adams, N.E., and Beyer, J. 1977. Cognitive processes mediating behavioral change. *Journal of Personality and Social Psychology* 35: 125–47.

Beck, A.T., Rush, A.J., Shaw, B.F., and Emery, G. 1979. *Cognitive therapy of depression*. New York, N.Y.: Guilford.

Billings, A.G., and Moos, R.H. 1981. The role of coping responses and social resources in attenuating the impact of stressful life events. *Journal of Behavioral Medicine* 4: 139–57.

– 1982. Psychosocial theory and research on depression: An integrative framework and review. *Clinical Psychology Review* 2: 213–37.

– 1983. Social support and functioning among community and clinical groups: A panel model. *Journal of Behavioral Medicine* 6: 161–74.

Blazer, D.G. 1982. *Depression in late life*. St. Louis, Mo.: C.B. Mosby Co.

Brown, G.W., and Harris, T.O. 1978. *Social origins of depression: A study of psychiatric disorder in women.* New York, N.Y.: Free Press.

Campbell, A., Converse, P.E., and Rodgers, W. 1976. *The quality of American life: Perceptions, evaluations, and satisfactions.* New York, N.Y.: Sage.

Cassel, J. 1976. The contribution of the social environment to host resistance. *American Journal of Epidemiology* 104: 107-23.

Cobb, S. 1976. Social support as a moderator of life stress. *Psychosomatic Medicine* 38: 300-14.

Costa, P.T., Jr., and McCrae, R.R. 1982. An approach to the attribution of age, period, and cohort effects. *Psychological Bulletin* 92: 238-50.

Coulton, C., and Frost, A.K. 1982. Use of social and health services by the elderly. *Journal of Health and Social Behavior* 23: 330-39.

Coyne, J.C., Aldwin, C., and Lazarus, R.S. 1981. Depression and coping in stressful episodes. *Journal of Abnormal Psychology* 90: 439-47.

Curran, J.P. 1985. Social competency training. In *Competence development: Theory and practice in special populations,* edited by H.A. Marlow, and R.B. Weinberg, 146-76. Springfield, Ill.: Charles C. Thomas Publisher.

Dean, A., and Lin, N. 1977. The stress-buffering role of social support. *Journal of Nervous and Mental Disease* 165: 403-13.

Dohrenwend, B.S. 1978. Social stress and community psychology. *American Journal of Community Psychology* 6: 1-14.

D'Zurilla, T.J., and Nezu, A. 1982. Social problem solving in adults. In *Advances in cognitive behavioral research and therapy,* Vol. 1, edited by P.C. Kendall, 201-74. New York, N.Y.: Academic Press.

Eckenrode, J., and Gore, S. 1981. Stressful events and social supports: The significance of context. In *Social networks and social support,* edited by Benjamin H. Gottlieb, 43-68. Beverly Hills, Calif.: Sage.

Feinson, and Thoits, P.A. 1986. The distribution of distress among elders. *Journal of Gerontology* 42(2): 225-33.

Fleming, R.C. 1981. Cognition and social work practice: Some implications of attribution and concept attainment theories. In *Promoting competence in clients,* edited by A.N. Maluccio, 55-73. New York, N.Y.: Free Press.

Ford, M.E. 1984. The concept of competence: Themes and variations. In *Competence development: Theory and practice in special populations,* edited by H.A. Marlowe, and R.B. Weinberg, 3-49. Springfield, Ill.: Charles C. Thomas Publisher.

Frerichs, R.R., Aneshensel, C.S., and Clark, V.A. 1981. Prevalence of depression in Los Angeles County. *American Journal of Epidemiology* 113: 691-99.

Fry, P.S. 1986. *Depression, stress and adaptations in the elderly: Psychological assessment and intervention.* Rockville, Md.: Aspen Publishers.

– 1988. Mediators of stress in community-based elders. Paper presented at the XXIV International Congress of Psychology, Sydney, Australia, Aug. 28 - Sept. 2, 1988.

– 1989a. Mediators of perceptions of stress among community based elders. *Psychological Reports* 65: 307-14.

- 1989b. Mediators of stress in older adults: Conceptual and integrative frameworks. *Canadian Psychology* 30: 636–49.
- 1989c. Main gaps in knowledge in the area of preventing mental ill-health among elderly persons: Key priority areas. In *Knowledge development for health promotion: A call for action*, edited by Health Services and Promotion Branch, Health and Welfare Canada, 67–76. Ottawa: Health and Welfare Canada.
- 1992. Major social theories of aging and their implications for counseling concepts and practice: A critical review. *The Counseling Psychologist* (monograph). 20(2): 246–329.

Gore, S. 1981. Stress-buffering functions of social supports: An appraisal and clarification of research models. In *Stressful life events and their contexts* edited by B. S. Dohrenwend, and B.P. Dohrenwend, 202–22. New York, N.Y.: Prodist.

Gotlib, I.H., and Asarnow, R.F. 1979. Interpersonal and impersonal problem solving skills in mildly and clinically depressed university students. *Journal of Consulting and Clinical Psychology* 47: 86–95.

Gurland, B.J., Copeland, J., Kuriansky, J., Kellerher, M., Sharpe, L., and Dean, L.L. 1983. *The mind and mood of aging*. New York, N.Y.: Haworth Press.

Harel, Z., and Deimling, G. 1984. Social resources and mental health: An empirical refinement. *Journal of Gerontology* 39: 747–52.

Hatfield, A. 1985. Family education: A competence model. In *Competence development: Theory and practice in special populations*, edited by H.A. Marlow, and R.B. Weinberg 177–202). Springfield, Ill.: Charles C. Thomas Publisher.

Haug, M., Belgrave, L.L., and Gratton, B. 1984. Mental health and the elderly: Factors in stability and change over time. *Journal of Health and Social Behavior* 25: 100–15.

Heppner, P.P., Hibel, J., Neal, G.W., Weinstein, C.L., and Rabinowitz, F.E. 1982. Personal problem solving: A descriptive study of individual differences. *Journal of Counseling Psychology* 29: 580–90.

Heppner, P.P., and Petersen, C.H. 1982. The development and implications of a personal problem solving inventory. *Journal of Counseling Psychology* 29: 66–75.

Hirschowitz, R.G. 1976. Groups to help people cope with the tasks of transition. In *The changing mental health scene*, edited by R.G. Hirschowitz 171–88). New York, N.Y.: Spectrum.

Holahan, C.J., and Moos, R.H. 1981. Social support and psychological distress: A longitudinal analysis. *Journal of Abnormal Psychology* 90: 365–70.

Holahan, C.K., and Holahan, C.J. 1987. Self-efficacy, social support, and depression in aging: A longitudinal analysis. *Journal of Gerontology* 42: 65–68.

Holahan, C.K., Holahan, C.J., and Belk, S.S. 1984. Adjustment in aging: The roles of life stress, hassles, and self-efficacy. *Health Psychology* 3: 5–328.

Kahn, R.L. 1979. Aging and social support. *Med Care* 15: 47–58.

Kanner, A.D., Coyne, J.C., Schaefer, C., and Lazarus, R.S. 1981. Comparison of two modes of stress measurement: Daily hassles and uplift versus major life events. *Journal of Behavioral Medicine* 4: 1–39.

Kaplan, B.H., Cassel, J.C., Gore, S. 1977. Social support and health. *Med Care* 15: 47–58.

Kuypers, J.A., and Bengtson, V.L. 1973. Social breakdown and competence: A model of normal aging. *Human Development* 16: 181–201.

Lawton, M.P. 1983. The varieties of well-being. *Experimental Aging Research* 9: 65–72.

Lawton, M.P., and Nahemow, L. 1973. Ecology and the aging process. In *The psychology of adult development and aging*, edited by C. Eisdorfer and M.P. Lawton. Washington, D.C.: American Psychological Association.

Lehmann, H.E. 1981. Classification of depressive disorders, In *Prevention and treatment of depression*, edited by T.A. Ban, R. Gonzalez, A.S. Jablensky, N.A. Artorius, and F.E. Vartanian 3–17. Baltimore, Md.: University Park Press.

Lewinsohn, P.M., Mischel, W., Chaplin, W., and Barton, R. 1980. Social competence and depression: The role of illusory self-perceptions. *Journal of Abnormal Psychology* 89: 203–12.

Liang, J., Dvorkin, L., Kahana, E., and Mazian, F. 1980. Social integration and morale: A reexamination. *Journal of Gerontology* 35: 746–57.

Lin, N., and Dean, A. 1984. Social support and depression. *Social Psychiatry* 19: 83–91.

Lin, N. Simeone, R., Ensel, W., and Kuo, W. 1979. Social support, stressful life events, and illness: A model and an empirical test. *Journal of Health and Social Behavior* 20: 108–19.

Lowenthal, M.F., and Haven, C. 1968. Interaction and adaptation: Intimacy as a critical variable. *American Sociological Review* 33: 10–30.

Lowenthal, M.F., and Weiss, L. 1976. Intimacy and crisis in adulthood. *The Counseling Psychologist* 6: 10–15.

Luke, E., Norton, W., and Denbigh, K. 1981. Medical and social factors associated with psychological distress in a sample of community aged. *Canadian Journal of Psychiatry* 26: 244–50.

McLean, P.D. 1981. Behavioral treatment of depression. In *Behavior modification: Principles, issues, and applications*, edited by W.E. Craighead, A.E. Kazdin, and M.J. Mahoney, 223–42. Boston, Mass.: Houghton Mifflin.

Maluccio, A.N. 1981. Competence-oriented social work practice: An ecological approach. In *Promoting competence in clients*, edited by A.N. Maluccio, 1–24. New York, N.Y.: Free Press.

Monroe, S.M. 1982. Life events assessment: Current practices, emerging trends. *Clinical Psychology Review* 2: 435–54.

Murrell, S., Norris, F., and Hutchins, G. 1985. Distribution and desirability of life events in older adults: Population and policy implications. *American Journal of Community Psychology* 14: 523–72.

Nezu, A.M. 1984. Stress and depression: Assessment of major life events or current problems? Paper presented at the annual convention of the Association for the Advancement of Behavior Therapy, Philadelphia.

– 1985. Differences in psychological distress between effective and ineffective problem solvers. *Journal of Counseling Psychology* 32: 135–38.

– 1986. *Effects of stress from current problems: Comparison to major life events.* New York, N.Y.: Montrose.

Nezu, A.M., Nezu, C.M., Saraydarian, L., and Kalmar, K. 1984. Negative live stress and depression: The role of social problem solving. Paper presented at the meeting of the Eastern Psychological Association, Baltimore, Md.

Nezu, A.M., and Ronan, G.F. 1985. Life stress, current problems, problem solving, and depressive symptoms: An integrative model. *Journal of Consulting and Clinical Psychology* 53(5): 693–97.

Norris, F.H., and Murrell, S.A. 1984. Protective function of resources related to life events, global stress, and depression in older adults. *Journal of Health and Social Behavior* 25: 424–37.

Nuckolls, K., Cassel, J., and Kaplan, B. 1972. Psycho-social assets, life crisis and the prognosis of pregnancy. *American Journal of Epidemiology* 95: 431–41.

Overall, J.E., and Zisook, S. 1980. Diagnosis and the phenomenology of depressive disorders. *Journal of Consulting and Clinical Psychology* 48: 626–34.

Paykel, E.S. 1979. Recent life events in the development of the depressive disorders. In *The psychobiology of the depressive disorders: Implications for the effects of stress*, edited by R.A. Depue, 245–62. New York, N.Y.: Academic Press.

Pearlin, L.I. 1980. *The life cycle and llife strains. Sociological theory and research: A critical approach*, edited by H.M. Blalock, 349–60. New York, N.Y.: Free Press.

Pearlin, L.I., and Schooler, C. 1978. The structure of coping. *Journal of Health and Social Behavior* 19: 2–21.

Pfeiffer, E. 1980. The psychosocial evaluation of the elderly patient. In *Handbook of geriatric psychiatry*, edited by E. Busse, and D. Blazer, 107–44. New York, N.Y.: Van Nostrand Reinhold.

Romaniuk, M., McAuley, W.J., and Arling, G. 1983. An examination of the prevalence of mental disorders among the elderly in the community. *Journal of Abnormal Psychology* 92: 458–67.

Salzman, C. and Shader, R.I. 1978. Clinical evaluation of depression in the elderly. In *Psychiatric symptoms and cognitive loss in the elderly*, edited by A. Raskin, and L.F. Jarvik, 39–72. Washington, D.C.: Hemisphere.

Sarason, I.G., Johnson, J.H., and Siegel, J.M. 1978. Assessing the impact of life changes: Development of the Life Experiences Survey. *Journal of Consulting and Clinical Psychology* 46: 932–46.

Snow, D.L., and Gordon, J.B. 1980. Social network analysis and intervention with the elderly. *The Gerontologist* 20: 463–67.

Strain, L.A., and Chappell, N.L. 1982. Confidants – Do they make a difference in the quality of life? *Research on Aging* 4: 479–502.

Surtees, P. and Ingham, J. 1980. Life stress and depressive outcome: Application of a dissipation model to life events. *Social Psychiatry* 15: 21–31.

Uhlenhuth, E.H., Balter, M.B., Mellinger, G.D., Cisin, I.H., and Clinthorne, J. 1983.

Symptom checklist syndromes in the general population. *Archives of General Psychiatry* 40: 1167–73.

Ward, R.A., Sherman, S.R., and LaGory, M. 1984. Subjective network assessments and subjective well-being. *Journal of Gerontology* 39: 93–101.

Warheit, G. 1979. Life events, coping, stress and depressive symptomatology. *American Journal of Psychiatry* 136: 502–7.

Weinberg, R.B. 1985. A coping model of competence. In *Competence development: Theory and practice in special populations*, edited by H.A. Marlowe, and R.B. Weinberg, 83–100. Springfield, Ill.: Charles C. Thomas Publisher.

Williams, A.W., Ware, J.E., and Donald, C.A. 1981. A model of mental health, life events, and social supports applicable to general populations. *Journal of Health and Social Behavior* 22: 324–36.

Zarit, S.H. 1980. *Aging and mental disorders: Psychological approaches to assessment and treatment*. New York, N.Y.: Free Press.

CHAPTER FOURTEEN

Implications for Assessment, the Understanding of Social Etiology, and Intervention

PHILIPPE CAPPELIEZ AND
ROBERT J. FLYNN

In the opening chapter, we challenged the tendency of depression researchers to focus on currently stressful situations, as well as intraindividual factors, in their attempts both to understand the etiology of depression and to devise interventions. Our objective in this book has been to emphasize the larger social context of depression, by addressing its occurrence in selected groups generally overlooked in research and treatment studies. In this final chapter, we discuss a number of central issues in the areas of assessment, social etiology, and treatment. We make a number of links among the various contributing authors' statements, as well as suggestions for the future development of research on depression.

ASSESSMENT

Depression is a phenomenon of considerable range and complexity. Often associated with life experiences involving a personally relevant loss, it can range in duration from temporary coping difficulties to a chronic negative orientation toward life. Depression manifests itself in different domains, whether somatic, cognitive, behavioural, or emotional, and can range in severity from mild adjustment problems to psychotic symptoms. It is not surprising, then, that many of the chapters in this volume began with a discussion of the current issues in assessment and diagnosis related to the specific topic at hand. These discussions reflect the evolution in assessment and diagnosis that has taken place since the advent of the *Diagnostic and Statistical Manual of Mental Disorders-Third Edition* (DSM-III) (American Psychiatric Association 1980). Although aware of the potential for overlap between chapters, we decided early on to allow authors to address assessment questions pertinent to their particular topics. We worried that having a single chapter devoted to assessment issues common to all the groups covered in this book might, in fact, obscure potentially important relationships between depression and group-specific etiological variables or therapeutic interventions.

Diagnosed Depression and Depressive Symptoms

Depression researchers increasingly recognize that diagnosable depressive disorders and self-reported depressive symptoms constitute distinct and equally viable topics of inquiry. An episode meeting the diagnostic criteria for major depression is not merely an extension, in duration and severity, of a high score on a self-report inventory of depressive symptomatology. As Coyne and Downey (1991) recently pointed out, some evidence suggests that self-reported depressive symptoms and diagnosed depression are related to different life stresses, including those of a social nature. Coyne and Downey mention that poverty appears more systematically associated with a higher risk for depressive symptoms than for major depression (Weissman 1987). However, this position was recently challenged by longitudinal data indicating that previously "healthy" poor people are approximately twice as likely to develop mental disorders, including major depression, over a six-month period, as their wealthier counterparts (Bruce et al. 1991).

In this volume, Stoppard reviewed studies showing that controlling for socioeconomic differences largely eliminated gender differences in depressive symptomatology, but not in diagnosed depression. This distinction suggests that socioeconomic inequalities may be involved in the development of depressive symptoms, which themselves may reflect demoralization in the face of chronic socioeconomic hardship. Such an interpretation is also consistent with Flynn's chapter, in which financial strain consistently emerged, both in cross-sectional and longitudinal studies of unemployed adults, as an important mediator of the impact of unemployment on depressive affect.

A number of investigators have pointed out that depressive symptomatology and depressive disorder may have different relationships with life stress, broadly conceived (Breslau and Davis 1986; Brown and Harris 1978; Dohrenwend et al. 1986). Even though stressful life events have frequently been associated with the development of psychological distress, including depressive symptomatology, the relationship between stress and major depression is not so straightforward. In fact, Coyne and Downey (1991) interpret the available evidence as suggesting that clinical depression can be predicted by a small set of relatively disruptive life events, whereas depressive symptoms are related to a broader range of major and minor life events. Future research needs to determine which weighted pattern of social variables is best related to the development of depressive symptomatology and which is most predictive of major depression. It may be that some sources of stress are relevant to both depressive symptoms and major depression, whereas others are uniquely relevant to one or the other condition. Turner and Beiser (1990) recently reported that chronic stress was a risk factor for both depressive symptomatology and major depressive disorder among physically disabled persons.

It may also be useful to consider depressive symptomatology and depressive disorder as distinct constructs for other reasons. Recent research indicates that such variables as gender, personality antecedents or correlates, and dimensions of coping may be differentially related to these phenomena. Although Stoppard's chapter noted that most research shows women with higher rates of depression than men, regardless of whether depression was operationally defined as depressive symptomatology or as diagnosed depression, some very recent results are at variance with this finding. Lewinsohn and his collaborators (Lewinsohn et al. 1988; Rohde et al. 1990b), for instance, have reported that female gender predicted the future development of a diagnosed depression but not an increase in self-reported depressive symptoms.

A large body of literature has focused on the relationship of neuroticism and introversion with depression. In their review, Barnett and Gotlib (1988) found a consistent association between neuroticism and depressive symptoms. They concluded that neuroticism is mood-dependent, decreasing as depressive symptoms abate. On the other hand, they also concluded that a higher-than-normal level of introversion constitutes an enduring vulnerability to clinical depression, one that does not decline after recovery from depression. Neuroticism and introversion thus appear to be related in different ways to the issue of vulnerability to depression: the former being predictive of depressive symptoms, the latter of clinical depression.

Recent findings *vis-à-vis* coping with depression (Rohde et al. 1990b) provide an additional justification for maintaining a distinction between depressive symptomatology and diagnosed depression. Researchers found that behaviours incorporating a coping factor, identified as "ineffective escapism" (that is, avoidant, passive, helpless, or reckless coping behaviours), were predictive of both a higher depressive symptomatology and an increased probability of an episode of diagnosed depression. Use of such coping behaviours increased the likelihood of becoming distressed and eventually being diagnosed as depressed. On the other hand, the coping dimension of "solace seeking" (that is, spending time with others and engaging in enjoyable activities) was found to buffer the impact of stress, reducing the likelihood of a diagnosis of depression. No such role for solace seeking was found, however, in the prediction of depressive symptoms.

In sum, there is converging evidence that self-reported depressive symptoms and diagnosed depression are sufficiently distinct as constructs to warrant separate treatment by investigators. Researchers should exercise caution when generalizing findings from studies of depressive symptomatology to major depression, and vice versa.

Limitations of an Exclusive Focus on Diagnosis

Depression research has come to emphasize the adoption of formal diagnostic criteria. This recent development and its implications deserve to be critically evaluated. First, we readily acknowledge the usefulness of a system in which diagnostic concepts are operationalized and diagnostic criteria spelled out in terms of well-defined observable signs. We also believe that research and practice can derive much benefit from the methodological advance of adopting standard practices of classification and assessment. It is nevertheless important to realize that recent developments have sprung from a rather narrow perspective on the diagnosis of depression, one that stresses a dichotomic (present/absent) approach. In our opinion, an overemphasis on such a nosological (classificatory) approach may stand in the way of truly understanding the etiology of depression and its treatment. Indeed, in a critical review of similarities and dissimilarities between community and clinic cases of depression, Costello (1990) wrote about the usefulness of supplementing a categorical, case-finding approach with a dimensional approach in community studies.

The nosological approach favours the definition of a limited set of neatly differentiated depressive disorders, each with its own clinical features, course, causation, and treatment of choice. In the *Diagnostic and Statistical Manual of Mental Disorders-Third Edition-revised* (DSM-III-R) classification system, this approach has led to the definition of two basic diagnostic entities: major depression and dysthymia. This perspective encourages the view that the range of depressive disorders is exhausted by the two DSM-III-R categories and that depressive states not meeting the diagnostic criteria are of no clinical importance. There are several important reasons, however, for not dismissing the clinical relevance of depressive symptoms that do not meet all the diagnostic criteria. Besides involving undeniable personal distress, chronic dysphoria is increasingly recognized as a risk factor for depressive disorders (Depue and Monroe 1986; Lewinsohn et al. 1988; Rohde et al. 1990a). In fact, moderate and chronic demoralization, which may be reflected in an elevated number of depressive symptoms, is perhaps the principal risk factor for future clinical depression (Rohde et al. 1990a). In other words, high and nontransient levels of depressive symptoms may place individuals at risk for developing "diagnostic" depression, which itself may become chronic (Keller et al. 1986). Furthermore, a generally negative affective style characterized by depressive and anxious symptoms may be associated with the development of a broad range of physical diseases (Friedman and Booth-Kewley 1987).

The Diagnostic and Statistical Manual of Mental Disorders-Third Edition (DSM-III) (American Psychiatric Association, 1980) and DSM-III-R (American Psychiatric Association, 1987) criteria for the diagnosis of depression attempted to provide clearly defined, observable indicators – indicators minimally contaminated by etiological viewpoints – that would improve diagnostic reliability. It is therefore no surprise that these diagnostic tools are of little help in the identification of etiological factors. Paradoxically, however, they also detract from a precise assessment of symptomatology (their *raison d'être*). The consequences are several. First, because DSM-III and DSM-III-R consider only a subset of symptoms for a primary diagnosis, discarding other symptoms as irrelevant for this purpose, potentially useful information that could lead to the selection of an optimal treatment strategy is lost. As an illustration, a DSM-III diagnosis of depression precluded the possibility of a concurrent diagnosis of another condition. This lack of attention to symptoms other than those making up the diagnostic criteria of depression (a weakness that has been corrected in DSM-III-R) obscured the high rates of concurrent depressive and anxious syndromes that exist in both adults (Sanderson et al. 1990a; Sanderson et al. 1990b) and children (Fleming and Offord, this volume). It may also have masked the existence of concurrent depressive and personality disorders (Black et al. 1988; Phofl et al. 1984).

Second, as pointed out by van Praag (1990), variables such as the duration and intensity of symptoms and personality characteristics do not relate specifically to a particular depressive syndrome. Rather, they vary within syndromes. Thus, there is a need to assess such variables separately from a purely syndromal diagnosis.

Third, a strictly nosological perspective encourages the view that each syndrome has a specific set of causes and a preferred (even if not a single) treatment modality. Such a view does not square, however, with the fact that the presence of neuroendocrine markers or vegetative symptoms (evidence typically interpreted as supportive of the "endogenous/exogenous" distinction) does not greatly diminish the relationship of negative life events to diagnosed depression (Dolan et al. 1985). There is also no *a priori* reason to rule out psychotherapeutic intervention for major depression of the melancholic type, or biological treatment with antidepressant medication for a dysthymic disorder. Recent studies comparing psychotherapy and pharmacotherapy for depression, in fact, provide no clear-cut evidence that one modality of intervention is superior to the other for a particular depressive syndrome (Free and Oei 1989; McLean and Carr 1989; Robinson et al. 1990). Furthermore, the lack of consistent differences in the efficacy of various psychotherapeutic methods raises "the provocative possibility that diagnosis has much less impact on treatment response than previously assumed" (Robinson et al. 1990, 42). This line of reasoning clearly shows the importance of investigating the effects of different therapeutic modalities on specific depressive symptoms.

Concerns about Depression Early in Life

The very possibility that children and adolescents may exhibit a true depressive syndrome (as distinct from the turmoil that characterizes certain developmental phases of childhood or adolescence) has only recently gained acceptance. As a result, as Fleming and Offord and Kutcher, Marton, and Boulos state in their respective chapters, the systematic study of depression in children and adolescents is only just beginning. We have little firm knowledge, at present, about the relationship between childhood and adult depression.

For several reasons, increased attention to the assessment of depression early in life is important. First, depression tends to be a recurring condition, for which the occurrence of early episodes serves as a risk factor for the occurrence of later episodes. Second, recent epidemiological findings suggest that the peak period of onset of depression now occurs at a younger age than was once the case (Burke et al. 1990). Among females, for instance, current hazard rates for major depression peak between fifteen and nineteen years of age; among males, rates peak between twenty-five and twenty-nine years of age (Burke et al. 1990). Third, major depression in the early years is apparently related to the subsequent development of drug abuse or dependence (Christie et al. 1988). Finally, as Kutcher et al. and Tousignant and Hanigan point out (this volume), depression increases the risk of suicide, particularly among adolescents.

Concluding Comments on Assessment

A number of contributors to the present volume have stated that many of the clinical manifestations of depression are similar across the life span. Indeed, there is currently a consensus that age-specific criteria for the diagnosis of mood disorders are not required. Several of the chapters, however, indicate that social factors, especially culturally normative role expectations, shape the expression of depression and calls for help in age-appropriate ways. The depressive syndrome in children and adolescents, for example, is often manifested by absenteeism, negative behaviour, or academic failure at school, or by problems of conduct at home (Fleming and Offord, this volume; Kutcher, Marton, and Boulos, this volume). In adults, depressive symptoms are frequently related to unemployment or marital problems (Flynn, this volume; Stoppard, this volume). Among elderly persons, somatic symptoms, lethargy, and a lack of interest and involvement – all features consistent with widespread stereotypes of aging –

are distinctive features of depression in later life (Cappeliez, this volume; Fry, this volume).

Finally, it is useful to recall that most people who experience a depressive episode do not seek treatment (Vernon and Roberts 1982). Although many will eventually overcome their depression without professional help, a significant proportion will not. Barnes (this volume) points out that many of the latter group will seek assistance from their family physicians, who are typically untrained to identify or treat depression. In discussing the hidden part of what is a sizeable "iceberg," Barnes underlines the magnitude of the challenge of adequately identifying, and effectively treating, depression.

ETIOLOGY: RISK FACTORS IN THE SOCIAL ENVIRONMENT

Social and Economic Inequalities

The contributors to the present volume stress the necessity of viewing depression from the perspective of the larger social context in which it occurs, in order to transcend the individualistic bias of much current theorizing. Stoppard's chapter illustrates the limitations of contemporary explanations of even as basic a finding as the higher rate of depression typically found among women as compared to men. Her contribution directs our attention not to hypothesized cognitive vulnerabilities to depression but rather to the depressogenic influence of social and economic hardships encountered by many women in our society. In this regard, 59 per cent of Canadian adults living in poverty in 1987 were women (National Council of Welfare 1990). This proportion has remained unchanged since 1975, despite government initiatives to reduce social and economic disparities between women and men and an increase in the female rate of labour-force participation during the same period (from 53 per cent to 68 per cent of all women of working age). The situation of single mothers is especially difficult. Besides the lack of social support that many face, 75 per cent of those who were never married and 52 per cent of those who were previously married live below the poverty line (National Council of Welfare 1990).

As for women's increased risk of depression, Stoppard proposes a two-stage process. First come the socioeconomic inequalities, which increase the risk of distress as manifested in increased depressive symptoms; then come the stresses related to gender role (for example, child care responsibilities), which make it even more likely that a clinical (diagnosed) depression will ensue. The hypothesis that caring for dependents in a situation of social and economic deprivation is strongly linked with depression is also important. For many women, the responsibility of taking care of others extends well beyond the domain of child care. Numerous studies have demonstrated that informal caregiving in our society is provided mainly by women, regardless of the ages of the caregiver or care receiver. Garant and Bolduc (1990), in a report published by the Ministry of Health and Social Services of Quebec documenting the central role that women continue to play in the informal care of aging parents, found that, in 70 to 80 per cent of cases, women (that is, spouses, daughters, or daughters-in-law) bear the primary responsibility of caring for dependent older adults. Current health-care policies that encourage caring for older persons in their own homes risk increasing women's burden as well. In fact, Stoppard's hypothesis suggests that an increase in women's already disproportionate share of the care of others, particularly under conditions of poverty, will lead to a further rise in depression among women.

Social Support and Depression

A number of contributors to this volume have indicated that deficient social support is an important risk factor for depression. Cappeliez (this volume) and Landreville and Cappeliez (in press) examine the role played by social support in the etiology of, and recovery from, depression among elderly persons. Fry (this volume) makes an especially strong case for the role of instrumental social support (that is, practical assistance) in older adults' depressive conditions. Mohide and Streiner (this volume) describe the need for social support on the part of family members who provide most of the emotional and physical care received by chronically ill elderly persons. McColl and Friedland (this volume) document the influential role played by social support, particularly that provided by a close personal source, in the emotional adjustment to disability.

In line with this recurring theme, inadequate spousal support has been found to be a predictor of depressive symptoms among women (for example, D'Arcy and Siddique 1984; Ross and Mirowsky 1988). Young women caring for young children appear to be at high risk for depression (Lewinsohn et al. 1988). As well, the risk is higher among young women living in urban settings compared to rural settings (Crowell et al. 1986; Kovess et al. 1987). The same urban-rural difference has been reported for elderly samples (Kovess et al. 1987).

Overall, the positive influence of supportive social relationships on mental and physical health is well established (for example, House et al. 1988). Much remains to be investigated, however, beyond the evident correlation between perceived social support and well-being. The lack of well-articulated theoretical perspectives in a field until recently dominated by epidemiological studies has impeded progress in understanding the role of social support in depression (Sarason et al. 1990).

Given that levels of low social support are often a proxy for strained interpersonal relationships (Coyne and Bolger 1990), it seems likely that the next generation of social-support research will go beyond the general notion of perceived adequacy of social support and consider the varied ways in which interpersonal relationships shape adaptation and coping. Tousignant and Hanigan's research on risk factors for suicide among adolescents, presented in this volume, is a good example of this trend. They show that the crucial factor was not simply the lack of a social network (that is, objective isolation), but rather a sense of alienation and a lack of understanding. That is, vulnerable adolescents had people around them but were reluctant to ask for and use assistance. This alienation stemmed from a sense that nobody cared, itself a belief deriving from poor relationships within the family. The fundamental question would appear to be the following: Which aspects of relationships are supportive and a resource for coping with depression for a particular individual at a particular stage of the depressive experience? Cutrona's (1990) model, which considers an optimal matching of stress and social support dimensions, may prove useful in investigating the role of social support in depression.

A Comprehensive Taxonomy of Environmental Risk Factors

The fact that socioeconomic inequality and low social support appear to be depressogenic suggests the need for a systematic and comprehensive taxonomy of environmental features that are risk factors for mental health difficulties, in general, and for depression, in particular. A number of domain-specific perspectives exist for conceptualizing and assessing the social environment. In the field of health psychology, for example, Winett (1985) and Moos (1985) have advocated "ecobehavioral" and "biopsychosocial" frameworks, respectively, in which individual health behaviour is viewed within an environmental context. Winett (1985) suggests that environmental influences on health problems may be conceptualized and assessed on many different levels, including the individual, small group, small setting, organizational, institutional, and community levels. Moos (1985) conceives of the social environment as including life stressors and social network resources, with the latter encompassing the quantity, quality, and climate of social relationships. He also proposes that diagnostic and treatment information of an environmental nature is as important as biological and psychological data in approaching problems of health, adaptation, and well-being.

Warr (1987) has provided a simple yet comprehensive classification scheme (introduced earlier in Flynn's chapter) that permits a systematic analysis of the basic features of virtually any human environment – whether work, unemployment, family, retirement, hospitalization, or a person's lifespace as a whole – likely to have an impact on mental health. Warr calls these environmental features "vitamins," because they affect mental health in a manner analogous to the way vitamins affect physical health. In our opinion, Warr's model has considerable heuristic value as a source of hypotheses about environmental elements that may interact with personal factors (baseline mental health, demographic variables, personality characteristics, and abilities) to produce depressive affect and even clinical depression. Warr's (1987) approach is situation-centred rather than person-centred and also enabling rather than controlling (Gergen and Gergen 1982), such that individuals are influenced by, but can also influence, their environments. Warr proposes that environments of all kinds be assessed and compared in terms of the following interrelated dimensions, all of which are determinants of mental health:

1   *opportunity for control.* Mental health can be expected to be better in environments that allow individuals to exercise personal control over activities and events;

2   *opportunity for skill use.* Mental health is enhanced by environments that permit the satisfaction of using already acquired skills and the improved coping resulting from the acquisition of new skills;

3   *externally generated goals.* Mental health is fostered by the presence of environmentally generated goals, that is, by the "traction," sense of purpose, targets, expected behaviours, routines, and plans engendered by formal and informal social-role requirements;

4   *variety.* Mental health is promoted by environments that provide diversity and novelty in physical location and in role-related activities;

5   *environmental clarity.* Mental health is strengthened by environments that provide predictability, clarity about role requirements and expected behaviours, and feedback about the consequences of one's actions;

6   *availability of money.* Mental health is enhanced by the availability of adequate financial resources. The availability of money is also likely to affect other environmental features, including the opportunity for personal control or skill use (for example, poverty reduces the pursuit of enjoyable activities that require the expenditure of money) and personal security;

7   *Physical security.* Mental health is fostered by environments that protect persons against physical threats; provide adequate space, light and heat; and offer a sense of permanency;

8   *opportunity for interpersonal contact.* Mental health is promoted by environments that provide for contact with other people. Such environments meet friendship needs, foster social support (emotional, instrumental, and motivational), afford opportunities for comparisons between

oneself and others, and permit the attainment of goals through the interdependent efforts of several people; and

9   *valued social position.* Mental health is strengthened by environments that permit persons to occupy valued social positions and, thereby, earn esteem from others.

Warr's (1987) nine categories allow a comprehensive description of possible differences between social groups and an interpretation of the effects of transitions between environments. Even a cursory application of Warr's model to the life situations of the various groups considered in this volume is sufficient to suggest why many members of these groups are at risk of experiencing mental health problems, including depression. As noted earlier in this section on risk factors, environmental feature number 6 (availability of money) is often deficient: women (particularly single parents), unemployed persons, Native Indians, immigrants and refugees, disabled persons, and elderly persons are particularly at risk of being poor. As also noted, environmental element number 8 (opportunity for interpersonal contact) is frequently lacking as well: children, adolescents, young adults, women, the unemployed, Native people, immigrants and refugees, the physically disabled, the elderly, and caregivers of impaired elderly persons may be particularly vulnerable to a lack of adequate instrumental, emotional, or motivational support. In the same vein, members of these groups may experience environments that are deficient in other ways, in that their life circumstances

- allow only limited control over their lives (for example, many adolescents and young adults, women, unemployed persons, Native Indians, immigrants, or elderly persons);
- discourage the use of old skills or the acquisition of new ones (for example, many unemployed persons, Native Indians, or immigrants and refugees);
- provide too few externally generated goals (for example, many unemployed young adults or Native Indians);
- provide minimal variety (for example, many severely disabled persons, chronically ill elderly persons, or family caregivers);
- provide little clarity about role requirements and consequences (for example, unemployed persons, Native Indians, or immigrants and refugees);
- afford minimal physical security (for example, many children and adolescents in impoverished families, women or elderly persons in abusive relationships, or some Native Indians); or,
- provide little social status and esteem (for example, many unemployed young adults, Native Indians, or immigrants and refugees).

INTERVENTION

Taking the Social Environment into Account

Situations are sometimes more easily modified than people (Feather 1990). Warr's (1987) approach is a useful guide for formulating socioeconomic and human service policies that would improve the environments, and thereby alleviate the depressive experiences, of the groups discussed in this volume.

The present approach is directed towards the mental health of people in many different settings. It seeks not only to study mental health but primarily to provide a framework for its improvement. Through presenting a systematic categorical model, identifying causal processes, and suggesting measurement approaches, the approach aims to yield recommendations for enhancing mental health by changing those environments identified as harmful. That goal is shared by many different groups of practitioners, and the vitamin model might provide a broad perspective on the 'levers' of change, to be 'pulled' in the setting of concern to each group. (Warr 1987, 21)

In contrast to Warr's situation-centred enabling model is the coping paradigm, a model that has dominated theorizing about depression intervention since at least the late 1970s. The coping model, while not ignoring the negative aspects of a person's life circumstances, focuses primarily on providing the depressed individual with opportunities for developing cognitive, behavioural and interpersonal skills in order to adjust better to life situations. The implicit belief is that once the depression has lifted, the person will regain the capacity and motivation to tackle her or his life problems.

In keeping with its focus on social-environmental etiological factors, this volume suggests that the coping perspective is likely too narrow for effective intervention with many depressed persons. A number of contributors (for instance, Stoppard, Flynn, Armstrong, DaCosta, McColl and Friedland) have argued that mental health personnel need to go beyond their traditional therapeutic roles, to advocate for improved social policies in areas such as pay equity, accessible child care, employment, aboriginal affairs, immigration, access to mental health services, and disability. Such a stance implies a socially active role for therapists in helping depressed persons to recognize and alter chronically stressful situations and not merely to manage their short-term reactions to difficult life circumstances. It also implies that practitioners recognize that people are active agents with some scope for acting upon their environments, even in adversity.

In sum, mental health practitioners need to recognize the role played by social-environmental factors, such as those discussed in this volume, and integrate them into both their analyses of problems and their interventions. From a research point of view, and because the empirical literature has not addressed the processes and outcomes of depression treatment systematically, much remains to be learned in this regard.

Psychotherapy

Several recent outcome studies and meta-analytic reviews of the treatment literature (for example, Free and Oei 1989; Elkin et al. 1989; Hollon et al. 1991; McLean and Carr 1989; Robinson et al. 1990) have shown that depressed individuals benefit significantly from psychotherapeutic intervention and that these gains are, in general, comparable to those obtained with antidepressant medication. The consensus in the literature on the treatment of depression is that, of the psychotherapies evaluated to date in controlled trials, none shows any greater effectiveness than the others (Elkin et al. 1989; Robinson et al. 1990). This finding means that the various psychotherapies may be bringing about their equivalent benefits by means of similar core processes (Imber et al. 1990).

These findings have helped to establish psychotherapy as an alternative to pharmacotherapy in the treatment of depression. It is important to note, however, that current knowledge concerning the efficacy of psychotherapy and pharmacotherapy in the treatment of depression derives mainly from studies of relatively homogeneous samples of nonbipolar, middle-class, female outpatients in their mid-thirties, who have had moderate to severe depressive symptomatology. It is an open question whether the results obtained with such subjects also apply to depressed clients who are members of the groups discussed in this volume. The hypothesis of equivalent benefits through similar processes, for example, needs to be addressed by means of intervention studies with these populations. Although the research presented in some chapters of this volume suggests that generalization may prove possible, the small number of studies conducted with the various overlooked groups precludes any firm statement at present.

McLean and Carr (1989) suggested that the finding of comparable effectiveness of different psychological treatments may mean that only limited benefits can be derived from the application of single, unitary theories of depression. The development of integrated treatment packages that draw on compatible approaches and are adapted to the needs of special populations may be one way of maximizing therapeutic effectiveness. In a similar vein, several contributors to the present volume have suggested that psychotherapeutic treatments for depression have not taken adequate account of specific clients' or patients' needs. For example, Cappeliez notes that the role of ill health as a predictor of older adults' depression has yet to be addressed by psychotherapeutic interventions. Similarly, Kutcher, Marton, and Boulos suggest that subgroups of depressed adolescents should be distinguished on the basis of their differential response to different treatment modalities.

Stoppard points out the limitations of standard approaches in treating depressed women, arguing that such interventions do not adequately address gender issues. McColl and Friedland and Mohide and Streiner note that progress in intervening with depressed individuals confronted with a personal disability or the care of an impaired family member has been hampered by a considerable heterogeneity of needs, situations, and resources. Mohide and Streiner suggest that if, indeed, most caregivers suffer from demoralization rather than major depression, intervention should aim at improving the quality of their lives through supportive interventions as well as tangible help to restore a sense of control and mastery.

Finally, as Beckham pointed out (1990), psychotherapy research has often ignored the impact of stressful environmental events on the processes and outcome of treatment. Yet there is accumulating evidence that continuing life challenges negatively influence the long-term outcome of depression. In a unique study of the effects of psychosocial factors on the long-term course of unipolar depression, Swindle et al. (1989) reported that medical conditions and family conflict – stressors that persisted over the four-year period after the end of treatment of their depressed patients – constituted two important risk factors predicting poorer long-term outcomes. Research on the relationship between psychosocial factors and symptom outcomes may uncover variables that moderate the short-term and long-term effects of treatment in high-risk populations.

Mediators of Change

Current psychotherapeutic modalities are likely to need adaptation to the specific needs of the groups discussed in this volume. Several authors (for example, Frank 1982; Zeiss et al. 1979) have pointed out that such factors as clients' expectations of improvement, their acceptance of therapeutic rationales, and the quality of the therapeutic relationship may mediate change in psychotherapy. Research and practice with depressed clients from underserved groups would do well to focus on how to adapt present treatments to capitalize on these and other important ingredients of psychotherapy. It is likely that elderly, immigrant, native Indian, or adolescent clients, for example, differ considerably in terms of their beliefs about treatment credibility, expectations for improvement, preferences concerning the client-therapist relationship, and adherence to treatment. Such variables must be taken into consideration to maximize the power of our interventions (Cappeliez and Latour, in press).

Prevention of Relapse

Depression is a condition with a high likelihood of recurrence. As many as 20 per cent of community subjects who experience an episode of depression will continue to be depressed one year later (Sargeant et al. 1990). Thirty-six per cent of depressed patients may experience a relapse during the first twelve months after recovery from unipolar depression and 50 per cent during the first two years (for a review, see Belsher and Costello 1988). Yet relapse-prevention interventions have received little attention. This situation is unfortunate given that, as Belsher and Costello (1988) pointed out, the prevention of relapse may well represent a more feasible objective than the prevention of onset. Furthermore, there are indications that some modalities of psychotherapy, in particular cognitive therapy, may be effective in preventing relapse following successful treatment (for a review, see Hollon et al. 1991). Before we can devise more effective interventions, we need to know much more about the factors that maintain recovery and precipitate relapse. We must also know more about the effects of repeated episodes of depression and their consequences. To date, research on formerly depressed individuals' residual deficits, which could serve as the targets of preventive interventions, has been limited to a small set of predictor variables and has produced only meagre results. Rohde et al. (1990a) reported that formerly depressed subjects, compared with the never depressed, did not differ regarding such variables as stress, social support, social networks, or coping style. The formerly depressed were, however, more likely to report moderate and chronic demoralization. In a four-year follow-up study, Swindle et al. (1989) reported that the continuing presence of medical problems and family conflict signalled a worse prognosis. These results indicate the need for more intensive treatment and follow-up, even when initial symptomatic improvement has been obtained, of problems in these domains in which persistent difficulties occur. Future research should also examine such other variables as interpersonal dependence, tendency toward self-criticism, introversion and marital distress.

Training of Professionals

Several contributors saw improving the ability of mental health and other front-line professionals to recognize and treat depressive symptoms and clinical depression in groups-at-risk as an urgent need. Barnes (this volume) observes that most depressed adults are not seen by mental health specialists. Fleming and Offord (this volume) note that the situation was much the same for depressed children, most of whom are seen by family physicians. Given the multiplicity and interactive nature of the biological, psychological, and social factors involved in depression, it is imperative to encourage a comprehensive, multidisciplinary approach in the training of mental health and other professionals.

CONCLUSION

In a recent article on epistemological issues in psychology, Rogers (1990) wrote that "the success of the theoretical/scientific enterprise rests with its effectiveness as a practical device for co-ordinating social action. Only if the discipline actually informs the society of its 'ills' and 'potentials' and lays out guidelines for cure and control will it be deemed a success" (216). Rogers's words seem applicable to the mental health disciplines in general. We undertook work on this book because of an interest in the social-environmental roots of depression and in certain at-risk groups who, we felt, tended to be overlooked by researchers and clinicians alike. At the conclusion of our efforts, we are more convinced than ever of the need to take into account the impact of the larger social context within which individuals experience depression. We hope this book will prove useful as a source of insights and ideas for agents of change on many levels, from individual counsellors and therapists to policymakers in the mental health and other human service areas.

BIBLIOGRAPHY

Akiskal, H.S. 1989. New insights into the nature and heterogeneity of mood disorders. *Journal of Clinical Psychiatry* 50: 6–12.
American Psychiatric Association 1980. *Diagnostic and statistical manual of mental disorders*, 3d ed. Washington, D.C.: American Psychiatric Association.
– 1987. *Diagnostic and statistical manual of mental disorders*, 3d ed., rev. Washington, D.C.: American Psychiatric Association.
Barnett, P.A., and Gotlib, I.H. 1988. Psychosocial functioning and depression: Distinguishing among antecedents, concomitants, and consequences. *Psychological Bulletin* 104: 97–126.
Beckham, E.E. 1990. Psychotherapy of depression research at a crossroads: Directions for the 1990s. *Clinical Psychology Review* 10: 207–28.
Belsher, G., and Costello, C.G. 1988. Relapse after recovery from unipolar depression: A critical review. *Psychological Bulletin* 104: 84–96.
Black, D.W., Bell, S., Hubert, J., and Nasrallah, A. 1988. The importance of Axis II disorders in patients with major depression: A controlled study. *Journal of Affective Disorders* 14: 115–22.
Breslau, N., and Davis, G.C. 1986. Chronic stress and major depression. *Archives of General Psychiatry* 43: 309–14.
Brown, G.W., and Harris, T.D. 1978. *Social origins of depression: A study of psychiatric disorder in women*. New York: Free Press.
Bruce, M.L., Takeuchi, D.T., and Leaf, P.J. 1991. Poverty and psychiatric status: Longitudinal evidence from the New Haven Epidemiologic Catchment Area Study.

Archives of General Psychiatry 48: 470–74.

Burke, K.C., Burke, J.D., Regier, D.A., and Rae, D.S. 1990. Age at onset of selected mental disorders in five community populations. *Archives of General Psychiatry* 47: 511–18.

Cappeliez, P., and Latour, D. In press. La préparation des participants dépressifs âgés à la thérapie cognitive en groupe. In *Aspects neuropsychologiques, cognitifs et cliniques du vieillissement.* Paris: Presses Universitaires de France.

Christie, K.A., Burke, J.D., Regier, D.A., Rae, D.S., Boyd, J.H., and Locke, B.Z. 1988. Epidemiologic evidence for early onset of mental disorders and higher risk of drug abuse in young adults. *American Journal of Psychiatry* 145: 971–75.

Costello, C.G. 1990. The similarities and dissimilarities between community and clinic cases of depression. *British Journal of Psychiatry* 157: 812–21.

Coyne, J.C., and Bolger, N. 1990. Doing without social support as an explanatory concept. *Journal of Social and Clinical Psychology* 9: 148–58.

Coyne, J.C., and Downey, G. 1991. Social factors and psychopathology: Stress, social support, and coping processes. *Annual Review of Psychology* 42: 401–26.

Crowell, B.A., George, L.K., Blazer, D., and Landerman, R. 1986. Psychosocial risk factors and urban/rural differences in prevalence of major depression. *British Journal of Psychiatry* 140: 307–14.

Cutrona, C.E. 1990. Stress and social support: In search of optimal matching. *Journal of Social and Clinical Psychology* 9: 3–14.

D'Arcy, C., and Siddique, C.M. 1984. Social support and mental health among mothers of preschool and school age children. *Social Psychiatry* 19: 155–62.

Depue, R.A., and Monroe, S.M. 1986. Conceptualization and measurement of human disorder and life stress research: The problem of chronic disturbance. *Psychological Bulletin* 99: 36–51.

Dohrenwend, B.P., Shrout, P.E., Link, B.G., Skodol, A.E., and Martin, J.L. 1986. Overview and initial results from a risk factor study of depression and schizophrenia. In *Mental disorders in the community: Progress and challenge,* edited by J.E. Barrett, 184–215. New York: Guilford Press.

Dolan, R.J., Calloway, S.P., Fonagy, P., DeSouza, F.V.A., and Wakeling, A. 1985. Life events, depression, and hypothalamic-adrenal axis function. *British Journal of Psychiatry* 147: 429–33.

Downey, G., and Coyne, J.C. 1990. Children of depressed parents: An integrative review. *Psychological Bulletin* 108: 50–76.

Elkin, I., Shea, T., Watkins, J.T., Imber, S.D., Sotsky, S.M., Collins, J.F., Glass, D.R., Pilkonis, P.A., Leber, W.R., Docherty, J.P., Fiester, S.J., and Parloff, M.B. 1989. National Institute of Mental Health Treatment of Depression Collaborative Research Program: General effectiveness of treatments. *Archives of General Psychiatry* 46: 971–83.

Feather, N.T. 1990. *The psychological impact of unemployment.* New York: Springer-Verlag.

Frank, J.D. 1982. Therapeutic components shared by all psychotherapies. In

Psychotherapy research and behaviour change, edited by J.H. Harvey and M.M. Parks, vol. 1: 5–37. Washington, D.C.: American Psychological Association.

Free, M.L., and Oei, T.P.S. 1989. Biological and psychological processes in the treatment and maintenance of depression. *Clinical Psychology Review* 9: 653–88.

Friedman, H.S., and Booth-Kewley, S. 1987. The "disease-prone personality": A meta-analytic view of the construct. *American Psychologist* 42: 539–55.

Garant, L., and Bolduc, M. 1990. *L'aide par les proches: Mythes et réalités*. Québec: Gouvernement du Québec, Ministère de la Santé et des Services Sociaux.

Gergen, K.J., and Gergen, M.M. 1982. Explaining human conduct: Form and function. In *Explaining human behavior: Consciousness, human action, and social structure*, edited by P. Secord. Beverly Hills, Calif.: Sage.

Hollon, S.D., Shelton, R.C., and Loosen, P.T. 1991. Cognitive therapy and pharmacotherapy for depression. *Journal of Consulting and Clinical Psychology* 59: 88–99.

House, J.S., Landis, K.R., and Umberson, D. 1988. Social relationships and health. *Science* 241: 540–45.

Imber, S.D., Pilkonis, P.A., Sotsky, S.M., Elkin, I., Watkins, J.T., Collins, J.F., Shea, M.T., Leber, W.R., and Glass, D.R. (1990). Mode-specific effects among three treatments for depression. *Journal of Consulting and Clinical Psychology* 58: 352–59.

Keller, M.B., Lavori, P.W., Rice, J., Coryell, W., and Hirschfeld, R.M.A. 1986. The persistent risk of chronicity in recurrent episodes of nonbipolar major depressive disorder: A prospective follow-up. *American Journal of Psychiatry* 143: 24–28.

Kovess, V., Murphy, H.B.M., and Tousignant, M. 1987. Urban-rural comparisons of depressive disorder in French Canada. *Journal of Nervous and Mental Diseases* 175: 457–66.

Landreville, P., and Cappeliez, P. In press. Soutien social et symptômes dépressifs au sein des personnes âgées. *Revue Canadienne du Vieillissement*.

Lewinsohn, P.M., Hoberman, H., and Rosenbaum, M. 1988. A prospective study of risk factors for unipolar depression. *Journal of Abnormal Psychology* 97: 251–64.

McLean, P.D., and Carr, S. 1989. The psychological treatment of unipolar depression: Progress and limitations. *Canadian Journal of Behavioral Science* 21: 452–69.

Moos, R.H. 1985. Evaluating social resources in community and health care contexts. In *Measurement strategies in health psychology*, edited by P. Karoly, 433–59. New York: Wiley.

National Council of Welfare. 1990. *Women and poverty revisited*. Catalogue no. H68-25/1990F. Ottawa: Minister of Supply and Services.

Phofl, B., Stangl, D., and Zimmerman, M. 1984. The implications of DSM-III-R personality disorders for patients with major depression. *Journal of Affective Disorders* 7: 309–18.

Robinson, L.A., Berman, J.S., and Neimeyer, R.A. 1990. Psychotherapy for the treatment of depression: A comprehensive review of controlled outcome research.

Psychological Bulletin 108: 30–49.

Rogers, T.B. 1990. Toward an emancipatory psychology. *Canadian Psychology* 31: 215–17.

Rohde, P., Lewinsohn, P.M., and Seeley, J.R. 1990a. Are people changed by the experience of having an episode of depression? A further test of the scar hypothesis. *Journal of Abnormal Psychology* 99: 264–71.

Rohde, P., Lewinsohn, P.M., Tilson, M., and Seeley, J. R. 1990b. Dimensionality of coping and its relation to depression. *Journal of Personality and Social Psychology* 58: 499–511.

Ross, C.E., and Mirowsky, J. 1988. Child care and emotional adjustment to wives' employment. *Journal of Health and Social Behavior* 29: 127–38.

Sanderson, W.C., Beck, A.T., and Beck, J. 1990a. Syndrome comorbidity in patients with major depression or dysthymia: Prevalence and temporal relationships. *American Journal of Psychiatry* 147: 1025–28.

Sanderson, W.C., DiNardo, P.A., Rapee, R.M., and Barlow, D.H. 1990b. Syndrome comorbidity in patients diagnosed with a DSM-III-R anxiety disorder. *Journal of Abnormal Psychology* 99: 308–12.

Sarason, I.G., Sarason, B.R., and Pierce, G.R. 1990. Social support: The search for a theory. *Journal of Social and Clinical Psychology* 9: 133–47.

Sargeant, J.K., Bruce, M.L., Florio, L.P., and Weissman, M.M. 1990. Factors associated with a 1-year outcome of major depression in the community. *Archives of General Psychiatry* 47: 519–26.

Swindle, R.W., Cronkite, R.C., and Moos, R.H. 1989. Life stressors, social resources, coping, and the 4-year course of unipolar depression. *Journal of Abnormal Psychology* 98: 468–77.

Taylor, S.E. 1990. Health psychology: The science and the field. *American Psychologist* 45: 516–25.

Turner, R.J., and Beiser, M. 1990. Major depression and depressive symptomatology among the physically disabled: Assessing the role of chronic stress. *Journal of Nervous and Mental Disease* 178: 343–50.

van Praag, H.M. 1990. The DSM-IV (Depression) classification: To be or not to be? *Journal of Nervous and Mental Disease* 178: 147–49.

Vernon, S.W., and Roberts, R.E. 1982. Prevalence of treated and untreated psychiatric disorders in three ethnic groups. *Social Science and Medicine* 16: 1575–82.

Warr, P. 1987. *Work, unemployment, and mental health*. Oxford: Clarendon Press.

Weissman, M.M. 1987. Advances in psychiatric epidemiology: Rates and risks for depression. *American Journal of Public Health* 77: 445–51.

Winett, R.A. 1985. Ecobehavioral assessment in health life-styles: Concepts and methods. In *Measurement strategies in health psychology*, edited by P. Karoly, 147–81. New York: Wiley.

Zeiss, A.M., Lewinsohn, P.M., and Munoz, R.F. 1979. Nonspecific improvement effects in depression: Using interpersonal skills training, pleasant activity schedules, or cognitive training. *Journal of Consulting and Clinical Psychology* 47: 427–39.

Index

Adolescent depression: age-specific features of, 13; course and outcome of, 82–3; decreasing age of onset of, 7; effect of on social and personality functioning, 81–2; phenomenology of, 77–8; similarity of to adult depression, 77; and specific personality disorders, 81–2; theoretical perspectives on, 73–7. *See also* Anxiety; Assessment of depression; Biological aspects of depression; Canadian Native Indians; Childhood depression; Cognitive-behavioural interventions; Cognitive-behavioural theory; Cognitive psychotherapy; Depressive symptoms; Diagnosis of depression; Epidemiology; Etiology; Learned helplessness; Loss; Prevalence; Professionals; Psychotherapy; Research priorities; Risk factors; Suicide; Treatment

Alcohol abuse: and depression, 131; as "masked depression" in men, 130–1; and suicide in young adults, 97, 112, 114. *See also* Drug abuse

American Epidemiological Catchment Area Surveys, 262

Antidepressant medication: effectiveness of, 175; ethnic and racial factors in response to, 245; prevalence of treatment with, 171–4, 175; side-effects of, 175; toxicity of, 176; and women, 141. *See also* Pharmacotherapy

Anxiety: and adolescent depression, 77; and childhood and adult depression, 29–30

Assessment of depression: in adolescents, 79–81; in Canadian Native Indians, 224; in children, 14–22, 55, 56; current issues in, 395–401; in disabled persons, 262–5, 276, 280; in elderly persons, 333–41, 358, 373, 381; in family caregivers, 290, 291–315, 319–20, 324–5, 325–6; in general practice attenders, 152–61, 170–1, 176–8; in immigrants and refugees, 236–40, 245; in unemployed persons, 191–207 *passim*; in women, 128–31, 142. *See also* Assessment instruments; Diagnosis of depression; Diagnostic systems; Recognition of depression

Assessment instruments: Affect-Balance Scale, 198; Barthel Index, 319, 320; Beck Depression Inventory (BDI), 79, 85, 96, 152–66 *passim*, 171, 178, 193–204 *passim*, 263, 264, 294–308 *passim*, 312, 314, 325, 333, 337; Bellevue Index of Depression (BID), 17, 20; Bellevue Index of Depression-Revised (BID-R), 20; Brief Symptom Inventory (BSI), 206–10 *passim*, 296, 304, 310; Cantril Self-Anchoring Striving Scale, 319; Center for Epidemiological Studies-Depression Scale (CES-D), 95, 109, 127, 152–66 *passim*, 172, 173, 194, 263, 264, 292, 293, 298–314 *passim*, 319, 322, 323, 325, 333, 336; Center for Epidemiological Studies-Depression Scale for